CLASSIC Hand Tools

GARRETT HACK

Photographs by John S. Sheldon

The Taunton Press

Publisher
Jim Childs

Associate Publisher
Helen Albert

Associate Editor
Strother Purdy

Editor
Peter Chapman

Jacket and Interior Design
Carol Singer

Photographer (except where noted)
John S. Sheldon

Illustrator
Kathy Rushton

Indexer
Lynda S. Stannard

The Taunton Press
Inspiration for hands-on living™

Printed in the United States of America
10 9 8 7 6 5 4 3 2 1

Classic Hand Tools was originally published in hardcover
in 1999 by The Taunton Press, Inc.

The Taunton Press, Inc., 63 South Main Street,
PO Box 5506, Newtown, CT 06470-5506
e-mail: tp@taunton.com

Distributed by Publishers Group West

Library of Congress Cataloging-in-Publication

Hack, Garrett.
Classic hand tools / Garrett Hack; photographs by
John S. Sheldon.
p. cm.
Includes bibliographic references and index.
ISBN 1-56158-273-5 (hardcover)
ISBN 1-56158-507-6 (paperback)
1. Tools—Collectors and collecting. I. Title.
II. Title: Hand tools.
TJ1195.H12 1999
621.9'08'075—dc21 99-23719
CIP

To Robert and Renée,
who taught me about the most important tools

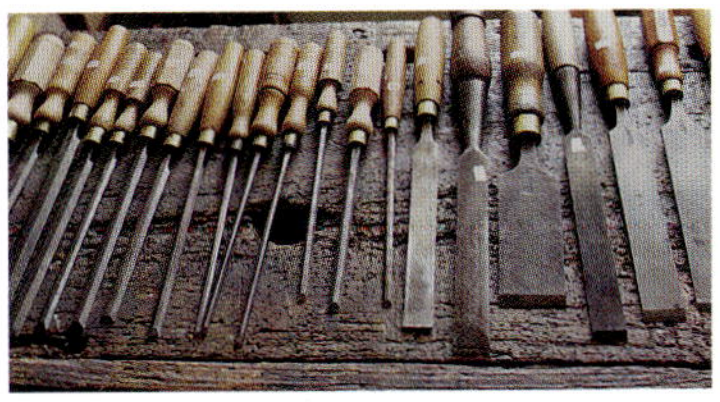

Acknowledgments

Writing this book has been a constant adventure. Tool lovers, collectors, and users are a far-flung lot. As I traveled looking for tools, often with my good friend John Sheldon, we never knew quite what each day would bring. As you can see, we discovered lots of tools, from those in the hands of craftsmen whose work we interrupted to others in collections of rare Stanley and unusual American and British tools. We also found many friends along the way, who shared their tools, their stories, and often their homes. I am sincerely grateful to the following people who made this adventure both fun and successful:

Roy and Julanne Arnold, Clarence Blanchard, Bridge City Tool Co., Henry and Susanne Bucki, Bill and Sarah Carter, George and Jean Derbyshire, Footprint Tools, Jerry Glaser, Ted Ingraham, Craig Jensen, Paul Kebabian, Leonard Lee and Lee Valley Tools, Steve Lamont and Phil Brown (and all at the Barnsley Workshops), Vincent Laurence, Larry Meyers, Tony Murland, Max Ott, Ray Pilon, Mark and Jane Rees, Dave Sawyer, David and Ian Stanley, William and Caroline Wilkins, and Anne and Don Wing.

For his quick mastery of English roundabouts, for his good humor despite the hour or the challenge, and for his photographic savvy, I owe a hearty thanks to John Sheldon.

Ultimately, the success of this project depended upon the many talented folks at The Taunton Press. For their steady support, creativity, and friendship I am grateful to Helen Albert, Jon Binzen, Jim Childs, Zack Gaulkin, Carol Singer, and Matthew Teague. A special thanks to Peter Chapman, a friend and gifted editor, who has nurtured my confidence as a writer as I have taught him more than he needs to know about woodworking tools.

John Green

Contents

Introduction

Hand tools are invaluable to me. Over the years of collecting, tuning, sharpening, and working with them, my hand tools have become natural extensions of me, linked with what I make and how I make it.

As for machines, I have everything you'd expect in a modest and efficient shop set up to produce the high-quality furniture that has been my living for more than 20 years. Although it's nothing that I ever consciously set out to do, every year I use those machines less and hand tools more. While the brute force of a machine is useful (if you don't mind the dust, noise, and danger), it is nothing like the intimacy and pleasure of working by hand. As I work, hand tools allow me the flexibility that I rarely feel with machines. And it's the subtle marks they leave behind that I find most beautiful.

Not long ago, all woodworking was done with hand tools alone. It took two men to saw lumber from a log, and then a square, hatchet, planes, and handsaws to work each board to width, length, and thickness. With an even greater variety of hand tools, different trades turned the boards into chairs, chests of drawers, coffins, and coaches. Over hundreds and in some cases thousands of years, the craftsmen who depended on these tools constantly refined them to be more efficient and accurate.

It is from these craftsmen that we have inherited an incredible wealth of hand tools. Which of these tools do you need, and how do you tell a good tool from a poor one? How do you tune and sharpen them? How do you use each tool, and what is it capable of? These are some of the questions this book will answer.

I started this book by making a list of all the hand tools I use, as well as some peculiar and interesting ones worth knowing about. The tools are organized according to their basic tasks, such as boring, sawing, and planing. I explain the most important tools in the greatest detail, including some of the stories about how they evolved or about the trades that adopted them. My favorites, planes, deserve a book in themselves (which is why I wrote *The Handplane Book*; The Taunton Press, 1997). You'll also find information about making your own tools, buying used ones and restoring them, and vignettes about contemporary tool makers and the best tool auction in the world.

I have two biases when it comes to tools. One is that I favor Western tools, because this is the tradition I learned within (I have also included some Eastern hand tools, however). My other bias is for older tools, beautiful shopmade or classic woodworking hand tools manufactured up until about World War II. Some are still available, although far fewer than the seemingly endless variety that once appeared on the pages of Stanley, Sargent, Miller's Falls, and other tool catalogs. Old tools have stories; I feel connected with their history through the handles polished over years of use, the patina of wear, and an owner's or maker's name stamped onto the tool.

Learning to use hand tools takes time and patience, but the rewards are enduring. With this book as your guide, I hope that you too will relish the pleasures of working by hand, at a friendly pace, in harmony with your tools and the material beneath them.

WESTFIELD TERRACE
SHEFFIELD
GENTLEMAN'S
OAK TOOL CHEST,
FITTED UP COMPLETE, WITH
Tools of Warranted Quality
NO. 3 CONTAINS
HANDSAW
HATCHET
HAMMER
MALLET
RULE
PINCERS
THREE BRADAWLS
THREE CHISELS
TWO GOUGES
THREE FILES
OIL STONE
MARKING AWL
PUNCH
TWO TURNSCREWS
SPOKESHAVE
SQUARE
CLAW WRENCH
COMPASSES
PLANE
FURNITURE, &c.

1

What Are HAND TOOLS?

Learning about hand tools and how to use them is part of the joy and pleasure of working wood. Hand tools are part of our rich and inventive history, just as useful today as they were vital to an 18th-century furniture maker working wood without machines. If there was a need to cut wood in some way, you can bet that someone devised a hand tool to do it. Their beauty only adds to the enjoyment of using hand tools.

Working with hand tools, I understand wood on a most intimate level—in a way I might easily miss working with machines alone. Each of my tools leaves its own texture upon the surface as one more detail, one further subtlety of the wood. It's no wonder that stunning planes, beautiful handsaws, and delicate chisels have become symbols of fine craftsmanship.

Marking gauges scribe fine lines parallel to an edge for laying out all kinds of joinery. The patented gauge on the right (1868) has two pivoting fingers for scribing around irregular curves; the one on the left (1864) has four stems for multiple settings.

Why Use Hand Tools?

With so many efficient woodworking machines available, why use hand tools? Quite simply, they are still the best tools for accomplishing many woodworking tasks. There are things that machines do well, such as surfacing and sizing rough boards to precise dimensions and cutting some joints, all with a lot less effort than would be required with a jack plane and other hand-powered tools. But it is the huge realm of working wood beyond machines—such as fitting common joints or cutting complex ones, planing surfaces to a polish, or splitting a log into parts for a chair and draw-knifing them to shape—where you can work more quickly, efficiently, and quietly with well-tuned tools powered by hand and body and guided by eye.

This might seem like a romantic vision of woodworking, and perhaps in a way it is, yet using hand tools is utterly practical. Generations of craftsmen have used and refined these tools, and I have no doubt that future generations will be using them as well. Learning what these tools are and where they came from is part of understanding hand tools. The rest is learning the skills and, by using them, gaining the confidence to pick up a dovetail saw and cut accurately to a line, to pare a tight-fitting joint with a chisel, or to plane a tabletop flat. Mastering one hand tool leads to success with others, and gradually to whole new ways of thinking and working.

Many hand tools will do multiple tasks, some better than others. I might pick up a shoulder plane to fit a joint, for example, while you might choose a paring chisel, and someone else a file. Each tool has advantages; no single tool is best. What tools you choose and how you use them is a matter of experience and personality. Few people use a tool in exactly the same way, or even agree on the basics of sharpening and tuning it. For me, this is what makes woodworking fun—to learn some new trick with a tool I thought I knew well, or to discover a clever tool I never even imagined.

Types of Tools

One of the advantages of hand tools is their versatility. Of course, some have very specific functions, but just as three woodworkers might pick up three different tools to fit a joint, most hand tools can do a range of different work. Still, they can be broadly grouped according to the work they perform: marking and measuring, striking, chiseling, planing, scraping, boring, and sawing. (This still leaves plenty of gray areas:

for example, dowel pointers and auger bits driven by a brace actually cut like little planes or chisels.)

MARKING AND MEASURING TOOLS

Marking and measuring tools—rules, squares, compasses, dividers, levels, marking gauges, bevel gauges, and chalklines—are the tools a woodworker uses to lay out cuts or joints. As construction proceeds, they are used for checking dimensions, aligning parts, or squaring up a frame or opening. Accuracy is important no matter what you are building, and marking and measuring tools are reliable guides.

STRIKING TOOLS

What could be simpler or more basic to woodworking than a hammer or an ax? But which hammer or ax is the right one to choose from the incredible variety? There are many such striking tools: wooden mauls for driving wooden nails into heavy frame construction; common claw hammers; axes and adzes for hewing and shaping; ball-peen hammers for metalsmithing, veneer hammers that aren't even used like hammers, and many others. Few of the specialized hammers and the trades that used them survive, but there are some new ones around, such as deadblow hammers and others with fiberglass heads and handles.

CHISELS

Chisels are all-purpose cutting tools. Chopping mortises and tenons, cutting recesses for hinges,

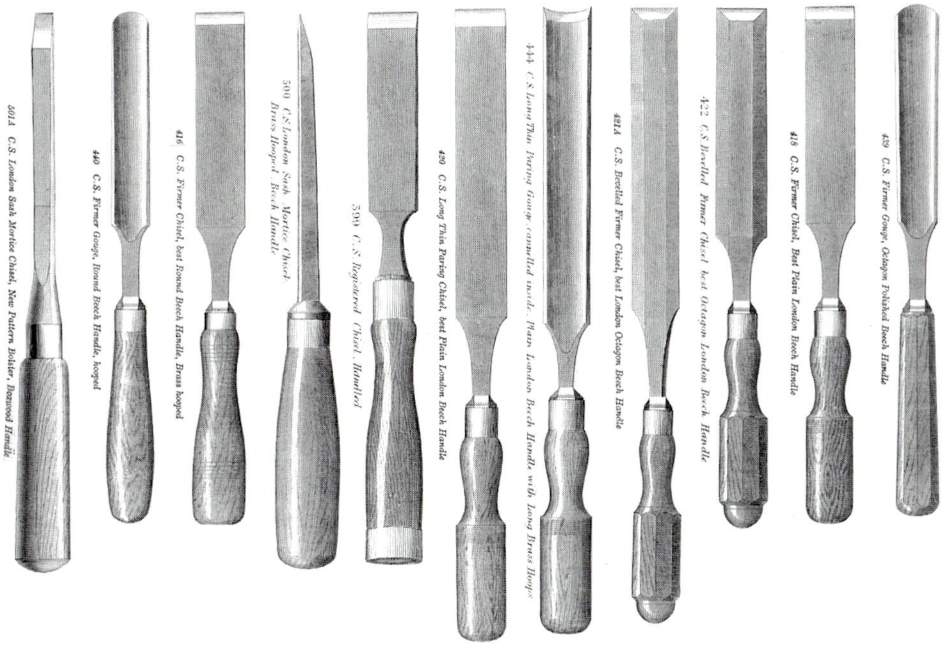

Chisels cut and fit joints and shape wood. The Sheffield Standard List of 1864 advertised a variety of first-class chisels with fancy handles, as well as carving gouges with curved cutting edges.

Planes are the most useful and beautiful of hand tools. These bench planes, which include a Norris #A6 smoother and Stanley Bedrocks #604, #605, and #607, can make delicate fitting cuts, shoot long straight edges, or flatten a surface to a polished sheen.

The rich texture of these hammer heads and handles belies the utilitarian function of this most basic tool. From dainty tack to persuasive sledge, hammers pound nails, yank bent ones, pick bungs (corks) out of barrels, clinch rivets, tap chisels, drive wooden pegs to attach shoe heels, and on and on.

Norris bullnose, shoulder, and chariot planes for fine-tuning joinery are among the most beautiful planes ever made—and the most rare today.

and doing all sorts of paring and fitting involved in woodworking joinery are just a few of their many uses. Curve a chisel's cutting edge and you have a gouge. A gouge is primarily a carving tool, but it can also be used for making or refining moldings, for coping joints, or for creating small details, such as pulls. Lengthen the cutting edge of a chisel, add two handles at right angles, and you have a drawknife, a tool indispensable to chairmakers and anyone who works green wood.

PLANES

Planes are sophisticated chisels. Take a chisel-like iron and wedge it into a wood or metal body and you have a plane, capable of everything from cutting rough boards into dimensioned stock to smoothing any surface to a glasslike polish. Planes are used to cut and fit a variety of joints, as well as to create decorative moldings and to do much more. An 18th-century joiner would have used wooden planes; the planes we use today have long-wearing metal soles and easy-to-use adjusters. Planes are not easy tools to master, but they are arguably the most useful hand tools ever devised for working wood.

SCRAPERS, FILES, AND RASPS

Instead of a plane's chisel iron and knifelike approach to the wood, scrapers work at a much higher angle with a tiny, hooked cutting edge burnished—not honed—onto the steel. The most basic scraper is simply a piece of flat steel about as thick as a handsaw blade, with either a straight edge for smoothing level surfaces, or profiled for scraping curved shapes, such as moldings. A scraper blade can be secured in a wood or iron holder (much like a

A scraper is as simple and versatile a tool as you can imagine. This elegant ebony spokeshave scraper, easy to hold and control, is ideal for smoothing a curve.

plane body) with a sole to guide the cut and handles for a good grip. Scrapers are simple and incredibly versatile tools, well worth learning the tricks to sharpen and use.

Files and rasps cut with a scraping action, employing everything from micro-fine file teeth to the pointed barbs on aggressive rasps. I use files mainly for sharpening and tuning other tools, and rasps for shaping curves or cutting in tight places where it's awkward to work with a plane or chisel.

BORING TOOLS

The ability to drill straight, smooth, and consistent holes is easy to take for granted, but for centuries simply devising the bits that could do this was a challenge in itself. Creating the turning power was never the problem—the simplest T-handle attached to an auger works fine, and sophisticated bow drills have been used since antiquity. The problem was designing an auger bit that could cut accurately, quickly, and without tremendous effort.

Inventive minds took up the challenge, improving early spoon-shaped and cylindrical nose bits to create twisted augers with spurs and chisel-like cutting lips and later modern brad-point and Forstner bits.

While power drills today are far more common than hand drills, a brace is still the best tool for drilling deep holes into bed rails for bed bolts, for driving screws when you need a lot of power, or for any boring where maximum control is

This elegantly boxed set of Russell Jennings "Precision Shank" twist bits (1855) slip securely into the ratcheting brace for boring quick and accurate holes.

From a tiny clockmaker's hacksaw to the sweeping blade of a Japanese pitsaw, handsaws are among the most versatile woodworking tools, able to cut with the grain or across it, in a straight line, or around a tight radius. They can cut everything from veneer straight from a log to the smallest keyhole.

essential. Chairmakers use bit braces to power hollow augers for cutting round tenons, and hand-driven dowel pointers for easing their ends.

SAWS

From the finest-toothed backsaw for cutting dovetails to coarse-toothed pitsaws for ripping logs into boards, no other woodworking tool does quite as much work as the simple handsaw. The teeth cut like miniature knives or chisels, slicing the fibers and chiseling out the waste. Disston, the most prolific of American saw makers, once made many hundreds of different saws and tooth configurations for every imaginable wood-cutting need.

Learning to use a saw efficiently and accurately is vital to becoming a skilled woodworker. Yes, you can rely on a table saw or bandsaw, as I do, for much of the drudgery of sawing. But build anything complex and you will immediately see the limitations of machines and the simplicity and beauty of a handsaw. The same can be said for any of these hand tools.

STEP BACK 3,500 years and hand a modern saw to an Egyptian carpenter. He might remark about its flexibility, its sharp teeth, and the unusual material for the handle (plastic), but he would know exactly how to use it. The same would be true for many other hand tools. Of course, there have been changes along the way, with constant tinkering and incremental improvements, but the fundamental designs have changed remarkably little over the centuries.

From Stones to Stanleys

Handsaws haven't always cut accurately and effortlessly; it's taken thousands of years to refine the temper and composition of the blade and the shape of the teeth. Such has also been the case with augers, planes, braces, axes, and even with tools as simple as hammers. Some evolved in a spurt of ingenuity—an entirely new tool took shape—but mostly they improved slowly, one step at a time, and even a step backward now and again. It's harder to see, but the process is just as dynamic today as it ever was, for someone will always be looking for a way to pry just a little bit more efficiency from a tool.

All tools were hand tools until quite recently. The first were undoubtedly pounding tools—hard rocks with the right shape and heft to chip other rocks into axes and scraping tools. Lashing the ax heads to a piece of bone or wood, man extended the natural movements of his hand and arm for greater force, and so evolved the first woodworking tools.

From there, the evolution of tools followed in the wake of a growing knowledge of metallurgy—the ability to smelt first copper and then copper and tin into bronze cutting edges. Neither made particularly

Oversized hand tools were sometimes used as advertising props, but all of these tools are capable of extra large work, such as filing the huge bearings of a steam engine.

Sometimes the line between hand tool and machine is hazy. This interesting device probably was made by a cooper, who cleverly attached a round-soled plane to rails in order to make his efforts hollowing pail staves more efficient and uniform. In the background is a stoup plane for doing similar work freehand.

Joiners and cabinetmakers took pride in their tools. Many carved and dated them, although rarely to the degree of this Dutch plane dated 1752.

durable edges, but amazingly—and this was about 5,000 years ago—Bronze Age man fashioned workable saws, chisels, augers, and adzes. Once mastered, the ability to smelt iron ore, heat and hammer it into wrought (worked) iron, and then harden it in a delicate tempering process yielded tough tool steel. Ultimately, this led to modern hand tools as we know them.

Well into the 19th century, until the beginning of the Industrial Revolution, a carpenter's tool kit was basic: a few chisels and gouges, three or four planes, a few saws, a hammer, an ax and a hatchet, an adze, and some measuring tools. These would have been wooden tools with few metal parts. Ironically, just as hand tools were being replaced by machines—planers, molders, and saws driven by water or steam—the Golden Age of hand tools flourished. Creative minds modified old tools and invented new ones (and patented them) to suit the factory worker.

The second half of the 19th century saw the growth of factory production and industrial know-how, spurred in part by the Civil War. New manufacturing processes such as casting, milling, and making batches of identical parts changed the way tools were designed and made. It didn't take long for Stanley Rule and Level Company to put this technology to work making its famous line of cast-iron Bailey bench planes, and Stanley was not alone. The onset of the industrial age produced an offering of woodworking tools more varied than we will likely ever see again. Hundreds of patents were taken out for tool improvements—from better chuck designs to the auger bits they held—and for whole new tools born of the mere challenge of designing them.

Particularly amusing are the all-in-one tools that tried (but usually failed) to do it all—a combination tool that included a hammer, pliers, screwdriver, wire cutter, wrench, pry bar, and leather punch, for example, or a single compact tool handle that came with various

The quality craftsmanship of an 18th-century joiner is all the more impressive when you consider how few tools he had to work with and how crude and simple they seem.

The Civil War introduced factory production and the manufacturing of multiple parts (25 different ones in this Bedrock #604 alone). This technology made Bailey and Bedrock planes, manufactured by Stanley Rule and Level Company, not only possible, but economical.

Footprint Tools of Sheffield, England, still makes some hand tools the traditional way, by pounding red-hot steel beneath mammoth drop hammers.

A TOOL FOR ANY POCKETBOOK

THE GOLDEN AGE of hand tools—the decades between the Civil War and World War II—not only spawned a huge variety of tools but also produced different versions of the same tool in a range of qualities and materials to suit any taste or pocketbook. Take, for example, what could be a simple tool: a gauge for spacing clapboards. A carpenter could fashion a perfectly adequate one from wood. For the masses, Stanley manufactured a shiny nickel-plated, adjustable steel gauge with the nice feature of a handle that turns sideways to push out a small tooth to hold the gauge and clapboard in place. A gentleman could buy a fancier version still, such as Nester's patented model made of walnut and golden brass. It had a graduated rule for fine adjustment, a built-in spirit level, and a marker for cutting clapboards tight to trim.

Hand tools were once offered in a range of materials to suit different tastes and budgets. The three versions of the clapboard gauge shown here are shopmade (right), nickel-plated steel (center), and a gentleman's model made of walnut and brass with built-in level and rule.

screwdriver bits and other small tools as attachments. A factory worker need only carry one of these multipurpose gadgets instead of the many tools they were meant to replace. The ultimate combination tool was Stanley's famous #45 and later #55 planes with interchangeable cutters that did the work of dozens of individual planes. These tools were dubiously successful, but the understanding of metallurgy and factory precision that made them possible also transformed common tools. Metals replaced wood, allowing previously impossible innovations, such as ratcheting corner braces and adjustable iron spokeshaves.

Hand tools have steadily improved, with more precise and easier adjustments, longer-wearing parts, stronger steels, and even a successful new design now and again. Tool improvements are still going on, although I didn't feel this way 25 years ago when I started buying tools. Back then the only good tools were secondhand Stanleys, long out of production as machines further shriveled the hand-tool market. I knew of only one hand-tool catalog, and almost nothing of the few tool companies still hanging on here and in England. Now it seems every year I hear about some new company starting to make specialty tools—and thriving. I still love my classic Stanleys, but there are some mighty appealing tools in all those catalogs I get these days. Maybe the Golden Age isn't quite over.

Charpentier. *Gravure de G. Vogel. XVII° siècle.*

Seventeenth-century French carpenters used crosscut saws to cut logs to length, broad axes to shape the heavy timbers, and chisels to cut mortises. Other carpenter tools lying against the logs to the right include a hatchet, squares, a bowsaw, and a chalkline for marking the cuts.

How HAND TOOLS CUT

Woodworking is all about cutting wood. It's no mystery, then, that most hand tools are cutting tools. Saws, planes, chisels, drill bits, and rasps all cut wood in some way: by sizing, smoothing, joining, or shaping. Yet as different as the tools and the work may seem, they're really not that different at all. The cutting edge of a chisel is the same as that of a plane, a drawknife, a drill bit, or an ax. That edge either cuts the fibers of the wood or splits them apart.

Cutting the fibers is far superior to splitting, which is difficult to control. Whether along the fibers (long grain) or across them (end grain), a cutting action produces the smoothest surface. But while it might be the ideal, some splitting is inevitable. The challenge is to keep it to a minimum.

Planes, especially tight-mouthed smoothers, favor controlled cutting of the wood fibers over splitting, producing an exceptionally smooth surface on the hardest of woods.

Aggressive chiseling with the grain is likely to split away some fibers rather than cut them, leaving a rough and uneven surface.

Cutting Dynamics

Many factors affect the results you will get with a tool. It might not be the right tool for the job. You might be using it ineffectively. The cutting bevel—the angle of the cutting edge—might be too fine or too large, or the cutting edges might not be sharp. A general understanding of how a tool cuts, with a beveled edge peeling off a shaving, will help you avoid some of these problems.

A sharp edge slices the fibers, whereas a dull one drives into them like a wedge. (Only in true splitting tools such as an ax or a froe is semi-sharpness a virtue.) A thin, knife-like cutting edge is ideal for slicing the fibers without wedging and splitting them apart. But a thin, sharp edge is also fragile and prone to chipping. Conversely, a large bevel is tougher, but it wedges and splits the fibers apart before the actual cutting edge does much cutting. A large bevel also takes considerably more force to drive into the wood. The compromise between these two extremes—the ideal bevel angle—depends on what kind of work you expect from the tool.

Take chisels, for example. A paring chisel has the finest of bevels (as small as 15°) because it is designed for light cuts and to be pushed gently and carefully by hand. A mortise chisel needs a greater bevel (about 30°) to cut tough end grain and withstand powerful mallet blows. Somewhere between the two are firmer chisels, which are pushed by hand and driven by mallet. In just about every wood-cutting tool, the

CUTTING DYNAMICS

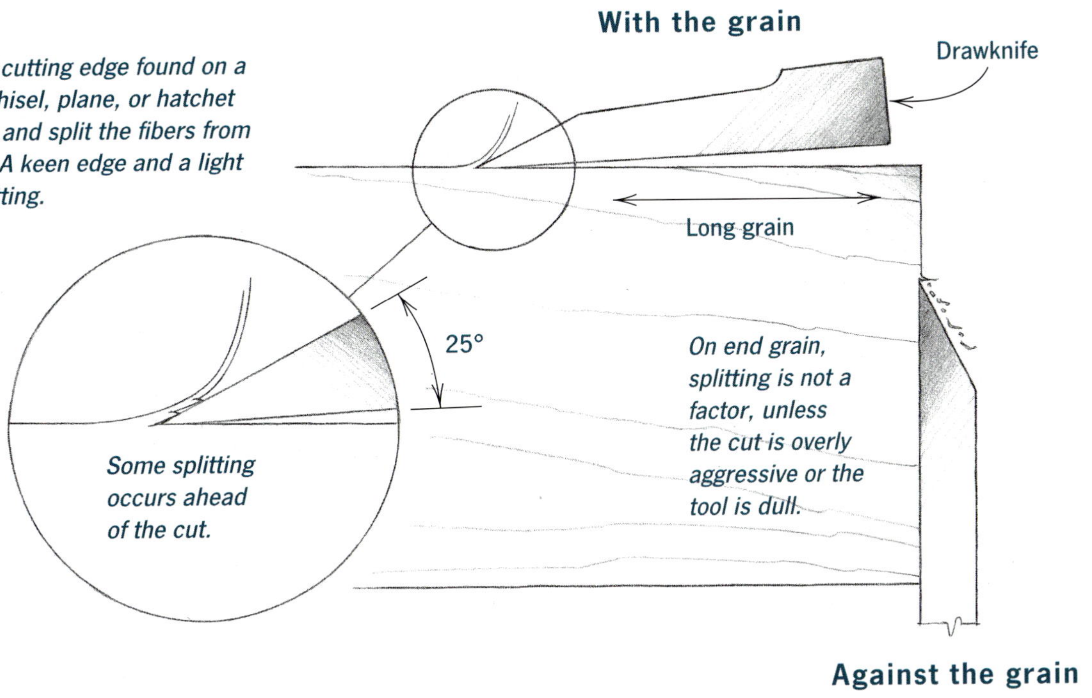

ideal cutting bevel lies somewhere between the two extremes of 15° and 30°, for the simple reason that the physics of cutting wood remain constant (see the photo on p. 16).

Plane irons have similar bevel angles as chisels, but the way the wood experiences the bevel gives them a higher degree of cutting control. The difference is that the iron is wedged into place at an angle to the guiding sole: the bed angle. Some planes have a low angle, nearly equal to a chisel, and some have high angles, 60° or more (see the photo at left on p. 20). Common bench planes have a bed angle of 45°. The wood experiences this bed angle no differently than a cutting-edge bevel angle of 45°, with the same resistance to the cut and potential for splitting. But what is not the same is that a plane has a throat, which effectively controls the cutting action.

As the shaving is cut, it's driven into the throat of the plane. The iron acts as a ramp for the shaving, levering it against the front of the throat. This levering action breaks the shaving repeatedly, which is what makes the shaving curl (see the photo at right on p. 20). Equally important, the sole of the plane ahead of the throat pushes down on the fibers, reducing the potential for splitting ahead of the cut. The actions of the sole and throat together favor cutting over splitting, explaining why planes can leave a smooth

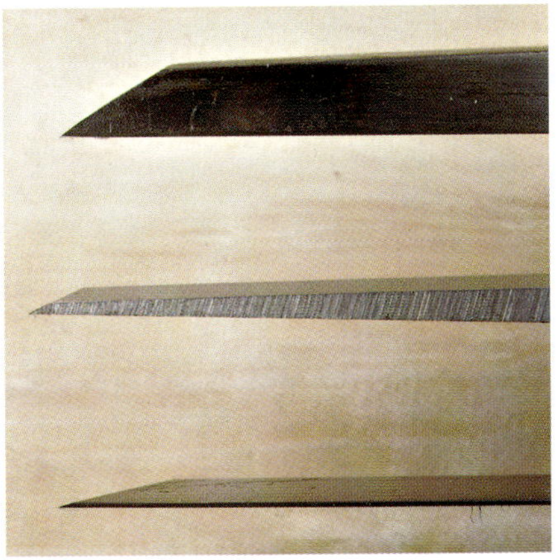

Chisel bevel angles range from a 15° bevel for a delicate paring chisel (bottom), to a tougher 30° bevel for a mortise chisel (top), used for chopping hard end grain. A firmer chisel (center) has a bevel angle somewhere between the two for varied bench work.

Plane bed angles vary, from an extremely low angle for slicing end grain (foreground) to a high angle for tough hardwoods (center), or somewhere in between the two for general-purpose bench work (rear).

As a shaving is cut and forced into the throat of a spokeshave, the cutter levers it against the front of the throat. The shaving breaks repeatedly (noticeable as tiny parallel ridges) and curls.

finish. In tough hardwoods, a high-angle plane is ideal—it curls and breaks the shaving more abruptly, with even less chance of splitting or tearing.

In theory, a low bed angle would seem to be an advantage, especially in softer woods. This is often the case, but what can also happen is that the iron drives into the fibers and some splitting goes on before the shaving can be levered and broken. As a result, low-angle planes are designed to cut end grain, where splitting is less of a problem and a low cutting approach is an advantage.

Many other tools have chisel-like cutting edges. The cutting lips of an auger bit are actually tiny chisels (you have to look closely to see them), and a ripsaw has chisel teeth, too. With each saw stroke the chisel-like teeth scrape and pare tiny shavings from the bottom of the kerf. Those same teeth are less effective across the grain, because they cut and tear at the fibers in exactly the same way as a chisel cutting across the grain. This is why the teeth of a crosscut saw are not chisels, but rather beveled knives that score and slice the fibers. An auger bit, on the other hand, must cut across the grain half the time and with the grain half the time. The chisel-like lips would tear out badly cutting cross-grain if it weren't for an added bit of sophistication: small knifelike spurs similar to crosscut saw teeth, that score the fibers ahead of the cut.

SKEWING THE CUTTING EDGE

There are no rules when it comes to choosing the best tool, although experience helps. Ultimately each piece of wood is different, and you won't know exactly how it will respond to a tool until you start working it. But whether you are cutting long grain or end grain, skewing the cutting edge introduces

Skewing the cutting tool (in this case, a drawknife) adds a slicing action for a better cut with less effort.

a slicing action that is almost always an advantage.

With tools such as an auger bit or an ax, you've got little control of the cutting edge once it's started into the cut. But with a chisel, plane, or drawknife, you can angle the cutting edge in relation to the force and direction of the cut. Simply skewing 10° requires noticeably less effort and produces less tearout.

A skew cut is not directly into the fibers (it's askew), adding the valuable element of slicing. It's no different than cutting a carrot with a kitchen knife with a forward and downward slicing action, which is much smoother and easier than chopping straight down. A skewed chisel or plane iron isn't taking quite as wide a cut as it could, so there is less pressure against the cutting edge. Less force is needed to drive the tool. Plus, the wood "sees" a slightly lower bevel angle (because the cutting force is diagonally across the bevel and not directly into it). It's like angling your way across a steep slope rather than attacking it straight up.

Sharpening

Dull tools are nothing but constant frustration. They work poorly, tire you needlessly, and on top of that, they can be dangerous (because you will push too hard and possibly slip). It should go without saying, then, that the only way to gain confidence with hand tools is first to become confident at sharpening them. You will need a few good stones, a comfortable sharpening station, a basic knowledge of what you are after and how to get there, and a fair bit of patience. It helps

A sharpening station should be a place you don't mind getting a little messy. You should have everything you need close at hand: a grinder, stones, honing oil or water, rags, and good light.

This quiet honing station has excellent natural light and enough space for both waterstones (left) and oilstones (right). The large bottle contains soapy water to lubricate the waterstones.

to relax, too. Your first attempts may not be perfect, but unless you are overzealous with a grinder, you're not going to ruin any tools by trying.

Some days I'll sharpen half a dozen times, spending only a few minutes each time to hone a few chisels or a couple of plane irons. I can't say it's my favorite part of woodworking, but I never fail to notice how much better a sharp tool feels, and how much easier it is to use. Sharpening often—and sharpening a few tools at once—is more efficient and makes this task less of a chore.

You can learn a lot about sharpening by careful observation. Before you start grinding or honing, look at the bevel angle of the cutting edge. Try to think about how the tool is designed to cut. Recently I was sharpening an old reamer, and even though I knew that the beveled outside edge does the cutting, I didn't know the proper angle. Understanding the basics of how the tool works and following what was there, I sharpened the bevel to cut respectably. Sharpening this way sometimes can be a bit of trial and error, gradually tuning the tool until it works for a particular task. Luckily, the range of what works is quite wide.

Whether you are working with a new tool or a secondhand one, sharpening usually proceeds in stages: from grinding the bevel to lapping the back and finally honing the bevel and back to a polished, sharp edge. What follows is general enough to apply to many tools; more specific sharpening tips are included in each chapter.

If sharpening is comfortable and convenient, you'll be more likely to stop what you're doing and sharpen or just "touch up" your tools. Create a sharpening station close to your workbench with everything you need (see the photos at left). Ideally, you should have a separate area that can get a little messy (it will), excellent light, a mechanical grinder, and a few benchstones.

GRINDING THE BEVEL

Like other machines in the shop, a mechanical grinder speeds sharpening by doing the heavy work that can be tedious by hand alone. You can get by without a grinder, doing the work on a coarse stone, a diamond lapping plate, or a fine file (for softer axes and adzes), but tool steel is tough. Save your time and energy for when it counts: honing the edge to sharpness on a benchstone.

There are plenty of commercial grinders on the market, ranging in quality and cost, and any one of them probably will work fine. I've used an oil-lubricated horizontal grinder, a benchtop version of an old sandstone clunker, and many common commercial grinders, all with good results. My current grinder is basic, even funky, but entirely functional. It's nothing more than an old ¼-hp motor from a washing machine that drives a simple arbor with a pair of coarse and fine stones. The tool rest is wood. It's just a little more advanced than the ancient, foot-cranked sandstone wheel lubricated by the steady drip from a tin can suspended above it, which I use for large tools such as my broad ax and drawknives.

A grinder is useful for bringing a dull tool (or one with a chipped edge) back to sharpness quickly. In addition to sharpening, a grinder can also shape a cutting edge (a cambered plane iron or scratch tool, for example) or restore the proper bevel angle. (A quick guide to a basic 25° bevel is a 2:1 ratio of bevel length to the thickness of the iron.) Besides sharpening, I use a grinder for tuning other metal parts on my hand tools and machines, and sometimes for making new ones.

Hollow grinding

A grinder speeds sharpening, particularly honing, by grinding a slight hollow across the edge bevel. Honing then becomes a task of removing metal from the cutting edge and the heel of the bevel, rather than across the entire bevel. The argu-

WHEN CHOOSING a grinder, look for a few basics: a slow speed (1,750 rpm, if possible) so there is less chance of overheating the tool from friction; a solid, adjustable rest; and coarse and fine stones at least 6 in. to 8 in. in diameter. Buy yourself a diamond or less expensive wheel-type dresser for keeping your stones true and sharp. If you have some money left, buy a couple of cool-grinding white aluminum-oxide wheels.

HOLLOW GRINDING

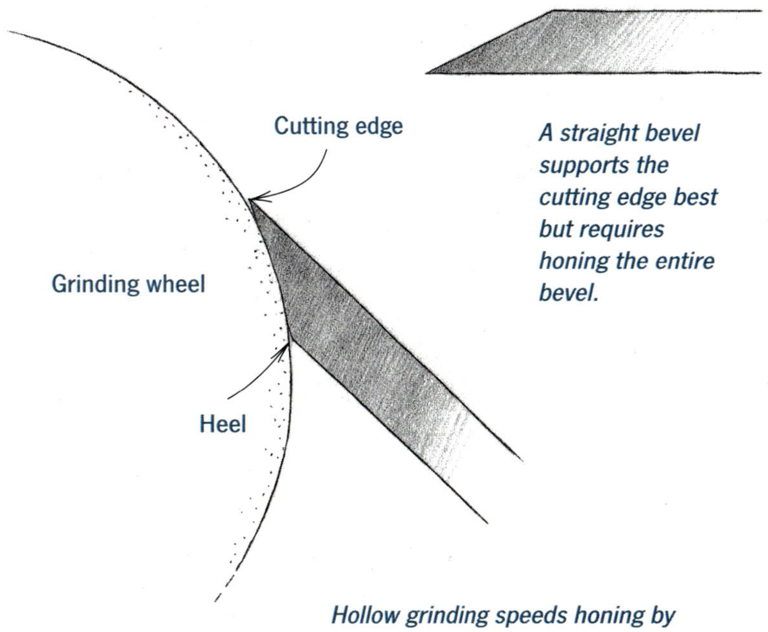

A straight bevel supports the cutting edge best but requires honing the entire bevel.

Hollow grinding speeds honing by removing metal in the center of the bevel, while preserving the overall bevel angle and the honed cutting edge.

The chisel on the right is ready for a light grinding to renew the hollow across the bevel. The one on the left is just off the grinder. Grind as little as possible for the longest tool life.

ment against hollow grinding is that if the hollow is too deep, such as one cut by a small-diameter grindstone, the cutting edge will be thin and weak. This is especially true with Japanese laminated edge tools, where the very hard steel cutting edge needs the support of a wide, flat bevel.

With any tool, my approach is to grind close to the cutting edge but leave some of the polished edge remaining. This preserves the shape of the edge, if there is any (such as a gently cambered smoothing plane iron), and it minimizes the amount of steel removed so the tool lasts longer. It also leaves a bevel wide enough to support the cutting edge.

LAPPING THE BACK

Every cutting edge has two faces: a beveled side and a back. The beveled edge gets all the attention, even though the back makes up half the cutting edge. Therefore, the back should be every bit as polished as the bevel (see the photo below), and in most tools it should be flat. There are exceptions, of course, such as axes sharpened with two bevels and drawknives that some craftsmen prefer to round slightly on the back for better control. Even with curved cutting edges, such as a gouge, the back is still flat, even if it might be curved along the length of the tool.

ONE WORD OF CAUTION about grinding: It's easy to ruin a cutting edge quickly. If you heat the edge enough to discolor the steel, you will alter the temper. The edge might sharpen, but it won't last. Grind only until the tool begins to warm (the fine edge heats most quickly) and then let it cool in the air. No part should be uncomfortable to the touch. Avoid the need to quench in water; this causes microscopic cracks in the cutting edge.

For a truly sharp edge, the back or nonbeveled side of a cutting edge should be just as polished as the beveled side.

A flat back serves at least two purposes. In a chisel, the flat back guides the tool in a straight line. If the back was even slightly bowed from handle to cutting edge, the chisel would tend to cut in a curve and would be difficult to control. A flat back also makes sharpening chisels, plane irons, and other cutting edges easier. There is no guesswork to laying the back flat on a stone and honing away.

To maintain a flat back on your cutting tools, you will need a lapping table. Think of a lapping table as a large, coarse bench stone. It can be used not only for flattening the backs of cutters but also for maintaining the soles of planes and benchstones. Lapping tables can be as simple as a sheet of 120-grit aluminum-oxide paper (or finer) stuck with spray adhesive to a piece of ¼-in. (or thicker) plate glass. An alternative is to sprinkle silicon-carbide grit on the glass and lubricate with water or kerosene. Plate glass should be dead flat, but use your lapping table on the bed of a table saw or jointer for extra support.

Start lapping your plane iron or chisel with 120-grit aluminum-oxide paper. Move through successive grits so that at each stage the back has a uniform polish at least ½ in. wide behind the cutting edge. Use light pressure to avoid deforming your cutter (which is possible), and keep the back flat on the lapping table (avoid the temptation to tip the tool to polish closer to the cutting edge). Bring the back to a higher polish on your sharpening stones in the same way.

TWO BEVELS OR ONE?

ALL CUTTING EDGES have two faces, and most of the time only one face is beveled. The other is honed flat to optimize its ability to cut and, in the case of a chisel, to guide the tool in a straight line. But there are some tools that cut with two bevels, such as axes, froes, and knives. Two edge bevels are quicker and easier to sharpen, because you don't have to worry about honing the back flat.

So why not do the same on a plane iron or drawknife? You can hone a back bevel by lifting the cutter slightly, rather than keeping it flat on the stone. A tiny back bevel (in a tool such as a bench plane, which cuts with the bevel down) can even be an advantage in cutting figured woods, because it steepens the angle of the cutting edge in relation to the work. The problem is that it is easy to get lazy and hone the back bevel a little higher each time, gradually changing the cutting dynamics for the worse.

HONING THE BEVEL AND BACK

Honing the bevel and back on benchstones is the final stage in sharpening a cutting edge. An edge off the grinder, coarse stone, lapping table, or fine file can feel sharp, but magnified it looks serrated and rough. Using progressively finer stones, any grinding marks and microscopic grooves left by the previous stone are honed away, creating a smooth, sharp and long-lasting edge.

Not long ago all stones were natural, quarried from the earth for their particular ability to cut tool steel. Natural stones have uniform and tough grit particles weakly bonded together so that new abrasive particles are constantly exposed (but not so soft that the stone will erode easily with wear). Buy new

A lapping table made with silicon-carbide powder or a sheet of abrasive paper on plate glass is ideal for flattening chisel backs, plane soles, and sharpening stones.

SHARPENING STONES

NATURAL STONES, man-made oil or waterstones, ceramic stones, diamond stones, and diamond paste on a cast-iron plate—there is certainly a bewildering variety of sharpening possibilities. Are they all that different? Not really. Some cut faster, some wear quickly and require frequent maintenance, some are messy, but the truth is they all share the ability to sharpen and polish cutting edges. Try different ones. Learn to use what you choose—how to get a good edge on them and how to maintain them. Most important, use them often.

Natural stones are found all over the world, with exotic names to match: Washita, Turkey, Charnley Forest, Tam O'Shanter. Even the little New England town where I live has an outcropping of novaculite slate (similar to better-known Arkansas stones). Natural stones have a consistent, silky feel and work wonderfully. Their only disadvantage is that they can be quite expensive. (Keep your eyes out at a flea market for an old one that just needs a good cleaning and flattening.)

Some of the many stones the author uses: black Arkansas, Belgian, and other natural stones, along with man-made India and diamond-impregnated stones. Some work with light oil, others with water.

Less costly and nearly as impressive are man-made stones manufactured from synthetic or natural grits. Man-made stones designed to work with oil as a lubricant tend to wear more slowly and need less maintenance than fast-cutting and quick-wearing waterstones. You can buy special honing oils, use kerosene as I prefer, or even try olive oil or light machine oil.

Diamond stones have a layer of microscopic diamonds bonded to a steel plate or other backing. They come in a range of mostly coarse and medium grits well-suited for lapping the backs of cutters, flattening other stones which have worn hollow, and restoring nicked edges. Diamond stones stay flat and last a long time (monocrystaline diamonds longer than polycrystaline), but they don't last forever. Lately I have been making my own diamond stones from 10-micron and 4-micron diamond paste spread on a cast-iron plate.

Ceramic stones are relatively new. They have the look and feel of porcelain, are quite fine, and are best suited for the final honing and polishing of an edge. These stones need no lubricant and maintenance other than an occasional flattening and rinsing with water.

stones today and you're more likely to get man-made stones that mimic natural stones, or diamond-impregnated "stones" (they're not really stones at all). Whether a stone is natural or man-made, it usually requires some sort of lubrication, generally water or oil, to flush the surface of spent grit and steel particles (*swarf* as it's known). Both water- and oilstones, whether natural or man-made, have their advantages and disadvantages (see the sidebar above). Whatever you choose, you will need a coarse, medium, and fine grit and individual lidded boxes to keep them clean and protected.

Natural or man-made slipstones hone curved or small edges such as gouges and molding-plane irons. Many useful shapes are available, but if need be, you can shape your own against a diamond stone.

Honing is the hardest part of sharpening to master. The challenge is to hold the cutting bevel at a consistent angle to the stone while moving it back and forth. Some rocking around is unavoidable, but this slows sharpening because sometimes you're honing on the back of the bevel, sometimes on the cutting edge. With large tools such as a drawknife, it's easier to hone by bringing the stone to the tool. And for honing curved cutting edges, such as gouges and molding plane irons, you'll need a few shapes of slipstones. (You can make your own by wrapping a dowel or other shape with a strip of fine abrasive paper.)

I've seen some wild honing techniques, from long back-and-forth strokes to jitterbugging all over the stone. Whatever technique you use, it's important to relax. I start by rocking the tool on the stone to feel the bevel, then I loosely lock my arms and wrists when I feel I am right on it. I then start stroking in loose figure eights up and down the stone, using nearly all of the stone to wear it evenly. A natural tendency is to work in the same pattern which, over time, puts a slightly skewed edge on the tool rather than a square one. This isn't necessarily bad, but in some planes, any skew makes the cutter harder to set parallel with the sole. Simply working in a reverse figure eight half the time keeps the cutting edges square.

Some craftsmen hone on a small "microbevel" (about 5°) on the cutting bevel by lifting the cutter slightly and honing the very tip of the edge more heavily. It's a natural thing to do anyway, and speeds sharpening somewhat. The advantage of a microbevel is that the cutting edge is tougher, albeit steeper, but the overall bevel has not changed.

With the bevel honed, hone the back of the cutter by keeping it dead flat on the stone. Resist the temptation to lift the rear of the cutter and hone just the cutting edge. I've seen this done with plane irons—essentially honing on a back bevel—but if you do this with a chisel, it will not cut true. Once the back is evenly polished on your finest stone, there should be no reason to go back to a coarser stone.

As you might expect, there are all kinds of jigs and fixtures available to take the guesswork out of honing, but I don't think you need any of them. Honing will feel awkward at first, but down the road relying on your hand and eye to guide you will be every bit as accurate, and much faster.

A piece of leather charged with rouge, an extremely fine abrasive, makes a good strop for the final honing of curved or straight cutting edges.

WORKSHOPS, *Benches, and Clamps*

For most craftsmen, there's no place they'd rather be than in their workshop. It's a place to be creative, to make piles of shavings and scraps, or to seek quiet refuge from the demands of daily life. You too will need a shop space, for no matter how wonderful your collection of hand tools, they're not worth a lot unless you have a place to use them. A shop for using hand tools doesn't have to be big, as long as you have good lighting, a sturdy workbench, and a convenient way to store your tools.

A bench is the heart of any shop, the most useful of all tools. A few planks or a sheet of plywood on sawhorses can suffice for a simple bench—at least until you get around to building a proper one. For that, you'll want to install a vise or two and learn a few tricks with clamps and specialty vises for holding unusual projects.

Light from skylights reflects off the white walls to illuminate the bench and sharpening station (at left). Tools are stored on shelves, in an old chest, and hung from nails and racks.

clamps on wall racks, drawers of hardware and more tools, and all of the things I need less often. My bench is in a corner about 4 ft. from each wall, lit from two sides by four large windows. The organization and layout of my workspace took many years to refine and it's still evolving. Some days I think about how nice it would be to have a bench area completely separate from all the dusty machines.

Whatever your circumstances, take the time to create a good working environment for yourself; it is the key to working productively with hand tools or machines. Whether you are there to make a living or just for the pure pleasure of being creative, make your shop a place you want to spend time.

Workshops

Workshops are as different as the craftsmen that use them and the work they do there. I've been in tiny shops so organized and efficient that every cubic inch was used. Others I've seen have been as vast as small factories. Two advantages of working with hand tools are that they take up less space than machines, and they are so quiet that even a spare bedroom could be made into a workshop. But no matter how much space you have to work with, you'll need some basic organization of your space, your tools, and your materials.

The most important element of any workshop is your bench and the area immediately around it. While a bench secured to a wall is sturdy, a freestanding bench allows you to work around all four sides, which comes in handy for large projects. Give yourself enough space to joint long boards without running into anything. A large area nearby is ideal for a couple of sawhorses to set work upon, or to spread out parts in various stages of construction. This leaves your bench uncluttered. Make your tools accessible: Put them in hanging cabinets nearby, in drawers built into the base of your bench (which adds to its stability), on shelves, or in banks of drawers along a wall.

My shop is divided in half, with a bench and extra space for ongoing projects at one end. At the other end are my machines, wood storage,

LIGHTING

Lighting in a workshop is often an afterthought, but it shouldn't be. Good lighting is vital to working with any tools, but especially hand tools. Choose a spot for your bench that has the best natural light. Long before my shop was finished, I knew exactly where I wanted to put my bench—in the southeast corner that has consistent light all day long.

Natural light is preferable for a number of reasons. It is the most even light, especially when you have more than one window. Even lighting creates few shadows and best illuminates your tool and your work, allowing you to do things by day that are far more difficult with artificial light at night. Natural light also is more restful, even though at times it can be glaring and hard to

TOOL STORAGE

ONCE YOU HAVE a workbench and you start to use hand tools—even if you use machines primarily—you'll need to store all the tools you accumulate. It's best if they are near your bench; after all, that's where you'll use most of them. And while there are lots of creative storage solutions—whole books on the subject, in fact—they basically can be broken down into drawers, shelves, and hanging racks.

Drawers, shelves, and racks make every cubic inch of this tool chest accessible and organized. Cabinet doors seal out dust.

The traditional solution is a tool chest with many fitted compartments and drawers for specific tools. It's a great idea, but not always easy to use. I prefer drawers—lots of drawers of various depths to suit tools of different sizes and heights. Tools stored one deep are easy to find quickly and can be protected from one another by simple dividers (strips of wood glued to the drawer bottom, for instance). Tools in drawers stay clean and are somewhat protected from moisture and swings in temperature that will cause metal parts to sweat and rust.

Shelves are like open drawers and are just as useful, except that your tools will get dusty. Shelves are a great way to store planes, when all you need to see is the end view to choose the right one. As with drawers, make shelves of different heights and not more than one or two tools deep. A couple of tips from experience: It's easier to find a tool on a shelf when it is well below eye level, and shelves made from closely spaced dowels stay cleaner because they allow shavings and dust to pass through.

Hanging tools from racks or nails driven into the walls near your bench works fine, too. Racks with holes are better for small tools, such as chisels and auger bits, and you can see at a glance when tools are missing. Peg racks are an easy way to store saws, drawknives, spokeshaves, and anything else with a hole in the handle. At one end of my shop I have a huge rack specifically for all the different clamps I use.

control. Make natural adjustments to your habits. After spending some time at your bench, for example, you will discover when the lighting is best for cutting dovetails. Every shop should have some natural light, even if it is nothing more than a couple of high narrow windows throwing light into a basement shop. On a purely emotional level, even one window gives you a view to rest your eyes and sense the day outside.

Even if you have fantastic natural light pouring into every corner of your shop, you'll still need some artificial light. Overhead light is a

and down the entire length there are holes for bench pins or dogs. Made of beech, the top is almost 3 in. thick, heavy, and solid. I bought the hardware for the end vise, which took me as long to build and fit as the entire bench took to make. The legs have strong mortise-and-tenon joinery and they are well braced. The only maintenance it needs is an occasional flattening with a jointer plane, and a coat of linseed oil every year.

A bench's height—typically between 34 in. and 36 in.—is more important than its other dimensions. A bench that's too high will be uncomfortable for hand-planing for any length of time. It will also be more tiring, because less of your upper body will be providing power. On the other hand, bench height for chiseling and sawing is less im-

good start. Fluorescent lights are the least expensive and produce an even light, but I prefer incandescents, which mimic sunlight more closely. At times you'll also need a raking light to see surface details—when planing across a tabletop, for example. For sawing dovetails, I prefer light from behind. A light on a movable arm right over the bench works well, as does a clamp-on light. It's best to have a few options for the most flexibility.

Workbenches

Everyone has an opinion about what makes the ideal workbench. Some woodworkers are content working on a large flat table and using clamps instead of a vise. Others prefer a long bench with multiple vises. Nevertheless, there are a few bench basics most would agree on: a flat top of modest width but long, rock-solid construction, and at least one but preferably two vises. Many modern benches are based on a versatile traditional European woodworking bench, which has a large side vise, an end vise with dogs for clamping work flat upon the benchtop, and a narrow tool till or recess running the length of the bench.

I built my own bench based on the one I learned upon, because at the time I knew no better design. It's 7 ft. 8 in. long, 29 in. wide (including a narrow tool till running the entire length), and 35 in. high. On the front, at one end, I have an old cast-iron side vise. At the other end, there is a heavy end or tail vise,

The large end or tail vise on the author's bench clamps work securely between wooden dogs, leaving him with both hands free to control the tool.

portant. There are certain rules of thumb about the proper height of a bench—one is that the bench should be as high as your wrists when you're standing with your arms hanging—but it really comes down to personal preference. Try out a temporary bench with sawhorses and boards, or work at different table heights to see what feels comfortable. A bench too low is better than one that's too high—and it's easy to remedy by jacking it up with a board or two under the legs.

A bench doesn't have to be fancy to work well, so don't think you have to spend a small fortune to buy the best. I know cabinetmakers who work on the most basic of benches half the size of mine. You can make a perfectly acceptable bench by laminating plywood or planks together to build up a couple of inches (or more) of thickness. Set this on some legs that are mortised, bolted, or securely nailed and braced together, and you've got a strong and stable work surface. You can buy a ready-made benchtop, too. Just be careful that you don't make the bench too long without bracing the top (or making it thicker), because it could sag and cause you endless problems. I highly recommend building your own bench—it's a wonderful project.

Don't do heavy pounding or mortising in a vise—you risk damaging it. Instead, put the work on top of the bench, a much more stable surface. In this case, two clamps—a handscrew and a holdfast—secure the work.

BENCH VISES

The purpose of a vise is to secure your work in the right position so that you have two free hands to power and control the tool. A vise can also serve as a clamp for gluing or assembly. The simplest vise is a side vise, a two-jawed affair that bolts onto the side or end of a bench and clamps shut with either a quick-action screw or a traditional screw. The advantage of the quick-action screw is that, with a half-turn of the handle or lever, you can slide the movable jaw in or out, and then crank it up tight. There are lots of other versions of this vise, with wooden screws instead of metal, double screws, or one or more bars to guide the vise parallel with the fixed jaw.

You don't need a massive side vise, nor one that opens more than 8 in. to 10 in. Do buy the best vise you can afford, however, not one of the small homeowner types you're likely to find in a local hardware store. Add wooden jaws, not only to avoid marring your work but also to save a tool edge if you slip. My side vise gets a lot of use holding boards on edge so I can joint edges, mortise in hinges, or pare a joint—all relatively light cutting with generally parallel-sided stock. A side vise is also ideal for holding boards with curved or uneven edges that would not lie flat on a bench. Heavy pounding on a vise can ruin it, so

Pairs of half bench hooks are a stable way to hold boards just above the benchtop for sawing tenons or planing tenon shoulders. You also can butt work against wooden dogs that fit into the holdfast holes.

Protect your benchtop from sharp tools by using a board or bench hook for chiseling small pieces (such as this inlay). The raised back makes a nice stop for planing, sawing, or chiseling small work.

If you are holding work in one side of a vise, place a scrap block on the opposite side for even clamping pressure and to avoid racking the screw. To help support large panels, add a bar clamp across the benchtop.

for work such as chopping joints, use the top of your bench; it is more stable, anyway (see the photo on p. 33). And for tapered work or awkward shapes that require creative shimming to secure in a side vise, clamp them to your benchtop with bar clamps or a holdfast.

I do a lot of light sawing in my side vise, such as cutting dovetails with the work clamped upright. A common problem with this setup is that most of the time the board has to be clamped to one side of the vise screw. As soon as you snug up the jaws, they rack out of parallel, stressing the screw. The jaws don't hold anything very securely this way, either. One solution is to clamp a block, about the same thickness as your work, in the other side of the jaw, as shown in the bottom photo at left. (Drive a brad into the block to keep it from falling out every time you loosen the vise.) I keep different sizes of blocks on hand in my bench till (this is one good reason to have a till). If you do a lot of this type of work, you might consider buying or making a two-screwed side vise large enough to clamp wide boards between the screws.

Whatever side vise you choose, make sure to mount it with the fixed jaw flush with the front vertical edge of your benchtop. That way you can clamp a long board into your side vise (for jointing, for instance; see pp. 115–118) and the front edge of the bench will give the board extra stability. This also allows you to clamp the far end of the board against the front edge of the bench with a bar clamp.

Besides a side vise of some kind, benches in the European tradition have an additional end or tail vise. After working with one for as long as I can remember, I cannot imagine an easier and more stable way to clamp work upon a benchtop. The clamping action is between two bench dogs or pins, one in the end vise and the other somewhere along the bench surface. (This is why a long bench is helpful.) The sliding end vise also forms a small but powerful clamping vise within the benchtop (see the photo on p. 32).

You can make or buy end vises with double screws and double pins or buy just the hardware and make your own. Either way, you'll need to mortise or drill holes for bench dogs about 6 in. apart. The dogs can be as simple as a length of 1-in. dowel, or rectangular dogs with a built-in spring to hold them at any height. Stick with wooden dogs over metal ones; they are easily shaped to fit odd work, quickly replaced, and a lot gentler on tools.

No matter how well made or well fitted an end vise, the wooden jaws will eventually sag slightly below the surface of the benchtop. You can level everything with a jointer plane, although a little sag isn't a big problem, as long as any work clamped to the benchtop is supported on the bench and not on the movable jaw of the vise. It is more stable this way, too. Sometimes this setup requires taking up slack with a scrap block between the movable jaw and the work (see the photo on p. 32). When using any vise (especially an end vise), just snug the vise enough to hold the piece; too much pressure can easily deform your work.

Holdfasts and bench stops are alternatives to an end vise. A holdfast is a quick-clamping arm mortised into holes along the benchtop to secure work on the top of the bench (see the top photo on p. 36). A stop is simply a fixed bench dog that

A VERSATILE VISE

THE EMMERT VISE is an unusual side vise that's a useful addition to any shop, especially if you work with a lot of oddly shaped pieces, as patternmakers do. (The wooden patterns they make for casting metals can be almost any shape imaginable.) The jaws of this vise clamp out of parallel, and they have double bench pins for clamping large pieces flat on the benchtop; the entire vise rotates 360°, tilts, and locks in any position. Versatile, you might say.

The Emmert patternmaker's vise swivels, tilts, locks in any position, and clamps odd shapes with pivoting jaws.

A holdfast is a quick and secure way to hold work upon the benchtop. Traditional holdfasts slide into a hole and hammer tight; this one works quietly with a screw.

A small carver's vise such as this benchtop model has a table with a screw for attaching the carving. The table turns and tilts, locking at any angle you need. The ebony block ready to be carved will be a decorative finial.

works as a single point to butt work against when planing or chiseling. You can use it alone or in combination with a holdfast for added stability. There are steel stops, sometimes with little teeth to help grip the work, that are mortised into the benchtop (usually on the left end) and flip down when not in use. The simplest is a tight-fitting wooden dog that can be tapped up or down. Bench stops take some getting used to, but they are a wonderfully quick and simple way to hold work.

SPECIALTY VISES

If you plan on doing some carving or making a Windsor chair, it's worth knowing about carver's vises and shaving horses. Three-dimensional carvings (as opposed to flat carvings, such as signs) are often too awkwardly shaped to clamp easily onto a bench. The simplest solution is to use a carver's screw that fastens into the bottom of the carving through the bench or a board (one is shown in the engraving on the facing page). A more versatile solution is a carver's vise that swivels, rotates, and locks in any position. (The work is mounted onto the vise with a screw, as shown in the bottom photo at left.)

A shaving horse is a vise and a bench in one. You sit on the shaving horse and push against a foot pedal to clamp your work between the wooden head and an angled shelf. The harder you push, the more clamping pressure you apply. To reposition the work, simply let up on your foot. It's the ideal place for

Chairmaker Dave Sawyer uses a shaving horse for drawknifing and spokeshaving the fine tapered spindles that form the back of his Windsor chairs.

KEEP ALL CLAMPS clean and free of dried glue and rust, wax the bar, and occasionally oil the screw. It's easy to distort a clamp by applying more pressure than it was designed to handle, so either use more clamps—which is better for even pressure anyway—or find a bigger, stronger clamp. Keep the length of the screw that extends from the head to a minimum by taking up slack with scrap blocks or by snugging up the movable head before applying pressure. Use nonmarring pads or pieces of leather on the clamping heads to protect finished work.

using a drawknife, or for shaping anything from chair spindles to shingles. You can customize the clamping head with leather (as shown in the photo above) to protect delicate work, or cut a small groove in the head to grip chair spindles.

Clamps

You can never have too many clamps. I've done complex laminations when I've used just about every clamp in the shop—and believe me, I have a few—and I still could have used more. Glue-ups are just one of the many uses for clamps. Think of them as an extra pair of hands (or several extra pairs) to hold work while you drill, chisel, saw, or plane.

Traditional clamps come in a few basic types: bar clamps, handscrews,

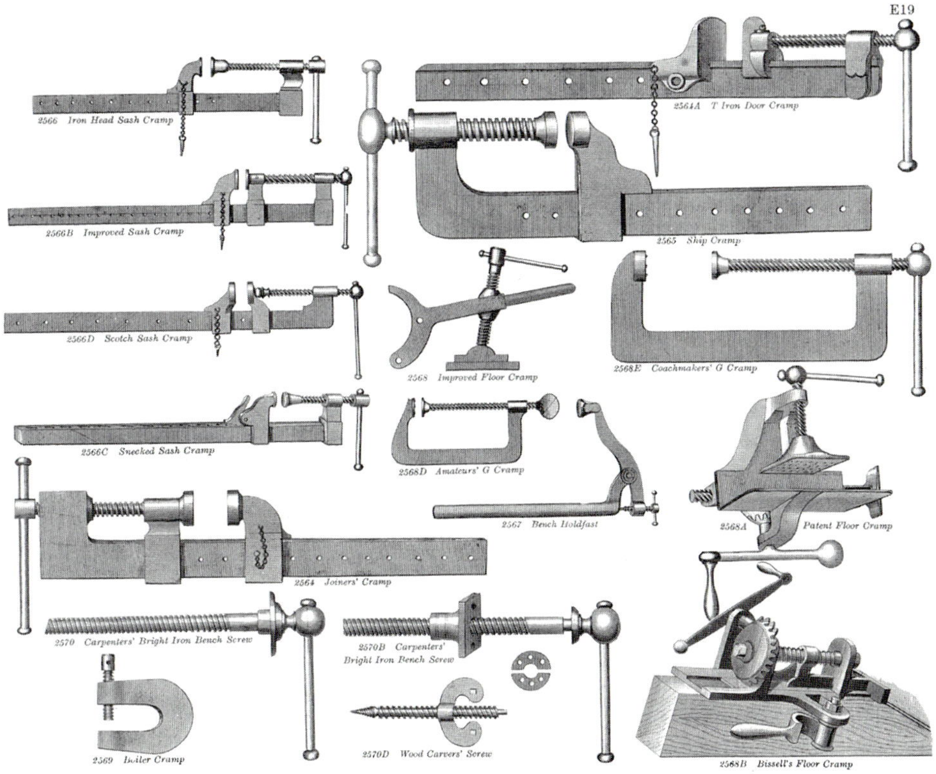

You can buy an interesting assortment of clamps today, but certainly nothing like the variety once offered in the Sheffield Standard List, which contained everything from floor clamps to coachmaker's clamps.

C-clamps and spring clamps are ideal for securing small work or for use in tight places, although they can be quite large and powerful, too.

C-clamps, and spring clamps. Few woodworking tools are as simple as a clamp with a screw or spring to deliver pressure, and a frame to hold the work and direct the pressure. Most clamps are made of malleable (slightly flexible) iron or steel, although handscrews and shopmade bar clamps are often wood. Clamps differ in their construction, their rigidity (which affects how much pressure they can apply), their size, and the depth of their jaws.

Bar clamps have a modest reach, they adjust quickly, and they have the advantage of a rigid, straight bar to keep large panels and carcases flat and true during glue-ups. The clamps I usually reach for in my shop are light-duty bar clamps, 6 in. and 12 in. long, which I use for small glue-ups and for holding jigs or work to my bench. I also have heavier ones—36 in. long and even longer—with larger screws and deeper jaws, and I use these nearly as much. You can buy clamping heads and make your own wood or pipe clamps any length you need. Pipe clamps can be threaded together to make extra-long clamps.

Wooden handscrews have three useful features: they can clamp securely with the jaws out of parallel, the wooden jaws don't damage work, and they have a deep reach.

Taper the legs of a staple into opposing wedges and you have a pinch dog, a simple and useful clamp for aligning parts or clamping joints.

Part clamp, part shooting board, a miter jack was once a common shop tool that helps to plane an exact 45° miter—or 90° using the rear face. The planes are unusual Spiers miter planes.

C-clamps are best for small work and modest clamping pressure. I have some with 1-in. openings and larger ones with deep jaws. C-clamps adjust slowly, however. To speed up adjustment, I either slip in a scrap block to shorten the distance I have to adjust the screw, or I grab the end of the screw and spin the clamp. Spring clamps, which are really just oversized clothespins, come in a range of sizes and clamping pressures for all kinds of light clamping work. They work quickly, but not very positively. For very delicate work, clothespins work just fine, too.

Wooden handscrews have largely been replaced by other clamps, which is a shame considering how useful they are for clamping odd shapes and for holding work in their large jaws with even pressure. Handscrews have two screws: Use the screw that goes through the middle of the jaws to snug the clamp in position and the end screw to apply the pressure. To open or close the jaws quickly with the clamp off the work, hold the two handles and pedal it like a bicycle.

Clamping odd shapes, such as coopered cabinet doors, is an interesting challenge. If the curve is shallow, some creative jigging along with a bar clamp might work. Much simpler is a pinch dog tapped into the end grain, straddling the joint. Pinch dogs are like heavy-duty staples, with wedges for legs, that draw the joint tighter the farther they are driven into the work. They are a wonderful example of a simple solution to a difficult problem.

Marking and MEASURING TOOLS

4

If you remember anything from your high school shop class, it's probably the old adage "measure twice and cut once." Not only is this good advice to help avoid errors, but it also speaks to how basic measuring and marking out is to every aspect of woodworking. From the initial drawing to the completed project, marking and measuring tools make the work easier and more accurate.

A rule and square are the most important measuring tools. After you master them, add others, such as dividers, mortise gauges, bevel gauges, and angle dividers. While there is a certain degree of precision inherent in each of these tools, bear in mind the degree of accuracy required. A ¼ in. one way or another might suit a barn frame, but the slightest gap looks sloppy in a fine piece of furniture.

Marking knives and awls are superior to pencils for marking out joinery because they cut a fine, distinct line, sever the fibers (preventing chipout), and provide a groove for seating a chisel edge or saw.

Tools for Marking Out

There are all sorts of options for marking out your work: Some craftsmen like to use a micro-point mechanical pencil, others a ballpoint pen or a sharply pointed awl. Pencils are fine for much marking out work. A pencil line is easy to see and erases easily, but even the thinnest line is not as distinct and fine as a knife or awl mark.

I prefer a marking knife for two reasons: First, it cuts a tiny groove that is perfect for holding the edge of a chisel (or some other cutting tool) dead on the line. Second, it scores the fibers to reduce chipping. A marking knife should be sharpened to a point, with a fine bevel. For extremely thin knives, a double-bevel works well, but for the greatest accuracy a single bevel is better (use the flat of the blade against a rule or square). I own a few different knives, one of which is narrow and long for marking in tight spaces.

For marking the face of a board or its position in a glued-up panel, where I want bold marks to avoid making a careless mistake, I use a red or blue lumber crayon, available at any hardware store. Lumber crayons are also useful for marking out cuts and potential matches (faces and edges), and for marking grain direction during the milling process.

Rules

Rules are as old as antiquity. As early as c. 2500 B.C., Egyptians had developed standardized measurements (based on the length of a human foot or an outstretched hand or arm), which they used in the first rules, made of stone or wood. The Romans had bronze folding rules, but they were rare and the average craftsman had a knife-marked lath—a straight wooden rule he probably made himself. Not until the 17th century were rules graduated into inches and then quarters, and it was a full century later before eighths and sixteenths came into common practice.

As the scales became more sophisticated, rules in common use also started to fold. Beginning in the 17th century, and roughly every century since, rules folded first twice, then four times, then as many as 15 times with long Stanley Zig-Zag Rules. Now we have the

FOR ABOUT 500 YEARS, since it was decreed by King Edward I of England, an inch was three dry barley corns (grains) laid side by side. In the 19th century, rules were standardized for inches and feet, but still every major trading center in Europe had a slightly different foot. Not so long ago manufacturers made rules with a Paris foot on one side and an Amsterdam or a London foot on the other. This shouldn't seem odd: today we still can't agree if we will measure in millimeters or inches.

A useful collection of shop rules includes straight metal rules of various lengths, a folding rule with an extension end, an architect's rule, and a flexible rule for laying out curves.

ultimate folding rule—a tape measure. But some carpenters will tell you that folding rules are still the best—easier to use than a tape in awkward places, such as measuring the inside of a wide door opening. Some rules have another nice feature: extension or caliper ends for accurate inside dimensions and depth measurements.

Fine rules traditionally were made of boxwood with brass joints. One notch higher were ivory rules with German silver fittings. Boxwood may not be as fancy, but it is a logical material for making a rule. It is extremely fine-grained and stable, and its light color displays the rule markings well. Ivory is a questionable choice for rules. Although it shows off the markings clearly, it is a decidedly unstable material that swells and shrinks quite readily with changes in humidity. At a cost six times that of boxwood, many ivory rules must have been gentlemen's tools, more for status than use. Occasionally you may run across an ebony rule.

In keeping with the ingenuity of toolmakers, there are lots of rules that not only measure length but also do some of the thinking for you. Take, for example, a "shrinkage rule" used by patternmakers (one of these rules can be seen on the far left of the photo on p. 40). The wooden patterns they make are for casting metals that shrink about 1% of their total volume as they cool after being poured into the mold. For example, a 2-ft.-long shrinkage rule for cast iron, which shrinks ⅛ in. per foot, actually measures 24¼ in. Likewise, sawyers have lumber rules that, when laid across the diameter of a log, calculate the number of board feet of lumber that the log will yield. "Wantage rules" measure liquids in barrels and tell you how many gallons are "wanted" to fill it. There are many other clever rules.

It's useful to have a few straight rules of various lengths. Steel rules can take rough use, and the markings are easy to read (especially on bright steel). They can be used as straightedges, flexed to lay out shallow curves, or you can clamp two together for accurate inside measurements. A 36-in. steel rule is useful for making drawings and layouts, but perhaps too long for daily bench work; 12-in. and 24-in. rules are about the right length, and a 6-in. rule is handy for measuring in tight places.

For the greatest accuracy, be sure to read a rule with its edge—not its face—against the work. Straight rules can do things other than simple measuring, too. One useful trick you can do with a straight rule is to divide a board into equal segments across its width (for laying out dovetails, for example). To divide a 6-in. board into eight equal parts, I place the rule diagonally across the board, with the "0" on one edge and the "8" on the other, and mark off a

DIVIDING A BOARD INTO EQUAL PARTS

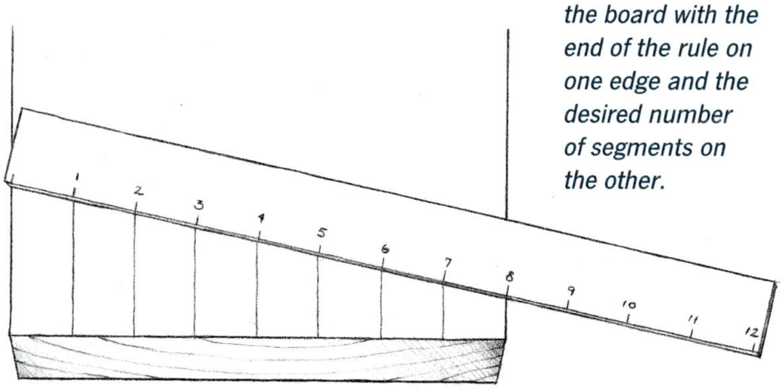

Eight equally spaced parts

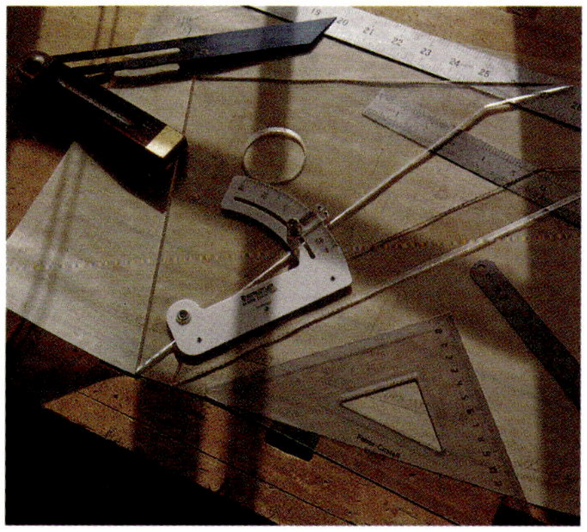

Stiff steel rules and plastic triangles aid in drafting accurate patterns and drawings, and for transferring measurements. Use a bevel gauge (top left) to transfer angles from a drawing to the work.

Patterns and story sticks are simple devices for transferring dimensions and helping you avoid errors commonly made when repeatedly measuring with a tape or rule. They also store those dimensions for later use.

segment at each inch marking (see the drawing on the facing page). This method works for any number of equal parts, depending on the scale you choose.

Patterns and story sticks are extremely useful measuring tools that can save a lot of time in the layout phase. A good pattern can be used again and again to lay out cuts, a more accurate method than measuring repeatedly, which can introduce small errors into your measurements. A pattern can be as simple as the first piece you cut, a cardboard template, or a story stick. A story stick is a thin strip of wood, as long as you need, with pencil marks at important reference points. They tell a story: for example, every element of a cabinet, from rail widths at top and bottom, to panel height, overall height, toe space, and so on.

Squares

It's ironic that so many woodworking cuts are at 90°, or square, considering there is nothing square about the trees we get our lumber from. Nevertheless, we live in a rectangular world. When building almost anything, you will have to make sure some part lies square to

WORKING BY EYE

TRY BUILDING a piece of furniture someday without your square, rule, and marking gauge—just use your eyes. Forget about inches and feet for a while and look at each element: its proportion to the parts around it and its relation to the whole. The wonderful results of working this way are that you'll begin to trust your eyes, and your work will have a freshness, and perhaps a bit of asymmetry, just on the edge of precision that says, "this was handmade."

Working from reality is a similar idea. You can "measure" one piece against another by eye, such as the width of a tenon against its mortise. No measuring tool is more accurate. Of course, you can't work by eye or from reality all of the time. Most woodworking has tight tolerances that you must adhere to, and it's far easier to lay out a cut or a joint with the aid of a square, rule, bevel gauge, or compass. But you'd be surprised by how well you can do without them once in a while.

These squares speed the layout of large work. The house framing square (top) has engraved rafter tables and a pair of adjustable gauges for laying out stair stringers; the unusual bridge builder's square is used to lay out large mortises and tenons. The square below it is hand-graduated and stamped 1804. A 12-in. square (bottom) is a useful size for a shop.

TRUING A FRAMING SQUARE

TRUING a framing square is a surprisingly easy thing to do. Whether the square is new or you've dropped it a time or two, check to see if it is square. Line up the tongue (the shorter of the two legs) against the straight edge of a piece of plywood and make a fine pencil line along the long leg. Flip the square over so that it is on the opposite side of the line and draw a second line parallel to the first. If the two lines are exactly parallel, your square is dead on. If they are wider apart at the bottom, your square is more than 90°; if it is narrower at the bottom, it is less than 90°.

The trick to correcting an out-of-square square is to move some of the metal along the imaginary miter between the blade and the tongue. Rap a center punch smartly on the inner corner to spread the square apart slightly, or on the outer corner to bring the legs of the square together. Punch a few times if necessary, but check your square after each punch so you don't push it too far the other way.

This framing square is not accurate, as shown by the two test lines. You can spread the legs of the square by tapping a center punch on the inside corner. To bring the legs closer together, place the punch on the outside corner.

some other part, and most likely you will be doing a lot of this. As a result, you'll need the following: an accurate try square or combination square for bench work (preferably both a 6-in. and a 12-in. size), and a framing square for larger work, such as laying out cuts on plywood sheet goods.

You can establish the squareness of a rectangle (such as a carcase or large panel) by measuring the diagonals; if the diagonals are equal, the rectangle must have square corners. You also can check squareness with a framing square (for large work) or a smaller try or combination square (for work at the bench). A framing square has one blade or "body" 24 in. long and 2 in. wide (useful for laying out mortise-and-tenon joinery in timber-framing) and a narrower "tongue" 16 in. long and 1½ in. wide (also for timber-framing). I have one with a 12-in. blade, a very useful size. The name "framing square" comes from its common use framing houses, as evidenced by the complex table of rafter lengths stamped onto the face of some squares. In theory, one could lay out all of the dimensions of a complex roof with a square alone. You can make a square of any size if you remember Pythagoras' rule that the three sides of a right triangle are in the ratio of 3:4:5.

Bench squares can be metal combination squares—meaning they have a 45° face for checking miters—or they can be wood and metal "try squares" (so-named because they "try" the squareness). The

For bench work, a small square is useful: either an elegant wood and metal try square (top), a metal square with movable rule (center), or a fixed engineer's square (bottom left).

A beautiful collection of squares, miter squares, and winding sticks (bottom left) is fitted into the till of a 19th-century joiner's tool chest. The care with which they are fitted both protects them and speaks of their value to an unknown craftsman.

wide blade of a try square is fixed at right angles to the body, whereas combination squares have a movable blade graduated as a rule. (In a pinch, a combination square works as a marking gauge, as shown in the photo at right.) Both squares can be accurate, but older try squares are the more beautiful of the two, often made with rosewood bodies, steel blades, shapely brass rivet plates, and edges trimmed in brass.

To mark a square cut with these tools, hold the body of the square tightly against the work and use a pencil or knife to mark along the blade. To check the squareness of the end of a board or joint, hold the square the same way and sight under the blade; the amount of light you see clearly shows the degree to which the edge is out of square (provided your square is accurate). Squares are delicate instruments and can easily lose their accuracy, so be careful not to drop them or otherwise manhandle them. If they're not true, they're not worth much.

A combination square and pencil make a quick marking gauge, but it's almost as accurate and faster to wrap a couple of fingers over the corner of the board for gauging a pencil line.

For transferring one or two angles, the St. Johnsbury Tool Co.'s cabinet-maker's bevel gauge (bottom right) has two blades locked in position by a thumbscrew. The A-shaped L. C. Stephen's patent folding inclinometer rules with spirit levels (top and bottom) are for measuring angles such as roof pitches.

Bevel Gauges

If you work with anything other than square edges, you'll need a bevel gauge. A miter square is one kind of bevel gauge, fixed at exactly 45° for miter cuts. A sliding bevel gauge, on the other hand, is adjustable. As with squares, there are many variations of bevel gauges: some are wood, some metal, and some are beautiful combinations of the two. All have an adjustable straight blade and stock. By tightening a nut at one end, the blade can be locked in any position; when loosened it folds into the stock. One variation has a small steel square for a blade that makes the tool even more flexible in transferring angles.

Most bevel gauges will do a serviceable job, but there are some things to look for when you're buying one. Avoid gauges with a nut or tightener proud of the stock where the stock and blade join—this gets in the way and makes them awkward to use. Better are bevel gauges with a wing nut on the end of the stock. They feel more positive, the nut is not in the way, and you can tighten the bevel no matter what side is up (not so with the first type).

A bevel gauge works like an adjustable square. You can set it with a protractor, from a drawing, or from the work itself. Tighten the nut just slightly before setting the blade so it will hold its position, and then cinch it down when you have it set where you want it. (Make sure the blade is flush or proud of the stock above the joint to get an accurate

Fancy combination gauges for the well-heeled craftsman are bevel gauges, levels, squares, and inclinometers all in one.

A miter square is fixed at 45° for consistent and accurate miters. The modern steel Japanese miter square in the foreground is used no differently than the traditional English one at top.

Set a bevel gauge from the work, from a drawing, or from a protractor. The Italian brass protractor is marked 1701 and has scales for laying out polygons of up to 12 sides. A combination protractor and bevel gauge (top) is an extremely useful tool for all layout work.

A quality metal rule is an accurate straightedge for checking the sole of a plane or the flatness of a jointer bed.

MARKING and measuring tools generally don't need a lot of tune-up—either they are accurate or they are not. You can adjust a framing square, but not other squares, at least not very easily. Start with quality tools and try not to bend them or drop them, especially on concrete floors. The most maintenance you should have to do is to keep your marking knife, and the pins of your marking gauge, compass, and dividers, honed sharp.

measurement.) When I have to keep track of multiple bevels, I use two bevel gauges. (Shipbuilders, who work with bevels constantly, use bevel gauges with two blades.) Once set, treat the tool gently, so you don't run the risk of changing the setting. It's also a good idea to transfer important angles to a board for later reference, or to keep track of many bevels. One of the nice features of a bevel gauge is that it gives you an angle and its complement, which can be helpful when setting a table saw for a bevel cut.

Similar to a bevel gauge are angle dividers, which look and work like bevel gauges with two blades, but the blades are connected to the stock so that they open and close in unison. Just as the name implies, the tool bisects any angle and yields the appropriate miter angle. Angle dividers are not that common anymore, but they come in handy for coopered work or for fitting woodwork in old houses with out-of-square corners.

Straightedges

Shop straightedges come in two types: precisely machined metal straightedges for checking the flatness of a plane's sole or a machine setup, and wooden straightedges used as fences to guide tools or to test the flatness of large work, such as doors, where precision is less critical. A good metal rule 24 in. or 36 in. long is accurate enough for much of the work in the first category. To see if a straightedge is straight, hold the edge against a known flat surface, such as a jointer bed or saw table, and then rotate the straightedge end for end to see if they agree. The faintest sliver of

A chalkline need be no more complicated than a spool of line and a hunk of chalk. Chalklines are used to mark out a long straight line, such as the one along the wany edge of this board. Also shown are traditional wooden line reels, and a modern one that also functions as a plumb bob (on the board).

light is about 0.001 in. wide, but if you want to be precise, you can measure any gap with a feeler gauge.

You can buy hardened metal straightedges (of any length) machined to whatever tolerances your budget will allow. A hardened edge is nice if you are going to use the straightedge for cutting veneer, because the edge will hold up to a stray knife cut. Another option is to make a straightedge. Buy a piece of cold rolled steel roughly ¼ in. by 1¼ in. (from any steel supplier), belt-sand the faces clean, and take it to a machine shop to mill one edge straight.

Simpler yet are shopmade wooden straightedges. For short work I use my metal straightedges, but for longer work I use 54-in. or 96-in. wooden ones. The 54-in. straightedge is an old quartersawn oak board with one good edge trued with a jointer plane; the 96-in. one is a plywood offcut. Both are accurate enough to get a fair idea of the flatness of a large cabinet or tabletop. I occasionally check them against each other, or alone by tracing the profile of one edge on a piece of paper or plywood, then flipping the straightedge end-for-end to see how the edge aligns with the pencil line. Any errors will appear twice as big. I hang the wooden straightedges when not in use to keep them from warping.

Chalklines

A chalkline marks a straight line much as a straightedge does, but the advantage is that it allows you to mark any length you need. It is simply a reel of cord that you charge with chalk, stretch between two points, and snap sharply to leave a line. Some versions use ink instead of chalk for a sharp, distinct line. Most chalklines store the cord and powdered chalk inside a case; you merely pull out the chalked cord as you need it. The simplicity of the system is that as long as the cord is stretched tight, the line will be straight. If I'm snapping onto an uneven surface or if the line is long, I'll hold it tight against the work at the midpoint and snap each half separately.

A lot of the lumber I work with has what is known as "wany edge," which means that the bark was left on one or both edges. It takes more work to mill wany-edged lumber to size, but the advantage is that you can get wider boards (and less wood goes into the scrap pile). To create a straight edge on wany-edged lumber, I use a chalkline; although the line is nowhere as fine as one made with a straightedge and pencil, it's entirely adequate to follow with a bandsaw. For the most part, however, a chalkline is a carpentry tool for marking lines to install shingles or to lay out lines for nailing.

Levels and Plumb Bobs

To determine whether a surface is level (horizontal) or plumb (vertical) you can use a level. To test or establish long verticals, the better tool is a weight on a string, or a plumb bob. At one time they were made of lead (hence *plumb*), but more modern plumb bobs are usually brass or iron with steel tips. (Some are quite ornate and beautiful, further examples of the tool maker's art.) Ancient Egyptians combined the ideas of plumb and level in an A-shaped wooden tool, where the chord between the two legs of the A was level when a plumb bob suspended from the top of the A hung exactly in the center of the chord. Another version has a plumb bob hanging along one leg of a square. When the bob is centered on the leg, the square is both

Hang a plumb bob on a line and gravity does the rest. A smooth profile and dense weight are important so the bob does not flutter in the wind.

Levels come in many styles, from the fanciful cast-iron Davis level (second from top) to the practical modern level with digital readout (center). At the top is a brass-bound rosewood level (with level sights for use as a transit); in the foreground are various small levels (including one that clamps onto a square) and a circular level for measuring an incline.

Levels are among the most beautifully made tools. The inclinometer level at center was made by L. L. Davis Level and Tool Co., and the brass-bound and rosewood levels are by Stratton Bros. of Greenfield, Mass.

plumb and level—a simple use of gravity.

Spirit levels, the common levels of today, use another aspect of gravity: the fact that liquids will form a level surface. The variations in such levels are endless, from tiny pocket levels to carpenter's levels 6 ft. long. The most beautiful are made with exotic woods and bound in brass to preserve their square and straight edges. Their precision is due to the slightly curved glass vials nearly filled with alcohol (hence "spirit") or antifreeze, which are set in plaster parallel to the length of the level or perpendicular to it. When the bubble inside the vial floats to the center (encouraged by the vial's curve), the level is exactly horizontal or vertical. This simplicity makes it easy to imagine small levels that clamp onto squares, levels that measure a fixed angle, or "variable-pitch adjusters" that clamp onto one end of a level for laying deck joists or plumbing at set angles.

Dividers have two stiff legs with a thumb screw for locking them in place, and sometimes the handy feature of an additional screw for fine adjustment of the setting. Use them to transfer dimensions or "step off" equally spaced increments.

Trammel points, which can be fitted to a wooden beam of any length, can scribe large circles or arcs, or transfer long dimensions. For fine-tuning the distance between the points, the standing pair has a screw adjustment. Trammels were commonly shopmade or school projects, and few are identical.

Compasses, Dividers, Calipers, and Trammel Points

For drawing a circle, transferring dimensions, or measuring dimensions on a turned piece, compasses, dividers, and calipers are essential. Each of these tools has two adjustable legs and some method to hold them at this setting—either a stiff hinge, a spring with threaded rod and nut, or an arm between the legs that can be locked in position with a thumb screw. These interesting tools range in size from the tiny to the huge, and in material from shopmade wood to precisely machined steel.

On a compass, one leg usually has a sharp steel point and the other a pencil point to draw circles or arcs of circles, or to scribe lines parallel to an edge. Whenever you have to fit a piece of wood to an uneven wall, you can scribe it with a compass. Hold or clamp the wood tightly in position against the wall, open the compass as wide as the biggest

Hand-forged or manufactured from cast steel and decoratively filed, calipers measure inside and outside dimensions. Some hold their setting through friction of the hinge alone; others have a spring joint between the legs with a screw adjuster to hold them in position.

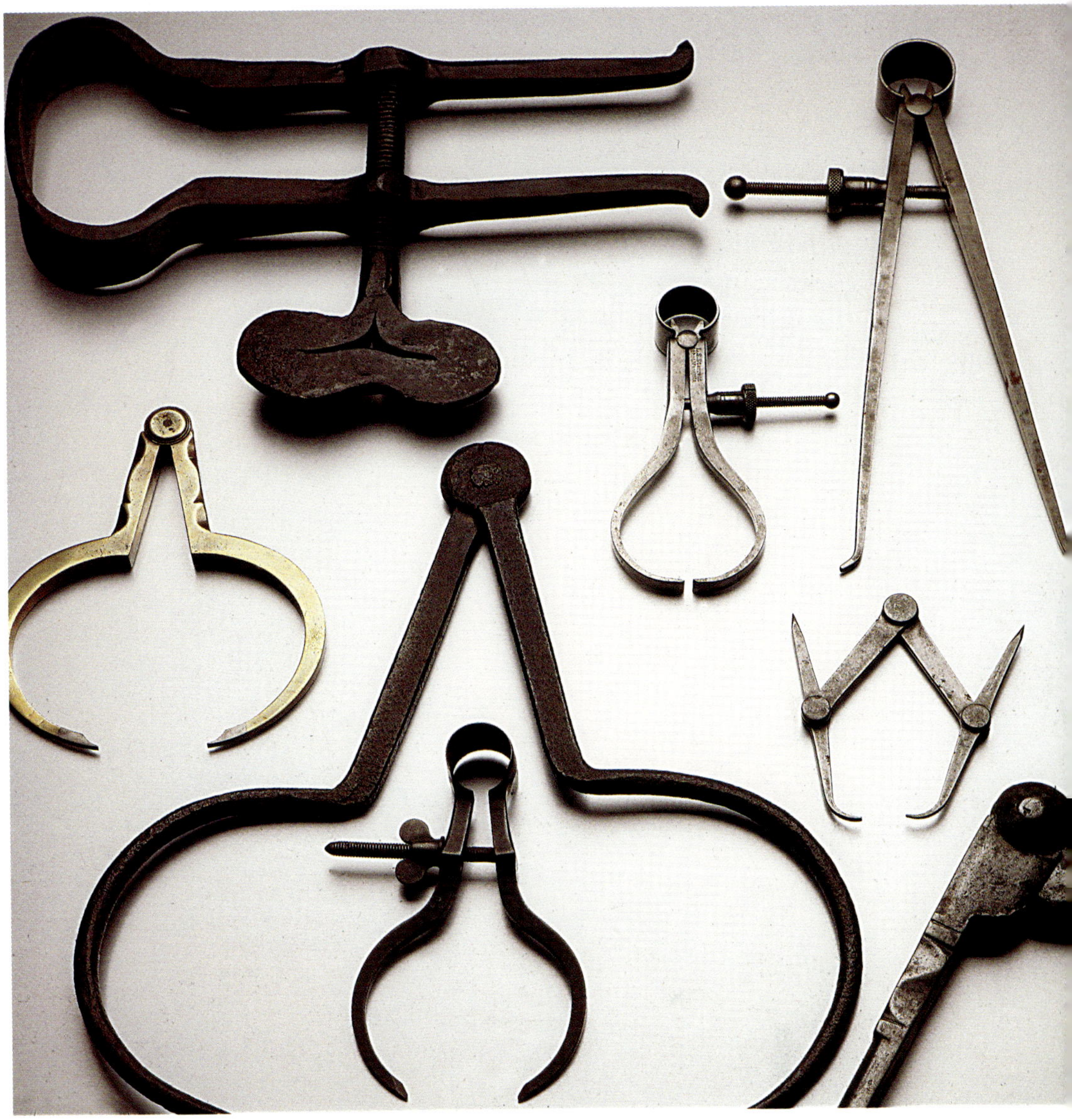

IT IS EXTREMELY difficult to accomplish most woodworking tasks without a good rule, a square, and a few other basic layout tools, but several of these tools you can fashion yourself. You can make a workable compass, dividers, or trammel set from a scrap of wood and a couple of nails or pencils. Likewise, a simple wooden or plywood pattern can substitute for a bevel gauge.

gap and—keeping the compass in the same orientation—guide the point along the wall. The pencil point will draw a line on the piece, perhaps a cabinet or a molding, that parallels every irregularity. Log home builders and timber-framers use this technique to fit parts and to lay out joints.

Unlike a compass, dividers have two sharp points (no pencil). They can do the same work as a compass, but what they do best is transfer dimensions accurately, when laying out dovetails, for example, or when marking a board for equally spaced holes. Prick the dividers into the wood and walk one leg after the other down the length along a straight line. You can see right away if the spacing works, readjusting the dividers if it doesn't. Dividers are also an accurate way to transfer a dimension from one place to another, such as from a full-scale drawing to the workpiece. I hone divider points on a fine stone to keep them needle sharp.

Proportional dividers have two legs that form two pairs of dividers joined end-for-end with a common movable hinge point, similar to a pair of scissors. By changing the hinge point (making one set of dividers half the length of the other) you can transfer dimensions and, at the same time, double or halve them.

Trammel points are half a set of dividers, you might say. They come in pairs and generally are used on a strip of wood (any reasonably rigid scrap will do). Some trammel sets have two steel points and are used as dividers for transferring large dimensions; others can be outfitted with a pencil for drawing large circles or arcs of circles (and many come with both options). Some are unique, with beautiful brass details and fine adjusters to move the points. I don't own any trammel points, mainly because an alternative is so easy to make: To scribe a large circle or arc, I drive a nail into one end of a stick and drill a hole for a pencil the right distance out (the radius). A notch in the side of the stick for the pencil point also works, with the advantage that I can fine-tune its position by cutting to one side or the other and move the apex of the notch just a little.

A set of dividers and a compass have straight legs; calipers usually have curved ones. They work the same way your fingers do when pinching something and are used for measuring the diameter of a turned table leg or the thickness of a bowl. Reverse the pinching action, and that's how some calipers measure inside dimensions accurately, especially in places you can't reach (and certainly a lot more easily than with a small rule). Perhaps to prove that tool makers have a sense of humor, they've made dancing calipers, with shapely female legs or a dancing couple; the toes measure inside and the arms outside. Because calipers often were customized by blacksmiths for some particular purpose, there are many variations for specific trades, with double openings for two separate dimensions or with rules that convert a caliper's opening to a measurement, or vice versa.

With a single setting a vernier caliper measures the thickness of a tenon and the width of its mortise, or a tenon length and mortise depth. A depth gauge (center) that is also a small bevel gauge is another useful measuring tool.

Why make a plain tool when you can have some fun with the design? Calipers with fanciful and shapely legs have toes for inside measurements and arms for outside dimensions. The leg on the marking awl is a pocket clip.

Patternmakers rely on inside and outside calipers for transferring dimensions from drawings to accurately size the round section of wooden patterns for casting anything from gears to shafts and wheels.

Designed with multiple functions, the A. Williams patented marking gauge (bottom right) combines a single-pin marking gauge with a double-pin mortise gauge, and a knife-pointed slitting gauge. The G. Kenny gauge behind it does all this and is a trammel set, too.

The caliper I use most often is a vernier caliper (see the photo at right on p. 54). It's really more of a machinist's tool, able to measure 0.001 in., which is impressive but not the main reason I like it. Rather, it is because the jaws open 6 in. and give three measurements simultaneously: inside dimension, outside, and depth. This allows me to measure a tenon thickness with the outside jaws, and without changing anything, I can test the mortise width with the inside jaws. I can also check a tenon length and mortise depth without actually measuring either, reducing the possibility for error. I have a little depth gauge that also does this job (shown in the same photo), but a vernier caliper is more versatile. Because its jaws are deep and parallel, I can use it to check whether the two cheeks of a tenon are parallel, or to see if a long mortise is the same width at both ends.

Marking Gauges

Marking gauges include a variety of tools, all with a similar function: to scribe or cut one or more lines parallel to an edge. There's one type of marking gauge, called a mortise gauge, that works on a similar principle to my vernier caliper: With one setting I can lay out both the

A large panel gauge marks out the width of a board parallel to an edge in preparation for ripping.

tenon thickness and mortise width. It consists of a sliding beam with a fixed and movable pin, and a head that clamps on the beam with a thumb screw. It scribes two lines parallel to a face or edge, much more accurately than a pencil.

Other gauges do similar layout work, such as a marking gauge with a single fixed pin for dovetailing, a much larger panel gauge for marking the width of a board parallel to one edge (used when boards were ripped by hand), and a cutting gauge with a knife in place of the pin. There are plenty of other unusual gauges made by Stanley and other manufacturers—butt gauges with multiple pins for marking out mortises for butt hinges, and metal gauges with thin wheels in place of pins, to name two. At a minimum you will want a mortise gauge, one of the most common and versatile.

When woodworking was done by hand, every shop had a number of gauges, purchased from catalogs or made in the shop from ebony, rosewood, or beech, sometimes with brass inlay at points of wear. Because they were such important tools, someone always was tinkering with the design to produce a tool that combined multiple tasks or worked more accurately and easily. Some designs were patented, but most were as individual as the craftsmen who used them.

The shape of the pin or knife further distinguishes the different gauge designs. Naturally, you would expect a cutting gauge to have a knife. If you are going to use one for cutting veneer strips for inlays as

DIVIDING TAPERS

PROBLEM: how do you mark the centerline of a tapered workpiece? A similar problem: How do you mark the four equal bevels on a square and tapering piece (such as a pencil post) to shape it into an octagon in section? Careful measuring is one tedious but workable solution, but there is an easier way.

Take a scrap of wood and drill a hole in the middle for a pencil. Then hammer a 16d nail an equal distance to either side of the pencil so they project at least 1 in. Straddle the gauge over the stock so the two nails ride along the edges as the pencil marks the center.

For dividing square or tapered stock into an eight-sided piece (for the posts on a pencil-post bed, for example) use two pencils spaced from the pins in the ratio of 5:7:5. The divider will mark the location of the bevels for shaping the octagon. With a little bit of creativity, you can use this idea to make similar gauges for many marking tasks.

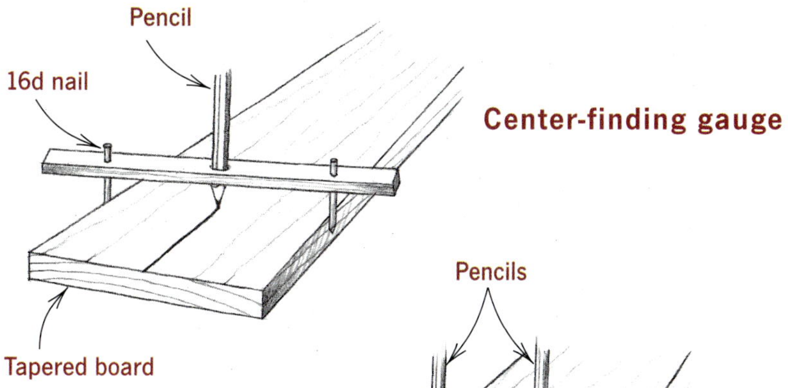

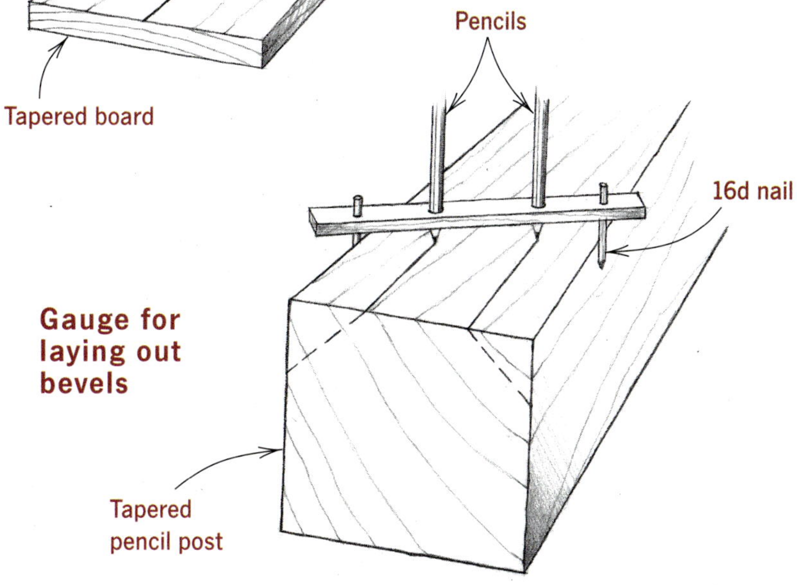

A gauge with a pin works well for cutting with the grain, but across the grain a knife scores the fibers more cleanly.

(A shallow mark is easier to plane away if you don't want it to show.) Be aware that the knife will tend to follow the grain. To avoid or at least lessen this tendency, sharpen the point so it angles away from the fence. If you do this, the knife point will pull away from the edge, drawing the gauge tightly to the work. This works just as well if you decide to push your gauge.

A marking gauge is used whenever you need a line parallel to an edge. It can be used for inlay work, for dimensioning a board to a consistent thickness by hand, or for cutting dovetails. For marking out mortises and tenons, set the two pins of your marking gauge as wide as the chisel you will use to chop the mortise. Don't rely on the rule on the beam of some gauges, but rather set the gauge by measuring the distance between the pin and head. Or better still, set it directly from the work.

I do, a rounded knife cuts more gently than a finely pointed one. For marking across the grain, a knife (think marking knife) is superior to a pin (think awl) for cutting the fibers. With the grain, a pin works well. Rather than having a number of gauges, I sharpen my mortise gauge with slipstones until I get a knife edge that works well in most circumstances.

A marking gauge is designed to be pushed away from you, but I've always found pulling less awkward. The point need only project 1⁄16 in. or so from the surface of the gauge. To scribe a line, rest the beam on the work, hold the fence tightly to the edge, and drag the point along. You can control the depth and size of the line by rotating the beam, from the point fully buried in the wood to just the faintest scribe line.

The fine steel fingers of a profile gauge conform to any contour, producing both a positive and negative profile.

Profile Gauges

Working with moldings—or with any shapes for that matter—there are many times when you need to transfer complicated contours or profiles. Wooden patterns are one solution, but they take time to make. A good alternative is a profile gauge, a stack of thin metal (or plastic) fingers bound together yet able to slide past one another and conform to almost any shape. One side is the negative of the profile, the other the positive (see the bottom photo on the facing page). The more fingers per inch, the more detail it captures.

The whole idea behind a profile gauge or any gauge, or for that matter any of the marking and measuring tools discussed in this chapter, is to improve your accuracy and efficiency. Making gauges is something I do quite often when building a piece of furniture: a dovetail gauge of a certain pin angle made from a beveled scrap of wood and fence glued together, or a small story stick for setting my router to cut evenly spaced grooves. They aren't fancy and they usually don't take a lot of time to make. Most of the time I use them once, so I don't want to spend a lot of time making them.

The beauty of knowing how to use hand tools—and being able to improvise new ones when you need them—is that it allows you to work to whatever degree of precision you desire. Many times 1⁄16 in. is accurate enough (that's all some rules can measure anyway). At other times, the precision of an engineer is called for. Don't forget that you're working with wood, a material with a personality of its own, and one that will change dimension no matter what you do.

A jack-of-all-trades, a Stanley Odd Job will do the work of many tools, including a level, plumb, square, miter square, marking gauge, depth gauge, and compass.

5

STRIKING TOOLS

Axes built America. Facing a seemingly endless forest, settlers used axes to clear land and hew trees into fences, stockades, homes, barns, and ships. To make all the wooden necessities of daily life, from barrels to water pails, wagon wheels to ox yokes, an ax or adze did much of the work, hewing parts out of a log and shaping them to size.

While a hatchet is still an ideal tool for shaping wood quickly, machines have largely replaced the work of axes and adzes. Similarly, air nailers and screw guns have diminished a carpenter's reliance on his most basic striking tools: the hammer and mallet. But no machine can replace the sensitivity and the pleasure of swinging a hammer—setting a nail or nudging a part into place—or the feel of a well-balanced mallet driving the wooden handle of a chisel.

Bronze Age tools, such as these axes and knife from Luristan, Persia, show the sophistication of tools made nearly 3,000 years ago. The cast ax at the top, with reinforced edges on the tapered blade and a cross-hatch decoration, would have needed constant whetting to maintain a sharp edge on the soft metal.

Axes vary in weight and width for many tasks: felling trees, shaping them into timbers, and cutting joints. British designs that arrived with the colonists, such as those illustrated in the Sheffield List (below), gradually evolved into a new American style with a heavier poll for better balance and more power.

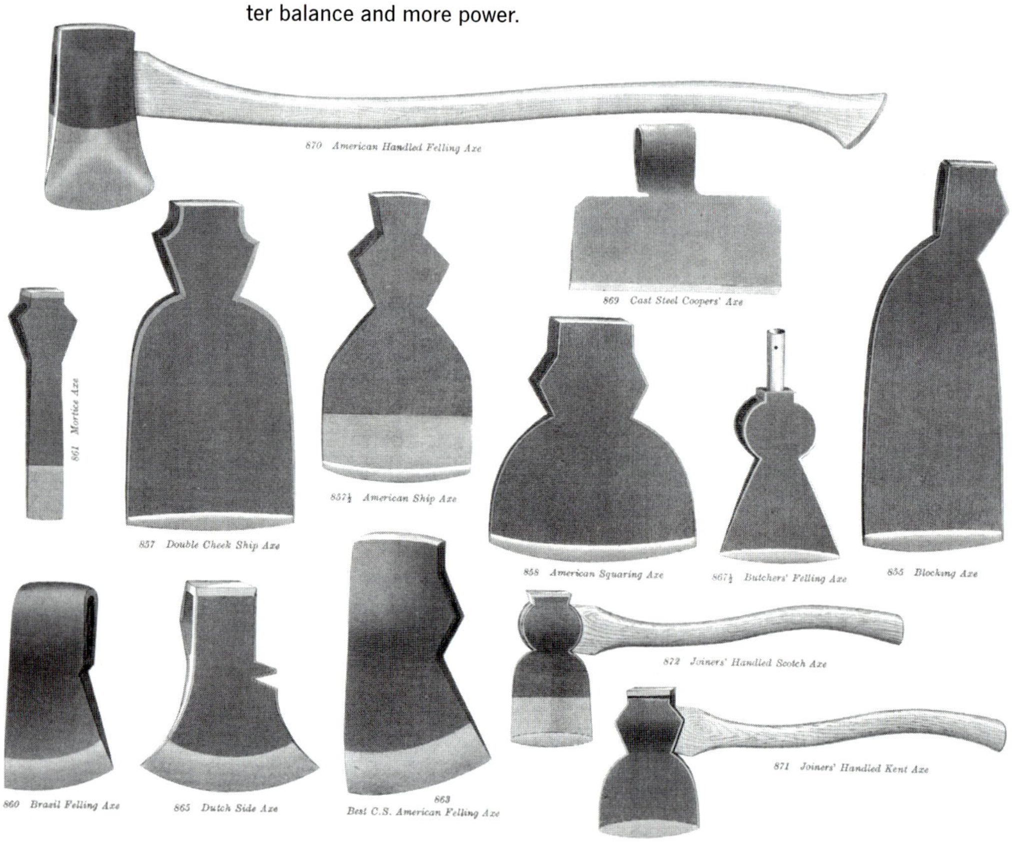

Axes

The first tools were surely stone hammers of some kind. By chipping a flint cutting edge with a hammer and lashing it onto a split wooden or antler handle, man made an ax. To work well, the ax head had to have enough weight, which stressed the connection with the handle. During the Bronze Age, in one of the more curious detours in the development of modern tools, ax heads were cast with an open end perpendicular to the cutting edge, not parallel with it as is typical today. This design strengthened the connection between the ax head and handle, but it meant that the handle had to be L-shaped to orient the ax head properly. Naturally, the

Early continental broad axes had long blades, as shown in this 1493 illustration of the building of Noah's Ark. The axes were probably harder to control than later, more symmetrical designs.

durability of the tool now depended on the strength of the handle.

It was not until the Iron Age that the prototype of the modern ax emerged, a design made possible by bending a rectangular strap of wrought iron in half, forming a handle hole parallel with the cutting edge. Steel was so valuable it was reserved for only the cutting edge welded between the sides. When it wore down, which it did, a blacksmith "rebit" it at the forge with a new steel edge.

Little has changed since then, although the size of the tool and the profile of the cutting edge have certainly evolved. Axes for felling trees need weight for powerful blows, a slim profile to cut deeply with each stroke, and a relatively narrow cutting edge with two equal bevels. Splitting axes work best with a more pronounced wedge shape and a stout bevel. On the other hand, axes for hewing and squaring timbers to size—called broad or side axes—are more efficient when they have a long cutting edge. Beveled on one side only, and with a handle slightly bent to give your hands clearance when working close to a surface, a broad ax is capable of paring wood nearly as flat as a plane.

An ax is the most basic woodworking tool. In skilled hands it is capable of a range of work, from splitting parts from a log to sizing and some joinery. A 17th-century settler could build a house with an ax alone and—I am exaggerating only a little—much of the furniture, too. If you look closely at barn or house beams, or the back of an 18th-century cupboard, you will see the distinctive marks left by an ax or its cousin, the adze. By the late 19th century, when machines began to replace hand tools, catalogs still offered an impressive range of axes, each having a slightly different weight or edge to suit the various trades: wheelwright, shipwright, cooper, carpenter, and woodsman. Each was named for the localities or trades that favored that style: Kent, Kentucky, Canadian, Norfolk, and Newcastle.

HATCHETS

Unless you are going to do a lot of green woodworking or hew a house frame out of logs, an ax is not going to be a tool you'll use that much. A hatchet is another story. Hatchets are light axes, less than 3 lb., with similar variations in shape and function. The one I use most often is an old multipurpose shingling hatchet. It has a blade for splitting shingles to size, a hammer head, and a small notch for pulling nails. It's similar to a lather's hatchet, which is used for nailing plaster lath and making the

REPLACING A HATCHET HANDLE

WOOD IS THE IDEAL material for handles. It's easy to shape and has just the right amount of springiness to absorb vibration. But wooden handles can split or snap, leaving a broken stub in the head. To work the stub out, drill a number of closely spaced holes into the wood with a metalworking twist bit (which won't be damaged by running into the metal wedge likely to be there) and punch out the stub bit by bit.

Use hickory or ash for the new handle. The white sapwood makes better handles than the darker heart, as do handles split rather than sawn. Bandsaw and drawknife the handle to shape using the broken handle or another favorite as a pattern. Fine-tune with a rasp or spokeshave.

Using a favorite handle as a pattern, split out the stock for a new handle and shape it to fit your grip perfectly with a drawknife and spokeshaves.

Fit the handle by trial-fitting it in the head repeatedly and shaving down the high spots (they'll show as dirty areas from rubbing inside the head). Check that the head and handle are in the same plane by sighting down the handle. When the handle fits the head snugly and is about ½ in. from going fully home, saw a kerf for a wedge across the long axis and nearly as deep as the head.

Drive the handle into the head by rapping hard on the opposite end while holding the handle vertically. Hammer in a hardwood wedge and saw off any excess. Start a slot with a chisel at right angles to the wooden one and drive in a metal wedge. Finish the handle with a scraper and sandpaper and wipe on a coat of boiled linseed oil and varnish.

lath by splitting a wide board from each side and opening it up like an accordion (a lather's hatchet is shown in the engraving on p. 71).

For rough sizing work, rounding a piece of wood to spin fairly true on a lathe, or wasting the bulk of a bevel cut along the underside of a curved tabletop, a hatchet is a remarkably quick and accurate tool. Mastering this tool is much easier than gaining the confidence to take a whack at your work with a tool you know can also do a lot of damage. As with any tool, accuracy comes with practice. Swing a hatchet with your arm and not your wrist. A hatchet sharpened with two equal bevels, like a felling ax, works well for most work. Sharpened with a single bevel and a flat back, a hatchet is more accurate for paring to a line or cutting a flat surface, such as a large tenon on a timber or that beveled table edge. In this case, a hint of a back bevel is recommended. In either case, the overall bevel can be as small as 20°.

SHARPENING AN AX

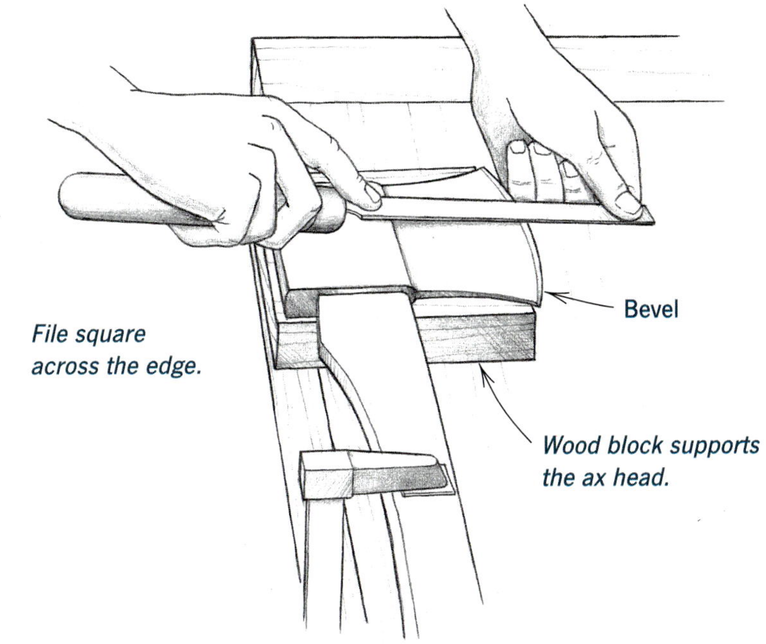

Hatchets are useful tools for rough shaping and quick removal of excess wood. Here, a chairmaker is rounding a leg billet with a hatchet before turning it on his lathe. The chopping stump has two levels, so that he can work at a comfortable height whether shaping long or short pieces.

SHARPENING AXES AND HATCHETS

Axes and hatchets are sharpened the same way. Often, the steel is soft enough to be cut with a file (a softer edge will hold up to the shock of chopping, especially into a hard knot). A file is the best tool to establish the overall shape and bevel. You can also use a grinder, but be sure to use a grinder with a large-diameter wheel; a small bench grinder leaves a hollow ground and a somewhat fragile edge. (If this is all you have, use the side of the wheel.)

File square across the edge, either away from it or into it, if you feel brave. Sight down the cutting edge to see that you are keeping the bevels equal. Finally, hone the edge by bringing the stone to the tool. Sharpen a broad ax or side hatchet the same way, only keep the back flat and polished. Hone just the slightest back bevel onto the edge to encourage the tool to angle out of the cut with every stroke. This will give you a bit more control over the tool.

Adzes

Turn the cutting action of an ax 90° and you have an adze. A short-handled adze is swung like a hammer for close-in shaping work. Adzes with longer handles are used the same way you might chop with a pickax. In sure hands, an adze is

TWYBILLS

TWYBILL, TWO-BILL, and mortising ax all describe variations on an ancient tool—a cross between an ax and a chisel. Some twybills are swung like a small double-bitted ax with the cutting edges at right angles to one another. They are used for chopping and picking out the waste from large mortises (probably drilled out beforehand). Other twybills are like huge chisels, or single-bitted axes, with long chisel-like cutting edges. Continental woodworkers used them—and still do—but for some reason they were never popular with English and American craftsmen.

One twybill I've seen was an iron bar over 4 ft. long, flattened at one end into a 1$\frac{1}{2}$-in.-wide paring chisel. The other end was a stout mortise chisel, and in the middle was a short hollow socket just the right size for a wooden handle—or at least you might think so. But if a hapless apprentice had been sent in search of such a handle (along with a left-handed hammer, to the amusement of his coworkers), the search would have ended in vain because such a twybill never had a handle. A handle would have made the tool ungainly and impossible to swing. Instead, a workman would rest the bar against his shoulder, grasp the short socket and, using the weight of the tool, chop out a mortise with one end and then pare it to size with the other.

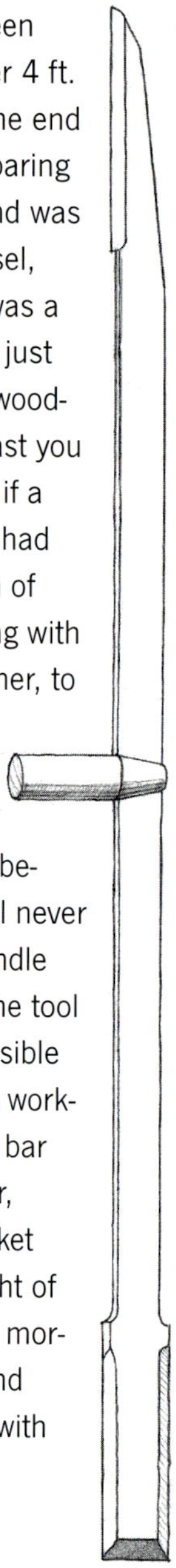

capable of accurate shaping and flattening, but it also is a far more dangerous tool. Swung like a hoe, the blade of a foot adze finishes cutting near or under your toe. It's easy to see how a moment of inattention could have disastrous consequences. No wonder it is said that the adze is the only tool the Devil is afraid to use.

A sculptor's adze has two blades of different curvature for roughing out a chair seat and then shaping it to a smooth, finished surface. The oval handle ensures a secure grip; choking up on it provides a measure of added control.

Until recently, I thought foot adzes were obsolete. So I was surprised to find a shipwright at Mystic Seaport, Connecticut, straddling a 60-ft.-long log of purpleheart, hewing it to a taper to form the keel of a reproduction of the schooner *Amistad*. Nearby was another shipwright shaping a massive rear stem with a broad ax. A century ago this would have been a common sight in any shipyard.

Hand adzes, although no longer common, are useful and still available both new and used. Many trades still use them, such as chairmakers to hollow seats, coopers to cut a consistent bevel on the inside of the barrel staves, and wheelwrights to shape the curved parts for wheels and wagons. The "poll"

Adzes combine the heft of an ax and the curved cutting edge of a gouge to quickly hollow everything from bowls to barrel staves or to flatten a surface as smooth as if cut by a plane. The narrow adze to the right is called a "joug adze" and is used for shaping wooden bucket yokes.

or hammer face of the adze is used in place of a hammer to knock parts into alignment or to drive nails. The long, round poll of a shipwright's adze is used to drive spikes or nails deep below the surface, well out of reach of the cutting edge. Some of these adzes have a straight cutting edge for leveling wide surfaces. Others have turned up ends, or a pronounced curve to the cutting edge like a gouge, for severing and paring the fibers when the tool is worked across the grain.

SHARPENING ADZES

Sharpen an adze similarly to an ax. On a foot adze, the handle gets in the way of sharpening, so quite cleverly the handle is wider toward the end that fits in the "eye" of the adze head and can be driven out and removed. The eye is quite deep, for a strong connection between tool and handle, especially important since the handle isn't permanently wedged into place. You can then grind, file, and hone the edge. An overall edge bevel of 25° is a good place to start. Because the back of the tool forms part of the cutting edge and guides the paring cut, it should be flat and polished, with only a slight back bevel. As

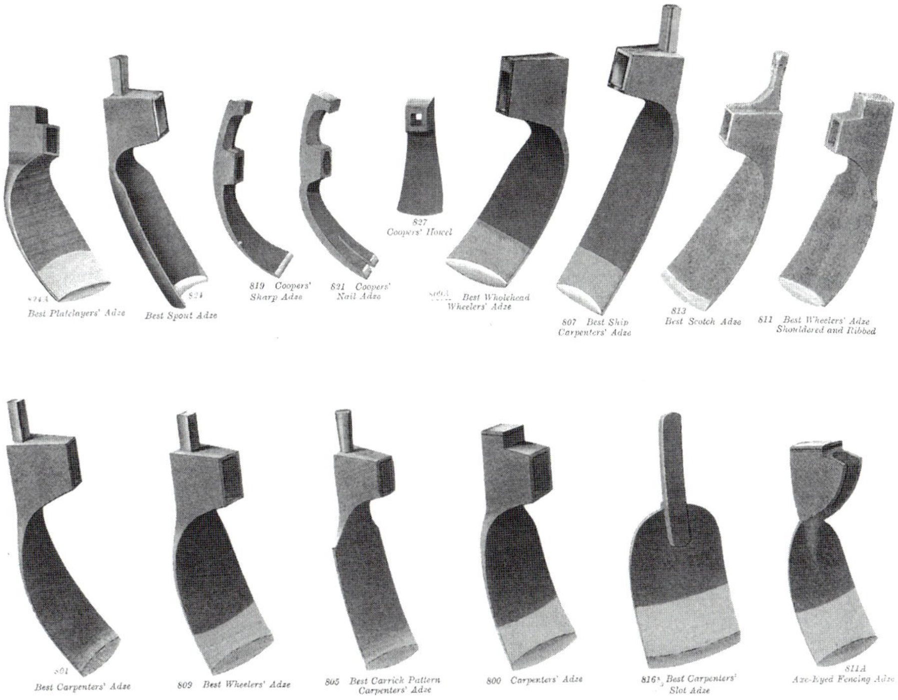

Adzes are used by every trade: shipwrights, coopers, wheelwrights, gutter makers ("spout adzes"), and carpenters. The hammer-like polls on some are useful for banging parts into alignment or for sinking a nail below the surface and out of range of the cutting edge.

Struck with a mallet, a froe splits a log into chair parts or tool handles with minimum waste and, most important, along the grain for maximum strength.

Using the froe as a lever or wedge helps open the split. Because the split wants to run out to the weaker side, pressuring against the heavier side of the bolt keeps the split running true.

with a side ax, the back bevel provides added control as it guides the edge out of each chopping cut. The curve of the blade also helps.

Froes

Imagine a long steel blade with an eye forged into one end for a perpendicular wooden handle, and you have a froe. It could be mistaken for an ax, and is used along with one, but it isn't a true striking tool. Rather, it is struck with a wooden club that drives it into the end grain of a block for splitting out anything from chair parts to shingles. Because it splits rather than cuts the fibers, semi-sharpness is all that is required.

Splitting parts from a log has a few advantages. For one, it's quicker than sawing for producing straight parts such as chair rungs and legs (provided the stock has straight grain). Using a froe and club only, chairmaker Brian Boggs can split the 15 parts he needs to build a chair in about 20 minutes. Another advantage is that the parts will be stronger than if they had been sawn, because the splits follow the grain. In a quality log, hardly any of the wood is wasted (there is no saw kerf), and when it comes to shaping with a drawknife, split parts work far more easily. A cooper's curved froe has one further advantage: The curved blade splits out staves partially shaped to the curve of the barrel or pail.

A froe might be a simple tool, but using one takes skill and strength. The split is started by hitting the top

Wooden mallets are gentle on wooden chisel handles. These simple, shopmade ash mallets have tapered handles that slip into a mortise in the head, wedging the handle in place. The striking faces are angled about 10°, in line with the arc of a natural swing, and they are large so there is less chance of missing the target.

of the blade with the club, driving the froe into the end grain. In a good log, it is then just a question of using the froe to lever open the split, tapping when necessary, and working the split to the end.

It gets tricky when the pieces get smaller—the thinner of the two parts bends, and the split drifts toward the bent side, cutting the piece progressively thinner. One solution is to split a large "bolt" or blank in half (or quarters, if necessary), so the pieces are close to equal in size and will tend to split evenly. You still may need to resort to another solution: pressuring against the thicker side, so that it bends slightly and the split works toward that side. To do this, lay a bolt heavy side down and push down as you lever, using gravity as much as you can (see the bottom photo on the facing page). Or you can hold the work as it is traditionally done: in a tight fork of a tree known as a riving break.

Mallets

The wooden club used to drive a froe is a type of mallet, similar to one a carver might use for driving chisels. The simplest mallets are nothing more than a limb of hardwood, gnarly burl, or root, with one end shaped into a comfortable handle. Large wooden "beetles" or "commanders" are for driving together house and ship frames, where a lot of heft is necessary. A length of tree trunk with a few feet of a limb attached for a handle works quite nicely. The beauty of these simple mallets is that they are easy to make and, for the effort, they last a long time.

The most common mallets are wooden hammers, 1 lb. or so in weight, with large striking faces more gentle on wooden handles, treenails, and furniture parts than the face of a metal hammer. Take a hammer to a chisel handle (other than a steel or plastic one), and you will probably split and ruin it. The larger head of a mallet also gives you a good chance of delivering a stout blow while watching the work (and not the mallet or chisel handle). In the case of driving a mortise and tenon together, a mallet, unlike a hammer, won't mar the wood.

There are two common types of traditional carpenter's mallets: They can be rectangular with slanting faces, similar to a chunk of beam, or cylindrical with a wedged handle at

PART OF THE RICH heritage of woodworking hand tools is the wonderful names that some of these tools carry. Among striking tools alone, there are names such as the curious "beetle," the imperious "commander," and the persuasive "go-devil." Some tools aren't content to have a single name—a "twybill," for example, also goes by the name of two-bill, mortising ax, and grubbing ax.

right angles to it. Both use tough end grain for the striking face. The handle in a rectangular-headed mallet fits in from the end and tapers wider, so it wedges into the head and stays tight. It also has the ergonomic advantage of slanting faces perpendicular to the arc of a natural swing. This delivers a solid, square blow with maximum force. One of the more interesting of the cylindrical-type mallets is a caulker's mallet—a very long, narrow, and iron-bound mallet for driving oakum caulking into the seams between a ship's wooden planking.

Modern mallets usually have rubber or rawhide heads, if they are not made entirely out of plastic. Their main purpose is for assembling woodwork, although a hammer and block of wood work just as well. For all-around chisel work, I still prefer a round carver's mallet made from a dense wood such as lignum vitae. Because it is round, any way you hold it works. Choking up on the handle close to the head gives me maximum control when chiseling or carving, while still producing quite a bit of force. Gripping the mallet farther down on the handle, I have the power for heavier work, such as driving a mortise chisel into oak.

A turned carver's mallet is the ideal tool for all sorts of chiseling and carving work.

Once you get practiced at it, tapping with a mallet rather than working freehand will increase your control. Push a chisel by hand, and there is always a chance of slipping and making large mistakes.

Never hit metal with a mallet or you risk damaging the head. Reflatten a worn head with a block plane and chamfer the edges well. The steady pounding on the long-grain fibers of a carver's mallet eventually separates them (in much the same way that a basketmaker pounds along an ash log to detach long, thin strips for weaving). Turn a new mallet out of any dense wood and, if you want, bore a hole in the end of the head for lead shot or pennies to add to its mass.

For assembling furniture parts, or disassembling trial fits, mallets with rubber, rawhide, or plastic heads deliver hefty blows without marring wooden surfaces.

TO FASTEN HOUSE FRAMES together, an 18th-century carpenter would have used "treenails" or wooden pegs driven into place by mallets or stout, iron-ringed "commanders." For even though hammers were common, iron nails were not. They were handmade and so valuable that when families moved, houses were sometimes burned to recover the nails. Only during the last 100 years or so have nails become so abundant and available in such variety—from tiny brads to huge spikes—that we almost take them for granted.

Every trade had its own special hammers, used for everything from driving wooden shoe pegs to punching holes in roofing slates. Few of the dozens illustrated in this early-20th-century catalog—or the trades that used them—survive today.

Hammers

There will never come a day when hammers are obsolete in the carpentry trade, because there is no more versatile tool than a claw hammer for driving nails, pulling bent ones, knocking things into position, or prying them apart. Hammer designs may have changed in subtle ways since antiquity, with fiberglass or tubular steel handles replacing wood and bone, but they are still the most basic of tools that combine the very different functions of pounding and levering.

During the 19th century, hammers blossomed into a multitude of different forms and functions and, like axes, they were named after specific trades or functions, or for the towns that originated the particular pattern. Naturally each trade favored a certain type of hammer—its weight, or some variation in its shape or size. Some had claws, others two faces of different shape, for driving nails and light riveting, for example. Handles were wood, light and delicately shaped for gentlemen and ladies, sometimes 4 ft. or longer for reaching way up on walls for a bill hanger's hammer, or stout for heavy sledges.

No hammer is more basic than a claw hammer, so-called because opposite the head is a curved or straight claw—ingeniously designed for pulling the nail you just bent over. The opening in the claw tapers toward the head and its inner edges are modestly sharp to get a good grip on a wide range of nail shanks.

A curved claw has better leverage for pulling nails, due to the way it rolls on the claw as you apply pressure to the handle. Straight claws have their advantages too, mostly to carpenters for all kinds of prying—much like a wrecking bar.

The connection between hammer head and wooden handle must be strong and rigid to hold up to constant pounding and levering. The eyes of early hammer heads were round, which were easy to make but not as strong as an oval or rectangular eye common today. And while tapered wooden handles have wonderful flexibility and can absorb vibration, they leave less wood for the handle-to-head connection. Moisture changes also take their toll—as the wooden handle shrinks and swells against the confining eye of the hammer head, the fibers eventually compress and the handle becomes loose.

Making a strong connection between a handle and hammer head has always been a challenge, but especially so on early hammers with narrow heads and shallow eyes. One solution was to rivet a pair of straps to the handle and then clinch them over the head. A more secure method was to forge straps as part of the head (second from left).

A solution that originated in the Middle Ages was to forge two long straps to the head and rivet these to the handle, or to clinch straps through the eye after the head was forged. For rugged small hammers—such as a grocer would use as much for hammering as for prying open cases—another solution that led to modern Stanley and Estwing hammers was to make the head and handle in one forging. In 1840, David Maydole, a blacksmith in Norwich, New York, took yet another approach. By forging a much deeper eye like that of an adze, he created a so-called adze-eye hammer, which became the design for nearly all claw hammers since.

For general-purpose shop work, a curved claw hammer from 12 oz. to 16 oz. is ideal. It's a compromise, but this size can drive a brad and also deliver a good whack to seat a tenon in its mortise. (Having both a light and a heavy hammer is a better solution.) Round faces are the most common, although an octagonal face is an advantage when working in a corner.

One of the few specialty hammers still available and favored by

These unusual hammer heads might seem like playful mistakes, but the designs are surprisingly useful. Double claws make practical sense—the extra claws give you a choice if you need more leverage. The head with two claws (and no apparent striking face) is possibly a shingler's hammer. Notice the head with the corrugated face (far left) for a good grip on the nail.

Veneer hammers are not designed to be swung but rather pressed across a veneered surface to squeeze out trapped air and excess glue. The hammer at left is shop-made with a brass edge; the cast hammer at right has a poll for setting pins that hold the veneer in position.

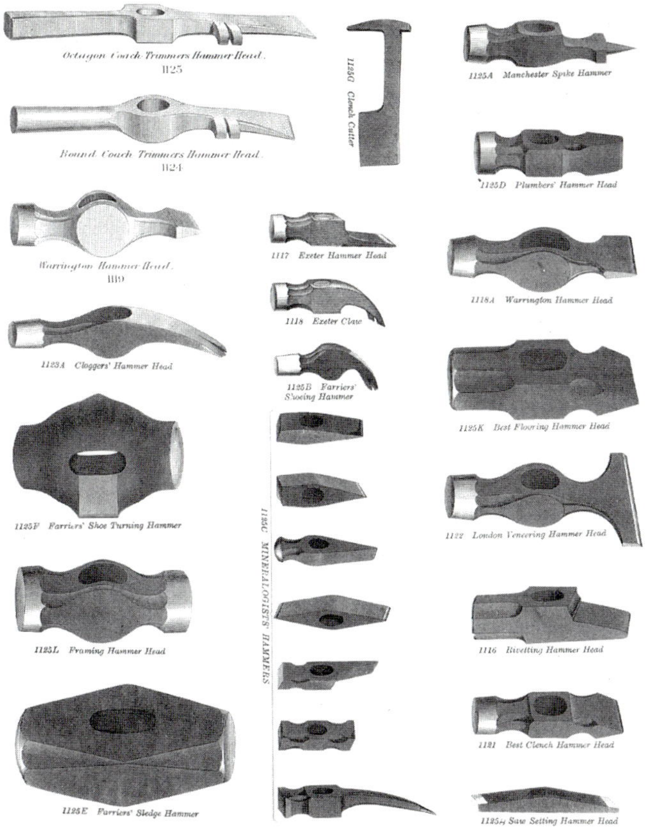

From massive sledges to a delicate coach-trimmer's hammer with a tiny side claw, hammers are as varied as the tasks for which they were designed. Contrast this array of hammer heads from the mid-19th century with the varieties sold in hardware stores today.

Designed in the same vein as handles with interchangeable tools popularized in the Victorian era, this modern hammer patented by George Derbyshire has interchangeable heads stored in the handle: a stainless-steel head for nails, lead and plastic heads for dead-blows, a copper head gentle on metal, and a ball-peen head for riveting and light forging.

One common use for a sledge is to drive a wedge for splitting a log. A wedge or froe allows you to direct the split more easily than with an ax, especially if the split is defined with a saw kerf first.

some cabinetmakers is a Warrington pattern hammer (one is shown in the engraving on p. 73). Instead of a claw, it has a wedge-shaped cross peen an inch or so wide, with a slightly rounded face. You'll appreciate this narrow head the first time you try to start a tiny brad; you may even find it easier to use than a claw hammer with a larger face. A Warrington hammer is also a good riveting hammer and ideal for tightening the knuckle of a knife hinge or tapping in a steel bolt when doing machine maintenance. A ball-peen hammer is another useful machinist's hammer for riveting and metalwork.

As the old joke goes, when things are really going together hard, you just need a bigger persuader. For driving big spikes, a 20-oz. (or larger) framing hammer with a long handle for maximum leverage is one solution. Another is to have a sledge or two. A 3-lb. sledge with a short handle is perfect for giving something a good whack and still maintaining control. For splitting logs (for chair parts or tool handles), a heavier sledge, along with a few wedges, is the best tool.

TUNING A HAMMER

If there was ever a tool that needed little or no tuning, a hammer is it. That isn't to say there is nothing you can do to make your bench hammer a bit more useful. On cheap hammers and well-worn ones, the claws are no longer sharp

Glazier's hammers are used to set small "points" to secure a pane of glass in a window. The large flats of the head ride along the pane of glass. Two styles are shown here, one with a fixed head and the other with a rotating head. The other glazier's tools include a square, pliers for breaking glass, a glass cutter, and modern pliers for setting points.

enough to grip the shank of a nail (only the head). Sometimes filing along the back curve of the claws will sharpen them, or you could try a small file between them. Then file the end of one of the claws into a chisel-like edge, so you can reach into tight cracks and pry things apart.

TOOLS USED WITH HAMMERS

In my shop in a typical week, I could be working on a piece of furniture one day and tuning a machine or making a piece of hardware the next. Besides different hammers, the variety of the work requires an assortment of punches, nail sets, and cold chisels. Look for them at tool sales or buy them as the need arises.

It's impossible to do blind nailing without a nail set. This is the tool for setting the tiny head of a finish nail below the surface of the wood (see the photo on p. 77), or for driving one in an awkward place. Rather than risk marring the wood,

For many woodworking and metalworking tasks, especially for making and repairing tools, you'll need some small cold chisels of different sizes (at right) as well as (from left) a center punch for marking drill holes, nail sets, punches, and a ball-peen hammer.

I often use one for driving a nail the last ¼ in. You'll need at least two: a nail set with a very small tip for fine nails and brads, and a slightly larger one for common finish nails. New nail sets have a concave tip, supposedly to grip the nail head better. A flat point works okay, but better yet is to grind the end to a blunt point and it will prick into the nail head like a center punch and stay put.

A center punch is another essential tool used with a hammer. It pricks the location of a hole before drilling, to prevent the bit from wandering by giving it a place to start. Center punches are usually metalworking tools, but they work just as well with wood, especially for such work as marking pilot holes for hinge screws. A similar punch with a flat end and a long, tapered shank is sometimes called a drift pin. It is ideal for driving out stuck bolts, hinge pins, or a broken-off handle in a hammer head. Another useful tool you should always have on hand is a cold chisel, which can be used for cutting metal, too (such

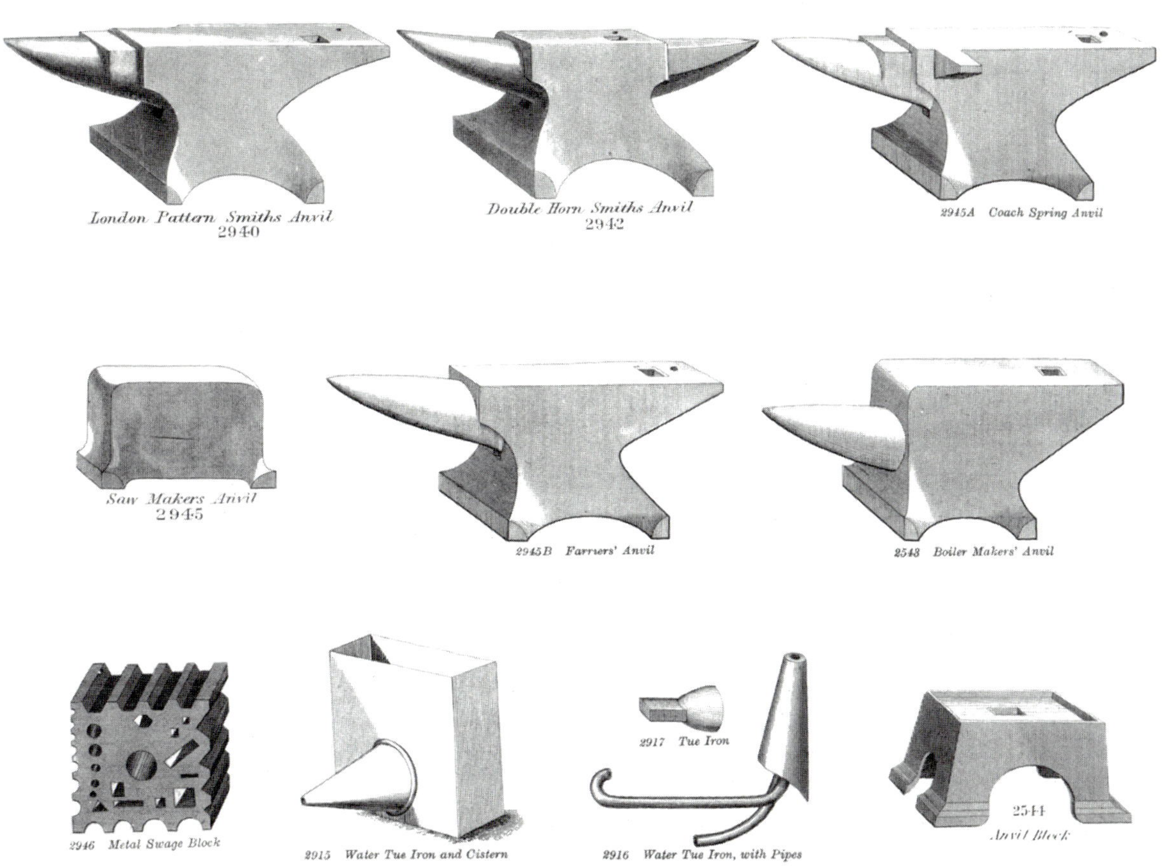

Anvils used to be available for every conceivable trade. A large floor anvil or even a smaller bench model is good for forging, riveting, flattening a bent hinge leaf, or driving a new handle into an ax or hammer head.

as a nail in an awkward spot or to enlarge the slot in a damaged screw). You should have a few sizes, and keep them sharpened.

Somewhere along your woodworking road you'll probably need an anvil—the equivalent of a workbench for metalworking. A good machinist's vise often has a flat area behind the jaws that works well as a small anvil. (A machinist's vice is useful to have for any number of holding and sharpening tasks away from your woodworking bench, where you can afford to be a little messy.) Better yet is a bench anvil, a small, portable anvil that can take heavier pounding. Meanwhile, keep your eyes out for a 125-lb. (or heavier) floor anvil. With a round, tapered horn and a large flat surface, this is the right tool for hot or cold forging, or for lighter work such as flattening a bent hinge leaf or peening over a rivet.

IF YOU EVER WANT to upset an overconfident carpenter, wax the face of his hammer. The hammer will slide off the nail head every time, no matter how good his aim. For the opposite effect, sanding the face of a hammer gives it a bit more grip. For this reason, a shingler's hammer is almost always checkered, and Stanley once offered hammers with corrugated faces.

Use a nail set to sink the small head of a finish nail below the surface. A slightly pointed tip (similar to a center punch) pricks the nail head and stays put. A finger or two against the wood surface helps steady the nail set.

CHISELS, *Gouges, and Drawknives*

A chisel is a simple tool. It's a blade with a beveled cutting edge and a handle to hold, guide, and drive the tool. Essential to hand woodworking for paring a joint to fit, chopping joinery of all kinds, or shaping wood, a chisel is simple in design but not necessarily simple to use. All of the control comes from the skill and coordination of the user, not from the design of the tool.

Gouges and drawknives are simple tools as well, with the same chisel-like edges, except that they are curved, or in the case of a drawknife, elongated and powered by two handles rather than one. As with chisels, you can vary your technique within a single stroke to go from cutting a coarse shaving to making a fine, paring cut.

A typical set of bench chisels, ranging in size from ⅛ in. to 1¼ in., for chopping mortises, cutting tenons, or paring joints. This set was made by Buck Brothers, of Millbury, Mass., one of largest and best-known makers of chisels and gouges.

Chisels

Chisels and chisel edges show up everywhere in hand tools. A plane is a sophisticated chisel, a saw or file a series of chisel teeth, an auger a chisel turning around a center point, and an ax or adze a chisel swung from a long handle. In its most basic form, a chisel is a rectangular steel blade sharpened to a beveled edge and connected to a handle. As with all the basic woodworking hand tools, there are endless variations for specific purposes.

Making sense of the various types of chisels can be bewildering, especially when it comes to choosing a set of chisels for everyday bench work. Which of the various types do you need? Is one style or length more useful than another? The questions can go on and on, because even with fewer choices than there once were, there are still many types of chisels available. In Sheffield, England, the historic center of edge-tool manufacturing, makers such as Robert Sorby, William Marples, and Ward and Payne offered an array of chisels. American makers such as Buck Brothers of Millbury, Massachusetts and Peck, Stow & Wilcox of Southington, Connecticut, among many others, at one time offered dozens of various types and sizes of chisels. Naturally, the many woodworking trades favored particular styles of chisels, each with a slightly different shape, length, weight, or handle.

Chisels can be divided into three types: firmer, mortise, and paring. Each type comes in a range of sizes from about 1⁄16 in. wide to 2 in. wide or even wider (except for mortise chisels, which are usually under 1 in. wide). Firmer chisels are the ones that spring to mind when you think of "bench chisels," and for good reason—they are generally the most useful. They have modestly long blades, a beveled or flat top face, and a cross section with enough steel to hold up to mallet blows. Mortise chisels are stout, deeper in section than their width to withstand the heavy work of cutting mortises. The longest and lightest in section are paring chisels. They are pushed by hand alone and are far less common than they once were.

All chisels have either flat faces or, on better chisels, bevels parallel with the long edges. Beveling the face was once a laborious process of hand grinding on huge water-powered grindstones, which added to the cost but makes for a more beautiful tool. Bevels also lighten a chisel without sacrificing strength and reduce its profile so that it can work in tight places, such as inside a dovetail, where the thicker edge of a flat-faced chisel may not fit. Cabinetmaker James Krenov grinds the faces of his bench chisels into two wide bevels, giving them a triangular profile. Even some mortise chisels have a slight bevel along the sides to give the blade a bit of relief when working in a tight mortise.

Vital to the strength of a chisel, especially one worked hard with a mallet, is a strong connection between the blade and handle. The simplest, yet by no means the easiest to make, is a blade forged into a tapering tang and driven into a wooden handle. (Skill is involved forging the tang strong enough to take the stress, yet not so hard that it becomes brittle, or so soft that it bends.) A brass or steel ferrule around the handle resists any splitting action caused by the tang. An improvement on this system was to forge a "bolster"—a widened area at the base of the tang for the handle to butt against and help absorb the force from handle to blade. Mortise chisels have large bolsters, paring chisels much smaller ones. On good chisels, a leather washer between bolster and handle further absorbs some of the shock of a mallet blow.

The most costly chisels have a superior method of joining the handle and blade: with a forged, tapered socket instead of a tang. The end of the handle has a mating taper, so that the harder the chisel is driven the tighter the connection. No fer-

Chisels vary in size, handle style and material, and blade shape (either beveled or tapered in thickness). This array of common chisels includes (from left) a timber-framing chisel, a small mortising chisel, a paring chisel, a Japanese firmer chisel, and two beveled firmer chisels.

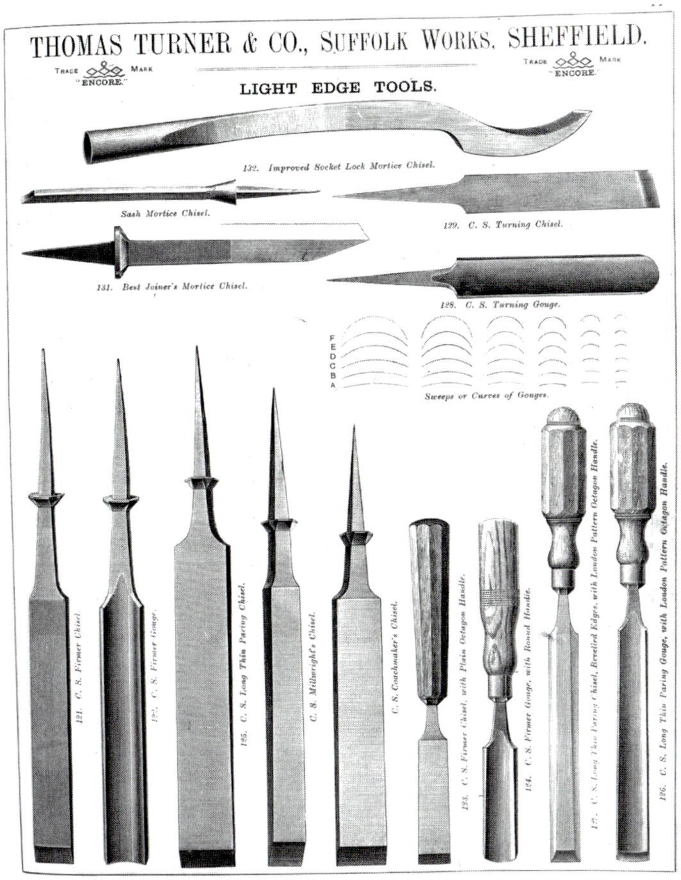

Quality chisels and gouges such as the ones advertised here have tang construction, which would have been fitted into handles either bought separately or made in the shop.

Chisel blades are designed for specific types of work: the short, tapered, and beveled blade of a bench or firmer chisel (top) provides careful control; the long and thin blade of a paring chisel, sometimes beveled, guides fine cuts (middle); and the thick, tapered, and square-edged blade of a mortise chisel is for hard chopping (bottom).

rule is required, since the end of the handle is captured in the socket. On heavy-duty chisels such as framing chisels, the top of the handle is sometimes "hooped" with a steel ring that keeps it from mushrooming over, or it is fitted with a leather washer to cushion mallet blows. Unfortunately, it is common to find used socket chisels with the handles long gone and the socket deformed by years of abuse with a hammer. If the socket isn't split or excessively deformed, it can probably be restored.

There are no simple generalizations about handle styles: it's a personal choice. Most are round, some are oval, often they taper for a more comfortable grip or have flat facets for the same reason (and so the chisel doesn't roll off the bench). Because handles were sold out of the same catalogs that sold chisels (and in just as much variety), a cabinetmaker could fit a favorite handle style to all his chisels. The most prized (and the ones usually fitted to the finest chisels) are those made of boxwood, sometimes delicately turned and detailed with incised rings. Ash and beech handles are more common.

Secondhand or new, there are many different chisels to choose from. One approach is to buy a set of new firmer chisels (or used firmer chisels in a range of sizes) and add a few mortise chisels or paring chisels as you find them or need them. Everyone has their own opinions about which chisels are best, but as with many tools, learning to tune and use what you have is more important that owning a wide variety of tools.

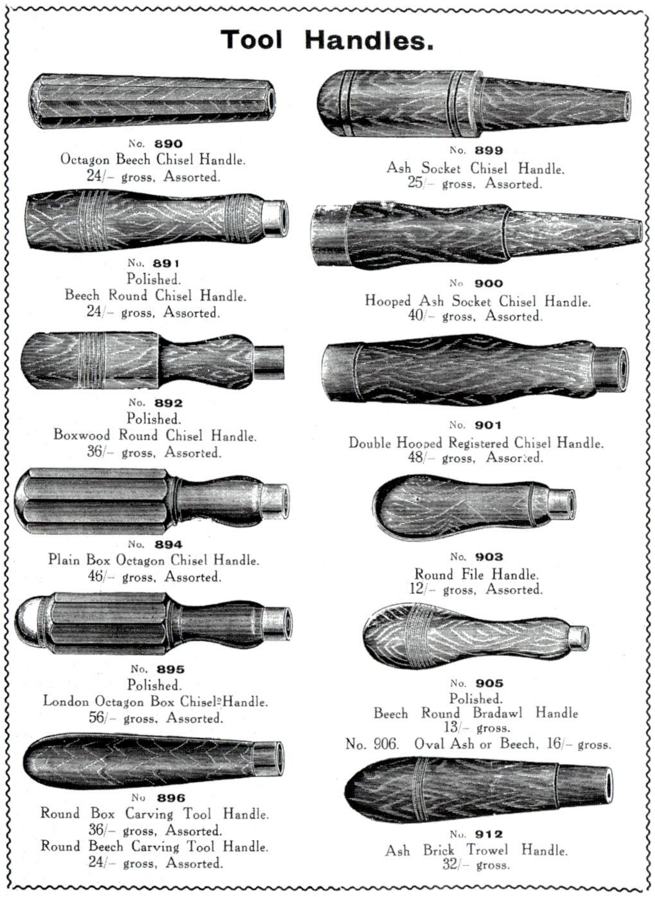

In the old days, you could buy tool handles from a catalog if you needed a replacement and you chose not to make your own. Such handles came in all sorts of styles, from octagonal beech to fancy boxwood handles, for socketed chisels or those with tanged blades.

FIRMER CHISELS

Firmer chisels are general-purpose bench chisels. Speculation as to where the name came from—perhaps a corruption of "former" or "forming"—suggests the importance of firmer chisels for the preliminary shaping and cutting of joints. In fact, they are well suited to contemporary woodworking, where most work is done first by machine and then at the bench with chisels or other tools. As something of a compromise between the stoutness of a mortise chisel and the fineness of a paring chisel, they will do either task adequately.

There is such a range of firmer chisels that it is hard to get too specific about what they look like (it is easier to say that they do not look like mortise or paring chisels). The blade can be as long as 8 in., which isn't much shorter than some paring chisels. The body of the blade is modestly thick, enough to hold up to being driven with a mallet, but not so thick that the chisel feels heavy. Yet on framing chisels, a type of firmer chisel, the blade is quite thick for cutting joints in large timbers.

THE SET OF Swedish firmer chisels the author bought more than 20 years ago has 13 sizes, from ⅛ in. through 1½ in., graduated roughly by eighths. Today you are lucky to find a set with any more than seven or eight sizes. The advantage of having many sizes to choose from is flexibility—you have more choices when cutting a mortise or spacing the pins on a set of dovetails.

"EVERLASTING" CHISELS

SHORT FIRMER CHISELS are known as butt firmer chisels. These are the style of the Everlasting line of chisels that Stanley produced early in this century, with blades as short as 3 in. and heavy steel-buttressed handles (to take the shock of a hammer, rather than a mallet, used by a careless carpenter). They were advertised as ideal for cutting butt and other hinge mortises, but in fact they have another advantage. The short blade means your hand stays close to the edge, giving you a lot more control than chisels with longer blades. The disadvantage is that butt chisels are useless for any sort of deep mortising or paring, because the blades just aren't long enough.

Stanley "Everlasting" beveled firmer chisels are easy to control, and the design of the tang makes for a very rugged chisel that can withstand hammer blows.

MORTISE CHISELS

Mortise chisels have a distinct shape that sets them apart from firmer and paring chisels: a thick cross section, often quite a bit deeper than they are wide. They need to be massive to take the constant beating of a mallet. They also need to be thick to give the cutting edge plenty of support. Lighter versions of this design, for more delicate mortising, are called sash mortise chisels. Before there were routers and mortising machines—the tools most likely to cut mortises in a shop today—a mortise chisel was the tool for the job. To cut a ½-in.-wide mortise, all you needed was a ½-in. mortise chisel and a mallet.

In softwood, a skilled cabinetmaker can cut all four mortises for a small cabinet door, by hand, in 10 minutes or less. I've seen it done. To work this fast with a simple tool takes skill and flawless technique. But there are subtleties of the design of a mortise chisel that help. Generations of joiners have refined these tools to make them easier to use, with more predictable results.

Mortise chisels have thick tapered blades, large bolsters with leather washers to cushion mallet blows, and oval handles for a comfortable grip for twisting the blade into alignment with the mortise. They sometimes are sharpened with a rounded bevel, making it easier to lever out the chips.

The long blade of a paring chisel, sometimes so thin it's slightly flexible, guides the cut as if it were a plane's sole. Fancy London pattern handles are typical on such fine cabinetmaker's tools.

When chopping a mortise, one cut follows another along the length, going deeper each time and levering out the waste. Understanding this helps to see another virtue of the deep profile of the blade: A thick blade helps guide the chisel in a straight line, cutting a mortise of consistent width. Some mortise chisels have a slight bevel from back to face, giving the blade clearance and allowing for some twisting of the blade to keep it on course. And because a large part of the work with a mortise chisel is levering out the waste, rounding the bevel is a small refinement that works like a rounded hammer claw, for when you're levering with the bevel down.

PARING CHISELS

Paring chisels are the most refined. They are lighter, with wide face bevels, and often ornate boxwood handles. Used mainly by joiners, cabinetmakers, and patternmakers, paring chisels have long, thin blades—some even flex slightly—for delicate paring and fitting, and for getting into tight places unreachable with a shorter chisel. One variation on a typical paring chisel has a handle offset from the blade, known as "cranked" or trowel-handled, for such work as paring the bottom of a long groove. Paring chisels should never be struck with a mallet, but driven by hand alone.

One of the more unusual paring chisels is called a slick. Slicks are heavy and huge, as big as 4 in. across, with long handles bulging into a knob for placing a shoulder or palm against. A canoe builder I know uses a slick for every sort of cutting task imaginable—in fact, it's one of the few tools he uses—from paring joints between planking to fitting ribs and decks. Traditionally, slicks were used by house joiners and shipwrights for the same sort of careful fitting of large parts. A slick's weight and balance turn what might seem like an ungainly tool into one capable of precise paring or aggressive shaping. A slick is sharpened no differently than a paring chisel, except that the cutting edge is shaped into a slight curve for maximum control.

With blades as wide as 4 in. and handles 12 in. or more in length, slicks are the largest chisels, but they are capable of finer work than their size suggests. They were traditionally a shipbuilding tool, used to pare, level, and fit decking and frames.

Japanese bench chisels typically have short blades for precision work and backs ground hollow to make the chore of flattening them easier.

EASTERN CHISELS

In terms of function, Japanese chisels are not much different from their Western counterparts. But it doesn't take a very close look to see that Japanese chisels are, for the most part, much shorter and stockier. The handles are connected differently, the blades are laminated, and the backs of the chisels are flat only around the edges (they are ground hollow in the middle). I have a few Japanese chisels mixed in with the rest of my hand tools, and I use

As much for decoration as function, high-quality Japanese bench chisels sometimes have multiple hollows ground into the back. For a strong connection with the handle, they have another characteristic feature: a combination socket and tanged blade. A Japanese paring chisel (second from right) looks short compared to its western counterpart (right).

them regularly. As Japanese tools have become more available in the past 20 years, many craftsmen have adopted them, and while some are more qualified to explain the subtleties of these tools, I offer these observations.

For one accustomed to Western chisels, the most noticeable difference in Japanese chisels is their shorter, stockier blades, more like short butt chisels than typical long-bladed firmer chisels. The advantage of this design is that your hand is closer to the work, giving you more control and reducing the amount of blade through which you must transfer the force. The handles are rigidly connected by a combination of tang and socket. A heavy tang unites the blade and handle, with a long socket-shaped ferrule fitting between them. Below the ferrule the tang widens into the same tapering shape and functions as a bolster.

A profound difference between Eastern and Western chisels is in the forging of the blades. Rather than being cut from one piece of high-carbon steel, Japanese blades have a hard steel cutting edge forge-welded to a softer, wrought-iron back (the soft steel sometimes is made from old anchors or anchor chains). The softer back absorbs most of the cutting stress, enabling the cutting edge to be quite a bit harder than Western chisels. Such edges stay sharp longer, but they are more brittle and require a stouter bevel angle.

Because you can't use more than one chisel at a time, tool designer George Derbyshire made a single handle with interchangeable blades (right). On the left is a prototype for an ergonomic handle that encourages a firm grip for both paring and chopping.

The key to sharpening a chisel is flattening the back, either on a lapping table or working from coarse to fine stones. The hollowed Japanese chisel (right) illustrates that the entire back need not be flat, only the area near the cutting edge.

SHARPENING AND TUNING CHISELS

To work properly, the back of a chisel must be dead flat and polished. A flat back mainly serves to guide the cut, but it is also half of the cutting edge. For shorter chisels, the last inch or so should be flat; on longer paring chisels, at least a few inches. For either, the area close to the cutting edge must be flat. While this sounds easy to do in theory, getting the back of a chisel flat—even a brand new one right out of the box—takes patience. Take heart in knowing you'll only flatten the back once.

To flatten the back, you'll need a lapping table (see p. 25). The most difficult chisels to lap flat are those that have a back that is slightly con-

SOCKET VS. TANG

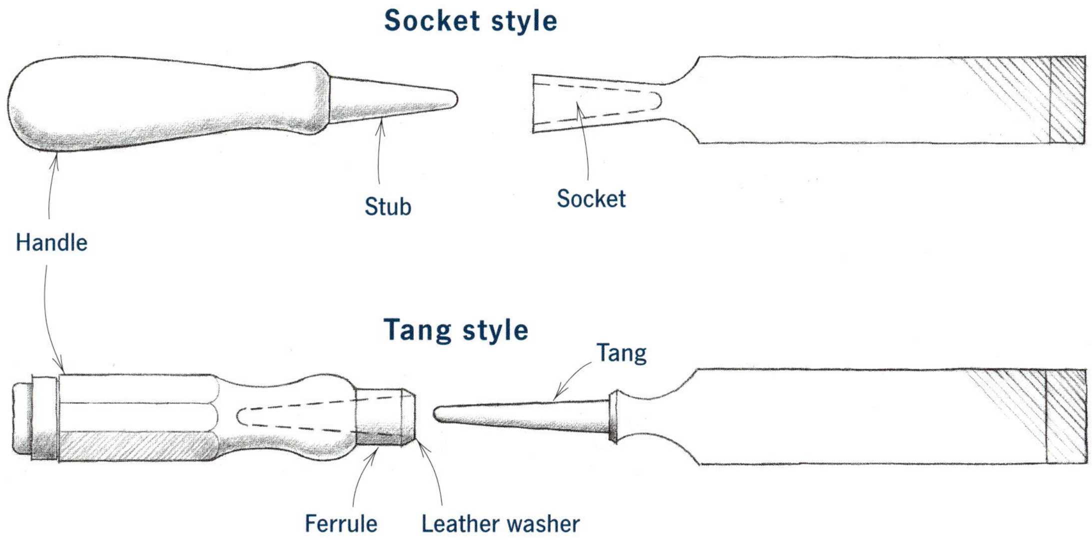

vex along its length (chisels with a concave back are considerably easier to flatten). On these chisels, you must remove most of the high area toward the middle first, in order to flatten up to the cutting edge (and the chisel will rock around while you do this). Japanese chisels have hollow backs to make flattening easier, but for Western chisels, it's a matter of persistence, moving from a coarse to a finer grit, and finally honing the back on ever-finer sharpening stones. If there is any pitting near the cutting edge, you'll need to lap it out. Finally, with your finest stone, dull the corners of the blade along the sides. They can be extremely sharp, and you will come into contact with them regularly.

Sharpen the bevel as you would any other—straight across, except in the case of a slick, when a bit of camber helps. Bevel angles vary from as low as 15° for paring chisels, 20° to 25° for firmer chisels and everyday bench work, and 30° for mortise chisels. As with tuning any edge, these bevel angles are guides—good places to start. Don't be afraid to fine-tune your chisels to the specific work you do, if you are so inclined. Use a lower overall bevel and hone on a 5° microbevel if you want easier sharpening and better performance. Just be careful with mortise chisels for use with hardwoods. This is heavy work that demands a stout edge. Don't hollow-grind mortise chisels, but rather hone the edge with a modest microbevel, or convex, to give the cutting edge extra support.

> **HOW DO YOU TELL if a chisel is really sharp? There's the old fingernail trick for testing a sharp edge—seeing if it grabs rather than slides along a fingernail—or you might try shaving some arm hair. But the best test is to use the chisel on wood: Only a truly sharp edge will easily pare pine end grain and leave a glass smooth surface. A less than perfect edge will tear out fibers and leave noticeable streaks where areas of the edge are the slightest bit dull.**

Replacing a chisel handle

Chisel handles usually don't need much tuning, but the handles on your workhorse chisels may need replacing from time to time. Socket chisels are the easiest to replace, es-

Bevel up or bevel down? Keep the bevel up to the waste side for paring or, as shown here, chopping the waste from a mortise. Turn the bevel down to use the chisel in the same orientation as a plane iron, or for levering out the waste.

The most accurate way to cut to a line is to use the widest chisel that will fit and creep up on the line slowly. Waste as much as possible this way so that the final cut just pares to the line. A knife line, seen here on this tenon shoulder, also helps by creating a tiny groove to hold the chisel's edge.

pecially if you have access to a lathe. Remove the broken stub by drilling it out. The only tricky part is sizing the tenon to the socket. I measure the diameter of the socket at the top, its depth, and guess the diameter at the bottom. I then turn the tenon to these dimensions, scraping and fitting by hand from there.

Every trial fit leaves marks on the handle where the high points rub. You want the two parts to mate closely to keep the handle firmly connected. But be sure to leave a small gap between the top of the socket and the corresponding shoulder on the handle, and cut the handle shy of the bottom so that, over time, the handle can seat more fully into the socket.

To replace a tang-type chisel handle, shape it to suit your hand and turn one end to the inside diameter of your ferrule. I cut my ferrules from brass pipe, thin-walled for light chisels and thicker for heavier chisels. You can cut the ferrule with a hacksaw or pipe cutter and file the inside smooth.

The hardest part of fitting the handle is drilling a hole along the centerline to receive the tang. If you are adept at turning, you can do a lot of this drilling on the lathe after turning the handle; otherwise, set the handle upright in a vise. I drill a hole with three diameters: one the full depth of the tang and equal to its smallest dimension; the second about half as deep and equal to the dimension of the middle of the tang; and the third hole ½-in. deep, and just a bit smaller than the largest part of the tang. The wood will compress to accommodate the tang, but you don't want to split the handle either. Cut a leather washer for the tang and drive the handle on.

Simple jigs can make laying out and cutting complex joints quicker and more accurate. This pair helps cut matching haunched mortises and tenons.

USING CHISELS

Much of woodworking involves the use of chisels. Some chisel work is careful fitting, some is aggressive chopping; no single technique works for it all. Even a simple task such as chopping a mortise has endless variations depending upon how you learned and what you are after, so I am going to leave descriptions of cutting dovetails and joinery to books better suited to that subject. Instead, I'll describe some techniques that will improve any work you do with chisels.

The first question that typically comes up is whether to use a chisel bevel up or bevel down. The simple answer is bevel up, or to the waste side, but it really depends upon the work you are doing. When paring or chopping accurately to a line, the flat back of the chisel against the line guides the cut. If the back has any sort of back bevel or a back that's not truly flat, you won't have this reference surface to help guide you.

However, if you are paring the bottom of a groove, or cutting with the chisel angled off the surface, the flat back is no longer a useful guide. Besides, it's hard to use a chisel that way—the angle of approach is too high and all the chisel wants to do is dig in—so turn it around with the bevel down. Use the bevel to guide the cut, and adjust the cutting

BUYING USED CHISELS

THERE'S NO EASY way to tell a good chisel—or any edge tool for that matter—from a mediocre one. The quality of the steel used in the chisel is paramount, but you can't just look at the steel and tell much about it. The composition of the steel certainly affects how a chisel will sharpen and hold its edge, but far more important is how the steel was forged and heat-treated. Short of sharpening and using the chisel, though, you won't know if it was tempered too hard (meaning it will be brittle), or if it is too soft and will dull quickly.

But buying a used chisel isn't entirely a shot in the dark. You can tell a lot just by looking at the chisel. Does it appear as though it was carefully forged and finished? Are the bevels consistent? Is the socket (if the chisel has one) robust and in line with the blade? Is the back of the chisel flat? If necessary, check it with a straightedge.

Craftsmen usually made their own handles, so the quality of the handle isn't always a reliable guide. However, if a chisel has a shapely handle that looks like it has seen much use, you can bet that someone valued it. The best guide to quality is to look for particular manufacturers with stellar reputations: Reliable names include T. H. Witherby; James Swan (number one in my mind); Peck, Stow, and Wilcox (marked as P, S & W); L. and I. J. White; Underhill Edge Tool; and Charles Buck (Buck Brothers is better known but has an uneven reputation for quality).

For cutting angled mortises accurately, a wooden block with a fence makes a good guide for your chisel. Use a chisel with a long blade, as wide as possible, and take paring cuts.

A chisel functions as a flat-backed knife for light paring cuts, such as trimming the end of a delicate table leg. Use your thumb for leverage and a slicing or skew cut. Chamfer the edges first to prevent breaking out the fibers.

depth by raising or lowering the chisel handle and levering against the bevel.

The first impulse when cutting to a line (when chopping a mortise, for example) is to put the edge of the chisel right on the line and start chopping. Resist this temptation—it's impossible to work accurately this way. Because of the shape of the cutting edge, pressure against the beveled face drives the back of the chisel hard against the work. Chop deep enough and the pressure will be so great the chisel will compress the fibers and drift beyond the line. The only way to overcome this is to creep up on your lines, wasting what you can before getting close, and finishing with as light a paring cut as possible.

I prefer to mark out with a knife or mortising gauge because it gives me a very fine groove to locate the cutting edge for this final cut. For a straight, true cut (on a tenon shoulder, for instance), work with the widest chisel that will fit. You also can hit a wide chisel more aggressively than a narrow one. Be careful of one last thing: When cutting all the way through a piece, cut from both sides rather than just one—you'll be less apt to split out the fibers.

Chiseling with a mallet is usually more controllable than working by hand alone. The exception is paring. When paring a surface, use both hands—one hand pushing and the other guiding the blade, especially when working close to an edge, where the back of the chisel has little support. When you have no choice but to work against the grain, pare with a light cut for the smoothest surface. Another way I like to pare is to use a curving and slicing action, with the chisel flat on the work, using my thumb for leverage. The trick is to take a light cut, using a corner of the cutting edge and skewing it across the work.

SOME UNUSUAL CHISELS

While firmer, mortise, and paring chisels will perform the bulk of your chiseling needs in the workshop, there are a few unusual chisels that can come in handy. These include skew chisels, scraper chisels, drawer-lock chisels, and lock-mortise chisels.

A bench chisel ground to a skew, anywhere from 10° to 20°, makes an incredibly useful chisel for paring the waste out of dovetails or other fine joinery where space is tight. Grind a right and a left skew for the most versatility.

A chisel ground with a very steep bevel (70° to 90°) might seem too blunt to be useful, but such a chisel works like a high-angle scraper, for controlled paring such as truing the bed of a wooden plane. The flat back helps guide the cut.

Skew chisels

Skew chisels are similar to paring chisels, except that they have a skewed cutting edge rather than a square one. It always strikes me as curious that I've never seen a used skew chisel—and I've only recently seen them in catalogs—because this is a very useful tool. Woodturners use skews, but evidently not many joiners. I made one many years ago from a broken chisel I found in a discount bin at a woodworking supply store. By chance, the blade was snapped off at about a 20° skew, so I sharpened it that way to see how it would work. For paring end grain in tight places, no other chisel is quite as handy. While you can now buy a pair with opposing skews, you can also grind any chisel with a skewed edge.

Scraping chisels

A scraping chisel is another simple idea. The tool couldn't be easier to make and is capable of the most controlled scraping and cutting. Instead of a 25° bevel, a scraping chisel is ground and honed closer to 90° (as low as 70° also works). Such an edge is anything but blunt if sharpened well. For trimming a haunch in a mortise, or for its traditional use—cleaning up the bed of a wooden plane—a scraping chisel produces fine, consistent shavings without digging into the wood. The flat back provides excellent control.

CUTTING CORNERS

TOOL MANUFACTURERS love to make tools and sell them with the promise that they are just what we need to increase our speed, improve our accuracy, or both. Take corner chisels, for example. Made to chop the corners of mortises perfectly square in one pass, they're really no faster than a firmer chisel and far more difficult to sharpen. Trying to get a single bevel sharp is one thing, but honing two bevels—side by side with no room between them—can drive you crazy. No matter how you do it, one edge will be either slightly longer than the other, out of square, or you will leave a little hook in the corner. Corner chisels might be useful for chopping large mortises (although I doubt it), but they are certainly superfluous in furniture making. Stick with your simple and versatile bench chisels.

Corner chisels are designed to create perfectly square corners by cutting adjacent sides of a mortise simultaneously. Although great in theory, in reality they are difficult to sharpen and align in the mortise, making them no more efficient than a firmer chisel.

In this cutaway view of a mortise, a lock-mortise or swan's-neck chisel levers against the side to pare the bottom—a task difficult to do with a bench chisel. Originally these chisels were designed to cut a deep lock mortise through a door stile and into the tough end grain of the rail, but they are just as useful in any deep mortise.

Drawer-lock and lock-mortise chisels

Very different, but just as useful for those unusual chiseling jobs, are drawer-lock and lock-mortise chisels. They are related only in that both have uses chiseling mortises for locks. A lock-mortise chisel (or swan's neck chisel, as it is also called, because of the gentle curve of the blade) can cut with the same sort of scraping action as a scraping chisel. Imagine a deep mortise for a lockset, so deep you have to cut into the end grain of the lock rail. A lock-mortise chisel is designed to lever from the sides of the mortise and neatly pare the end grain away. Sharpen the blunt edge as you would for scraping, or with a fine bevel for paring long grain in the bottom of deep mortises.

What do you do when you want to fit a lock to a small drawer after the fact, or chisel in an area too small even for a butt chisel? A drawer lock chisel is the answer. Z-shaped and struck with a hammer, it has two chisel ends at right angles to one another, so it is able to cut at right angles or parallel to an edge. I've never seen a new one offered anywhere, but it would be simple enough to forge one yourself.

A drawer-lock chisel works in the tightest spots, as when retrofitting a lock to a small drawer. Both ends of the Z-shaped tool have flat chisel blades at 90° to one another. The chisel is hit at the bend with a hammer or mallet.

Gouges and Carving Tools

Carving is a skill with its own special techniques and tools, and entire books have been written about the carving cousins of chisels—gouges and other carving hand tools. As a generalist when it comes to furniture making, I carve as little as I need to get by. Nevertheless, I use a number of carving tools, especially gouges. Think of them as curved chisels, useful for shaping curved joints, fairing the transition between moldings, and adding small decorative touches.

Gouges come in two basic types: in-cannel or paring gouges sharpened with the bevel on the inside,

A typical set of gouges has blades of different curvatures, with bevels on the inside for curved paring cuts (or copes, as seen in background), or on the outside for carving. The two cranked patternmaker's gouges (right) will smooth the bottoms of long troughlike shapes.

Gouges did and still do come in a dizzying array of shapes and curves, known as their sweep. Sweeps are classified as flat, middle, scribing, and fluting. In today's catalogs, they are more likely to be identified by number, with higher numbers for greater curvature.

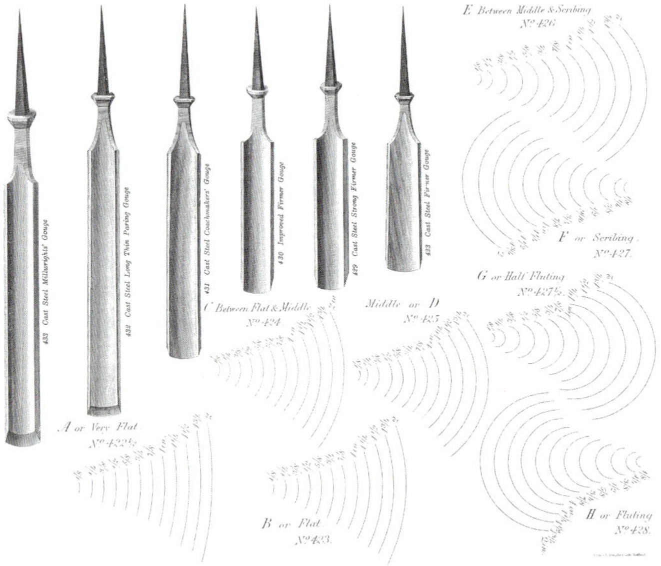

and out-cannel or firmer gouges sharpened with the bevel on the outside. The way they cut is very different and they are not interchangeable. An out-cannel gouge is probably the one that comes to mind first. This is used for carving into a surface, with the bevel down as with a bench chisel. It also can make convex cuts, for paring or coping, which is a way of joining two moldings together by cutting one to fit over the shape of the other (see the facing page).

An in-cannel gouge works like a paring chisel, for shaping and concave coping cuts. Gouges are further classified by the sweep or curve of the cutting edge (regular, middle, or flat) and the shape of the blade (bent, spoon, back bent, fish tail, and on and on). A serious carver might have a few hundred carving tools, although a dozen or more can do the lion's share of the work.

TUNING AND USING GOUGES

Gouges and all the common carving tools are sharpened like chisels, the only difference being that most of them have curved edges. Ideally, you'll need a few different shapes of slipstones, although you can get by

Owning even a few carving tools gives you the ability to add decorative touches to your work, such as carved knobs and pulls. This assortment of carving tools includes V-groove, fishtail, spoon, and straight gouges.

with fine abrasive paper wrapped around different-sized dowels (or other shapes). Follow the shape of the existing edge as much as you can, as least as a start. As with a chisel, bevel only one face of the edge and keep the other as flat as possible. It is not important that the edge be straight across. For out-cannel tools, rolling the bevel across the stone is a good way to hone it consistently.

In addition to their obvious uses for carving, gouges are a necessary tool for coping, a method of joining two moldings more securely than is possible by mitering (see the photos at right). A coped joint is a relatively quick joint to cut and it stays tight as the parts move with changes in humidity. To cope quarter-round moldings meeting at an inside corner of a cabinet door, first miter one side with a wide chisel (or a backsaw, if you prefer). Then, with an in-cannel gouge close to the same curve as the molding, cut vertically along the molded edge of the mitered surface. The other side of the joint needs no coping, and when fitted together should slip fully within the coped profile.

Putting a gouge to work on a scrap of softwood such as pine or basswood is the best way to understand how they cut. From there it isn't a big leap to carving little touches in your work, such as pulls, knobs, or moldings. These are details that only the curved cutting edges of carving tools can accomplish.

A coped joint will stay tight despite the inevitable shrinkage of the parts. Start by mitering the side that will be coped with the aid of a mitering jig and a wide chisel.

Working vertically and using your fingers to guide the cut, cope or pare the back of the miter to a knife edge with an in-cannel gouge. A slight undercut is okay.

The uncut side should slip into the coped recess for an invisible joint. The advantage of this joint over a simple miter is that it will stay tight even as the wood shrinks or moves.

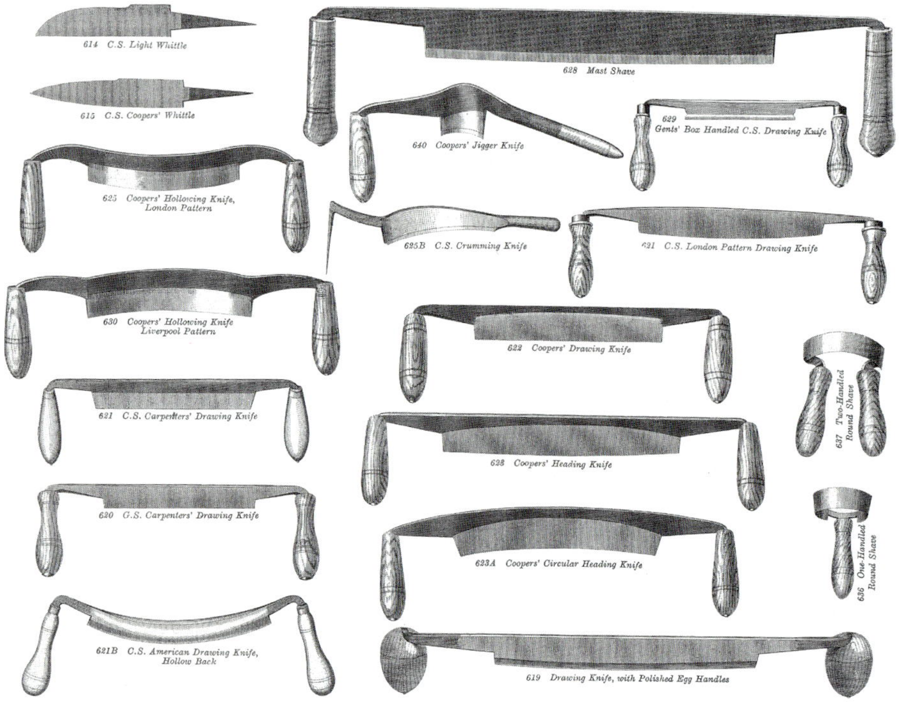

Coopers used many drawknives: one for beveling the head and bottom of the barrel, another for shaping the staves inside and out, another for leveling an area for the head (a cooper's jigger), and yet another for smoothing the inside of the barrel.

There's no better place to use a drawknife than at a shaving bench or horse with a large jaw to hold the work securely.

Drawknives

When I started this chapter extolling the virtues of simple tools, I had drawknives in mind. Here is a tool that in the right hands can hog great jagged shavings, and on the next stroke pare so fine that the shaving almost floats off the edge. There is no magic to this tool—it has the same edge as a chisel. The advantage of a drawknife is that it is used two-handed, with handles at right angles to the edge for maximum power and leverage.

Coopers, spar makers, chairmakers, wheelwrights, shingle makers, and many other trades adopted drawknives and altered them to suit their particular work. Some have long, wide blades, others are shorter and narrower, or have blades curved to work in unusual places, such as inside a barrel. Carpenters created an ingenious variation with handles that fold over the blade, protecting both the tool and its owner when he reaches in his toolbox.

I have three common drawknives, all of which have a role in my furniture making. One is for the roughest of work, like taking the bark off the waney edge of a board. I use a smaller knife with a 6-in. blade for wasting large chamfers, such as on the facets of a pencil-post bed or the bevel along a curved tabletop. I also have a very small gentleman's knife with a blade only 4 in. long, which I use for the most delicate chamfers and shaping. All three knives cut more quickly than a plane and, with care, produce just as beautiful a surface.

TUNING AND USING DRAWKNIVES

Whether to use a drawknife bevel up or bevel down is a matter of some debate. I use them bevel up for most work and bevel down only when I am cutting within a concave area, when it seems to work better that way. Sharpening has something to do with my choice. Basically, a drawknife is sharpened like a chisel with about a 20° bevel, except I hone on a very small back bevel that gives me extra maneuverability working bevel up. No longer does the cut have to follow the flat of the back: I control the cutting depth by lowering or raising the handles.

To hone the bevel (and the back bevel), it is easier to bring the sharpening stones to the tool. There isn't much else to tune on a drawknife, except to replace a broken handle (as you would a tanged chisel). To tighten a loose handle, try peening the end of the tang coming through the handle. If this fails, try squirting some Super Glue adhesive into the tool end of the handle.

Chairmaking is one of the few trades left that depend upon the versatility of drawknives, from working up rough legs and other parts, to their final shaping and fitting. While you can work at a vise or bench with a drawknife, a shaving horse is designed just for this kind of work. You can sit, shave, quickly reposition the work or clamp in a new piece, all at a comfortable height to deliver the most power and control to the tool.

SCORPS

Some chairmakers use an unusual form of drawknife called a scorp or inshave for hollowing and shaping a plank seat. Essentially a curved drawknife, a scorp works like a two-handled gouge. Coopers used them to smooth the insides of barrels, as did wooden shovel and scoop makers. True to the ingenuity of craftsmen who relied on hand tools, I've seen an interesting variation—a one-handed scorp. The interior between the curved edge was filled in with wood like the sole of a wooden spokeshave, giving much more control by transforming a simple cutting tool into a more complex plane.

Sharpen a drawknife as you would a chisel, with about a 20° bevel and slight back bevel. It's easiest to hold the tool steady on a surface and bring the stone to the blade.

Hand-forged scorps or inshaves are used one- or two-handed for hollowing plank seats, scoops, or for smoothing the insides of barrels.

BED ROCK

7 PLANES

Imagine a time when nearly everything was made by hand. Not just furniture and houses, but every necessity of daily life, from kitchen utensils to farm wagons. The labor and sweat to make even the simplest piece of furniture was enormous; every board had to be flattened to a uniform thickness, then sized by hand with a jack plane. Planes were easily the most important hand tools in any shop, and they still are. It's no wonder they have become symbols of fine woodworking and meticulous craftsmanship.

Integrating planes into your routine will get you thinking in new ways about how you make things. And you will enjoy the process far more, because there are few pleasures as wonderful as curling up translucent shavings, smelling their aroma as they float to the floor, and feeling a surface so polished it shines.

This iron miter plane from the late 17th century is not much different from a Roman plane of 2,000 years ago or a modern low-angle bench plane. Even the construction is ancient: The sole is connected to the body with two large tenons that are peened and clinched.

A Legacy of Planes

Woodworking made a great leap forward when planes appeared. You would think that a tool as vital as a plane might have been around forever, as far back as the dawn of woodworking, when man started chipping stone scrapers and chisels. The Egyptians left no evidence of having used planes, though it is amazing that they made such intricate and sophisticated furniture without them. They used adzes instead, and it's not too hard to imagine some craftsman who eventually started pushing his adze instead of pulling it, and then lengthened the body into the sole of a crude plane. By mid-morning, historically speaking, the first planes appeared. Some were found in the ashes of Pompeii (A.D. 79), quite rusty and missing wooden parts, but still with all of the important elements of the design.

Through the Middle Ages and up to the 18th century, planes were quite basic. A joiner's or carpenter's kit contained a number of wooden planes: a smoothing and longer jointer or jack plane for general work, a few molding planes, and some joinery planes such as a plow

Until the Civil War, a joiner or carpenter relied on wooden planes for preparing and sizing stock, smoothing surfaces, and jointing long edges. Fashioning his own planes from wood, he could make any length needed.

Patternmakers adapted (and in some cases made themselves) an unusual molding plane with interchangeable soles and irons. Compact and efficient, such a tool was used to cut hollows or coves in wooden patterns for casting metals.

and rabbet plane. Either because of the conservative nature of craftsmen or because such planes served their purposes, changes during this time were slight and usually just affected the shape of the handle or body of the tool rather than the way it functioned.

All this started to change in the 18th century. Rising wealth and a growing middle class with a taste for fine furniture, elaborate houses, carriages, and other consumer goods created a demand for skilled craftsmen. This, in turn, created a demand for the tools—especially planes—to make such craftsmanship possible. Joiners and cabinetmakers needed fancy molding planes for house trim and casework, a greater variety of bench planes for sizing and shaping, heavier smoothing planes for working the difficult timbers suddenly in vogue, and more accurate planes of all types for cutting joinery, raising panels, and plowing grooves. For every trade, planemakers supplied the planes needed, and although new in some ways, they were still only variations on the same basic wooden tools of centuries before.

Things likely would have continued this way except for the scientific and mechanical curiosity spurred

LEONARD BAILEY

LEONARD BAILEY left his mark—sometimes quite literally—on nearly every cast-iron bench plane ever made. Many of the features that make modern planes so easy to use, features we almost take for granted, were his invention: an adjustable frog, a knuckled lever cap that holds the iron in place, a vertical adjuster for the iron, and rosewood for handles and knobs. When he started tinkering, cast-iron planes were a novelty—wooden planes ruled. He knew cast iron would make a superior and economical plane, as long as he could devise a simple way to clamp the iron in place and adjust it.

In 1855, at age 30, Bailey took out his first patent for a rocking adjuster later used in Stanley's cabinet scrapers and scraper planes. Thirteen years later he had a line of a dozen cast-iron planes in production (plus another dozen spokeshaves and combination cast-iron/wood planes) with most of the features we have come to know. When he joined forces with Stanley a year later, his reliable designs—coupled with Stanley's marketing savvy—hastened the acceptance of Bailey bench planes as the preferred plane throughout the world.

Advances in technology spurred by armament manufacturing during the Civil War helped companies such as Stanley Rule and Level produce cast-iron planes with long-wearing soles and simple adjusters for the iron (top and bottom). Meanwhile, British makers such as Thomas Norris refined smoothing plane designs (center).

by the Industrial Revolution, and later the Civil War. While water- and steam-powered factories turned out millions of wooden planes, inventors and small-town mechanics tinkered with ways to make planes easier to use. They created new adjusters and better mechanisms for holding the iron in place, and they began to use cast iron for longer-wearing soles.

Leonard Bailey and Stanley Rule and Level are the two names we most associate with these changes, transforming the humble plane into a tool for every man. Ironically, while Stanley engineers devised more and more sophisticated planes for every conceivable need, they couldn't overcome a market that was steadily shrinking as thickness planers and other woodworking machines replaced hand craftsmanship. What remains of this Golden Age is our rich legacy of classic planes.

Types of Planes

Leaf through any tool catalog and you're apt to see a couple dozen or more planes offered. Any good used-tool shop might have a hundred or more classic Stanleys and others for sale. I've seen collections of nearly a thousand planes. How are all these planes different from one another, and what are they used for? And what exactly distinguishes them as planes?

Planes are complex tools. Think of them as sophisticated chisels, where the design of the tool controls the size and quality of the shaving.

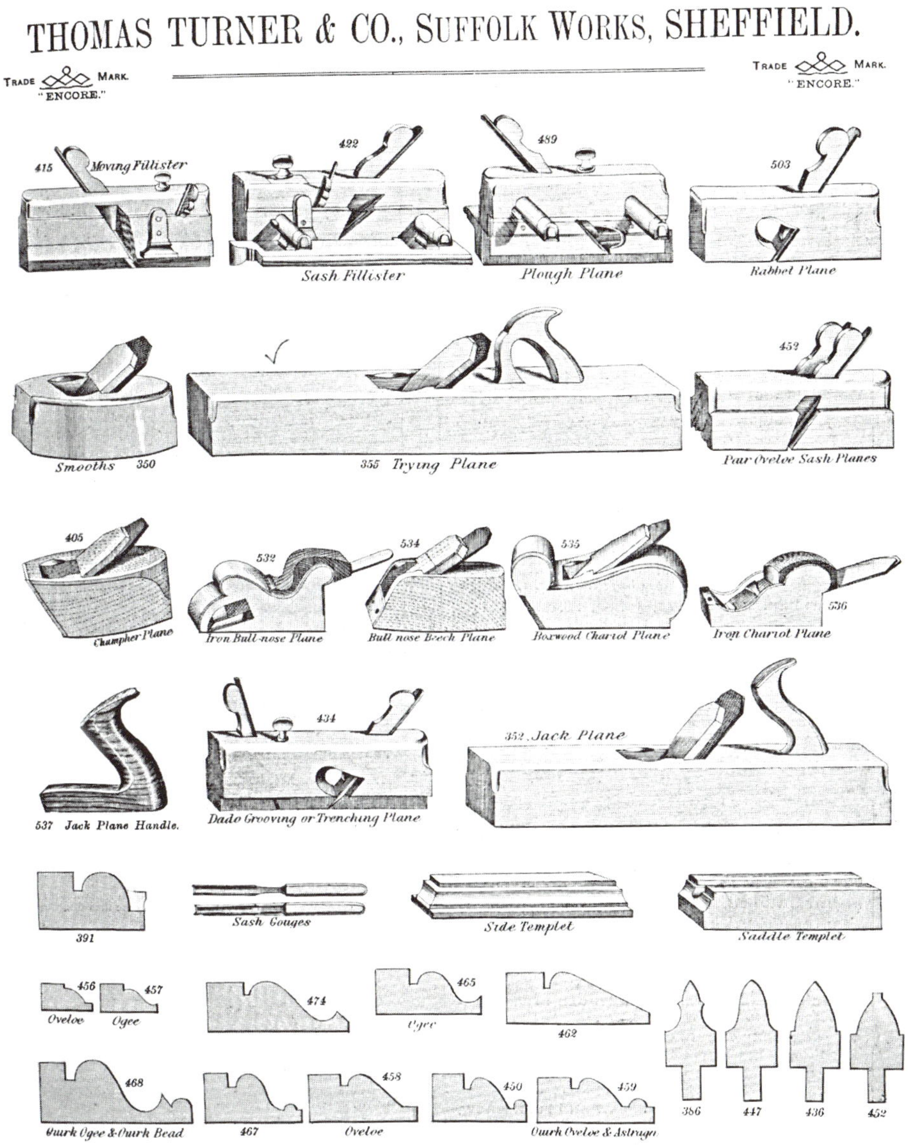

This page from an 1890 catalog offers a typical array of workaday wooden planes for every shop task from sizing and smoothing stock to cutting joinery, moldings, and window sash.

Specialized planes designed for a single purpose can be hard to categorize, such as this witchet and rounding tool, which cut round tenons.

The important elements are a sole that guides the cut and regulates its depth; a slender mouth that accepts the shaving, which is then curled against the cutting iron; and the pitch or angle of the iron to the work, which determines how fast the shaving is bent and curled. There is a little more to it, but essentially it all adds up to a self-regulating tool that's relatively easy to use.

As for what a plane can do, so far plane designers have had no trouble thinking up new and interesting ways to make planes that can cut everything from dovetails to ornate cornice moldings. This variety can be distilled into four basic tasks: sizing and preparing stock, cutting joinery, flattening surfaces to a smooth polish, and shaping curves and decoration. There are also specialized planes, usually associated with a specific trade and designed for a single purpose, such as cutting round tenons or half-round core-boxes. And while it would be interesting to organize planes into one of these groups, many are capable of multiple tasks.

PLANES FOR SIZING AND PREPARING STOCK

When you picture a plane, it's probably a bench plane, for the simple reason that they are the hardest working and most common of all planes. Named for their work at the

These late 19th-century bench planes by Mathieson of Glasgow, Scotland, do not have cast bodies but are made of steel plates dovetailed together. Combined with an overstuffed wood infill (like over-risen bread), they are massive enough to work figured or ornery timbers more easily than comparable Bailey planes.

bench (where most planes are used), bench planes range from the tiny Stanley #1 to the #8 jointer, and include low-angle planes, block planes, and scrub planes. Bench planes are general-purpose planes. They were the thickness planers and jointers of an 18th-century shop, used for sizing, smoothing, cutting tapers, rough-surfacing parts, or performing any of the varied tasks involved in preparing stock.

While Bailey-pattern cast-iron bench planes are the most common (many sizes are still in production), wood-bodied planes are preferred by some craftsmen for their sweet action of wood upon wood. At one time, Stanley made a line of transitional bench planes, a combination of wooden body and metal mechanical parts, which have some of the advantages of both wood and metal planes.

STANLEY NUMBERING SYSTEM

STANLEY'S PLANE numbering system has had collectors confused for decades. While it might appear orderly, some numbers seem to have been assigned as much by whim as by logic. How do you explain why a #5½ is larger than a #5, but a #5¼ is considerably smaller than both?

It all began with the first catalog of January 1870, which offered a line of cast-iron bench planes numbered 1 through 12 and wood-bottomed planes numbered 21 through 37. As new planes were developed they were generally given new whole numbers, unless they were intermediate sizes of existing planes, or nearly identical with only slightly different features (such as tilting handles). That's why we have a #4½, #9¾, and #10¼, to name just a few.

At least twice Stanley gave different planes the same number (#80 and #90), while for some reason #14 and #38 were never used. As the first hundred slots filled, Stanley used a new numbering logic: Similar tools jumped by 100, such as routers #71, #171, and #271 (and we have a #71½, too). The Bedrock line jumped to #602, #603, #604, etc., the Stanley Victor was banished to the 1100s, and the Handyman to the 1200s. This left plenty of classy numbers such as #444 to assign to the only dovetail plane on the market.

PLANES FOR CUTTING AND FITTING JOINERY

Once the stock is flattened and sized, joinery planes are put to work. We're more apt to use a table saw or a router to cut joinery today, but a cabinetmaker of the past relied on a variety of specialized joinery planes: plows for cutting grooves; rabbet and dado planes for cutting rabbets and grooves across the grain; dovetail planes; shoulder and bullnose planes for fitting tenons; and low-angle miter planes for trimming end grain. Some of these planes are still in production—and for good reason. No matter how you actually cut a joint, they are still the best tools for adjusting and fitting the parts.

PLANES FOR SMOOTHING

A third type of plane, a smoothing plane, is used after the joinery is cut. Smoothing planes have a single purpose: to plane a surface to perfect smoothness. No other tool leaves a surface with the clarity, depth, and shine of a well-tuned smoother. The best of these planes are uniquely designed for this demanding work, with thick irons to resist chatter, short massive bodies to hold the plane on the work and firmly support the iron, and narrow throat openings for the finest shavings.

Some of the most beautiful and efficient of the smoothers are steel Norris or Norris-type planes with dense rosewood or ebony infill (see the photo at left on p. 106). The #3 and #4 bench planes are also considered smoothing planes,

For plowing grooves and other joinery, every woodworker used to have a plow plane. Few, however, were as fashionable as this one of rosewood with ivory stop nuts and a set of eight irons by the Greenfield Tool Co., Greenfield, Massachusetts (c. 1872).

Before the advent of mechanical routers, craftsmen would make hand-powered ones from a worn plow-plane iron and a shapely body of beech or ebony. Stanley and competitors such as Record made an adjustable nickel-plated version (#71), which is useful for adjusting the depth of a groove or cutting a hinge recess.

As efficient as it is stunning, the Norris A6 has all the attributes of an excellent smoothing plane. This plane has soul!

and while they work fine on well-behaved woods, they need some special tuning to produce a flawless finish (see p. 122).

A small collection of hollow and round molding planes (plus a quarter-round, ogee, and ovolo at rear) can cut a wide range of decorative profiles. Molding planes were made by the thousands until the turn of the century.

PLANES FOR DECORATION AND SHAPING

The fourth task that planes perform is cutting decoration and shaping. The variety of planes and type of work this includes is enormous: spokeshaves for shaping; compass planes for cutting along curves; panel-raising planes; chamfer planes; and molding planes of every description. No other hand tools can cut such details as quickly or easily, from a small bead along a table apron to bold crown moldings.

When you consider the sheer number of molding profiles and the planes needed to cut each one—plus all the other shaping planes—this is easily the largest group of planes. Fortunately, you can do most of this work with a few spokeshaves, a dozen or so basic molding-plane profiles, and your bench planes. What you can't accomplish with these you can with easily-made profiled scrapers known as scratch stocks (see pp. 132–134).

There is one other form of plane that might be considered a fifth type: scrapers. Some look like bench planes, others resemble spokeshaves, and others are simply a piece of springy steel, yet they have all the characteristics of a plane. Scrapers smooth or shape with a high-angle scraping action as opposed to the slicing cut of a plane. They cut slowly, but they also work highly figured or difficult woods better than most other planes. They deserve separate attention (see Chapter 8).

Each of the boxwood spokeshaves in this unusually fine set cuts like a small plane, shaping curves such as the top of a headboard, a cabriole leg, or a table apron laid out with the aid of one the French curve templates (top).

Tuning Planes

Choose any type of plane—bench plane, rabbet plane, smoothing plane, or molding plane—and, while they may have different shapes or lengths (and other obvious differences), they share some basic elements. They all have a sole (flat or shaped); a chisel-like iron (also straight or shaped); a wedge or lever cap holding the iron in position; a throat (sometimes called a mouth); and a handle or some way to grip the tool comfortably and to control the cutting direction. Working in harmony, the parts add up to a tool that regulates the cutting depth and the cutting dynamics for you. The trade-off is that planes can be tricky to tune. Think of a plane as a kit, all the elements of which need to be tuned together for the best results.

I suspect that many woodworkers avoid planes because they don't understand how to tune them or fear they will ruin the tool if they try. Adding to this frustration is the expectation that a tool right out of the box is going to work perfectly—it rarely does. You can expect a new chisel to work well enough after a light sharpening (and better after a thorough one), but it's a much simpler tool than the combination of

You might not think of a hollow auger (used for cutting round tenons) as a plane, but it has many of a plane's characteristic features, including an iron held in position, a throat, and a sole. Driven by a brace and adjustable for various diameters, hollow augers were used by wheelwrights and chairmakers.

TUNING AT A GLANCE

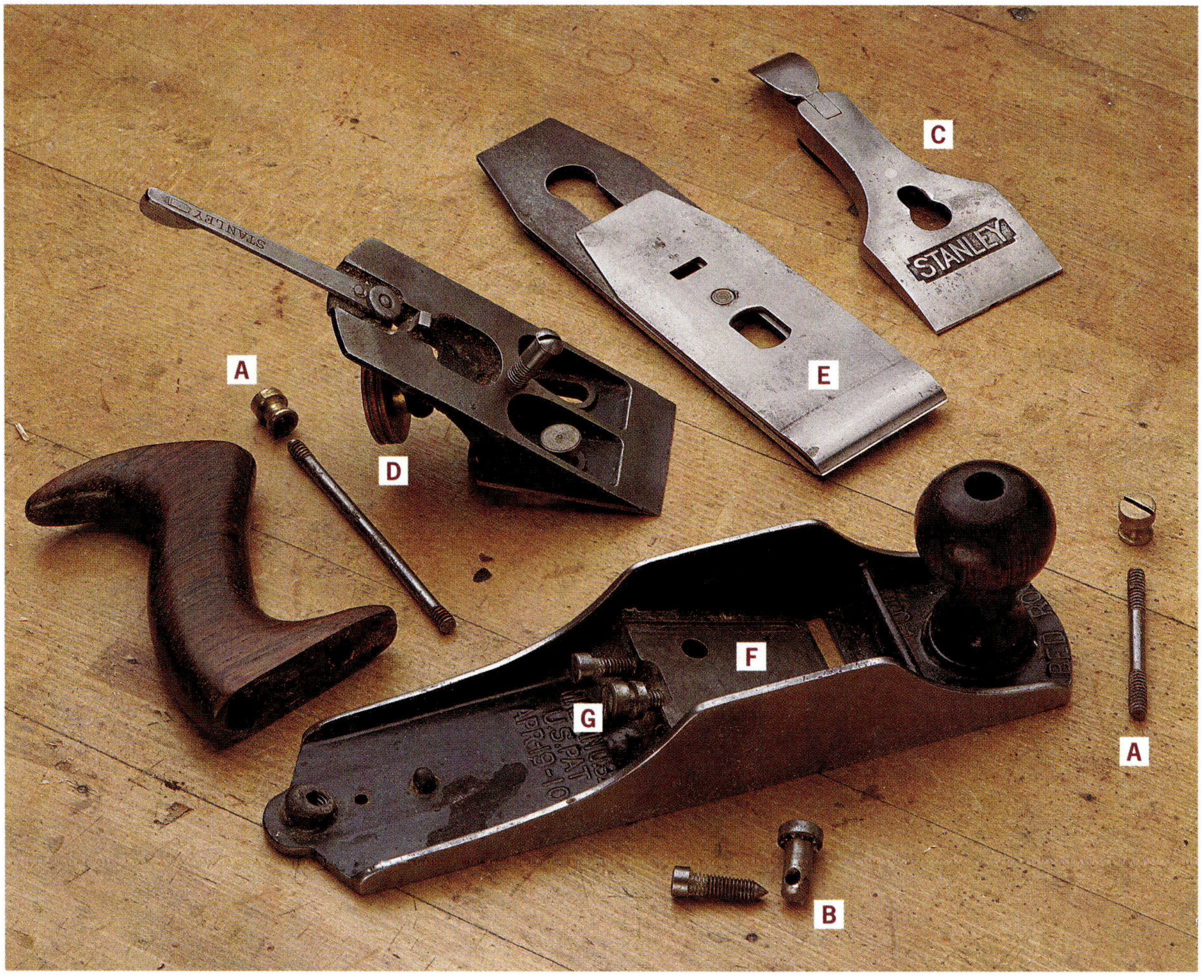

A The threaded rods that secure the rear handle and front knob to the plane can be ground slightly shorter to take up any looseness.

B Two screws or pins (as for this Bedrock plane) secure the adjustable frog to the sole; loosen them to move the frog with screw G.

C The lever cap holds the iron and cap iron (E) in position by locking down on the screw in the center of the frog. Don't tighten it too much—just enough to hold the iron but still adjust it smoothly.

D The depth adjustment for the iron should need little tuning other than a wipe of paste wax.

E Position the cap iron as close as practical to the cutting edge.

F Make sure the surface where the frog beds with the sole is flat and clean.

G Adjust the position of the frog—and the throat opening—with this screw.

parts that make up a plane. Buy any plane, other than one from a high-end specialty maker, and you will have to do some tuning; a flea-market find may require a major overhaul. Tuning is not difficult, but it can be time-consuming. The upside is that you will understand more about the subtleties of how the tool works and be able to tune it for specific situations or troubleshoot problems. You will appreciate the results of that tuning every time you use your plane.

How much tuning you do depends on what you are starting with, how finicky you are, your patience, and what kind of work you expect from the plane. A rough jack plane obviously needs less tuning than a smoothing plane. Small joinery planes that need to be accurate might fall somewhere between the two. Even in the case of a new bench plane of mediocre quality right out of the box, it's possible to turn it into an accurate and predictable tool if you follow all the tuning steps (and replace the standard iron with a thicker one). No matter what type of plane you're tuning, the general principles are the same—more or less.

Among the tiniest planes are the violinmaker's hollowing planes for shaping the arched back and top of stringed instruments. A tail handle that snuggles into the palm of the hand helps give the user a firm grip.

HANDLES

Start by tuning the handles (on those planes that have them) for a quick and very satisfying improvement. Bench planes have two wooden handles: a rear tote and front knob. They attach with a threaded rod through the handle into the iron casting and are tightened with a brass nut. The castings sometimes have a raised boss to receive the handle, giving it a more secure seat. Over time and with use the handles work loose. This can be frustrating when you are relying on the handle not only to hold the plane but also to control its direction and apply some downward pressure.

The easiest fix is to tighten the brass nut that secures the handle. This has probably been done before (and probably the nut has run out of threads). If this is the case, slip a washer under the nut (leather works well) or remove the threaded rod and grind or cut off ⅛ in. or so.

IF YOU DID NO OTHER tuning than replace your bench-plane irons with thicker ones, the results would still astound you. Whether it's in a top-of-the-line Bedrock or a low-end Handyman, a thick iron is stable and cuts far more smoothly. Thin Stanley irons are easy to hone, but they're not stiff enough for the demanding stresses of planing hard woods. Many catalogs sell replacement blades and a two-part cap iron for a turbocharge of your planes you will really feel.

As the plane cuts, a shaving is bent upward against the ramp of the iron, which levers the shaving against the front of the throat, breaking it as it goes. The area of the sole in front of the throat presses down on the fibers, and the repeated breaking of the chip prevents splitting ("tearout") and curls the shaving.

You might want to replace the ugly plastic handles on new planes with rosewood aftermarket handles or shopmade ones. No handles quite compare to the beauty and ergonomic perfection of Stanley's classic rosewood styles, polished by years of handling. Unless it is a historically significant plane, don't hesitate to smooth or shape any handles (or the body of wooden planes) or strip off the varnish to make them more comfortable. An occasional light rubbing of paste wax or linseed oil will polish the wood to a beautiful and protective finish.

FLATTENING THE SOLE

Very few planes—new or old—have a truly flat sole, and although they will work, they will work better with some flattening. More important than overall flatness is flatness at important points along the sole. At the very least, the area at either end of the plane and in front of the mouth should be flat. Flatness at the extremities of the sole takes full advantage of its length to guide the plane.

Understanding how a plane cuts explains why it's also critical to make sure the area in front of the mouth is flat. As a shaving is forced into the mouth against the ramped iron, the shaving is levered and bent against the forward part of the mouth (see the photo at left). This area of the sole exerts pressure on the wood fibers so splitting away (or tearout) is kept to a minimum. It can do this only if the sole ahead of the mouth is in firm contact with the surface of the wood.

The first step in flattening any sole is checking it with a straightedge. Hold the sole up to a bright light and sight under the straightedge. Depending on what you want to accomplish with the plane, it might be fine as is, or you may have many hours of flattening ahead. For a long plane such as a jointer, used for shooting accurate straight edges, expect to flatten the toe, the heel, and the area in front of the mouth to give the sole good support to cut a flat, straight surface. On planes with smaller soles—joint-cutting planes, for example—the entire sole should be close to flat. There is actually some advantage to a small amount of hollow in the sole for reducing friction. Corrugated or grooved soles supposedly slide more easily, and Japanese craftsmen purposely shape areas of their planes' soles hollow.

There are no shortcuts to lapping a sole flat, unless you are a machinist or know one you can trust to surface-grind the sole. Surface grinding is tricky, to say the least. Not only is it hard to grip the awkward shape of most planes without a lot of jigging, but the mere act of clamping can also distort the sole. It's slower but safer to stick with hand lapping on a lapping table, as shown in the photos at right.

Be sure the iron is clamped in place but pulled well back from the throat—the iron exerts pressure on the sole, which should be taken into account when lapping. If lapping seems like too big a job, just do a little. When the spirit moves you again, do some more. Give the lapped sole a wipe of paste wax for an almost frictionless glide.

TUNING THE IRON AND CAP IRON

The easiest way to improve the performance of almost any plane instantly is to replace the standard iron with a thicker one. This is especially true for smoothing planes and those

Flatten the sole on a lapping table made from ⅜-in. plate glass sprinkled with silicon-carbide powder and lubricated with oil or water (front). You can also use sheets of silicon-carbide or aluminum-oxide paper glued to the glass (rear). Retract the iron and use a back-and-forth motion with even downward pressure.

This sole needs more lapping. Much of the sole, including the important area in front of the throat, shows lap marks, but the toe and heel are still low spots.

BEVEL ANGLES

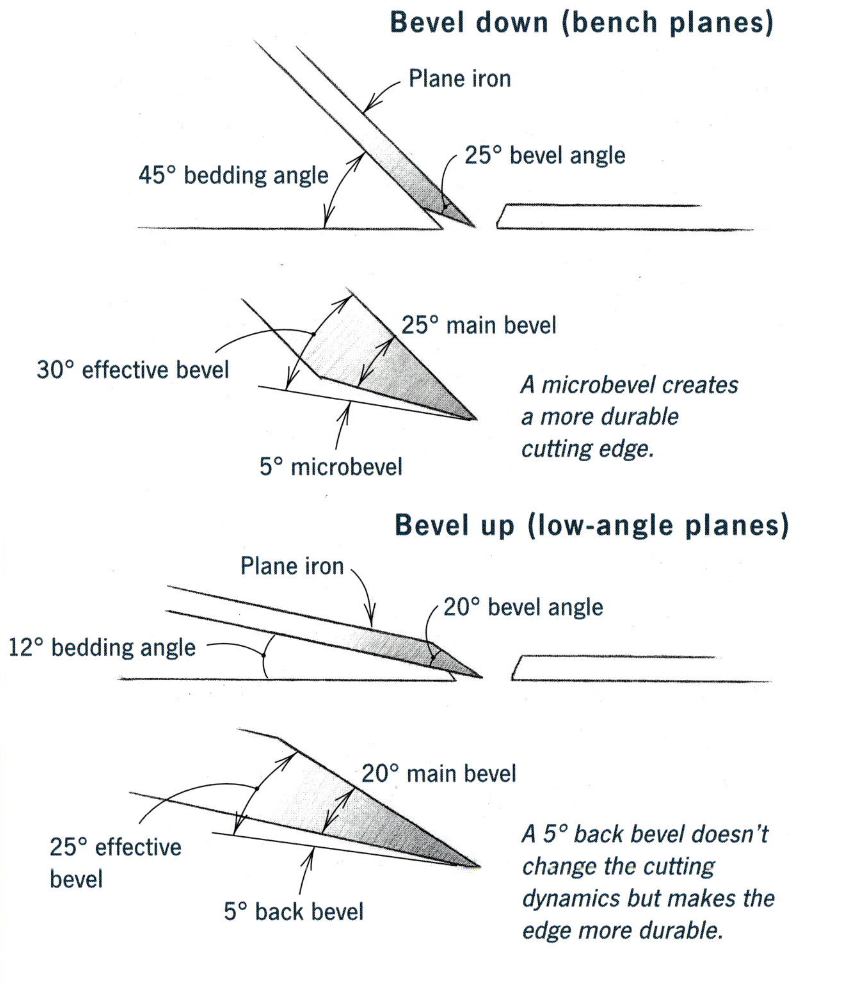

For a truly sharp cutting edge, flattening the back of the iron to a polish is every bit as important as honing the bevel. Start on a lapping table for backs that are rusty or warped, and work up to your finest stone.

that you use on difficult woods. The thin iron typical in most bench planes, particularly Stanley and Bailey planes, is quicker to hone but entirely too flexible to stand up to the considerable stresses at the cutting edge. Remember that these planes were originally made for carpenters working soft woods, and not the hard woods typically used in a shop today. The cap iron helps stiffen the iron, but still not as well as a thicker iron. Find an old iron (old wooden planes are a great source) or buy a new thick replacement iron—it makes a world of difference.

Sharpen the iron as you would a chisel. Generally a bevel of 25° is a good compromise for most planes. (The width of a 25° bevel is about twice the thickness of the iron.) The exceptions are low-angle planes, where the lowest cutting angle possible is used for shaving end grain (see the drawing at left). For these, a 20° bevel is worth trying, or even lower (though you run the risk of chipping the delicate cutting edge). The back should be polished and flat. If you want, hone on a microbevel or a back bevel (see p. 27).

Most of the time the cutting edge is straight, but there are some advantages to a cambered or curved edge. On jack and scrub planes, a well-cambered iron cuts like a gouge for removing wood quickly. Rounding the corners slightly on a smoothing plane helps feather the strokes (see the drawing on the facing page).

Bench planes and some other planes have double irons: an iron and a mating cap iron. The cap iron supports the cutting edge and curls the shaving as it rides up the iron.

IRON PROFILES

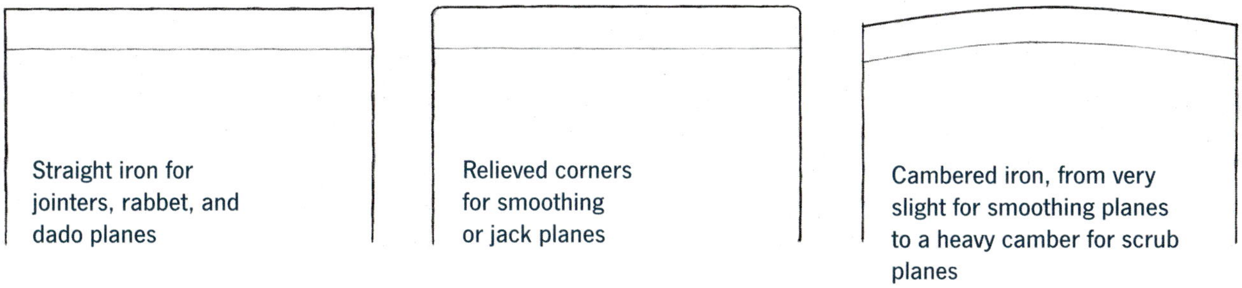

When you are tuning up your plane, smooth the top of the cap iron with fine emery paper and wax it. Then take the cap iron onto a stone and flatten the tip where it mates with the iron. Trial-fit the two and sight between them; there should be no gaps for a shaving to wedge itself. There need not be a lot of tension between the cap iron and iron; in fact, too much tension can curl a thin iron and cause a whole new set of problems. There should be just enough tension that the cap iron stays in place when you rap the end of the iron gently on the bench.

The most difficult part of tuning a molding plane is honing the iron to the same profile as the sole. Work with shaped slipstones, maintain a typical 25° bevel, and test the iron in the mouth to see where its shape differs from the sole.

How you set the cap iron in relation to the cutting edge depends on how the plane will be used. The closer it is to the edge, the more support it provides and the faster it can curl a shaving. A good rule of thumb is to set the cap iron back the thickness of the shavings you expect to cut. On planes doing the most exacting work—smoothing planes and some bench planes—the cap iron is quite close (if the edge has any camber you can't set the iron as close). For a general-purpose jack plane, set the cap iron and iron as much as a 1/16 in. apart (see the photo at right on p. 114).

BEDDING THE IRON

The final area that needs attention is the bed of the iron—or the "frog," as this piece is called in bench planes. The frog is separate from the body casting for two reasons: It simplifies the casting of the body and allows you to fine-tune the position of the iron and, in turn, the throat opening. I don't know where the unusual name came from, but it

The multiple irons in these complex molding planes are much easier to sharpen and tune than a single, large iron.

One rule of thumb for positioning the cap iron is to set it as close to the cutting edge as the shavings you will cut. Set it extremely close for a smoothing plane (right) and with about a 1/16-in. reveal for a cambered jack-plane iron (left).

Bailey-type planes have two adjusters: a lateral adjustment lever that engages with the slot in the iron and pushes it right or left, and a brass adjuster wheel that slides the iron in and out by pushing against a slot in the cap iron.

does resemble the frog of a horse's hoof (or perhaps it originates from the old saying about a frog in your throat). On well-made old planes, the frog probably needs no tuning. The frogs of newer planes (except high-end ones) probably do because expensive milling is usually kept to a minimum. A frog needs two types of tuning: one is to fit it firmly to the sole of the plane, the other to make sure the area the iron lies against is flat.

First, take out the frog and the screw that tightens the lever cap and run over the bed with a fine file. To get a solid fit between the sole and the frog, coat one side of the mating surfaces with a dye called engineer's blue. When you assemble the parts, the color transfers and you can see where the high spots are.

File the high spots and tighten the screws carefully to avoid stripping them when re-attaching the frog to the sole. Start with the frog positioned in line with the bevel and gradually work it forward, tightening up the throat after you see how the plane performs. One virtue of Bedrock planes, Stanley's premier line of bench planes, is that you can move the frog with the iron in place, although chances are you'll set each of your planes and leave them that way.

By now you've tuned every part of the plane except the depth and lateral adjusters, and the lever cap that secures the iron. A drop of oil on the working parts of the adjusters is all they really need. The lever cap should be smooth and waxed to easily pass the shavings over it. Adjust the tension on the screw through the cap just enough to hold the iron and still adjust easily.

To set the working depth of the iron, turn the depth-adjuster wheel, either while looking at the throat (with the plane turned over) or by feeling the iron's position with a finger. Using the lateral adjuster, position the iron parallel with the sole, testing it in the same way. It's safer to start with a shallow cut and deepen it after you see how the plane performs. You'll be amazed how much a little tuning improves the way your planes feel and work.

Using Planes

The planes you'll use the most are bench planes: a #3 or #4 smoothing plane, a #5 jack, and a #7 or #8 jointer. How you use them depends a lot on what you make, but it's sure to involve the basic techniques of cutting true edges or jointing surfaces for such work as edge-gluing boards, smoothing narrow surfaces, trimming parts to exact width and length, and fitting parts together. From there, it isn't much of a leap to using joinery, molding, or other specialized planes. The best place to start is with an easy-to-handle and versatile #4. Put it to work and get a feel for the way it cuts. It's time to make some shavings.

For efficient planing you need a sturdy bench at the right height (see pp. 32-33). Planing takes effort, and you will work up an honest sweat some days; a bench just makes it easier by transferring your energy to the work (and holding it for you). If you are going to plane a lot, you'll want a lower bench to get the weight of your upper body over the plane. There is no single correct body position, but it should feel natural and comfortable. Spread your feet for stability. Think about moving your body along with the plane (when jointing a board, for example), while keeping it balanced and cutting evenly. All of this might feel awkward at first, but in time it will become second nature.

JOINTING

Trimming a drawer face to width, cutting a bevel on the underside of a drawer bottom, shooting the edges of two boards to be glued together or the four sides of a tapered leg are all variations of typical everyday jointing. Think of it as a kind of smoothing, cutting a surface (usually narrower than the width of the iron) flat and true so that two such edges can be joined together seamlessly. Smoothing larger surfaces is different and covered later.

For the most accurate jointing, use the longest plane practical. The longer the plane, the better the ability to ride over the hollows and plane off the high spots. (A shorter plane would fall into the hollows

Efficient planing can't be done without a good bench and a vise or two to hold the work while you concentrate on controlling the plane. Work at a height that allows you to get your upper body over the plane and settle into a comfortable stance.

To joint a long board, clamp it against the edge of your bench in a side vise or upon a board jack (at knee level near the far end of the board) so that the top edge is at a comfortable height. Balance the plane on the edge, extend a few fingers from your front hand to stabilize it, and walk along as you plane from end to end.

Edge-joint thin boards by folding them together and planing both edges at once. If you plane on a slight bevel, which is quite natural on such a narrow edge, it will be the same for both boards (complementary) and cancel each other out.

and would have more trouble planing the surface straight.) A long plane also has more mass, which helps power the tool through the cut. This said, for cutting a beveled drawer bottom or tapered leg, where perfect flatness end to end is not vital, a #4 bench plane would be less tiring to use.

Clamp your board on edge in a side vise, on the top of the bench, or whatever way keeps it steady and well supported. Position the plane on the edge with the iron about to start cutting. The front of the sole guides the cut at the beginning, so keep pressure on it and merely support the rest of the plane with your hand on the rear handle. As you begin cutting, shift some weight toward your rear hand.

Completing the cut is the opposite, with the pressure shifting to the area of the sole behind the iron. If you put pressure on the heel of the plane at the start of a stroke and on the toe at the end, you will gradually cut a convex surface. No matter what plane you are using, keep the pressure focused over the part of the sole in contact with the wood.

There are a number of things to concentrate on all at once while jointing: You've got to balance the plane, keep your weight over the correct area of the sole, and apply some downward pressure as well. A heavy plane helps, as does the forward slant of classic plane handles. Balance comes with time. To joint an edge true, start by making it slightly hollow, since this is an easier condition to flatten than a convex one. (Even a long jointer plane will

SPOKESHAVES

SPOKESHAVES are the gliders of the plane world, able to loop the loop over the curves of a headboard as easily as skim along a cabriole leg. Graceful handles—their wings—afford a good grip. With hollow, round, or flat soles (and everything in between), spokeshaves can cut along nearly any curve, in the tightest of places. Wheelwrights found them indispensable for fairing and smoothing spokes, as did chairmakers, coopers, basketmakers, and furniture makers for shaping everything from chair seats to pail staves.

Wooden spokeshaves are quite common secondhand. Their blades are shaped like a small drawknife with two tapering square tangs bent at right angles that wedge into the stock. To set the depth of the cut you tap on the tangs or blade; more sophisticated shaves have captive nuts threaded onto the tangs. Often bone or brass is inlaid in front of the mouth to prevent wear. The beauty of these simple shaves is their very low cutting angle—a noticeable advantage planing end grain—and their ability to cut easily and aggressively.

When interest turned toward tools made of cast iron in the mid-19th century, Leonard Bailey and others re-engineered spokeshaves. Their blades are steeply bedded, like miniature bench planes with handles. They cut with less tearout, at the cost of greater effort to power the tool. Some versions have blade adjusters. My favorites, Stanley #53 and #54, have a thumbscrew that rocks a yoke to close the mouth and lighten the cut. On nonadjustable shaves, set the blade slightly deeper on one side for the widest range of cutting options.

The trick to using a spokeshave is learning to rock it to the best cutting angle, while following the changing contour of a curve. Push or pull—the choice is yours—and skew the tool slightly for the smoothest cut.

Spokeshaves are small planes capable of shaping concave or convex curves. One of the author's favorites is the Stanley #53, which has a simple depth adjustment to alternate between aggressive shaping and light cuts, such as chamfering this chair spindle.

A useful collection of spokeshaves includes some with different sole shapes: concave, convex, and flat. Close cousins to spokeshaves are scraper shaves (at rear) for a slower yet controlled cutting action shaping surfaces.

follow a convex surface, but it will cut the ends of a hollow until the surface is flat.) To do this, take a few cuts from the center only and sight down the edge to see how you are doing. If it is slightly hollow, cut end to end, and when you cut a full-length shaving, stop. Do the same thing on another edge, and with any luck, the two boards will fit together seamlessly. When I am jointing two boards, I usually take an extra shaving from the middle to hollow-joint the edges for a stronger joint.

A technique that helps with narrow boards is to joint them at the same time (see the bottom photo on p. 116). Fold them together, inside to inside, clamp them as one board, and joint them the same way. The thicker edge gives the plane better support, and any slight bevel will be canceled out. A shooting board is a jig that also helps shoot true edges, especially for jointing thin veneers (see the drawing and photo below).

When it all comes together, you'll be able to joint two edges for a glue joint superior to anything produced by machine. For one thing, a plane-cut surface is perfectly smooth and free of machine marks; it is flat and true, with fibers cleanly severed for good glue absorption. And for long boards that are always awkward to machine, bringing a plane to the work is far easier.

PLANING END GRAIN

Cutting end grain has its own challenges, although the basic planing technique is the same as for jointing long grain. Bench planes, with their

SHOOTING BOARDS

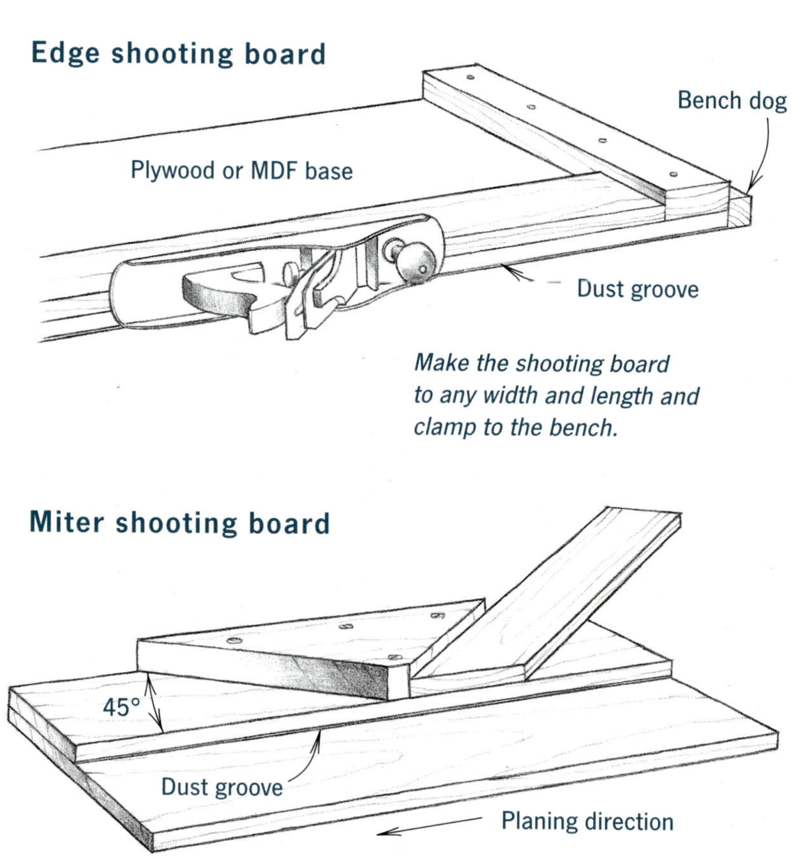

Use a shooting board to accurately joint any edge, but especially thin stock such as veneer. A shopmade wooden handle turns this #7 jointer into a shooting plane and makes it easier to hold while planing with it on its side.

Shoulder planes, which are rabbet planes with low-angle irons and sides milled perfectly square with the sole, are designed for truing and fitting tenon shoulders. Shown here are the Stanley #93 (in use) and the #92 (on the bench).

Overshooting the end while planing end grain is likely to break out fibers unless you back them up with a scrap block clamped in place. Alternatives are to work from both ends toward the middle, or to cut a fine chamfer on each end.

high-pitched irons, cut end grain well—in some situations a #5 is my preferred tool—but generally planes specifically designed for working end grain are short and have low-pitched irons. End grain is tough; a low cutting angle is ideal for slicing the fibers like a knife. Tearout is much less of a concern, because the shavings are so fragile they break up, so there is no need for a narrow throat or a cap iron. And because a low pitch orients the cutting forces in line with the cutter (rather than partially against it as in a higher-pitched iron), chatter is less of a problem.

Trimming the end of a drawer face, cutting the shoulder of a tenon, and truing a mitered corner are all typical end-grain tasks. A block plane is the ideal tool for this type of work. The lower the cutting angle, the easier it will work and the smoother the surface will be. Hone

Position the iron in a rabbet plane so it is slightly proud on the working side (the side into the rabbet) and parallel with the sole. For precise cross-grain rabbets, set the nicker a hair deeper than the iron, so it will slice the fibers ahead of the cut. (The nicker is not set in this photo.)

One of the more common rabbet planes, a Stanley #78 is useful for a variety of rabbet work, such as fitting a panel to a groove (shown here), cutting a rabbet or shiplap joint between two boards, or planing a rabbet for a door.

With a minimal sole ahead of the iron, this Stanley #90 bullnose rabbet plane is a good tool for working into tight corners or for truing up small areas, such as these mitered shoulders.

a bevel close to 20°, and find a plane with a 12° bed angle for the lowest overall cutting angle. For planing longer end-grain surfaces such as a tabletop, Stanley made a low-angle jack plane and smoothing plane, basically just elongated block planes with bench-plane handles. Although it takes a little more effort, a common jack plane works almost as well.

Block planes are terrific tools, but they are useless for working into a corner, when trimming a tenon shoulder, for example. This is when you need a plane with a rabbet mouth, where the iron extends all the way to the side of the plane. Rabbet planes come in an assortment of shapes and sizes, although shoulder planes with heavy bodies and precisely ground sides and soles are the best for working end-grain shoulders. They are low angle and are tuned in the usual way, except that the iron should be positioned ever so slightly beyond the edge of the plane. This is the same with all rabbet planes. There is usually little space for moving the iron laterally, so you'll have to keep the edge honed square to do this.

No matter what plane you use, it's easy to split away the end grain fibers by overshooting an edge. The simplest way to overcome this is to chamfer the edge slightly. Clamping a block against the edge does the same thing; the block splits out but not the workpiece (see the top right photo on p. 119). A shooting board or bench hook is useful for planing end grain because it holds the work and backs up the fibers. A light cut,

SPIERS AND NORRIS PLANES

SPIERS PLANES are one of Britain's best-kept secrets. By about 1845, at least 15 years before the better-known Thomas Norris set up shop, Stewart Spiers in Ayr, Scotland, was devising the building methods and patterns for some of the most exquisite planes ever made. Besides dozens of styles and sizes of smoothing and bench planes, he made specialty planes, such as a shoulder rabbet and thumb plane, as well as custom planes to any pattern a client desired. The enduring quality of Spiers planes is in the dovetailing that joins the sides and sole, so expertly done that the joints are often invisible.

Shoulder planes such as the four shown here are typical of the work of Stewart Spiers, an early maker of stuffed planes. Two of the planes have unusual double irons for two cutting positions.

Norris readily copied Spiers methods and designs—right down to the shaping of the sides, screw cap, and rosewood infill. Why then are Norris planes so eagerly sought after and not those of Spiers, the more prolific, and according to many opinions, the better maker? It all comes down to one feature—a single lever depth and lateral adjuster for the iron—that Norris fitted to his planes after 1914. American craftsmen accustomed to Bailey bench planes and their easy-to-use adjusters naturally prefer adjustable Norrises. Spiers planes never went out of favor with British craftsmen, who appreciate their impeccable performance and a price tag often half to two-thirds that of a Norris.

skewing to slice the fibers for the least amount of pressure against them, also works. Working from both sides toward the middle avoids the problem entirely.

A shoulder plane and block plane are two basic planes that should be in any well-equipped shop. For real versatility, look for a Stanley #90, #92, #93, or #94; they all break apart into useful chisel planes, and can cut tenon shoulders and small rabbets (see the top left photo on p. 119). Block planes fit your hand just right for many trimming tasks, not all of them end grain. They also make great little smoothing planes with only minor adjustments.

SMOOTHING SURFACES

Machines have taken over many of the mundane tasks of working wood once done by planes—quite thankfully. They do their work well, too. But no machine can match the surface cut by a smoothing plane. The flat plane and cleanly sliced fibers cut by a sharp iron have a clarity and brilliance that is unsurpassed. If this weren't justification enough to start using planes to finish surfaces, consider how efficient they are. It takes just minutes to plane all of the parts for a modest

Sight over a pair of winding or "winking" sticks to tell if a surface is flat—the sticks are parallel—or twisted (in "winding"). Two straight scraps work, but it is easier to sight differences if you make them from contrasting woods or inlay holly sights.

cabinet door or a small tabletop to a finished polish.

Stanley #3 and #4 bench planes are considered smoothing planes and they will smooth some woods, but the best smoothing planes are designed and tuned specifically for this demanding work. You want a plane with lots of mass to give the iron rock-solid support. The thicker the iron, the more stable it is, especially against the extreme cutting pressures of figured hardwoods. A long plane isn't necessary, because you're not trying to level the surface (although you do somewhat), but smooth it to a polish.

TO STORE their planes more compactly in a chest, joiners once removed irons and wedges. I store my planes in drawers or on shelves with the irons set, ready to go to work—just as I rest one on my bench while working. To protect the exposed iron, either lay a plane on its side or raise the toe on a scrap of wood. For that matter, it's good practice to lay any cutting edge—saw, auger, chisel, or file—propped on a piece of wood and out of harm's way.

My favorite smoothing planes are the stunning planes made by a man named Stewart Spiers in Ayr, Scotland, before 1900 (see the sidebar on p. 121). Many of his designs were continued by the better-known Thomas Norris. All of these planes combine a steel body dovetailed together with rosewood infill for the handle, front knob, and iron bed, which adds mass to the tool. With irons two or three times as thick as a standard Stanley iron, they are perfectly suited to their task.

Tuning a plane for smoothing is so specific that you should think about using a dedicated plane just for this task. Buy the best plane you can afford; if you are like me, you will use it plenty to make it worth the cost. Wood-bodied smoothers, often made of beautiful tropical or fruit woods with thick irons, make great smoothing planes. Flatten the sole with another plane and inlay a throat plate into the sole to narrow the opening as much as possible. Similarly, adjust the throat on a cast-iron smoother as narrow as possible and keep the cap iron close to the cutting edge. Find the thickest iron that will fit in your plane. Hone it with the slightest camber or round the corners to feather the smoothing strokes seamlessly together.

In all woodworking there are surfaces to smooth. Use the same basic planing technique as for jointing with a few minor changes. Take a very fine cut and plane parallel with the grain as much as possible.

Complex molding planes such as the two shown here were too expensive for most 18th-century joiners (who made do with hollows and rounds). Their wide irons, sometimes as wide as 5 in. or 6 in., were tricky to tune, but they could quickly cut yards of identical moldings.

Skewing the plane often leaves a better surface and is an advantage around areas of difficult grain. Start cutting at one edge and plane to the opposite edge in one stroke; stops and starts leave noticeable marks. Overlap strokes as you move across the width of the surface so that they blend together. If you have to start or stop mid-stroke, glide in or out slowly. If things are working right, you'll be sending up billowy light shavings and leaving a surface that you can almost see your reflection in.

Smoothing beautiful surfaces—or any planing really—is easily the most satisfying part of working wood, but not the most easily mastered. Only experience can teach you how to read the grain or which tool to choose for a particular situation. This chapter offers just the barest hint of the possibilities of planes; for more detailed information on all types of planes, see *The Handplane Book* (The Taunton Press, 1997). Finally, there is no better way to learn about planes or gain more confidence using them than by picking one up, tuning it, and making some shavings.

SCRAPERS,
Files, and Rasps

More mystery surrounds scrapers than any other hand tool. The tools themselves are not unusual; they resemble spokeshaves or planes, and the simplest is no more complicated than a rectangle of thin and springy steel. There is no confusion in what the tools are capable of—cutting gossamer shavings from the most figured and challenging woods. The mystery surrounds the sharpening: how to burnish on the tiny hooked edge that allows a scraper to perform its magic.

Files and rasps are also scraping tools, but they cut with hundreds of little teeth that shave the surface like tiny planes. Files will sharpen the metal cutting edges of some hand tools, or smooth curves and flat surfaces in wood. Rasps cut more aggressively, like coarse sandpaper.

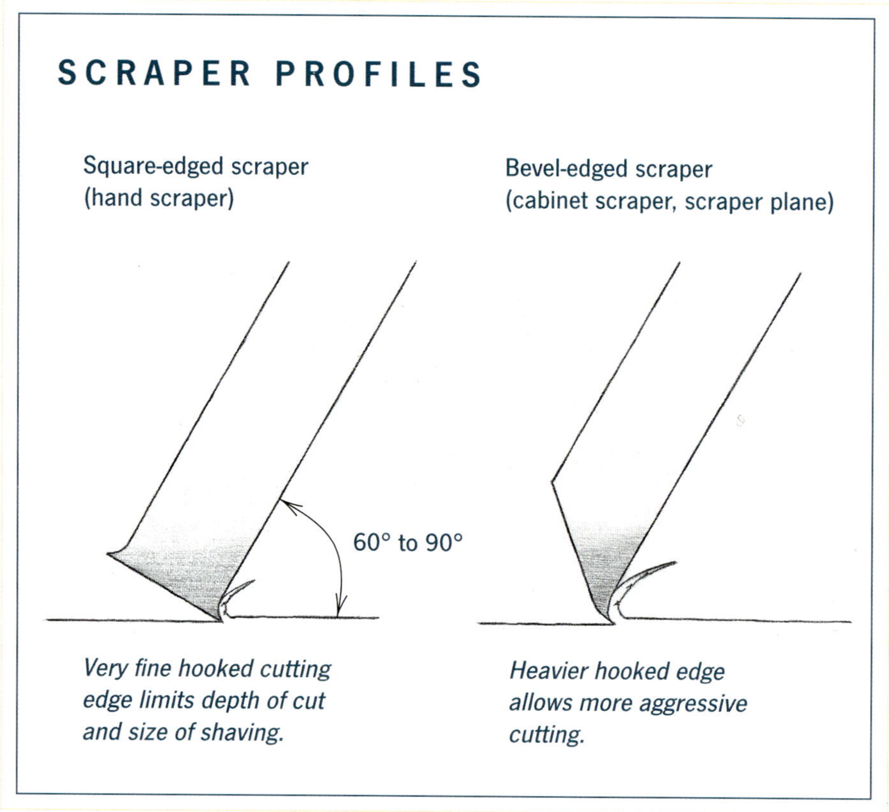

Pieces of a heavy hacksaw blade make excellent scrapers, stiffer and easier to use one-handed than a flexible hand scraper. Bevel one edge and sharpen as you would a cabinet-scraper blade.

Scrapers

Scraping is such an unflattering description of the finesse and precision possible with a hand scraper. We're not talking here about tools for scraping off old varnish or peeling paint from the hulls of wooden boats—although scrapers are certainly capable of this. Rather, we're talking about finely tuned tools with minute cutting edges for curling up delicate shavings.

These tools are classified as scrapers because they cut with a high cutting angle, a different sort of cutting dynamic than the slicing cut of planes. Yet scrapers are also planes, in a way, and are just as versatile for cutting anything from small moldings to finished surfaces, although they cut slowly due to the nature of the cutting edge. When it comes to working highly figured woods—something scrapers excel at—that same feature causes less tearout than a plane. A smoothing plane is still my preferred tool for creating a nearly polished surface, but I usually finish the job with a few strokes of my hand scraper to smooth out the small amount of tearout that is inevitable.

Most planes demand special tuning and adjustment to work well. They are complex tools. A hand scraper is the simplest of the lot, and handled scrapers, known as a cabinet scrapers and scraper planes, aren't far behind. Sharpening aside (this is the crux of making any of these tools perform), using scrapers couldn't be easier. Once you get the right cutting angle—by feel alone—a scraper can work into the tightest corner to scrape out some dried glue, skew over the most contorted figure and leave the wood almost polished, or fair a tight curve to a smooth and finished surface. When you get the hang of it, the versatility of a hand scraper is unmatched by any other hand tool.

This sleek ebony spokeshave scraper with comfortable handles, a thin scraper blade, and a microscopically fine throat will smooth and fair curves.

CABINET SCRAPERS AND SCRAPER PLANES

If a simple hand scraper is so useful, why use a spokeshave-like cabinet scraper or scraper plane? The main advantage of both of these tools is that they have soles (like a plane) that help level a surface, and the tool holds and tensions the scraper blade so it is less tiring to use when smoothing large surfaces. With a hand scraper, your hands become the holder and the sides of your palms the sole, which makes it easy to change orientation or cutting angle but also makes this task fatiguing. Heavy scraping also builds up heat, which conducts right to your thumbs. A cabinet scraper or scraper plane eliminates this problem.

The most common cabinet scraper is the Stanley #80, although Stanley made a number of versions and so did other manufacturers (see the photo on p. 128). Some have wooden soles, others are cast iron. Stanley also made four scraper planes, three of which are among the most sought after of the Stanley line. All will take a toothed blade for "toothing" veneers (to give them

A chairmaker uses a few sizes of specialized shaves, or "devils," for smoothing round parts such as spindles and legs. Placing a few fingers under the spindle helps to stabilize it and damp out vibration.

Cabinet and scraper planes have the advantages of a flat sole for scraping a true surface, comfortable handles for good control, and a blade held in position at an effective working angle. From the top: a bronze Lie-Nielsen based on a Stanley #212; a Sargent cabinet scraper with rosewood sole (like a Stanley #12½); a Stanley #112 scraper plane; and a wooden holder for a hand scraper (which keeps the edge stiff and less likely to dish a surface).

a good glue bond) or for leveling ornery woods (much like a scrub plane). The main advantage of a scraper plane is a long sole and a bench-plane handle or two for comfort and control. (If you invest in a good smoothing plane and learn to use other scrapers, however, a scraping plane isn't essential.)

The blades in both a cabinet scraper and a scraper plane are heavier for more aggressive scraping, and the blades are beveled like a plane iron to help burnish on a larger hook. A minor disadvantage of cabinet scrapers and scraper planes is that instead of four usable edges as in a hand scraper, you have at best only two, or even just one edge that you can sharpen (requiring more frequent sharpening). The angle of the bevel is not critical: 30° to 45° works well.

SHARPENING AND USING SCRAPERS

The cutting edge of a scraper is a fine hook that feels slightly smaller than the burr you naturally hone onto a chisel edge when sharpening (before removing it on a finer stone). A scraper will work as well without the hook—with a square but sharp edge, in other words—but the edge will not last as long. The larger the hook, as typically used on cabinet scrapers and scraper planes, the more aggressive the cut and the larger the shaving. A small hook works fine, though, and leaves a very smooth surface.

The sharpening process is essentially the same for all of the scrapers, with some small differences between a hand scraper—in some ways the hardest of the lot—and a cabinet scraper or scraper plane. Sharpening is like filing a saw—you don't have to go through every step each time. If it isn't very dull, you can begin part way through and end up with a nicely sharpened edge. The concept perhaps hardest to grasp is that you can burnish down the hook on a scraper and then roll up a new cutting edge. But let's start at the beginning with either a brand new scraper or one ready for a totally new edge.

SCRAPE, PLANE, OR SAND?

WHAT'S THE difference in the final surface depending on whether you scrape, plane, or sand? All three techniques can smooth a surface that feels and looks polished, yet there are subtle and distinct differences. A planed surface has the most depth, clarity, and shine. A scraped surface has nearly as much, and a sanded surface—even one sanded with a fine grit—can appear slightly dull. A finish helps hide these differences, but they will still be there.

Under the ideal circumstances of a perfectly sharp iron and working with the grain, a smoothing plane cleanly slices the fibers and cuts a flat surface. It has clarity and shine due to the consistent way it reflects light. An ideally sharp scraper cuts as cleanly, although in reality the fine hook edge degrades quickly due to the high-angle cut, and some fibers get torn rather than sliced as a result. The wood feels smooth, but it doesn't have the consistent radiance of a surface cut by a plane.

Sanding combines a little of both: It tears fibers while cleanly slicing them, too. Unfortunately, as the sandpaper dulls, a lot more tearing goes on. The finer the grit, the smoother the wood feels, but the surface is still irregular enough that it doesn't reflect light with quite as much sparkle.

Sharpening hand scrapers

Hand scrapers are usually rectangular, although I have about a dozen filed to various curves, including a few commercial "gooseneck" scrapers with a variety of edge shapes (all great for fairing moldings). Sharpening is the same, but for the sake of simplicity let's stick with a typical hand scraper.

The first step is jointing the two long edges with a fine file (and the short edges, too, if you want to sharpen all four sides). An 8-in. bastard mill file is commonly available and works well. The goal is to shape an edge square with the sides and straight, although a slight convex shape is fine. Clamp the scraper low in a machinist's vise with soft jaws (or in a side vise at your bench) and lightly file the edge from end to end. Try to cut the edge square to the sides, using the vice jaw as a visual guide. If this seems too difficult, run a saw kerf in a scrap just big

A gooseneck scraper has curved edges of different radii to scrape moldings and shaped parts. It's faster than sanding, cuts a more consistent profile, and leaves a smoother surface.

The first step in sharpening a new or dull scraper is filing the edges straight and square, either freehand with a bastard mill file or with a shopmade jointer (made from a scrap with a file-sized saw kerf in it).

Hone the edges on a fine stone to polish them. Either work upright with a zigzag motion, or flat on a board against the side of the stone. Only when the edges feel very sharp (they should curl up a fine shaving) are you ready for the next step: burnishing them with a triangular or oval burnisher (foreground).

Lubricate the burnisher with a couple drops of oil, lay it flat on the scraper, and wipe it up and down to draw the metal out slightly and work-harden the edge. Use modest pressure and do all four sides.

The magic in a scraper is the tiny hooked cutting edge burnished onto it. Work with a light touch; stroke the burnisher from end to end starting at 90° to the edge and gradually lower it to 80° by the third pass.

enough for a file, slip in the file, and use this as a jointer (see the top photo at left).

Hone the edges next, to polish them straight and square. It's easiest to hold the scraper upright and hone back and forth on the stone, although this can wear a groove in the stone if you are not careful (especially a soft waterstone). Use light pressure and work from a medium through a fine stone. Hone the flat sides of the scraper, too. Another method is to hone the edge of the scraper against the side of each stone, guiding the scraper by sliding it along a flat board. This is a sure way to hone the edge at 90°, and by varying the thickness of the board, you won't wear a groove in one place. Hone a curved scraper the same way, except roll it perpendicular to the stone.

At this point the edge should feel sharp, and it should be sharp enough to curl up a fine shaving. Try it out on a piece of hardwood. Grip the scraper in both hands, thumbs behind tensioning and curving the flexible blade into an arc, tip it slightly forward, and push. You should be able to feel subtle differences in the way the tool cuts by tipping the blade forward, or angling it more upright. If you are scraping up dust, then the edge is still not sharp; hone it some more.

This is called a hookless edge, and it is fine for delicate scraping work—leveling inlays or smoothing veneered surfaces, for example. Putting a hook on the edge makes it longer-lasting and more aggressive. To create the hook you'll need a burnisher, a polished steel rod that can be triangular, round, or oval in cross section. A round or oval burnisher is easiest to learn to use, because it glides along the edge and disperses the force over a wide area. On edge, a triangular burnisher applies a concentrated force.

The first step to produce a hooked edge is to draw out the steel that will form the hook. Apply a drop or two of oil to the burnisher, and with the scraper flat on a board and the burnisher flat on the scraper, stroke back and forth along the edge a few times. Keep the burnisher flat on the surface of the scraper (resist the temptation to tip it down). Do both sides of each long edge (for four working edges). This step does two things: It work-hardens the edge ever so slightly, and it draws out the metal to be formed into the hook. If your scraper is only slightly dull, this is where you can start the sharpening process, by burnishing the edge to lay down the old hook in preparation for the new.

Hone the beveled edge of scraper-plane and cabinet-scraper blades as you would a chisel, then burnish up a hook along the edge with slightly more pressure than for a hand scraper. Start along the bevel angle and finish at about 15° to 20°.

The trickiest part of sharpening is the next step, actually turning up the hook. Hold the scraper in one hand, the burnisher in the other, and stroke along the edge with light pressure. Slide the burnisher as you stroke the scraper so you don't wear it in one place. Make your first stroke at 90° to the edge, the next one at 85° or so, and the third one at 80°. You can roll up a more obvious hook by tipping the burnisher even more, but you will then have to tip the scraper well forward for it to cut—and risk burnishing your knuckles while you scrape. The smaller the hook, the easier it is to renew without having to file and hone. When you finish one edge, roll up the hook on the next.

If you have been successful with sharpening, using a hand scraper is a pure joy. The tool will amaze you. You can scrape in any direction, although working with the grain (and at a skew angle) leaves the smoothest surface. It doesn't take a lot of pressure or tension to bend the scraper into a tight curve in your hands. Curving the scraper stiffens the cutting edge and lets you concentrate on scraping small areas with precision. The more relaxed the curve, the wider area you can scrape in each pass.

Experiment with different cutting angles; often a lower angle is less aggressive but not quite as smooth. As with a smoothing plane, try to glide in and out of each stroke to minimize noticeable cutting marks. The only thing to be aware of is scraping the surface out of level, so go at it carefully and check with a straightedge, scrape large areas around knots or tearout with long strokes, and switch to a cabinet scraper or scraper plane if you are worried about keeping the surface absolutely flat.

Sharpening cabinet scrapers and scraper planes

Sharpening a bevel-edged scraper is much the same as sharpening a square-edged hand scraper. File and hone the beveled edge and the back face of the blade (the way you would a chisel or plane iron) and work-harden the edge with a burnisher laid flat against the back of the blade. Turning the hook is nearly the same, except that you use a little more pressure. Stroke first along the bevel and then two or three times more, so that you finish about 15° to 20° from perpendicular (see the photo on p. 131). In the #80 Stanley scraper, the bed for the blade is fixed, but in many of the other cabinet scrapers and planes it is adjustable. A fixed bed means that the hook angle can't vary much from 15° to 20° or the tool won't cut well—a small disadvantage over a versatile hand scraper.

To set the blade at the correct depth, slide a piece of paper under the sole ahead of the blade, then clamp the blade in place. In the #80 scraper, tension the wing nut behind the blade to set the depth: more tension pushes the blade into more of an arc, making it cut deeper. In other cabinet scrapers, cutting depth is changed by rocking the movable bed forward (for a deeper cut) or backward (for a lighter cut). The threaded arm that adjusts it locks against a post with two nuts (see the photo on p. 128). With any of these tools, take a light cut for the smoothest finish.

Scratch stocks are versatile scraping tools for cutting anything from inlay grooves to small moldings. They are no more complicated than a profiled blade secured in a simple wooden holder that also functions as a fence.

SCRATCH STOCKS

In a family of unusual tools, scratch stocks stand out. Furniture making can be challenging enough; any little tricks or tools that make things easier are favorites with me, and these tools are among my favorites. Scratch stocks essentially are reverse profiled hand scrapers with a fence of some kind to guide the cut. Stanley made a cast-iron version, the #66 beader, with a dozen different cutter profiles. Scratch stocks cut with the same gradual scraping action, so they aren't the best tools for cutting large moldings. But in figured woods, around curves, or for minute details, they shine. The ease with which one can be fashioned only adds to their appeal.

Any piece of old hacksaw, hand scraper, or bandsaw blade works for the cutter. Hacksaws and bandsaw blades are hard, so you have two choices if you want to work with them: either soften them and file the profile, or grind and hone them to shape. Filing is usually faster, but for the most durable edge, you'll have to reharden the blade. Don't bother with this unless you expect to use a specific profile a lot. Soften the blade by heating it red hot with a torch or stove burner, then cool it slowly. Needle files work well for shaping the profile. Reharden the blade by heating it red hot again and quickly quenching it in water.

To cut well, the sides of the blade (the cutting edges) must be honed square and polished, similar to a honed hand scraper ready for burnishing. Use slipstones for the curved edges. You can bevel the edge and even turn up a small hook, although it will work fine if you don't. Stick with sharp square edges and the scratch stock will cut in either direction—a real advantage in figured woods where the grain is apt to change orientation.

Cut a saw kerf in a scrap of wood for the fence and drive the cutter into it. This lets you tip the cutter forward for the best cutting angle (or backward while pulling the scratch stock). The flat sole of the #66 beader is nice for guiding the depth of cut, but it is not as versatile as this simpler version.

To make a scratch stock, start with a scrap of old hacksaw, plane iron, or scraper blade. Heat it red hot and cool it slowly to soften or anneal the steel so you can file the profile. (For shallow profiles you can grind the hard steel to shape and bypass this step.)

Needle files or chainsaw files work well for filing the profile, in this case a series of five reeds first marked out on the steel with dividers. File straight across to create square edges. (A small machinist's vise fastened to a block and clamped in a side vise is a secure way to hold the small blade.)

Hone the flat faces of the blade with a benchstone and the profile with slipstones, creating polished and square edges. For a fence, saw a scrap with a kerf slightly smaller than the thickness of the blade, and drive the blade into position.

The scratch stock cuts smooth and consistent reeds along the curved leg of a Regency chair in a matter of minutes.

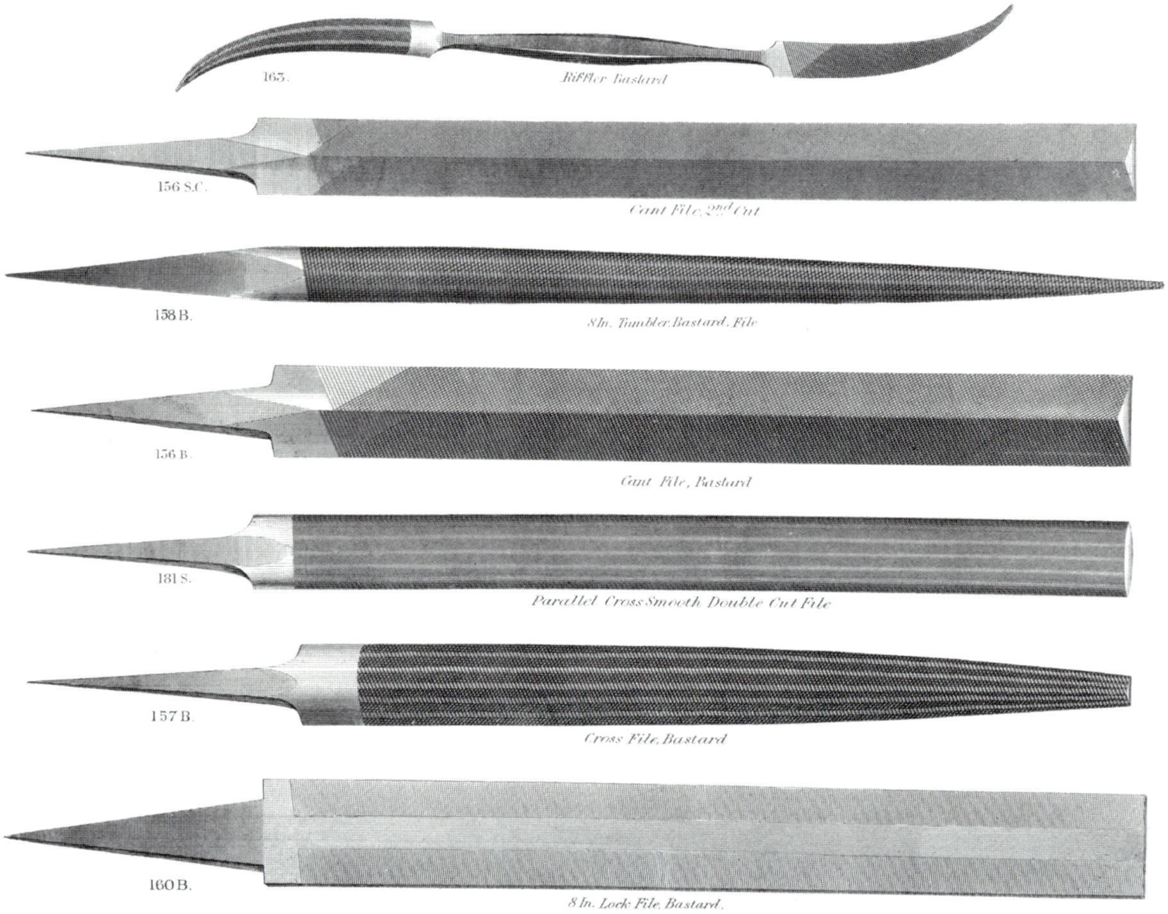

Files have uses for sharpening metal cutting edges and tuning tools but also for shaping curves or smoothing small parts like knobs and pulls. Their teeth vary from extremely fine to aggressively coarse.

Files and file handles come in all styles and sizes. The shop-made split handle (center) has enough spring to grip the tang—no ferrule is needed.

The key to unlocking the potential of scratch stocks and scrapers is no different than with other tools: good sharpening technique. You'll know when you get it right—when you feel the slightest resistance against the cutting edge and see the lightest of shavings curling up.

Files and Rasps

Files and rasps are a scraper's handy cousins when it comes to shaping wood or metal. While the primary use of files in a woodshop is for tuning the metal parts of hand tools and sharpening saws and other cut-

Among these filesmith's tools are a hammer with an ergonomic head for working close in to the body, two chisels for cutting files, and a pointed punch for rasp teeth. The hand-cut rasp (by Thomas Brammall, dated 1787) has random teeth, which cut more smoothly than the more ordered pattern of a machine-cut rasp.

ting edges, a fine-toothed file can also cut flat or curved wood surfaces, and do it surprisingly well. The teeth are cut at an angle across the file, so almost any way you hold the tool it will cut with a clean shearing action. Rasps are simply coarse files with random teeth, for aggressive shaping or smoothing. Somewhere between the two are floats, with their large file-like teeth and smooth cutting action, and cabinet files that cut faster than common metal files.

The variety of files and rasps is staggering, with hundreds of combinations of shapes, patterns, tooth designs, and lengths. It's easy to become confused about which ones to use where. It doesn't have to be confusing, however, because a small kit of a number of common files and rasps will do nearly every task you will face (and will save you from having to find a specialized tool dealer).

Over the years I have collected a number of files and rasps at flea markets, where I always seem to find at least one dealer selling surplus files with a few good rasps mixed in. While I can't tell you the names of most of them, nor does it really matter, I do know how aggressively each cuts and the finish to expect. After a little bit of experience and a good look at the teeth, you'll know the same thing about any file or rasp.

FILES

The most common shop file is the mill file, so named by the sawyers that used them for filing lumbermill saws. These are the files you are likely to find at any hardware store, 4 in. to 16 in. in length (excluding the tang), flat with square sides, and tapered gradually toward the tip. Other common patterns are triangular files for sharpening saws, and half-round and round files for shaping curves. The teeth on any of these files can be uniformly angled

MAKING FILES BY HAND

FILEMAKING was once a specialized trade, allied with similar metalworking trades such as saw and edge-tool making. With special hammers, chisels, and punches, a filemaker would sit at an anvil and punch-form the teeth at about 80 per minute, making 20 files in a day.

A file blank was first prepared from high-quality steel by rolling and forging it to shape. The steel was left soft so it could be worked and so the faces could be ground as flat as possible for the most uniform teeth. Holding the file against an anvil with leather straps looped under his feet, the filemaker punched up row after row of teeth with a special hammer and a wide chisel similar to a cold chisel. It took angling the chisel at just the right angle (close to plumb) and giving it a blow only learned by experience.

By guiding the chisel against the ridge of the last tooth, the filemaker found the position for the next cut. The heavier the blows, the higher and farther apart the teeth, and the coarser the file. Round and half-round files were made with many rows of straight cuts, while rasps were created by chopping one tooth at a time in a random pattern with a chisel-like punch.

Hardening the file to make it useful demanded equal skill. To protect the vulnerable edges of the teeth in the heat of the fire, the file was first dipped in a sticky mixture, such as beer grounds, and then salt. When the salt melted, the file was withdrawn from the furnace and quenched in water, using a different technique for each file pattern to prevent warping. Today, the process is done by machine, but the quality of the finished file still depends on the same process, from preparing the blank to hardening and quenching.

A filemaker hunches over a small anvil, a file blank held in place with two leather straps looped under his feet, as he punches up row after row of skewed teeth. He uses no guide other than his eye and the previously cut tooth.

in one direction, known as *single cut,* or they can have another set of teeth crossing it, known as *double cut.* To complicate things further, each file pattern or shape—of which there are dozens—comes in a range of grades (from coarsest): coarse, bastard, second-cut, and smooth. Furthermore, a longer file of the same grade has coarser teeth.

Naturally, the finer the tooth pattern, the slower the file cuts and the smoother the surface. But fine teeth clog easily, especially on wood and nonferrous metals. Single-cut files clog less quickly than double-cut, and they cut faster, but they wear out faster, too. Both leave an equally good finish.

Files, floats, and rasps were once made in far greater variety of tooth patterns and cuts than you are likely to find today, as shown in this catalog from the mid-1800s. The larger the teeth, the more aggressive the cut (and the more space for holding and carrying off sawdust).

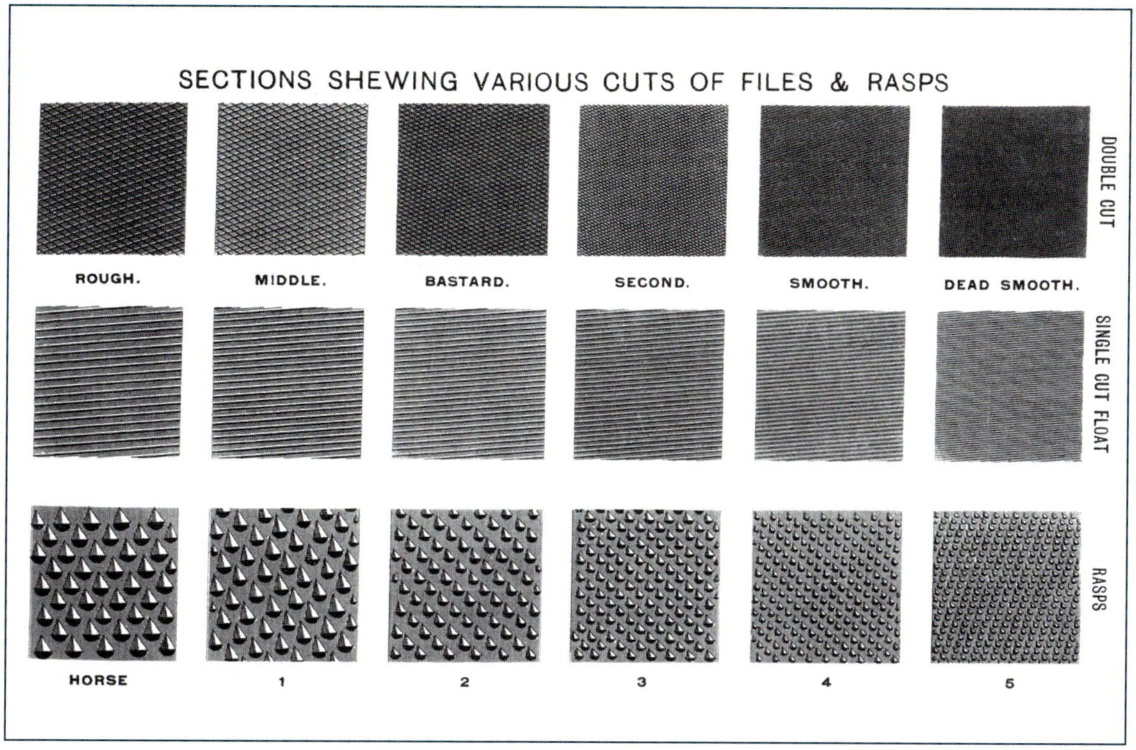

No file (or rasp) is going to cut well or leave a very good finish unless the teeth are kept clean of the small pieces that inevitably clog them. I dislodge them by rapping the file flat against my wooden bench every few minutes, or I use a file card or brush with short stiff bristles (but soft so they don't damage the teeth). A toothbrush or brass brush also works. What material remains you can pick out with the point of a small nail. Files (and rasps) will last longer and stay sharp if you store them hanging up or in a shallow drawer with dividers, so they don't bang together and knock off the brittle cutting edges.

Every tanged file should be fitted with a handle for two reasons. First, the tang can be quite sharp, so covering it with a handle protects your hand. Second, a handle extends a file's usable working length, while giving you more control over the tool at the same time. The farther apart your two hands are when filing, the more precise you can be. The handle doesn't need to be elaborate—a scrap of pine with the corners planed off works as well as a turned rosewood handle with a brass ferrule—although a nice handle only adds to the joy of using a file. (See pp. 200-201 for more about making and fitting handles.)

SOME FILES have edges with no teeth (known as safe edges). This feature lets you cut right up to a corner without also filing into the corner. An auger-bit file has two safe faces on one end, and two safe edges on the other, specifically for the tricky work of filing the spur and cutting lip of an auger bit, but not at the same time.

Using a file properly is not as easy as you might think. Like a chisel, all of the control over the tool comes from good hand-eye coordination, plus the little bit of guiding the length of the file provides. Because the teeth cover most of each face of a file, it cuts continuously, despite small shifts in your hand or body position.

Filing a truly flat surface is the hardest task, mainly because the joints of your arms and hands want to rotate and not remain stiff. For flattening wood, a plane is a better choice, anyway. There is a subtle way a mill file (the best choice for flattening) is made that also helps.

The center is slightly thicker so that even if it warps during heat-treating, both faces will be a bit convex in their length. This is a better shape to use for flattening, rather than a concave face, which would cut the outer edges more aggressively.

The natural rotation of your arms and wrists is an advantage in shaping or fairing curves with a half-round or round file, or a rasp. With either tool, the smoothest cut is a combination of a slightly skewed forward stroke (to give your file the widest bearing) with some downward pressure and a rolling action (to prevent clogging the teeth). Filing straight across tends to chatter and rip the fibers and concentrates the cutting in only one place. Instead, file with a skew motion into each stroke as you slide the file along the curve to fair it. Sensitivity to the way the tool cuts will guide you to a comfortable and natural motion.

RASPS

The variety of rasps is much narrower than that of files, but the two tools are similar. Whereas a fine file might be my first choice for smoothing odd surfaces, such as the top of a chair leg or relieving the sharp corners of a drawer opening, a rasp is a better tool for rough shaping. While the individual teeth of a rasp scrape, they also tend to tear the fibers. The same could be said of some files—cabinet files, for instance—that are nearly as coarse as a fine rasp. The most important idea is not what the tool is called but whether the fineness or coarseness of the teeth suits the work you want to do.

Because rasps are most useful for shaping curved surfaces, half-round and round rasps are the most com-

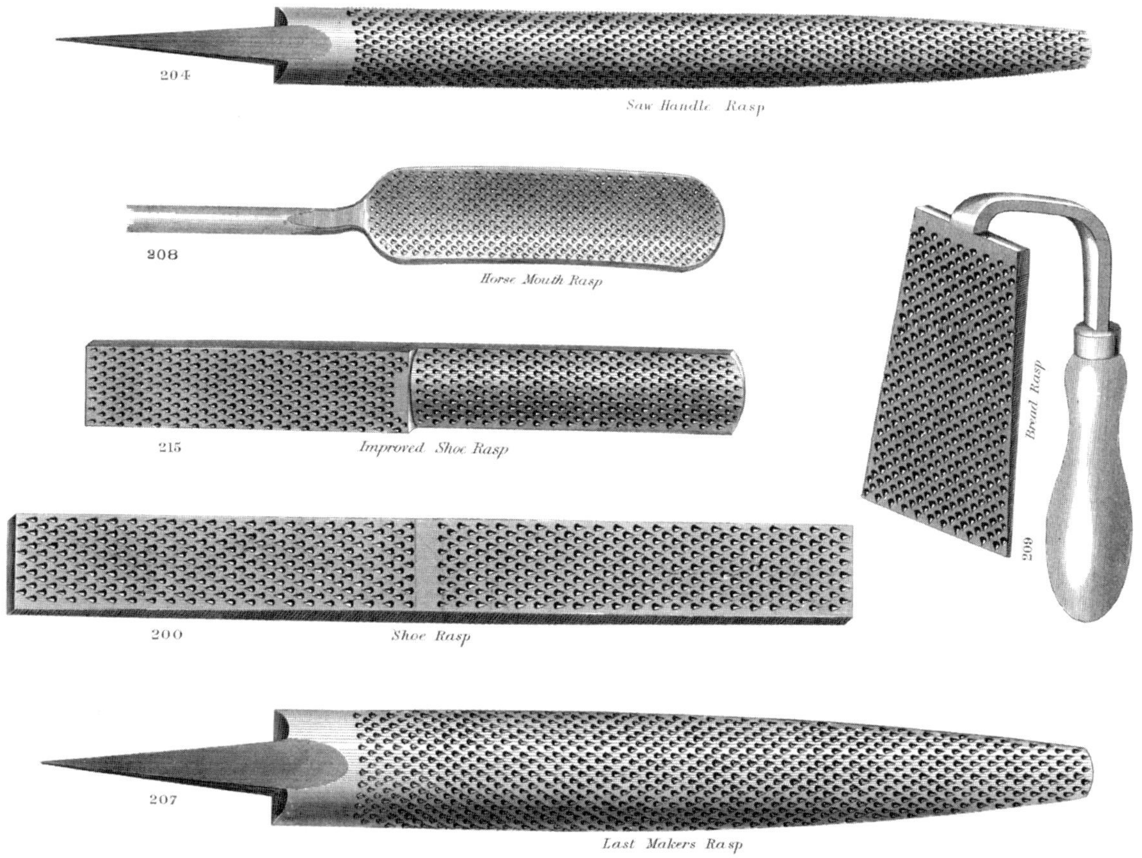

Many trades relied on rasps, from saw-handle makers to "last makers" shaping curved wooden shoe lasts (forms). Even cooks used rasps—for scraping the burned crust off the bottom of a loaf of bread.

mon shapes. Nicholson patternmaker's rasps #49 and #50 (slightly finer) are two readily available and versatile rasps. Hand-cut rasps have an enduring appeal that has lingered despite the reality that most rasps are now cut by machine. The allure is the randomness of their teeth for the smoothest cutting action. Rifflers are small curved and double-ended rasps (sometimes they have file teeth) for working in tight places and for carving.

Use a rasp like a file, with the same forward and rotating motion. The more downward pressure, the more aggressive the cut. To protect my fingers from the sharp teeth and to give me a comfortable place to grasp the tip, I always wrap it with a few layers of masking tape. Then, if I am working a flat surface (such as filing proud dovetails), the tip rides along on the tape and doesn't dig in. Use a half-round rasp for cutting or fairing a curve. Cut close to the line and then switch to a cabinet or finer file. For the smoothest surface, finish with that most versatile of hand tools—a hand scraper.

One of the best rasps still on the market is the #50 patternmaker's rasp made by the venerable Nicholson File Co. of Providence, Rhode Island. It's the ideal tool for making light, controlled cuts, such as filing away high spots to fit a tapered leg to its mortise.

Somewhere between a plane and a rasp are Surforms, with their individual razor-sharp teeth that cut like miniature planes for aggressive shaping and smoothing. They never need sharpening—you merely replace the blade.

Sheffield
METALLIC FRAME
PATENT BRACE

BORING TOOLS

Not long ago a brace and bits could be found in every tool kit in every woodworking shop, because every trade had a need for drilling holes. A carpenter drilled holes for cutting mortises and pinning their tenons; a shipwright bored holes for the long treenails that joined planking and ribs; a wheelwright drilled the holes for spokes and reamed tapered holes in the hub, all by hand with augers, braces, and an ingenious variety of bits.

Electric drills and drill presses bore holes quickly and accurately and have largely replaced augers and braces. I appreciate and take advantage of these tools. But for drilling holes at compound angles, for working with maximum sensitivity and control, or just for the pure pleasure of using the tools, I still prefer my classic Miller's Falls brace and hand drills.

Augers, Braces, and Drills

Many tools bore holes—augers, braces, hand drills, push drills, and bow drills, to name several. They supply the rotational energy needed to penetrate wood, and some of them provide considerable mechanical advantage for cutting large holes. The bit is what actually cuts the wood. Bits are as different from one another as a small screw hole is to a tapered bung hole in a whiskey barrel. While the bits evolved in a logical way from simple sharpened points to sophisticated and accurate twist bits with multiple cutters, the same can't be said for the boring tools that power them. Typical of many hand tools, augers, braces, and various kinds of drills evolved to meet the needs of specific trades in an interesting but not always linear way.

Boring is both simple and complicated at the same time. Boring a small hole is not difficult—the rather blunt point of a nail makes an adequate drill that wears its way through the wood as much as it actually cuts. Twisting a chisel-pointed bradawl into the wood cuts and divides the fibers, making a crude but entirely adequate hole.

Drilling larger, more accurate holes is more complicated. It takes more power to remove a greater volume of wood. And with every revolution the bit is cutting long grain half the time and end grain the other half. The bit must be able to cut cleanly in both situations, while also cutting straight, despite knots and irregular grain. Clearly the design of the bit is important, balanced with the speed and power of the brace, drill, or auger.

BORING WITH BRADAWLS

THE SIMPLEST and quickest way to pierce a hole is not with a drill bit but with a bradawl. This small, screwdriver-like tool has a round blade with a chisel point. Merely pushing the awl into the fibers and giving it a half twist makes a pilot hole for nails or screws.

A similar tool with a tapered, pointed blade and square cross section can cut a hole quite close to an edge without danger of splitting the wood. This square-pointed version is also known as a birdcage awl for its use in boring the holes for the wire framework of a birdcage.

The chisel tip of this bradawl severs—rather than just parts—the fibers as it is pushed and twisted into the wood to drill a small hole for a screw or nail.

AUGERS

Augers are the simplest boring tools. They are no more complicated than a handled bit. They range in size from a large shipwright's auger, with its long wooden handle that fits through an eye forged at the top of the bit (and interchangeable with other bits), to tiny gimlets used to make pilot holes for nails and screws. Each clockwise turn of an auger handle spins the bit a single revolution. Augers don't cut very fast, but they are powerful enough to handle the largest holes. Wheelwrights, carpenters, and shipwrights were just a few of the many tradesmen who relied on augers for boring and reaming.

You can add a handle to any drill bit to make an auger, which might lead you to believe that augers were the first boring tools, evolving just behind early copper or bronze bits. Interestingly, Egyptian and Roman craftsmen used far more complex bow drills for the simple reason that augers are frustratingly slow for drilling small holes—at least with the crude sharpened point bits then available. A bow drill has all of the advantages of rapid speed, forward and backward.

Eventually bits became larger and more sophisticated, with lead screws on some and cutting lips that both pulled the bit into the hole and improved cutting performance. Adding handles was a logical step, to deliver the greater power necessary to turn larger bits. With its many styles of handles and bit shapes, augers became the most important boring tools for centuries.

Many years ago, I built a house from an old barn I took down, repaired, and moved. There weren't many nails holding the barn together, but each joint of the massive frame was a variation on a mortise-and-tenon joint, pinned together with wooden treenails. When I rebuilt the barn, I cut many more such joints, some with mortises 8 in. deep and 2 in. wide. I could have rented a generator and a powerful electric drill to waste the wood from the joints, but instead I used an old wood-handled auger. It was hard work and I got a lot stronger

To drill out mortises and peg holes in the heavy frame of a barn, bridge, or house—or for any strenuous drilling—a carpenter would once have used (and still might) a large T- or crank-handled auger. With the slick he would pare tenons and pegs to fit.

This 17th-century reamer, with a large T-handle bound with two iron rings to stand up to hard work, would have been used by a wheelwright to taper the inside of a large wheel hub to fit snugly onto an axle spindle.

that summer, but it was quite amazing how quickly the auger hogged out a hole, quietly, and without any electric cords to get tangled.

The diminutive cousins of T-handled augers, gimlets are ideal for drilling small holes or starter holes for screws, especially deep in barely accessible places. Various bits fit into the large T-handle for both drilling a hole and cutting a countersink.

Ancient yet sophisticated in concept, a bow drill (top) uses the sawing action of a bow to rapidly spin a pointed bit forward and backward to drill small holes. A push drill (center), this one made by Goodell Bros. of Greenfield, Mass., works on the same principle, only with an internal spiral screw in place of the bow.

GIMLETS

Augers have all but disappeared, but gimlets, their tiny cousins, have survived. Gimlets are versatile and practical for everything from drilling small holes in awkward places to boring quick pilot holes for screws. With a superior twist-bit design and small screw feed, a gimlet bites into the wood and carves out a hole. Bell hangers once used gimlets as long as 36 in.—as a phone lineman today uses extra-long twist bits for installing phone lines—and brewers and vintners used gimlets for making small holes to taste wine or vent beer kegs.

When making and repairing furniture, there are plenty of times I want to add a small screw after assembly—usually somewhere difficult to reach. Other drills might work as well (a push drill for instance), but not as simply as my old gimlet with its worn and polished applewood handle. A few turns of the wrist are all it takes.

BOW DRILLS

The complexity of Egyptian furniture is all the more amazing when you consider how basic craftsmen's tools were three or four thousand years ago. When drilling holes for inlays and typical joints held together with wooden pins, for example, they relied entirely on bow drills. The bit was simple enough—a sharpened and flared point—but the drill itself was quite a sophisticated idea. The bow supplied power and rotation to the bit by back-and-forth "sawing" of a string wrapped around it. Meanwhile, the craftsman held the bit shaft by its head, which spun freely, in order to guide and apply pressure to the bit.

BRACES

Hints of the modern brace and contemporary hand drills first appeared in a variation of the auger known as a breast auger. It looked no different than any other handled auger, except that it had a large and loose head for leaning against, hence the name. The idea originated with shipwrights, who not only needed to drill large holes but also worked in tight places. The loose head let a shipwright get the weight of his upper body against the tool, while still being able to turn the handles. At around this time—late in the 10th century—bits were shaped like a gouge and needed considerable pressure to cut a hole of any size.

Logically, a simple brace should have preceded the more complex bow drill, but it didn't. Just by adding some sort of crank arm to an awl or pointed bit, such a brace would have allowed continuous drilling motion as opposed to the backward and forward motion of a bow drill, and the stops and starts of an auger. But such is the history of braces: What seems obvious to us today actually took until the 15th century to develop. But when it finally happened, braces had the important elements of a loose head and a cranked arm.

The chuck that we take for granted today—the piece of hardware that holds a wide range of bits securely in the brace—was also a long time in coming. Attempts to perfect a chuck parallel the trials and errors that planemakers were going through in the first half of the 19th century, as they tried to improve the mechanics of wooden and cast-iron planes. Many ingenious minds were at work.

Typical of early shopmade braces, this small piano maker's brace is sawn and shaped from a single piece of beech. It has bits fitted to separate pads that merely jam into the tapered chuck.

NOT ALL DRILLS bore round holes. A passer drill can bore a square, diamond, or any shape hole, much like a modern-day router. Power is provided by a bow, which twists the bit—two steel rods welded together at one end with flattened cutting tips at the other—within a template pierced with the desired hole shape. The springy legs of the bit follow the outline of the template and rout out the hole. One of the drill's uses was to rout diamond recesses for decorative rivets on try squares.

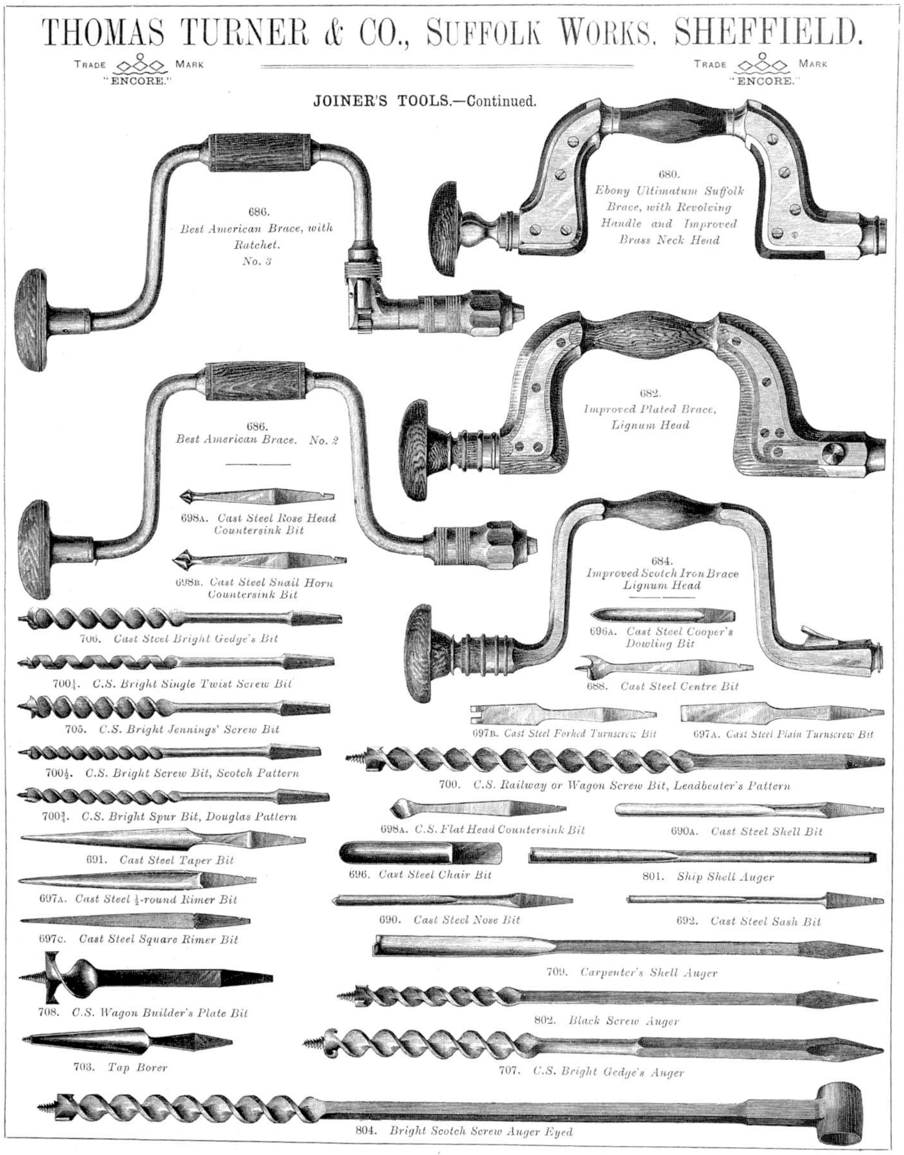

Advertised alongside a selection of bits and fancy English braces with three different chuck designs (from top: push ring, button, and lever) are streamlined American steel braces (top left), which eventually dominated the market due to their positive shell chucks and ratcheting drives.

The simplest chuck solution, one adopted by chairmakers who needed a limited range of bit sizes, was to fit the bit permanently in the brace. Because braces were wooden and shopmade anyway, a chairmaker merely made additional braces. For workmen who traveled to the job site, a far better solution was to have one brace and individual bits fitted to wooden pads that either wedged into the tapered chuck or had a wooden spring similar to a clothespin that locked the pad in place.

The problem was never holding the bit while drilling—downward pressure kept the pad in place—but preventing the pad from falling out when retracting the bit to clear the shavings. A later variation had an internal spring (with a button to release it) that engaged with a notch filed in the end of each bit. The only problem was that each brace was different, so that each set of bits had to be fitted individually.

Many other solutions were tried, but none were as successful as the "shell" design patented by William Barber in 1864. This is the chuck you will undoubtedly find on any new brace, and quite likely any one made in this century by Miller's Falls or Stanley, the two biggest manufacturers. The two internal jaws that hold the tapered rectangular shank of the bit are forced together by a threaded shell that screws over them (hence the name "shell"). By simply screwing and unscrewing the shell, bits of different sizes could be slipped into place and held securely.

While Americans were tinkering with better chucks and designing clever braces that could drill around corners, in tight spots, or with ratchet drives, British makers were refining the brace into a high art. A typical craftsman still worked with wooden braces—or metal ones for trades such as coachmaking, where the tools got hard use—but for the master furniture maker there was the grandly named "Ultimatum." William Marples was only one of many makers of these exquisite braces, which, typical of

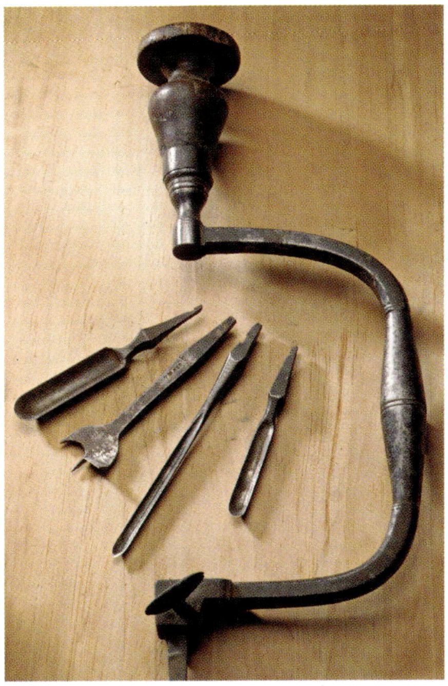

Compared with stripped-down, mass-produced American versions, this fancy English gentleman's brace—with its shapely head, incised lines on the bulging handhold, and chamfers along the frame—displays the kind of art and elegance that often went into handmade tools.

Drilling holes in tight corners or around obstructions is never easy, although many designers tried innovative solutions. From top: Stanley corner ratchet bit brace with a flattened head to lie tightly against a wall or floor; a right-angle corner brace with a universal joint by Dumont Tool Co., and a Miller's Falls brace with a detachable cornering handle and gear.

British tools, combined exotic woods, such as ebony, rosewood, or boxwood, with a metal frame (usually brass) and other details, such as an ivory ring inlaid in the head. Ultimatums once cost as much as the best smoothing planes—about a week's wages. American braces were far less beautiful, but their ingenuity and effective chucks won over workmen throughout the world.

Brace basics

Braces have so few moving parts that they last a long time. Any tool shop or flea market is bound to have at least a few classic braces, both wood and metal. Stick with a metal brace: it's stronger and will have a better, more user-friendly chuck. Barber's shell chuck is still quite common, although you might find a Spofford brace with a split chuck tightened with a wing nut on the side (see the photo on p. 149). This is a good design that fits the tapered tang of most bits.

While there are subtle variations in details, the most obvious difference between braces is the length of the cranked arm. The larger the sweep—the diameter of the circle the arm makes—the more power you can deliver to the bit. Watchmakers used braces with tiny sweeps, and carpenters ones in the range of 4 in. to 14 in. Ten inches is a good compromise—a brace big enough to turn a large bit without bumping into your chest if you happen to lean over the tool while you

Before cordless and electric drills, egg-beater and breast drills such as these Yankee drills by North Bros. Mfg., Philadelphia, Pa., did all the small to modest drilling jobs—boring screw holes, countersinking, and even driving screws. Their workaday chucks hold modern brad-point, twist, and countersink bits.

Among these unusual hand drills is one in the shape of a pistol made by Ruger Manufacturing Co., an Archimedean double-screw pump drill, and a T-handle that converts an ordinary twist bit to a small auger (here with a depth stop).

work. Another feature to look for is a head with ball bearings for the smoothest boring action. (In this type of brace, there will be a small oil hole under the head to lubricate the bearings.) Before you buy any brace, take the chuck apart to check if any internal parts are worn or missing, and to see how they work together. There should be two jaws, a spring between them, and an outer shell. Before using a used brace, be sure to clean and oil everything.

Along with the chuck came another invention: a ratchet mechanism for drilling in tight spots. The ratchet has three positions. The center one is for positive drive both clockwise and counterclockwise. To either side of this is a position for all clockwise or all counterclockwise ratcheting rotation. This is a nice feature for drilling large holes, where you can get maximum leverage by short, ratcheted swings.

HAND DRILLS

Braces are ideal tools for boring modest to large holes, but what about small holes for screws, nails, wooden pins that lock joints, and all of the light drilling tasks typical in a shop? Hand drills or egg-beater drills, as they are sometimes called, are invaluable for this sort of work. Most have a lightweight cast-iron frame with gears and shapely rosewood handles. They are light, have an easy-to-use and positive three-jaw chuck, can turn slowly or fast enough to drill metal, and can drill in tight places. Often the side handle is removable for just this purpose.

Chairmakers favor venerable spoon bits for practical reasons: Without a lead screw you can change the cutting angle as you drill, cut as aggressively as you want, and leave a smooth exit hole with its gouge-like cutting action. The Spofford brace powering the bit has a simple and universal split chuck tightened with a wing nut.

Not all hand drills are small. I have one made by Miller's Falls that has a breast plate, ratcheting gears, two speeds, a large chuck, and enough mechanical leverage to drill a fair-sized hole. (It's essentially a hand-powered drill press.) Stanley made more than a dozen different models, as did Miller's Falls, including a combination of brace and hand drill. Portable electric drills can drill circles around hand drills and have largely replaced them, yet a hand drill is still my preferred tool for drilling extra slowly, or when I need maximum precision and control.

PUSH DRILLS

A push drill is another small drill for light drilling tasks, similar to a Yankee screwdriver, with an interesting mechanical system that transforms pumping action into rotation (see the bottom photo on p. 144). It works with an Archimedean screw, a spiral-fluted shaft, and a nut in the hollow handle that engages with it, so that every push and release turns the shaft. The advantage of this design is that there are no handles to turn, so it will drill a hole in the tightest space.

Push-drill bits are unique, similar to straight router bits with two cutting flutes, except that one flute cuts on the push, the other on the release (when the shaft turns in the opposite direction). Push drills are quick, not very powerful, and best used for small screw and nail holes.

Bits

The best brace or drill is worthless without a collection of bits, the business end of the tool, so to speak. Straight and clean holes—and twist-bit designs that eject the shavings effortlessly—are easy to take for granted. Such improvements, however, are relatively modern. For centuries, craftsmen had to make do

Bits have evolved from sharpened points to sophisticated cutting tools. Shown here (from left to right) is a reamer for enlarging and tapering holes, a countersink, early nose and shell bits similar to spoon bits, a center bit with single spur and cutting lip, a single-twist auger without cutting spurs, and a double-twist auger with cutting spurs.

with less efficient bits that demanded considerable pressure for effective cutting. They cut roughly, or had to be withdrawn frequently to clear shavings.

Early bits were spoon-shaped, with a round tip to start the cut and sharpened sides to enlarge it. The more pressure applied, the faster the shavings curled up inside the hollow center. The design has survived, and for good reason. Unlike bits with a lead screw, you easily can change direction when drilling with a spoon bit by starting a hole perpendicular to a surface and gradually shifting to an oblique angle. This is a technique common among Windsor chairmakers. Because spoon bits can cut slowly or rapidly, and along their sides as well as at the tip, they don't split out the backside of a hole (the way a twist bit might). They are also the only bit that will cut a pear-shaped hole—a further subtlety of locking the parts of a Windsor chair together.

An 18th-century carpenter had an interesting variety of other bits to choose from. Among them were nose bits, which resembled spoon bits, except they had a flattened end sharpened into a single cutting flute; shell bits with a gouge end; and pod bits with a gimlet's twist or two at the end. This small twist at the end of a pod bit, used on long pump augers for drilling out logs for water pipes, helped the bit cut fast and straight. Without any lead screw, nose and shell bits were hard to position without first gouging out a depression, much as we center-punch a hole before drilling.

Where today we use Forstner bits, an 18th-century craftsman would have used a center bit to drill a flat-bottomed hole. A center bit

Although they express beauty beyond their function, every detail of the shape and cutting edges of these large gimlet-point and Scotch-eyed augers is designed to cut wood fibers and spiral the chips away.

AUGER-BIT HEAD

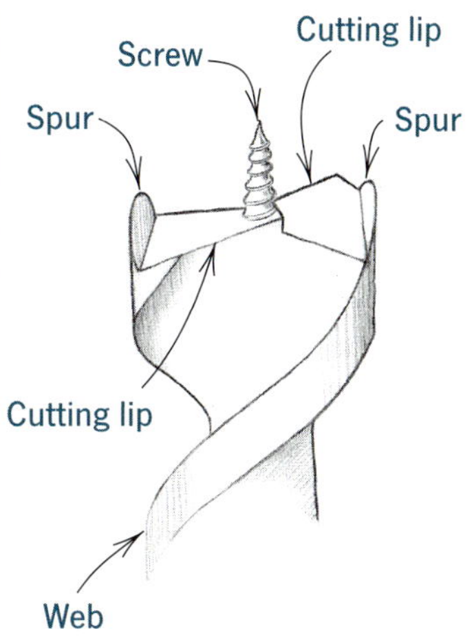

was also used to drill holes at modest angles, and for drilling in thin wood where its point is less apt to split the wood than the wedging action of a lead screw.

Today, the most useful and common twist bits have the improvements of a lead screw to pull the bit into the cut, cutting spurs and chisel-like lips that score and pare a shaving, and a spiral shank to eject the shavings. A drill bit might seem like a fairly simple cutting tool, but it is actually quite sophisticated—it combines different types of cutting actions simultaneously.

As with other hand tools, many creative minds worked on perfecting the design, each contributing some improvement. Russell Jennings was one who made a seemingly small change in the mid-1800s, yet it established the design of twist bits since (including modern brad-

DOING THE TWIST

THE PROCESS of forming the spiral shape and cutting edges of a twist bit by hand and machine is an interesting bit of manufacturing history. A bit starts as a blank of hot-rolled cast steel, forged flat for the twists and round for the shank. To eliminate confusion through the rest of the process, the tang is stamped with the bit size. (The standard marking is a number, 7 for instance, for a 7/16-in. bit.)

The twists were once formed in a hand-cranked lathe with the steel red hot, and later with dies, rugged molds that shape the hot steel under the pounding of a very heavy hammer in a process known as drop forging. The cutting head is formed in a separate die, the drill is heated and annealed, and then machined to cut the threads, cutting lips, and spurs. All of the forging and pounding of the steel increases its density, and careful annealing in small batches eliminates stresses, making a more durable bit.

In a process once done by hand, auger twist bits are now formed in dies or molds and drop-forged to shape. First a blank of cast steel is twisted into an accurate spiral, and then the cutting lips, spurs, and center screw are forged to shape. After hardening and tempering, the cutting edges and screw are precisely ground and filed to sharpness.

Whether powered by hand or machine, brad-point drills (left and right) are a woodworker's first choice for small holes. For easy shopmade depth stops, use a snug block twisted along the shank into position, make a loose sleeve out of wood to the correct length, or wrap the bit with a piece of tape.

Jacks-of-all-trades and masters of none, many expansion-bit designs have been devised to cut a range of small to large holes, although none do it very easily. All have a large center screw to pull the bit into the work, and one or more adjustable spurs and lips to score the fibers and pare them out.

point bits). Instead of placing the spurs in line with the cutting lips, where the lips were thinnest and weak, he pushed the spurs back. The result was a stronger spur and one that didn't interfere with the cutting action of the lips.

A "Jennings pattern" bit is what you are likely to find new, although a look through a box of old bits at a flea market will turn up quite a variety of other designs. Some of these bits might have a single twist in the shaft, with a single spur and lip, while others have double twists and two spurs and lips. You can find twist bits with coarsely threaded lead screws for rapid drilling into softwoods, or ones with fine screws for hardwoods. Irwin, the largest modern bit manufacturer, still makes another variation, a solid center bit with a single twist for rugged drilling. A subtlety of most of these bits is that the spiral—or "web" as it is known—is slightly smaller than the width of the cutting lips, to give the drill clearance.

While twist bits are the best choice for holes larger than about ½ in., two similar types of bits—brad points and common metalworking twist drills—work better for smaller holes. Brad-point bits have spurs and cutting lips, plus a sharp center point in place of a lead screw. Twist drills have two cutting lips and no center point or screw, and were designed for drilling into metal, although they also work well with wood. While both are designed for a drill press that could turn the bit quickly, they cut more slowly but just as cleanly in a geared hand drill. Just be careful using a hand drill, because it is easy to wobble just a little and snap a fine twist drill in two.

At the other end of the spectrum, adjustable "expansion bits" are used for large holes. Augers are an alternative, of course—this is the work they are designed for—but with a single compact expansion bit you can cut any hole up to 3 in. Most expansion bits have a simple design—a single spur and cutting lip adjustable for different diameters. I find them awkward to use; they feel unbalanced and don't drill accurately in anything other than softwoods. They also need a brace with a large sweep to deliver the considerable power required for all but the smallest holes.

SHARPENING BITS

If you can sharpen a chisel, sharpening a boring bit is no more challenging. The cutting edges all are variations on the familiar chisel edge. Understanding the physics of how the bit cuts also helps with sharpening, but so does looking at the bit closely and simply tuning what's there, at least as a start. Bits other than twist drills are soft enough that they can be filed easily. Auger files are designed just for this task, with two tapered ends and safe edges on two sides and two faces so you can safely file one cutting bevel at a time. Needle files also work.

Twist bits are ideal for learning how to sharpen, because they are big enough to work on and their cutting edges are obvious. Watching how the bit cuts explains a lot about

To better understand sharpening the various parts, twist an auger bit into a piece of softwood to see how the lead screw pulls the bit into the wood, the spurs score around the hole, and the cutting lips chisel out the chips.

Sharpen the lips as you would a chisel, at about a 25° bevel angle, using small needle files or a special tapered auger file. File or hone the underside if possible.

File the cutting spurs as little as possible to prolong bit life, and only file on their inside face or you will change the cutting diameter of the bit and cause it to bind. The lead screw should need no tuning.

Useful for more than just drilling holes, braces can turn hollow augers, such as this one by A. A. Woods, used for cutting the round tenons on the ends of the bowback on a Windsor chair.

To help drill straight, Stanley at one time made a bit level that pinches the drill shank, or you can sight against a square (or two) placed on the work. Slip a piece of paper between your work and a waste block and you'll know you're through when you see bits of paper in with the chips.

Drill at a compound angle by sighting against a square and bevel gauge set to the required angle. A ruler establishes a sighting plane against the square, to keep the bit angled yet plumb. Steady yourself by planting your feet, leaning against the bench, and locking your upper body.

sharpening the various edges: As the lead screw pulls into the wood, the spurs are the first to cut (see the top photo on p. 153). They score around the hole, the horizontal cutting lips pare some chips, and the twist of the web spirals them out of the hole.

The spurs are the widest part of the bit, establishing the diameter of the hole. File them on the inside only, or you may alter the clearance of the bit. The spurs should be the same length and sharp on their leading edges. Both lips should cut equally, too. Turn the bit into soft wood to see that they start cutting at the same time. File the lips along the top bevel, being careful not to cut into the lead screw or spurs.

The back of the bevel is harder to sharpen; work it with a small file or a slipstone. Think of it as a small chisel, and file as little as possible to extend the life of the bit. A properly sharpened bit should work smoothly, sending up consistent chips with clean round edges. Unless you use a bit often, you might go years without having to resharpen.

Learn to sharpen a twist bit, and a spoon bit or gimlet isn't much harder. Avoid any filing and instead hone the outside and inside edges that you can reach with a slipstone. The technique with both bits is to roll or rock them across the stone. Sharpening a spoon bit is similar to sharpening a gouge, except that you have to hone the rounded tip at a higher angle to the stone. Look at a teaspoon for the proper shape.

While a simple piece of tape or a wooden sleeve works for a depth stop (see the top photo on p. 152), Stanley manufactured two positive versions that clamp to the bit: the #47, which clamps to the drill shank, and the #49, which clamps to the spiral web.

Using Braces and Hand Drills

Don't think of braces and hand drills merely as tools to bore holes. While this is what they do best, a brace is also a powerful tool for setting large screws or removing them, countersinking or reaming holes, cutting round tenons with a special tenon cutter, and even pointing their ends. As for drilling a few holes, a brace or hand drill is a pleasing alternative to an electric drill. It is not much slower and offers a lot more control. Learning to drill straight, on the other hand, takes practice.

Dowels make a quick and fairly strong joint, but the mating holes must be accurately drilled. This Stanley #59 doweling jig clamps square to an edge and holds various sizes of hardened bushings and drill bits. A shopmade alternative is to drill a length of hardwood (center) and use it as a guide.

Securing a bit in a brace might seem like a basic place to start, but it is not quite as simple as it appears. For the longest time I shoved bits into the chuck and just tightened down the outer shell, only to have the bit loosen after a few turns of

Driven with a brace or by hand, dowel pointers cut like a pencil sharpener (which also works) to bevel the ends of dowels or any round part, such as a turned leg.

The simplest and quickest way to make dowels is to rough blanks through a dowel plate, a thick piece of steel with various sizes of holes drilled through it. Point the blank first with a dowel pointer or pencil sharpener (at center).

the brace. The trick is to pull the bit up so that the squared tang engages in the grooves of the jaws, and then tighten down the shell. In a pinch, a brace chuck will hold bits with smooth shanks, although a three-jawed chuck common in hand drills is more positive.

Drill bits vary in size so much (most twist bits are actually $\frac{1}{64}$ in. oversized) that drilling a test hole is always a good idea for the most accurate work. With an expansion bit it is vital. A properly sharpened bit should take only modest pressure to cut in long grain but far more into end grain. If more force is required, you can lean over the head of a brace, pressuring it with a chest or thigh, or whatever works in some of the awkward positions you may find yourself when drilling holes in difficult places.

Start slowly, letting the spurs score the hole for a clean start. If you can, clamp your work to a bench or use a vise so you can concentrate on drilling. Back up your workpiece with a scrap, if possible, not only for a cleaner exit hole, but also for a place for the lead screw to bite into to finish the cut. Put a piece of paper between the two and when you see bits of paper in with the chips, you'll know you're through. Or you could drill until the point just pokes through and finish by drilling from the other side.

Drilling straight with a brace or hand drill is challenging, but it's no more difficult than with an electric drill. I find it easiest to drill perpendicular when working vertically. Try to set your work up and stand so that you can see in both planes, and set up a square or bevel gauge on the work to sight against. Stanley made a little level that clamps onto the shank of a drill that helps, or you can make your own (see the top right photo on p. 154). For accuracy when drilling deep holes, drill from both sides toward the middle, if you can.

Sometimes I need to drill an accurate hole at an angle—a pocket hole for a screw, for instance—or a perpendicular hole for a knob and lockset on a door already hung. A hole drilled in a scrap at the right angle (best when done with a drill press) becomes an accurate jig when clamped to the work to guide the bit. Doweling jigs work on the same principle, only with hardened bushings for guides (see the bottom photo on p. 155). Drilling a series of holes in a piece of hardwood works as a doweling jig for one-time operations such as drilling a row of dowel holes in mating parts.

Dowel pointers are designed for easing the ends of dowels (on table-leaf pins, for instance) or round tenons. The pencil-sharpener action of a dowel pointer works best with a few slow and careful cranks using a brace (see the photo at left on the facing page). I find that countersinks work best this way, too, especially when countersinking holes already drilled. An electric drill simply cuts too fast and often with lots of chatter.

Countersinks come in a variety of patterns, from roseheads with multiple cutting flutes, to clean-cutting metalworking countersinks with a single cutting edge formed ingeniously by drilling an oblique hole through the head. This latter design also works well for counterboring holes for plugs. Reamers are similar tools turned by hand or by brace, still used by chairmakers for tapering or enlarging holes to an exact diameter.

Chairmakers use round, tapered tenons and mortises for the leg-to-seat joint for a snug fit that tightens under pressure (but can be disassembled for repair). A reamer pares the mortise to a consistent taper and also can fine-tune the leg angle.

Most countersinks make dust rather than shavings and cut less than perfect holes. This unusual design, used mainly by machinists, cuts very cleanly and quickly no matter the speed or rotation and will counter-bore for a plug.

Use a hand drill or brace for reaming, boring, countersinking, or turning in a row of screws, and you will quickly appreciate its slow speed and the control you will have over the tool. Of course, electric drills and drill presses have their own advantages, earning them a place in any shop. Hand boring takes practice to master and can be slow, but then there are plenty of times when working a little slower suits me just fine.

10

SAWS

Before the advent of water-powered and electric saws, cutting wood to size was sweaty, hard work. Imagine the labor involved sawing logs into boards with a heavy 7-ft.-long pitsaw, one man on top and the other below under a steady rain of sawdust. Cutting the boards to size required rip and crosscut handsaws, or a large frame saw to shape them into chair seats, headboards, and curved wheel felloes. Joinery called for fine-toothed, brass-backed saws, and a host of specialty saws were used by carpenters and other tradesmen.

Even with contemporary machines, there is still a need for handsaws. Make a chair, join a curved apron to a leg, or cut a complex joint and you'll quickly see the versatility of sawing by hand. There's no better choice than a handsaw for superior control when making the most complicated cuts.

Before routers, the recesses in stair stringers for treads and risers were cut by hand with a stair saw and chisel. A hole the same diameter as the tread nosing gives a place to saw into. The beech body of the saw (top) by E. C. Atkins stiffens the narrow blade and acts as a depth stop. The saw in the foreground is blacksmith-made from a piece of old scythe blade.

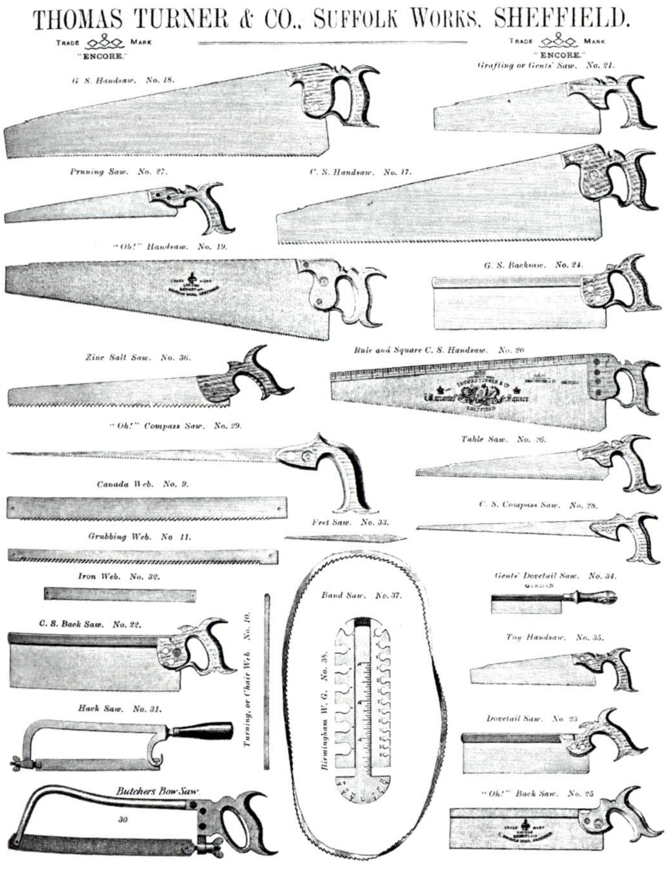

While the physics of saws has changed little in 4,500 years, the variety of sizes, shapes, and functions has grown enormously—from the tiniest fretsaws to large ripsaws and specialized salt saws with noncorroding zinc blades.

Bygone Saws

Unlike many other hand tools, saws haven't changed much in 4,500 years. There aren't many Bronze Age saws around to compare with a modern handsaw, but enough to see the similarities. Both have thin metal blades, the teeth are only slightly different (even allowing for millennia of deterioration), and the bronze blade is curved like a pruning saw and narrower than the straight, wide blade of a steel handsaw.

The bronze saw even has some of the subtleties of later saws, such as finer teeth filed into the toe of the saw to help start a cut. Likewise, to overcome the weakness of the thin blades, ancient saws cut on the pull stroke, like Japanese saws. Early saws probably didn't cut all that rapidly, but all of the physics were there.

Bronze is a sufficiently malleable material to form into wide, thin sawblades, but this wasn't the case with iron, a superior material, until the metallurgy of steelmaking was mastered. The difficulty was forging a blade strong and stiff enough to cut on the push stroke without buckling. Pushing lets you get your body behind the stroke, and it's a big advantage for holding the work simply and firmly—against a sawhorse, for instance. (Remember, this was before fancy benches and vises, when lashing a board to a tree was one holding strategy.)

One solution to overcome the buckling problem was to forge a narrow blade and tension it in a wooden frame. Eventually, master smiths in places like Sheffield, England, developed the means to make sheet steel for flexible and strong handsaws in many shapes and styles. There have been only minor changes since, such as refining the shape of the teeth for more efficient and rapid cutting.

Saws cut wood in one of two ways: along the grain (ripping) or across the grain (crosscutting). Chisel-like rip teeth (bottom) pare curly shavings, whereas the beveled knives of crosscut teeth (top) score and cut the ends of the fibers into a fine dust.

HOW SAWS CUT

For all their numerous variations—from coarse-toothed pitsaws to tiny coping saws—handsaws cut wood in only two ways: either along the grain (ripping) or across the grain (crosscutting). How they cut depends primarily on the shape of the teeth, and to a lesser extent on the fineness of the teeth. A ripsaw will cut across the grain, but not very efficiently, just as a crosscut saw will rip. You can file a saw to cut both ways modestly well (as I explain later). This is useful for joinery, for instance, where you might make a rip cut one minute and a crosscut the next.

To see the differences between the teeth of a ripsaw and crosscut saw, you have to look closely. Because cutting with the grain is no different than planing or chiseling along the fibers, ripsaws have the same chisel-shaped teeth, square

RIP TEETH VS. CROSSCUT TEETH

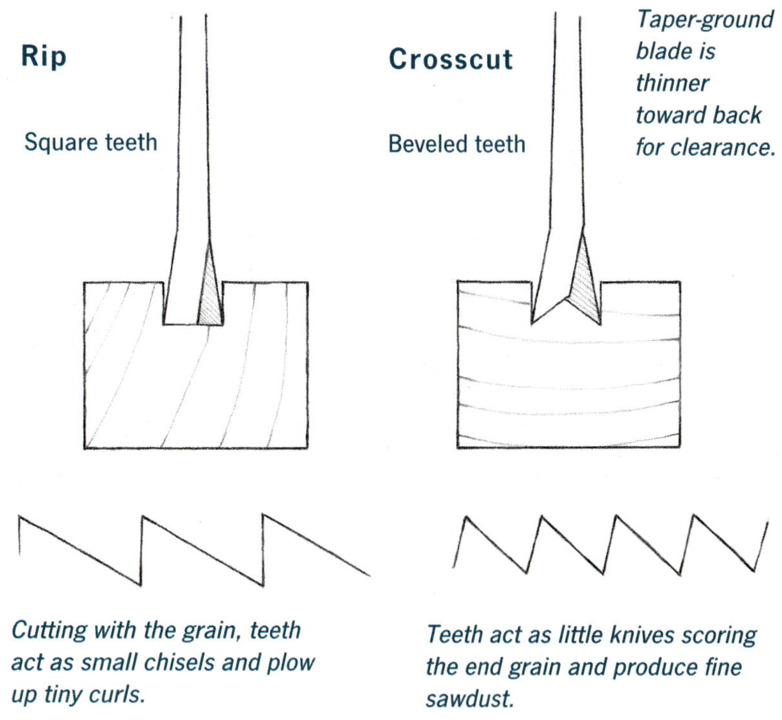

Tooth set and a taper-ground blade prevent the blade from pinching in the cut.

The coarseness or fineness of a saw is measured in the number of tooth points per inch, always one more than the number of complete teeth per inch. The fewer the teeth, the quicker and rougher the cut.

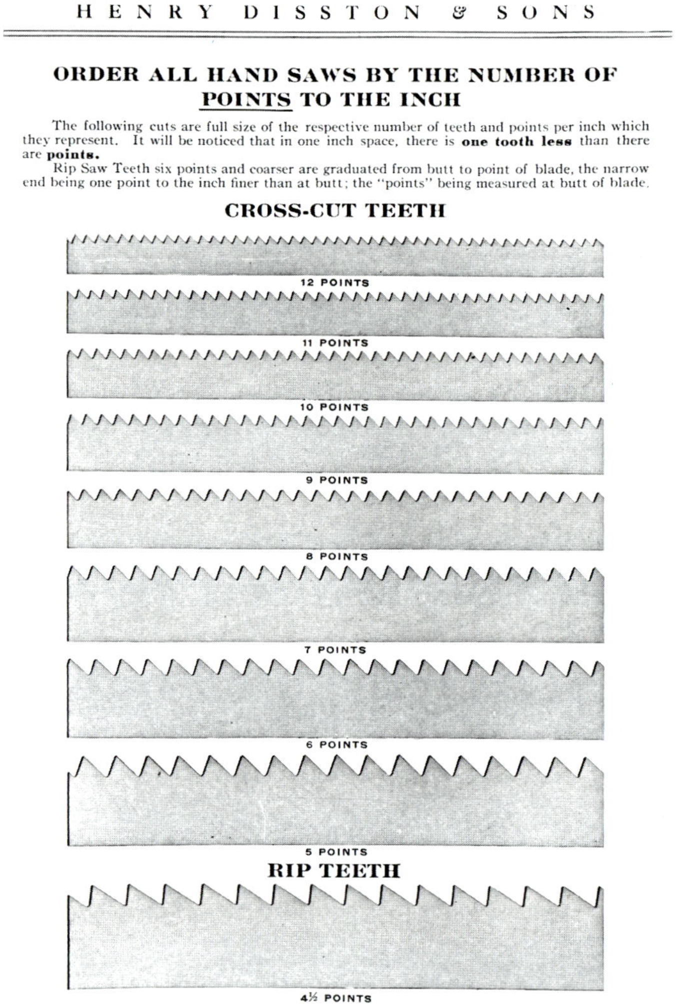

HENRY DISSTON & SONS

ORDER ALL HAND SAWS BY THE NUMBER OF POINTS TO THE INCH

The following cuts are full size of the respective number of teeth and points per inch which they represent. It will be noticed that in one inch space, there is **one tooth less** than there are **points.**

Rip Saw Teeth six points and coarser are graduated from butt to point of blade, the narrow end being one point to the inch finer than at butt; the "points" being measured at butt of blade.

CROSS-CUT TEETH

RIP TEETH

Setting, or bending the tips of the teeth alternately outward and slightly wider than the thickness of the sawblade, creates the necessary clearance to prevent the blade from binding.

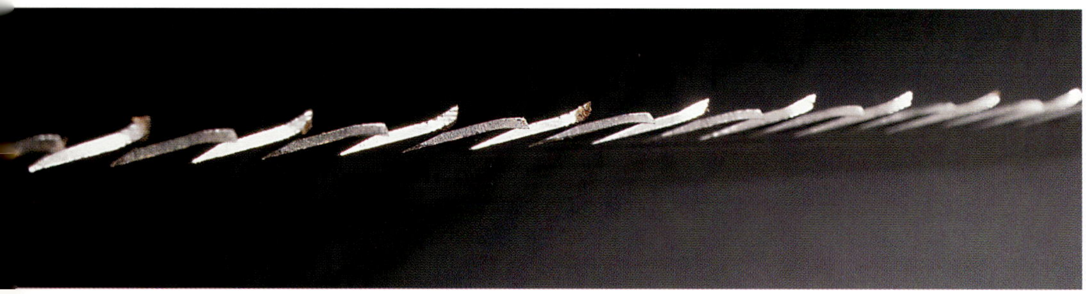

with the direction of the cut. They plow up little curls—miniature shavings—quite different from the fine sawdust from a crosscut saw. Rip teeth cutting across the grain cut roughly, tearing up the fibers much like a rabbet plane without a nicker. Crosscut teeth are filed into little knives that score the fibers on each side of the cut. The bits of weak grain between them break away and are swept out by the teeth. The "gullet" or valley between each tooth holds the sawdust. In a fast-cutting pulp saw, the gullets are large and special raker teeth clean the sawdust out of the saw cut, or kerf, as it's called.

In addition to the shape of the teeth (and there are many variations of the basic shapes), saws are further distinguished by the number of teeth—more specifically, the number of tooth points per inch (which is one point more than the actual number of complete teeth found in one inch of blade). This number can range from as few as 2 points in a ripsaw to as many as 25 points in fine dovetail and coping saws. (The number of points is often stamped on a handsaw blade below the handle.) Large coarse teeth cut quickly, especially in softwoods, whereas in hardwoods more teeth per inch are desirable for a smoother cut.

If the teeth were merely filed onto the bottom edge of the sawblade, the saw would bind in the cut after a few strokes. My father, who understood little of the subtleties of saws, used to liberally swab a saw with oil before using it, in order to prevent binding. So did pit sawyers. It's a messy solution to a simple problem: The teeth don't have enough "set," or slight outward bend, which allows them to cut a kerf slightly wider than the thickness of the blade. You need a lot more set sawing green wood than dry hardwood; in fact, fine dovetail saws work best with almost no set at all.

Some saw manufacturers added a further refinement to their best handsaws that also prevents binding: They taper-ground the blade thinner toward the back and the tip. In

Sheffield, grinders pressed sawblades (backed by a flat board) against huge water-powered stones all day, flattening and taper-grinding them. Not only do such handsaws work sweetly with a minimum of set, but in musical hands such saws can also be "played" to sound like a violin.

Whether for playing or cutting wood, no single saw, or even two or three, will do it all. You could get by with one set of chisels or a single brace, but you will need more than a couple of saws because there are just too many different ways to saw wood—crosscutting or ripping boards to length and width, cutting curved parts, or cutting joinery, inlays or fretwork, to name just a few. There are special saws for every woodworking task, varying in size, shape, and tooth pattern, as well as quite different Japanese saws that have become increasingly popular. Depending on what kind of work you do, you might need specialized saws such as veneer and flush-cutting saws. Machines can do a lot, but so far they haven't replaced all of these saws.

Types of Saws

There are easily dozens of types of saws, and dozens of variations within each type. Some variation is purely the result of different saw designs for different cutting tasks; for example, huge pitsaws and crosscut saws—yesteryear's sawmills—compared to tiny backsaws for cutting fine joinery. Other differences can only be explained as regional tastes or the preferred saw styles of certain trades. American and British craftsmen loved backsaws; Continental craftsman preferred bowsaws. Between the two groups dozens of variations of both types of saws evolved, however subtle in their differences, to suit the work exactly.

PITSAWS AND CROSSCUT SAWS

Sawmills have replaced the pitsaws that once cut every board and plank by human power alone and with tremendous effort. Today, from our machine-dominated perspective, it's

Only slightly exaggerated, the two Japanese sawyers in this print by Hokusai Katsushuka (1760-1849) rip boards from a balk resting on a trestle with huge, coarse-toothed *maebiki-nokogiri.* Two men pitsaw, while another man sits at a stump filing and setting their saws.

Loggers once felled and cut trees to length with one- and two-man crosscut saws, yesteryear's chainsaws. Given colorful names such as Lightening, Lumberman, and Great American, each saw had a different tooth design to cut more quickly or smoothly.

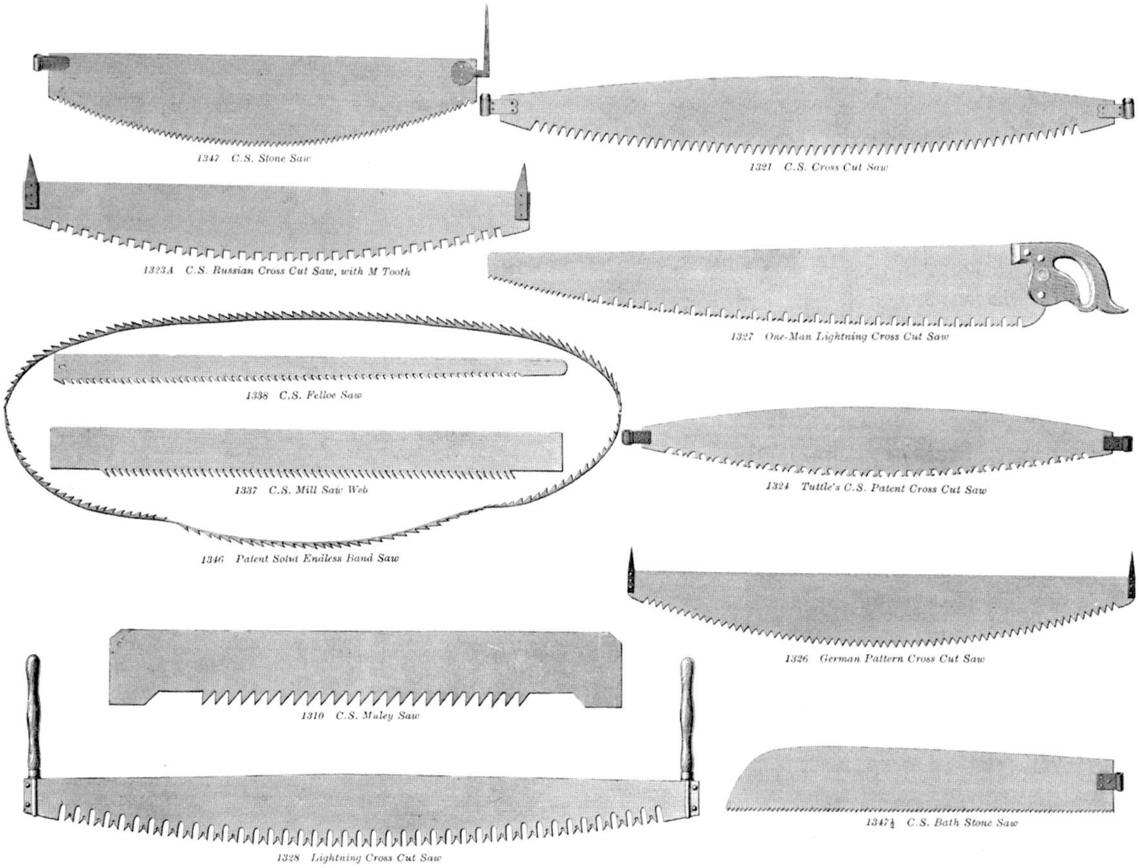

hard to appreciate the importance of the pitsaw and its partner, the crosscut saw, for felling trees and bucking them to length. Yet these are some of the most important tools of our woodworking heritage, tools that in one sense made all other woodworking possible.

Not all lumber was sawn over a pit, but it certainly was a common and not overly complicated way to work logs into usable lumber. Besides boards and planks, shipwrights pitsawed large curved futtocks (ribs), knees, and stems, and wheelwrights felloes and wagon parts from crooked logs. All that was needed was a 6-ft.-deep pit 12 ft. to 14 ft. long, with a couple of logs across the top for support. Roll a log on, snap a few chalklines down its length to mark the cut, and saw away.

Early pitsaws were of the framed type with a narrow blade, 4 ft. to 5 ft. long—the only shape possible with the limited knowledge of iron metallurgy. Later versions resembled long handsaws, up to 10 ft. in length, with coarse teeth, a tiller handle on one end, and a removable box handle (so it could be slid into or out of the log) for the pit man to grab. (A pitsaw's other name, "whipsaw," gives a sense of the narrowness and flexibility of the blade.)

Nathaniel Dominy of the well-known Dominy family of craftsmen was probably typical of 18th-century furniture makers in that he owned a pitsaw with others and shared its use. Eventually, water power replaced manpower and single pitsaws were ganged together to slice a log into many boards at once.

Axes and crosscut saws were the tools of the logger for felling trees and sawing them to length. Used by one or two men, crosscut saws (sometimes as long as 16 ft.) improved upon the shape and design of pitsaw teeth to work faster, to clear the kerf of sawdust more easily, or just to cut more sweetly. These tools live on at lumberjack contests, where savvy contestants know to start sawing on the shaded side of a log or risk breaking off the sharp points of their saw teeth on the sun-hardened side. Both pitsaws and crosscut saws also survive in the poorest and most remote areas of the world, where there is a need for lumber and no sawmills to supply it. Chainsaws are rapidly replacing these venerable old tools.

Essentially a hand-powered bandsaw, a turning saw was the choice of chairmakers and wheelwrights for cutting curved seats and wheel felloes. Just like a deep throat on a bandsaw, the large ash frame allows plenty of maneuverability, while the ram's-head nuts maintain blade tension.

FRAME SAWS

Once the lumber was sawn from the log, smaller versions of the framed pitsaw were used to cut it to shape or to resaw it into thinner stock (for drawer bottoms, for instance). The frame design is ancient, originating with the Romans. The blades are narrow and thin, the frames rigid enough to tension the blade to keep it running true and make it less apt to buckle.

A thin blade was an advantage for sawing veneers, where less of the valuable wood was wasted in sawdust. For curved parts commonly used by chairmakers, wheelwrights and a whole host of other trades, a narrow blade was used for cutting along a tight radius. From large chairmakers' saws to smaller bowsaws, these were the bandsaws of a hand-powered shop.

Once the technology needed for producing high-quality steel plate for handsaws was mastered, British and American craftsmen adopted the handsaw, and its many variations, over frame saws. Continental craftsman continued to use framed saws of some kind, and still do. I understand why. It's partly a matter of custom and the conservative nature of woodworkers clinging to the tools they learn with and know, and partly the efficiency of the tools themselves. There is not much cutting resistance with a thin blade. It will cut straight lines as easily as it will cut curves (something handsaws don't do as well). I've seen dovetails—waste and all—cut in one continuous motion with a bowsaw. I still use a bowsaw for curved work too large or awkward to carry to a bandsaw.

For sawing smaller logs into veneer or thin boards (for drawer bottoms), or for extra thick parts such as bed posts, craftsmen used a frame saw. The thin blade held in tension in a stiff frame cuts a thin kerf, wasting less wood and cutting more easily than a thicker blade.

A framed bowsaw can cut dovetails as easily as it can follow a curve. Steady the blade against a fingernail to start, shift to sawing with both hands on the front handle, and use smooth, full-length strokes.

ASK A HUNDRED woodworkers if they know what a table saw is, and you can bet that all will describe the stationary machine found in workshops everywhere. But through the last half of the 19th century, a table saw was a handsaw—an enlarged version of a compass or keyhole saw—with an open handle and a long, narrow blade. The "hand-table saw" is no longer in use, and there remains some confusion about what it was actually used for. Some believe that it was for cutting round table tops, while others think that it was used in fitting the mating surfaces (or "tables") of a scarf joint.

Think saws and classic rip and crosscut handsaws likely come to mind. Among the more unusual (left to right) are a saw with a shapely handle carved in the profile of a panther, a Disston combination saw complete with level, plumb, square, and awl, and a Disston practical double-sided saw—two saws in one.

You could build a bowsaw quite easily, in a style and size that suits your needs, and get a great amount of enjoyment doing it. A simple design has loose mortise-and-tenon joints to join the stretcher with the sides. The blade is attached to turned handles that rotate for cutting at different angles and is tensioned with a simple toggle and twisted cord. You can buy narrow blades or make your own by refiling a piece of a bandsaw blade.

HANDSAWS

In the English tradition, handsaws rather than bowsaws are the tools that most quickly spring to mind when imagining a saw. With flat blades tapered heel to toe and shapely handles so comfortable you can almost forget you are grasping them, classic handsaws are elegance

Among the rarest of the rare and prized by every saw collector is a panther saw by Woodrough and McParlin Saw Company of Cincinnati, Ohio (c. 1880). Flowing from the shapely lines of the handle and incised decoration is the head of a growling panther.

itself. Before power saws, handsaws were the most used saws in any shop. They were used for ripping boards to width, crosscutting them to length, and, with an unusual variation called a table saw, for cutting around modest curves as well.

"Handsaw" is quite a general term for saws that vary from 1 ft. to 2½ ft. in length, some with coarse teeth and others with fine teeth. What distinguishes them from other saws is their wide, thin blades unsupported by any frame or thickened back, and a single handle with a closed or open grip.

As ancient as saws are, the design is relatively modern, able to be made only after it was possible to manufacture large and flexible sheets of steel. The earliest (and for a long time the best) handsaws came from makers such as Spear and Jackson in Sheffield, England, with its long tradition of making high-quality edge tools and superior cast and spring steels. Henry Disston learned the

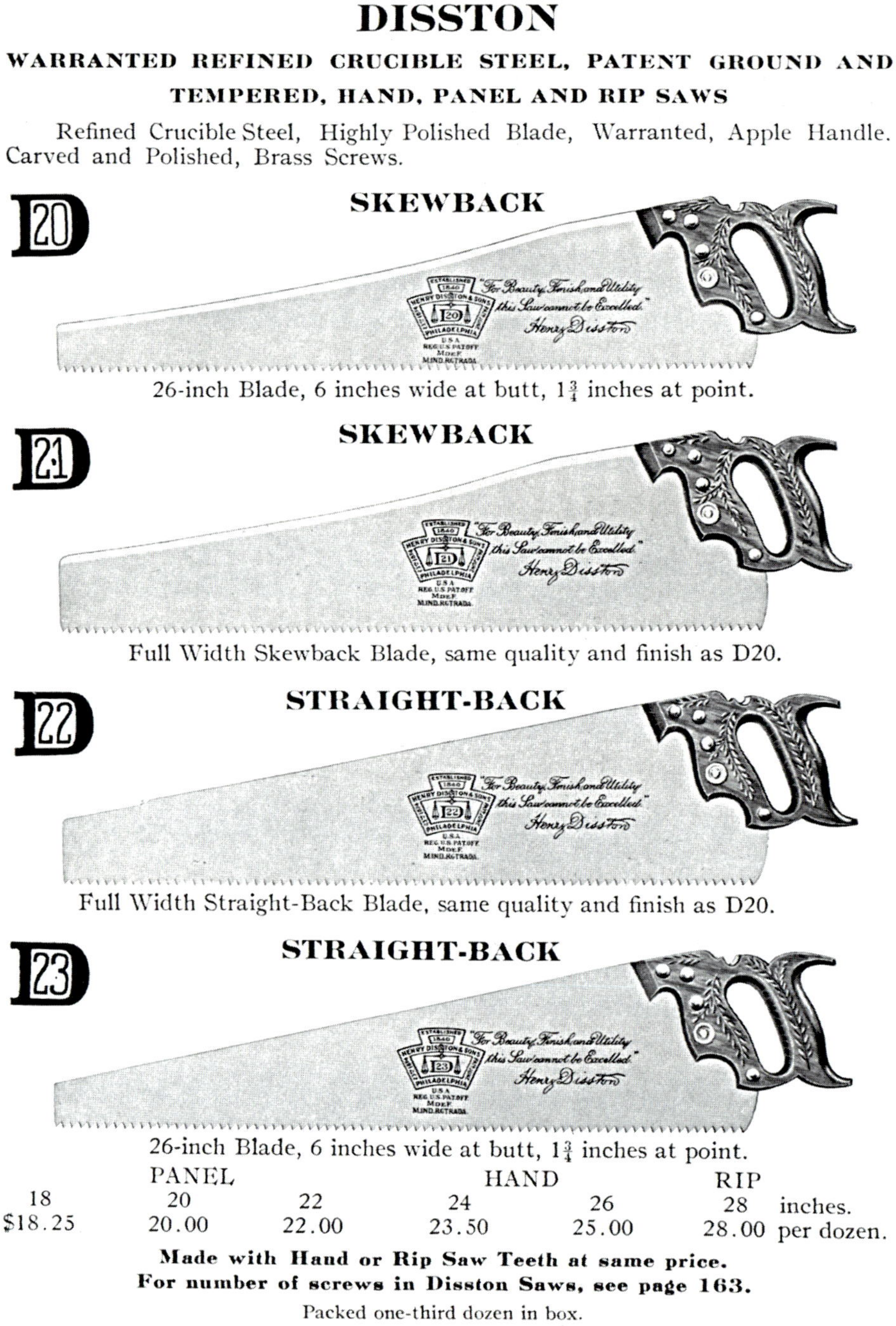
DISSTON

WARRANTED REFINED CRUCIBLE STEEL, PATENT GROUND AND TEMPERED, HAND, PANEL AND RIP SAWS

Refined Crucible Steel, Highly Polished Blade, Warranted, Apple Handle. Carved and Polished, Brass Screws.

D20 **SKEWBACK**

26-inch Blade, 6 inches wide at butt, 1¾ inches at point.

D21 **SKEWBACK**

Full Width Skewback Blade, same quality and finish as D20.

D22 **STRAIGHT-BACK**

Full Width Straight-Back Blade, same quality and finish as D20.

D23 **STRAIGHT-BACK**

26-inch Blade, 6 inches wide at butt, 1¾ inches at point.

	PANEL		HAND		RIP	
18	20	22	24	26	28	inches.
$18.25	20.00	22.00	23.50	25.00	28.00	per dozen.

Made with Hand or Rip Saw Teeth at same price.
For number of screws in Disston Saws, see page 163.

Packed one-third dozen in box.

America's largest saw manufacturer, Henry Disston & Sons, improved on English designs to produce a skewed-back handsaw for a lighter, more flexible, and graceful saw. It was just one of hundreds of different saws offered in their catalog of 1914, and, in this age of handsaws, sold by the dozen.

HANDSAWS come in many different lengths—24 in., 26 in., and 28 in., to name a few. Why so many sizes? One obvious answer is that small tasks require smaller saws, but there is more to it than that. Each of us has an optimum saw length related to the distance of our natural sawing stroke. Use too short a saw, and it will jump out of the cut. Use one too long, and you won't use all of the blade, wearing the teeth unevenly as a result. Pretend you are sawing and measure a comfortable stroke to determine the best saw length for you.

trade at Spear and Jackson, emigrated to America with his knowledge, and in 1840 started his Keystone Saw, Tool, Steel, and File Works. Disston grew to be the largest maker of saws in the world, producing almost 200 different types of handsaws in a typical year. More than likely, any used saw you find will be a Disston.

Other than the shape of the teeth, there is no difference between a rip and crosscut handsaw. Ripsaws generally have fewer points per inch, since they are cutting with the grain and can cut quite aggressively without tearing out the fibers. I use a 4-point ripsaw infrequently, but it's the best saw for timber framing or for ripping a valuable board that is too awkward to cut with a bandsaw. It cuts a narrow kerf, and the wide blade guides the cut. On the other hand, I have a number of crosscut saws—with 6, 8, and 10 points—and I use them often for cutting boards roughly to size, or for cutting long or heavy parts to length at my bench. Numerous machines can do the same thing, but it is often easier to reach for a saw, mark out the cut, and quietly start in.

WHAT'S THE NIB FOR?

WHAT'S THE PURPOSE of the little nib on the end of fine handsaws? Is it there for decoration, as some suggest, or is it a place to secure a cord to tie on a saw guard? Is it a special tooth for starting a cut? If it's important to the function of the saw, why do some saws have it and others do not?

While a nib is useful for holding one end of a saw guard (a slotted cover, usually wood, that protects the teeth), its origins go back to the earliest handsaws. Late-17th-century Dutch handsaws had quite fanciful decorative curls where we find a nib today. Less elaborate nibs must have been on English saws at about the same time, because Moxon, one of the earliest writers about various trades and tools, illustrates one in 1683. Disston and others carried on the tradition.

The little nib on the end of fine handsaws has sparked much curiosity about its function and origins. It's a vestigial decoration dating back to the 17th century.

Outwardly, modern saws don't look much different from classic Disstons. The teeth might have a more aggressive shape influenced by Japanese saws, they might be impulse-hardened (electrically made extremely hard but unfileable) to hold up to manmade materials, and the handle may be plastic rather than wood.

Some cut easily, but using them is nothing like the experience of an older saw. For one thing, the balance feels different. Disston's skew-back saws—some of the most graceful—feel light even though the blade is long. Taper-grinding further lightens the blade, giving it flexibility and a sweet cutting action with minimum set. The handles are beautifully polished apple, beech, or figured maple that conform to the hand with a place for every finger. Every detail of an older saw speaks of a tool designed to be used day in, day out.

BACKSAWS

Backsaws, a variation of handsaws, will never become obsolete in any shop doing challenging high-quality work—or in one where you enjoy working quietly by hand. For cutting joinery or any fine sawing task, a backsaw is versatile and accurate. A backsaw has much finer teeth than a typical handsaw, along with a thinner blade stiffened with steel or, on the best saws, a brass rib folded

For cutting joinery accurately, a backsaw combines the virtues of fine teeth and a thin blade, which is stiffened by a brass or steel rib folded over the top edge. A snug-fitting wooden sleeve protects the blade from getting bent and the delicate teeth from getting damaged.

Possibly the oldest dated tool in England, the dovetail saw at top is dated 1756, though it is no different from a good modern saw. Below it is an uncommon table saw with a long flexible blade, and a long carcase saw for sawing large joinery.

over the top edge. The rib prevents the saw from cutting very deeply, but it is a perfect design for cutting a narrow kerf right to a line.

At a minimum you will want to have at least two different sizes of backsaws: a 12-point tenon saw, 12 in. to 16 in. long with a handsaw-type handle either open or closed; and a smaller, finer dovetail saw (15 or more points per inch), with a straight-turned handle known as a "gent's" handle. Unless you are cutting thin wood, it's not an advantage to have finer teeth on your dovetail saw; they cut more slowly, giving you more chance to wander off your line.

For exacting work, I have a bead-saw with extremely fine teeth. This kind of saw can be used for slicing inlays, or for sawing around a shoulder of a dry-fit mortise and tenon to fit it exactly. A shop of a century ago would have had a number of other sizes of backsaws: a carcase saw, sash saw, and long miter saw used in a miter box. These saws vary only in length, blade width, and in the fineness of their teeth.

Cutting the cheek of a tenon is a rip cut; cutting the shoulder is a crosscut. Because these two joinery tasks are common, the backsaw you use will be more useful if you can file it to do both types of cutting. This certainly is a subtlety, considering how difficult it is to file the small teeth of a backsaw anyway, and it doesn't improve the quality of the cut, just the cutting speed. Nevertheless, I explain this along with filing and setting fine-toothed saws later in this chapter.

Among the author's collection of everyday joinery saws are fine-toothed dovetail saws with both closed and turned "gent's-style" handles, a half-backsaw with a blade flexible enough to be used for flush cutting, and unhandled bead saws with very fine teeth.

The extremely thin blade and unset teeth of a Japanese flush-cutting saw allow you to flex it flat to saw off screw plugs, proud tenons, or pins locking a joint, without marring the surface. The wooden-handled version in the background has teeth set only on the top side for the same reason.

FLUSH-CUTTING AND VENEER SAWS

First cousins to backsaws are flush-cutting saws—useful for cutting off proud through-tenons, screw-hole plugs, or pins locking a joint—and veneer saws. In most variations of these saws, a thin flexible blade has a partial back to stiffen it, and the teeth are set on one side only (sometimes, as with Japanese saws, they have no set at all). This allows a flush-cutting saw to cut flat against a finished surface (unset side down) without scoring it.

When trimming veneer to size, a veneer saw is usually guided against a straightedge. The unset teeth against the straightedge will not dull, or wear the straightedge. Uneven set has another advantage: The saw cuts toward the set side and away from the straightedge, or finished surface, in the case of the flush-cutting saw. Because the blades are thin and flexible, they most often cut on the pull stroke.

JAPANESE SAWS

At one time all saws cut on the pull stroke, for the simple reason that the blades were not strong enough to resist buckling and bending if they were pushed. As soon as it was possible to make flexible steel for sawblades, Western saws got turned

It's safer to cut veneer with a saw guided against a straightedge than with a knife that can follow the grain. A veneer saw has fine teeth set on only one side to avoid dulling them against a steel straightedge.

Japanese saws, designed to be pulled, are very different from their Western counterparts. A pulled blade is in tension, which means it can be thinner, less flexible, and the steel can be tempered harder. Add in complex tooth bevels, and you have saws that work easily and stay sharp a long time.

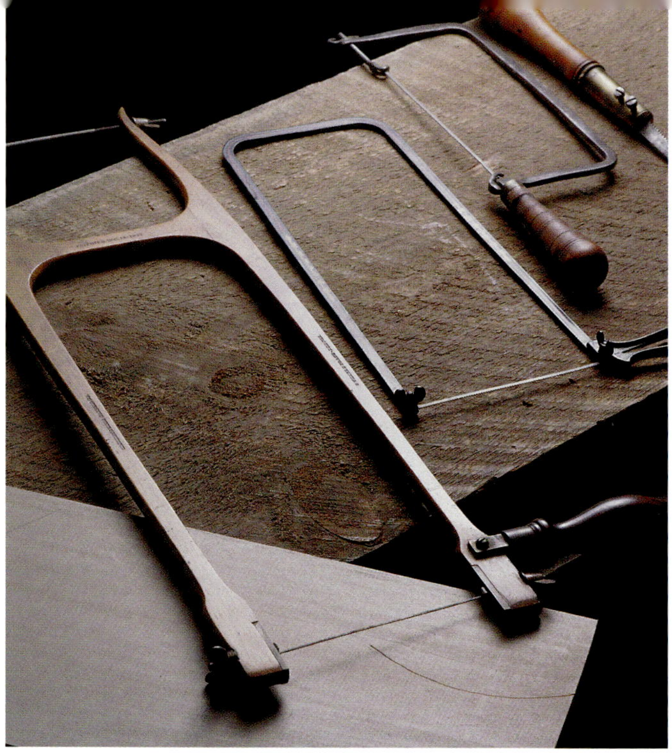

Call them fretsaws, coping saws, or jigsaws (front to back), they are all small frame saws with fine and narrow blades for cutting along tight curves, coping a joint, or cutting inlay and marquetry. A keyhole or pad saw (rear), a close cousin, has a wider, stiffer blade.

around so that almost all of them cut on the push stroke. The Japanese, on the other hand, never gave up pulling their saws. One explanation is that Japanese craftsmen work from a sitting position, in which case pulling is more powerful. On the other hand, sawing from a standing position allows the whole upper body to power the push stroke.

Whether used sitting or standing, the advantages of Japanese saws are compelling enough that many craftsmen who use no other Japanese tools are likely to have a *dozuki* or *ryoba*, two common types of Japanese saws, for cutting dovetails and joinery.

A blade that cuts on the pull stroke can also be very thin, since it will be in tension and not subjected to the buckling forces of pushing. A thin blade cuts with less effort than a thicker blade, removing less wood to cut as deeply. For both reasons Japanese sawblades can be tempered harder than Western saws. Hard blades mean hard teeth, which stay sharp longer. Japanese saws also have more sophisticated tooth shapes, with different patterns depending on whether you are cutting hardwood or softwood. You can now buy Western saws with Japanese-style teeth, diamond-cut and sharpened.

For someone learning to saw dovetails or tenons, there are definite advantages to using Japanese saws. Right out of the box they are generally better tuned and thus more accurate than a new Western saw. Pulling feels quite natural—that is, unless you have pushed a saw all your life, as I have. Once you get the feel, controlling the blade right to a line is not difficult. Particularly nice is the fine kerf they cut. The only disadvantages are that you cannot sharpen your own saws (unless you are a *metate-shokunin,* a master saw sharpener), and the hard teeth are brittle and quite easy to snap off.

COPING, FRET-, AND COMPASS SAWS

When it comes to coping saws and fretsaws, both framed saws with very fine blades, the debate over pushing versus pulling still goes on. Sometimes I push; other times I pull. It all depends on how fine a blade I am using and whether I am cutting horizontally or vertically.

Coping saws and fretsaws are simply small bowsaws, sometimes called jigsaws. Their blades are fine-toothed, in the range of 14 to 30 points, and so narrow that it is easy to cut around curves—the most important function of these saws. Blades can be removed easily so you can shift from pushing to pulling, or start a piercing cut within a drilled hole.

As with other framed saws, the frame gives the blade stability by holding it in tension. The blade in a coping saw can swivel 360° so that you can saw in any direction and not have the frame in the way. A fretsaw has a fixed blade, but often a much deeper throat.

Whether you push or pull, the side you are cutting toward may splinter out slightly. This can obscure your line. Coping two moldings or cutting out the waste from a set of dovetails—typical uses for a coping saw—I can see my lines clearly if I push, and it feels natural to me.

Really thin blades break or don't track well when they're pushed, so I pull them and try to saw vertically, handle down. I support the work flat on my bench, overhanging it just enough to work the saw. For delicate work, such as cutting out decorative fretwork or marquetry, I clamp a board with a V-cutout in my vise to support the work. Sawing on the pull stroke (within the V), I can see the line clearly.

Pad or keyhole saws were often shopmade from a piece of broken sawblade fitted to a handle. A Japanese keyhole saw (on the bench) that cuts on the pull stroke gives good control cutting delicate keyholes or working into tight places.

The fine, narrow blade of a coping saw allows you to change direction easily, when sawing a tenon and haunch in one continuous motion, for example. The blade pivots in the frame (note the levers front and back) for even more maneuverability.

Compass, pad, and keyhole saws are all names for similar long and narrow-bladed saws without any frames. They will also cut around curves, although not as well as a coping saw or fretsaw. They can cut anywhere with just a drilled hole to get started in. Because the blade is tapered, you can saw tighter curves and reach into very small openings (such as keyholes) by using just the tip. The handle of a pad saw is hollow, so just as much blade as you need can be exposed. The teeth on all of these saws are quite coarse, and the blades are too thick (so they don't buckle) to cut a smooth hole. But when you need one, there's no other choice.

Usually the first step in tuning an old saw is cleaning off surface rust with emery cloth and fine steel wool to restore the blade close to its original shine. An occasional wipe of paste wax (on the blade and the handle, too) will keep your saws working sweetly and prevent rusting.

The bolts that secure the handle to the blade screw into one another. To eliminate any handle looseness, tighten each bolt with a thin-bladed screwdriver. (They sometimes bottom out before they are snug, so file the bolt shorter if necessary.) A small carriage bolt makes a good substitute for any missing handle bolts.

Saw Maintenance

Other than sharpening—no small feat to master—most saws need little maintenance or tuning. Any saw works best with an occasional waxing, the handle bolts must be kept snug to keep the handle secure, and the inevitable kinks should be straightened out. When it comes time for a sharpening, the details of which are explained on pp. 175-181, once you learn the basics you can sharpen nearly any saw you own.

TUNING

The brightly polished steel blade of any saw will rust, especially in a damp shop or in one that experiences large swings in temperature (because the steel will sweat). Most secondhand saws have some rust. I would avoid buying one that's pitted, although you can restore it to usable condition with fine abrasive paper and steel wool. Keep your saws rust-free and working sweetly by giving them an occasional wipe with paste wax. Wax or oil the handle and other wooden parts.

Saw handles can break or work loose. You can't control a saw with a loose handle. Making a new handle is fun and not very difficult—and it's a perfect place to use that exotic scrap you've been saving. Chapter 11 includes some patterns for beautiful and comfortable handles (see p. 200).

Special two-part bolts secure the handle to the saw (one part screws into the other for a flush finish on the handle); a high-quality handsaw has four or five bolts. Tighten the

A kinked blade will not saw straight. Sight down the blade to find any kinks, mark them with chalk or tape, and then bend them out against a hard edge such as your bench, using concentrated pressure with your thumbs and slightly less with your palms.

bolts with a screwdriver (older ones use a special slotted screwdriver). Unfortunately, missing bolts are not easy to replace without stealing some from another handle, and even then they are likely to be a different size. A small carriage bolt makes a serviceable (though not elegant) substitute.

Sometimes a saw binds, flexes too much, and kinks. It can happen because the saw is dull, there is too little set to handle the damp wood you're sawing, or because you are working too aggressively. Even stiff backsaws will kink. Sawblade steel is flexible enough to take some bending, but bad kinks can crack a blade (and, with Japanese saws, break off a few teeth).

However bad the kink, as long as the blade is not cracked, you probably can work it out (and will have to or your saw will not cut straight). First, find and mark the kink by sighting down the blade. Bend the saw over the edge of your bench to straighten a mild kink. You'll need to hammer out a severe one. In this case, lay the saw on your bench or anvil and flatten the kink with a ball peen hammer. Unfortunately, any kink weakens a saw just enough that it will likely kink again in the same place. The best you can do is keep it properly set and sharp.

SHARPENING

Sharpening a saw is tricky and time-consuming but no more difficult than tuning a plane or sharpening a chisel. I find that the hardest part isn't jointing, setting, and filing the saw but simply seeing the teeth, especially on fine saws. So start with a 5- or 6-point handsaw whose teeth are clearly visible, but don't use your best saw until you get the feel for sharpening.

If you protect your saws with blade guards when not in use, and keep them from running onto hardware, they will stay sharp a long time, and you won't need to file them very often. In the 20 years I have had the same dovetail saw, I have sharpened it just twice. Not everyone will want to sharpen their own saws, but if you do they will cut effortlessly and accurately.

A couple of caveats: You can't sharpen Japanese saws (at least most

SAW STEEL is spring steel, with a certain amount of elasticity. For the same reason that a frame saw holds its blade in tension, and Japanese saws are pulled (tensioned) as they cut, a traditional handsaw will work best if the cutting edge is in tension. Saw doctors (the specialists who make and tune saws) use hammers with slightly crowned faces to tension the blade. By spreading the steel in the center of the sawblade, putting it in compression, the edge is put into tension. Circular saws work in a similar way: As the blade heats up and expands, a slight amount of tension along the edge helps keep the cutting edge stiff.

Careless sharpening results in misshapen teeth of different heights, so that no matter how sharp they are, only some are cutting. It's time to joint the teeth level, file them to a consistent shape, and set and sharpen them.

The key to sharpening is good light—bright natural light against the far side of the blade is ideal—along with a sturdy saw vise, such as this shopmade one with wooden screws, cushioning leather washers, and holes for storing files.

of us can't, because the tooth geometry is too complicated). Nor is it worth your while to file a coping saw—just replace the blade. First, I'll describe a method that works for any saw up to about 12 points per inch, and then another method for fine-toothed saws that speeds up sharpening considerably and creates a combination tooth suitable for both ripping and crosscutting.

Sharpening a saw is similar to tuning a hand scraper (see pp. 129–132). Just as you can burnish down the edge of a scraper blade and roll it back up again without going through the whole process of jointing and honing, the same is true with a saw. File the teeth lightly and stay away from nails, and you can delay a complete overhaul. This involves jointing the teeth so all the points are the same height, reshaping them to the same size with the proper angles, setting them, and then filing them sharp.

To do any sharpening, you'll need a saw vise of some kind (you can make one from two boards clamped in a side vise), good light, a mill file for jointing, and a double, extra-slim, tapered saw file (one 6 in. to 7 in. long for handsaws and one 4 in. long for fine-toothed saws).

The key to the whole sharpening process is good light. You have to be able to see each tooth clearly and the glint from the sharpened bevels. For me, this means natural light, morning light if possible, against the far side of the saw. If you rely on electric lights, a clip-on light shining right where you are working helps greatly.

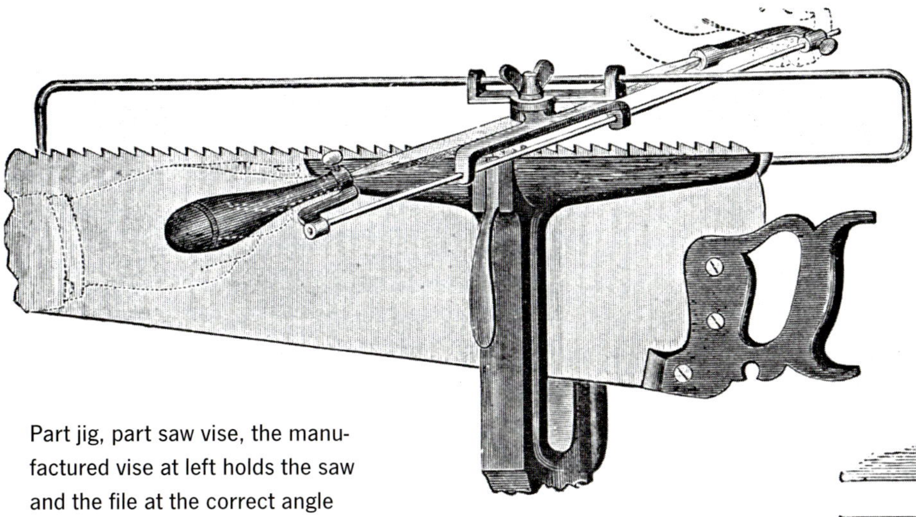

Part jig, part saw vise, the manufactured vise at left holds the saw and the file at the correct angle and tilt. The ball and socket of the vise at right allows you to rotate it to a comfortable angle.

The first step in sharpening is to joint the teeth to a consistent height, leaving the edge slightly crowned end to end. With a manufactured jointer or a simple shopmade one, file just enough to create a small flat at the top of each tooth.

Jointing the teeth

Assuming you have worked out any kinks and your blade is straight, the first step is to joint the teeth to an even height. I always make a light jointing pass, even if I am just filing the teeth. Even teeth cut smoothly.

The same wooden block with a groove for a mill file that you use for jointing a scraper works for a saw (see p. 130), or you can use a manufactured jointer. Good saws have a subtle crown to the cutting edge, just enough to be noticeable when you sight down the blade. Run the jointer over the teeth from end to end, crowning it by working the ends slightly more, until you just see a bright flat spot at the top of each tooth.

Shaping the teeth

The next step—shaping the teeth—is definitely the trickiest part of sharpening. Even careful filing cuts more off one tooth than another, until after a couple of filings the teeth are not identical. They don't really have to be, but your saw will work noticeably better the closer they are. The best guide is to follow the existing tooth shape. (Go by the ones near the handle; they are the least used and sharpened.) This is also the time to fine-tune the angle of the teeth for a more aggressive hook, if you want.

It's no accident that a sawtooth gullet is a 60° notch, the same angle as a triangular file. Running the file in the gullet you can cut both the back of one tooth and the front of another. Ripsaws and crosscut saws have different tooth shapes, which you will need to keep in mind during this step. Rip teeth slant backward about 3°, and crosscut teeth about 15° or more. The angles are approximate and a matter of preference, although the smaller the angle the more aggressive the tooth. To help maintain this angle, I make a simple guide from a softwood scrap with the appropriate angle marked on it, which I drive onto the tip of the file. If I keep the guide level, I know the front angle of the teeth will be the same.

The saw should be in a vise for this step, with the teeth just above the jaws. Grab the file in both hands, one hand on the handle and the other at the tip guiding the cut, and hold the file in a horizontal position. Feel the gullet with the file and stroke across. By pressuring the file forward, backward, or down, you can cut more off one tooth than another to shape each one. The flats jointed on the tops of the teeth also guide you. Try to leave an equal flat on the top of each tooth and the gullets an even depth.

Setting the teeth

The next step is setting the teeth. Traditionally this was done with a saw wrest, a steel tool with different-width slots slipped over the tooth and levered to bend it. Another method is to use a special hammer and anvil, bending one tooth at a time. A pliers-type set (available new) is the easiest to use and is very consistent.

How much set you bend into each tooth is a matter of experience and knowing what kind of work you will be doing with that saw. You need a lot of set to saw green wood, but in dry hardwood only the smallest amount is required. A good

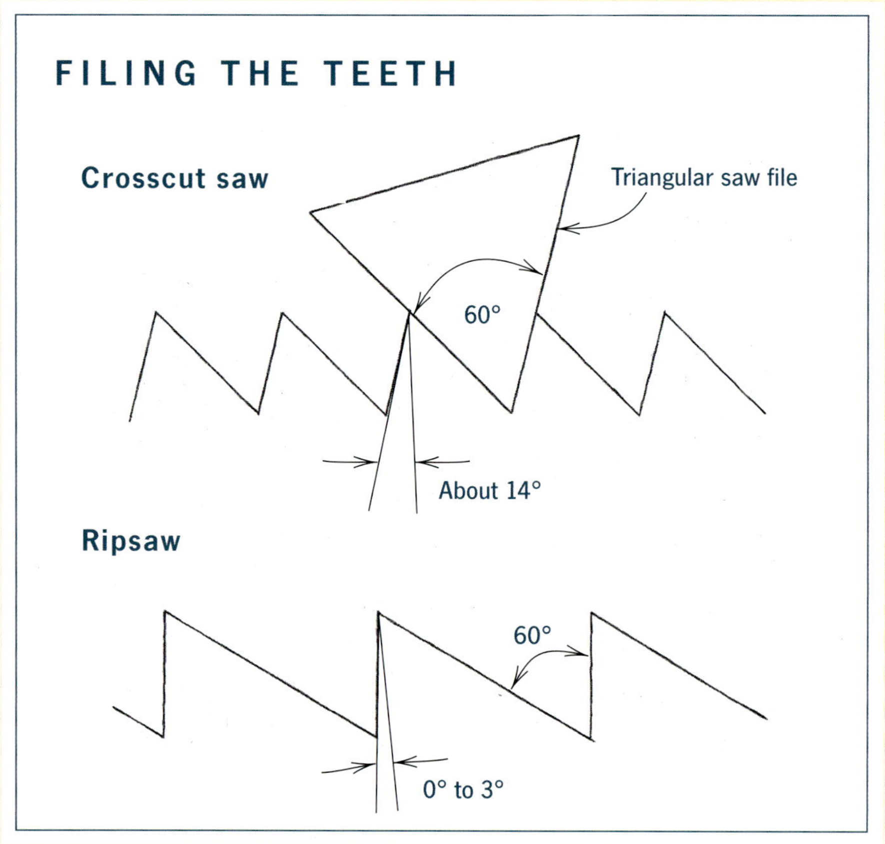

Traditional methods of setting saw teeth include slotted saw wrests (at right) that slip over each tooth to bend it over slightly, H. Aikens patent (1830) anvil set struck to bend each tooth (bottom), or a wooden saw-setting block with a plunger hit with a setter's hammer that works on the same principle (top).

Each squeeze of the handles of this pliers-type saw set presses the top third of a tooth between a small plunger and a beveled anvil, bending it a uniform amount. The anvil adjusts up or down for more or less set and for larger or smaller teeth.

rule of thumb is an overall set equal to 1½ times the thickness of the blade.

Bend just the top half or third of each tooth. I like to hold the saw in my lap while setting, so that I can easily move it to get the best light where I am working. Follow what is there and work from one end to the other setting half the teeth one way, then back to the other end to set the other half.

Filing the teeth

If your saw is only somewhat dull, you can skip all of these steps and go right to filing the teeth sharp. Sharpening is similar to shaping the teeth, with distinct differences between filing a ripsaw and a crosscut saw. The front edge of a ripsaw tooth is nearly vertical and square across. A crosscut tooth, on the other

File the back face of a tooth set away from you and the front face of one set toward you—straight across for a ripsaw and at an angle of 60° to 75° for a crosscut saw. Lock your wrists to keep the file face cutting a rip tooth vertical and a crosscut tooth slanted back 12° or more. File every other tooth, then turn the saw around to file the rest.

The final step in sharpening a saw is to lightly run a stone flat along the side of the blade to even out the set and hone off any burrs created by filing.

Hacksaws, which come in a range of tooth sizes, make accurate patterns for reshaping fine backsaw teeth. Clamp the two blades together; the harder hacksaw blade will keep your file cutting a consistent depth and shape.

Clamp a dovetail saw between two boards with beveled top edges both to hold the saw and to keep track of where you are filing (and how deep). Each file stroke should leave a consistent mark in the wood. Tap a wooden block onto the end of the file as a guide to maintain the same tooth angle.

hand, is slanted back 15° or more, and beveled at an angle of 60° to 75° rather than straight across. The more square to the saw you file, the smaller the tooth bevels and the longer they will last in hardwood. Use a greater angle for saws used mostly for cutting softwoods. You can also use the same wooden guide for sharpening as you did for shaping.

Starting at the handle end, file the back face of a tooth set away from you and the front face of one set toward you, and file *every other* gullet. Keep an eye on the jointed flat and the faces of each tooth, and pressure the file forward or backward to maintain tooth shape. At most, file only half of the flat away. File down one side of the saw, turn it around and file back the other way. The best technique is to file each side twice, just creeping up to sharp points. This helps keep the teeth evenly shaped.

Finish sharpening by running a stone flat against the teeth from end to end on both sides of the saw. This evens out any teeth with too much set. If you've done well, your saw will cut smoothly, with just a whisper.

SHARPENING DOVETAIL SAWS

The most challenging part of sharpening a dovetail saw is seeing the small teeth. I'll explain a couple of tricks that help. I usually don't worry about shaping the teeth, jointing them to a uniform height, or setting them (filing creates enough set), but focus on filing the points sharp. Most dovetail saws are so inexpensive that you can replace them after a few filings if things get way out of tune.

Hacksaw blades have fine teeth perfectly cut by machine in a range of point sizes. They make good guides for either refiling a dovetail saw with fewer points (10 to 12 points are an advantage for faster cutting) or for shaping existing teeth. Clamp the two sawblades together with the gullets lined up. Use the hacksaw as a pattern, which is hard on your file, but foolproof.

The key to filing fine teeth is having a pair of wooden jaws clamped right at the bottom of the gullets. Each file stroke leaves a groove on the wood that helps you keep track of position, cutting depth, and filing angle. I use a wooden guide on the end of the file for maintaining the angle of the front of the teeth, just as I described for handsaws. With these aids I can see where I am working without having to actually see each tooth.

Because I am aiming for more of a rip tooth, I try to keep the front face of the teeth slanted backward about 5° or so. I create a small bevel by filing at an angle of somewhere between 5° and 10° across the saw. Use a single stroke in each gullet to cut the teeth evenly. Otherwise, the filing process is no different: up the saw filing every other tooth and back down filing the remaining ones.

On very fine-toothed saws, which include dovetail saws, the burr formed on the tooth from filing creates enough set. A new saw probably has too much set to begin with. To find out, make a cut 1 in. deep in a scrap and then turn the saw on end and insert it in the kerf. Quite likely there will be a lot of slop.

To remove some of the set, lay the saw on a flat surface and with an oilstone (harder and less apt to be scored than a waterstone) lightly hone a stroke or two flat along both the sides of the blade and teeth. The idea is to hone away some of the set, which has the additional benefit of sharpening the teeth noticeably. Make another cut and try the saw in it. Hone again if necessary, until the saw cuts a kerf just barely snug against the blade. Now you're ready to go cut some dovetails.

A new dovetail saw is likely to have far more set than you need, which only lets the blade wobble around in a wide kerf. The three trial cuts show (from left) an untuned saw, partially tuned, and tuned so that the saw just fits the kerf.

Lay the saw flat on a board and hone off some of the set with a fine oilstone (a soft waterstone would get scored by the teeth). Take one or two light passes on each side and make a trial cut. Honing the teeth also sharpens them noticeably.

To get started in the cut, hold the blade to the line against a thumbnail and pull the saw back to create a small kerf. Use a few light half-strokes until the saw is engaged in the cut.

Using Saws

There is no one right way to saw, but it should feel natural, and your arm, shoulders, and body all should be relaxed. Think only about guiding the saw, not pressuring it into the cut, and let it cut at its own pace. A few careful strokes to get started straight is far easier than fighting the saw to your line for the next dozen strokes. To help get started, visualize how the stroke of your arm and the saw (as an extension of your arm) aligns with the cut. You can hear when a saw is cutting well; when everything is right, it sings. When it's not, it will chatter and squeal in a most unmusical way.

Hand-powered miter boxes such as this classic Stanley might be slower than motorized chopsaws, but they are ideal for working high up on staging when mitering large cornice moldings, or for quietly cutting accurate frame miters back in the shop.

No matter the saw or the task, clamp your work in a comfortable position, one that lets you see your lines. Holding strategies can be as simple as clamping a board in a side vise, using a pair of bench hooks to hold work flat on your bench, or working on a pair of sawhorses and clamping the work with your knee. The more comfortable you are, the more you can concentrate on sawing accurately. Crosscut saws are designed to cut best at an angle of 45° to the surface, and ripsaws at a higher 60° angle. But use them at any angle or hand position that works, including sawing backwards when you need to.

For careful work, such as sawing the cheeks of a tenon, clamp the work upright in a side vise and position yourself to see two of your lines at once. Saw vertically if possible. Over time, working with any tools, you develop an internal plumb, so take advantage of it when you can. Saw only the lines you can see, not the back side you cannot. Turn the work around to complete the cut.

I like to use the fingernail of my thumb as a rub block for getting the cut started right to a line (see the top photo on p. 181). Go easily or you risk having the saw jump out of the kerf. Draw the saw back, then ease it gently forward. Use full strokes once the kerf is started. To reflect some added light onto tricky sawing, clamp a piece of white paper in the vise sticking up above the jaws a few inches and creased away from you work. For precise work, leave a little of the line to plane or chisel away. For difficult or repetitive cuts such as miters or bevels, a shopmade or manufactured miter box is quicker to use and more accurate than sawing freehand.

Miter Boxes and Trimmers

At one time, large crown moldings and all manner of house trim were cut with long backsaws guided in wooden and iron miter boxes. Today, chopsaws rule. Tilting-arbor table saws and radial-arm saws also have pushed classic miter boxes aside, but not entirely, at least not yet.

A miter box is a simple solution to a timeless problem: cutting accurate bevels and miters. Without a chopsaw, there are plenty of times I need to cut a large molding either deeper than my table saw will handle, too awkward to cut safely, or while I am working on staging. For

Simple wooden miter jigs or miter boxes (rear) are easy to build and make sawing identical cuts or at specific angles quick and accurate.

For the greatest accuracy sawing small parts or precious inlays where the width of every saw kerf counts, make a wooden miter block to hold the work snugly, or a one-sided jig for cutting miters (foreground).

very small parts, such as fine strips to secure glass in a rabbet (which are hard to cut by machine without splintering) or for slicing inlays where every millimeter counts, I make special miter boxes for my finest backsaws.

A miter trimmer works on the same principle as a miter box, only with a knife and guillotine action. The knife shears as it cuts, slicing off the thinnest shaving much like a plane, cleanly and without splintering. For mitering small moldings, picture frames, or cockbeads around a drawer, or for miters at odd angles, no machine matches the accuracy and efficiency of a miter trimmer. Fortunately, there are plenty of tasks where the same could be said of handsaws. Any tool that has survived more than 4,000 years with few changes must have earned its keep along the way, and likely will continue to do so.

The shearing knife cut of a miter trimmer cuts a face as perfect as if it were planed by the Stanley #9 miter plane in the foreground. This hand-powered machine is the ideal tool for cutting small or delicate parts likely to splinter on a table saw.

NORRIS
LONDON
Carter
Carter
LONDON AND LEICESTER

11

Making and Restoring HAND TOOLS

Bill Carter saws and files away in a little shed at the end of his garden, cutting dovetails to join together another of his exquisite planes (photo facing page). Fifteen years ago he hadn't made a single tool—never even thought about it—and today he's one of the best toolmakers around.

You too can make beautiful tools; maybe not dovetailed planes to start, but simple tools like a marking knife or a square. If you don't feel up to making tools, consider repairing them. Flea markets are full of orphaned tools in need of repair. Shape a new iron and heat-treat it or make a shapely handle that fits your hand perfectly, and you're on your way to more complicated repairs. You may even decide to make a tool. For people who love tools, making your own is merely the next step.

Coachmakers often made many of the unusual tools their work required, such as these tools for routing grooves, planing a V-groove, or cutting a small cove around a curved coach frame.

Over the years, the author has made a number of specialty tools (for inlay work, for example) which he couldn't find new or secondhand. Among those shopmade tools are tiny chisels and wooden gauges with small scrapers for cutting the grooves for string inlays.

Toolmaking

All tools were once made by hand—often by the same hands that used them. Two hundred years ago, a carpenter or joiner wouldn't have given much thought to making a jack plane or frame saw. For the iron or sawblade—or for an ax or drawknife—he would have gone to a local blacksmith. A craftsman could also order special tools or those of the highest quality—a brass-ribbed backsaw, a fancy brace, or a set of carving chisels—from long-established toolmaking centers such as Sheffield, England.

Through the 19th century and into the 20th, toolmakers such as Stanley, Sargent, and Miller's Falls grew to dominate the world tool market by producing catalogs of tools to suit every need or desire. For the most part, craftsmen stopped making their tools and bought them instead. Why make a tool that you could buy inexpensively, made of cast iron and more durable than one you could produce yourself, made of wood?

When toolmakers mastered cast iron, it became the favored material for parts of tools or for the entire tool, such as Stanley's line of planes. Steel replaced wood in braces, saws, marking gauges, and rules. The strength and durability of these new materials allowed innovations in design: new patterns, and tools that were lighter, easier to use, and easier to adjust. But while a small shop could make wooden tools, as many continued to do, cast iron and steel required complex manufacturing methods.

English toolmakers didn't immediately embrace cast iron, although they had long accepted the advantages of metal for plane bodies. To avoid the complex technology of casting planes, they devised hand methods of dovetailing flat plate sides and soles together. These methods survive today—the only machine Bill Carter uses is a grinder. Otherwise he works with a hacksaw and files, cutting dovetails much as you would to join two pieces of wood. You can make a great variety of planes this way, as handsome and functional as you could ever desire, with the hand tools you already own. If you can cut dovetails in wood, cutting them in metal is easier, because you can spread the metal to fill any gaps.

Over the years I have made a number of tools, from planes to small forged hammers. Some, such as scratch stocks, took hardly any time to make (see pp. 132–134). Other tools I have made because I couldn't find them—for inlay work, for instance—or because the one I found didn't suit my needs as well as something I could make. Still others I've made simply because of the challenge of making them and the satisfaction of using them. Toolmaking is a lot less difficult than you might think. Sometimes finding a

BILL CARTER, PLANEMAKER

ENGLISH planemaker Bill Carter makes exquisite planes entirely by hand using common shop tools. He employs his woodworking skills to lay out, cut, and fit the dovetails that join the brass sides and steel soles of his small miter planes. He uses a ball-peen hammer to spread the metal into gaps between the tiny dovetails, securing the joint (photo below).

The old Spiers jointer plane (at top in the photo at right) is constructed with dovetails. The dovetail sample (foreground) shows a small bevel filed in the dovetail. When the metal is peened and spread to fill the beveled area, the joint appears as though it is dovetailed on both sides.

A MODERN TOOL DESIGNER

"INNOVATION IN TOOLS" might be their motto, but "we can do it" is easily the motivation behind Veritas, the woodworking arm of Lee Valley Tools of Ottawa, Canada. It all started in 1979 when Leonard Lee, the company's inspirational leader, couldn't find some framing chisels or a broadax for a log addition he was building. He believed that there must be a need for at least one Canadian supplier of such tools, so he started one himself. Since then, Veritas and Lee Valley have grown enormously by redesigning some familiar old tools, developing new ones, and winning design awards for their efforts along the way.

Leonard Lee's long experience using hand tools and his keen observations of how they work or might work better (he has written *the* book on sharpening) is often the beginning of a project for one of Veritas' team of engineers. Inspiration is just as likely to come from a customer's suggestion, Lee's gene pool of old tools he's collected over the years, or something he's found at a flea market or among the 50 tons of salvage hardware he just purchased.

Some Veritas designs are inspired by a desire to overcome the limitations of a user's skills: jigs to help solve the problems of sharpening, honing, and using cabinet scrapers. Other designs are new takes on old tools: a chisel plane that's simply a plane body with a bench chisel for the iron, or a set of scribing dividers with bubble levels and articulating arms. The engineers make and test prototypes, and Lee challenges them at every step along the way.

A typical problem Lee tackled involved Japanese handsaws. He understood the advantages of their thin kerf and razor-sharp teeth, and how cutting on the pull stroke helps some novices saw more accurately. These saws work amazingly well in softwoods and fine in hardwoods, at least until the teeth start breaking. So Lee went to Japan, first to learn how the saws were made, and then to work out a tooth redesign that would hold up to cutting hardwood. He ended up with a new line of saws and satisfied customers.

No design challenge is too big—so far. The next frontier is bench planes, and already Lee and his engineers have been collecting planes with interesting designs, including ones from eastern Europe and the Paragon line of planes Veritas once made. How can they make a plane easier to use or more accurate, to improve upon a design essentially unchanged from Leonard Bailey's clever ideas of well over a century ago? Judging from their successes so far, this modern-day Leonard just might.

At Lee Valley Tools, the process of designing and refining the prototype for a new chisel plane involves drawings, wooden models, and plenty of close inspection of older tools such as this Stanley #97 and an anonymous cast-iron plane for inspiration. (Photo by Ray Pilon.)

good iron or a beautiful chunk of rosewood inspires the rest.

With only modest woodworking skills—and ideally a tool to copy—you can make the wooden parts of almost any tool. Tempering useful blades and the metalworking side of toolmaking is not as familiar to most woodworkers. For this reason, I have only lightly addressed the woodworking aspects of toolmaking in this chapter. Instead, I focus on metalworking techniques.

No matter what tools you make, you'll need to have the right tools at hand, suitable materials, and an understanding of heat-treating the cutters. If you find your interest piqued, there are books about every aspect of toolmaking, from making wooden planes to forging chisels (see the Bibliography on p. 214).

Isolate the dirt and mess of toolmaking on a separate bench, preferably with a metal top, a large metalworking vise, a grinder, a buffer, and the necessary hand tools nearby.

TOOLS FOR MAKING TOOLS

A well-equipped woodshop has all the tools you need for making your own tools. Ideally, you should have a separate area for metalworking so that the mess of metal filings doesn't dirty your woodworking bench. A machinist's vise is the most versatile way to hold everything from small parts to entire tools. Attach one to your bench or to a platform that can be clamped in a side vise and adjusted to a comfortable height (see the bottom photo at right).

A small machinist's vise is handy for holding metal parts. Mount the vise on a sturdy wooden platform and clamp it in a side vise or in the jaws of a larger metal vise at a comfortable height.

I have a small vise attached to a maple block that I clamp in my side vise for delicate work, such as filing a cutter for a scratch stock. Metalworking vises have an anvil behind the jaws for riveting and flattening

Shears are quicker than a hacksaw for cutting hand scrapers, durable patterns, or tool parts from thin-gauge metal. Modern shears often have leveraged jaws, which are considerably easier for cutting tough materials than these antique shears. (Also shown is an early metal rule that pushes into a revolving cup inside the case.)

A small bench anvil is a handy work surface for flattening parts, peening rivets, or bending sections around the round horn. An assortment of needle-nose pliers and nippers is useful for bending, holding, and cutting.

parts. A pin vise for holding small parts and a bench anvil are also useful, as is a large floor anvil if you decide to take up forging.

You'll need a hacksaw, various files (especially needle files for fine shaping), pliers in assorted shapes and nose configurations, nippers, shears, taps and dies for metal, punches and countersinks, a few cold chisels, a good assortment of twist drills, and at least one ball-peen hammer. Many of these tools you may already have. If not, they are readily found. Taps and dies (for wood threads) are not as common. I have found a few smaller sizes (⅜ in., ½ in., and ¾ in.) useful in toolmaking—for making small clamps or locking screws on marking gauges—as well as for securing knobs in my furniture making (Peugeot Freres made some of the best). Always buy a matching set of tap and die.

One other tool that you are not likely to have is a set of letter and number punches. Not only are they useful for stamping your name, initials, date, and any other revelation that might occur to you (Bill Carter stamps "Diana" and "Carter, Planemaker to the Gentry" on his planes), but it's also a good way to keep track of parts and their position. A stiff whack with a hammer makes a clear mark in end grain or soft steel that won't be mistaken. On many British planes, the cap irons, irons, and infills are stamped with the same number, so as the parts are made they will find each other during assembly.

MATERIALS

Wood is a perfect material for fashioning tools. Take away the steel cutters, brass wear plates, and a few other small metal parts and, for many tools, all you will have left is familiar old beech, birch, rosewood, or perhaps even apple. Beech is the favored wood for many tools because it is tough, fine-grained, and works easily, although any stable hardwood is just as good. I prefer the beauty and polish of rosewood, ebony, and boxwood.

Working steel into cutters and blades is not as familiar to woodworkers as making the wooden parts of tools. But you don't have to be a metallurgist to make blades for common tools (and you can even buy some of them new from catalogs). To make your own cutters, you first need to find good steel that can be hardened and tempered to an edge that will hold its sharpness. High-carbon steel, sometimes stamped "cast steel," is what you should look for.

Old plane irons, chisels, handsaws, worn-out bandsaw blades, heavy hacksaw blades, and files are all made of good steel. I know black-

Taps and dies cut consistent wooden threads and mating nuts for such tools and tool parts as clamps, saw vises, and locking screws. An older hand-cut tap is at top; a modern continuous thread is in the foreground.

With a set of number and letter punches, you can impress your name (or any other inscription) into the wood or soft metal parts of a tool.

The high-quality steel in old rasps and worn files can be forged or ground into practical new tools, such as rugged timber-framing chisels (with rasp teeth clearly visible), a lathe tool, a burnisher, and a drawknife.

Early tool steel, known as blister steel, was made by heating pure Swedish bar iron with charcoal in a closed chest, where only the outer layer of the bar absorbed carbon (visible in the engraving). Depending on how it was forged, the steel was then used for making everything from shears to chisels.

The simple wooden details of these gauges—sliding arms that lock in place with wedging keys or a wooden thumbscrew (top)—lock positively, are easily made, and are worth keeping in mind when designing more complex tools.

A lucky find—a Sheffield spokeshave cutter—inspired the author to make a boxwood shave with a horn wear plate (at rear). The ebony scraper, with a blade cut from a hand scraper, is a copy of a traditional tool.

smiths who forge tools from old leaf springs. You can also buy flat ground stock in a wide range of widths and thicknesses specifically for toolmaking. And if you want to go that far, there are special alloys such as A11 or M4 for making cutters with incredibly long-lasting edges. They are available through steel retailers, who can tell you the specifics of each.

Just by looking in flea markets, junk shops, and tool shops, I have found a complete inventory of toolmaking supplies: brass stock, bits of ivory or bone for wear plates or other details, cast-steel irons of every vintage, knurled knobs, ferrules, and parts from other tools. And these are good places to get inspiration, to see tools that work well or construction details that might come in handy someday. If you get serious about toolmaking, you'll need to have more than just the materials. You'll need a basic knowledge of metalworking techniques, including riveting and, even more important, heat-treating.

Some modern toolmakers make complete (and working) tools only an inch or two long. Among these miniatures by Paul Kebabian are an ebony plow plane, an ivory bow saw, a brass and ebony Ultimatum brace, and tiny coachmaker rabbet planes.

HEAT-TREATING

Nearly all woodworking tools (rules and squares being notable exceptions) have a cutting edge or edges. Hardening and tempering those steel edges give them durability. You can make tools without heat-treating them—by careful grinding you can make new blades from old ones and preserve the original temper of the steel. But it's a lot easier to soften or *anneal* the steel first, and then saw and file it to shape. Restoring the steel to a harder state then requires heat-treating. Not all steels heat-treat, so make sure you start with high-carbon steel, a known alloy, or old blades. The best way to learn is to experiment.

Beyond the physical composition of the steel, which is out of your hands, the durability of an edge (and its ultimate usefulness) depends upon heat-treating. This involves heating the finished blade until it is red hot, quenching it rapidly to make it very hard, then drawing some of the hardness out by heating it to 350°F or so. Commercial heat-treating is done in special ovens, with scientific control for predictable results.

Japanese tools are testimony that a small forge and experience can do the job just as well, if not better. Sometimes I use a small riveter's forge, especially when I also want to

The first step in making a marking knife (on the bench anvil) is to anneal or soften the blade so it can be filed to shape and drilled for the rivets. Heat the blade red hot and let it cool slowly. Harden the finished blade the same way, only quench it rapidly in water. (Photo by Jon Binzen.)

Each cutting tool has an optimum tempering range, visible by the color the steel turns as you apply heat. The more heat you apply, the darker the steel colors and the softer the resulting tempered edge. A softer edge will also be less brittle.

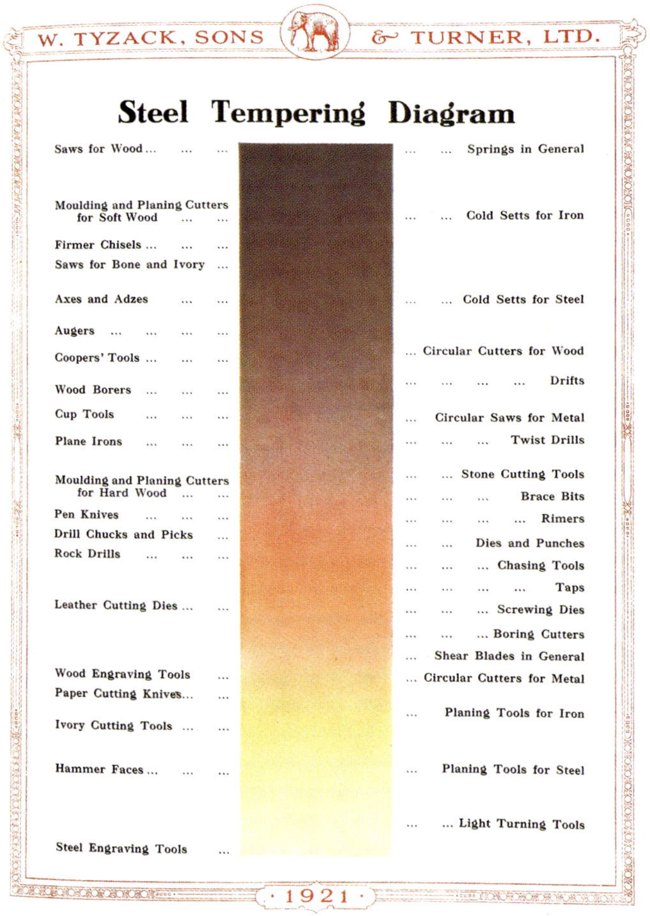

forge a tool, but otherwise a propane torch works for heat-treating all but the heaviest irons.

The first step in making a cutter is annealing it to a soft and ductile (workable) state. If the blade has any sort of profile, such as a new molding-plane iron, annealing the steel allows you to file it to shape easily. Play the torch over the business end of the blade until it is uniformly bright red, then bury it in a can of warm ash or fine sand, allowing it to cool slowly.

It helps to work in subdued light, as "smithies" often do, to see the subtle color changes of the steel as it heats. Sometimes I throw a blade into a dying fire in my wood stove with just enough heat left to get it to red hot, letting it cool as the coals burn out. If a file cuts the steel easily, it's annealed. This is the time to complete all of the forming and shaping of your cutter. But annealed steel is useless as a cutting edge until you take it through the next step of hardening it once again.

To harden it again, heat the steel to cherry red and quench it rapidly, edge first, in a pail of warm water. Agitate the steel in the water to shake off any steam bubbles clinging to the surface that prevent it from cooling quickly. The internal structure of the steel is now frozen, you might say. It's hard and brittle, quite different from its "relaxed" state while annealed. Water is the easiest and safest liquid to quench in, although some steels require oil. (Any steel alloys you buy will be noted "W" for water hardening,

Screws are best for adjustable or replaceable parts, such as the throat plate fitted to the smoothing plane and the sole of the spokeshave (foreground). Rivets can be nearly invisible, such as those through the wear plates of the marking gauge, and they can hold steel cutters in wooden handles securely (see the reamer at left). (Photo by Jon Binzen.)

Two brass rivets hold the finished blade snugly in place. Work on a stable, flat surface like this bench anvil, and tap the rivet carefully to mushroom a head on both ends without splitting the wood. (Photo by Jon Binzen.)

"O" for oil hardening, and "A" for air hardening, which requires a special oven.)

If you ever overheated a cutting edge while grinding—and who hasn't?—then you already understand a little about tempering. Any part that turned blue will no longer hold an edge very well; much of its hardness has been tempered out. If you reheat the blade in a controlled way, you're tempering it, or drawing out just enough of the hardness to make the edge tough. Any shiny area of the blade will show a progression of colors from light straw to blue as the steel heats. Apply heat well back from the edge, along the entire width of the blade, and watch for the colors as they run toward the edge.

Where you stop and quench is a matter of experience, but as with most things it's a compromise and depends on how the tool will be used. Apply just a little heat and the edge will be very hard yet brittle (good for a cold chisel). More heat will leave a tough edge, but one that will not hold its sharpness as long (good for an ax or adze). Temper woodworking edges to light straw, at least as a place to start. Test your blade, and if the edge chips in use, soften it slightly by retempering it with a bit more heat.

RIVETING

If heat-treating mystifies you, riveting is a piece of cake. Rivets are a metalworker's nails, available in nearly as many sizes, shapes, and materials. Nails themselves even make serviceable rivets. To join metal to wood—brass wear plates or the handles of a marking knife, for instance—rivets are strong, easy to make and, in some situations, nearly invisible. You can make a movable "knuckle joint" between two wooden parts with a rivet.

Rivets are also great for joining pieces of metal together. While not as strong as welding or soldering, they avoid any potential problems of

FOOTPRINT TOOLS

ONE OF THE LAST in the long tradition of making hand tools for the world's tradesmen, Footprint Tools carries on in Sheffield, England. As the largest privately owned manufacturer, their production includes wood and cold chisels, auger bits, hammers, joiner's tools, and planes.

The day I paid a visit to Footprint Tools, two 20-ton drop hammers were vibrating the entire factory (and probably everything else for blocks around). Each deep thud shaped a 2-lb. ball-peen hammer head. Smashed between matching molds or dies (drop forging, as it is known), the red-hot round stock was roughly shaped with one whack, and another whack in an adjacent die refined it. A third thud sheared off the glowing head; a neighboring ancient machine punched out the eye for the handle as easily as you'd core an apple. Finally, the hammer faces were heat-treated and ground smooth.

Everywhere in the factory were cart loads of tools in various states of manufacture. Men at smaller mechanical forges worked each woodworking chisel, much as they would have a century ago. Nearby, finished chisels were tempering in special ovens, and the woodworking shop was turning out dozens of plane and saw handles.

Two whacks of a 20-ton drop hammer and the red-hot round stock is neatly forged in matching molds, or "dies," into the shape of a ball-peen hammer head.

As the eyes for the handles are punched out, the red-hot heads fall into a metal bin to cool.

Woodworking chisels begin as Swedish steel bar stock forged to shape in dies. The chisels are then hardened, tempered in ovens, finish-ground, and finally fitted with handles.

Dozens of knobs come off lathes, are lacquered red, and are then fitted to block planes.

heat. Modern glues are certainly another alternative, although I put more trust in the mechanical connection of a rivet or screw.

Why rivet and not screw? Screws are best for parts of tools that will need to be disassembled, replaced, or loosened to make adjustments—fences and depth stops, for instance. The problem with screws is that, over time, the threads lose their grip on the wood, so that the connection is no longer as secure. You always can tighten a rivet, however, with a few taps of a hammer. Rivets also are smaller than screws and less apt to weaken the narrow cross sections typical of many tools.

Whether you use nails, brass rod, or commercial rivets made of steel or copper, the rivet must be annealed so you can peen the metal into a head. (Anneal brass by heating it dull red and quenching.) The hole for the rivet must be no smaller than its diameter, and hardly any bigger. To set a rivet flush (making it invisible, if the materials are the same), countersink the hole slightly. Securing the rivet is then a matter of forming a head on both ends with many light blows using a ball-peen hammer.

One method is to cut the rivet long, clamp it in a vise, and peen one end into small head. Tap the rivet into place (into the wood side first, if you can), cut it off just proud of the surface, and peen a head on the other end. Work both sides and back up the work on an anvil. Be especially careful of the side set into the wood to avoid splitting. The connection will be stronger if you use a small washer under the rivet head (as you commonly see on old knife handles).

If you countersunk the hole on the metal side of your joint (or on both sides) and peened the rivet to fill it completely, you can then file the surface flat and have an invisible connection (or repair). Whether you are trying to hide a rivet or true a metal surface flat, proper filing technique is critical. It's no different than using a rasp or file on wood, as explained in Chapter 8.

Any woodworker with modest skills could restore these flea-market finds with some basic repairs, such as shaping a new handle, replacing a missing wedge, or piecing in the charred heel of the round plane.

Restoring Tools

Restoring some venerable old tool to usable service can be just as challenging and satisfying as making a new one. Make a new blade or a new handle, and you're using all the same skills. At least with an old tool you have something to start with, even if it's hidden under years of dirt.

A stiff brass brush, fine steel wool, and a mixture of boiled linseed oil and beeswax will clean and polish both wood and metal surfaces.

CLEANING

If you buy many secondhand tools, you'll quickly become adept at cleaning. Beneath typical paint spatters, grime, and surface rust there's probably a beautiful tool just waiting for you. Exactly how much to clean is an ongoing debate among collectors and users. This is not a problem with common tools—manufactured ones such as molding planes or Stanley tools—but if you are overzealous in cleaning a rare or historically significant tool, you risk irreversible damage.

You might remove tool marks that indicate how it was made, the patina of years of use that make it so appealing in the first place, almost certainly devaluing it considerably. Old tools have a soul that too much cleaning only diminishes. My guide is to clean a tool to a condition to be used—to make it look the way it would if I had found it on a past owner's bench.

The first step in cleaning a tool is to take it apart so you can get into every crevice filled with grime. Everyone has a secret formula for cleaning: a solvent (such as kerosene or turpentine) and a gentle abrasive. I use 0000 steel wool, a small scraper, and a fine brass or steel brush—all gentle enough to clean surfaces and protect the patina. For stubborn gunk I use 00 steel wool, and for surface rust I sometimes reach for 400-grit wet-and-dry paper (or coarser if necessary).

Work as little as possible on gunmetal parts to preserve the beautiful color that only time can produce. A good rubbing with paste wax (I mix beeswax and boiled linseed oil) brings up the shine and prevents rusting. Nothing polishes a tool better than using it. (The same wax or thinned boiled linseed oil is a good universal finish on any wood.)

REPAIRS

While it can be tricky to repair the wooden parts of some tools, the skills involved are not beyond the means of any capable woodworker. Add basic metalworking skills to your repertoire, and you might succeed with a more complicated repair: drilling out a sheared-off bolt and retapping for a larger one, restoring damaged threads by some delicate filing, or fabricating a missing part. This is all part of the thrill of making a tool whole again, especially if you can buy it for a bargain price. But when it comes to repairing cracked or broken cast iron, you have to be careful.

If you work with old cast-iron tools, you are bound to drop one, as I have done more than once. Cast iron is tough but brittle. If you are lucky, a dropped tool might only chip or crack, but it could also split in half. Tools become rare for this reason alone. It's also why there is a lively market for tool parts. I've seen some ingenious handyman repairs on cracked tools, with rivets and plates that are not much to look at but that saved an old friend from an early demise.

Really good repairs—gas welds that are almost invisible—are expensive, and sometimes more than the tool is worth. Brazing is another option and often less expensive. (You could even try a tough, modern epoxy, although it won't be as durable a repair.) Most repairs are noticeable, which is not usually a concern for a tool that's going to be used, but the alignment of the repaired handle or the flatness of a

Cast-iron tools are tricky to repair. The gas weld to the Bedrock #604½ (top) is very good, a similar repair to the block plane (middle) is utilitarian, and the brazing on the #78 rabbet plane (foreground) left the front part of the sole twisted.

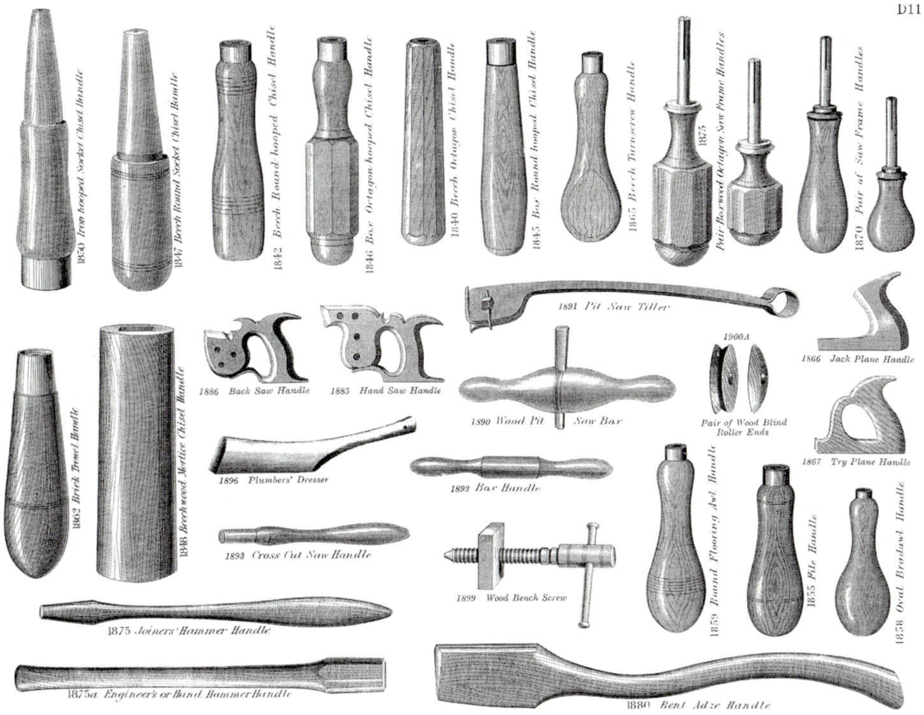

Any of these traditional handles would be a good model for making your own, for repairing a broken handle, or for fitting a new one to a file, rasp, or chisel.

SAW-HANDLE PATTERNS

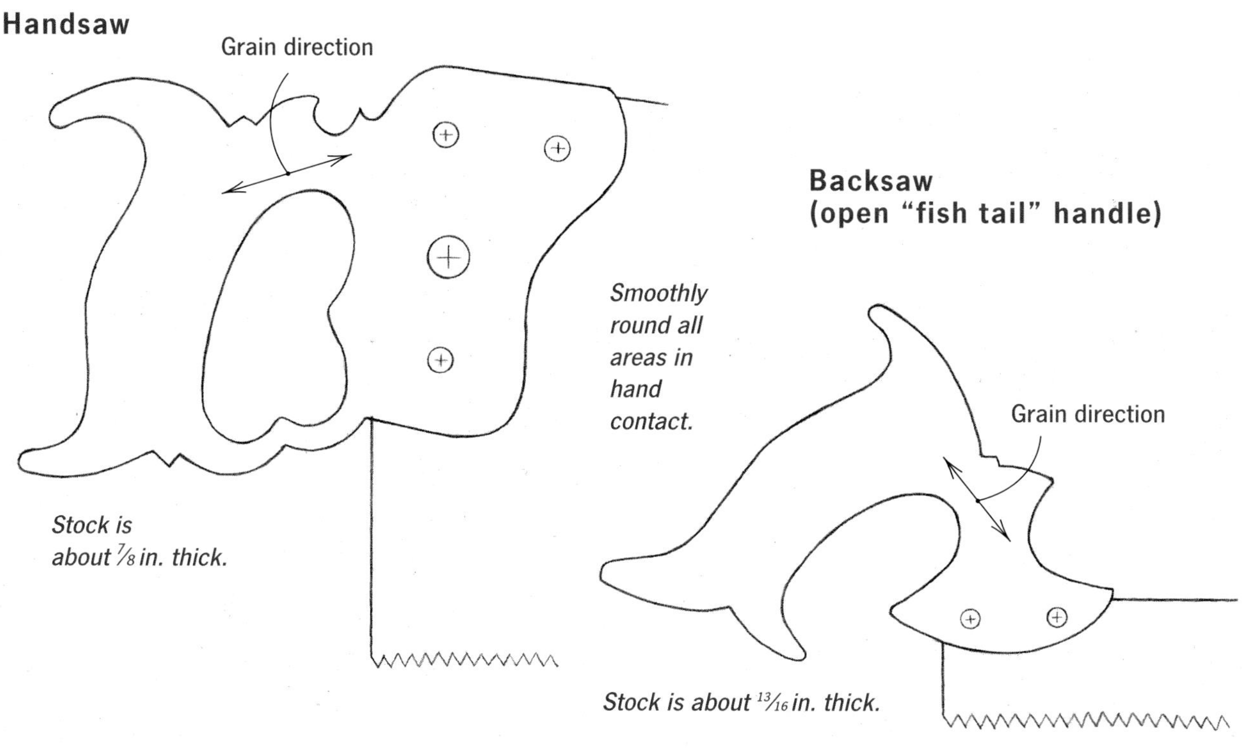

plane's sole with a repaired side might never be the same. Certainly don't go looking for broken cast-iron tools—at any price—but when you drop a favorite tool, think long and hard about your options. Your old friend might end up with just a scar—or a limp.

Making handles

One of the easiest repairs is to make a new handle for a chisel, saw, drawknife, or any number of other tools. Considering how long most woodworking projects take, making a handle is quick and satisfying. Of course, it takes longer to shape a saw handle than to turn a round one on a lathe, but either handle will be better than anything you can buy, and it will fit your hand comfortably.

Rosewood, boxwood, beech—any hard and fine-grained wood can make a stunning handle. I save scraps of exotic or wildly figured woods just for handles. Every round handle needs a ferrule to keep the wood from splitting where the tang enters, and for heavy-duty framing chisels and other tools apt to be hit often and hard, a steel hoop on the opposite end is a good idea. Flea markets are good places to look for brass and steel tubes of various diameters and thicknesses, and you may even find old ferrules with special details, such as knurling or cap ends. You can also find orphaned handles at flea markets for a few dollars at most.

A lathe is the simplest way to shape round handles. You can also use a plane, rasps, and scrapers, with the advantage that you can cut an oval handle just as easily as a round one. For a fine gent's backsaw or a rasp—tools you tend to hold in the same orientation to the work—an oval handle provides a more positive grip than a round one. You can also plane a round handle into an octagon for a comfortable grip (and to prevent the tool from rolling off your bench).

On the lathe, size the wood for a snug fit for the ferrule and hoop, and flush with the rest of the handle. Tap either into place with another piece of pipe of similar diameter. Drive the hoop lower than the top of the handle so that the wood can mushroom out and hold it on. If you planned well, the lathe center will be the start of a hole for the tool's tang. For more tips on drilling the handle and fitting the tang, refer back to pp. 87-89.

Making a new saw handle is more time-consuming, but you'll appreciate the results every time you grasp it. Apple, curly maple, and cherry are my favorite woods for saw handles. For a pattern, use either of the ones shown on the facing page or another favorite handle; just make sure to plan for the saw bolts. If you have them, measure the length of your saw bolts to determine the thickness of the handle. Pay attention to the grain orientation to give the fine tails of your handle maximum strength.

I like to rough out the shape, saw a kerf for the blade with a tenon saw (or whatever saw you have that cuts a properly snug kerf), and fine-tune the handle's position before getting too caught up in the shaping. Cut the details with either a bandsaw or a coping saw, and then rasp and scrape the edges into comfortable and flowing curves. Embellish with some carving.

To transfer the location of the holes for the saw bolts, hold the blade in the correct position on the handle. If you are lucky enough to have the right bolts, measure them for the proper counterbore to sink them flush. If you don't have any bolts, soft copper rivets work nicely. Who knows, your handle might be so comfortable it will encourage you to use a saw more often.

Whether you make just the handles or entire tools, the tools will certainly become favorites. Getting started is the hardest part, and there is no better way to get inspired than by looking at old tools. The next chapter explains where to look and what to look for.

Cut out a new saw handle with a bandsaw or coping saw, and refine and smooth it with rasps and files. All three handles on the bench were turned on a lathe and fitted with old ferrules. (Photo by Jon Binzen.)

TO HELP determine the diameter or length of a handle, measure other handles that feel particularly comfortable. I prefer simple shapes, with a bulging center section and tapering ends. A dip and then increased diameter just above the ferrule gives a nice place to get a thumb and finger behind for extra leverage when pushing, for tools such as paring chisels and carving tools.

602
"ODD-JOBS"
No. 1
BIT & SQUARE
LEVEL
No. 84
STANLEY
PLUMB
BOB
1
STANLEY
LEVEL
SIGHTS
2
FOR IRON LEVELS
STANLEY RULE & LEVEL CO.
NEW BRITAIN, CONN. USA
ONE
STANLEY'S
No. 67
UNIVERSAL
Spoke Shave.
STANLEY'S UN
By changing the
used equally well for Circ
Movable Gauge is used in ra
detachable and either of them ca
on top of the Stock, thus enabling the owner to work in
Corners or Panels where other spoke shaves cannot be used.
Both Handles
screwed into a Stock

BUYING USED
Hand Tools

Twenty-five years ago I didn't know a Bedrock from a Bailey, a Sargent from a Stanley, but secondhand tools were cheap and I bought plenty. I was a carpenter, I needed tools, and these were far better than anything I could have purchased new. Every detail—from shapely rosewood handles to sturdy parts—spoke of quality, of tools designed to work day in and day out. After I found my first Norris smoother at a flea market for $125, I was hooked.

Until the recent renaissance of quality toolmaking, buying secondhand was the surest way to build a shop of good hand tools. For unusual tools it still is. Even if you rarely buy anything, looking is half the fun—the thrill of hunting through boxes at flea markets, haggling with dealers, or feeling a tingle of adrenaline counter-bidding at an auction.

Where to Look

You never know where you'll find tools besides all the places you would expect: yard sales, tool auctions, antique stores, and, of course, flea markets. A couple of years ago I met a woman at a church supper, and in passing I mentioned that I was a furniture maker. Recently, she called to tell me that she was selling her father-in-law's house, and he had some tools I might be interested in. Knowing almost nothing about tools, she described worn wooden bench planes and some iron tools bought at auctions over the years.

Ever curious, I went to investigate. But no, this story doesn't end with the find of a rare early patented plane among that jumble of iron, although it could have. Instead, I found a clean Stanley #53 spokeshave and a small bench anvil—both of which I put right to work.

As beautiful as Christmas tree ornaments, finely turned plumb bobs are common finds at flea markets. Every carpenter once had one in his tool kit.

No matter where you find used tools, look them over carefully for cracks, damaged or missing parts, and rusted cutters or adjusters. Even the best price is no bargain if the tool is unusable.

I've heard plenty of stories, though, of similar outings ending in great finds: a Spiers miter plane found in a bucket at a country auction for $4 (value $1,000), a going-out-of-business sale at a hardware store where a Stanley #164 was thrown in with a lot of junk (value more than $3,000), and the earliest marked wooden plane found in Maine for $12 (value at least $10,000, if not more).

It might seem that with more interest in collecting tools and more education about them through price guides and books, these sorts of lucky discoveries are a thing of the past. They aren't. The lure of the unexpected and the minor triumphs along the way keep the hunt interesting.

FLEA MARKETS

Nowhere is the hunt more unpredictable than at flea markets, yard sales, and secondhand stores. You never know what might turn up, but there's a good chance you can find some bargains. The drawbacks are that the hunt takes time, and you have to wade through a lot of junk—sometimes entire boxes of rusty tools and hardware—for the chance of finding a complete tool in restorable condition.

Wherever you look for tools (but especially at flea markets, auctions, and tool dealers), knowledge about what you are buying is critical. It doesn't matter how great a bargain you get if the tool is missing important parts, or if it's entirely wrong for the work you want to do. Just looking a tool over very carefully is a good start. Experience is still the best teacher; expect to make a mistake or two along the way. Buy a reprint of the Stanley #34 catalog (1915 edition) or other catalogs and learn what you can about tools that interest you (see the Bibliography on p. 214). How else will you know that the rusty piece you found is a rare beader for a Stanley #72 chamfer plane?

DEALERS

Dealers are a more reliable source for tools. Some have entire stores filled with classic hand tools of every sort, which you can examine and even try out before buying. Many put out catalogs several times a year, with each tool photographed and fully described, or they might have a Web site updated more often. Woodworking catalogs are another source (although more limited) for new tools in classic patterns. The only disadvantage of buying from dealers is that you'll pay the market price. But for this you also get a number of benefits.

The best dealers have a love and respect for the tools born from a long history with them—as collectors and users—and a ready knowledge of their details that they are glad to share. They are the inside circle of the tool market, connected to its ebb and flow and to each other. This network can find any tool, especially the rare ones not easily found other ways. They'll answer your questions, sometimes even take tools you no longer need in barter, and, of course, they will dicker. You will pay more than flea-market prices, but you get the assurance (and sometimes a guaran-

You never know what treasured tool you might find in amongst the old crockery, tinware, and common household junk at a flea market.

The three golden planes and a handsaw mark the modest shop of tool and book dealer Roy Arnold in Needham Market, Ipswich, England. Over the years, many of the best British tools have passed through his hands.

Inside Roy Arnold's shop there's everything from a Holtzapffel engine lathe to hundreds of new and used books about the once-common woodworking trades, and workaday tools just waiting to be tuned and put back to work.

tee) of a complete tool in working order. Buying from dealers might not be as exciting as attending auctions or prowling junk stores, but they are dependable sources for excellent tools.

AUCTIONS

If you are willing to pay the price, you could buy a whole shop's worth of tools in just a couple of days at a large regional sale. Dealers and collectors congregate from all over for the same reason that attracts you: the chance to see lots and lots of tools in one place. There are a number of regional sales in this country and abroad, in addition to organizations such as the Midwest Tool Collectors Association, which gathers twice a year to sell tools and swap stories.

In researching this book, I headed off to Harrisburg, Pennsylvania, where the rare, the unusual, the pristine (sometimes in an original box)—in short, the best of the best—are on the block. And then for a comparison to this granddaddy of the domestic auctions, I went to a most prestigious auction in England (see the sidebar on p. 209).

Harrisburg International Tool Auction

Imagine a huge hotel ballroom filled with row after row of dealer tables. Some are piled high with usable tools of every sort—planes, handsaws, braces, sets of chisels—with more filling shelves and boxes on the floor. Spread over other tables are levels and boxwood rules, old tool catalogs, rare Stanley planes, British tools (including many gleaming Norrises and Spiers), hammers, and axes.

Four 50-ft.-long tables are spread with more than a thousand tools ready for auction, with the most valuable and smallest guarded in glass cases. Then there are the buyers, two or three deep, filling every aisle. Such was the busy scene for the dealer show and preview of the Saturday auction. The action at this event continues late into the night over dinner, in hotel rooms transformed into tool shops, and anywhere two tool lovers chance to meet.

WHY ARE THERE so many more inventive tool designs found in the United States than in England? The answer lies partly in the conservative nature of English craftsmen, working with familiar tools. English guilds stifled change by their strict control over every aspect of a trade, including its methods and tools. Guilds and tradition were much less important in colonial America, where ingenuity flourished.

The key to success at any auction is to read the catalog and carefully preview the tools. Make notes, narrow your focus, and set your highest bids before the action begins.

Even the best catalog description doesn't tell you as much as a hands-on inspection of a tool that interests you. Disassemble a tool if need be to see all its details.

Bud Brown started this auction in 1983; Clarence Blanchard, a down-home Mainer with a long history of collecting Stanley tools, has run it out of his home since 1997. It takes a full year to put together, to find everything from entire collections to consignments of a single high-ticket item such as a Thomas Falconer coachmaker's plow plane, the highlight of the 1998 auction that I attended (the plane sold for $22,500).

Also up for sale were almost three dozen Scottish planes—unusual and beautiful examples of the planemaker's art—from the collection of Ken Roberts, an early collector of hand tools and a prolific writer about them. And among the 762 lots were the usual selection of Stanley tools, plow planes, molding planes, and unique tools from many trades.

Clarence gathers a cross section of tools that will appeal to a wide variety of collectors and users, and then writes a catalog enticing them to come and bid. A tool might not look like much, until you read in the catalog where it was made, by whom, and other details that set it apart from similar tools, as well as information about what trades used it, its condition, and an estimate of its value. Many bidders never appear, instead submitting bids by mail based on the thoroughness of the catalog alone.

In the tool world, this is certainly an auction for the big boys, drawing collectors from all over the world.

The rare and unusual tools at any auction attract all the attention, which leaves plenty of common tools for the alert (and prepared) buyer to snatch up for a song.

Every chair is taken, every catalog open, and every eye follows the action at the start of the 15th Annual International Auction in Harrisburg, Pa., the granddaddy of domestic tool auctions.

The centerpiece of any collection and, at $22,500, one of the highest-priced hand tools ever sold, an extremely rare Falconer's plow plane was on the auction block for less than two minutes.

To look over the crowd, though, you have little idea who has deep pockets and who, like myself, is there to watch and learn. And what an education it is. The auction is a good excuse for tool guys (and gals) to get together and swap stories about their particular tool expertise. There's no better source to learn about the subtleties and history of tools than from these long-time dealers and collectors who have handled, owned, or in some cases spent a lifetime working with them.

Just being among all those tools is an education. Some museums have tools, but even the best have just a handful compared to the incredible variety that are on offer at auction. And no museum will let you handle and take apart its tools, to see the details of how they were made and how they work. I doubt I'll ever see another Falconer plow, but I'll remember the way this one felt in my hands as I imagined cutting a groove along the sinuous curve of a coach. I might think back to the details of the cutters someday, perhaps when I need to make a tool for inlaying along a curve.

The big event is choreographed, orchestrated. Beginning with the auction preview, bidders plan their strategies, trying not to look too interested in tools they desire. Catalogs are out, and everyone is scribbling notes in the margins. I had my eye on a couple of Scottish planes, but seeing a constant knot of admirers handling them, I gave up hope of owning them. I might have a chance with one later in the sale, an old beauty covered with a century of grime, which would be a discouragement to others. Or at least I hoped.

No matter what type of tool you're buying or selling, ones in top-notch condition with the name of the maker clearly marked, always bring a high dollar—rare tools even more so. Common tools sell in cycles, way up one year and leveling off or dropping the next. Braces are way down from a few years ago—as much as a third the value—and Bedrocks and Norrises are way up due to a strong user market. It's a quirk of the auction scene that British tools can sell for considerably less here than in England, and

AN ENGLISH TOOL AUCTION

DAVID STANLEY and his son Ian run an international tool auction twice a year in Leicestershire, England. The tools are similar to those offered at American auctions: many Stanleys and tools by their English competitors, Record and Preston; molding planes; plows; rules and levels; axes and adzes; unique tools from bygone trades; and dozens of those planes dreams are made of—Norrises, Spiers, and Mathiesons.

The crowd is relatively small, and there are no tables for dealers; the auction is the action. Yet there's plenty of competition. One man I meet owns 161 Norrises and is still going strong. Another has a shop filled with what must have been many years' worth of production of the planemakers he collects and uses. To promote the auction worldwide, the Stanleys produce a lavish catalog, with color pictures and descriptions of almost 2,000 lots—more than twice as many as at the Harrisburg auction. More than three-quarters of the lots are sold to absentee postal bidders or their agents.

Emphasis on postal bids is just part of what sets English auctions apart. Unlike American auctions, each item has a reserve, a minimum selling price set by the seller. As an agent of the seller, the auctioneer can bid against you if he chooses (and quite surreptitiously) to raise the price to the reserve. No tools are held up at the opening of each lot, and a digital display tracks lot numbers. Add to this a rapid-fire pace—287 lots an hour, or less than 15 seconds for each—so you better stay focused.

On the block were whole shops of tools belonging to clogmakers, coachmakers, coopers, basketmakers, patternmakers, sailmakers, furniture makers, carvers, and carpenters. The variety in this one sale was far greater than at Harrisburg. Handwork survived longer in Britain and on the continent than it did in the United States, and so did the spectrum of woodworking trades and the tools they used.

Where we had mass-produced Stanleys and a great many tools, a British tradesman typically used far fewer tools (and still does). Yet each was beautifully made with striking details and the personalized touches that speak of small makers or the owner himself. Only by seeing the rich variety of these and American tools together at such an auction could I begin to understand the influences they had on one another over the past three centuries.

The action slows but hardly stops. After hours, hotel rooms turn into instant tool shops as auction-goers gather to hunt for last-minute bargains and to swap stories.

Stanley items for as much or more there. Such isn't the case today; the first Scottish planes come and go, and I never even get off a bid.

Most purchases are headed for collections, so you're competing against this high-end market. And collectors are serious about it. Buying a long-sought-after tool for what might seem like a ridiculous price can bring forth tears. But not all these tools sell for unreal prices. Some do, but there are also plenty of user tools that don't arouse much interest. Since many attendees fly in and out with their loot, heavy or large items can be bargains, such as two nice workbenches that sold for $120 and $125.

Back at the auction, everyone is waiting for the Falconer plow. The auction has to build the proper mood for such a sale through a series of smaller crests: a wooden thread-cutting engine for $8,000, a Tidey double-beveling plane for $11,000 (below estimate and far below an ebony Tidey sold for $27,500 two years earlier), and a Stanley #164 for $4,700.

Until Don Rich's recent death, the Falconer was the premier piece in his collection of coachmaker's plows, a tool he had desired for years but sadly owned only a short time. One of only three known and the only complete version of this unusual plane, it started at $18,000 and a minute later was gone, headed to another collection and never to be used again.

The room all a-titter with speculation about the mystery postal bidder, the grimy Spiers panel plane came up. Not everyone was distracted and it was only by my classic "Statue of Liberty"—bid card firmly planted in the air—that I was the successful bidder. For myself and others it was downhill from here, as more and more seats emptied and only the hardy remained to pick up some bargains.

The end of one auction is the beginning of the next, as high prices bring out more tools from collections, the sellers hoping to get the best prices. Yes, there is a bit of greediness in all this accumulation and chasing after the highest price. But then such sales also attract friends like Craig and Larry who come every year. They spread blue cloths on their hotel beds and cover them with tools—a temporary tool shop with parts of their collections for sale. But the tools are really only a come-on to swapping stories with other tool lovers and enjoying themselves.

TWO USEFUL TOOLS to bring along on tool-hunting forays are a combination square with a 12-in. blade, and a flat-bladed screwdriver. Take things apart. Check the squareness of parts such as the sole and sides of a rabbet plane, the flatness of a bench plane's sole, the backs of cutters and chisels, or the straightness of a backsaw's spine.

What to Look For

The surface pitting on the sole of this Spiers miter plane would turn off a collector and make the tool all that much more affordable for a user. But beware of deeply pitted cutters and rusted-together parts that can ruin a tool.

You don't have to go to a big auction to get caught up in the euphoria of finding and buying old tools. The problem is getting too carried away in the beginning and bringing home boxes of useless junk. The difference between a worn-out or unusable tool and another with generations of life left in it is not as great as you might think. For a tool bought to be admired in some collection it doesn't make much difference. But if you are looking for tools to tune and put to work, missing parts, cracked bodies, or rust-pitted irons are discouraging and disappointing. They are also part of the learning process. Educating yourself about quality tools and gaining experience finding them takes hard work and time.

Buy the tools you need. Most will be common tools, manufactured in large numbers, and these are affordable. Condition and rarity establish their selling price. Take planes for instance: Two #4 bench planes in the same condition can sell for very different prices. A collector would value the rarer earlier type, a user the less expensive later plane with a lateral adjuster. Chipped japanning, dings, surface rust, or other minor defects can turn off a collector while making a perfectly usable tool more affordable. Bear in mind, if you buy a tool in top condition you will pay more, but you can also get a better price if you decide to sell it again.

Repairs usually devalue tools and can even ruin them, such as the #10 rabbet plane in the foreground with a repaired body and a sole that's now warped. Adding a side handle to the #9 (middle) makes the tool easier to use as a shoot plane but unappealing to a collector. Despite the good repair to the side of the #604 (top), holes in the sole diminish its value.

A complete tool is not much more expensive than an incomplete one, but without a good tool guide or lots of experience, you wouldn't know whether the #45 (top) or the #78 (bottom) is complete.

Tools marked by the maker are no more usable, but they are worth more when you sell them. The otherwise identical square on the right marked "Stanley" is worth 10 times the unmarked square next to it; the common bevel gauge is worth a fraction of the Southington below it.

Broken tools aren't a bargain unless you can fix them, and this just adds to the cost. Repairing the wooden parts of tools is not that difficult, nor are basic metalworking repairs (see Chapter 11). If you are willing to take the time, you can learn a lot in the process and end up with a tool that might not have much collector value but is wonderfully pleasing to you. There is one major exception—cracked cast-iron bodies and parts are not easily repaired. Look these sorts of tools over carefully; good repairs are expensive. Look for hidden cracks and tap on the body and hope for a nice high ring.

Is the tool complete? Empty tapped holes might mean a missing part, but unless you are familiar with the tool you might not know. The downside of multipurpose tools—of which Stanley made many—is that parts like fences, cutters, and side handles used infrequently are easily lost. Many common tools have such parts, and because Stanley used unique thread pitches, any missing parts are hard to replace except from a similar tool. Mismatched parts are common and harder to spot, although they don't necessarily affect how the tool functions. To use up its inventory of parts, Stanley was even known to send out new tools with parts of different vintages.

Rust kills tools. You can sand off surface rust, but deep rust welds parts tight and pits cutters so badly they become useless. Some cleaning is inevitable with used tools, but any rust alerts me to look further. Do the adjusters work smoothly over a complete range? Are the screws that secure parts frozen with rust? Look over chisels and cutters carefully, especially the back that will need to be polished flat for a truly sharp cutting edge. Given the will and lots of time, most rust can be lapped out. It's hard work. Do it once and the next time you might look a little further and find an equal tool with little or no rust for nearly the same price.

More planes by late-18th-century cabinetmaker John Green than you are likely to see anywhere else, this collection took a lifetime to assemble, one piece at a time.

Embark on the next level of buying tools, seeking the less common or unusual for many hundreds of dollars per item, and you are verging on collecting. You will need even more education about what you're buying, you will have to look harder, and because of the sums involved, be more wary. You'll be in competition with other collectors and dealers, although they might turn up their noses at a totally usable tool if it's less than perfect. Be patient, as even the rarest tools continue to show up. Investment also becomes a factor, as you wonder how the value of your tools will change over time.

If you buy tools that appeal to you and they are in great condition, they will hold their value or, more likely, grow in value. The overall tool market is fickle enough that prices rise and fall, but the best of the best still increase steadily year after year. But don't think of tools as a retirement hedge. Selling takes patience and luck to find the buyer who appreciates the same beauty you saw in that well-worn cooper's croze. The more unusual the tool, chances are the more difficult it will be to sell. But I still believe that in 10 or 20 years we will look back and say how reasonable tools are today—and maybe even wish we'd bought a few more.

I prefer to think about the tools that I have collected over the years as a different kind of investment. Having the best tools has inspired the best in me, to hone my skills and work in ways I couldn't with machines alone. To earn a living with such beautiful and ingenious objects is a further dividend. Having good tools also encourages my sons' love of woodworking, for while they are too young to use machines, they can quite confidently plane, saw, and carve. Have fun looking for tools, buy the best, and learn to use them well. The rewards will last a lifetime.

Bibliography

Bridgewater, Alan and Gill. *Mastering Hand Tool Techniques.* Cincinnati, Ohio: Betterway Books, 1997.

Dunbar, Michael. *Restoring, Tuning, and Using Classic Woodworking Tools.* New York: Sterling, 1989.

Goodman, W. L. *The History of Woodworking Tools.* London: G. Bell and Sons, 1962.

Graham, Frank D., and Thomas J. Emery. *Audels Carpenters and Builders Guide #1.* New York: Audel, 1946.

Holtzapffel, Charles. *Turning and Mechanical Manipulation, Volume 2: Construction, Action, and Application of Cutting Tools.* London: 1875. Reprint, Mendham, N.J.: Astragal Press, 1993.

Hummel, Charles. *With Hammer in Hand.* Henry Francis duPont Wintertur Museum, Charlottesville, Va.: University Press of Virginia, 1968.

Jackson, Albert, David Day, and Simon Jennings. *The Complete Manual of Woodworking.* New York: Knopf, 1989.

Kean, Herbert P., and Emil S. Pollak. *Collecting Antique Tools.* Morristown, N.J.: Astragal Press, 1990.

Kebabian, Paul B., and Dudley Witney. *American Woodworking Tools.* Boston: New York Graphic Society, 1978.

Kingshott, Jim. *Making and Modifying Woodworking Tools.* East Sussex, England: Guild of Master Craftsmen Publications, 1992.

Korn, Peter. *The Woodworker's Guide to Hand Tools.* Newtown, Conn.: The Taunton Press, 1998.

Lampert, Nigel. *Through Much Tribulation: Stewart Spiers and the Planemakers of Ayr.* Pascoe Vale, Victoria, Australia: Oliver Pub., 1998.

Lee, Leonard. *The Complete Guide to Sharpening.* Newtown, Conn.: The Taunton Press, 1995.

Odate, Toshio. *Japanese Woodworking Tools: Their Tradition, Spirit, and Use.* Newtown, Conn.: The Taunton Press, 1984.

Rees, Jane and Mark. *Tools, A Guide for Collectors.* Suffolk, England: Roy Arnold, Ipswich Book Co., 1996.

Salaman, R. A. *Dictionary of Woodworking Tools.* Newtown, Conn.: The Taunton Press, 1990.

Sellens, Alvin. *The Stanley Plane: A History and Descriptive Inventory.* Albany, N.Y.: Early American Industries Association, 1975.

Underhill, Roy. *The Woodwright's Companion, Exploring Traditional Woodcraft.* Chapel Hill, N.C.: University of North Carolina Press, 1983.

Watson, Aldren A. *Hand Tools, Their Ways and Workings.* New York: Lyons Press, 1982.

Wearing, Robert. *Hand Tools for Woodworkers, Principles and Techniques.* New York: Sterling, 1997.

TOOL CATALOGS

The Cutting Edge: An Exhibition of Sheffield Tools. Sheffield, England: Ruskin Gallery, 1992.

David Stanley Auctions. Osgathorpe, Leicestershire, England. Various catalogs, 1995-1998.

Sheffield Standard List, Illustrated, Containing Prices & Patterns of Machinery, Files, Rasps, Saws, Joiner's Tools, Light and Heavy Edge Tools, Lancashire Tools, Machinists', Plumbers', Tinmens' Tools, Spades, Shears, Anvils, Bellows, Wire, and Other Sheffield Goods. Sheffield, England, 1864.

Stanley Rule and Level Co. *Catalog #34, 1915 Edition.* Reprint Westborough, Mass.: Stanley Publishing Co., 1985.

Thomas Turner and Co. Suffolk Works, Sheffield, England, 1890 catalog.

Tool Shop Auctions. Needham Market, Suffolk, England. Various catalogs, 1996-1998.

W. Tyzack and Sons and Turner, Ltd. Sheffield, England, 1921 catalog.

Index

T

U

V

W

THE COMPLETE GUIDE TO

SHARPENING

THE COMPLETE GUIDE TO

SHARPENING

Leonard Lee

The Taunton Press

COVER PHOTOGRAPH: ROBERT MARSALA

The Taunton Press
Inspiration for hands-on living®

10 9 8 7 6

Printed in the United States of America

ISBN 1-56158-067-8 hardcover
ISBN 1-56158-125-9 softcover

A Fine Woodworking Book
Fine Woodworking® is a trademark of The Taunton Press, Inc., registered in the U.S. Patent and Trademark Office.

The Taunton Press, 63 South Main Street, Box 5506,
Newtown, CT 06470-5506
e-mail: tp@taunton.com

Distributed by Publishers Group West

Library of Congress Cataloging-in-Publication Data

Lee, Leonard.
The complete guide to sharpening / Leonard Lee.
p. cm.
"A Fine woodworking book"—T.p. verso.
Includes index.
ISBN 1-56158-067-8
1. Woodworking tools. 2. Sharpening of tools. I. Title.
TT186.L43 1994 94-37677
684'.08'028 – dc20 CIP

■ To Lorraine, who not only makes it all possible, but so enjoyable

ACKNOWLEDGMENTS

Some years ago, Tom Hurley of Toronto and I set out to write a book on sharpening but (through no fault of Tom's) got mired down along the way. Very little of the prose from that earlier effort survived to be included in this book, but some of the photographs did as well as a variety of jigs that Tom had developed or modified to make shop sharpening easier and more accurate. These photos and jigs are most evident in the chapters on drill bits and saws, although there are several elsewhere in the book as well. Thank you, Tom, for permission to use this material.

Of all the other people whose contributions should be acknowledged possibly the first should be the hundreds of customers over the years who asked "Why?" They provided the reason to write.

A number of people were instrumental in enabling me to write. Peter Sewell of the National Research Council of Canada patiently and cheerfully photographed dozens of tools and stones through an electron microscope. This was critical to understanding materials and processes. Dorothy Liberty of Forintek (Ottawa) provided key library services. Sandy Stewart (Mississippi Forest Products Laboratory), Vincent Farengo (Everlast Saw Company) and Roger Comer (Eagle Carbide) took turns educating me about carbide cutting tools. Norm Franz of Vancouver and Bill McKenzie of California and Australia were generous with answers, advice and photographs, a small portion of which is presented in Appendix 1. The Canadian Conservation Institute took a number of photographs under some time pressure.

On the editing side, Jerry Glaser applied the whip of precision to many technical matters, as well as making available a wealth of material from his library. Brother Bob answered dozens of grammatical questions, and Peter Chapman at The Taunton Press helped substantially with sequence and flow while excising many lumpy passages and smoothing others. Donna Curtis typed everything, sometimes through the fourth or fifth revision, but always cheerfully.

On the business side, the staff at Lee Valley Tools and Veritas Tools frequently took up the slack caused when I dropped normal duties to play author. To all of those above and those unintentionally missed, I offer heartfelt thanks.

On the home front, I was an indifferent companion at the best of times as the book was being written, and variously testy, distracted or too busy to be fit company at the worst of times. For tolerating all of this plus three other decades of my aberrant activity, I thank my wife, Lorraine.

And, finally, I owe the most to my parents, William and Winnifred Lee, who spent most of their lives ensuring that their children would have the opportunities that had been denied them. From a hardscrabble homestead in northern Saskatchewan they saw their children through all the education that could be absorbed, while they denied themselves all the luxuries of life and some of the basics. This is a debt that can never be repaid, only acknowledged.

CONTENTS

INTRODUCTION

Woodworkers tend to believe that the only thing separating them from the masters of the craft is another piece of equipment. Since this widely held belief has provided me with a living for many years as president of both a tool-manufacturing company and a tool-retailing firm, I should not even attempt to change it. But from time to time a missionary zeal seizes us all, and I am so seized with the relationship between sharp tools and good woodworking.

Although good sharpening technique alone is not sufficient to make you a master of the craft, it can allow you to maximize whatever innate skill you have. For truly talented woodworkers, it can elevate their work to a level from which they would otherwise be forever barred; only sharp tools can create the crisp detail and fine joinery that their minds are capable of conceiving and their hands of constructing.

I became interested in sharpening for two reasons. First, I mistakenly thought that it was the only thing separating me from the masters because I owned almost every conceivable tool, and, second, I was embarrassed by the endless stream of customer questions that I could answer only hesitantly. Pride is a great motivator.

The specific event that triggered a decade-long analysis of sharpening materials and techniques was the introduction of Japanese water stones to the Western world. Like most woodworkers, I was an oil-stone user and initially looked askance at these oriental intruders: they were just so untraditional. Besides that, they seemed to wear much faster than Arkansas stones, another reason to mistrust them. But they gave wonderful results. In the coarse grits they cut faster than anything I had used before, and in the fine grits they gave a better finish than any other stone. Why? What made them so effective?

Fortunately, I found a scientist at the National Research Council of Canada who had the two necessary ingredients to help unlock the mysteries: boundless curiosity and tremendous skill in using an electron microscope. As fast as I could provide the stone samples and chisels sharpened on them, he photographed them and helped interpret the results.

Within a year, we had covered the Japanese stones, the Arkansas stones and a wide selection of Western man-made stones, as well as a selection of honing compounds. Many of the mysteries of sharpening stones were unlocked. But how could this information be applied to creating a durable edge of the correct shape? I wish the answers were as straightforward in this area as they are in the field of abrasives, but they aren't. Maintaining the keenness of an edge depends on many factors, the main ones being the technique of the user, the material being worked and the nature of the metal in the tool. All will be dealt with in this book.

The first five chapters cover theory and equipment; the rest of the book deals with various tool groups by category. Throughout, emphasis is on the most effective combination of edge shape and keenness for each tool. Overriding all is the nature of the work required of each tool, because edge shape flows from this requirement.

I hope to convince you that sharpening can be done competently and economically by anyone. You can even make some of your own sharpening equipment. But most important, I hope this book will make your woodworking more enjoyable by removing yet one more barrier between you and mastery of the craft.

CHAPTER 1

THE MEANING OF SHARPNESS

(Photos courtesy National Research Council of Canada)

In the last 2,000 years, Western civilization has used at least three standard references for sharpness. For the first 1,500 years, the standard was a serpent's tooth. As serpents went out of vogue, the expression became "sharp as a tack," a modern equivalent of the serpent's tooth. For the last 100 years or more, both "sharp as a tack" and "sharp as a razor blade" have served as standards in everyday speech. Since there is little call for tools that just puncture wood, both the serpent's tooth and the tack can be set aside as standards in woodworking. The razor blade makes a more useful reference standard.

SHARPER THAN A RAZOR BLADE?

Back in the 1970s, the question of sharpening received a lot of attention in woodworking circles when Japanese water stones were introduced to the West. There had been little new in bench stones since man-made stones had taken most of the market from natural stones some decades before. Debate raged over the effectiveness of these new Japanese stones that used water instead of oil to clear away swarf.

Top left, a standard craft razor blade and a human hair; top right, the same razor blade at increased magnification; bottom left, a Wilkinson Sword razor blade; bottom right, a chisel sharpened on a 6000x water stone then honed with chromium-oxide honing compound. The difficulty of using a human hair for comparison is that it is huge in relation to the details that we want to look at. Accordingly, the photomicrograph showing the hair and craft razor blade is shown at a reduced magnification. If it were shown at the same magnification as the other three, the diameter of the hair would be almost the width of the page. The bar in the bottom right-hand corner of each photomicrograph gives the scale in microns, indicated by the Greek letter µ (1 micron equals one millionth of a meter).

As both an amateur woodworker and a seller of sharpening equipment, I was interested in the new stones and tried out a wide variety of them. I found that they not only cut quickly but that the finer grits seemed to give an even better edge than the natural Arkansas stones that I had been using. But it seemed to me that some comparative standards were necessary to underpin these trial results or it would forever be a matter of opinion.

It occurred to me that a good standard of comparison would be a razor blade. Could you actually sharpen a chisel or plane blade as sharp as a razor? Fortunately, I was able to interest a scientist at Canada's National Research Council in the question. Dr. Peter Sewell, an expert in laser technology, was very skilled in the use of an electron microscope. He agreed to photograph a series of edges sharpened on different stones, both natural and man-made. The results were fascinating.

Early in the game, Peter photographed some razor blades. At the time, Wilkinson Sword razor blades were giving Gillette a hard time in the market, so a Wilkinson blade was photographed as well as one of the standard craft razor blades, the single-edge type suited to freehand use. The photomicrographs of the two blades showed a substantial difference in edge refinement (see the photos on the facing page). The craft blade had a great wire edge that looked like a cresting wave. The Wilkinson blade had a much better defined edge, but even this had a wire edge in places.

And so the fun began. Peter photographed a hair from his head for size comparison, and then he photographed dozens of chisel tips that we sharpened in exactly the same manner on a variety of stones. To minimize the variables, we used chisels of the same type and size that came from a single factory run at Marples. In this manner, we tried to eliminate the effect of different alloys and different hardnesses. To our surprise and pleasure, we found that a number of our test chisels were in fact sharper than razor blades. One is shown here; a greater variety is shown in Chapter 4.

All of this proved that, with basic modern equipment, every woodworker could produce edges sharper than at least the two razor blades photographed. But anyone who has used a razor blade to cut wood knows its limitations. It can be used for incised cuts only; even slight lateral pressure will cause the edge to crumble or even snap the blade. There has to be some relationship between the sharpness and shape for different uses.

THE IMPORTANCE OF SHAPE

Sharpness for a cutting tool could be defined as two surfaces meeting at a line of zero width. That might be fine theory but could result in bad practice. To be effective, a cutting tool not only has to have an edge of zero width, but the angle at which the two surfaces meet must accommodate the intended use of the tool and the material from which the tool is made. The intended use part is straightforward. Most people know what they intend to use a tool for or they wouldn't bother sharpening it. Metallurgy presents a more difficult problem. Seldom do we know the specific alloy of a tool and, even if we did, it would mean little to most of us. But we usually know whether the tool is made of tool steel, high-speed steel, or carbide. These and other categories will be covered in more detail in the chapter on metallurgy (see pp. 18-27), but the vast majority of woodworking hand tools are made of high-carbon tool steels so we will deal only with them for the moment.

Despite the wide variety of tool steels used to make chisels and plane blades (chrome vanadium, tungsten vanadium, D-2, etc.), they all function within a narrow performance band as far as brittleness is concerned, and brittleness is a basic concern when you are shaping an edge.

A razor blade is shaped to cut hair, not wood. The steel can be very hard, very thin and sharpened at a very acute angle. It need only cut small-diameter pieces of presoaked protein. A woodworking chisel made from the same type of steel at the same hardness would need to be thicker (for strength and rigidity) and sharpened at a more obtuse angle; otherwise, it would never withstand the forces that it would be subjected to. We could use exactly the same abrasives on the chisel and get the same keen edge as the razor blade (better, I hope); the only difference would be the angle at the junction of the two meeting surfaces.

This is a roundabout way of leading you back to the proposition that a reasonable definition of sharpness should include not only the keenness of the edge but also the suitability of the shape of the edge considering both the nature of the steel and the intended use of the tool. Therefore, throughout this book the word "sharpening" will be used to describe what are really two different activities—giving the edge keenness and giving it shape.

To illustrate the importance of shape, consider a length of steel with a cross section like an isosceles triangle,

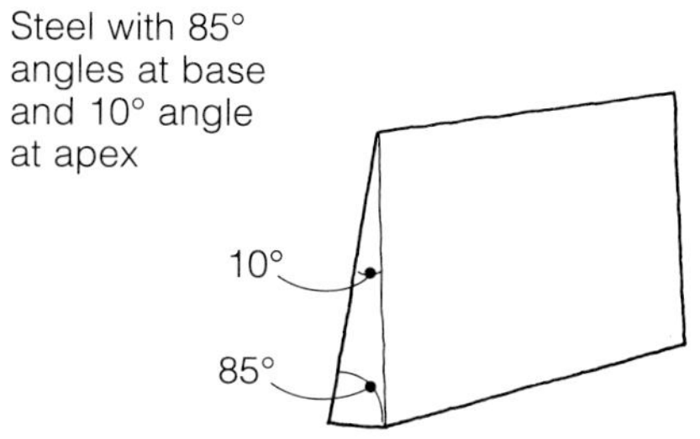

with base angles of 85° and an apex angle of 10°. If all three sides were carefully ground and honed to create three perfect edges, which edge would you least want to have dropped on your finger? The three edges might be equal in keenness but not in effect.

And so it is with woodworking tools; keen edges that do not consider other factors are of limited use.

UNDERSTANDING SHARPENING

To sharpen woodworking tools effectively you have to understand how to shape an edge that will cut cleanly and repeatedly while staying keen. In turn, this requires an understanding of:

- the physics of severing wood fibers (see Chapter 2);
- the strengths and weaknesses of different alloys (see Chapter 3); and
- which abrasives will cut the fastest and still give you the quality of edge you need (see Chapter 4).

With a basic knowledge in each of these areas, you can confidently select and sharpen tools to perform any woodworking task. More important, once you have a grounding in each of these areas, you can get the most value out of your tools. You will select them more intelligently, use them more efficiently and sharpen them more quickly than you did before. You will also use a lot less sandpaper when you get to the finishing stage of any project.

SHAPE AND FUNCTION

Most people ask questions that are impossible to answer when they are in search of sharpening information. One such question is, "How should I sharpen an ax?" The answer depends on how the ax is to be used. If it is going to be used as a felling or notching ax, it would be sharpened one way. If it is for splitting firewood, it would be sharpened another way. But even more basic in this case is the design of the ax. It is impossible to sharpen a felling ax to split wood effectively; the basic shape is wrong. A splitting ax is equally bad for felling. Each ax is shaped for its individual function and does not become interchangeable through any magic of sharpening technique. One is designed to sever fibers and the other to divide them. Their basic shapes reflect these facts (see the photo on the facing page).

If an ax happens to be "dual purpose," it can be biased to perform one function better than the other but it will always lack the core property to perform either function well; it will lack proper body shape. Fortunately not all tools are as intractable as axes. Many general-purpose tools can be shaped to meet a specific need.

So the first consideration in sharpening is always, "Can I shape this tool to do what I want it to do?" To answer that question you need an understanding of wood and how it reacts to a cutting edge, the first of the three basic knowledge areas. Knowing how wood reacts will let you select the most effective edge shape. For example, if you want to shape a chisel to chop mortises in hardwood, you will know that the wood will exert substantial bending force on the tip of the chisel. The bevel angle you select will reflect that knowledge.

But there is no need to extend that bevel angle all the way to the back of the blade. You want a strong edge, a chisel that will not flex, yet a wedge shape as slim as possible so that it will penetrate a reasonable depth with a single mallet blow. If you need a 35°

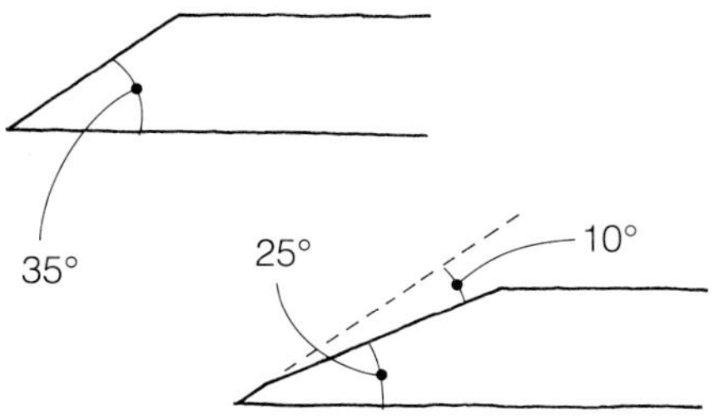

bevel angle to stop edge crumbling or folding, rather than grind the entire chisel tip at 35°, you can grind the chisel at a basic angle of 25° and put a 35° angle on only the last 1⁄16 in. or so. You now have a chisel that holds an edge well, is just a bit more flexible, but penetrates more easily. You have changed the way the tool works. Just how much change you make in it depends on your personal technique and on the metallurgy of the chisel.

METALLURGY

As three quick examples of the importance of metallurgy, consider:

- a traditional Japanese chisel, high-carbon-steel-hardened to Rc62, laminated to a wrought-iron base;
- a high-carbon-steel Western chisel hardened to Rc58-60; and
- a chisel alloyed to reduce brittleness and to increase ease of manufacturing. It might have both chrome and vanadium in significant quantities as well as carbon.

The Japanese chisel will take a wonderfully keen edge but will need a beefy bevel angle (35° to 45°) to prevent crumbling. A high-carbon steel hardened to Rc62 is relatively brittle as woodworking tools go (see pp. 36-37 for a discussion of hardness scales), so the bevel should be continued at the same beefy angle at least to the lamination line to benefit from the damping action of the wrought iron. To a great extent this negates any advantage of a double bevel because the chisel would not be driven into the wood past the first bevel in normal use.

The high-carbon-steel Western chisel will be less brittle at Rc58-60 (and will probably not take quite as keen an edge) but might still need a steep bevel angle for some distance back from the edge to give the edge sufficient strength.

The alloy chisel, being able to flex more without failure, could be shaped for better penetration and still hold its edge. As the three examples show, unless you understand how each alloy type reacts to the forces experienced, it is impossible to design the most effective, yet durable, tip without a lot of experimentation.

BEVEL ANGLES

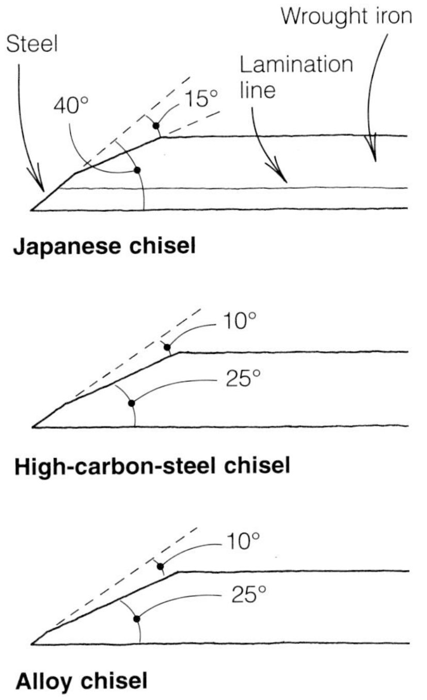

The three axes shown here (from left to right, a dual-purpose ax, a splitting ax and a felling ax) illustrate that there is more to sharpness than a keen edge. Equally important is the basic shape of the tool: the angle at which the cutting surfaces meet must accommodate the intended use of the tool.

ABRASIVES

Finally, to arrive at the desired edge shape efficiently, you need a general understanding of abrasives and the techniques of using them. You want to be able to sharpen quickly, using coarse abrasives for shaping and fine abrasives for honing, but if you use the wrong abrasives or the wrong technique, you could end up with a keen edge that has been fatally flawed in the process of creating it.

The most common error in shaping a high-carbon-steel tool is to overheat it, thereby softening the edge. Regardless of how well you then hone that edge, it will degrade quickly in use. You will have ruined it with your technique. A less common error, but equally damaging, is to use a hard abrasive on a sensitive steel. Traditional Japanese chisels, for example, are among the hardest chisels (at Rc62 or more) that most woodworkers will encounter. They cannot be treated as casually as their Western cousins because they are more brittle. You can actually cause minute fractures in the steel by shaping them on a power grinder or on a diamond bench stone. (In general, only soft stones are used with Japanese chisels.) The edge might appear to be perfect after honing, but the tiny fractures would cause it to chip quickly in use.

So, a definition of sharpness has to include all four factors: the material to be worked, the metal in the tool, the technique of the user and the suitable use of abrasives.

In view of all this, a sharp tool can be defined as one that has a keen edge that will hold its shape in repeated use for a given material and technique while producing a good surface finish on the wood. Throughout the remainder of this book, the themes of tool composition, intended use (both materials and technique) and suitable abrasives will occur repeatedly. That is what sharpening is all about.

CHAPTER 2

THE PHYSICS OF SEVERING WOOD FIBERS

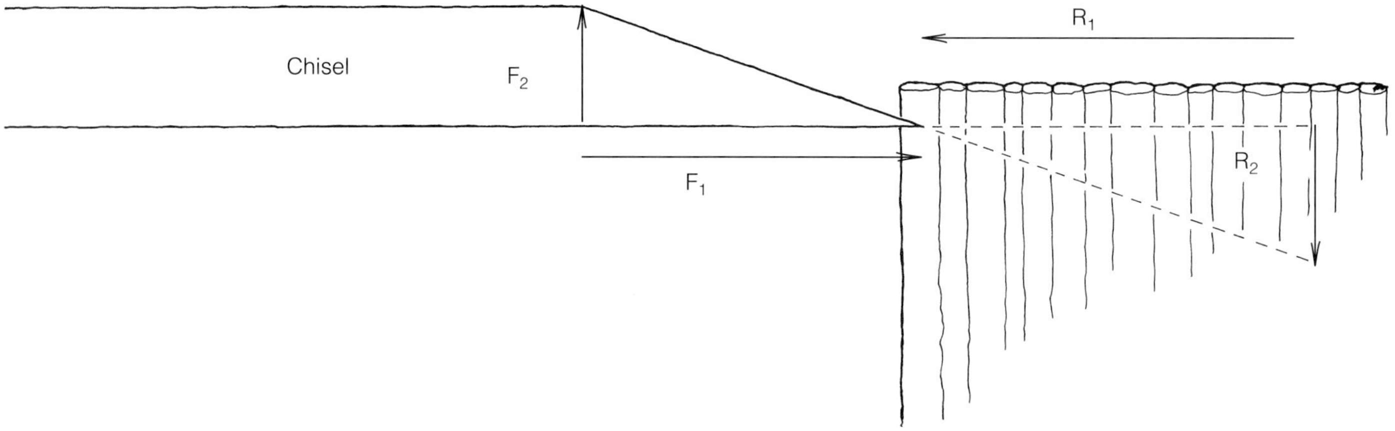

I know. You want to go directly to tool sharpening without having to go through a course in physics. Well, you can do that if you wish, but if you read this chapter you will do a lot better job of sharpening anything that cuts wood because you will understand how wood reacts to cutting tools, dull or sharp.

THE NATURE OF WOOD

For a good understanding of the nature of wood, I can recommend no better book than Bruce Hoadley's *Understanding Wood* (The Taunton Press, 1980). This very readable book is a classic in the field, and a virtual necessity for anyone who intends to do any serious woodworking. The material that follows is an over-simplification of the structure of wood, but it is sufficient to describe the major factors at play when wood and cutting tools interact.

To start the oversimplification, consider wood to be a bundle of straws held together by glue. The straws are cellulose and the glue is lignin. This could be a fairly loose, fragile bundle (like some species of cedar) or an extremely strong, rigid bundle (like cherry). The primary differences between the two are the amount of force required to separate the fibers and how readily the fibers will crush or tear when a cutting force is applied to them.

If you remember your high school physics texts, the assumption was often made that there was zero friction in a process. I'm going to ask you to accept the same assumption now, because taking friction into account at this stage adds many complications without adding much information. Ignoring friction, therefore, the approximate forces at play when you begin to cut end grain with a chisel (see the drawing on the facing page) are as follows:

F_1 = the force required to begin to cut fibers

F_2 = the force required to begin to raise the chip

R_1 = the resistance of cell walls to being severed

R_2 = the resistance of the chip to being lifted

These represent the equilibrium forces just before the wood begins to be cut. As soon as the force applied to the chisel becomes greater than the resistance of the wood, cutting starts.

HOW WOOD REACTS TO CUTTING EDGES

Wood can be cut many ways in relation to both grain and annular rings. The force required for different cuts can be quite different. A landmark study in the cutting forces in woodworking was the doctoral thesis of Eero Kivimaa presented to Finland's Institute of Technology in 1950. Using a knife sharpened to the industry standard of the day and cutting Finnish birch at 12% moisture content, he got the results shown in the drawing below.

Cutting end grain (A in the drawing) requires nearly three times the force that it takes to cut parallel to the grain (B). In turn, it takes more force to cut parallel to the grain (B) than it does to cut cross grain (C). These forces change with different woods and different moisture contents, but the ratios hold well over most temperate wood varieties. Recognizing the difference in these forces becomes as important as the different hardness of the species that we use. We know that it will always take more force to cut end grain than parallel grain or cross grain. Combined with this difference is the different way fibers react as we try to cut the three different ways.

END-GRAIN CUTTING

If we look at the cutting action a bit more closely, we begin to see the relationship between edge shape and what is going to happen to the wood. Consider one fiber being cut. The chisel is a wedge passing through the fiber, virtually prying the fiber apart. As it

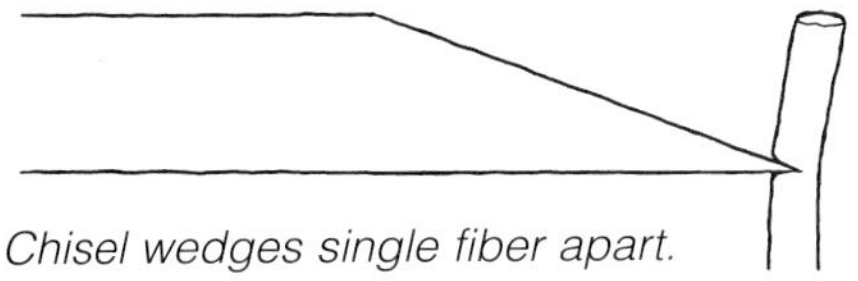

Chisel wedges single fiber apart.

enters the fiber wall, the fiber begins to bend because the chisel is wedging it apart on one side while the other wall is still intact. If the wood is sufficiently elastic it will tolerate this division without tearing. But wood is not very elastic. It can be compressed much more readily than it can be stretched. Even in steam bending, when the fibers are at their most flexible (softened with water and the lignin in a plastic state), most fibers can be extended less than half of one percent before rupturing.

FORCES REQUIRED FOR DIFFERENT CUTS

	Instance 1			Instance 2		
Cutting direction	A	B	C	A	B	C
Main cutting force (F_1) in kgf/cm	7.75	2.90	1.65	8.35	3.15	1.85

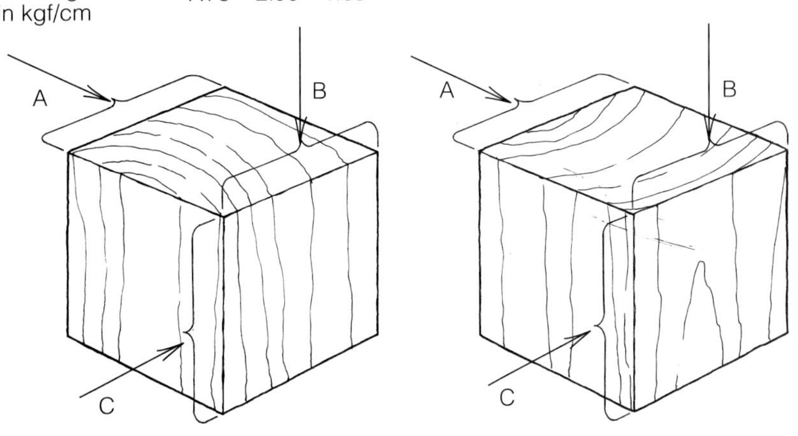

FIELD OF STRESS

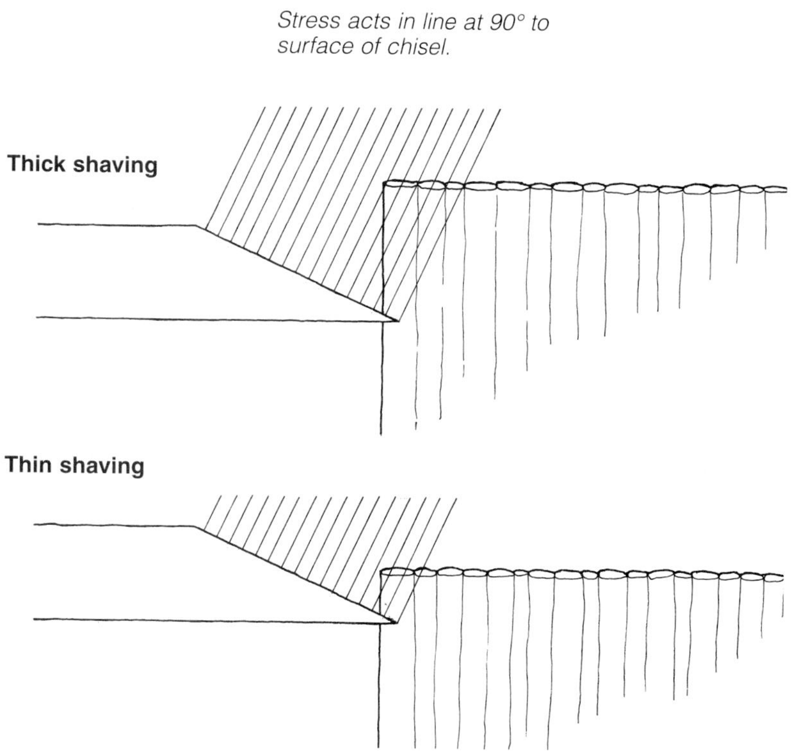

REDUCING INCLUDED ANGLE

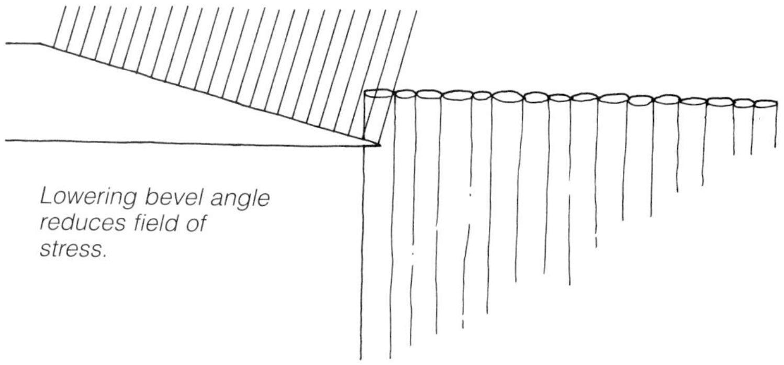

Wet or dry, the stresses at the cutting plane become so great that the fibers begin to tear apart. The phenomenon we like to think of as cutting becomes, if we are lucky, a controlled tearing process. If we are unlucky (and the intent of this chapter is to tell you how to control your "luck"), it becomes a series of uncontrolled tears that can leave a very rough surface.

But the process is actually more complicated than what has just been described. Wood is a bundle of such fibers all glued together with lignin. What we do to one fiber affects the surrounding fibers. If we consider the fiber immediately behind the one being cut, it is being subjected to stress before the blade even reaches it. So is the one behind that. We have a chain reaction affecting a number of fibers.

It quickly becomes apparent that we want an edge shape that will cause the minimum amount of tearing stress as the blade passes through the wood. There are several ways we can reduce the stress.

The most obvious one is to make the wedge more efficient by reducing the included angle (see the bottom drawing at left). Since the bending stress acts in a line at 90° to the surface of the wedge, if we reduce the bevel angle we restrict the field of the stress. In this example, we would reduce the field to a single fiber. This solution would be fine if we had tool steel that would not bend or break at such a low bevel angle, but the practical limit for a chisel is about 15° for end-grain work in most hardwoods. Even though reduction of the bevel angle reduces the force component needed to lift the chip (or, conversely, the resisting force of the wood tending to bend the chisel tip downward), it is not a simple relationship; the practical limit is governed by the thickness of the chip, the nature of the wood and the steel in the chisel. If the bevel angle is lowered too much, the edge will break or fold, effectively dulling the chisel.

A dull chisel creates a whole new set of problems. Fibers start to crush instead of being cut. These immediately create a false edge that is more rounded (duller) than the actual edge. Instead of being severed, fibers flatten and are stretched on both sides of the cutting plane. Highly uncontrolled fiber breaking takes place well below the cutting line. The crushed fibers build up ahead of the edge until the density is increased

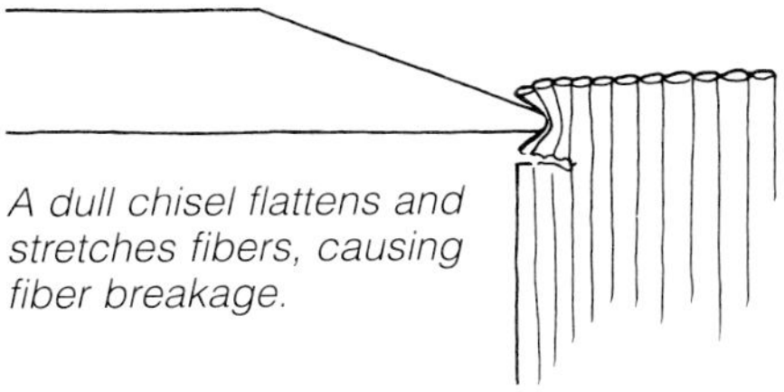

A dull chisel flattens and stretches fibers, causing fiber breakage.

to the point that they are finally severed. The process immediately starts again, and you get a "cheesy" surface that shows this repeated pattern (see the photo at right).

You can do four things to make end-grain cutting easier. First, you can keep the edge of a chisel as keen as possible (see Chapter 6). Second, you can take lighter cuts. When you reduce the chip thickness enough, the telegraphing of stress to adjacent fibers is minimal since the field of stress has been restricted to very few fibers. The chip also breaks more easily since a shorter section of cell wall is involved; it presents less resistance than a longer section. The cut almost becomes like shaving off a series of whiskers, since the shaving breaks very frequently.

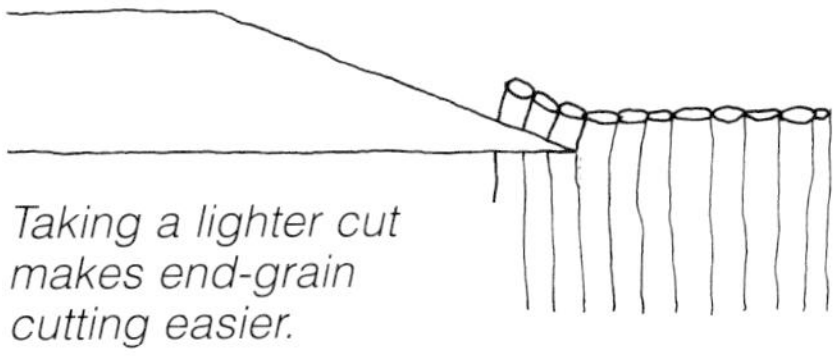

Taking a lighter cut makes end-grain cutting easier.

Third, you can keep the included angle (or bevel angle) of the chisel as low as possible consistent with edge retention. This is a matter of trial and error with a tool. You start with a low bevel angle and increase it only if you get edge failure. The failure is quickly evident by the scratches on the end grain (as shown in the photo at right). Keep increasing the angle by honing at a higher micro-bevel angle (see p. 62) until the edge holds its shape.

Fourth, you can skew the chisel. Instead of cutting directly across the grain, hold the chisel askew the path

The two outer wood samples show the effects of an imperfect chisel edge. The cheesy surface at left was produced by a dull chisel; the scratched surface at right by a chisel with edge failure. The middle sample shows a cleanly cut surface. (Photo by Susan Kahn)

SKEWING THE TOOL

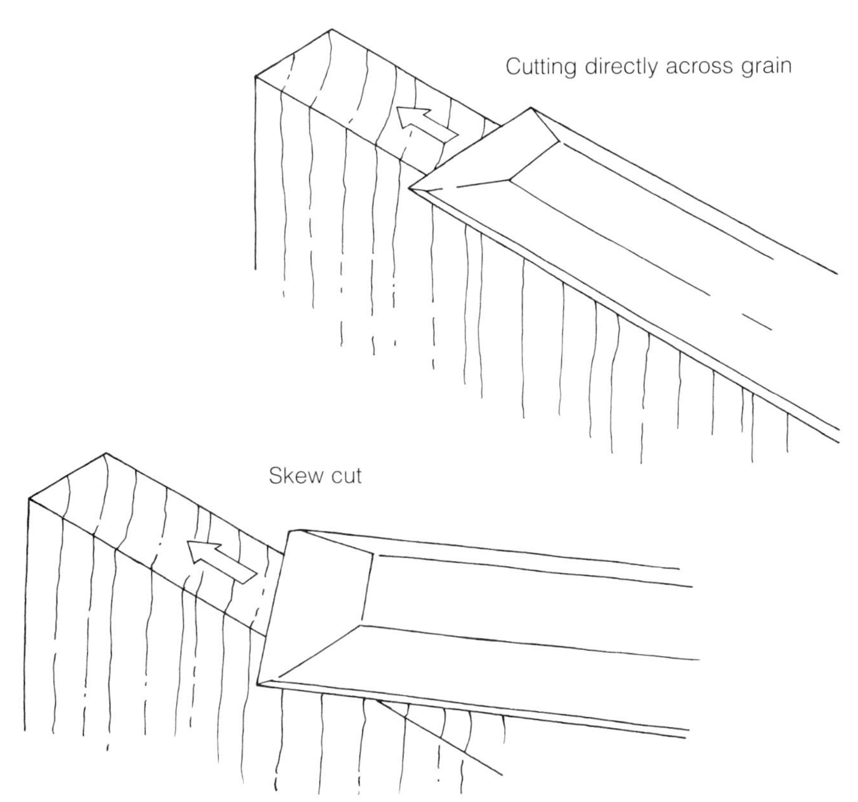

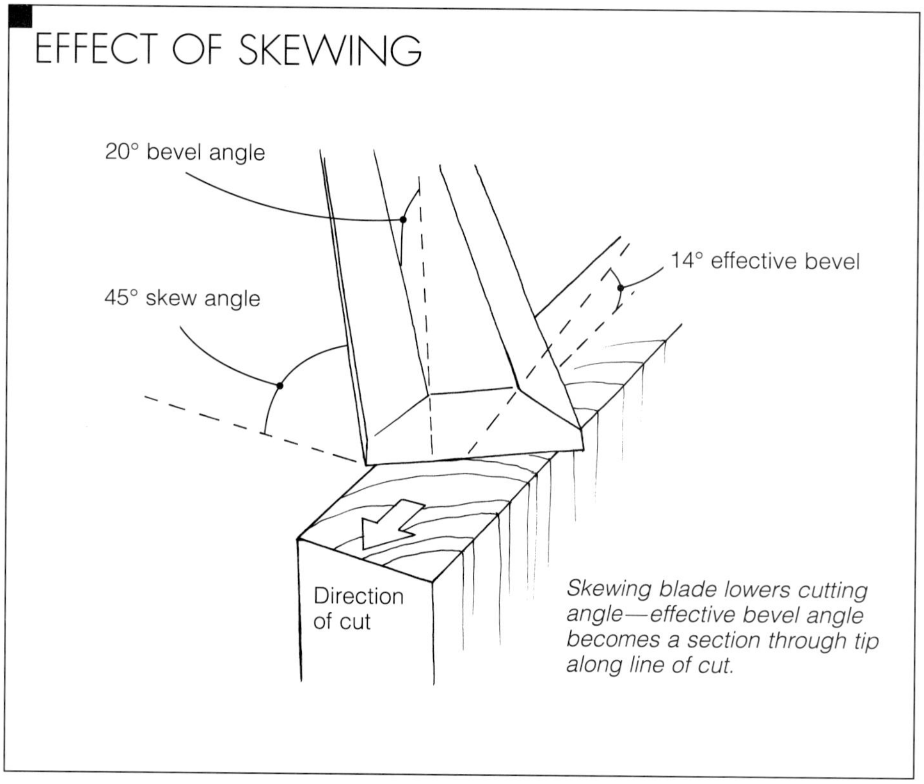

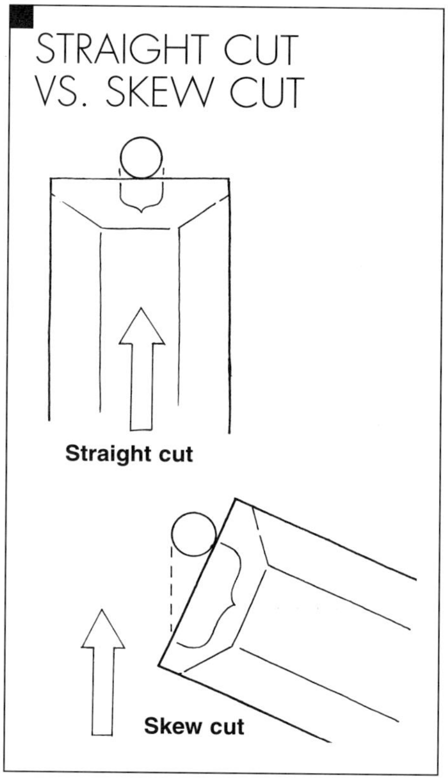

of travel. This has exactly the same effect as lowering the bevel angle, because it lowers the cutting angle. If you have a chisel with a 20° bevel angle, by rotating the chisel 45° and taking a skew cut, you will get the same cutting action that you would if you had lowered the bevel angle to 14° (see the drawing above). If you skewed the chisel even more, say to 60°, you would get a cutting angle of 10°.

But, you may ask, "Why doesn't the edge fail at this cutting angle?" It does not fail because exactly the same amount of distortional force is being applied over greater blade width. Consider the drawing at right above, showing a chisel cutting a single fiber: one cut is square across the fiber; the other is in the same direction, but with the chisel skewed so that the force of severing the fiber is distributed over much more blade.

In the straight cut, the resistance of the fiber to being cut is concentrated on about one fifth of the chisel edge. In the skew cut, the same force is distributed over half of the blade. In fact, there is *less* distortional force per unit of blade length with the skew cut than with the square cut. This leads directly to one of the little-known facts about tool technique—a blade used at a skew can be sharpened at a lower angle than a blade used to cut squarely across the wood, and the skewed blade will still retain its edge. This is part of the magic of the "slicing" cut (see p. 14) that is widely talked about but little understood.

Taken in combination, the above explanation of forces also leads to one of the basic tenets of tool sharpening. A chisel should always be sharpened at the lowest bevel angle consistent with edge retention. Such a chisel will cause the least tearing and leave the smoothest surface in every instance, except when cutting against the grain in parallel-grain cutting.

PARALLEL-GRAIN CUTTING

As we know from experience (and as Kivimaa showed in his study), cutting parallel to the grain is easier on tools than cutting end grain because it takes less force. The reduced cutting force means that the opposing force acting on the tool is similarly reduced. The distortional forces on the tool are lower. But the process is similar. Where we were aiming for controlled tearing with end-grain cutting, we now have to concentrate more on controlled splitting. The objective is always to cut, not split, but the wood often will not cooperate.

First of all, because the forces are more moderate, parallel-grain cutting immediately implies lower cutting angles. But chip formation in parallel-grain cutting is quite different from chip formation in end-grain cutting. There is a tendency for running cracks to develop in the chip, a problem that is

PLANING AND BLADE DIRECTION

When planing with the grain, any splits are above the intended cut line.

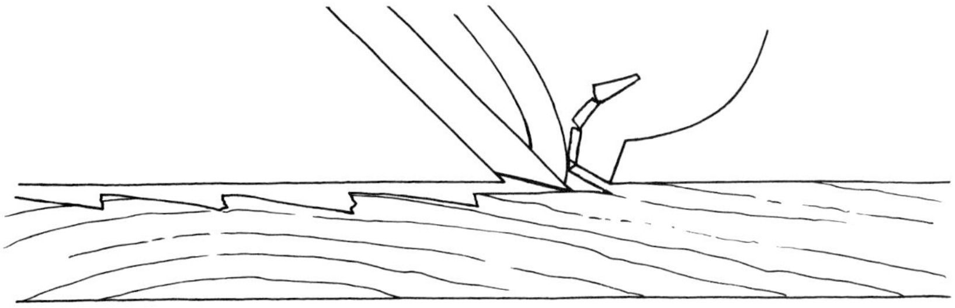

Planing against the grain leaves a jagged surface, because running cracks are below the intended cut line.

not present in end-grain cutting. For this reason, you should always plane "with the grain," that is, when the grain is rising up and away from the direction of cut.

Because parallel-grain cutting is associated more with planes than with chisels, a plane will be used as the cutting tool in this explanation. When you are cutting with the grain, planing is easy. The wood may split in front of the blade but the splits are above the intended cut line and do not cause a problem. The split runs into the waste wood and actually helps chip formation. The shaving comes away as a linked series of broken chips as fibers are cut until a crack develops (see the top drawing above). Then the crack runs out until the chip becomes thin enough that it breaks, or until the shaving is levered up on the cap iron causing the chip to break just at the mouth of the plane. This process is all very easy and pleasant. All you have to worry about is keeping a keen edge on the plane blade.

THE WORK OF DR. NORMAN FRANZ

Most woodworkers take plane-bed angles for granted; it does not occur to them that changing the cutter angle might contribute more to a smooth surface than honing the blade. Nearly 40 years ago, Dr. Norman Franz of the University of Michigan studied how shavings were formed, using a carefully controlled cutting process and a high-speed camera. Among many other things, he found that the type of wood surface generated by planing could be changed by changing the cutting angle. Appendix 1 on pp. 229-234 covers some of the highlights of Dr. Franz's work.

Dr. Norman Franz and his apparatus for recording the process of chip formation.

CHIP BREAKING

A cap iron on a plane is also called a chip-breaker. Cutting against the grain, it is important to break the chip into pieces as short as possible. The longer the chip, the rougher the finish will be because it will break deeper below the cut line. To get the best chip-breaking action, you should:

1. Keep the blade as sharp as possible so that it cuts into the fibers instead of just wedging them apart.

2. Keep the cap iron close to the cutting edge. This forces the most rapid change in direction of the chip, causing it to break sooner.

3. Close the mouth of the plane to just greater than the thickness of the chip to reduce the length of the levered portion of the fiber. The front of the mouth is holding the fiber down and the blade is lifting it. The closer they are together, the shorter the broken pieces will be.

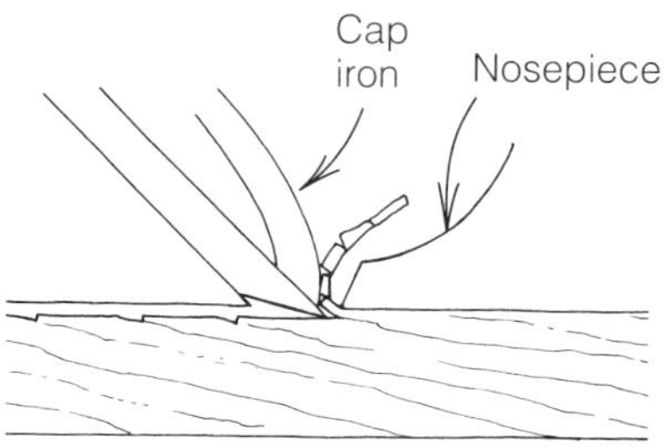

Tight mouth, fine shaving, close cap iron

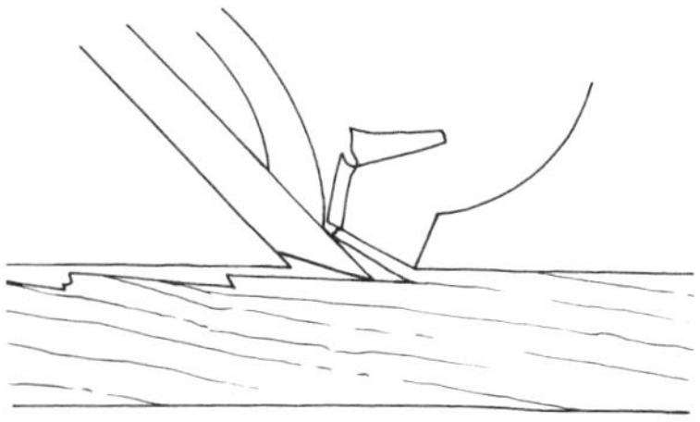

Wide mouth, coarse shaving, cap iron set back

4. Take thin savings. A thin chip breaks more readily than a thick one. It also lets you keep the plane mouth narrower.

5. Where possible, skew the plane.

Since true parallel grain almost never exists in the real world, we can move from planing with the grain to planing against the grain. The transition will be through that very small amount of parallel grain that does exist in real woodworking, associated as it always is with one of the other two types.

Planing against the grain is never fun. Wood fibers are always more willing to divide longitudinally than be severed transversely; as Kivimaa has shown, about three times as willing. As a result, planing against the grain becomes a process of controlling the running cracks that begin at the blade edge and follow the grain to some point below the intended cut line. As the plane moves forward, the chip is pried up by the blade and cap iron until the chip breaks, partially beneath the cut line. The result is a finish with a series of jagged fiber breaks (see the bottom drawing on p. 11). Since it is virtually impossible to plane against the grain and get a silky finish, the objective becomes one of getting the least rough finish possible.

One obvious solution is to close the mouth of the plane so that the chips will break more frequently and leave a smoother rough finish (see the sidebar at left). If the plane has an adjustable nosepiece, it should be brought back so that there is just room for a shaving to pass between the blade and the front of the mouth. If the plane has a non-adjustable mouth, a sheet of brass or soft iron can be fitted under the plane blade to bring the blade forward as far as needed to tighten the mouth (as shown in the drawing above).

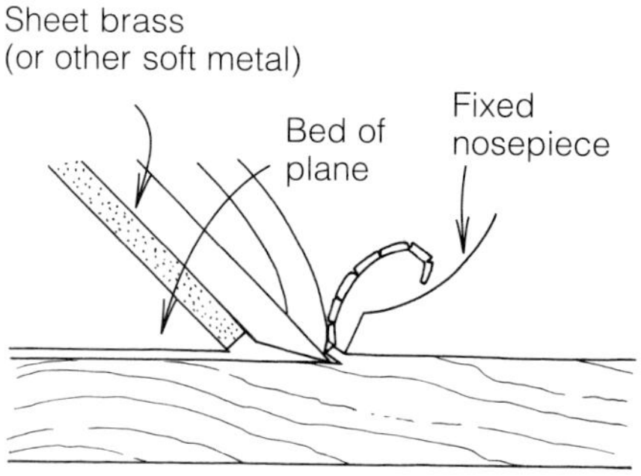

Of course, taking a lighter cut helps as well. The thinner the shaving, the more easily it breaks. Similarly, the thinner the shaving the tighter you can make the mouth of the plane. The tighter the mouth, the more frequently the shaving is broken and the shorter the running cracks will be.

But the best solution is to tighten the mouth, take a light cut *and* skew the plane. By skewing the plane you materially change the forces at work as you sever fibers. Consider how the fibers are arranged when you are planing against the grain. It is really just a variation of end-grain planing. The fibers are at an angle to the surface, not 90° to be sure, but still presenting themselves partially in cross section. A close-up of a portion of the surface would look something like the drawing below. By straight planing you are plucking up the fiber ends, creating the running cracks that are then broken off to create a rough finish. But if you skew the plane, part of the force on the fibers becomes lateral to the grain not in line with it.

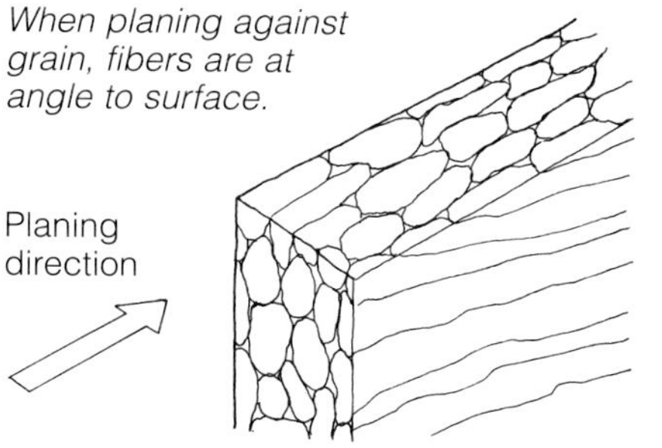

As with the skewed cut in end grain, the force of severing the fiber is distributed over greater blade width, but in this case the fiber is lifted less because it is being forced up a ramp of lower slope (see the drawing on the facing page). The distance A is twice as great as the distance B. The effective cutting angle in the skewed cut is only half the cutting angle in the straight cut, so there is less tendency to create a running crack. More important, the lifting or wedging force on the fiber is now acting at an angle to the grain, not parallel to it. Instead of plucking up the tip of the fiber, the blade enters the fiber from the side, creating a lateral force as well as a longitudinal force.

STRAIGHT CUT VS. SKEW CUT

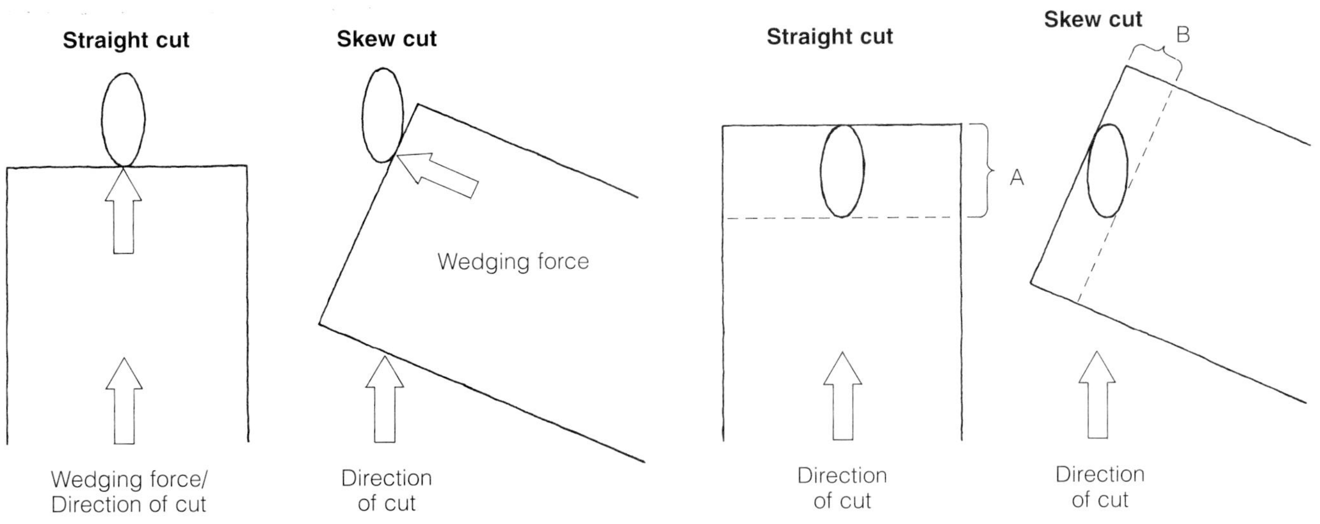

Not only is the fiber not plucked up, as it is in straight planing, but the fiber is actually being held in position by part of the cutting edge as the blade passes through it.

In practice, the forces do not conform to theory as predictably as they do in the other examples given in this chapter. A lower bed angle in the plane is indicated, but as the bed angle is lowered, the relative forces change; there is more compressive force on the fiber and less lifting force. But at the same time, the lower angle encourages fiber separation since it is now reducing the angle at which the fiber is bent. The fiber is less liable to break and more liable to develop a running crack. But the more the blade is skewed to the angle of the grain, the more the splitting tendency is reduced. The forces become lateral to the fiber, forcing it against adjacent fibers rather than lifting it. It requires a great deal of experimentation to determine just when the combination of forces changes in your favor to give a cleaner cut. This is an area requiring much more research (see the sidebar at right).

THEORY VS. PRACTICE

I fell in love with the tight-mouth, light-cut, low-bed-angle theory but found that it did not work as well on wood as it did on paper. This might have been because too little research was done or that it was done poorly. One of the test planes used is shown below. It had an alarming tendency to grain-follow. This could have been for several reasons (e.g. wide mouth, flexible blade, etc.), but even a finely tuned #60½ low-angle block plane showed a similar tendency in certain grain configurations.

To date there has not been an opportunity to do the sort of controlled testing that would indicate whether the theory is flawed or whether it just has limits. Meanwhile, I strongly recommend that you read Appendix 1 on different chip types and keep your cabinet scrapers handy.

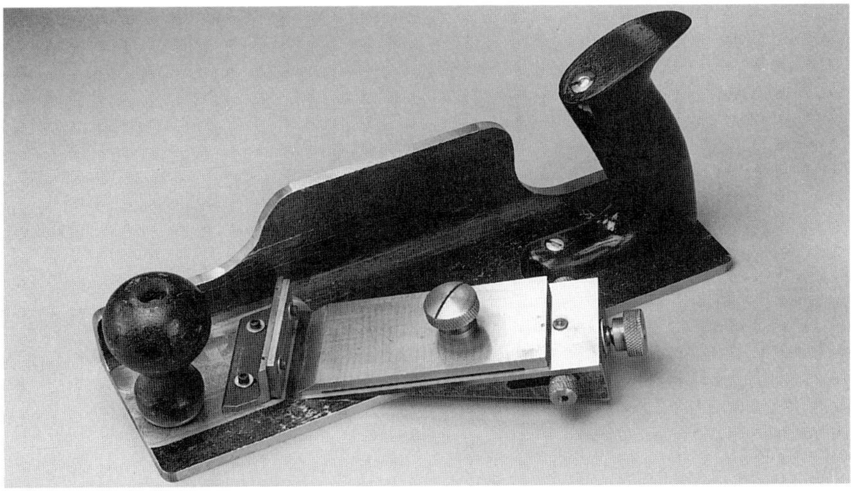

This low-bed-angle plane was developed to test the theory that a skewed blade gives a cleaner cut when planing against the grain.

SKEWED BLADES IN CARVING

There are many instances when skewed blades are used in carving, but often the carver does not realize that it is the change in forces caused by skewing that produces the desired result.

Fred Cogelow, a top North American carver from Willmar, Minnesota, designed a set of skew gouges for working difficult grain. He designed them to allow limited cutting against the grain, since it is nearly impossible to cut with the grain on larger pieces without getting into awkward tool positions or awkward rotation of the piece being worked. As is necessary with skew chisels, the gouges are available in pairs, one left-hand and one right-hand. These gouges, as well as some designs of chip-carving knives, show the direct application of skewed blades to carving.

Making a roll cut with a gouge

For a smooth finish, carvers will often roll a gouge as they push it through the wood. Anyone who has ever carved end-grain basswood knows how effective a roll cut can be. Instead of forcing the gouge directly through the fibers, the rolling action is a dynamic way of skewing the blade, effectively reducing the cutting angle, reducing the force per unit of blade width and reducing fiber tearing. It is not at all obvious, but the roll cut is a skewed-blade cut.

Making a slicing cut with a knife

Using a knife on the same end-grain basswood, carvers know that they get a smoother finish if they draw the knife across the wood with a slicing cut. Once again, the geometry of the skewed blade is at work. Just like the roll cut, the slicing knife cut is exactly the same as skewing a plane or a chisel in use. In this case, the amount of skewing is much greater but the effect is the same.

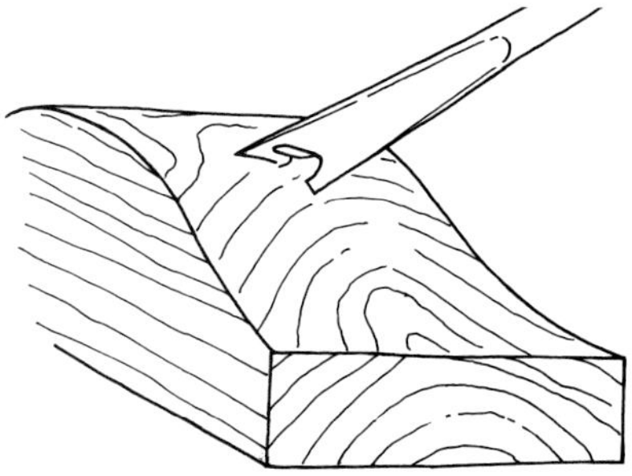

Skew gouge for carving difficult grain

Rolling a gouge has the same effect as skewing a blade.

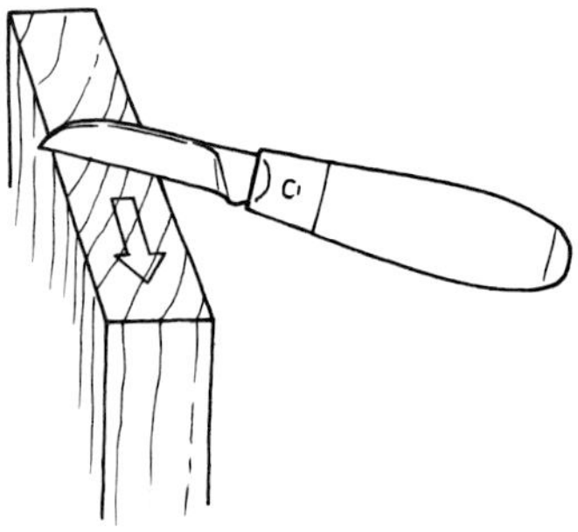

Drawing a knife across the grain with a slicing cut is a method of skewing the blade.

A roll cut (at left on the end-grain surface) produces a much smoother finish than a straight cut (at right).

CROSS-GRAIN CUTTING

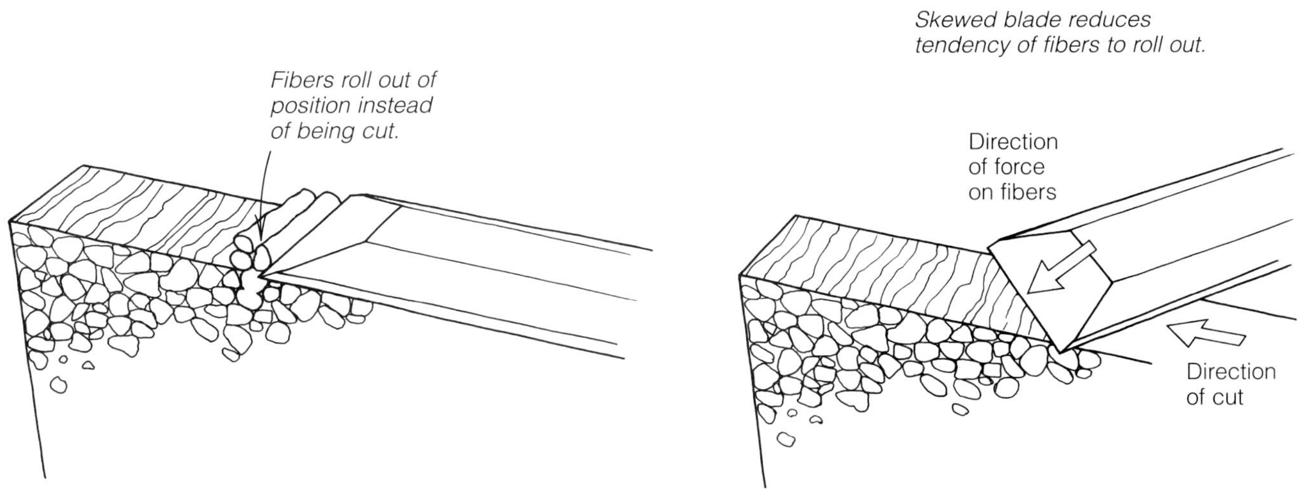

CROSS-GRAIN CUTTING

The results of a skewed blade are much more apparent and much more easily controlled when cutting across the grain. If you have ever tried planing directly across the grain, as you might when making raised panels, you know that there is a tendency for the fibers to roll out of position rather than being cut. The result is a reasonably level but rough finish.

When planing directly across the grain, the plane blade is applying both shearing and lifting forces on a fiber. In fact, the fibers react in groups, not as single fibers. Instead of only a single fiber being sheared or rolled out of position, a bundle of fibers will be affected, breaking away where the cell walls are weakest. When entire groups of fibers break away, the break line often will dip well below the intended cut line; this is the cause of the rough finish.

But when a blade is skewed, not only are the total forces acting on a single fiber or bundle of fibers reduced, but the direction of the forces changes to act partly parallel to the fiber instead of completely transversely. Skewing the blade reduces tearout, but there is also another helpful factor at play. As the blade moves across the wood, the fibers are actually being held in position by one part of the blade while another part of the blade continues to cut them. The smoothness of cut is further enhanced by a tight mouth and a low cutting angle, the same as with end-grain cutting.

But the skewed blade is the most important factor in this instance. It is for exactly this reason that a skew chisel pares tenon cheeks more smoothly than does a square chisel and that panel-raising planes have skewed blades.

CLEARANCE ANGLES: A CASE OF APPLIED PHYSICS

As described earlier, fibers deform a certain amount before they submit to being cut. In the case of end-grain cutting, the deformed fibers tend to right themselves as the cutting edge passes. For this reason, there is always a recommended clearance angle for plane blades (see the drawing on p. 16).

The amount of clearance required is governed by many factors: the nature of the wood, the depth of cut, the sharpness of the blade, whether or not the cut is end grain or cross grain, and so on. You will read and hear all sorts of conflicting advice on appropriate clearance angles for bench planes; I have seen recommendations from as low as 3° to as high as 15°. While I am a fan of low clearance angles because they allow lower cutting angles, I am not going to enter the fray by making a flat declaration that any particular angle is best because there are too many variables at play.

The main factor to consider is that you need enough room to accommodate fiber springback or you will find your plane porpoising in use, making a series of scalloped cuts. Consider an end-grain cut with a low-

TOOL GEOMETRY

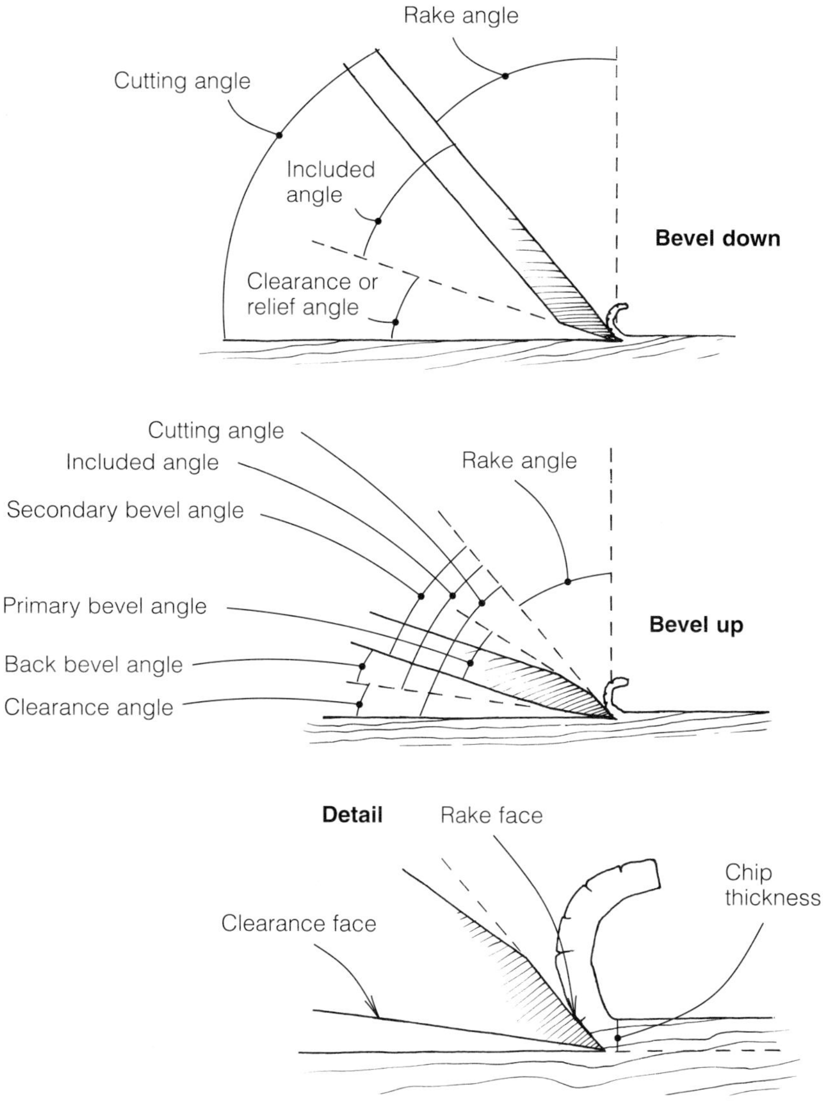

Cutting angle The total included angle of the cutting tip plus any clearance or relief angle. The complement of the rake angle.

Rake angle The angle between a line drawn normal to the cut surface and the rake face of the cutter. Always the complement of the cutting angle.

Included angle The angle formed by the rake face and clearance face of a cutter tip.

Clearance/relief angle The angle between the clearance face and the cut surface.

Primary bevel The basic grind angle of a tool.

Secondary bevel A bevel at a slightly steeper angle than the primary bevel next to the cutting edge. A micro-bevel is a very narrow secondary bevel.

Back bevel A bevel on the clearance face equal to the included angle minus the secondary bevel angle (or minus the primary bevel angle on a cutter that has no secondary bevel).

angle block plane. The fibers are bent forward slightly before they are cut. When they then spring back, they return to a level that is slightly higher than the line of cut (see the drawing on the facing page). A heavy cut increases fiber distortion, causing the fibers to bend more before being cut. When they spring back, they spring back to a higher level than they would with a light cut. For light cuts therefore you can live with a smaller clearance angle.

It is not just fiber springback that causes blade porpoising: Blade distortion contributes to it as well. Just before fibers fail (i.e., are cut), there is maximum stress on the blade. The resistance of the fibers to being cut causes the blade to flex into the wood, essentially taking a deeper cut than intended. When the fibers fail, the blade straightens at the same time as the bent fibers straighten. The two activities are reinforcing in nature.

A related factor affecting the amount of springback is the basic cutting angle. As shown in the drawing on the facing page, the cutting angle is 37° (the 12° bed angle plus the 25° bevel on the plane blade). The reason for developing the low-angle block plane in the first place was to have a plane that had a lower cutting angle than standard bench planes, which are usually 45° (Common pitch) or 50° (York pitch). As shown earlier (p. 8), the lower cutting angle creates less stress on the fibers so they will deform less.

Standard bench planes are all used with the blade "bevel down," so the cutting angle is always the bed angle. But block planes are normally used with the blade "bevel up." This leaves a lot of latitude for tinkering with cutting angles. We don't have to accept some arbitrary cutting angle (like 37°), but can raise it or lower it if we want to.

A lower bevel angle is usually functional for planing many softwoods (cedar, pine, etc.). If light cuts are taken, a good plane blade will support a 20° bevel angle. This will lower the cutting angle to 32°, and cause less fiber distortion and less springback. In many woods this lower bevel angle and reduced springback leaves more than enough clearance at 12°.

FIBER SPRINGBACK

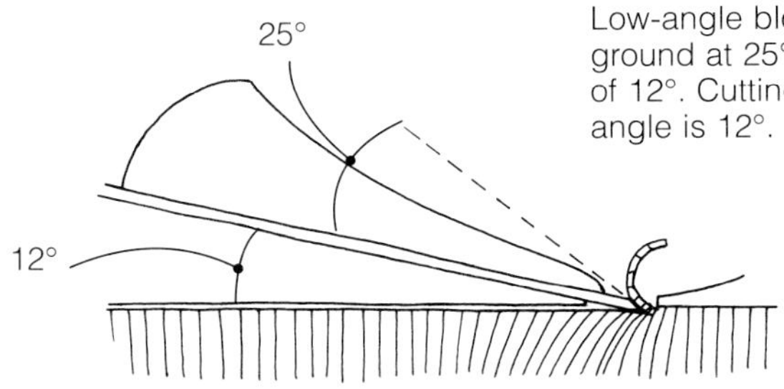

Low-angle block plane with blade ground at 25° and standard bed angle of 12°. Cutting angle is 37°; clearance angle is 12°.

Detail at cutting edge

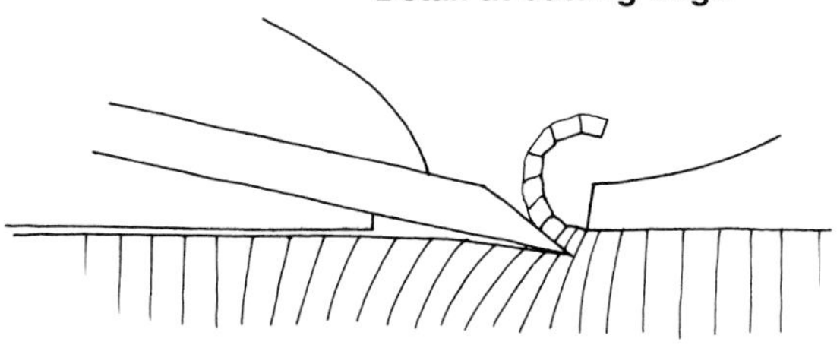

Fibers are bent forward before being cut, then spring back to a level slightly higher than line of cut.

SETTING ANGLES: THE 1-IN-60 RULE

No honing guides currently available readily allow you to put 5° of bevel on anything; the angle is beyond their range. This is not a problem, however. If you want to set an angle of less than 20°, use the basic rule that a 1° angle subtends an arc of 1 unit at a radius of 60 units. The 1-in-60 rule is close enough for many purposes, particularly sharpening at low angles. You'll find that a 10-unit rise in 60 units is about 9½° and a 20-unit rise in 60 units is about 19°.

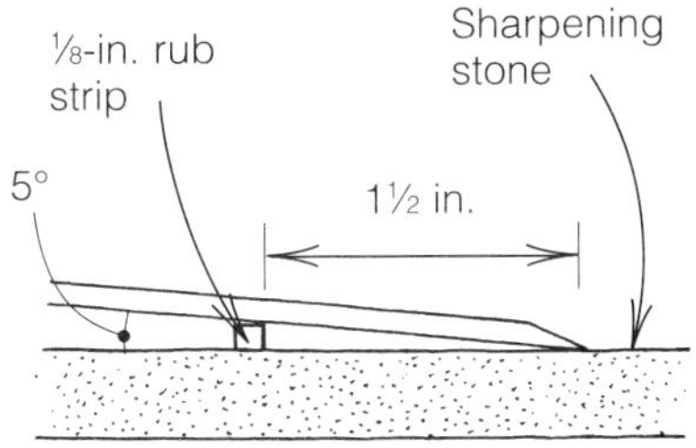

If, for example, you want a 5° back bevel on a blade, simply place a rub strip ⅛ in. thick at a point 1½ in. back from the blade edge. A scrap of steel or even hardwood attached with double-faced tape will serve. Using the rub strip as a guide, you can confidently stone a back bevel on the blade knowing that you are within minutes of 5°. The back bevel does not have to be very wide—somewhere between 1/64 in. and 1/32 in. is fine—but it should be as finely honed as possible.

This rationale automatically leads us to another easy modification. Let's assume that the plane blade is not the best on the market and we experience some edge folding or crumbling at a 20° bevel angle. Rather than increase the bevel angle, we can reduce the clearance angle, not by changing the bed but by putting "back bevel" on the blade. As explained in the sidebar at right, it is a simple matter to put a 5° back bevel on the blade, which will substantially increase edge strength without affecting the forces on the fibers during cutting. All we have done is use some of the unnecessarily large clearance angle.

You will find that you can easily live with this reduced clearance angle on woods that have little springback (any dense, fine-grained hardwood). But on these woods you may find that you may have to beef up the basic bevel a bit to retain your edge. Even if you do, you can still end up with a 5° advantage over an unmodified blade. With a good blade used on softwoods with a light cut you will probably find that you can sneak a few more degrees off the primary bevel onto the back bevel, keeping the total included angle at the edge the same but further lowering your cutting angle.

This whole discussion of relief angles has completely avoided recommending any one angle, because bevel angles and relief angles are a function of what sort of blade you have, what woods you usually work and how aggressively you attack them. With an understanding of the interaction between fibers and the cutting edge, though, this is the typical sort of problem you can solve for yourself, customizing your tools to suit your work. Now, aren't you glad you didn't skip this chapter and go straight to sharpening something?

CHAPTER 3

METALLURGY

Once mankind learned to control fire, the development of metal tools was almost inevitable. Nearly 5% of the earth's crust is iron, and, sooner or later, some tinkerer was going to melt the right rock.

The progression from iron tools to steel tools was more complex. There are many varieties of iron ore in the world, but most of them contain numerous contaminants that would frustrate a tool maker. The principal iron ore is hematite (Fe_2O_3), the ore of the great Mesabi Range bordering Lake Superior. The main contaminants of hematite are oxygen, sulfur, phosphorus, silicon and carbon. Carbon combines with the oxygen, and the addition of lime during the smelting process encourages the sulfur and phosphorus to combine with the slag for easier separation, leaving a reasonably pure cast iron at 3% to 4% carbon content.

But the most historically significant iron ore in the tool business is magnetite (Fe_3O_4). A hard black stone with natural magnetic properties, it is the richest and purest ore. It has an iron content in excess of 60%, is free of sulfur and contains little phosphorus. Although it occurs in significant quantities in Norway and North America, the great magnetite ore body in northern Sweden was the first to be developed, and it was iron from this source that made Swedish steel famous. Iron from this ore, first converted to wrought iron and shipped in that form, also underpinned the fame of Sheffield steel. Modern metallurgical techniques can overcome the problems of lower-grade ores (such as hematite), but the European edge-tool business depended almost exclusively on the pure Swedish wrought iron in the 1700s and 1800s.

WHAT IS STEEL?

Basic steel is a combination of iron with a small percentage of carbon. Mild steel has 0.15% to 0.25% carbon, medium-carbon steel 0.25% to 0.50% and high-carbon steel above 0.60%. Most tool steels are in the range of 0.80% to 1.20%. For centuries, carbon was the only alloying element commonly used with iron. The primary problem in the early days was ridding the iron of unwanted elements, not searching out new ones to add. In common usage, plain carbon steel is not called alloy steel, even though it is an alloy of carbon and iron. The term "alloy steel" is normally reserved for iron with two or more alloying elements (such as chromium, tungsten, etc.).

Iron alone is relatively soft. It does not hold an edge well, wears quickly and has little resistance to bending. But the addition of a bit of carbon to iron has a marvelous effect. The carbon combines with the iron to form hard carbide platelets (Fe_3C) cemented together in a matrix of iron. The combination is resistant to wear and to bending.

Carbon is normally added when the iron is liquid; a melt will be charged with the appropriate amount of carbon (usually in the form of high-carbon steel) for the steel type being made. But early steels were not made by adding carbon to a melt; they were made by a type of case hardening, a process whereby iron bars were packed in charcoal, heated in an airless chamber, and the carbon in the charcoal was absorbed by the iron. The steel had to be packed in an airtight chamber because in the presence of air the charcoal would burn. The iron would also oxidize to form ferrous oxide (FeO). In short, it would rust. Although case hardening is an antique process, it is still often used today when a very hard surface is needed on thin stock that must still retain shock resistance (for example, on beading-tool blades). The unhardened core retains toughness in support of the hardened cutting surface.

SECOND-CLASS STEEL

There is ample evidence that the British colonies had more than "taxation without representation" to be concerned about in the 1700s. Sheffield had an unwritten policy of shipping low-grade steel to the colonies while it supplied domestic manufacturers with the better-quality steel made from Swedish wrought iron. There is also evidence that even the finished products shipped to the colonies contained lower-quality steel. It could just as justifiably have been chisels that were dumped in the Boston harbor that fateful day rather than tea.

MAKING STEEL FROM IRON

Although crude forms of steel have been made for 3,000 years, controlled methods date back only to the 1600s. The earliest controlled method was the cementation method. Swedish wrought-iron bars, interleaved with charcoal, were packed in earthenware boxes, sealed and placed just above a furnace in a tall chimney. The iron was heated to a bright yellow, kept there for a week and then allowed to cool very slowly (to keep it from hardening) for another week. The bars were then cut up, brought to a welding heat and forge-welded together. In this layering process, the uneven carbon content was minimized. Only the very pure iron from the Swedish magnetite ore made this process practical; otherwise, impurities would have ruined the steel.

In 1856, Henry Bessemer built the first furnace that could purify otherwise unusable iron by blasting air through the molten iron to burn off impurities and excess carbon. The price of steel dropped by 75%. The Bessemer process was quickly followed by the open-hearth process (which allowed better carbon-content control) and then the various electric furnaces that contributed to the even finer control needed for alloy steels. The use of tungsten to develop high-speed steel was discovered in 1868; manganese steel was developed in 1888, and stainless steel in 1913.

On many old tools you will find the declarations "Cast Steel" or "Silver Steel." These are leftovers from the early days of steelmaking.

Cast Steel

In the early 1700s a British clockmaker, searching for a better steel for clock springs, discovered that if he took steel made by the cementation method and melted it in a crucible, he had steel of far greater consistency. In essence, by melting it, he ensured that the carbon would be evenly distributed in the steel. In turn, this allowed him to make much more predictable clock springs. They had no soft spots. The process quickly spread among other craftsmen, and steel treated this way became known as "Cast Steel" or "Crucible Steel."

Silver Steel

This mark is most commonly found on old handsaws. One of the most irritating problems with early saws was the difficulty of keeping the steel bright, clean and relatively frictionless in a kerf. Plain carbon steels rust quickly, as anyone who has left a carbon-steel tool outside during a shower knows. The other problem was dealing with the constant trade-off between hardness and toughness. If the blade was hardened to the point that the teeth stayed sharp for an extended time, the steel was usually too brittle, causing the blade to crack or break under stress. When it was discovered that adding a percentage of chromium to high-carbon steel not only increased the hardness and toughness but also gave the steel a bright silvery finish that improved rust resistance, the alloy was quickly dubbed "Silver Steel" by some enterprising vendor. Needless to say, there was no silver in the alloy.

HEAT TREATMENT

Just as critical as the carbon content of steel is the heat treatment it receives. It has to be heated, forged, hardened (quenched) and then partially softened (tempered) in a very controlled manner to ensure fine grain, good distribution of carbides and toughness. In some respects the heat treatment process is more important than the alloy itself.

The same is true in the sharpening of tools. You can have the finest chisels in the world but still ruin them with bad grinding technique. If you overheat an edge when grinding, it will turn blue. The blueness is evidence of two things. First, it indicates that you have burned the thin edge. The heat will have freed the carbon to combine with oxygen. You will now have iron, not steel, at the tip of your chisel. Second, just adjacent to the burned part, you will have annealed a section of the tool, reducing hardness so that it will no longer hold an edge. What you do next is very important. If you ignore the blue band, go ahead and hone the tool, carefully lapping off the blue mark, and pretend that nothing happened, you will be like the majority of woodworkers and will deserve the bad service that tool will give you from that day forward.

If, on the other hand, you quietly remonstrate with yourself for a moment then go back to the grinder and, taking care not to overheat the tool, grind it

TO QUENCH OR NOT TO QUENCH?

As a general principle, quenching tools during grinding is a substitute for good technique. The drawing below shows what happens to a quenched tool.

1. Tool at room temperature before grinding. The thin edge heats and cools very rapidly in comparison to the main blade body.

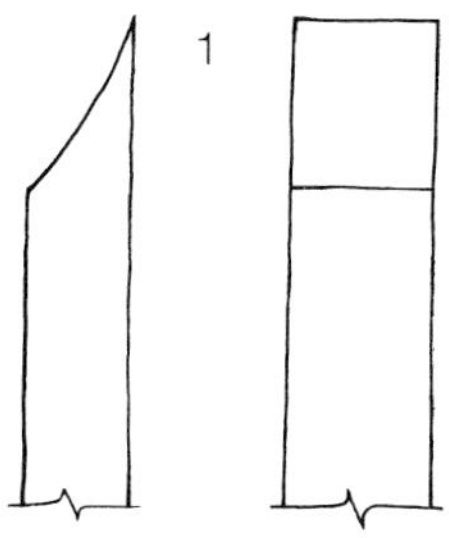

2. As the tool heats up during grinding, it expands.

3. If the metal were perfectly elastic, this is what the tip would look like as it first hit the water and the thin tip cooled more rapidly than the rest of the blade.

4. But metal is not perfectly elastic, and as it shrinks, tiny cracks are created in the edge.

5. When the entire blade has cooled, the cracks may become invisible but they will be there.

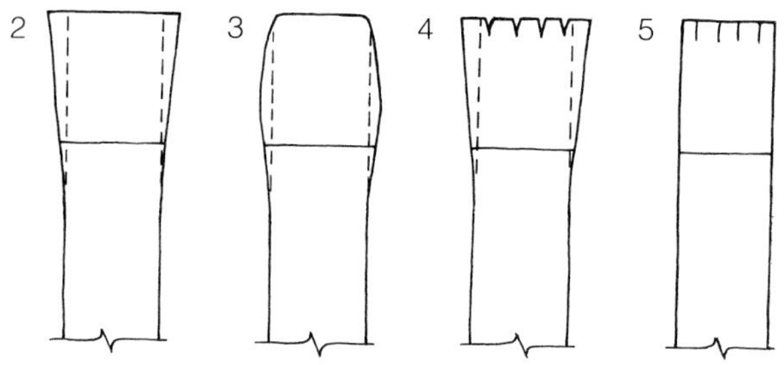

Dotted lines show normal width at room temperature.

ALLOYING ELEMENTS

Chromium
Increases high-temperature strength and shock resistance; increases hardness through formation of chromium carbide; reduces tendency to warp during heat treatment.

Cobalt
Increases red-heat hardness of high-speed steel; refines the grain; increases tensile strength.

Manganese
Increases hardness, tensile strength and resistance to wear.

Molybdenum
Increases hardness and tensile strength; makes steel easier to machine.

Nickel
Increases toughness, hardness and corrosion resistance.

Silicon
Increases hardness, tensile strength and elastic limits.

Tungsten
Refines the grain; increases heat, wear and shock resistance as well as tensile strength.

Vanadium
Used only in combination with other elements (often chromium) to increase hardening ability, refine grain and resist softening on tempering.

back to sound steel, you will have grown immeasurably as a craftsman. While I may have mildly overstated the case, there is no question about what you should do with a burned tip. Be brave, take the extra ten minutes to grind out your error, and learn from your mistake.

ALLOYING ELEMENTS

You will frequently see tools that are marked with the main alloying elements. For example, a chisel might have "chrome vanadium" or "tungsten vanadium" etched on the blade. Without getting into the endless arguments about the qualities of different alloy steels, some of the reasons for adding various elements besides carbon are presented in the chart at right above.

Obviously there is considerable overlap in alloying characteristics. In addition, the percentages used are interdependent. Two or more of these alloying metals could be used in carefully controlled ratios to impart special qualities. Equally important, the optimum qualities of any alloy can be realized only if the heat treatment is carefully controlled. More than one craftsman has made bad furniture from perfectly good lumber. So it is with steel; only competent treatment of the alloy will result in a good tool.

THE SPARK TEST TO IDENTIFY METALS

When there were few alloys on the market, a spark test was a quick and accurate way to identify iron and basic steel types. With the hundreds of alloys now used in tools it is much less reliable, but it can still be used for rough classifications in many instances. It is still an effective testing process with older chisels and plane blades. The spark patterns shown are those that would be generated by grinding a tool on a powered dry wheel.

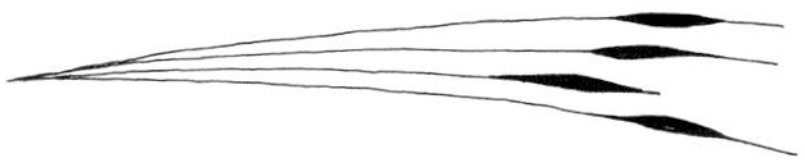

Wrought iron
Long yellow streaks, becoming leaflike in shape before expiring

Mild steel
More variety in streak length, with smaller leaves and some sparking

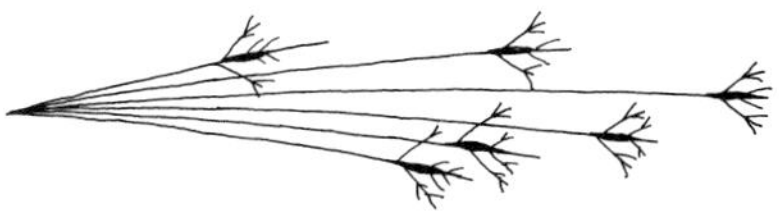

Medium-carbon steel
Almost no leaf, some forking, great variety of streak length, sparking nearer the wheel

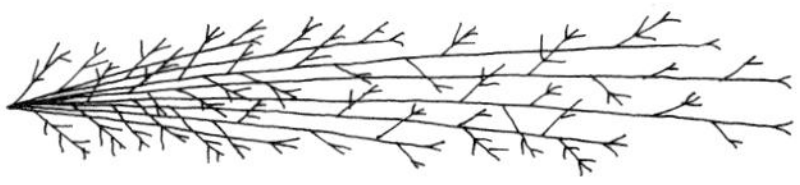

High-carbon steel
No leaf, bushy spark pattern, forking and sparking starting very close to the wheel; less bright than medium-carbon steel

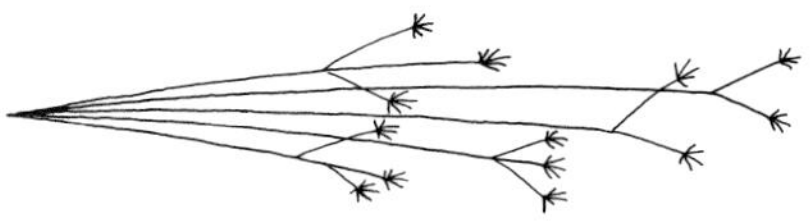

Manganese steel
Small leaf before streaks fork to form sparks

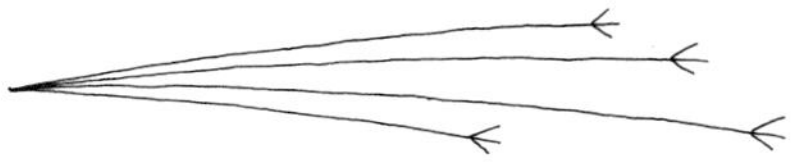

High-speed steel
Faint red streaks forking at the tip

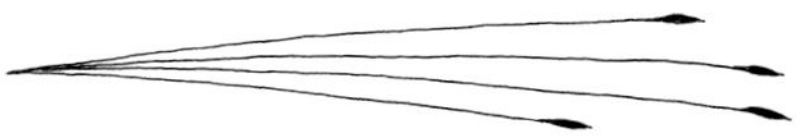

Stainless steel
Bright yellow streaks with a small leaf end

ALLOYS OF PARTICULAR INTEREST TO WOODWORKERS

Of the thousands of alloys in everyday use, only a few dozen are of specific interest to woodworkers. And of these few, some of the key ones are not steel but more modern metals developed to make edges as durable as possible.

High-speed steel (HSS) Alloys that will cut at high speed and high temperatures are particularly valuable in motor-powered cutting tools like drill bits. When it was discovered that tungsten alloys were air hardening (i.e., they required no quenching), the use of these alloys quickly spread to tools requiring "red-heat" strength. Typical tungsten alloys are T1, M1 and M2 (see the chart on the facing page).

Such high-speed steels are more costly to make and to machine than plain high-carbon steel, but they are truly the woodworker's friend. They are tough, durable and forgiving. Every time you remove a high-speed-steel bit from a scorched hole in a piece of cherry, you should be thankful that modern metallurgy has triumphed over your bad technique. The bit lives to cut again. A carbon-steel bit would have to be tossed.

Just as all tool steels are not created equal, neither are high-speed steels. There is a continuing trend to the use of high-speed steel in woodturning tools, but the difference in alloys is substantial. Some tungsten-based HSS tools have as little as 8% tungsten, others 18% or higher. In general, higher tungsten content reduces wear in use. This means longer periods of time between sharpenings.

Stellite Stellite is not a steel alloy, since it has no iron in it. A typical stellite composition is:

Cobalt	50%
Chromium	33%
Tungsten	10%
Molybdenum	5%
Carbon	2%

Tantung "G" has similar ratios of these elements and also includes up to 1% iron and 2% to 7% columbium. Extremely wear-resistant, both stellite and Tantung "G" are used in cutting tools and for other surfaces where wear resistance is important. Some high-quality knife-sharpening steels are made from stellite. This is a case where terminology has been overtaken by technology: There is no steel in a stellite "knife steel."

Tungsten carbide Tungsten carbide (which is strictly a compound, not an alloy) is increasingly important in woodworking tools as woodworkers look for tools that will hold an edge indefinitely in difficult conditions. Fine powders of tungsten carbide and cobalt or nickel are mixed together with binders, heated and hydraulically pressed into molds of various shapes. The shapes can vary from the tiny balls in the tips of ball point pens to the solid rods used to make some router bits.

Like steel, there is a near-infinite variety of tungsten-carbide compositions. Other components such as titanium carbide and vanadium carbide can be added to the mixture to achieve shock resistance, machinability, and so forth. The trade-offs are usually between the hardness and wear-resistance characteristics and the resistance to shock. Developments are so rapid in this field that it would be futile to describe the various compositions; they are superseded almost monthly by ever more versatile composites that have finer grain structure, greater shock resistance and lower price. At one time, a rough rule of thumb was that edge-durability ratios of plain high-carbon steel to high-speed steel to tungsten carbide were 1:10:100, but these ratios become a rougher measure every day. For example, the new micro-carbides with very fine grain structure and as little as 3% cobalt can outlast regular tungsten carbide in some cases by a factor of 10. (See Chapter 14 for more detail.)

Much as with steel, it is possible to make a poor-quality tungsten carbide cheaply; high-quality carbides are more costly. While price is never a wholly reliable guide, it is one of the few indicators you can use in this field unless you are willing to make a detailed study of the subject.

Stainless steel Most woodworkers do not appreciate how quickly rust can degrade an edge. Even when no rust is apparent to the naked eye, it can be quietly destroying a good edge (as shown in the photo above). The only place most woodworkers will come across stainless steel is in some carving knives (for example, sloyd knives). Even there, it is sometimes used to clad a steel core rather than being used for the cutting edge itself.

Makers of kitchen knives are particularly concerned about rust because knives are used to cut high-acid materials (fish, citrus fruit, etc.) that aggressively attack steel. One of the

ALLOYING ELEMENTS FOR HIGH-SPEED STEEL

	T1 Tungsten	M1 Molybdenum	M2 Molybdenum
Carbon	0.72%	0.80%	0.82%
Manganese	0.25%	—	0.25%
Silicon	0.25%	—	0.25%
Chromium	4.00%	3.75%	4.25%
Tungsten	18.25%	1.50%	6.25%
Vanadium	1.15%	1.15%	1.90%
Molybdenum	—	8.75%	5.00%

Although this blade looked mirror-bright to the naked eye, rust had started to form and was visible as bulbous clusters under an electron microscope. (Photo courtesy National Research Council of Canada)

Top: These Japanese plane blades clearly show their structure. A thin layer of steel has been welded to a much thicker layer of wrought iron. The unused blade at right shows the typical hollow grind of a Japanese blade. (Photo by Susan Kahn)

Above: The weld line on the ax at left is clearly visible. The ax at right has been whacked on the poll one too many times, distorting the cheek and causing the iron/steel weld to fail on one side. Both are turn-of-the-century heads.

favorite alloys of knifemakers is 440C stainless. It has six alloying elements:

Carbon	1.00%
Manganese	0.50%
Silicon	0.40%
Chromium	17.50%
Molybdenum	0.45%
Nickel	0.20%

When a tool-steel alloy has a chromium content greater than 10% (and usually less than 18%) it is referred to as "stainless." In fact, it is not stainless, only stain resistant. Over time, any stainless tool steel will rust to some extent. The time required is just much greater than it is for plain carbon steel.

Laminated steels Brought to welding heats, steels of different compositions (or iron and steel) can be welded together with pressure. Traditionally this was done by a blacksmith. The materials would be brought to welding heats at the forge, one metal would be placed over the other on an anvil and struck with a hammer to merge them. Before steel became a mass-produced product, most edge tools had steel edges and wrought-iron bodies. The price of steel dictated that it be used only where absolutely necessary in a tool.

There were advantages to this process. In plane blades, for example (or plane "irons" if you prefer, a term that indicates their origin), the iron backing dampened vibrations. The dead blade improved performance, reducing chatter in use. With axes, a worn cutting edge could be replaced, regenerating a tool that was otherwise sound. Tips of plowshares could be replaced with the same economy.

But the greatest advantage of the process was that an alloy that was ideal for a cutting edge (hard, wear resistant but probably brittle) could be limited to that part of the tool. The rest of the tool could be made from a material more suited to the structural strength required.

The process has been widely used in Japan for centuries and is still in use today. Traditionally, Japanese chisels had wrought-iron bodies with steel faces. They are still made that way today, although mild steel is used more often than wrought iron.

A JAPANESE BLADE MAKER

There are still a number of traditional plane-blade makers active in Japan, although mechanized methods have supplanted most of them. Some of these blade makers have been classified as national treasures, the embodiment of history.

Their workshops are invariably small with a tiny furnace/forge in one corner and a low-mounted anvil on a block of wood in the center. The other necessities of the craft are within easy reach of the craftsman, who usually sits on a small pillow by the anvil.

The shop arrangements vary, but the one constant is that you are sure to find a huge ship's anchor or length of anchor chain just outside the shop. Wrought iron, with its excellent rust resistance (because of the incorporated slag filaments), was prized for anchors and anchor chain. The old anchors and chains are now raw material for blade makers. It is hard to think of a more awkward form for the raw material. When the craftsman needs wrought iron, he has to hack it from a giant anchor weighing several tons or from a chain link that can be 5 in. thick. There is much to be said for the infinite variety and shape of rolled stock available to today's Western blade maker.

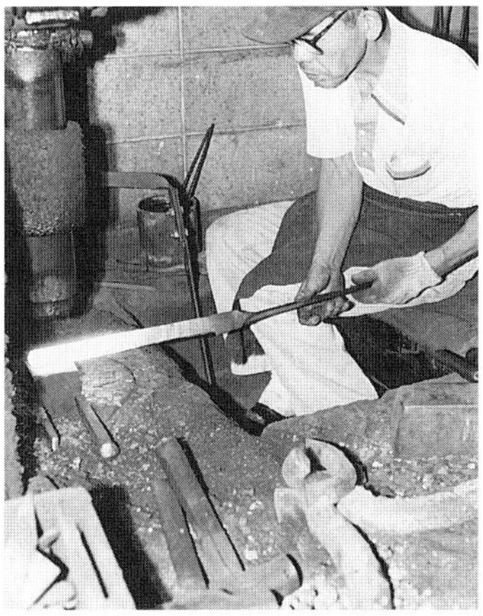

SEMI-MODERN CHISEL MANUFACTURING IN JAPAN

Iyoroi chisels are among the best made in Japan. They are manufactured in a small factory on a farm near Miki City. The owners, Mr. Iyoroi and his wife, live in the farmhouse near the factory. When three of us came to see the factory one day, Mr. Iyoroi, a gentle and slightly formal man, then in his 80s, welcomed us and suggested that we first see the plant and then have tea with him and his wife. As we left the house, he took us on a short side trip to a small outbuilding to see if the family duck had laid an egg that day. It had, and we took the egg back to the house before continuing the tour of the plant.

The inside of the plant was the Japanese equivalent of a Dickensian workhouse. Workmen squatted next to completely unguarded grinders with open pulley drives. The air was filled with the noise and dirt of industry. About a dozen men were engaged in the various processes of chisel making.

Steel rod was being cut, heated, forged, hammered, shaped and ground. But the most remarkable operation of all was the process used to incorporate the steel face in the laminated chisels. Forged chisel blanks were heated white hot at the tip, a sprinkling of flux was put on the recess for the steel blank, then a workman holding the hot blank in a pair of tongs with one hand would place the steel bit on the flux with his other (bare) hand. The bit and blank were then put in the open-faced furnace to bring the bit to a welding heat (somewhat lower than the blank), then forged together on an anvil with a few heavy blows followed by a series of tune-up taps on the sides and faces. The worker's thumb and the two adjacent fingers of the hand used to place the steel bit on the blank had only vestigial finger nails. The tips of the fingers had been killed back from years of exposure to intense heat whenever he placed a steel insert on a chisel blank.

Returning later to the house, we had tea, Mr. Iyoroi thanked us for our visit, and gave each of us a beautiful set of boxwood-handled carving tools made in his factory. No tools that I own today bring with them more vivid recollections in use than those carving tools.

Mr. Kozo Iyoroi. (Photos this page by Shiro Tanaka)

SPECIAL PROCESSES

In the search for ever longer tool life and more time between sharpenings, some unusual processes are being used to influence tool wear. These include supercooling, impulse hardening, laser hardening, titanium-nitride coating, diamond coating and magnetic fluxing.

SUPERCOOLING

Although little discussed today, in the 1980s there was great interest in the effect of supercooling on tools. Drill bits, saw blades (particularly saw chain) and even chisels and plane blades were being treated by supercooling. Some wild claims have been made about the effects of supercooling, but there is evidence that it was effective in many instances. Much like the proponents of the magical power of pyramids, however, the supercoolers often asked people to take the process on faith.

The known effect of supercooling is that it can convert austenite to martensite. Since martensite is much harder than austenite, supercooling can improve both the strength and wear characteristics of an alloy. For it to work, however, there must be austenite present in the first place, which is not the case with all tools. It has proved to be most effective with stainless-steel alloys where austenite is normally present.

AUSTENITE AND MARTENSITE

For several reasons, I have consciously avoided describing the exact chemical and physical transformations that take place in steel alloys during heating, hardening and tempering. The first reason is that it is difficult to explain succinctly. The second is that the process is tangential to woodworking; even if you knew the process intimately, it would have little practical application in a woodworking shop.

But having used two terms that are explained nowhere else in the book, I owe you some explanation of them.

Steel is heated to an austenitic state so that the carbon and other alloying elements become dissolved and can permeate the structure. The purpose of quenching is to convert austenite into much harder martensite. To maintain fine grain structure, quenching often must be done at a rate that leaves some austenite in the steel.

Cold treatment, sometimes as little as -76°F (-60°C), can convert the remaining austenite to martensite. The process is particularly effective with stainless alloys that have a high chromium content.

IMPULSE HARDENING

Most commonly used on jigsaw blades and handsaws, impulse hardening is a localized hardening process that hardens only the part of the tool that experiences wear. It is possible to make saws with very hard teeth (Rc60-70) while leaving the body at Rc40-50 as required for toughness. In conventional impulse hardening, a saw blade (hand, jig, band, etc.) is induction-heated and then immediately quenched with a blast of air or water. The impulse can be from 1/10 of a second to 5 seconds, and the hardening depth ranges from 0.020 in. to 0.100 in. There is usually some distortion involved.

A more sophisticated process using very high frequency pulses for much shorter times (1 to 100 microseconds) permits greater localization and shallower penetration (0.002 in. to 0.020 in.), still yielding extreme hardness on the wear surface but a softer and tougher core. It can be done with virtually no distortion.

You can usually tell which process has been used by the amount of discoloration of the blade. With high-frequency pulsing, only the top half of a tooth will be discolored. In regular impulse hardening, the entire tooth and a strip of the saw body will be discolored.

An interesting sidelight of the very high frequency process is that the steel can be heated so rapidly and in such a thin layer that it also becomes self-quenching. There is no need for a blast of air or water because the adjacent steel mass rapidly cools the heated film. The cooling can be so rapid that the film is not really a solid but a super-cooled liquid. The rapidity of the process prevents crystal growth and the layer is homogeneous, quite different from ordinary steel. It can be as hard as Rc70 and very resistant to wear. The process is roughly comparable to making plate glass. which is also a super-cooled liquid, not a solid.

Done well, impulse hardening can create very fine grain steel that can outlast conventionally hardened blades by a factor of 5 or more. It is a standard process now with most bandsaw-blade makers.

Impulse-hardened teeth are not usually intended to be resharpened (although it can be done with diamond files) because sharpening can remove the hardened surface, particularly in the case of high-frequency pulsing.

LASER HARDENING

Very controlled hardening of steel can be done with lasers. Unlike impulse hardening, which requires induction coils to be shaped to fit either side of the tool tip to be hardened, a laser beam can be focused on any surface, anywhere. By controlling the beam energy and duration, very precise hardening is possible. Much like high-frequency impulse hardening, lasers can be used to create very localized films of super-cooled liquid steel.

TITANIUM-NITRIDE COATING

Cutting tools are often surface-coated by a physical or chemical vapor-deposition process that creates a hard surface film. Titanium nitride is one such finish. It is particularly effective in metal cutting since it reduces the crater wear caused by the chemical interaction at the high-temperature interface of the tool and the material being cut. For woodworking tools, it is effective for its other properties, which are its hardness (30% or more greater than high-speed steel at Rc62) and its very low coefficient of friction.

DIAMOND COATING

For decades diamonds have been used on the tips of various tools, drills in particular. They were sometimes imbedded in a softened tip (so that they looked like chocolate chips in a cookie) and sometimes held in place with a metallic coating. Both processes required relatively large diamond crystals to be effective.

Currently researchers are working on a new diamond-coating process that holds much promise for woodworking. The process is one whereby diamonds are cultured right on the cutting tool. The crystal formation can be controlled so that crystals are aligned (adjoining and abutting), to create a virtually continuous smooth film. The different coefficients of contraction and expansion between the diamonds and the substrate have yet to be overcome, but a ceramic substrate is showing promise. It is probable that such diamond-coated router bits will be available at competitive prices in a very short time.

MAGNETIC FLUXING

Magnetic fluxing involves placing a tool (usually a cutting bit) in a small chamber that is bombarded with pulsed waves of magnetic energy. The tool actually vibrates momentarily until it is stress relieved. Increased tool life from the process has ranged from 30% to nearly 200% as reported by users.

The process is based on the principle of magnetostriction—the change in length of a ferromagnetic material when it is magnetized. The crystalline structure of steel is a latticework of separate magnetic dipoles; as the tool is magnetized, the dipoles are aligned causing the material to grow or shrink slightly. The rapid fluxing (developed by Innovex of Hopkins, Minnesota) changes the magnetic field unequally in the tool. The process begins at the surface and then permeates the tool, a sort of tidal wave of magnetostriction, creating shear forces within the tool that serve to equalize concentrations of residual stress. The process is similar to work hardening.

An interesting sidelight of this process is that some cutting-tool users have long recommended magnetizing tools because it increases the modulus of elasticity of the tool, extending its life. So whether or not you give your cutting tools the high-tech treatment, you may want to use a simple electromagnet to magnetize them for the benefit that the process gives. For tools like twist drills that will be used for cutting iron or steel, it is not a good idea since it causes chips to cling to the tool. However, for drilling non-ferrous metals or for woodworking, it would not cause this problem.

CHAPTER 4

ABRASIVES

The search for abrasives parallels the development of man's metallurgical skills. Before iron was discovered man had little need for abrasives. In the Stone Age, the best edge tools were made from flint, which was chipped to form a sharp edge. In the Bronze Age, tools made of copper and copper alloys were beaten to the required edge; this was readily done because they were malleable. To resharpen, the tools were hammered into shape. But iron tools (and later, steel) required some abrasive method of refining a forged edge and restoring it again after dulling.

Two water-bathed natural-sandstone grinders. The smaller one at right is a typical 'settler's' wheel, later featured in early Sears catalogs. The treadle-operated wheel has a well-designed stand with a splashboard and a hook-and-eye connection for the water trough so that it could be easily emptied after use.

NATURAL VS. MAN-MADE ABRASIVES

For most of modern history, only naturally occurring abrasives such as sandstone were used to sharpen tools. Only in the last hundred years have man-made abrasives come into common use, and only in the last fifty years have they been predominant.

Historically, abrasives for sharpening came in two basic forms: grinding wheels and bench stones. The wheels came in all sizes but in one predominant shape, a transverse section of a cylinder. Bench stones were most commonly rectangular slabs but also included dozens of specialized shapes for sharpening tools other than chisels and plane blades. The shapes and their uses will be covered in Chapter 5; in this chapter, the abrasive particles themselves will be examined.

BENCH STONES

Although natural grindstones have been supplanted by man-made stones almost universally at both lower cost and increased efficiency, the replacement of natural bench stones has been slower and more grudging. Partly this is for reasons of tradition and partly it is because the advantages of man-made bench stones are not as clear-cut as they are with grindstones.

There is not much argument about coarse bench stones. It is generally accepted that you get the best combination of cost, efficiency and predictability with man-made silicon-carbide and aluminum-oxide stones compared to the various sandstones that were once used. But in the area of finishing stones people who use Arkansas oil stones, Welsh slate, Belgian water stones or natural Japanese water stones would often rather fight than switch.

This historical attachment has led to the curious phenomenon where several current bench-stone manufacturers try to replicate as closely as possible the natural stone they are replacing. This is the case with the Arkansas Perfect stones now on the market, and also with the finer Japanese water stones. In the case of the Arkansas Perfect stones, the manufacturer grinds up natural novaculite and reconstitutes it to make the stones. In the case of Japanese water stones, the manufacturers adopted a resin bond (see below) to best mimic the soft bond of the natural Japanese stones. While they came close, I think that anyone who has ever used a top-quality Japanese natural finishing stone will tell you that no man-made stone feels quite the same. There is a softness to the abrasive action that is not replicated in the artificial stones.

WHAT MAKES A GOOD STONE?

Although all stones are abrasive to a certain degree, humans quickly discovered that some worked better than others, and the interminable argument about what makes the best sharpening stone began. Then, as now, the search probably included the five factors basic to selecting a sharpening stone: the size, shape, hardness and toughness of particles, and the type of bond that holds the particles to each other.

Particle size The size of particles in a stone is basic to the speed of abrasion. Within limits, larger particles remove larger chips of metal. Smaller particles remove smaller chips and give a finer edge. It is important that particle size be consistent so that abrasion results are predictable.

Particle shape Obviously, spherical shapes are not ideal for abrasion. Highly angular shapes are. Although early humans would not have known the shape of a particle, they would have known that a specific stone cut faster than some other stone that gave an equally fine edge. Particle shape would have been chosen intuitively.

Hardness The abrasive particle should be substantially harder than the material to be abraded. If not, it will become worn and rounded, unable to perform its function.

Toughness A particle can be so fragile that it may not survive long enough to become worn at all. Particles must have a reasonable level of shock resistance or they will too readily fracture in the abrasion process.

Bond The way particles are held together to form a stone is critical to the functioning of the stone. If particles are held in place too solidly, the surface of the stone will eventually be worn smooth and the abrasion rate will be reduced dramatically. If the bond between the particles is too fragile, particles will constantly be torn from the face of the stone and the stone will lose its shape and wear out very quickly.

HOW BIG IS A GRAIN OF SAND?

Some readers may remember the Monty Python skit about small rocks floating. It was probably a similar real-life situation that finally led geologists to agree on a classification system for particles found in nature that most of us call dirt and stones. The standard particle sizes are metric; approximate inch sizes are given for those who are more comfortable with the imperial system.

	Limiting Dimensions	
Particle Classification	**Millimeters**	**Inches**
Boulder	256 and larger	10 and larger
Cobble	64 to 256	2½ to 10
Pebble	4 to 64	5/32 to 2½
Granule	2 to 4	5/64 to 5/32
Very coarse sand grains	1 to 2	0.040 to 0.080
Coarse sand grains	½ to 1	0.020 to 0.040
Medium sand grains	¼ to ½	0.010 to 0.020
Fine sand grains	⅛ to ¼	0.005 to 0.010
Very fine sand grains	1/16 to ⅛	0.0025 to 0.005
Silt particles	1/256 to 1/16	0.00015 to 0.0025
Clay particles	1/256 and smaller	0.00015 and smaller

SANDSTONE

The reason that sandstones were the stones of choice for everything except fine honing for so many years was that they most ideally combined all of the above features. Sand deposits can have amazingly consistent particle sizes. As an example, there is a deposit at Ottawa, Illinois, that is so consistent that it was used over the years for various standards. Even today, it is still the standard material used in the "sand drop test" to determine the durability of applied finishes. This deposit not only has particle-size consistency but shape consistency as well.

But sandstone generally is not a consistent product. First of all, "sand" is descriptive of size, not composition. You might have a sand that is made of feldspar or a sand that is made of quartz. The sandstone that was used for grinding was usually quartz crystals that had been bonded together in nature by something else. The sandstone might have been formed when a bonding agent such as calcite was leached from overburden and deposited between the particles, cementing them together.

The variety of possible particle sizes, from 0.0025 in. to 0.080 in. (see the sidebar above), the angularity of the particles and the variety of bonding agents can create a wide variety of sandstones. The larger particles with a hard bond make a sandstone suitable for rough grinding of iron; smaller particles with a softer bond would be suited to the fine finishing of steel. The regularity of particle shape tends to be much more consistent than the bond, and, unfortunately, at 7 on the Mohs scale (see p. 37), quartz is only as hard as very hard steel. As an abrasive, natural sandstone eventually proved inadequate to the metallurgical developments of the 1800s.

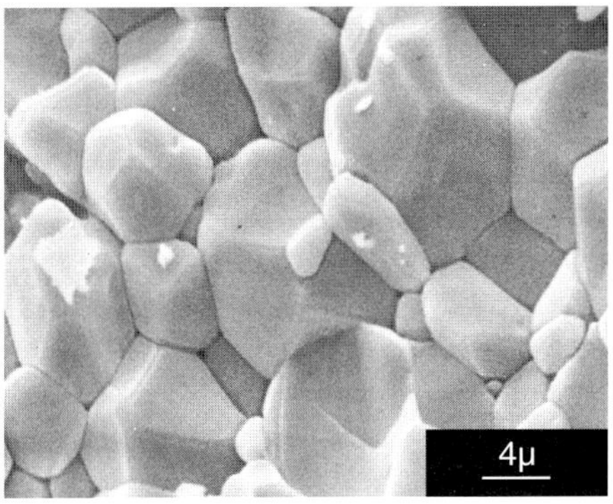

Washita stone

Soft Arkansas stone

Hard Arkansas stone

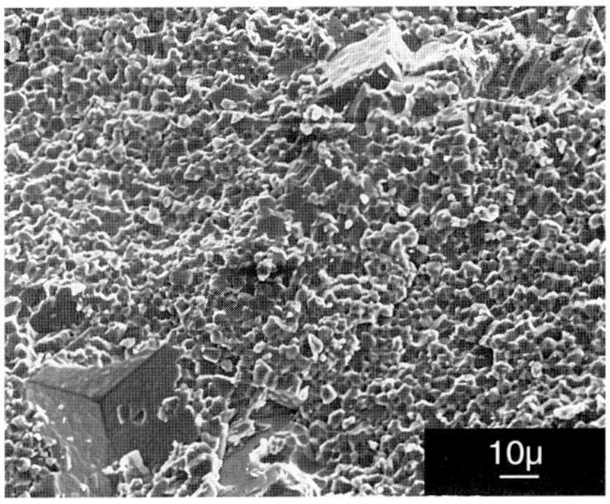

Black Hard Arkansas stone

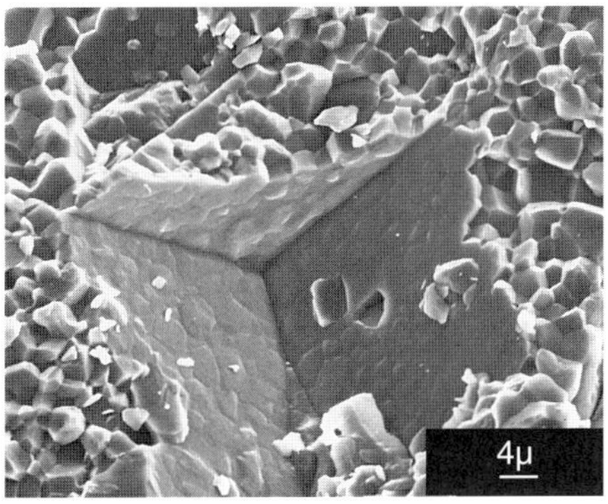

Anomaly in Black Hard Arkansas

Natural Japanese water stone (Photos courtesy National Research Council of Canada)

OTHER NATURAL ABRASIVES

The other natural abrasives did not lend themselves at all to power grinding, either because they were too fine or too weak structurally to be turned at any speed, but they were suited to use as bench stones. Among such bench stones both Welsh slate and Belgian water stones were used for fine finishing of steel edges, but the stone that dominated the bench-stone market for more than a century was the novaculite deposit in Arkansas.

The Arkansas stones were given various names, which has led to more than a little confusion over time. It is generally accepted that (from coarse to fine) they are graded Washita, Soft Arkansas, Hard Arkansas and Black Hard Arkansas. But anyone who owns one of the old Norton Lily-White Washitas can tell you that it is better than any Hard Arkansas marketed in the last twenty years. Similarly, the translucent Hard Arkansas that was traditionally used for surgeon's stones was extremely consistent, would give a very good finish and was generally held in higher regard than the Black Hard Arkansas. Over time, as the best parts of the deposit were mined, grades have become unreliable. It is very difficult to find top-quality Arkansas stones on the market today. Most that are currently sold have variable hardness and visible inclusions in the stone.

The highly regular shape of the novaculite particles is both a blessing and a curse. Viewed under an electron microscope, you can see how they nest together in a very tight and regular matrix. The photomicrographs shown above were taken ten years ago. Even then Arkansas stones were of highly variable quality. The Washita stone appears to have a particle size about the same, on average, as the Soft Arkansas and the Hard Arkansas stones. In fact, both the latter have at least one particle larger than anything seen in the Washita. Only the Black Hard Arkansas is clearly of finer grain. The regularity of particle size makes for a consistent abrasion pattern, but the tight nesting causes a problem: Worn particles are not easily released and the rate of abrasion is reduced appreciably. If you have ever lapped an Arkansas stone, you will know that a freshly lapped stone cuts much faster than one that has been used for a while. You can get a good edge on a well-used Arkansas stone, but it takes a while.

A further problem with the very tight nesting of the particles is that some of the bond lines are stronger than others and it is possible to get a large number of particles acting like a single particle. The photo in the center of the bottom row shows such a configuration in a Black Hard Arkansas stone. This is a freshly broken stone that reveals this anomaly, but you can sometimes see it with the naked eye in a bench stone. I have found this anomaly only in Black Hard Arkansas, not in any of the other

Arkansas stones. The first time I went looking for it was when I found that I was getting what appeared to be a very deep random scratch in an edge that I was honing. After cleaning the stone thoroughly I saw that light was reflecting from one spot in the stone. Since the facets on novaculite particles are so small that you could not normally see light reflect from any single particle, I examined the stone under an inspection scope and found an anomaly similar to the one photographed.

The photomicrograph at bottom right on p. 31 shows the structure of a natural Japanese water stone. Again the particle size is quite regular, but it is of completely different construction—it looks like a piece of flaky pastry. Unlike the particles in the Arkansas stones, the particles in Japanese water stones are not tightly nested. Neither are they as large. The shape does not look particularly aggressive, but it is, and the stone cuts quickly for such a fine finish.

This particular chip came from a stone owned by Toshio Odate, author of *Japanese Woodworking Tools: Their Tradition, Spirit and Use* (The Taunton Press, 1984). I have no doubt that it is one of the top-quality Japanese water stones. Although I did not use this particular stone, I have used other Japanese natural water stones and they have a wonderful feel to them. The cutting action is really quite soft, and I believe that they are uniquely suited to the very hard blades that are used in Japan.

CHISELS SHARPENED ON VARIOUS STONES

All of the chisels shown here but one (photo 1) were lapped on an 8000x stone to a mirror finish on the face before honing the bevel. This distorts the results somewhat by making the chisels whose bevels were honed on the coarser stones look better than they would if both the face and the bevel had been done on a coarse stone. So that you can appreciate what a difference this makes, the first photomicrograph below shows the bevel of a chisel that was honed and then finished on a strop charged with green compound. It would have had an excellent edge except the face of the chisel had not been lapped. The intersection of the grind marks on the face with the finely finished bevel leaves the chisel with a very jagged edge. The photo gives some indication of how irregular the edges would have been on some of

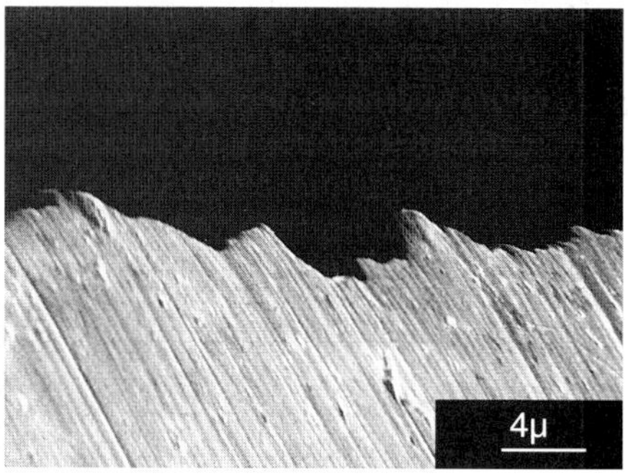

1. Bevel honed and stropped on green compound (face of chisel not lapped)

2. Bevel honed on a 400x aluminum oxide oil stone

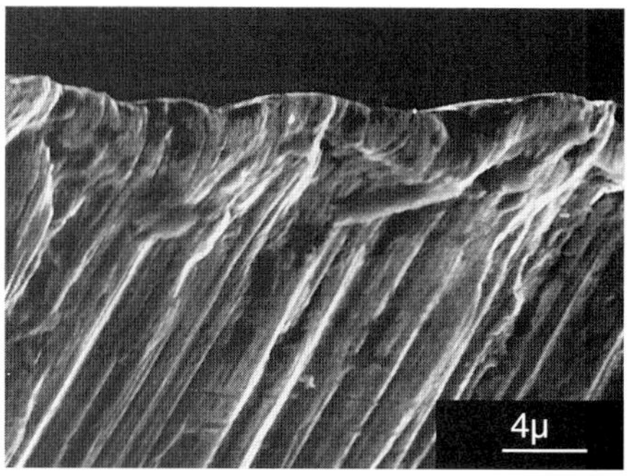

6. 800x water stone

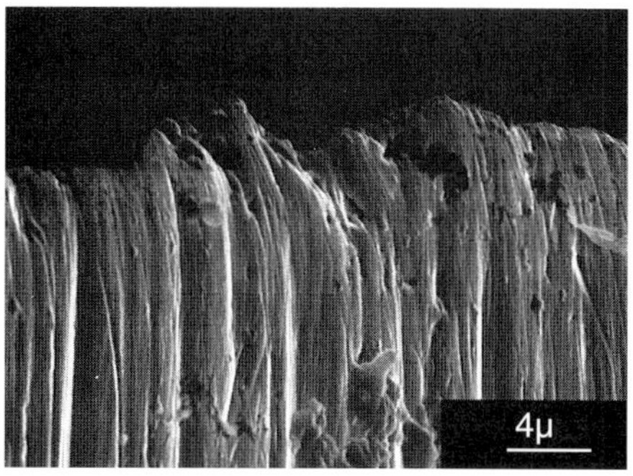

7. 1200x water stone

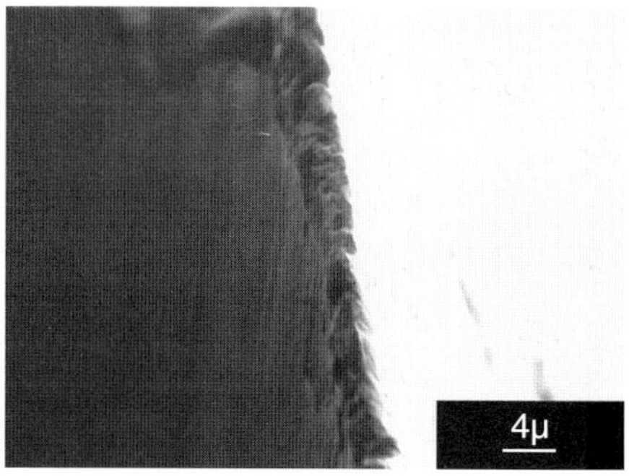

11. 8000x water stone

12. 8000x water stone honed with chromium oxide

(Photos courtesy National Research Council of Canada)

the coarser stones if the faces had been lapped on a coarse stone rather than finished first on an 8000x water stone.

The comparisons of the chisel edges are quite straightforward. The photos are shown at the same magnification, with the exception of photos 11 and 12, which are at about half the magnification of the others. Photos 13, 14 and 15 are repeated from Chapter 1 for comparison. Most photos were taken at an angle of 70° to the normal in order to capture as much of the chisel edge as possible. Photo 9 is photographed at 80° to the normal, which shows about twice as much chisel edge as the others but begins to cause focusing problems as well.

Photos 11 and 12 are exceptional in that they sight along an edge that was first honed on an 8000x water stone and then finished by stropping on a hone charged with chromium-oxide compound. Because of the sequential shots, this chisel could not be gold-plated before photography (as were all the others), thus the much greater glare in the photographs. Nonetheless, it very adequately shows the refining effect of stropping.

As a final point of interest, there is rust forming on the edge of the chisel in photo 4 (upper right-hand corner) and in photo 8 (both upper corners).

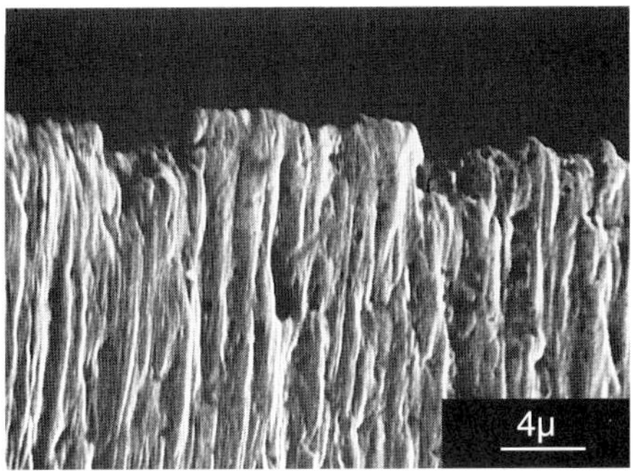

3. Soft Arkansas oil stone

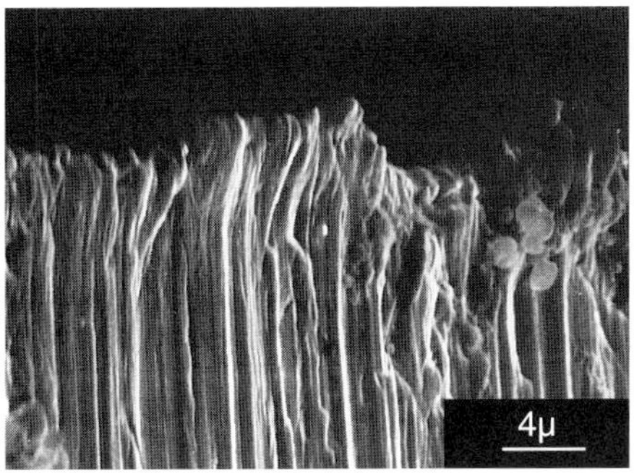

4. Hard Arkansas stone

5. Black Hard Arkansas stone

8. 6000x water stone

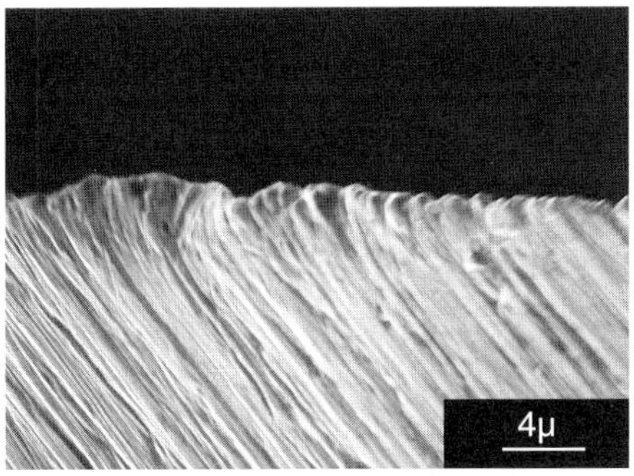

9. Natural Japanese water stone

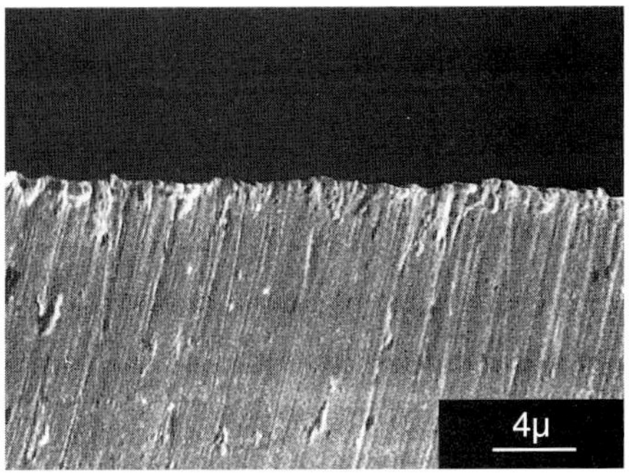

10. 8000x water stone

13. Standard craft razor blade

14. Wilkinson Sword razor blade

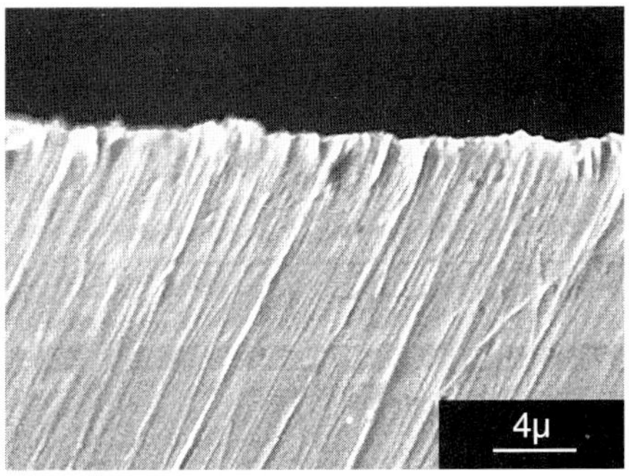

15. 6000x water stone honed with chromium oxide

ORIGINS OF THE VITRIFIED-BOND WHEEL

In the 1800s there was much experimentation with methods of bonding corundum to make grinding wheels. Shellac, animal glue and vulcanized rubber were all being used, but the most popular for a brief period was a silicate of soda bond developed by Gilbert Hart in Detroit in 1872.

Shortly thereafter, Frank Norton, a potter in Worcester, Massachusetts, encouraged two of his potters to try grinding-wheel manufacturing to augment the company product line. Legend has it that Norton bet a bucket of beer that Sven Poulson, one of his Swedish immigrant potters, could not duplicate the Hart wheel.

Poulson mixed emery with some pottery slip clay and fired three emery wheels; one was good. This is credited as being the first vitrified-bond wheel. After a number of false starts, serious production of the wheels began in 1878. Poulson had meanwhile become frustrated and left Norton, but his brother-in-law, John Jeppson, who had learned wheel making from Poulson, almost single-handedly brought Norton to industry dominance by 1890. Within 25 years, 75% of all grinding wheels sold in the United States were vitrified bond.

THE IMPORTANCE OF BOND

Of the five factors important to abrasive performance (particle size, shape, hardness, toughness and bond), the most critical over time has been bond. For centuries, sandstones were the only powered grinding wheels used because they were the only ones that would both hold together under centrifugal force and still release particles at a controlled rate to prevent glazing.

The common thread that runs through the development of decent man-made grindstones and bench stones is the problem of developing a suitable method of bonding particles together. The significance of this is highlighted by the fact that natural diamond was being used as an abrasive in the gem industry in the 1600s but did not become significant in the tool industry until this century when better bonding methods were developed. The same is true of some of the natural abrasives that were so significant in the last century.

Emery (imported from Asia Minor and Greece until a deposit was found in Massachusetts in the 1850s) is basically aluminum oxide, but it is contaminated with a fairly high percentage (25%) of iron oxide as well as lesser quantities of other material. Although widely used at one time, emery was so variable in particle size and structure that it was normally ground and sieved before either being applied to a soft metal wheel or a leather-covered wheel for surface finishing.

Similarly, corundum (first brought from India in 1825), which was nearly pure aluminum oxide and had better cutting properties than emery, suffered from the same problem. It was sometimes fixed on cast-iron wheels with glue, but the most successful bond was the resin bond that had been used in India. Of very limited strength, this was usable only in powered wheels of small diameter. The first real breakthrough in bonding was with the development of wheels using vulcanized rubber as a bond. For some types of wheels (notably the Cratex line) this bond is still used today.

But the development that led directly to most modern grindstones was the work of Sven Poulson, a Massachusetts potter, in the 1870s (see the sidebar at left). He fired a mixture of emery and clay to create the first vitrified-bond wheel. It was this process on which the Norton Company was founded.

THE MOVE FROM NATURAL TO ARTIFICIAL

By this time corundum had almost entirely replaced emery for grinding, but good corundum was scarce and expensive. Silicon carbide was developed in 1891 and artificial corundum (aluminum oxide) in 1897. By 1910, both abrasives were highly developed. Aluminum oxide was particularly successful, completely replacing emery and natural corundum in wheels. Because the nature of crystallization could be controlled, aluminum-oxide abrasives for a wide range of grinding purposes were developed.

It is important to note that not all aluminum oxides are created equal. The basic raw material for making aluminum-oxide abrasive is bauxite. The highest-quality bauxite yields the whitest and highest-quality wheels. You will often find that cheap aluminum-oxide wheels have a fair percentage of brown particles in them.

Man-made diamonds It is only in the last thirty years that man-made diamonds have become significant in tool sharpening. Diamond dust had been used for centuries in gem cutting and various lapping processes, but the generally prohibitive cost had prevented its use in grinding wheels. But in the last thirty years both DuPont and General Electric have developed methods of making diamonds. DuPont uses an explosive process that creates tremendous pressure to convert a mixture of carbon and metal powders to diamond crystals. General Electric uses a crystal-growing process of quite different technology.

The primary difference between the two processes is that the DuPont process creates polycrystalline diamonds whereas the General Electric process creates monocrystalline diamond. The difference is significant. In the DuPont process a microcrystalline aggregate is formed where the individual crystals are of angstrom size, that is as small as 0.0001 microns. They can be composed of just a few atoms, are highly faulted and are not 100% dense. Such diamond makes an ideal lapping compound since the aggregate breaks down in the lapping process creating ever-finer abrasive. The General Electric diamond, on the other hand, is monocrystalline and, like natural diamond, does not fracture as readily.

Except for lapping, diamonds have to be held in a metal backing; there are three ways to hold them. They can be soldered in position, as is usually done in making single-point wheel dressers (see p. 43). They can also be held in position physically by pressing them into a copper or aluminum base until the metal is crimped around them thereby trapping them. But the holding method you will normally see, particularly in diamond files of all types, is where the diamond is held to the metal backing by a nickel-plating process.

You will generally find that the monocrystalline diamond is appreciably more expensive than the polycrystalline. Wheels, bench stones and files made from single crystals are worth the extra money. The crystals are subject to wear and fracture over time but at a far slower rate than the polycrystalline diamond, which crushes quickly in use and continues to fracture until only the tiniest monocrystals are left. A general rule of thumb is that monocrystalline is best in bonded form and polycrystalline is best for lapping.

LAPPING AND POLISHING COMPOUNDS

There are many instances when you want an abrasive that is not solidly formed like a wheel or a bench stone. Lapping compounds are used between two surfaces; they tend to bed in the softer one and abrade the harder one. Polishing compounds are used just a bit differently: The compound is applied to a backing and then used to abrade something else. As a rule, lapping is used where flatness is paramount; polishing is used where speed and fineness of finish are most important.

Silicon carbide, aluminum oxide and garnet are all used as general industrial lapping compounds, but a woodworker need be concerned only with silicon carbide since it is the best for cast-iron and hardened-steel alloys. Aluminum oxide is used for mild steel, stainless steel and bronze. Garnet is used as a non-imbedding compound with glass and plastics.

Among the range of polishing compounds used for honing and stropping, only a very few apply to the sharpening process. These can be broken down into those for medium polishing and those for fine polishing.

The medium polishing compounds include black, red and white rouge, tripoli, quartz and levigated alumina. All except red rouge and tripoli have some application. The black and white rouge can be used to polish medium-hard materials, and the quartz and levigated alumina can be used on hard materials. The tripoli and red rouge are unsuitable for sharpening. Specifically, red rouge is for soft materials like brass and is not a good choice for hardened steel blades.

Among the fine polishing compounds, there are really only two that apply—tin oxide and chromium oxide. Pumice is used on soft metals, trichromium oxide on stainless steel and aluminum, and cerium oxide for optical glass. Tin oxide and chromium oxide can both be used across a range of metals and a range of hardnesses. Chromium oxide cuts the fastest and is definitely the best choice in a honing compound. For increased speed of

SIZING DIAMONDS

In diamond mining a great deal of non-gem-quality material is mined. Called bort, this has been used for centuries in lapping processes and in a more limited manner in grinding wheels and wheel dressers. Coarse bort is separated by a sieving process exactly the same as that used for other types of grit. The separation of lapping grades (everything that passes through the finest sieve) is done by a very unusual process. All of the fines are mixed with a high-grade olive oil, stirred and allowed to stand for five minutes. The oil is then poured into another container, and the material that has settled out is given the grade of the finest of sieves that was used.

Next begins the process of separating the various grades of diamond dust for lapping processes. The oil is stirred again and left to stand for ten minutes, after which it is poured into another container and everything that settled out in that ten minutes is labeled #1 lapping compound. The process is repeated according to the following table to get the other grades.

Grade of lapping compound	Settles in
#1	10 min.
#2	30 min.
#3	1 hr.
#4	2 hr.
#5	10 hr.
#6	until oil is clear

The process is not really one of sizing (although it tends to work that way for natural diamond because it is so blocky in shape) but rather a process that separates particles according to their mass and relative surface area. The same principle is used for water- and air-flotation systems for grading other abrasive particles.

A hardness tester is used to determine the relative hardness of various tool steels.

The depth of the dimple in the surface of the tool (right) indicates the hardness of the steel.

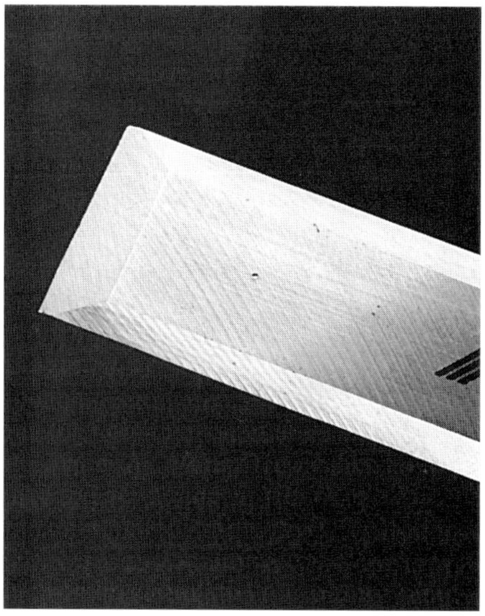

cutting, chromium oxide is sometimes mixed with very fine aluminum oxide as well. The aluminum oxide is harder and cuts more aggressively.

HARDNESS SCALES AND TESTS

Just as hardness is important in polishing compounds, so it is in all sharpening activities. You need adequate hardness differential between the abrasive and the tool being sharpened or you will get poor abrasion. Anyone who has tried honing a carbide bit with an aluminum-oxide stone knows the problem well.

The oldest hardness scale still in use is the Mohs scale developed by Friedrich Mohs in 1826. Based on the susceptibility of a material to being scratched, Mohs ranked ten materials from talc to diamond on a scale from 1 to 10, with talc at 1 and diamond at 10. The primary problem with the Mohs scale is that it is not consistent in any respect except the order of hardness of the materials. It has since been augmented by various tests that show relative hardness of materials so that you can determine not just whether one material is harder than another but also exactly how much harder.

There is still some complication in this field, however, because a whole series of different hardness tests are now in use, each suitable for specific materials. It is necessary to provide some correlation between the testing methods to make them useful.

For woodworking tools, the most commonly used test is the Rockwell Hardness Test. The Rockwell system uses a variety of scales (A, C, D, 15-N, etc.), but the most common is the C scale, indicated by the "Rc" or "HRc" you frequently see in literature on hardness of steels. The C scale test is based on the depth of penetration of a shaped diamond under a load of 150 kg into the surface of steel. You may have seen the telltale dimple that such a test leaves in tools (see the photo at left).

Other tests are Brinell (which measures penetration of a hardened steel ball at a load of 3000 kg) used on softer steels and Knoop (which uses an elongated diamond). Since the Knoop hardness is more applicable to minerals, it is combined with Rockwell C and Mohs in the table at right. It is apparent from the table why aluminum-oxide stones are not very effective on carbide bits. It is equally apparent why diamond wheels are used to sharpen all the carbides.

UNDERSTANDING GRINDING WHEELS

Only in recent times has a standardized international code been developed for grinding wheels. Although the quality of abrasive and the consistency of manufacture can still vary among various makers, you can have some confidence that stones with the same code will function similarly. And, unexciting though the subject may be, you need to know something about the composition of grinding wheels or you will inevitably ruin tools attempting to grind them on a standard bench grinder using no coolant.

To start with, the stones that come with the standard bench grinder can be put to better use as patio stones than for grinding chisels and plane blades. They are almost inevitably coarse, hard stones that will quickly burn any woodworking blade. You can use them to sharpen lawnmower blades or clean up your welding, but you shouldn't even think about grinding tools with them. It is those stones that have given dry grinding a bad reputation.

The following explanation of grinding-wheel codes will help to explain many of the recommendations that come later in the book. In the example on p. 38, a Norton code has been used. The only difference between this code and the code you will find on a wheel made by any other company is the "38" at the beginning and the "BE" at the end. The central part of the code is according to the ISO (International Standards Organization) code for grinding wheels.

RELATIVE HARDNESS OF SELECTED MATERIALS

Substance	Mohs	Knoop	Rockwell C
Talc	1		
Gypsum	2	32	
Magnesia	-	370	38 (cabinet scraper)
Apatite	5	430	42 (handsaw)
Nickel	-	557	51 (hand scraper)
Feldspar	6	560	
Most chisels, plane blades	-	690-776	58-62
Japanese chisels (laminated)	-	776-822	62-64
Quartz	7	820	64
Chromium	-	935	68
Zirconia	-	1160	
Berylia	-	1250	
Topaz	8	1340	
Garnet	-	1360	
Tungsten-carbide alloy	-	1400-1800*	
Zirconium boride	-	1550	
Titanium nitride	9	1800	
Chromium carbide	-	1820	
Tungsten carbide	-	1880	
Tantalum carbide	-	2000	
Corundum	-	2000	
Aluminum oxide	-	2100-2440	
Beryllium carbide	-	2410	
Titanium carbide	-	2470	
Silicon carbide	-	2480	
Aluminum boride	-	2500	
Vanadium carbide	-	2520	84
Boron carbide	-	2750	
Diamond	10	7000	

* In a matrix of cobalt or nickel; includes C1 to C4 grades.

GRINDSTONE CODES

38 A 80 - H 8 V BE

38 A 80 - H 8 V BE **Norton symbol**	The first number indicates the type of aluminum oxide that Norton used in this stone. Norton uses a number of other types as well but is reluctant to explain them to consumers.
38 **A** 80 - H 8 V BE **Abrasive**	A = Aluminum oxide C = Silicon carbide D = Diamond There are many codes for abrasives, but these are the ones of interest to woodworkers.
38 A **80** - H 8 V BE **Grit size**	Grit size can range from 8 to 500. The band from 60 to 120 is used in basic tool grinding.
38 A 80 - **H** 8 V BE **Grade**	Wheel grade is indicated by a letter from the following ranges: ABCDEFG – Very soft; HIJK – Soft; KMNO – Medium; PQRS – Hard; TUVWXYZ – Very hard A wheel is make harder by increasing the amount of bonding material. This reduces the volume of the pores and makes the abrasive particles more resistant to release. The wheel lasts longer but tends to grind hotter because it retains more worn particles than a softer wheel; this reduces the cutting rate and increases friction when grinding tool steel.
38 A 80 - H **8** V BE **Structure**	Structure describes the grain spacing. 0 1 2 3 4 5 6 7 8 9 10 11 12 Dense ——————————> Open In general, an open structure is cooler cutting because of entrained air and reduced friction. It also has reduced tendency to glaze. A dense structure is more durable but is hotter in use and more subject to glazing.
38 A 80 - H 8 **V** BE **Bond**	The most common bonds are: V - Vitrified (tool grinding) B - Resinoid (high speed, rapid metal removal) R - Rubber (high-pressure grinding) E - Shellac (where an elastic bond is needed) M - Metal (used with diamond and boron nitride)
38 A 80 - H 8 V **BE** **Bond modification**	An optional manufacturer's designation for some modification to the basic bond; in this case it indicates a modification to the basic vitrified bond.

Norton grinding wheel, code 38A80-H8VBE. (Photo by Susan Kahn)

The stone used as an example (38A80-H8VBE) is the best all-purpose stone for dry grinding in a woodworking shop. It cuts quickly with minimal friction but excellent abrasion. For very light grinding where a fine finish is important, such as with carving tools, a 100x or 120x stone can be used but the rest of the code should be the same. It is important to have a relatively soft bond and open structure.

SEEDED-GEL STONES

For more aggressive grinding, such as reshaping of high-speed-steel turning tools, the new SG (seeded gel) stones from Norton work well. The grit in these is an aggregation of submicron particles. The sieved grits are actually made up of many small particles much like polycrystalline diamond versus monocrystalline diamond. They, too, are self-dressing wheels in that particles will fracture under pressure rather than load up, but they are designed for greater grinding pressures than would be normal in grinding chisels and plane blades. These wheels also grind hotter because they are not available in a bond softer than "I." But this is less of a problem with high-speed steel, which has excellent red-heat hardness and can take higher grinding temperatures than regular tool steels without deteriorating.

The polycrystalline particles in the SG wheels are available in four concentrations: 100%, 50%, 30% and 10%. The balance would be standard 38A grit. The recommended concentrations for HSS turning tool grinding would be 50% or 30%. The codes for these would be, respectively, 5SG80IVS and 3SG80IVS in 80x and 5SG100IVS and 35SG100IVS in 100x.

CHAPTER 5

SHARPENING EQUIPMENT

For the purposes of this chapter, I'm going to assume that you want to sharpen tools as cheaply and quickly as possible. If cost is irrelevant to you and you have more money than you know what to do with, I will be glad to put on my tool vendor's hat for a while and quickly bring you to greater economic equality with your fellow man. If, on the other hand, you are the sort of person who insists on making all of your own tools, be forewarned that this chapter actually recommends buying some things. If you have ever tried to make a file, for instance, you will understand completely.

The second general bias throughout this chapter is that more time will be spent on simple sharpening equipment than on complex equipment. The basic principle here is that if you understand how to arrive at predictable results on simple equipment it will be an absolute breeze for you on equipment that has all the bells and whistles. Accordingly, the complex and costly will briefly be considered, and then more time will be spent on simpler equipment since it usually requires better technique because of the absence of jigs and fixtures.

Motorized wet grinders are available in vertical-wheel and horizontal-wheel designs. Note that the tool rest on the vertical-wheel model can be raised so that the tool being ground can slope downward, to prevent water from running down the blade.

POWERED SHARPENING EQUIPMENT

As is common in many areas, powered equipment does not necessarily do things better it just does them faster. In sharpening, powered equipment is most useful when you want to remove a great deal of material. This could be grinding back an entire edge to eliminate a nick, major reshaping of an edge to lower the bevel angle, or restoration of an edge deformed by bad honing technique. Most of this equipment can also be used for honing, an activity that can include minor edge shaping as well as general refinement—what you do when you are stropping, polishing or buffing. Incidentally, all of these terms are not mutually exclusive; just as grinding is basic edge creation or restoration, honing is edge refinement, which can be achieved in various ways including polishing, buffing and stropping.

GRINDERS

Grinders are usually separated into two categories, wet and dry. A wet grinder uses water to cool the edge being ground as well as remove swarf from the wheel to prevent glazing. A dry grinder is dependent upon the wheel bond structure to reduce heat buildup and prevent glazing. The boundary line between the two types can be a bit fuzzy. Some wet grinders use a transfer roller to pick up water from a reservoir and apply it to a rotating wheel. These might more accurately be called damp grinders. Similarly, some dry grinders are modified to have a fine mist of water directed at the edge of the tool being ground. These might also be called damp grinders.

These indistinct models highlight the basic problems with the two types. A wet grinder can be dirty and inconvenient if there is anything less than excellent water control when using the machine. However, the great advantage is that it is possible to remove material quickly without fear of overheating the tool and drawing its temper. Dry grinders are inexpensive, clean and compact but carry with them the constant risk of overheating an edge.

Wet grinders Nothing is safer than a wet grinder for shaping a cutting edge, whether it is a knife, a carving tool, a plane blade or a hatchet. With an ample supply of water, the edge stays cool and the stone is clear of all swarf, giving a very even cutting action. Wet grinders come in both horizontal-wheel and vertical-wheel styles (see the photo above). Since it is nearly impossible to get hand-powered wet grinders any more, I'll deal only with the much more common motorized versions.

Most horizontal-wheel wet grinders are made in Japan. Both coarse and fine wheels are available, although a single 800x (i.e., 800-grit) or 1000x wheel will accommodate virtually all shop grinding. Horizontal-wheel wet grinders are delightful to use in that you never burn a tool, but they are also disconcerting in some aspects. First, because the process is so smooth and quiet, you are lulled into thinking that metal is being removed slowly, which is not usually the case. Resin-bond wheels cut very quickly, and you can take 1/16 in. off the end of a chisel in a deceptively short period of time.

A freestanding commercial tool rest, grooved to accept sliding jigs and drilled for rotating jigs, mounts directly to the bench in front of a dry grinder (left). The tool rest in the photo at right is a shopmade fixture with a tilt mechanism and a jig slot.

Because they were originally developed for sharpening knives, horizontal-wheel wet grinders often have inadequate jigging for woodworking tools. This combined with the fact that most of them have flutter in the wheel makes them more suitable for freehand grinding than jigged grinding.

It is possible to take out the wheel flutter by truing the wheel with a single-point dresser (see p. 43), but then the wheel will usually run true only in a single shaft orientation. If you remove the wheel from the shaft and replace it, you will have to rotate the wheel to exactly the same spot it was at when trued or flutter will still be a problem.

None of this is very significant when sharpening knives, and the wet grinder can be a real pleasure with both knives and carving tools. Used with carving tools, though, it quickly gets a scalloped surface that reduces its usefulness for chisels and plane blades.

There are a variety of vertical-wheel wet grinders on the market, but some have wheels too small for use in sharpening woodworking tools (small wheels will undercut the bevel too much). A minimum acceptable wheel size is 6 in. diameter (8 in. or 10 in. is preferable). These grinders often have lateral wobble, which, although disconcerting, is not critical to their function at low rpm. Much more critical is what is called "hop," the lack of concentricity around the axis. Hop can be removed readily with a diamond-point wheel dresser.

As with almost all grinders, you should look carefully at the versatility and accuracy of the tool rest. It should be a stable, easily adjustable rest that is parallel to the face of the wheel. Another consideration for a vertical-wheel wet grinder is the position of the rest. With a bathed-wheel grinder, the tool rest must be mounted high enough that any grinding being done has the bevel as the lowest point so that the water will run off the tool back onto the wheel, not down the blade. (On wet grinders that use a transfer roller to pick up water from the trough and apply it to the wheel, water running down the blade of the tool is not a problem.)

Vertical-wheel wet grinders frequently come with vitrified-bond wheels, which are slower cutting than resin-bond wheels but also wear more slowly. Resin-bond wheels are available for many vertical grinders, as they are for horizontal grinders.

Of the two types of wet grinder, I prefer the vertical-wheel style, primarily because it is much easier to maintain a true wheel and also usually easier to build specialized jigs for. A horizontal-wheel grinder produces a flat grind, which I prefer to the hollow grind of a vertical wheel (see pp. 61-62), but the very low speed of a vertical-wheel grinder lets you safely use the side of the wheel where flatness is critical.

Dry grinders While there are some horizontal-wheel dry grinders, they are almost all for industrial use and beyond the budget of the average woodworker. The grinder that is most commonly found in woodshops is a vertical-wheel, double-spindle bench grinder for either 6-in. or 8-in. wheels. These are inexpensive and versatile machines, though virtually unusable as they come from the store.

The first problem is that the grinder will come with wheels that are totally unsuited to grinding chisels and plane blades or any hard, high-carbon tool steel. The grinder will probably have one fine and one coarse silicon-carbide wheel. Both wheels will have very hard bonds more suited to cleaning up castings or welding spatter than to sharpening tools. These wheels can be used for rough grinding but certainly not on any tool that you care about. I would restrict them to lawnmower blades and shovels. As recommended in the previous chapter, the best all-purpose wheel you can put on such a grinder is an A80H-8V (see pp. 37-39).

The second thing that has to be done with these bench grinders is either to replace the entire tool rest or remanufacture the one that comes with the grinder. Since the vast majority of these tool rests are not fixable, it is easiest to build or buy a freestanding tool rest that you mount in front of the grinder (see the photos on the facing page).

With the right wheel and a good tool rest, a dry grinder becomes a real workhorse in a shop. To my mind, it is second in usefulness only to a good belt sander.

Truing and dressing grindstones Truing a grindstone is the process of creating or restoring the stone to the shape you want. New stones are seldom perfectly true, and you should be prepared to true one as soon as you buy it. Although some abrasive manufacturers sell very hard abrasive sticks for truing wheels, a diamond dresser is both more accurate and easier to use.

The most common reason for having to true a stone is that it is out of round. To true such a stone, clamp a single-point diamond dresser (a ¼-carat model costing about $15.00 should outlast you) between two pieces of wood or in a grinding jig. The tip of the dresser should just touch the highest point of the wheel at an angle anywhere between 10° and 15° below the center point of the wheel, but never less than 5°. Angling the dresser in this manner will protect the diamond from destructive shocks.

Turn the grinder on and slowly traverse the face of the wheel, using the jig to control projection of the dresser (see the drawing on p. 44). For a second pass, tilt the dresser up until it is taking a cut of 0.001 in. or 0.002 in. (about the thickness of this paper).

GRINDER ACCESSORIES

Whether you buy a tool rest, make a tool rest or remanufacture the one that came with the bench grinder, as a bare minimum you want the following three features:

1. The face of the tool rest should be at 90° to the running plane of the stone at all settings.
2. The tool-rest table should be lockable in a variety of angular settings.
3. You should have a grinding guide in which you can clamp tools and slide them back and forth across the tool rest for grinding.

There are a number of specialized grinding guides and jigs that you can buy or make; these include jigs for radius grinding of skew chisels (see p. 127) or grinding of lathe gouges (see p. 124). But these are peripheral accessories; all you really need are the three core functions listed above.

A jig that clamps the tool and can be slid across the tool rest is essential for accurate grinding. Shown here are a commercial jig (left) and a shopmade jig (right). (Photo at left by Susan Kahn)

To true a grindstone, clamp a diamond dresser in a grinding jig and pass it across the face of the rotating stone. (Photo by Susan Kahn)

TRUING A STONE

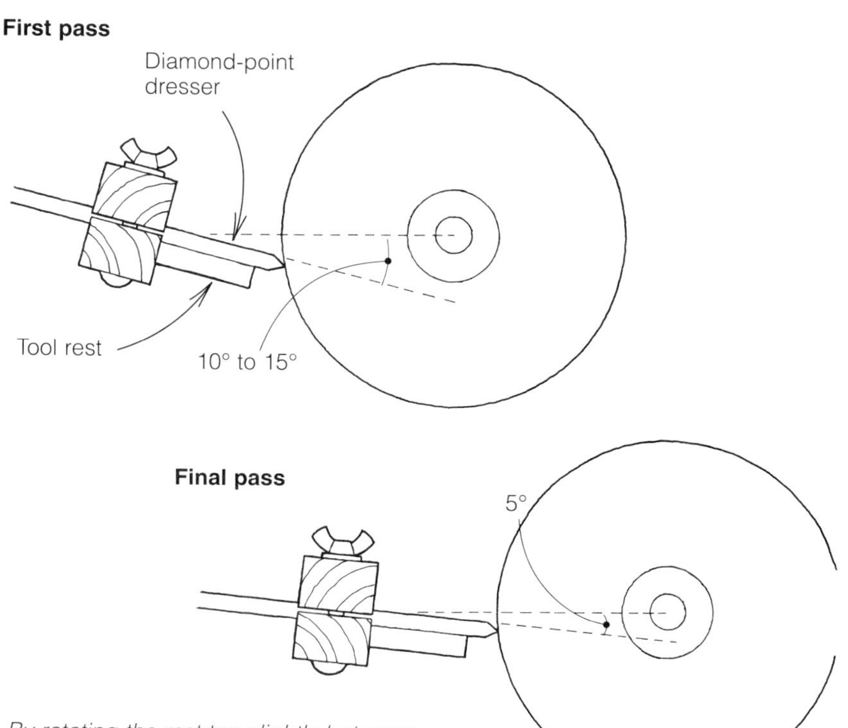

By rotating the rest top slightly between passes or laying strips of tape along the top front edge, just the right amount of cut can be taken at each pass.

Tools for dressing grindstones include a diamond dresser (which can also be used for truing stones) and star-wheel dressers. The cutters of the star-wheel dresser at right have been worn through frequent use and are long overdue for replacement.

Traverse the wheel again. Repeat the process until you have a perfectly shaped wheel or until you have reached the 5° angle. If you have reached 5° and the wheel is still not true, reset the dresser below 10° (but not more than 15°) and start again. This will give you a square-faced wheel parallel to your tool rest.

A grindstone needs to be dressed to restore its cutting ability, usually after it has been glazed through carelessness. This can be done with a star-wheel dresser or a diamond-point dresser (see the photo below). A star-wheel dresser is most applicable with hard wheels; it leaves a coarse, aggressive surface. I prefer a diamond point because it can be used both for dressing and for truing wheels. You will find that the only time you have to dress an A80H-8V wheel is when someone has misused it (for example, grinding brass or aluminum). Otherwise, it does not glaze and the only servicing it needs is occasional truing.

BELT SANDERS

The belt sander is probably the most underrated sharpening tool in the woodshop. It can be used for virtually any job where you might normally use a bench grinder and for a wide variety of jobs (such as knife sharpening) that a bench grinder cannot adequately perform. The entrained air in the belt combined with the length of the belt makes for cool cutting, but not so cool that you should not be careful of tool temperature. On a belt sander you have a choice of a long flat area, a convex area or a slightly concave area on which to sharpen. Each has its use at different times. If you wish, you can even add platens of greater convexity for specialized hollow grinding, which is something that knifemakers often do (see the drawing on the facing page).

Belts are relatively inexpensive and available in a wide variety of abrasives and grits. You can use belts as coarse as 60x for rapid stock removal and work up the range to very fine honing belts, which are now available as fine as 16,000x. Alternatively, you can buy a leather belt and charge it with honing compound for fine finishing.

A belt sander makes an excellent sharpening center. The narrow, 1-in. belt sander is ideal for sharpening knives and carving tools, while the 3-in. belt-sander attachment is handy for tools like axes and hatchets.

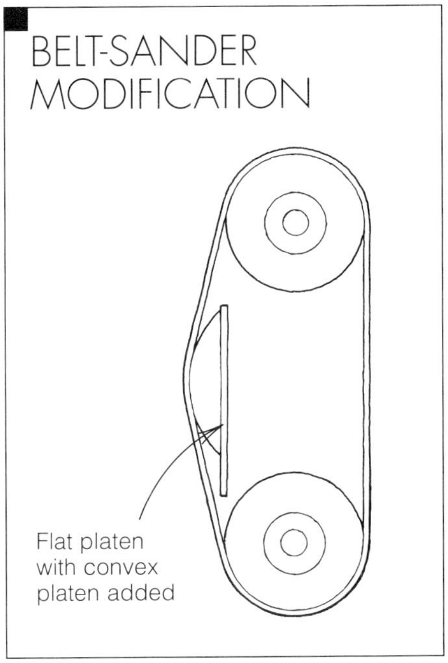

Much like bench grinders, most belt sanders suffer from inadequate tool rests, but it is even easier to build a suitable rest for a belt grinder than it is for a bench grinder because the work area is normally above the motor and unhampered on either side.

SANDING DRUMS

Sanding drums, which are inexpensive and available in a wide range of diameters (usually ½ in. to 4 in.), are ideal for sharpening in-cannel gouges, scoop adzes and cornering tools.

You can mount the sanding drum in a drill press (or in a hand drill clamped in a vise) and bring the tool to the drum, or put the drum in a flex shaft and bring the drum to the tool. For fine work, like small gouges, I prefer to use the sanding drum in a flex shaft and fix the tool in a vise. For something like a scoop adz, it is easier to have the sanding drum in a drill press.

A sanding drum mounted in a drill press is a handy tool for sharpening large in-cannel gouges (left). The sanding drum can also be mounted in a flex shaft (above). (Photo at left by Susan Kahn)

CHARGING A FELT WHEEL

Putting the initial charge of honing compound on a felt wheel is not easy. A new wheel is fuzzy and will tend to throw compound all over the shop rather than accept it. To complicate matters, the binders in bars of honing compound tend to dry out over time, so any bar that has been sitting on a store shelf for months will be less likely to stick to the wheel.

Professional polishers call this initial charging process "building a head." They use various methods, but a common one is to spray the rotating wheel lightly with diluted animal glue or fish glue. This creates a sticky base for the compound. Unless done very carefully, I find that this can harden the wheel too much. I prefer to singe the wheel* to remove the fuzziness then dress it with a bit of hard fat or mineral oil. It will then take a charge more readily. Once the wheel has been well charged once, it will readily accept subsequent dressings.

***Do this exactly the same way you would singe a chicken after plucking. You don't know how? Ask your grandmother.**

Charging a felt buffing wheel with honing compound.

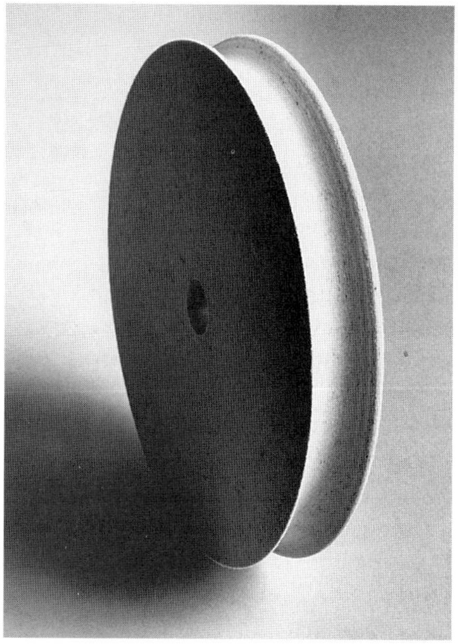

A shaped felt wheel is ideal for honing the inside of gouges and parting tools.

As with belts, sanding-drum sleeves are available in a wide range of grits and are inexpensive and effective. Used with a light touch, there is no reason ever to overheat a tool.

FELT BUFFING WHEELS AND BOBS

The use of felt wheels developed from the need to put a fine edge on a tool quickly. Until very recently, it was impossible to buy ultra-fine abrasives in belt or power-stone form. Since felt wheels could be charged with any one of a variety of fine abrasives, they became popular substitutes for fine-grit bench stones.

Basically you want to avoid the normal buffing wheel (which is made of cloth) and use a solid felt wheel instead. If you do use a cloth wheel, you need to put large stiffening flanges on either side; otherwise, it will be too soft to use with any sort of control. Even with flanges the wheel will round bevels, destroying the ideal geometry of the edge.

To call these buffing wheels is really a misnomer (buffing implies restoring or enhancing a surface by removing oxides or making a surface more consistent). A felt wheel, once charged with abrasive, will actually hone, removing material as it refines an edge. Charged with a good honing compound, it will remove material quite quickly. The mirror finish that is left by a fine compound has lulled people into using such wheels for polishing brass. Big mistake. It will leave a fine finish but strip off a substantial amount of brass in the process.

Felt wheels come in a range of densities, and only the harder wheels are normally used in honing tools. For carving tools, a shaped wheel is available, which is particularly handy for dealing with the inside of parting tools and gouges (see the photo at left).

Bobs are small, shaped-felt heads, usually mounted on an ⅛-in. diameter (or smaller) shank for use in a flex shaft. They are used for gouge flutes, incannel gouges or similar hard-to-hone shapes. They are charged in exactly the same manner as a felt wheel (see the sidebar above).

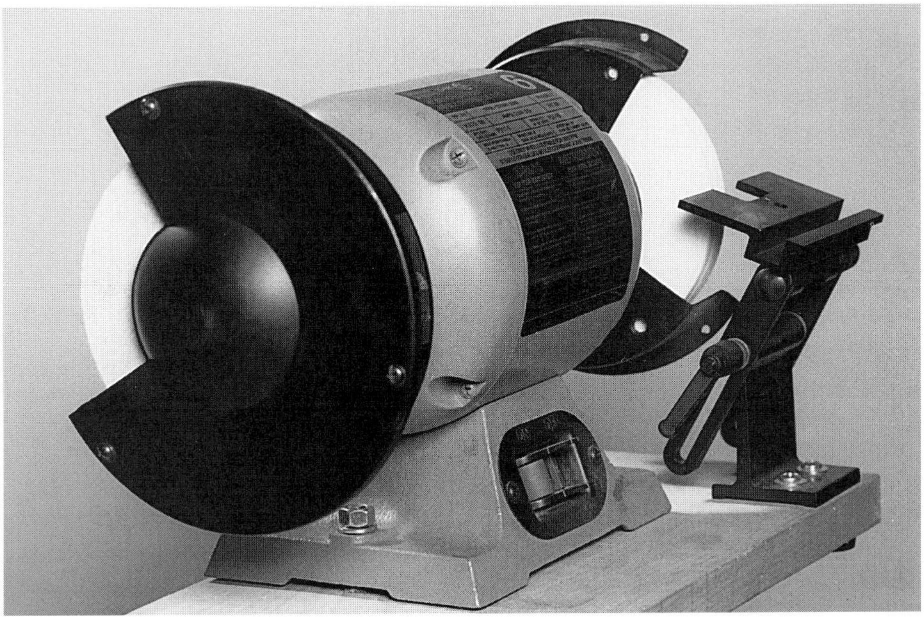

Mounting a grinder on a swivel base allows you to work with a grinding wheel and a buffing wheel running in opposite directions.

Felt-wheel setup Here, I would like to concentrate on the standard 6-in. felt wheel with a square face. The first consideration with this wheel is that it should be mounted so that it turns away from you at the top. This is just the reverse of the normal bench-grinder setup. You have at least four choices here. You can get accustomed to doing everything on the bottom half of the wheel and have it turn toward you, or you can mount your bench grinder on a swivel base so that you can rotate the whole grinder through 180° and lock it in position. This lets you have the grinding wheel on one end turning toward you at the top and, when rotated, a felt honing wheel rotating away from you at the top. But since either of these methods may be illegal where you live, I cannot actually recommend them to you. Check your local legislation to see what is allowable.

The third alternative is to have your grinder on an island stand where you can easily work on either side. This way you can have wheels properly shielded and still running in opposite directions. As a fourth alternative you can use a completely separate unit for buffing.

BENCH STONES

Although you can do everything from initial shaping to final honing with bench stones, very few people today would turn to a bench stone to restore an edge that had hit a nail. Some form of power grinding is normally used for major metal removal, and bench stones have been relegated to the work of edge refinement. Both natural and man-made bench stones come in a wide range of shapes and sizes.

NATURAL BENCH STONES

There are only two groupings of natural bench stones regularly available in North America: the Arkansas stones and the natural Japanese water stones.

The Arkansas stones were described briefly in the previous chapter. As a rule, the older the Arkansas stone, the better the quality. You can often find old Arkansas stones at flea markets; they may have to be trued but this is a small price to pay to get a good-quality stone. It is still possible to buy new Arkansas stones that are of good quality, but it is unusual to find any in bench-stone sizes. They are now usually only found in the smaller shaped stones. If you are convinced that a natural Arkansas bench stone is what you want and you cannot find one at a flea market, I recommend that you contact a dealer in antique tools. Dealers frequently get stones as part of lot purchases of tools.

Good-quality natural Japanese water stones are getting scarce as well, though you can still buy them from retailers specializing in Japanese tools. The best indicator of their scarcity is the price you will have to pay for a decent stone: A good stone will cost you several hundred dollars; a top-quality stone can cost $1,000 or more. Clearly, you need to be quite certain that you want a natural water stone before spending this kind of money. There is no question that a very fine natural water stone has a wonderful feel to it, but I would consider one only if I were using top-quality Japanese chisels and plane blades on a regular basis.

GRADING NATURAL JAPANESE WATER STONES

Fred Damsen (The Japan Woodworker) has done more than anybody I know to introduce traditional Japanese tools and Japanese water stones to the North American market. Fred describes the grading process as one of sniffing, scratching, tapping and spitting. It isn't exactly a voodoo art, but it is close to it.

Fred says that the primary features to look for are water-absorption rates and apparent material consistency. The fineness of the stone, as well as its porosity, particle shape, bond, and so on, are known to the miner. The wholesaler who buys from the miner will also have a good idea of the value of the stones from different mines. The final price will be struck in negotiation between the two. The stone then passes through the marketing chain with that relative price intact. As a consumer, it is very difficult for you to differentiate between stones, and there are no easy tests. Your best assurance of good value and a good stone is the reputation of the person selling the stone to you.

MAN-MADE BENCH STONES

Man-made bench stones can be entirely man-made, as is the case with a silicon-carbide stone, or they can contain a natural abrasive (novaculite, corundum, etc.) that has been crushed, sieved and rebonded to give the desired shape, particle consistency, bond and structure.

Oil stones The two most common man-made oil stones are silicon-carbide and aluminum-oxide stones with vitrified bonds. Although these stones are available in a fairly wide range of grits, most woodworkers use only the coarser grits. Both of these stones are fine for fairly rapid stock removal, but there are much better choices for fine honing.

As you can see from the photomicrograph of a Fine India (400x) stone at left below, the vitrified bond almost totally masks the abrasive particles. The bond overwhelms the abrasive particles. Such a stone cuts slowly and glazes quickly. Compare the structure to the Japanese water stone in the photo at right below.

For very hard steels and for high-speed steels a silicon-carbide stone is suitable, otherwise an aluminum-oxide stone should serve well for virtually all of your steel edge tools. A 90x stone is a good choice in either style for rapid material removal.

Water stones Man-made water stones from Japan first came into the North American market about twenty years ago. Although they are still not well known in the handyman market, they are probably used by 90% of professional cabinetmakers. With only minor exceptions, most of the Japanese stones have a resin bond, cut very quickly and wear more rapidly than Western stones. To my mind, they can be forgiven their tendency to wear rapidly, because of the speed of cut and the very consistent particle size in the stones. I find that an 800x resin-bond water stone cuts more quickly than a 90x aluminum-oxide oil stone. (The only time a 90x stone might cut as fast as a water stone is when the stone is brand new or just after it has been lapped.) Worn and rounded particles remain locked in position in the oil stone, but spall off a water stone at a controlled rate.

Looking at the photo at right below you can see a structure that is porous and does not mask the abrasive edges of the particles. There are globules of resin in sight, but they act only as a bonding agent since they are softer than steel and would be quickly removed if they came between a blade and an abrasive particle. In addition, a water stone gives a far finer degree of finish for the same cutting rate. In the very fine ranges, such as the 6000x or the 8000x Japanese stones, there is no comparable Western man-made stone.

The vitrified bond of an aluminum-oxide (Fine India) oil stone (left) gives the stone a quite different structure from that of a resin-bond Japanese water stone (right). (Photos courtesy National Research Council of Canada)

Reconstituted stones I find that Arkansas Perfect stones, which are reconstituted novaculite (see p. 29), function much like the natural Arkansas stones. The photomicrographs at right show a Washita and a Hard Arkansas stone in reconstituted form. They are more porous than the India stone shown in the photo at left on the facing page, but otherwise the particles are similarly masked. I do not recommend them.

Diamond stones As the hardest of all materials, diamond can be used on steel of any hardness, on carbides and, equally important, on other abrasives. This last point may sound odd, but a diamond stone is useful to have if only to flatten all your other stones.

Traditionally, diamond stones have been available only in relatively coarse grits (600x or less), but this is changing as ever-finer grits are demanded to touch up carbide cutters. 1200x diamond hones and files are now available.

Two things to look for in diamond bench stones are monocrystalline diamonds and a flat substrate. The vendor should be able to tell you whether the diamond is monocrystalline or polycrystalline type (see p. 35); you can check the flatness of the substrate yourself. You can expect to pay about twice as much for a good monocrystalline stone as you would for a polycrystalline stone, but you can also expect it to last much more than twice as long.

Ceramic stones Ceramic stones are a variation of vitrified-bond stones. Normally sold only in very fine grits, they are used for honing rods in knife sharpeners and other specialized shapes where structural strength is necessary. They cut well when new but have such a hard bond that the abrasive particles become rounded in time, and since they cannot dislodge the cutting action is reduced. To remain effective over time these should be lapped or refaced regularly. A good job for a diamond stone.

HONING OILS, HONING WATERS

The primary purpose of a honing oil is to keep a stone from glazing. It should provide enough lubrication to keep metal from bonding to the stone, but it should not mask the abrasive action. The honing oil also acts as a flushing agent to clear dislodged abrasive and metal chips. It should be a non-drying (or non-curing) oil that will not clog the stone. A light mineral oil is most commonly used, although something like diesel fuel will also serve.

With stones that have an open structure and a soft bond, glazing is caused primarily by crushed abrasive particles packing the pores. With such stones, water is all that is required as a flushing agent. Since many such stones also have resin bonds, only water should be used because many oils will attack the resin bond.

Some people like to use soapy water (instead of oil) with oil stones. A vitrified bond is impervious to almost everything except hydrofluoric acid, so it will not damage the stone. I have not experimented with this and cannot comment. But I would caution you never to use anything but water with water stones. People who have stored their water stones in antifreeze in the winter have found to their regret that some antifreezes dissolve resin bonds.

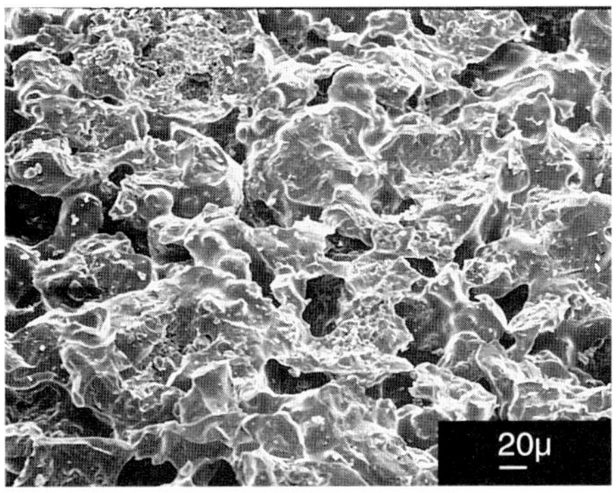

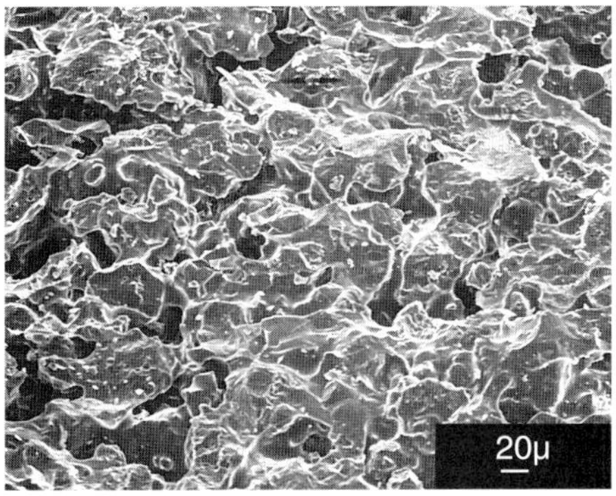

Reconstituted Washita (left) and Hard Arkansas (right) stones have a masked structure similar to that of an aluminum-oxide stone. (Photos courtesy National Research Council of Canada)

A monocrystalline diamond bench stone is a good stone for basic sharpening and excels as a tool for truing other bench stones.

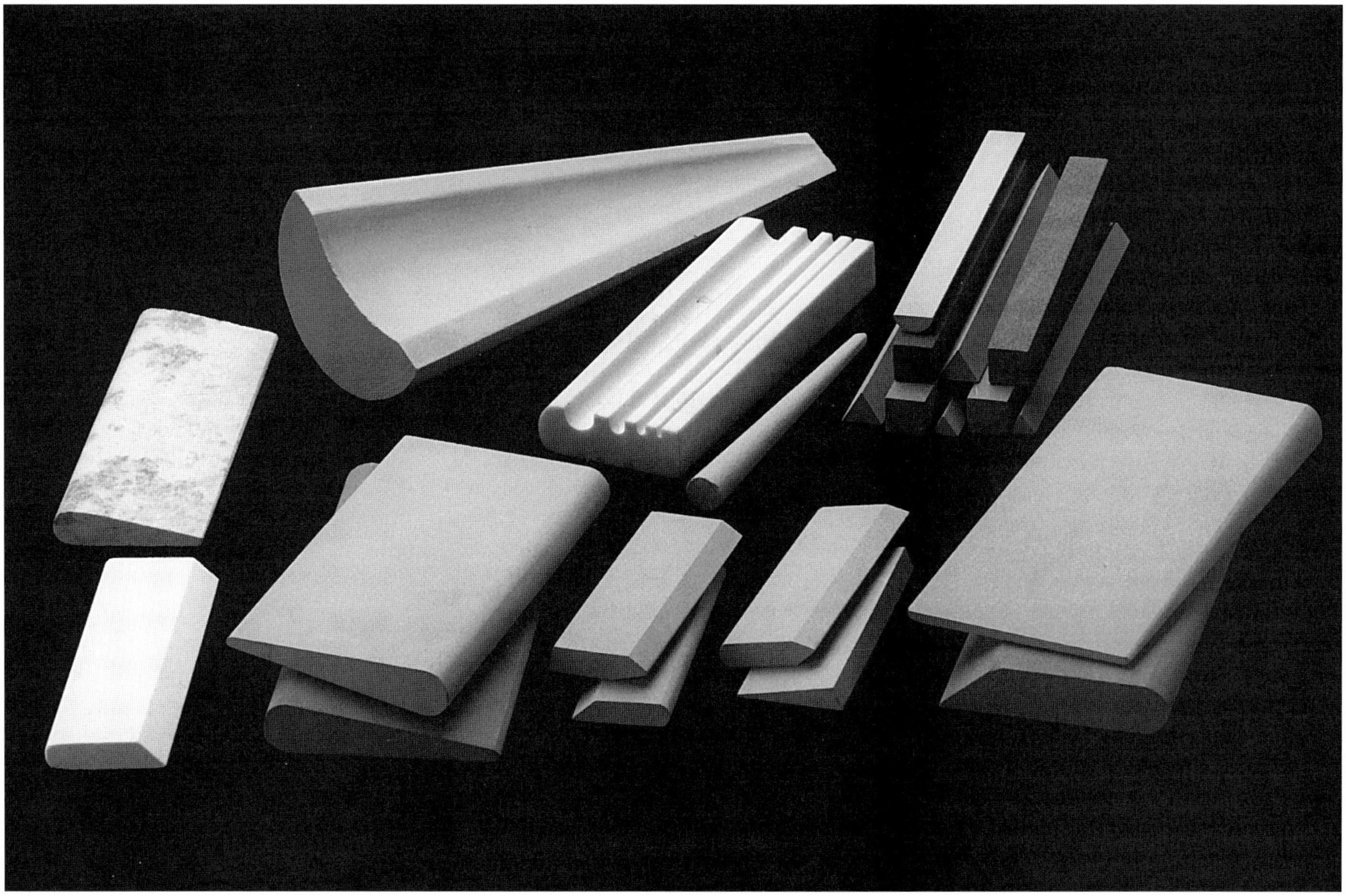

Shaped stones, available in numerous profiles and abrasives, are nowadays used primarily to sharpen turning and carving tools.

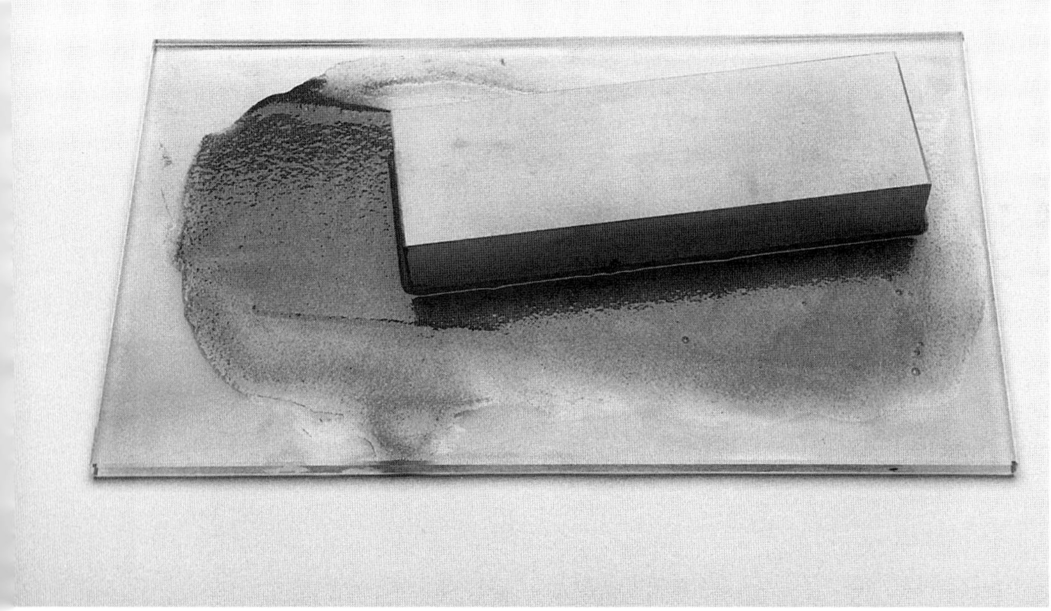

Lapping a bench stone on plate glass with loose silicon-carbide grit serves to flatten the stone as well as remove any glazed layer. (Photo by Susan Kahn)

SHAPED STONES

There are too many shaped stones on the market to do an adequate job of describing them all. There are gouge cones, slipstones, round, triangular and square-section stones. They are available in natural Hard Arkansas, resin-bond aluminum-oxide water stones, vitrified-bond aluminum oxide and silicon carbide, and an increasingly large number of diamond-coated shapes.

To a great extent, power-sharpening equipment has rendered many of these stones obsolete. In addition, many of the special shapes they were designed to sharpen are now made from tungsten carbide, and they are only sharpened with diamond. The ones that have continued to retain some popularity are the gouge cones among turners and the slipstones among carvers. Both are now available in either water stones or oil stones. With slipstones, resin-bond water stones are preferable but, just like the bench stones, they need more care since they wear more rapidly. The one place where the natural Arkansas still has a clear advantage is with stone files of the type used to touch up combination plane blades and filed edges like auger-bit chippers or two-man crosscut saw teeth. Water stones are too soft in these uses, and vitrified-bond stones are not available in fine enough grits.

KEEPING STONES FLAT

Eventually stones wear from use. If they wore evenly there would be no problem, but they tend to wear most in the center; eventually a stone becomes so dished that it is impossible to hone a straight edge on it.

The easiest and fastest way to flatten any bench stone is to use a coarse diamond bench stone. If you can afford one, it is a wonderful luxury. For the poor and the parsimonious, there are several other alternatives. Silicon-carbide paper on a sheet of plate glass works well, although the stones will quickly dull the sandpaper. Loose silicon-carbide particles on plate glass with a bit of water or WD-40 will also work as a lapping medium. It is even more effective if a hard plastic like Mylar is backed with plate glass and silicon-carbide particles put on the Mylar. They will bed in the Mylar and abrade the stone. On the plate glass alone they tend to roll around a bit too much, and the process takes longer.

Particularly with Japanese water stones, it is possible to true a finer stone with a coarser one. As an example, an 800x water stone can be used to true a 6000x or an 8000x stone. Using the stone with a circular rubbing motion, you can be reasonably sure that the coarse stone will stay flat as it is abrading the finer stone. You should be aware, however, that stones rubbed together will normally wear until they have mating surfaces. These surfaces will always be flat if you are using three stones in rotation. If you have only two stones to rub together, you can get mating surfaces but one might be concave while the other is convex.

WHAT SIZE STONE?

Although it can be tempting to buy cheaper, small bench stones, I recommend that you buy a stone that is at least 2½ in. wide by 8 in. long. You will find that the common size of 2 in. by 6 in. will often be too small. It is not only too short for an easy honing action in many instances, but it is too narrow for any blades wider than 1¾ in. I would prefer to own fewer stones and have them a decent size.

Whatever method you use to lap stones, it's a good idea to flush them completely since it is possible to get contamination from the lapping grit or the coarse stone that was being used. This is not a particular problem with coarse bench stones but is very much a concern with fine finishing stones, particularly those with a resin bond because particles will imbed in them more readily than in vitrified-bond stones. Fortunately, your fingers are sensitive enough to detect a rogue particle in one of your finishing stones.

Storing stones Another way to contaminate a stone is to store it badly. All stones should be kept in covered containers. Oil stones are usually kept in fitted wooden boxes; water stones are best kept submerged in a covered bath, unless they have wooden bases. Wooden-base stones may be stored upside-down in a shallow bath, keeping the wood well clear of the water, or they can be stored dry. It is generally best to keep water stones wet so that they are ready for immediate use (a dry stone can take several minutes to fill) and to avoid the salt deposits that can accumulate in the pores if you have hard water and allow stones to dry out between uses. You will find that very fine stones (6000x and finer) function well with just surface water on them, so they can be stored dry if desired.

One exception to these general recommendations is that water stones should never be allowed to freeze unless they are completely dry. A wet stone will burst when frozen. As a further word of caution to innovative woodworkers who think they can store stones in antifreeze, most antifreezes attack resin bonds.

HONING GUIDES

I recommend the use of honing guides with chisels and plane blades for two reasons: speed and accuracy. A good guide should let you select a honing angle, clamp the tool firmly at that angle for shaping a basic bevel, and then let you make a small angular adjustment for fine honing of a secondary bevel or micro-bevel. In addition, you should later be able to set the tool at exactly the same angles again when you need to resharpen it.

A system that lets you do all this will remove the least metal each time you have to sharpen a tool. Since metal removal is a function of time when you are honing, such a system is also therefore the fastest. Equally important, it provides the accuracy you want for maintaining bevels at their optimum angles.

There are only two honing guides on the market that meet these criteria, the Eclipse guide and the Veritas guide. At this point I am reminded of the qualifier that a publisher sometimes puts at the end of an opinion column in the financial press. It runs something like this: "Columnist X may own stocks or bonds discussed in this column." I declare such a conflict with the Veritas guide, but since I used an Eclipse guide for a decade before the Veritas guide was developed I think that I can deal with it as an old friend.

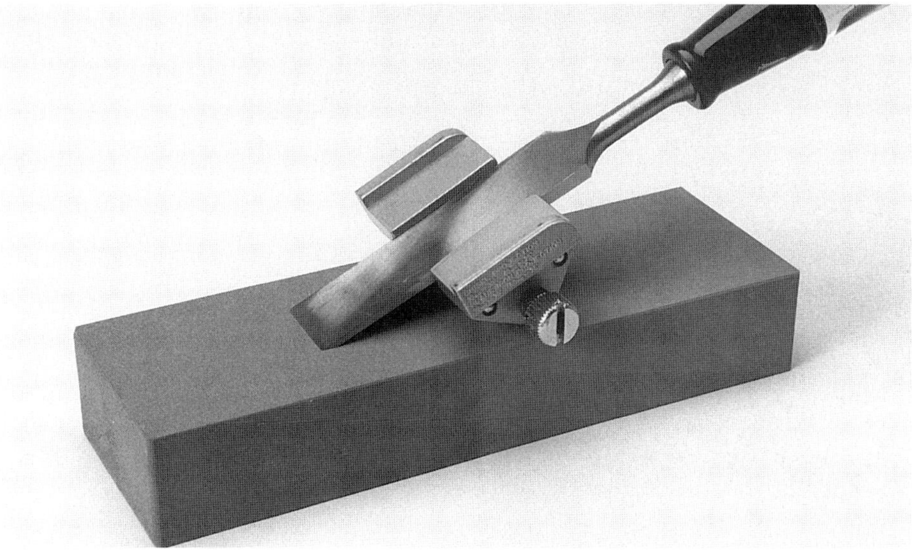

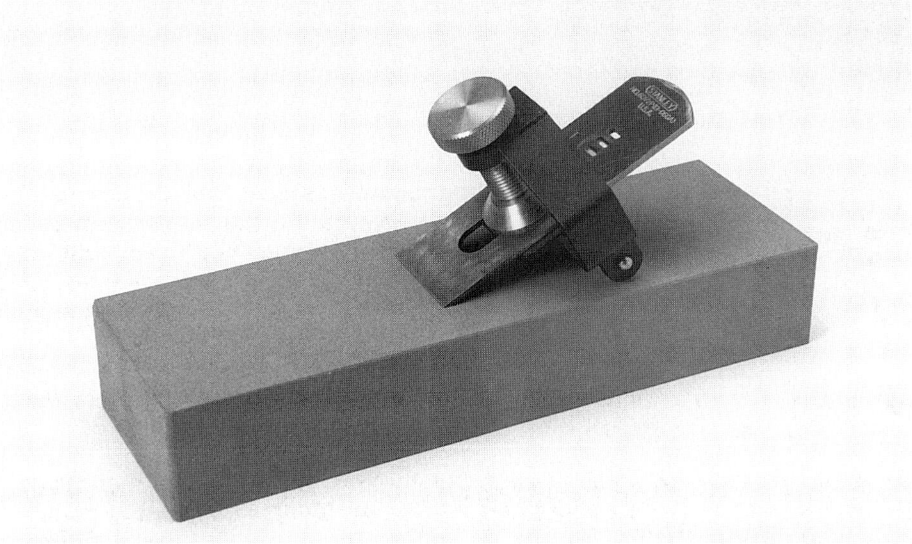

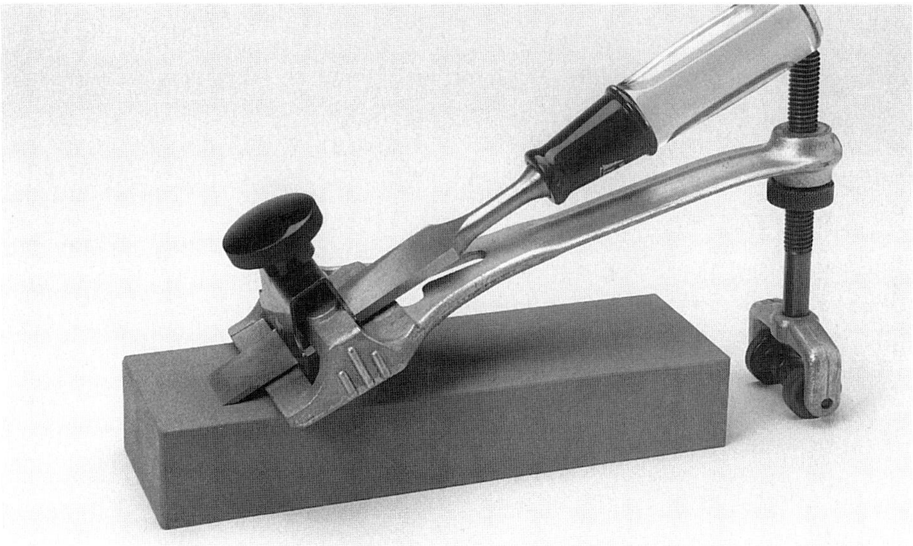

The side-clamping Eclipse guide (top) and the top-clamping Veritas (middle) are two of the most effective honing guides available. The General guide (above) is a dependable tool but does not provide good angular control. (Photos by Susan Kahn)

The Eclipse guide (see the top photo at left) is a side-clamping design that clamps firmly but cannot handle skew chisels, spokeshave blades or butt chisels at normal honing angles. The Veritas guide (middle photo at left) is a top-clamping model that clamps firmly (a hair less so than the Eclipse) and can handle skew chisels, spokeshave blades and Western butt chisels at normal grind angles but not Japanese butt chisels. It does not clamp very narrow chisels as well as the Eclipse, but, once clamped, they are easier to hone because of the wider and more stable roller on the Veritas. For different reasons, it is easy to get a tip off-square on a narrow chisel with either guide if care is not taken. On chisels wider than $\frac{1}{4}$ in., the Veritas guide holds blades so that they hone true; the Eclipse guide has a narrower roller with enough play in it to be a problem.

Finally, the Veritas guide has a cam roller that lets you adjust the bevel by 1° or 2° without unclamping the tool. With the Eclipse you can achieve the same effect by sliding a piece of plastic or metal under the roller. It restricts the range of travel of the guide, but since it is only necessary when honing a microbevel it is more of a nuisance than a limitation.

The Veritas guide is best used with the Veritas angle-setting jig (see the top photo on the facing page). So is the Eclipse. The setting jig has a pentagonal disc with five bevel angles on it from 15° to 35° at 5° increments. To set the bevel angle on a blade, the blade is clamped loosely in the jig, rolled up to the setting jig and then clamped tightly only after adjusting the blade until it is flush with the beveled face of the jig.

One serendipitous feature of the Veritas jig is that it automatically adjusts itself on a skew chisel. When the skew is set flush in the angle jig, with the cutting edge tucked into the join of the pentagon and the base, and a loosely clamped guide is allowed to slide down the chisel until the roller hits the base of the setting jig, it will automatically orient itself correctly. Just plain luck. It wasn't designed to do that.

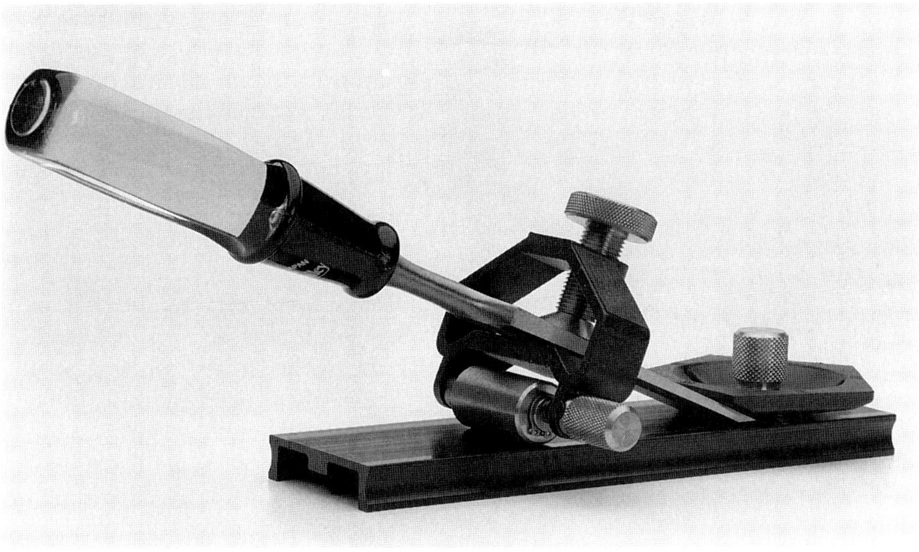

A commercial angle-setting jig, which can be used with either the Veritas or Eclipse guide, allows accurate setting of bevel angles from 15° to 35°.

Before leaving the subject of honing guides, brief mention of the General guide is in order (see the bottom photo on the facing page). This is a workmanlike guide that is suitable for occasional do-it-yourself use but unsuitable if you want good angular control. There is no easy way to set honing angles, never mind returning to them exactly when it is time to resharpen. But the General guide is quick to set up and allows you to use shorter stones because the roller runs on the work table, not on the stone.

WHY USE A MICRO-BEVEL?

The primary reason for using a micro-bevel is that it saves honing time. If you want a 25° bevel angle on a tool and you grind the bevel at 25°, you then have to hone the entire bevel in order to get a keen cutting edge. On a very fine stone, like an 8000x, this can take quite a while and wear away a lot more stone than if you grind at 24° and put on a 1° micro-bevel with a half-dozen strokes on the stone. The fine finish on the whole bevel makes no difference in cutting, it is only the last few thousandths of an inch that is important to the edge. (For more on micro-bevels, see pp. 62-63.)

SETTING ANGLES ON AN ECLIPSE GUIDE

If you want to use a wide range of angles with an Eclipse honing guide, you have to make a special setting gauge. The guide's instructions tell you how to set 25° and 30° by measuring blade projection from the guide, but this is both limiting and cumbersome. It is easier to spend a bit of time and make a setting gauge so that you can put the tool tip against the stop and slide the guide up to the gauge edge before clamping.

This same system will work with the Veritas honing guide if you do not have the Veritas angle-setting jig.

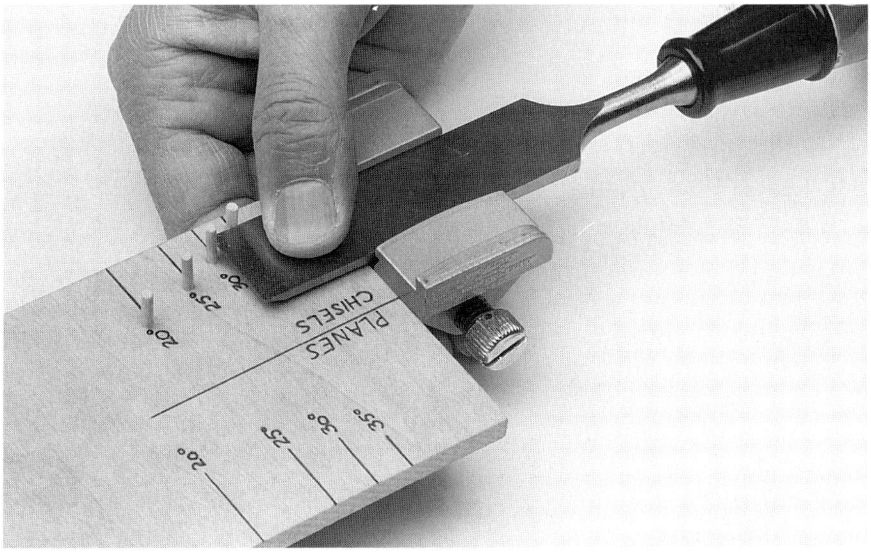

This shopmade angle-setting gauge for use with the Eclipse honing guide allows setting of bevel angles from 20° to 35°.

STROPS

The word "strop" is used ambiguously nowadays. Originating with the leather barber's strop, it was both verb and noun. Lately some writers have used it to describe any fine sharpening operation, whether or not the edge being sharpened is being passed in a trailing stroke (a "stropping" action) over the abrasive. But not here. To me, stropping always means the use of a trailing stroke, and a strop is something that could be accidentally cut with a leading stroke.

A strop is used to touch up an edge. Although a variety of materials can be used for strops, with very few exceptions the strops are normally charged with a stropping compound before they are used. This is certainly the case with strops made from cloth or wood, but not always the case with strops made from leather.

LEATHER STROPS

Many leathers contain a natural abrasive. Under a microscope it appears to be some kind of silica. Until recently, natural leather strops were in common use in barber shops. But the traditional barber's strop is not the type that would normally be used in woodworking, because it is too flexible. Flexibility was no problem for a barber, because a straight razor was hollow ground on the sides to maintain just the right geometry for stropping on a taut belt. In woodworking it is more normal to fix the leather to a firm backing such as a piece of wood in order to minimize bevel rounding during the stropping process. The leather is also normally charged with a chromium-oxide compound. It then makes an excellent strop for all kinds of edge tools, especially knives.

While not exactly strops, leather belts are available for some belt sanders. These are usually charged with a buffing and honing compound such as chromium oxide and are very effective with knives and carving tools.

WOODEN STROPS

The least publicized and probably the most useful strops of all are ones made of wood. A good chromium-oxide compound (one that has a small percentage of fine aluminum-oxide particles in it as well as chromium oxide) applied to a piece of wood makes a potent sharpening device. As an example, I no longer use slipstones with carving tools. Taking a simple gouge as an example, I do the basic sharpening with a power system and all the honing with wooden strops (see Chapter 9). Using a soft wood like basswood or pine, you cut a groove in the face of the scrap with the gouge that you want to hone and you then have a perfectly formed strop for the bevel (see the photo below).

Turning your attention to the edge of the piece of scrap, you also cut it with the gouge but to match the inside of the gouge. It takes only seconds, and you now have a strop that is matched perfectly to the tool that it is going to be used on. You will find that the wood is very easy to charge with chromium oxide and that the strop will cut quite quickly. More important, unless you are particularly careless, you readily avoid bevel rounding using strops like these.

The potential for wooden strops is obvious. Pieces of wooden dowel can be charged with compound; V-shaped pieces of wood can be used for honing the inside of parting tools. But the true magic of it all is that you can use the blade that you want to hone to form the piece of wood to shape. In seconds, you can make a wooden strop that is perfectly matched to any shape of tool you have.

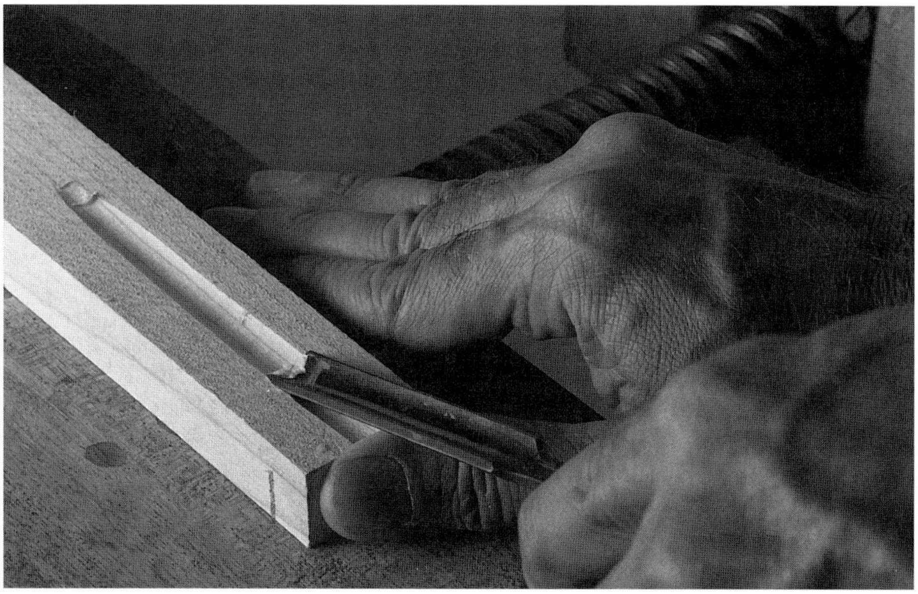

Cutting a groove in the face of a softwood block with a gouge produces a perfectly formed strop for honing the bevel of the same gouge. (Photo by Susan Kahn)

FILES

In sharpening, files are usually used for basic shaping. They are often followed by similarly shaped honing stones. Files are limited to tools that are relatively soft, usually Rc50 or less—tools such as handsaws, scrapers and axes. On tools like chisels or plane blades files are not only ineffective but will also dull very quickly.

Files that look alike can be dissimilar in use; the difference in performance usually reflects the difference in quality. A well-made file starts with a smoothly ground blank made from annealed steel. Sharp chisels are used to raise the file teeth before the file is hardened. If the blank is not smooth, the file teeth will be ragged and irregular. If the chisels are not sharp, the file teeth will have slightly rounded tops (like cresting waves) caused by the deformation of the blank as the chisels enter at an angle to raise the teeth. A well-made file looks smooth on the uncut portion and feels smooth along a single-cut ridge. It will also have sharply defined edges on all teeth. If it is not carefully hardened, the fine tips will lose some of their carbon allowing them to dull quickly.

It is getting increasingly difficult to find good files. Nicholson has always made good files but it has reduced its range substantially in the last decade. Most of its files are now sold under the Black Diamond brand, but at one time the company sold under all of the following brands, which can still often be found in old hardware stores—McClellan, K&F, Great Western, Superior, Eagle, J.B. Smith, Beaver, American, Arcade and Globe.

Files come in a bewildering array of shapes, sizes and cuts. While it is always pleasant to be able to chose from a wide variety, you really need only a very few files to handle 95% of all the sharpening jobs in your shop.

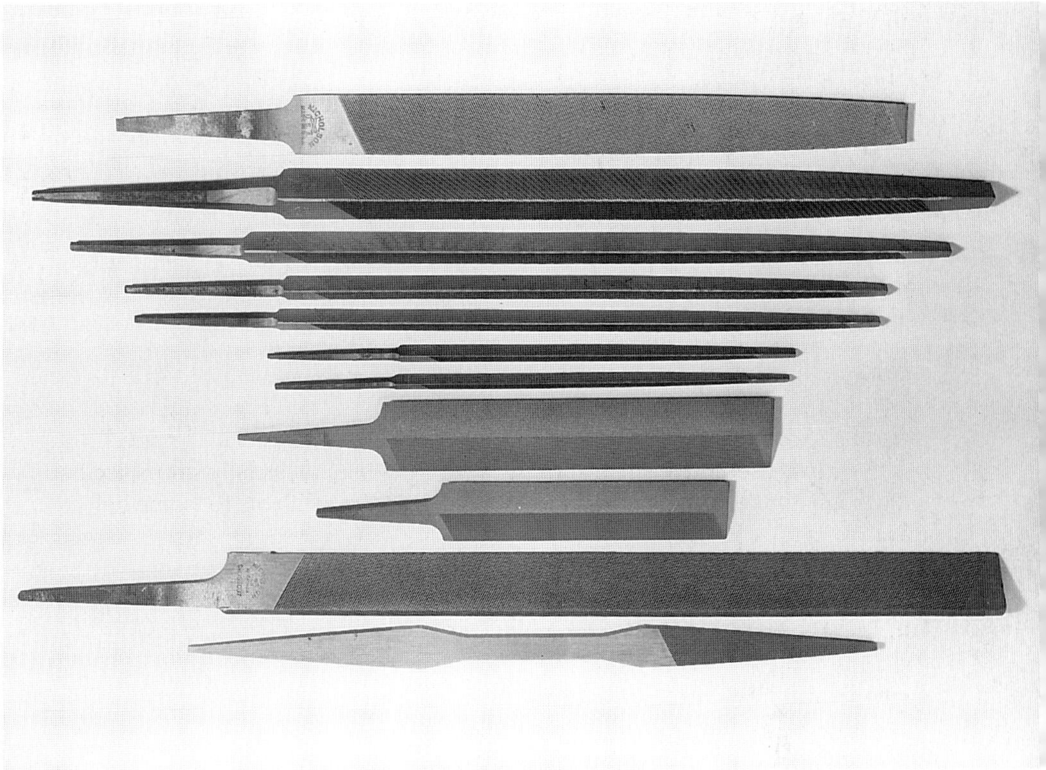

Files with specific sharpening applications include (from top to bottom) an 8-in. mill file, six triangular handsaw files, two feather-edge files, a Great American crosscut file and an auger-bit file.

MILL FILES

Mill files, so named because of their early use in filing circular saws in lumber mills, are absolutely indispensable in any shop. If you can afford only one, an 8-in. file is your best choice. It is the best compromise of fineness versus rapid stock removal. If you can afford them, a 6-in. file is handy for fine work, including jointing fine saws, and a 10-in. file is ideal for heavy stock removal in relatively soft steel that you might encounter in axes or many gardening tools. But an 8-in. mill file (bastard cut) is just about the handiest file you can have in the shop, and all the rest of those listed below cannot approach it in general usefulness.

The one thing you will notice in common with all the files discussed below is that the mill file is a single-cut file. In the Rc range from approximately 35 to 50, single-cut files remove steel fastest with the least clogging. They also wear more quickly than double-cut files.

TRIANGULAR HANDSAW FILES

Specifically for sharpening handsaws, triangular files are of limited usefulness for anything else in the shop except sawtooth bits. These are tapered files and are graded as regular, slim taper, extra-slim taper and double extra-slim taper. If you are uncertain about what file to use for a given saw, you should use one that has a flat that is at least double the length of the face of tooth that you intend to file. This is to ensure that you get three usable pairs of filing surfaces on each file (see p. 148).

At one time there was a saw file made called a Double Ender, which was tapered from the center toward both ends and was cut from the ends toward the center so that it gave six intersections. These files were about 7 in. long and, since you normally use only about a 3-in. stroke, it was like having two files.

WEB-SAW FILES, FEATHER-EDGE FILES

When Swede saws were popular, the file of choice for the cognoscenti was a web-saw file, a file no longer in production. Actually they were for use on any saw that had tooth tips more acute than 60°. Naturally, since they are no longer available, I attribute far greater utility to them than they ever probably had.

But they have an Eastern cousin, the feather-edge file, which is now fairly widely available in North America. This is the file that is used for sharpening Japanese saws, all of which have tooth tips more acute than 60°. Feather-edge files are a little thinner in the body than web-saw files but have the advantage of being available in a safe-face version as well as in a full-cut version. The safe-

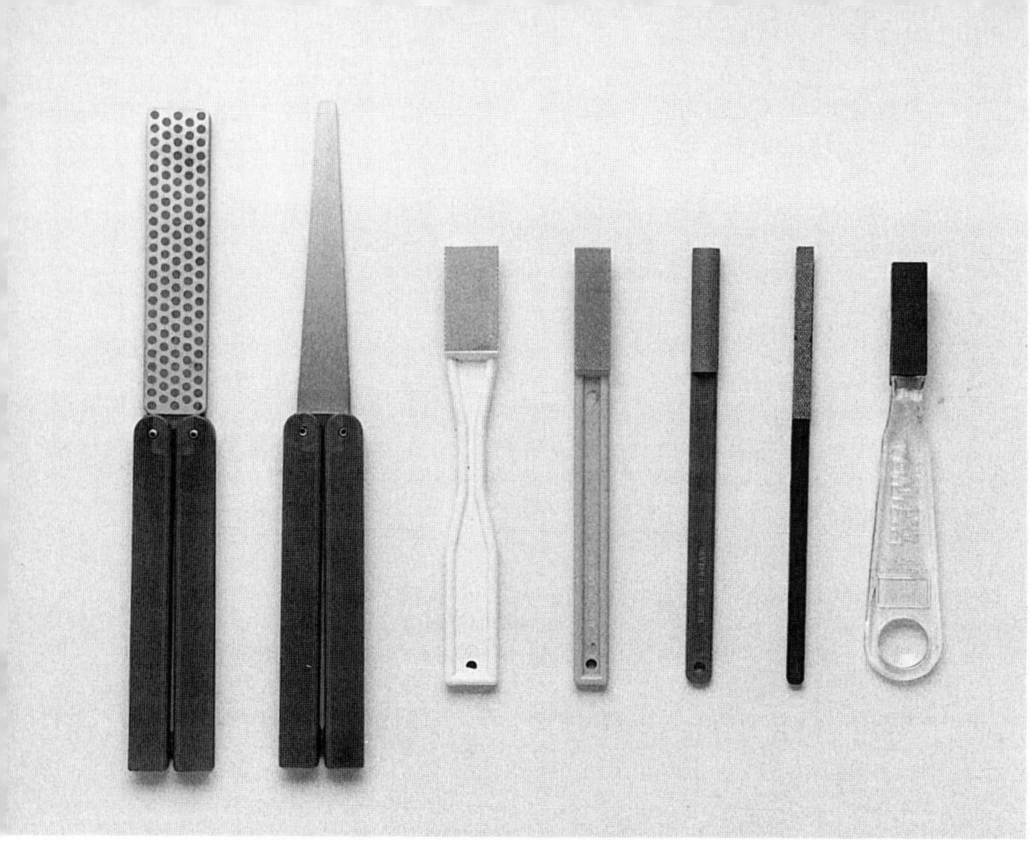

Diamond hones and files, shown here in a range of configurations and grit sizes, are used to sharpen tungsten-carbide-tipped tools. (Photo by Susan Kahn)

face version is cut on only one side, which means that if you accidentally slither off whatever you happen to be filing, the back of the file will not do random damage to anything it encounters. This is a very desirable feature when you are first getting accustomed to the intricate geometry of Japanese saws. Again, these are excellent fitting files.

GREAT AMERICAN CROSSCUT FILE

These files are certainly on the endangered species list and will probably not be manufactured much longer. A specialized type of saw file, it has a rounded back for gumming out between teeth. Between them, a feather-edge file and a chainsaw file will do the same job.

AUGER-BIT FILE

Specifically designed for sharpening auger bits, this file has one end cut on both faces but not cut on the edges; the other end is cut on the edges but not on the faces. It is designed this way so that you can file the chippers of an auger bit without marking the screw point or the lip. Similarly, you can file the inside of a spur without scoring the chipper. Although this file has a highly specialized purpose in sharpening, its greatest usefulness around the shop is for those dozens of fitting jobs where you want to be able to dimension one surface without affecting an adjoining surface. Perfect examples are when you want to file the inside bevels of a corner chisel, or dress off a high spot on a plane bed without scoring the cheek.

DIAMOND FILES, BORON-CARBIDE FILES

Only two types of abrasive deal effectively with tungsten carbide: diamond and boron carbide. Diamond files come in a variety of configurations, but a flat file is probably the most useful. Boron carbide is normally in block form glued to another type of backing. Diamond files are usually only available up to about 600x (although a 1200x file has just been introduced), and boron carbide up to 400x. A 400x boron carbide gives a finish about equal to a 600x diamond.

SANDPAPER

Sandpaper, dealt with in passing under belt sanders (see pp. 44-45), is an excellent sharpening material used on shaped backings of different types. A 600x wet/dry silicon-carbide paper mounted on a block of wood still makes an inexpensive fine stone for a chip carver. Combined with a simple stropping block with chromium oxide, it can be a complete sharpening system for someone.

Similarly, PSA-backed sandpaper can readily be attached to a wooden dowel for use with gouges. With a shaped surface, a spray-on adhesive and the right type of grit of sandpaper, you can make a sharpening device of almost any shape you want.

MICRO-FINISHING ABRASIVES

There are newer, finer abrasives coming on the market rapidly. One of the most impressive is the micro-finishing line from 3M. The regularity of the grit size and the aggressiveness of cut are exceptional. Probably most impressive in the line is the 0.5 micron chromium oxide on 3-mil Mylar. It will put a mirror finish on an edge faster than a stone that is five times as coarse. Considering that it is a 16000x abrasive, it is amazingly aggressive.

I believe that the effectiveness of the Mylar-backed abrasive is a result of the electrostatic charging process that 3M uses when bonding particles to the

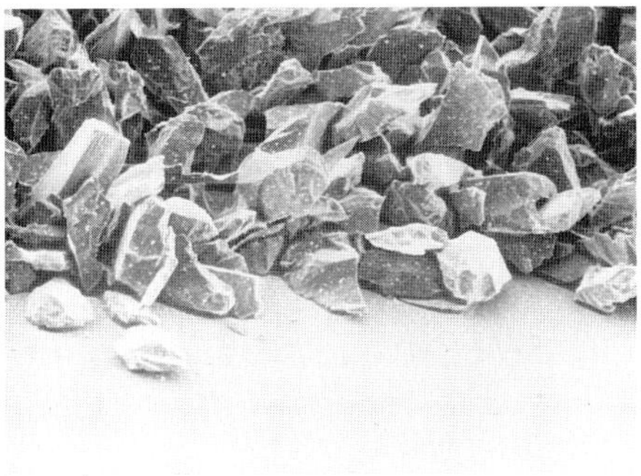

3M's diamond micro-abrasives on Mylar (top), paper (middle) and cloth backing (above). (Photos courtesy 3M)

A BASIC SHARPENING SETUP

There is such a bewildering array of sharpening gear available that it is difficult for a novice to decide what to buy first or even what to buy at all. If I were starting from scratch on a limited budget, I would buy products in this sequence:

1. 1000x/4000x combination water stone ($25.00)

This stone will let you sharpen all the high-carbon-alloy straight-edged tools (chisels, plane blades, knives, etc.) in your shop.

2. 8-in. mill file ($4.00)

For basic shaping of softer steel (axes, hatchets, drawknives, etc.) and the inevitable gardening tools.

3. Chromium-oxide honing compound ($6.00 to $20.00)

With this compound and scrap wood you can make a wide variety of hones to fit almost any shape of tool. Combined with sandpaper, it can become a basic sharpening system.

This is a watershed. From this point on you are buying speed, accuracy and specialization.

4. Honing guide ($12.00 to $30.00)

Either the Eclipse or the Veritas with the angle-setting jig. Chisels and plane blades are basic to the craft, and a guide not only saves time but introduces precision and control to the sharpening process.

**5. Grinder ($40.00 and up)
Stone (A80H-8V) ($25.00)
Diamond dresser ($15.00)**

Not only does a powered grinder introduce speed to the process, but it is a virtual necessity for many specialized tools, such as turning gouges. Besides tool grinding, it is hard to conceive of fixing anything in a shop without having a grinder at hand.

6. From here on it could be a good tool rest, a felt wheel, a belt sander, a leather strop, an 8000x stone, etc. What you buy next depends on your budget and on the nature of your woodworking.

Mylar. The particles are all standing up like iron filings on a magnet when they are glued in place. These microfinishing abrasives are available in belt, roll, disc and sheet form (the last two with or without PSA backing).

Because of the flatness of Mylar and the very regular application of grit, these leave a finer finish than similar grit on regular paper or cloth backings. To give an indication of the flatness of Mylar film, compare the three photos above, which are from 3M's diamond abrasive line.

With this discussion of abrasives and sharpening equipment behind us, the boiler-plate section of the book is complete. As Peter Drucker, the management guru, observed, sooner or later all planning must degenerate into actual work. We are at that point now.

CHAPTER 6

CHISELS

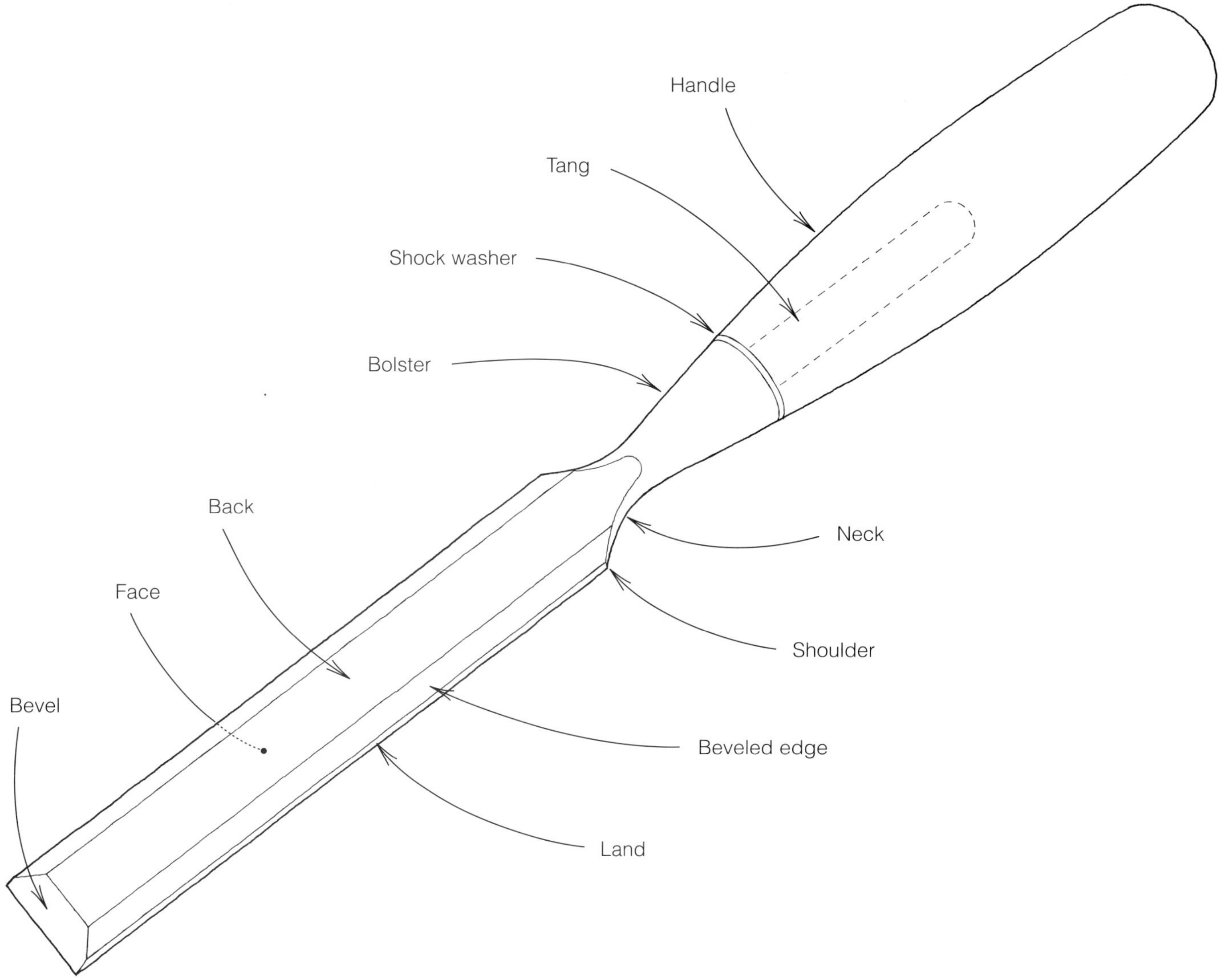

Somewhere in the mists of time man discovered that a wedge-shaped rock could be used to divide things. It was probably only a matter of days before he found that it was also a handy little prying tool, and probably only a matter of minutes after that when he damaged the tip prying something that really needed a bigger rock. The pattern for the use and abuse of chisels was set early in the tools' history.

A chisel comes from the factory with grinding marks on its face (top). These marks must be removed to create a sharp edge and to flatten the face (above).

GENERAL SHARPENING PROCEDURES

Chisels do not come from the store ready to use. Most have been ground to a basic shape, a few have been honed, none have been lapped and almost all have been dipped in lacquer to prevent rust. The first thing to do to your new chisel is to remove the lacquer.

REMOVING THE LACQUER

Lacquer must be removed from the face of the chisel and the bevel. On all except mortise chisels, it is not mandatory to remove the lacquer from the back and the sides, but my preference is to strip it all off up to the neck. Otherwise, you have scuffed lacquer on part of the tool, which not only looks ugly but also can give you a false sense that the tool is still rust-proofed. Lacquer thinner or paint stripper can be used to remove the lacquer. Be sure the thinner does not get on the handle, since it can soften some plastics and will strip lacquer off wooden handles.

LAPPING THE FACE OF THE CHISEL

In the condition it comes from the factory, the face of the chisel will have grinding marks on it, as shown in the top photo at right. If you did not first lap the chisel but devoted your attention only to the bevel, regardless of how well you honed that bevel, it would still be intersecting with a grooved face and the resulting edge would be ragged. So the first thing you have to do is remove these grind marks and make the face of the chisel as smooth as possible (as explained below).

CHISEL DEFECTS

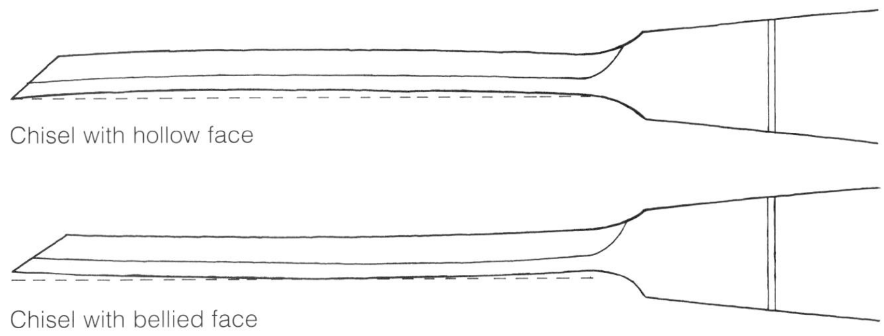

There is a second reason that lapping may be necessary; the face of the chisel may not be flat. Although a slight hollowness can be accepted in a chisel face, it cannot have any belly and still function well. A chisel with a belly in it should be returned to the vendor.

If that is not possible, initial flattening can be done on a belt sander (see the sidebar at left). Only when the face is very close to flat should you start working it with stones.

Most chisels made today are ground reasonably well. Two types that you should immediately be suspicious of are chisels that have been hand ground (several German styles) and chisels that have been polished. Hand-ground chisels are almost never flat, square or straight. Polished chisels almost invariably have the sides rounded and

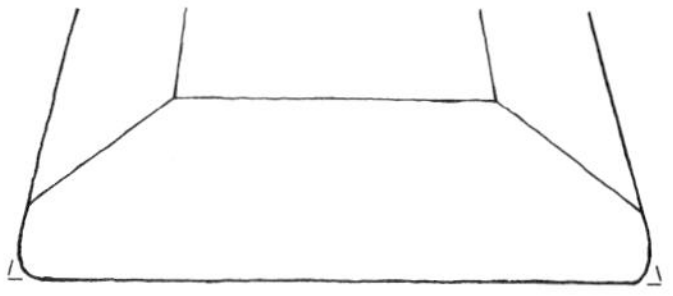

the face dubbed next to the bevel. The rounded sides (above) prevent you from getting a flat, full-width cut; the dubbed face (below), if uncorrected,

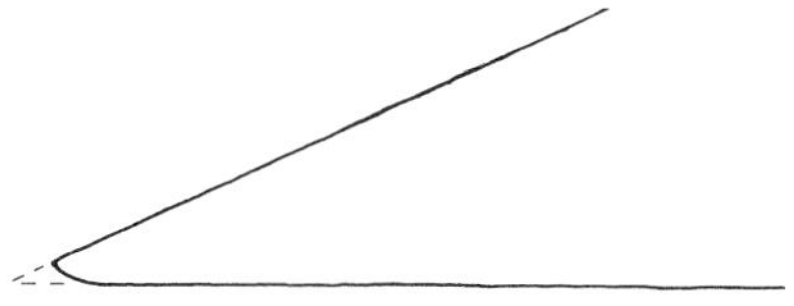

would mean that you would constantly have to tilt the chisel up to get it to cut. You would then have poor control of the tool.

To fix the dubbed tip, you usually have to grind about $\frac{1}{16}$ in. off the bevel. Lapping the chisel face will show when you have removed enough material. To true rounded sides, you can use a belt sander or dress them back on a stone. It is best to do such dressing on the edge of the stone, because you can quickly wear a groove in the stone when repeatedly rubbing a narrow edge in the same spot. The drawing at left shows a simple setup for truing the sides of a chisel as well as squaring the sides to the face.

For lapping most chisels you can start with an 800x or 1200x stone and then go directly to a 6000x or 8000x stone. This is one time you want to be absolutely sure that your stones are flat (see p. 51), because it is a fair amount of work to lap a chisel and you do not want to have to do it more than once.

FIXING A CHISEL WITH A BELLY

There are times when you have no choice but to fix a bellied chisel. If the chisel needs a great deal of work, I would start on a belt sander with a 120x belt. This assumes that you have a nice flat platen to work against as you hog off the bulk of the material on the belt sander (being ever conscious of the steel temperature). Check your work frequently by lapping the chisel briefly on the stone. The lap marks will tell you immediately where the high points are and how much you still have to remove.

These are guerrilla tactics but quite effective. You will find that you can do most of the straightening on a sander without taking off steel that you do not want to remove.

TRUING THE SIDES OF A CHISEL

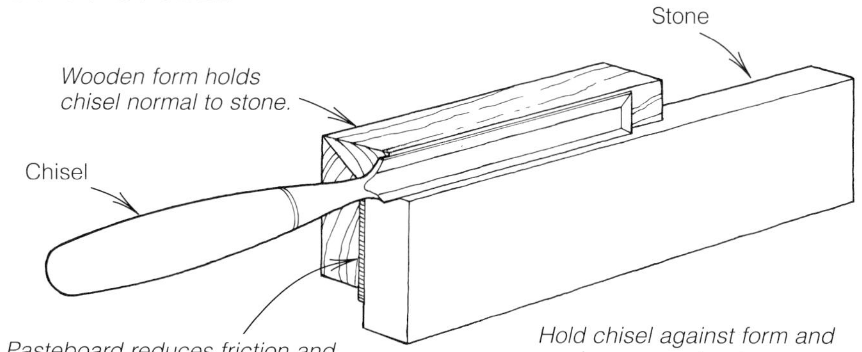

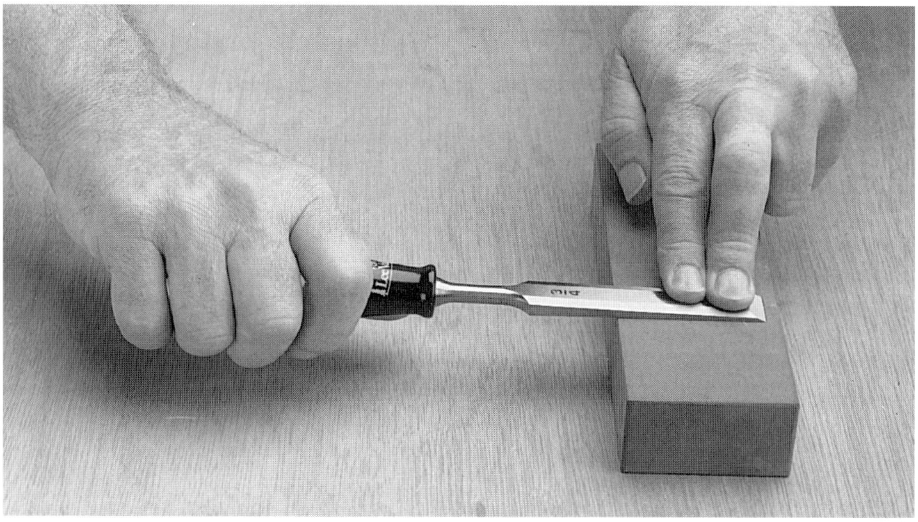

To lap a chisel, hold two fingers on the back of the tool while rubbing it back and forth on the stone. With a narrow stone you may need to skew the chisel to the line of travel to get most of the face on the stone.

It is not necessary to get the entire face of the chisel flat. Just as you can tolerate some hollowness fore to aft, you can tolerate some hollowness from side to side. If you have a chisel that is slightly hollow from side to side, you can stop lapping it as soon as you get the face to approximately the same configuration as most Japanese chisels, which are ground hollow on the face (see the bottom chisel in the photo at right). You do not have to be concerned that the edge will eventually reach the hollow portion. In the normal sharpening process the hollowness will slowly be eliminated as you remove a small amount of metal each time you sharpen.

If you are using a water stone, you can save yourself some time if you stop flushing your stone and let the crushed abrasive particles accumulate as you are approaching a satisfactorily lapped face on the coarse stone. This will slow the sharpening process by reducing the depth of scratch that the stone puts in the chisel, but the lost time will be more than made up when you move on to the fine stone. It will take you less time to refine the surface, because the scratches left by the preceding stone are shallower than they would have been from a flushed stone. This technique, which is frequently used with water stones, is a way of changing the effective grit size of a stone to your advantage.

SHAPING THE EDGE

There are two basic activities to shaping the edge of a chisel: setting the basic bevel angle and then honing it. The guiding principles you use here are that the bevel angle should be the lowest possible one consistent with edge retention in intended use, and that you want to spend the minimum amount of time resharpening. Under each chisel type discussed later in this chapter, there will be recommended basic bevel angles, as well as exceptions to the general process that I am about to describe.

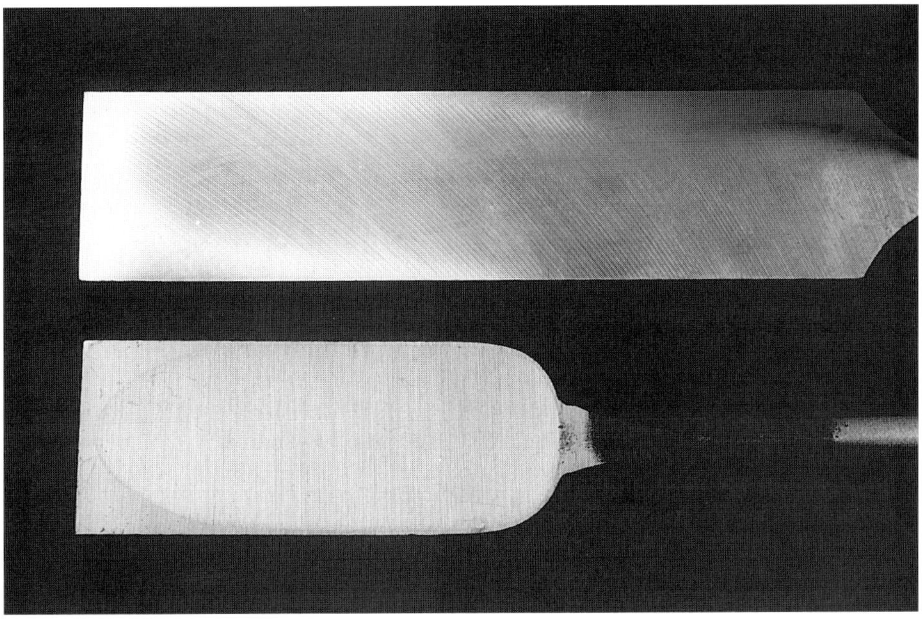

Most Japanese chisels (above) are ground hollow on the face, whereas Western chisels (top) are ground flat.

Hollow grinding For at least the past twenty years, various cabinetmakers have recommended using a hand or power grinder to put a hollow bevel on a chisel so that it can be rapidly honed. The basic principle is that you clamp the chisel in a simple jig that can be slid back and forth on the grinder tool rest to grind a regular hollow from one side of the blade to the other. When you then hone the chisel, only the very front and the very back of the bevel will ride on the stone. This makes it possible to hone blades without using a

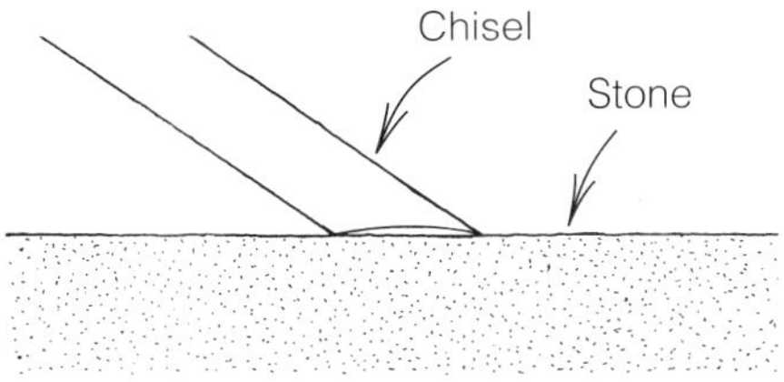

honing guide, since it minimizes the tendency of the blade to rock during honing.

While I am all for a method that reduces sharpening time, hollow grinding often does so at the expense of a strong edge. The undercutting of the bevel weakens the edge. Equally bad, if you hollow-grind at an angle that will give you the necessary edge strength, you have to hone at a higher

HOLLOW GRINDING

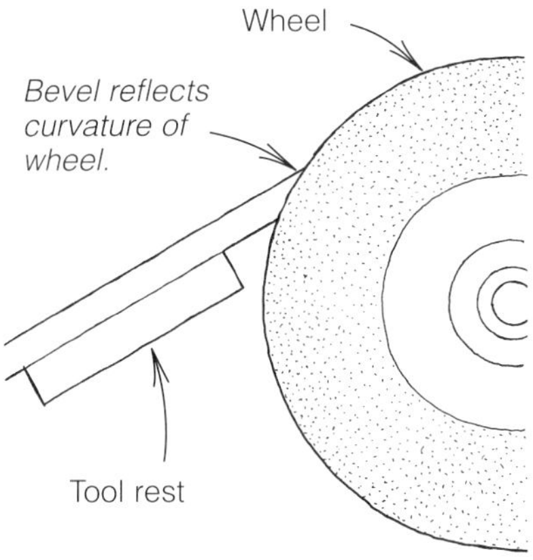

HOLLOW GRINDING

Hollow grinding creates a smaller real bevel angle than the apparent bevel angle. The effect is accentuated as blade thickness increases and/or as grinding-wheel diameter decreases. The table shows the effect for a limited number of examples.

Bevel angle	Grinding-wheel diameter	Reduction in bevel angle caused by hollow grind		
		1/8-in. thick blade	1/4-in. thick blade	1/2-in. thick blade
20°	4 in.	5.24°	10.53°	>20°
	5 in.	4.19°	8.41°	17.00°
	6 in.	3.49°	7.00°	14.10°
	7 in.	2.99°	5.99°	12.05°
	8 in.	2.62°	5.24°	10.53°
30°	4 in.	3.58°	7.18°	14.48°
	5 in.	2.87°	5.74°	11.54°
	6 in.	2.39°	4.78°	9.59°
	7 in.	2.05°	4.10°	8.21°
	8 in.	1.79°	3.58°	7.18°

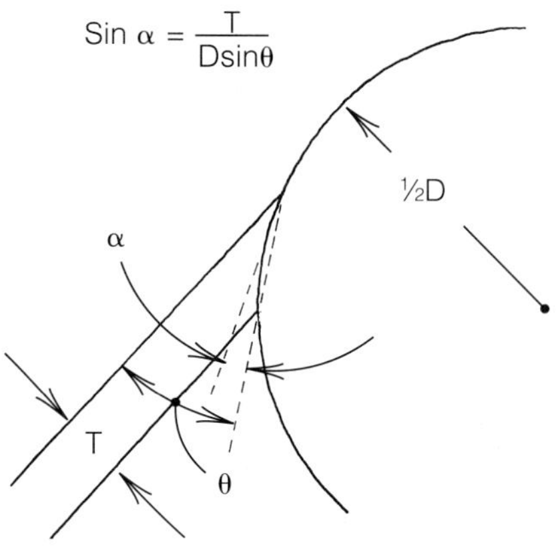

If you want to calculate the angular reduction (α) caused by hollow grinding at an apparent bevel angle (θ) for any blade thickness (T) and given wheel diameter (D), use the formula shown in the drawing above.

angle than is desirable for the best cutting action.

The problem is not nearly as acute if an 8-in. grinding wheel is used, but most shops are equipped with 6-in. wheels, which, in time, become 5-in. wheels or even smaller. The undercutting is a major problem with small wheels.

There is really nothing wrong with hollow grinding, but it should be limited to about half the bevel—the half farthest from the cutting edge. As an example, if you want to put a 25° bevel on a chisel, you can remove 2° or 3° more from the back half of the bevel to reduce your honing time substantially. For strength, you have only to worry about the front half of the bevel (with the exception of laminated chisels, which will be dealt with later). What you do with the other half of the bevel

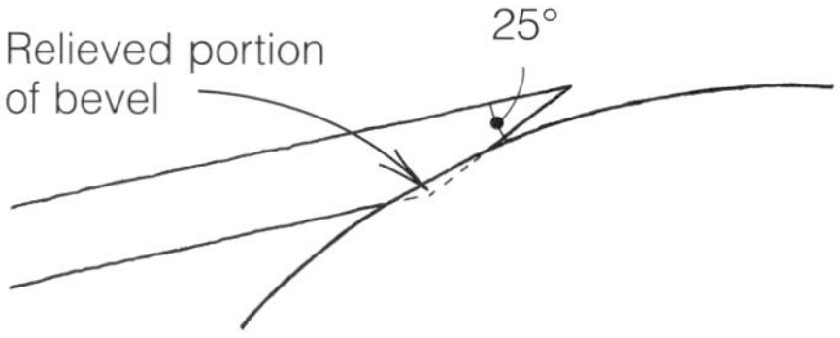

will affect rigidity, but it will not materially affect edge strength.

Removing 2° or 3° saves time in sharpening on bench stones because you have to deal with only the first half of the bevel. As this lengthens with repeated sharpenings, you can periodically relieve the back part of the bevel on a grinding wheel or belt sander.

Micro-bevels The best way to avoid a weak edge and still reduce your sharpening time is to use micro-bevels. A micro-bevel is a narrow secondary bevel at an angle slightly higher than the primary bevel. As an example, if you want to put a 25° bevel on a chisel, you would shape the basic bevel at 24° on a coarse stone and then hone on a fine stone at 25°. You need only a very narrow bevel on the fine stone, because the efficacy of the cutting action is determined only by the bevel angle and the edge keenness for any given chip or shaving thickness. Such a narrow bevel might only be 1/64 in. wide (see the top photo on the facing page).

The sole purpose of a micro-bevel is to get the finest possible edge in the shortest period of time. There is absolutely nothing wrong with grinding and honing the entire bevel at 25° if you wish to. The time it takes to do this though is substantial, and the performance difference is usually not detectable.

FRICTION ON THE BEVEL

Back in Chapter 2, I asked you to accept the assumption that there was no friction in the cutting process. Well, Dr. Norman Franz did not ignore friction in his work (see Appendix 1), and he found it to be a significant factor at low rake angles (high cutting angles). But he also found that surface roughness of the tool was relatively insignificant if the roughness was grinding serrations parallel to the path of travel of the escaping chip.

Since most of the sharpening procedures recommended here result in grooves being parallel to the path of travel of the escaping chip or shaving, and since we are dealing with high rake (low cutting) angles, we can still safely ignore friction.

Adding a micro-bevel at an angle slightly steeper than the primary bevel both strengthens the edge and reduces sharpening time.

For best control when honing freehand, hone with the blade askew the direction of travel on the stone.

For good angular control, you need to use a honing guide (see pp. 51-53 and the photo on p. 64). All of the honing guides are compatible with the micro-bevel technique. The Veritas guide has an integral cam in the roller for quick setting of micro-bevels, but the same technique can be used with all other honing guides with some sacrifice in their function but without having to unclamp the chisel from the guide. All you have to do is form the basic bevel on a coarse stone and then, when you switch to your fine honing stone, slide a flat piece of material of credit-card thickness under the roller. With a couple of honing guides, like the Eclipse, the range of travel is then limited to the distance between the roller and the point where the edge touches the stone. With guides like the General, there is greater range of movement.

Honing technique I recommend using a honing guide because you need good control of chisel bevel angles if you want to get maximum performance out of your chisels. Chisels work best when ground at the lowest possible included angle consistent with edge retention. Freehand honing does not give you that sort of control.

However, like everyone else, I do lots of freehand honing. I have a selection of chisels that are the true orphans of the tool world; they might be too soft, not straight, or rust pitted—maybe all three! Whenever I have to fix something like the barn door or the garden gate, I cheerfully grab one of these chisels, put a quick edge on it with the belt sander, touch it to the felt buffing wheel and go off to work in wood where dirt and nails lurk. But I would not do that with my bench chisels. I want them in top condition.

I keep a couple of 30° bevel chisels for cutting end-grain oak or similar destructive woods and the balance are shaped for softwoods or hardwoods, all with the honing angles marked on the tool somewhere: 15° for one paring chisel, 18° for another, skews at 20°, a great gathering around 25° and a few mortise chisels in the 30°s.

If I honed those chisels freehand, all the bevel angles would creep up and none would be as finely tuned nor work as effectively as is the case now. If you are determined to do all your honing freehand, all I can suggest is that you hone with the blade well askew the direction of travel on the stone. This gives you the best shot at good angular control.

SQUARING A CHISEL IN A HONING GUIDE

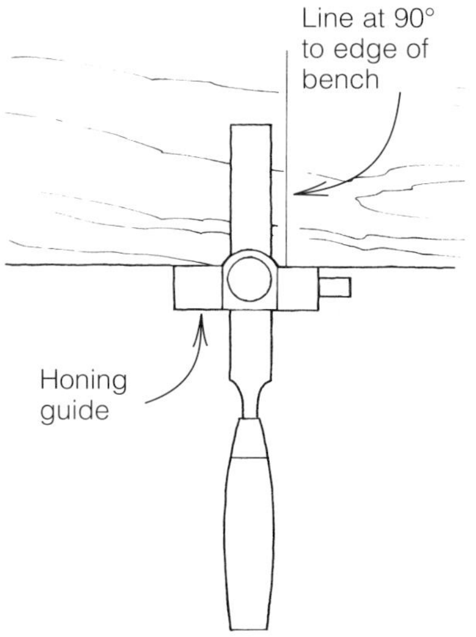

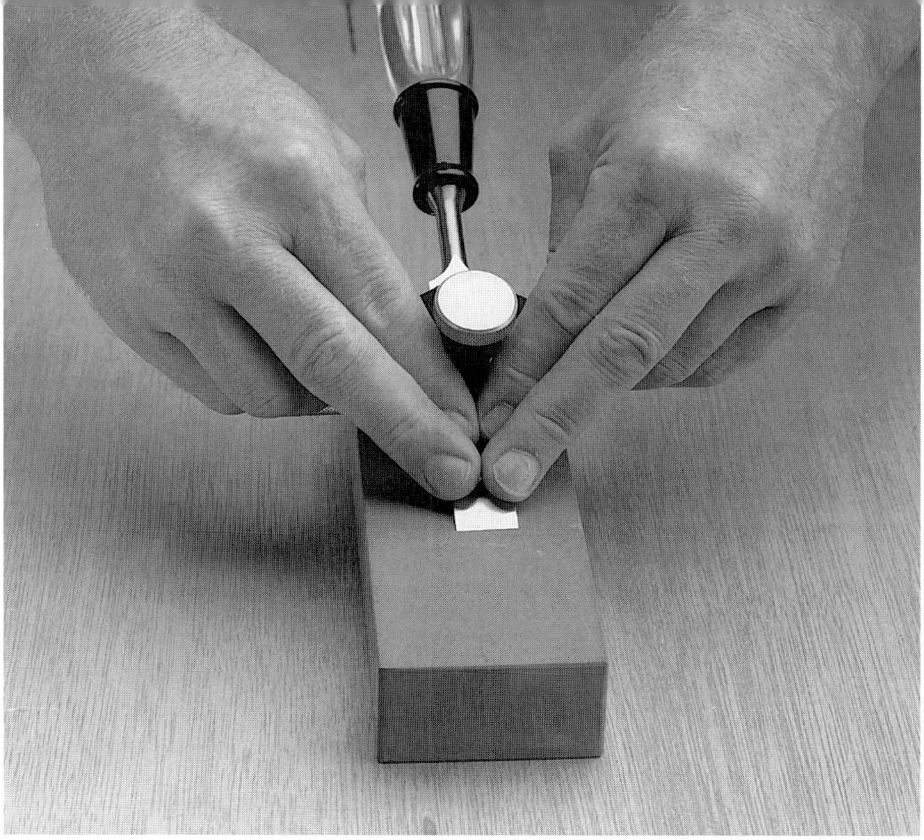

When using a honing guide, keep finger pressure well forward on the blade with thumbs hooked behind the guide. Use the whole surface of the stone for even wear.

When using a honing guide with a bench stone, there are only a couple of things that you have to be alert to: You should have the chisel set in the guide at the correct angle, and it should be set squarely. There are numerous ways to set the angle, and the instructions with your honing guide should tell you how to do it. It is an easy matter to square a chisel in a honing guide, since virtually all guides can be held against the edge of a bench while the chisel is aligned with a mark at 90° to the edge of the bench (see the drawing above).

When you are shaping the main bevel, you do not have to worry about forming wire edges. You just lean into your work and try and use as much of the stone surface as possible so that you keep the stone reasonably flat through even wear. Always keep finger pressure well forward on the blade with only your thumbs hooked behind the guide (see the photo above). The honing guide should be carrying almost no weight. It is only there as a guide and should have only enough weight on it to keep the roller in firm contact with the stone. As you work, flip the stone end for end every so often to be sure that you are giving it equal wear in all areas.

Once you have formed the basic bevel you have to exercise a bit more care. The first thing you should do is give the face of the chisel a few lapping strokes on the fine stone. This will remove or bend back any wire edge that has formed. You then go about forming your micro-bevel, which should only take a half-dozen strokes on the stone. Next take two or three lapping strokes on the face, and then take one or two more strokes on the micro-bevel using pressure only on the forward stroke. This sequence will eliminate wire edges. To check your work, run the newly sharpened edge along the tip of a thumbnail; if it feels frictionless, the edge is ready. If you feel any roughness, retrace your steps in the process to a point that will let you correct the problem.

When the chisel eventually becomes dull again, you do not have to repeat all the steps. The lacquer is off, the face is lapped, all you have to do is touch up the bevel. Depending on the dullness of the chisel, this might mean using only your finest stone to rehone the micro-bevel. Usually it is faster to go back to a coarser stone (800x to 1200x), renew the primary bevel and put a new micro-bevel on the chisel. Then follow the sequence from that point on.

RUST NEVER SLEEPS

A key to preserving the sharpness of tools is the prevention of rust—not just the visible rust that noticeably pits a blade but the slight rusting that comes from testing a blade with your thumb or finger. Rust like this, although visible only under an electron microscope (see the photo on p. 23), is already causing deterioration of the keen edge.

A pitted blade edge.

Where rust pits intersect the edge of the blade, you get a blade nick. Some old tools that have been allowed to pit deeply are hardly worth restoring. Unless the face of the tool can be brought to a mirror finish, the same as the bevel, you will continue to have problems when repeated sharpenings cause the receding bevel to encounter craters in the face.

SETTING THE GRIND ANGLE

You can set the grind angle by adjusting the tool rest to the correct angle, using a jig to ensure a square grind.

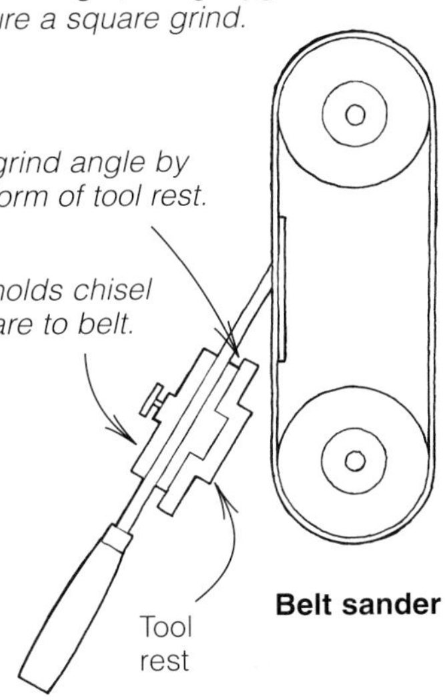

Alternatively, you can set the grind angle by adjusting the amount of chisel projection from the grinding jig (which again keeps the tool square to the wheel).

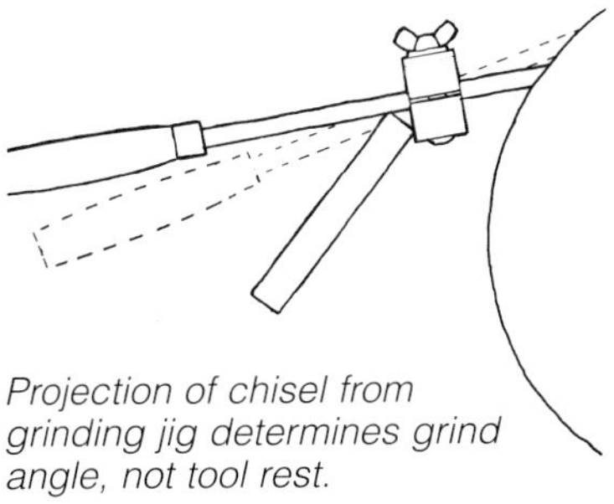

WHEN TO RESHARPEN?

There are several ways to tell when you need to resharpen a chisel. One is when you notice a difference in use. If the wood seems to be getting harder, check the chisel. Another is to look at the edge under a good light. A sharp edge reflects no light. But the most usual indicator is when you see scratches on your finished work. You know immediately that you have a damaged edge.

Fixing nicked chisels If you have seriously nicked a chisel, you may have to remove a fair amount of steel to eliminate the nick. You can do this with a coarse bench stone, but you should be prepared to spend a fair amount of time at it. Even aggressive bench stones take quite a while to work past a nick. It is faster to use a wet grinder, a dry grinder or a belt sander. In the case of the last two, you have to be very careful not to burn the tool or draw the temper.

If you are using a belt sander or a dry wheel, set your bevel angle either with the platform of the tool rest or by setting the projection of your chisel from the edge of the rest. In either case, use a simple grinding jig, which you can make or buy. With a belt sander, use only a coarse belt (80x is fine). With a dry grinder, use a soft-bond, open-structure wheel (such as an A80H-8V, see pp. 37-39 for details). With either, use a light touch and check tool temperature often. Both cut quickly but can overheat an edge.

For a very deep nick, the best approach is to mark a line across the chisel using a square and marker pen and grind back to the line. I first grind the edge square, right back to the mark, then re-form the bevel. This lets you work a bit faster with less danger of burning the edge, since you get good heat dissipation from the blunt edge to the main body of the tool. Heat dissipates more slowly from a thin section.

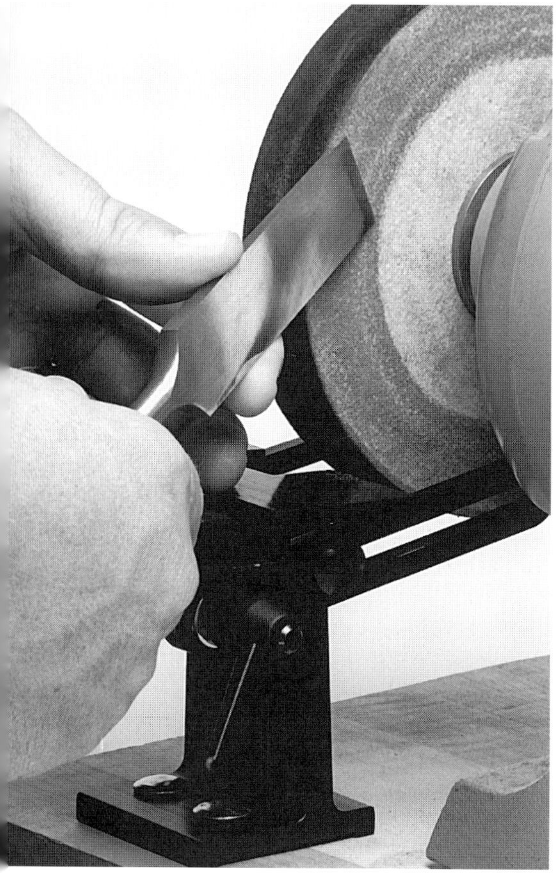

If you touch up chisels between sharpenings on a felt buffing wheel, use only the side of the wheel to minimize bevel rounding.

Do not try to grind material off too quickly. Check blade temperature frequently against the back of your hand, and when the blade starts to get warm cool it down by laying it on a slab of metal, which will act like a heat sink. This is better than dunking the tool in water (see the sidebar on p. 21). When you have formed the bevel, revert to your bench stones for the final steps.

BUFFING OR STROPPING CHISELS

Some woodworkers touch up their chisels between sharpenings on a felt buffing wheel or a leather belt on a belt sander; either would be charged with a buffing compound first.

There is nothing wrong with either system as a quick fix, but I recommend that you never buff the face of the chisel. Almost invariably you destroy the flatness. Similarly, you will find that you are not saving time at all if you round the bevel. I also recommend using only the side of the felt wheel to minimize bevel rounding. The bevel rounding caused by a leather belt on a belt sander is negligible if good technique is used (i.e., honing only over the platen where the leather can flex the least, and honing only at a small incremental angle increase). This method is all made even easier if a micro-finishing belt (see pp. 56-57) is used on the belt sander instead of a leather belt. There is no flexing, and the flat joins even eliminate bumping.

UTILITY BEVEL-EDGE CHISELS

Woodworkers who own only one style of chisels usually have bevel-edge chisels, the workhorses of the shop. This makes it a bit difficult to recommend sharpening angles, since the chisels will see use in all types of wood and in all activities from paring to mortising.

Usually a 25° bevel angle is adequate for these chisels, except in the smaller sizes. As you may have noticed, you will more frequently roll the edges on narrow chisels than on wide ones.

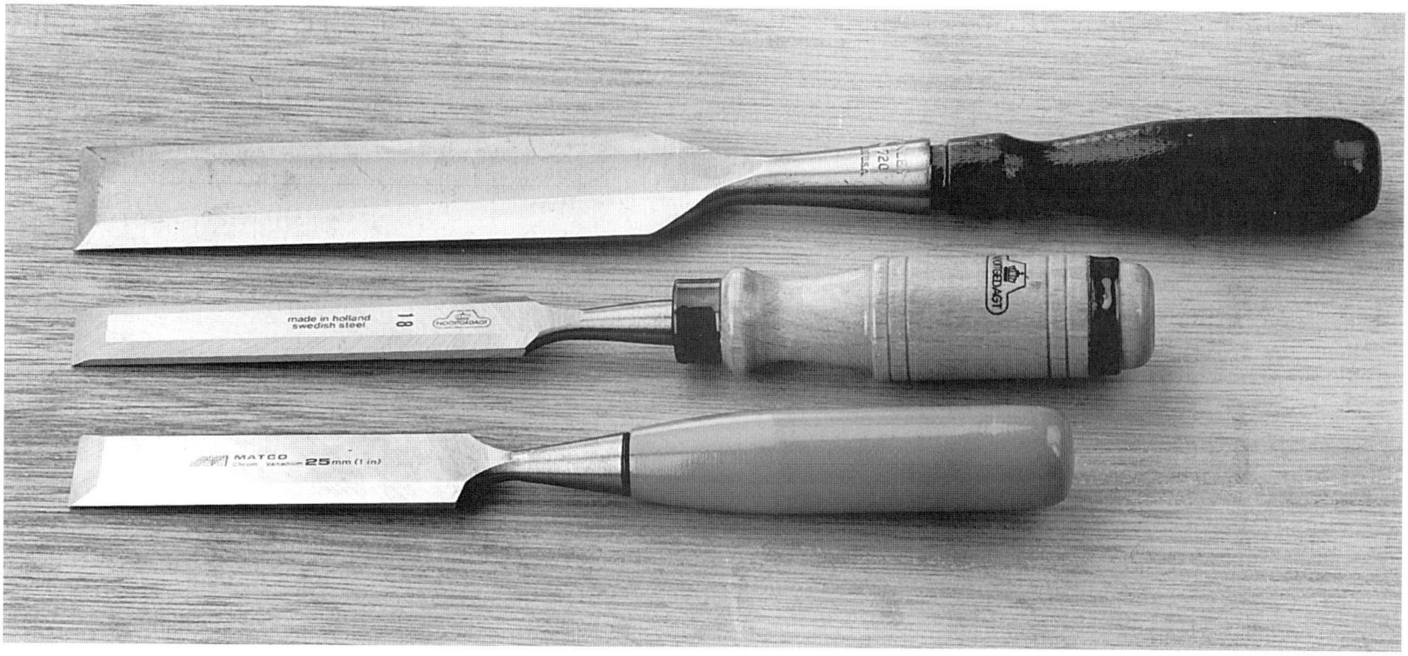

Utility bevel-edge chisels are the workhorses of the woodshop. At one time they were mostly socket chisels, like the old Stanley chisel shown at top. Now they tend to be tanged chisels, like the Dutch-made, Scandinavian style in the center or the ubiquitous plastic-handled type shown at bottom.

The reason for this is fairly straightforward. Assume that you are going to do some light mortising with a 1-in. chisel and a ¼-in. chisel. If you use mallet blows with the same force on the ¼-in. chisel as on the 1-in. chisel, the ¼-in. chisel will be subjected to four times the deforming force as the 1-in. chisel (see Chapter 2). Since we all tend to forget that the force of mallet blows should be modified according to the width of chisel we are using, we frequently overstress narrow chisels. Accordingly, it is a good idea to put a higher bevel angle on narrower chisels (30° is appropriate). Such narrow chisels are seldom used for light paring so this steeper bevel angle is justified for edge retention.

If you have only one set of chisels you might even consider putting a bevel angle as low as 20° on the largest chisel, remembering that if it is used for any light mortising, the mallet blows should be light as well. Since the largest chisel is most frequently used for paring this will give you the greatest versatility in a single set of chisels. If you never use your bevel-edge chisels for mortising and you have other chisels specifically for paring, you should be able to put a 25° bevel angle on all of them and be quite happy.

PARING CHISELS

Paring chisels are usually the same basic design as bevel-edge chisels, except that the blades tend to be a bit thinner and longer. Square-edge paring chisels are less common than bevel-edged ones but seem to be preferred by shipwrights. Possibly this is because shipwrights tended to use square-edge chisels in all of their other activities. Cranked-neck paring chisels (no longer common) are for use on large, flat surfaces where an offset neck is needed to prevent handle interference with the surface.

Since paring chisels are almost invariably used with hand pressure alone and not with a mallet, they are not subjected to the same forces as other chisels. In addition, as their name implies, paring chisels are usually used for very light cuts. As a result, they can be sharpened at bevel angles of 20° or less. For very fine work, a 15° bevel angle is not unusual. Otherwise, the general sharpening procedures described at the beginning of the chapter apply.

For information on sharpening slicks, very large paring chisels used in timber work, see pp. 74-75.

MORTISE AND FIRMER CHISELS

Mortising is just about the toughest test of a chisel edge. Cutting end grain subjects the chisel edge to nearly three times the force of parallel-grain or cross-grain cutting. The bevel angle on a mortise chisel has to be more obtuse than on other types of chisels to withstand these forces. For softwoods, mortise chisels should have a 30° bevel angle; for hardwoods, a 35° bevel angle. These recommendations are averages only. The steel in your particular mortise chisels may let you get away with somewhat lower bevel angles, or it may be relatively brittle and

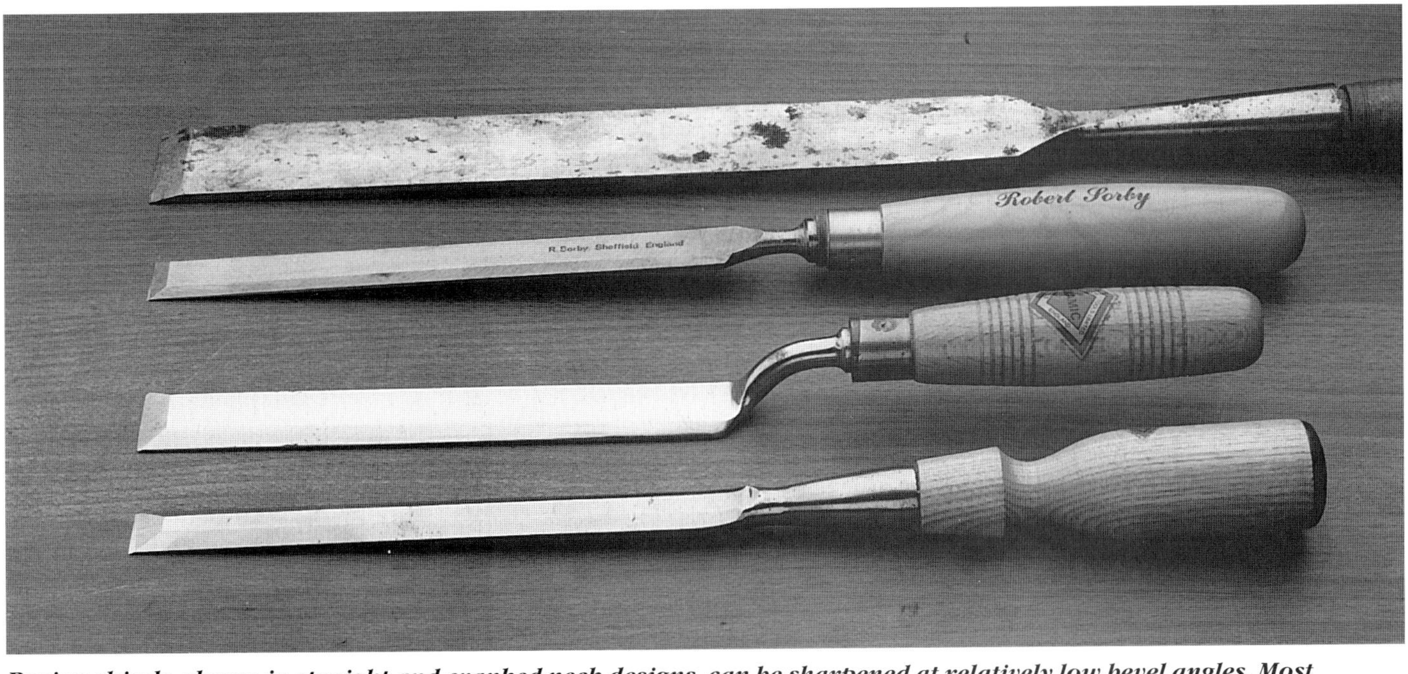

Paring chisels, shown in straight and cranked-neck designs, can be sharpened at relatively low bevel angles. Most people associate the term 'paring' with small, light chisels, yet there used to be much larger and heavier (but still slim) styles used in some trades—chisels like the shipwright's socket paring chisel shown at top.

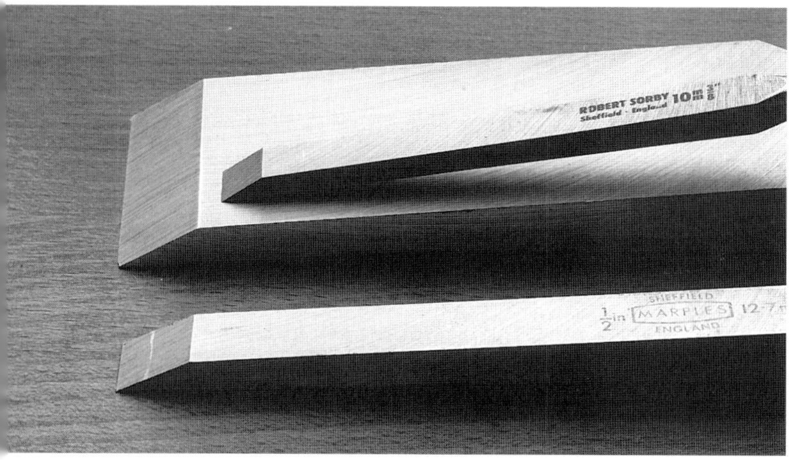

Mortise and firmer chisels require fairly steep bevel angles in order to withstand the force of cutting end grain.

BEVEL ANGLES FOR MORTISE CHISELS

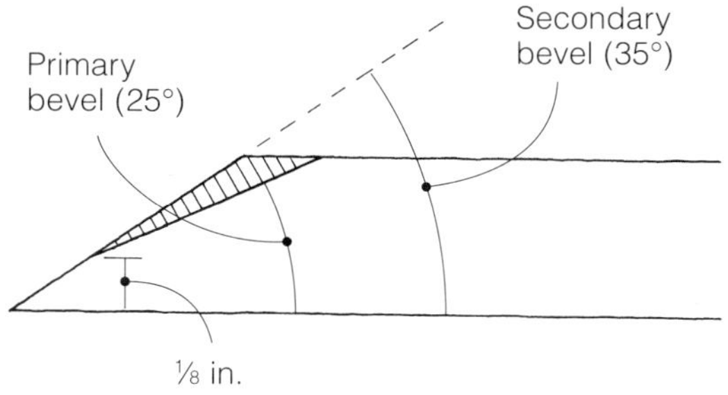

require somewhat higher angles. Your guide is edge failure; start at a low bevel angle and increase it only as much as required to prevent the edge from folding or chipping.

"Firmer" is a term used to describe utility chisels of sturdy build. They normally have square edges and since they are frequently used for mortising, they are lumped in here with the general recommendations for mortise chisels.

For speed of sharpening and best penetration, I recommend a primary bevel of 25° and a secondary bevel of 30° or 35°, as required, extending back to about ⅛ in. of blade thickness (see the drawing above). It is apparent that a chisel of this shape will penetrate more deeply than one that includes the hatched area. The wedging action is reduced.

The edge has a strong secondary-bevel angle extending well back; the only concern is the effect on rigidity. The reason mortise chisels are as thick as they are is only party to provide the rigidity needed to counteract the force. As the tip is deflected by the reactive force of the wood, a beefy blade is needed to keep the chisel from bowing and vibrating. But most mortise chisels are of deeper cross section than needed for rigidity. The extra depth is for alignment of the tool in the mortise. The minor modification of relieving the bevel angle detracts very little from overall blade rigidity; it is usually not noticeable in use.

ORIGINS OF THE MODIFIED TIP

For a long time after first modifying a mortise chisel for better penetration, I was quietly smug each time I used a modified chisel. I honestly thought that it was an original idea.

But when I was digging out some photographic samples for this book, I came across an old set of Greaves mortise chisels that I had bought many years ago because they were such good examples of their type. All of them still had their labels and were little used. The largest one had a wired handle to contain a crack; the great weakness of that style was the design of the handle and the lack of a shock washer. The handles were almost guaranteed to split in use.

However, you might be able to see the modified tips on some of them and the generally low bevel angles on all of them. I have been much less smug since noticing this and much more concerned about my memory.

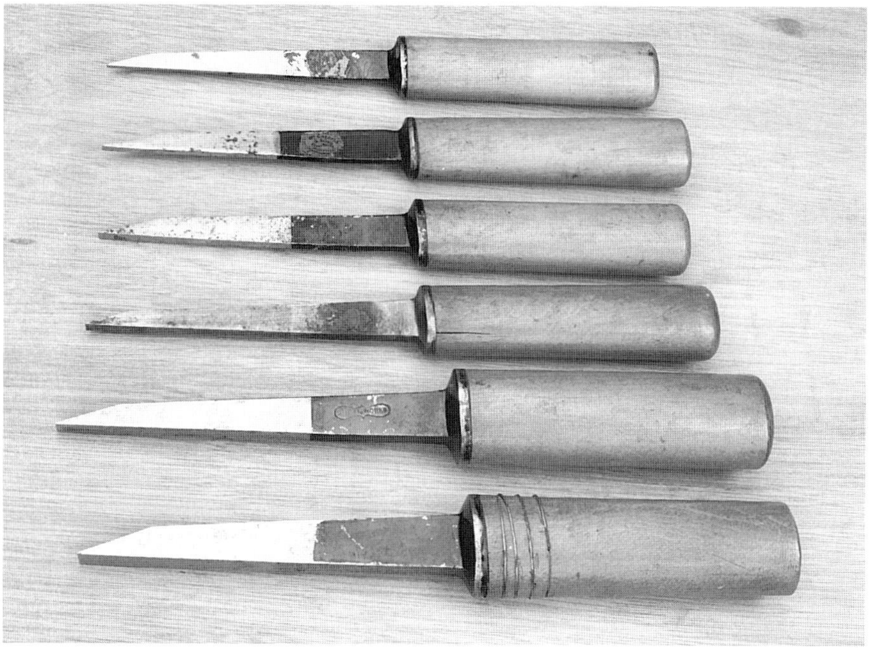

Greaves mortise chisels.

If you are constantly working softwoods like clear pine, the extension of the secondary bevel can be reduced from ⅛ in. to as little as ¹⁄₁₆ in of blade thickness. In fact, with clear pine you can also reduce the tip angle to less than 30° with most chisels.

SQUARE AND UNSQUARE MORTISE CHISELS

Most mortise chisels sold today have a rectangular cross-section. Some, particularly those made in Germany, are tapered from the face to the back, sometimes as much as ¹⁄₁₆ in. in total. The chisel is tapered to reduce friction in the mortise and to allow minor directional changes as mortising progresses. Good work can be done with either style, and the choice is largely a question of personal preference.

Unfortunately, mortise chisels are among the worst made of any modern chisels. Manufacturers do not seem to realize what the critical aspects of a mortise chisel are, and it is common to find blade sides that are not straight and that form an angle greater than 90° with the face of the chisel. Neither condition is acceptable.

If you have a chisels with these defects, you have no choice but to correct the faults before you use them. You can use a belt sander or disc sander to remove the major portion of the metal and finish off by lapping on a bench stone.

Few people actually use mortise chisels today since there are so many other ways to remove most of the wood from a mortise that it is possible to dress out the remainder with just about any chisel. Given this reduced market, I do not expect to see mortise-chisel manufacturing improve in the near future.

HOW DESIGN FEATURES GET LOST

The first time I visited the Sorby factory in Sheffield, England, in the 1970s, I asked the works manager why they were the only manufacturer to round the back of the bevel on their mortise chisels. He looked at me quizzically, drew himself up and said something like, "We have been doing that, man and boy, for the 40 years that I've worked here." Although that was not the answer I was looking for, I dropped the subject.

Thinking about it weeks later, after I had returned to Canada, I realized that rounding the junction between the bevel and the blade back would make it easier to lever waste out of a mortise. That particular part of the chisel is used as a fulcrum in the process and rounding it would prevent the corner from digging in.

I should have said something to Sorby at the time because the next year their catalog showed all mortise chisels with a sharp intersection between the bevel and the back. A useful design feature had been lost because nobody knew why it was there.

The old-style Sorby mortise chisel, with rounded bevel back, is shown in front of a standard mortise chisel.

MORTISE CHISELS

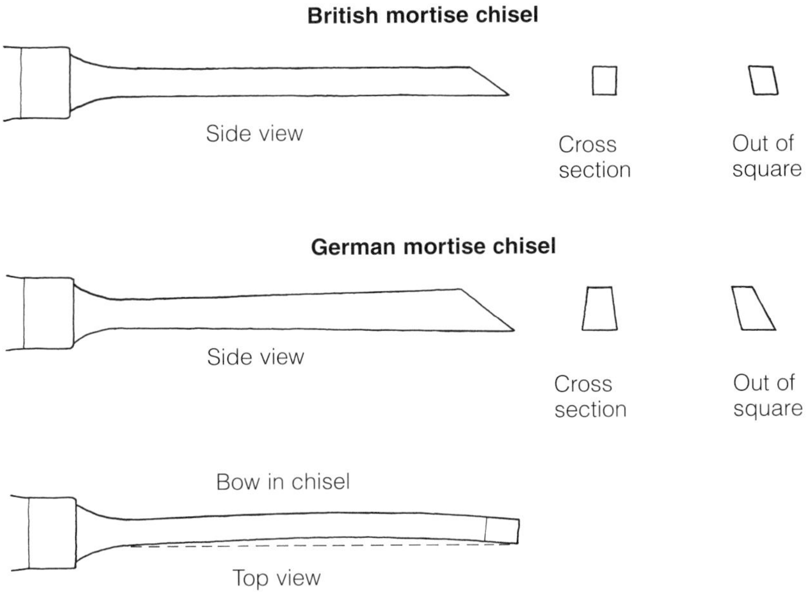

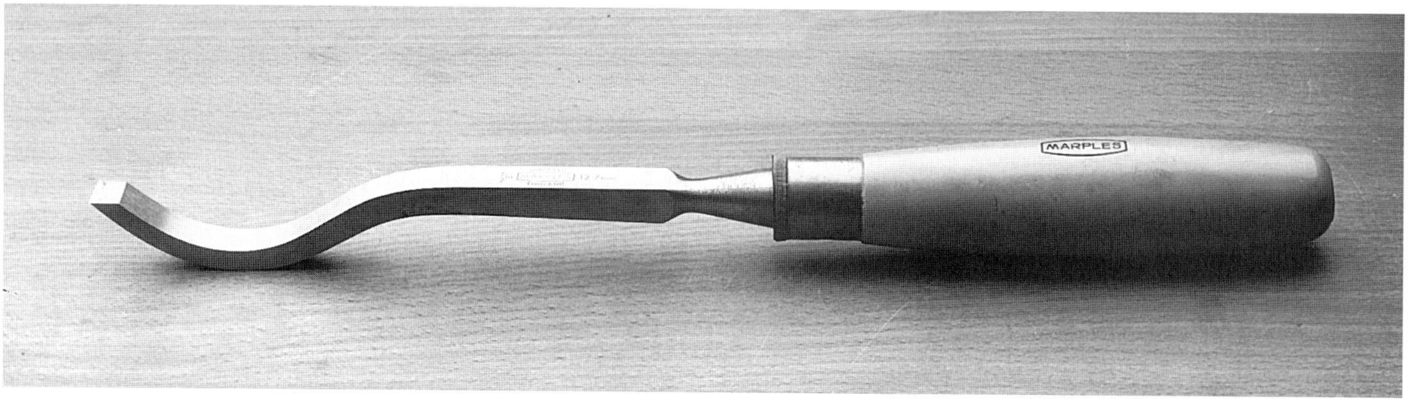

The bevel on a lock-mortise chisel is roughly in line with the axis of the handle.

LOCK-MORTISE CHISEL DEFECT

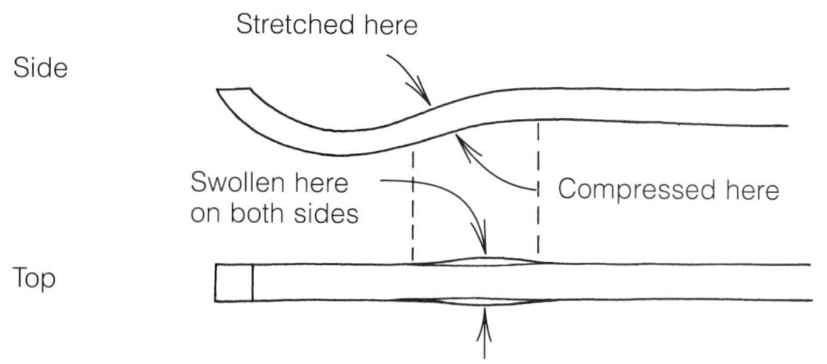

LOCK-MORTISE CHISELS

As the name implies, lock-mortise chisels are used for levering waste out of the deep mortises required to install door locks. They are essentially scraping chisels not cutting chisels and are usually ground and honed with the bevel approximately in line with the handle. Just like standard mortise chisels (and possibly for the same reason), lock-mortise chisels are almost invariably badly made.

They are usually made by bending square stock freehand. When you bend square stock, the steel is stretched on the outside of a curve and compressed on the inside of the curve. This causes a problem at the transition point from straight blade to curved blade. The sharp directional change creates two "hips" on the back of the chisel, and most manufacturers do not grind these off completely. Some manufacturers do not even seem to realize that the hips are a serious problem because they become the widest point on the chisel preventing it from entering the mortise past this point.

The hips can be ground off quickly on a belt sander or worried off on a coarse bench stone. This part of the chisel must be no wider than the face of the chisel. Whether or not you like using honing guides, this is one chisel that has to be sharpened freehand. It is easiest to clamp the chisel in a vise, bevel up, and hone the bevel in line with the axis of the handle. The actual bevel angle is not critical, it is the angle that the bevel makes with the handle that determines the chisel's effectiveness. Some lock-mortise chisels have quite a pronounced curve in them, while others have a relatively shallow curve. The latter will work deeper mortises.

SKEW CHISELS

Skew chisels are actually a variant form of paring chisels, though they are usually square-edged not bevel-edged. They are most effective in end-grain cuts and in paring the cheeks of tenons. Wooden-plane makers prized these chisels for working the beds of planes, since the square-sided skew would let them work next to the cheek without undercutting it, while at the same time avoiding the choppiness that could result from using a square-edged chisel on a plane bed. A skew chisel will not suddenly dig in, the way a square-end chisel will. For similar reasons skew chisels are ideal for paring the cheeks and shoulders of tenons. To understand their usefulness on tenon cheeks, refer to Chapter 2 on cross-grain cutting.

Skew chisels are usually sharpened with a bevel angle of 20° or less. Depending upon the equipment you have available, it can be a tricky process. Side-clamp honing guides are of no use with skew chisels, so you must either sharpen them freehand or use a top-clamp honing guide such as the General or Veritas guide (see the photo below). With either guide it is important that the cutting edge be exactly parallel to the transverse axis of the guide. This is not as easy to achieve as you might think. It is simple with square-edge chisels because you can set the bevel angle first and then fine-tune the squareness afterward. With a skew chisel you have far more opportunity to go wrong. And this is one case where you do not want to solve the problem with applied geometry.

If you are using the Veritas honing guide and angle jig, you will find that the best way to set the honing guide on a skew is to have it on the blade loosely as you set the blade in the angle jig and then just release the honing guide. It will slide down the blade and automatically align itself correctly.

If you are using the General guide, concentrate on getting the cutting edge of the skew chisel exactly parallel to the front edge of the honing guide (90° to the path of travel) and then adjust the tilt angle as required.

Skew chisels, available in left- and right-hand pairs, are specifically adapted to cutting end grain.

With the skew chisel held in a top-clamp honing guide, keep the cutting edge parallel to the transverse axis of the guide as you hone back and forth on the stone. (Photo by Susan Kahn)

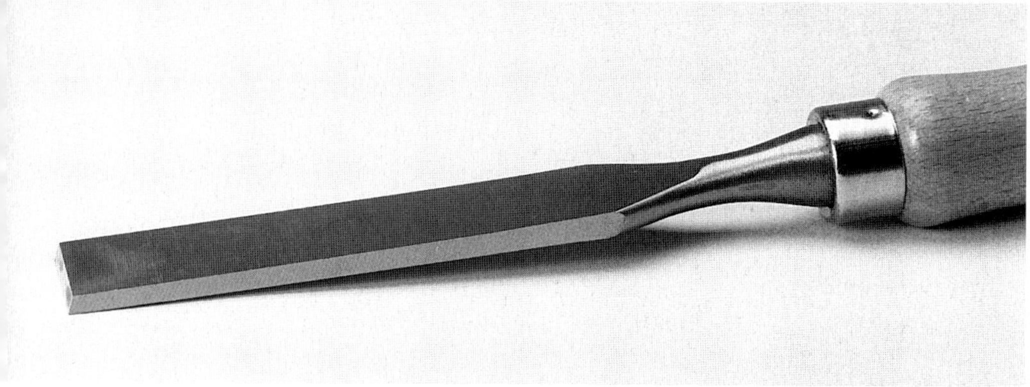

Scraping chisels, traditionally used in plane making, are sharpened at very high bevel angles, which increases control and prevents inadvertent digs in the work surface. (Photo by Susan Kahn)

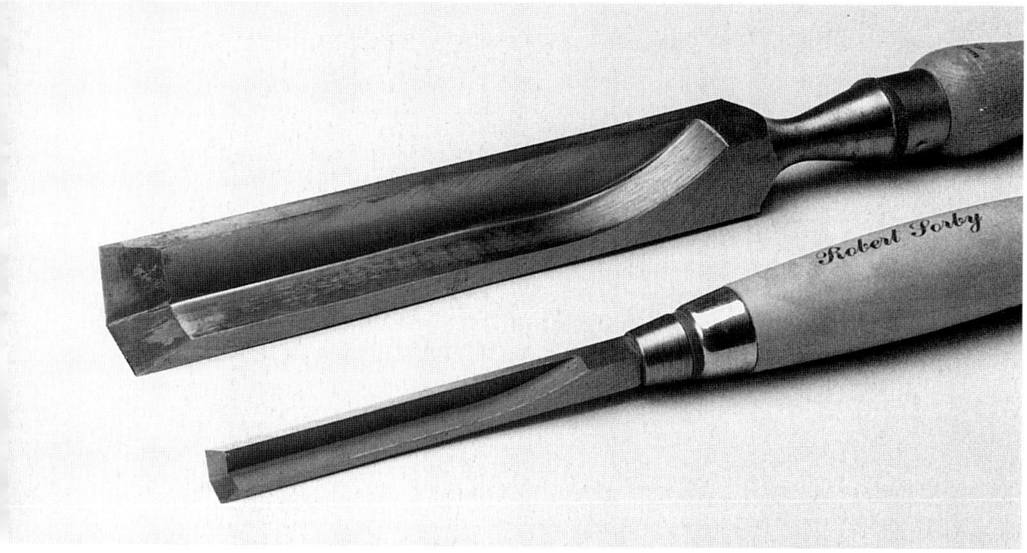

Corner chisels, shown here in 1-in. and 3/8-in. sizes, are used to clean the corners in mortises. (Photo by Susan Kahn)

SCRAPING CHISELS

Scraping chisels are almost never used any more, but at one time they were used by plane makers to make fine-tuning cuts on plane beds. They are a fitting chisel for end-grain work. Scraping chisels were traditionally sharpened at a 90° bevel angle, but looking at the research results of Dr. Norman Franz (Appendix 1) an argument could be made that they should have been sharpened at a 70° or 75° bevel angle. Either way, a high bevel angle increases control and ensures that there are no inadvertent digs. Maybe these forgotten tools will enjoy a resurgence.

CORNER CHISELS

A corner chisel is used to clean the corners in mortises or hinge gains. Large ones, usually 1 in. on a side, were very popular with wheelwrights, who called them "bruzzes."

These are truly the chisels from hell when it comes to sharpening. I used to think that sharpening a V-tool used in carving was difficult, but it is child's play compared to doing a first-class job on a corner chisel.

The first thing you have to realize with the corner chisel is that it has two faces not one. Both have to be lapped until decently flat and then polished. Turning your attention to the inside bevels of the chisel you will normally find one of two things. If it is a new chisel, the manufacturer will probably not have risked sharpening it well and you will find a square edge, but one that is very blunt. If it is a used corner chisel, the edge is likely to be fairly keen but it will probably neither be straight nor at 90° to the spine of the chisel. The first thing you will have to do in this instance is grind the end of the chisel square. When this is done you will now have reached the state where the used chisel will be exactly the same as the new chisel, a good square end but blunt.

For reasons known only to the world's corner-chisel manufacturers, I have always found corner chisels to be fairly soft, almost never harder than Rc58. Many antique ones are as low as Rc54 or Rc55. This means that they can readily be filed, and a file is unquestionably my first choice of sharpening tool for a corner chisel. You have the necessary control to sneak up on a sharp edge without overshooting it.

You should use a safe-edge file (see pp. 55-56) for the job; otherwise, you will cause yourself some problems in the corner. Although an auger-bit file has one end where the edges are safe and another end where the faces are safe, it is a bit small for most corner chisels. I recommend that you grind the edge off a 6-in. or 8-in. mill file and use it instead. For a chisel too hard for a steel file, you can use a diamond file. You'll almost certainly have to do some work on the edge of the diamond file, because the file face seldom comes out to the edge of the supporting backing plate. You'll have to dress the backing plate flush with the file edge.

A 30° bevel angle is fairly standard with corner chisels, though you will find antique ones with higher bevel angles. I suspect that this was partly an insurance policy on the part of the original owner who wanted to be absolutely sure that an edge didn't fold in use, and partly the tendency to increase bevel angles to save sharpening time. Given the nature of use of a corner chisel, it would seem that 30° should be about appropriate. I have used them only in softwood and 30° was fine. In testy woods like oak, 35° might be necessary.

Once the inside of the chisel is filed, it should be honed with a file-shaped stone, as fine as can be found. To finish off the tool, put some green buffing compound on the face of a stick and use it on the two bevels just as you would a file.

It is important to keep the two cutting edges at 90° to the spine of the tool. If they are swept backward, the heel of the tool will constantly be forcing its way through wood that is not yet free to be released. With the wings square or with slight forward sweep the wood will release freely. But realistically, if you get two straight edges that cut well, just leave the thing alone. Be glad you didn't get a hook in the corner.

Use a safe-edge mill file to sharpen the inside bevels of a corner chisel.

JAPANESE CHISELS

The traditional Japanese chisel is quite different from its Western counterpart. First, it is a laminated chisel with a very hard steel face (Rc62 to Rc64) laminated to a soft-steel or wrought-iron back. The use of very hard steel requires the soft back both for the damping qualities and to provide an element of toughness that the steel face alone would not have. Second, a traditional Japanese chisel has a hollow face for faster sharpening and to make it easier to maintain flatness. Japanese chisels are sharpened in the same manner as Western-style chisels but normally require higher bevel angles to avoid edge chipping.

Most traditional construction, cabinetry and interior trim in Japan is with softwoods. To avoid crushing of the fibers it is necessary to have particularly keen chisels, but there is no great toughness requirement since they are subjected to little distortional force from the softwood. The use of a very hard high-carbon blade makes sense

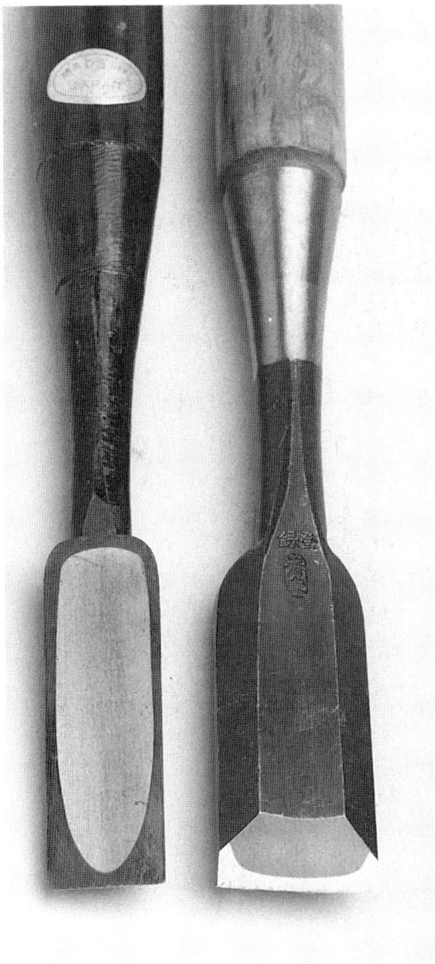

Traditional Japanese chisels, which have a hollow face (left), are usually sharpened at higher bevel angles than Western chisels. (Photo by Susan Kahn)

THE STEEL USED IN JAPANESE CHISELS

When people talk about traditional Japanese chisels, you may hear them say that the chisels were made from "white" steel or "blue" steel. Alternatively, they might say "white paper" steel or "blue paper" steel. These are not technical standards but refer to the color of the labels that Hitachi uses for some of their commercial grade steels. Among Japanese manufacturers, these become "Blue Label #1," "White Label #2," and so on. Both types are high-carbon steels in the 1.0% to 1.2% carbon range alloyed with silica (0.1% to 0.2%) and manganese (0.2% to 0.3%). The "blue paper" steels also have chromium (0.2% to 0.5%) and tungsten (1.0% to 1.5%) added for toughness. Japanese manufacturers routinely produce chisels from these steels in the Rc62 to Rc64 range, substantially harder than any Western-style chisels.

For the soft-steel back, they use a very low carbon steel (0.06%) with a bit of silica and manganese (both at 0.2%). The highest-quality tools still use wrought iron from old anchors or anchor chain as the backing material.

under these circumstances. The high-carbon steel will take a very fine edge if the brittleness can be tolerated.

If you intend using traditional Japanese chisels for Western hardwoods you are going to have to use higher bevel angles than you are accustomed to. For most purposes, an extra 5° should be sufficient, but for mortise chisels you may need as much as 10° more than you would use on a Western chisel.

It is perfectly acceptable to use the same micro-bevel sharpening system that you use normally, but I would not recommend relieving the back half of the bevel as earlier recommended for Western chisels (see p. 62). Neither should you use a modified tip on the mortise chisel, unless you make sure that the lowered angle is well back into the soft steel. Most Japanese chisels that I have used will take a wonderfully keen edge, but they are far more prone to edge crumbling than other alloys. Woods of inconsistent hardness (such as end-grain oak) can cause very rapid edge degradation. A pin knot can take out a piece large enough to make you weep.

With successive sharpenings the hollow face is going to get ever closer to the cutting edge. You do not want it to get much closer than ⅛ in. or you risk weakening the edge, particularly on a mortise chisel. You have two choices. You can lap the back of the chisel to effect the necessary recession of the hollowness, or you can try the Japanese method of tapping it out with a hammer. I use the lapping method for two reasons. First, I have not found the hollow face to be a discernible advantage in use and therefore am not concerned about reduction of the hollow through lapping. Second, I cannot bring myself to use a steel hammer on a chisel blade because I am convinced that I would do more evil than good.

But for those of you who are seized with the karma of Japanese tools, I can recommend two excellent books that will explain the process of hammering out the hollow: *Japanese Woodworking Tools: Their Tradition, Spirit and Use* by Toshio Odate (The Taunton Press, 1984) and *Japanese Woodworking Tools: Selection, Care and Use* by Henry Lanz (Sterling, 1985).

SLICKS

A slick is a very large paring chisel that is always used two handed, usually with shoulder pressure as well (see the top photo on the facing page). Traditionally, a slick was held much like a lance, the primary difference being that the butt of the handle nestled just below the shoulder and the tool was guided with the off hand. Because slicks are used for paring cuts, they almost never have a bevel angle higher than about 25°.

Slicks are sharpened in two different ways. For dovetail work in logs where the paring is almost invariably with the grain, the slick is sharpened with a square tip. For more diverse work, which could include lap joints and notches, a slick is usually sharpened so that there is a slight crown to the edge. On the 3-in. slick shown in the bottom photo at left on the facing page, the blade is crowned nearly ⅛-in. at the center. The amount of crown can vary according to personal taste.

There are two reasons for crowning the edge. First, a slight crown makes the slick versatile in use. Light paring cuts can be made that use nearly the entire width of the blade but still clip the end fibers, preventing any splintering and leaving a very smooth finish. Second, a crown makes the tool more controllable. The crown tends to keep the blade cutting directly in line with the applied force. It is much like a shallow gouge; it tends to maintain a cutting line through self-centering forces.

Most slicks (except Japanese ones) are soft enough to be filed. It is fairly straightforward to shape the edge of a slick with a file, but I strongly recommend that you file from the back of the bevel toward the front. You end up with a wire edge, which you could avoid if you filed in the opposite direction, but you also get to keep ten fingers intact.

Slicks are large paring chisels traditionally used by shipwrights, timber framers and other craftsmen for working large timbers.

Slicks for paring lap joints and notches are typically ground with a crowned blade. (Photo by Susan Kahn)

A crowned blade leaves a very smooth finish when cutting cross grain.

To file a regular crown I recommend filing the edge squarely back to a marked line, then filing the bevel until the edge is sharp. It is easier to achieve a fair curve the first time this way, rather than trying to strike the bevel and curve simultaneously.

The square-tipped slick would be sharpened in basically the same manner as any square-ended chisel. The only difference would be that it might be easier to bring the stone to the tool rather than vice versa. You can work the edge from whatever position you feel most comfortable. My preference is to have the edge of the tool just sticking over the edge of the bench and use the stone in a rotary motion.

Do not attempt to flatten the entire face of the slick. The vast majority of older slicks actually had a slight bend (or belly) in the blade about halfway along. Whether this was done intentionally or accidentally is uncertain. There is no question that some relief is needed for a slick to function easily, but the few users still around tend to be a bit vague on the reasons.

In any event, you will probably find it useful to sharpen your slick with a slight crown to the edge. The dead-square tip can be difficult to control, but once you get accustomed to using a slick you will be pleasantly surprised at how quickly your skill develops and by the versatility of the tool in any large-timber work.

CHAPTER 7

PLANES

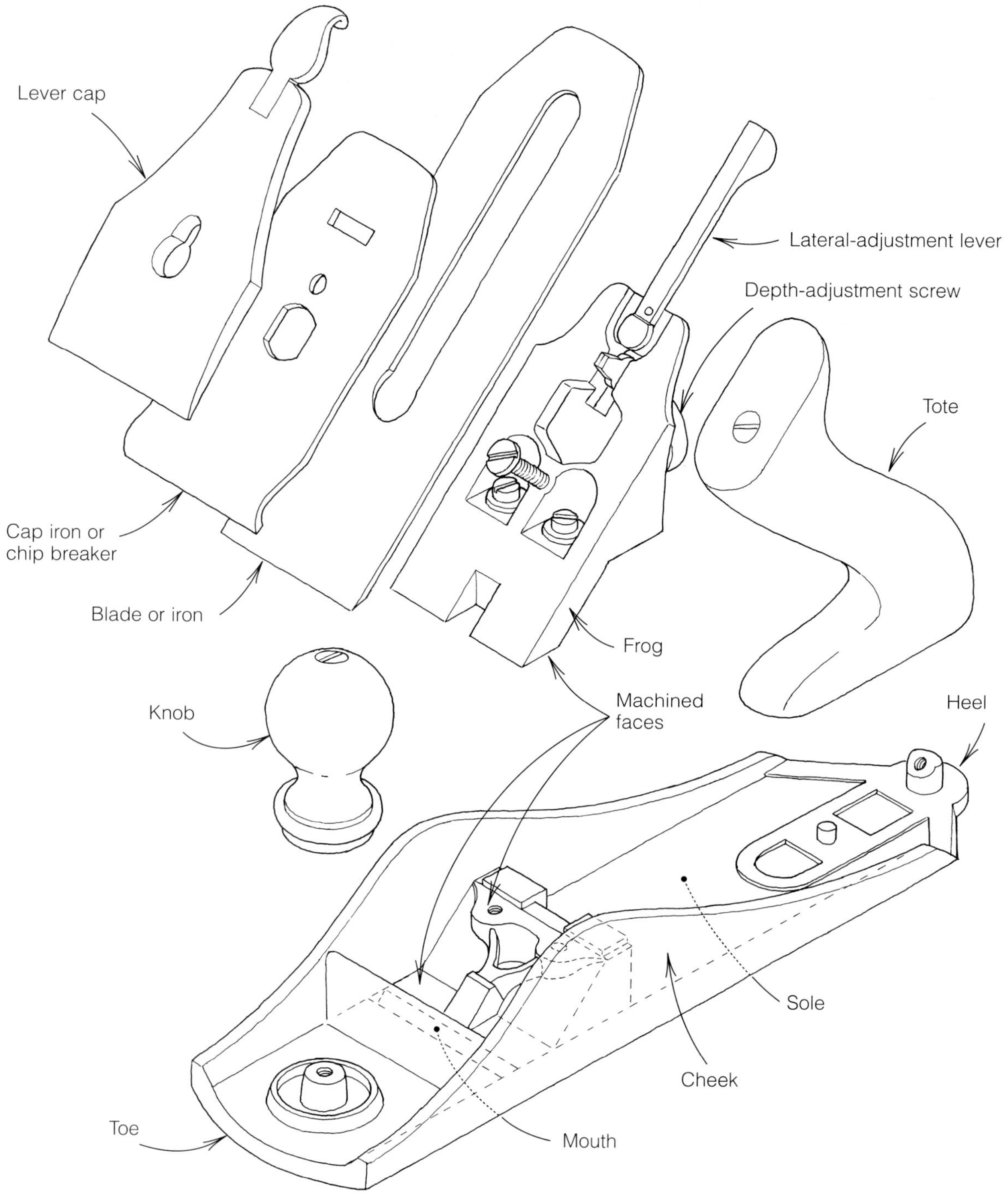

I doubt that there is any hand tool more satisfying to use than a finely tuned plane with a perfectly sharpened blade. The ease of use, the consistency of results and the general feeling of craftsmanship generated create one of the magic moments of woodworking.

Sharpening the blade perfectly is a relatively easy task compared to the fine tuning. The production process that is used for most bench planes today seldom creates an end product that is ready for use even if it came with a sharp blade—which it usually does not! When you buy a new plane you are usually getting a collection of parts that can only be converted into a fully functioning tool with a fair amount of thought and a substantial amount of work.

TUNING A PLANE

There is little point in sharpening the blade well if it is not going to be seated well on the bed of the plane or clamped in place in a manner that will minimize flexing of the iron in use. A quick checklist to put the plane in reasonable working order would include the following steps:

1. Strip off the lacquer First, remove any lacquer from the plane blade, the sole of the plane and the sides. It is only there to make the plane look good and prevent it from rusting until it is sold. After stripping, you can wax any parts you won't be abrading. The wax will prevent rusting and reduce friction.

2. True the sole With the blade in the plane and the lever cap in position tightened for use, lap the sole of the plane until it is flat. Lapping can be done in a variety of ways, but the most practical method in a small shop is to use silicon-carbide grit on a cast-iron lapping plate, or on a fairly firm plastic sheet such as Mylar fixed to a sheet of plate glass with spray adhesive.

Moving the plane in a figure-eight or circular motion, lap the sole with silicon-carbide grit on a sheet of Mylar-faced plate glass.

LAPPING THE SOLE

When the sole of a plane body is being milled (or ground), the plane is clamped on the cheeks. The clamping pressure causes the sole to arch outward. When the clamps are released after machining, the finished sole is almost invariably hollow. A bit of hollowness is of no great concern, but there are three places where you must be certain that the sole is dead flat after lapping—both tips and the front of the mouth, as shown below.

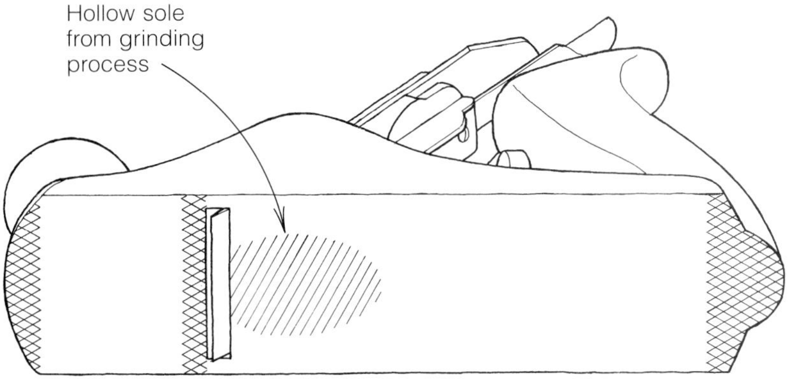

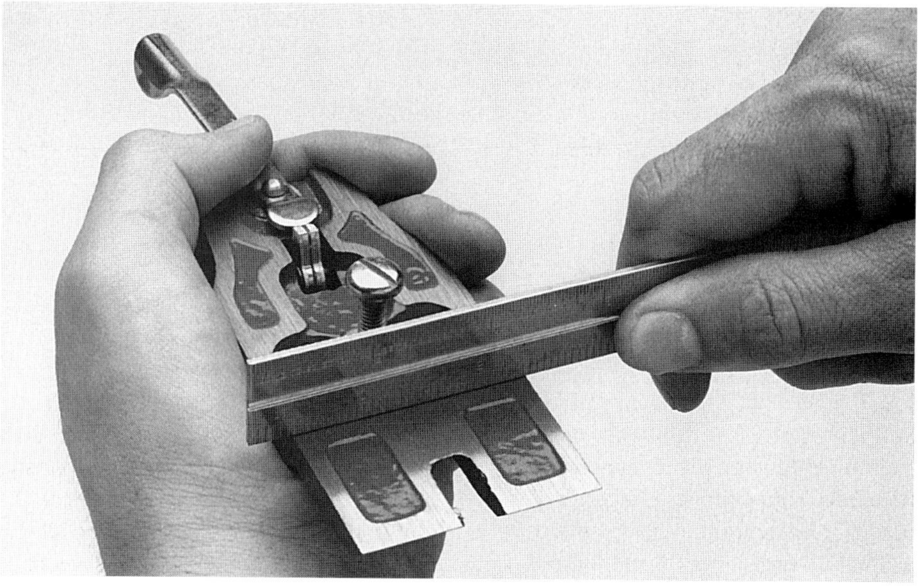

Use a straightedge to check that the machined surfaces of the frog are true. Check diagonally as well as transversely. (Photo by Susan Kahn)

DRESSING A BLOCK-PLANE LEVER CAP

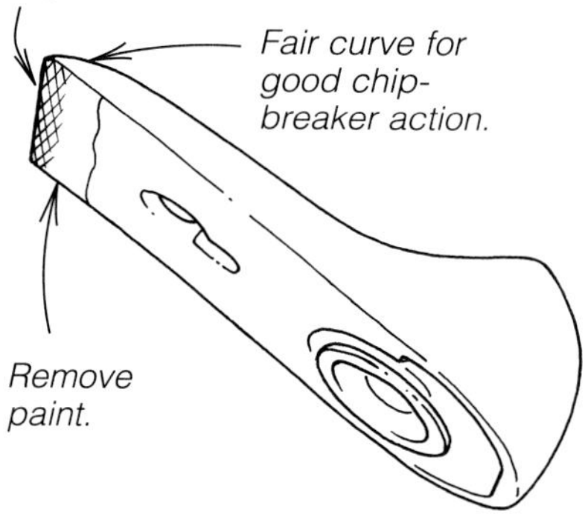

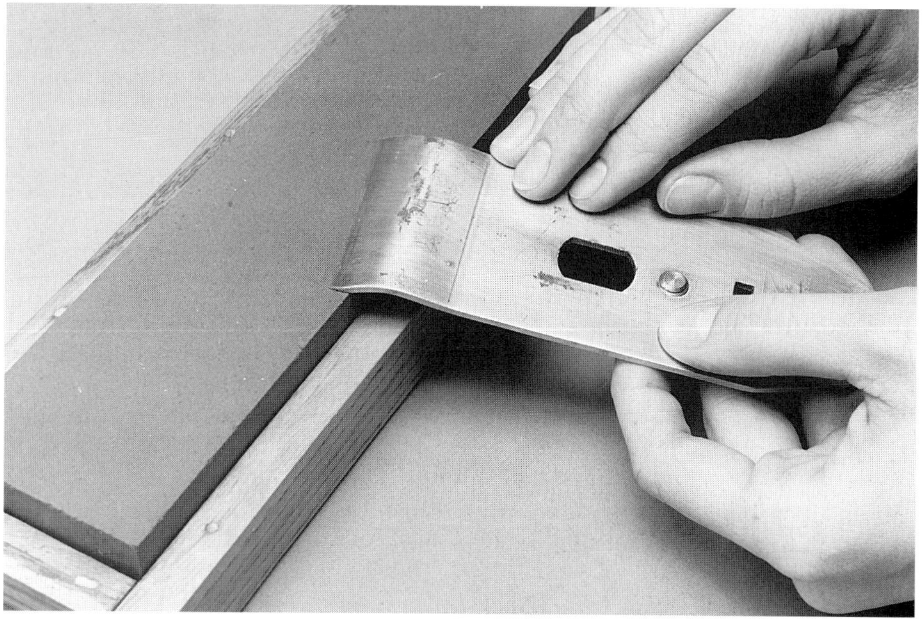

Dress the tip of the cap iron on a stone, with the opposite end of the iron held about ⅛ in. below the level of the stone.

The dressed cap iron should fit tightly across the width of the plane blade.

Start with about a 90 grit and do not move to a finer grit until the sole of the plane is flat in all critical areas. (Change to a finer grit only to get the degree of smoothness that you want on the plane's bottom.) Use a slightly circular or figure-eight motion in lapping to keep the grit evenly distributed under the sole. Take care to keep the pressure directly down on the plane with no tendency to tilt it.

Having the blade and lever cap in position and tightened introduces the permanent forces that the plane will experience. With these forces in place as the sole is being trued, you have some assurance that the sole will be flat when you really need it to be flat, that is, in use.

3. True the bed..The bed is everything that the blade rests on, including the frog and the machined surface adjacent to the mouth. The machined surfaces of the bed should be in a single plane from top to bottom and side to side. This may require some adjustment of the frog (if it is adjustable) or filing of the bed, with frequent test fittings of the blade using machinist's dye or carbon paper to indicate high spots.

This is exactly the same process that dentists use to test and then modify a new filling to suit your bite. With a plane, if you paint the blade with machinist's dye, the dye will transfer to the high points of the bed when the blade is pressed into position. If you use carbon paper, put the carbon side next to the bed before positioning the blade.

4. Dress the lever cap The first ⅛ in. or so of the lever-cap bottom should be lapped on a stone so that it will create a single line of contact with the cap iron, or with the blade itself on those models that do not have a cap iron. This is important since the lever cap has to fit well to tension the blade in the plane, minimizing chatter in use.

On a block plane, the lever cap also serves as a cap iron and should fit snugly to the blade across its entire width. To dress it, scrape the paint off the last ¼ in. of the bottom of the lever cap near the tip and lap a band about ⅛ in. wide on it (see the drawing on the facing page). You should also fair the curved tip so that shavings will slide over it smoothly.

5. Dress the cap iron The cap iron, or "chip breaker," should be dressed across its width at an angle that is just slightly less than one that would make it parallel to the plane blade. This will ensure that the nose of the cap iron fits tightly to the plane blade; if there are any gaps, shavings will inevitably lodge between the cap iron and the blade, choking the mouth of the plane. This dressing can easily be done freehand (see the middle photo on the facing page).

As long as the unground tip of the cap iron is held ⅛ in. or more below the level of the stone being used to shape the tip, you will have the right geometry to give you a tight fit. After the cap iron has been dressed and fastened to the blade, it should meet the blade all across the tip and be slightly canted away from it toward the arch (see the bottom photo on the facing page).

SHARPENING THE BLADE

Just as you would do with a chisel (see p. 59), the first thing you do with a plane blade is remove any lacquer or paint and lap the face of the blade. Lapping can be done on a medium stone (800x to 1200x) followed by a fine stone (4000x to 8000x). Unlike when lapping a chisel, you do not have to be concerned about the entire blade being flat at the perimeter. Any slight hollowness or belly in a plane blade is compensated for by the clamping pressures between the lever cap and the blade. Your primary concern is just to get a good smooth surface on the face of the blade near the cutting edge before turning your attention to the bevel.

After choosing the bevel angle (see the discussion of specific types of planes for recommended angles), I strongly recommend that you use a honing guide (see pp. 51-53) for the bevel-shaping process. The guide lets you apply greater pressure while holding the exact angle you want, and you get better results in less time than with freehand honing.

As with chisels, I recommend putting the basic bevel on the blade at 1° less than the micro-bevel (see p. 62). Basic shaping on an 800x stone and finishing on a 4000x to 8000x is suitable.

CHOOSING A BEVEL ANGLE

Choosing a bevel angle is a nearly limitless discussion area because of the nearly limitless combination of plane types, wood types and cutting processes. Many aspects will be covered under the various plane types detailed in the rest of this chapter, but the first major division is between those planes where the blade is used bevel down (the vast majority, including all bench planes) and those planes where the blade is bevel up—the block planes and low-angle special-purpose planes.

An unlapped blade (left) and a lapped one (right).

An adjustable mouth is desirable in any plane, but particularly in smoothing planes. The plane at top, of current German production, has a sliding insert in front of the mouth. The old smooth plane in the middle has an adjustable nosepiece much like modern block planes. The steel plane at bottom relies on a movable frog to open or close the mouth.

BENCH PLANES

Virtually all bevel-down planes have bed angles of 45° or 50°. In the areas of greater specialization, 45° bed angles are commonly used for softwoods and 50° beds for hardwoods. The bed angle is not significant to the choice of bevel angle in either case. Anything between 30° and 35° is quite acceptable. If you go much lower than 30° you encourage blade chatter; if you go much higher than 35° any wear dulls the blade much faster, but, more significantly, you could reduce the relief angle unacceptably, particularly on planes with a 45° bed.

Bevel-down planes as a group represent an exception to the general rule that blades should be sharpened at the lowest angle consistent with edge retention, because the bevel angle has no bearing on the cutting angle. A sturdy edge is wanted, and a basic grind angle of 30° to 35° will give you good blade stability and the least chatter.

Turning to blade shape, the general rule of thumb for standard bench planes (#3 to #8) is that the blade be sharpened square across unless you intend to be working wood wider than the blade; in this case, you would either round the blade corners, crown the blade or do a bit of both, depending on your intended use.

SMOOTHING PLANES (#3, #4½, #5½)

The #3 smoothing plane is usually used for the final smoothing of large flat surfaces. It is not used to take off much material, so it should be set for a very fine shaving. You want to the corners of the blade to be slightly rounded, so that overlapping passes of slightly different height will not have a distinct overlap line nor will you get any fiber tearing as would be the case with a square-edge blade.

Whether or not you use a honing guide, it is a fairly simple matter to put a straight basic bevel on a smoothing-plane blade and then bias the process first to one corner and then to the other to round off the last ⅛ in. or ¼ in. of blade. The rounding does not have to be substantial, since the plane will be used only for very light finishing cuts.

The #4½ and #5½ are planes designed for hogging off wood in the smoothing process. In normal use it is not enough to just round the corners of these blades, the entire blade should be crowned by $1/32$ in. to $1/16$ in. This can be done with a honing guide putting "English" on one side and then the other, but it can be difficult to get enough curvature this way. One easy solution is to keep a worn stone specifically for sharpening such blades. Such an out-of-true stone can be used only for the bevels and never for lapping. A better alternative is to use a simple jig to grind the crown, as shown in the sidebar on the facing page.

BLADE-EDGE SHAPE

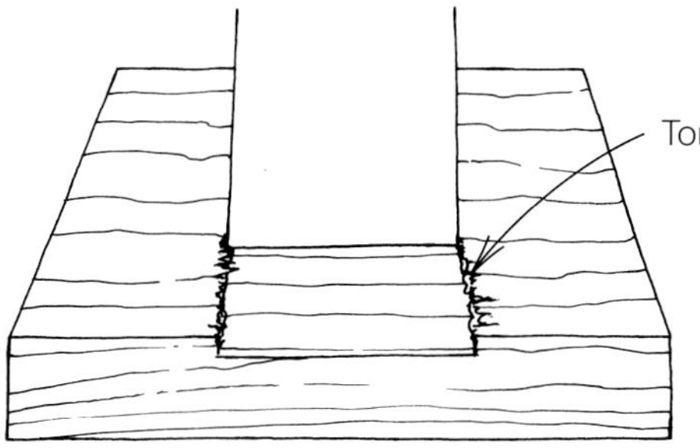

Square-edge blade

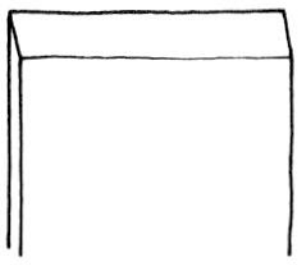

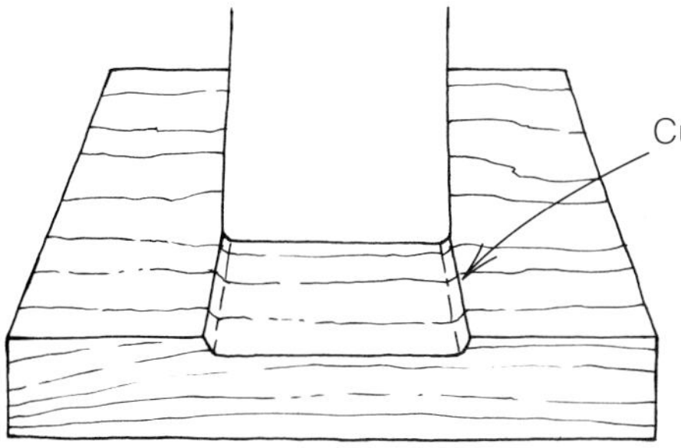

Rounded blade

Rounding the blade corners avoids fiber tearing at the edge of the cut.

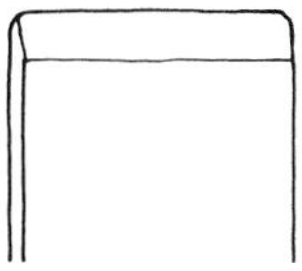

GRINDING A CROWN ON A BLADE

There are many ways to grind a crown on a blade. The jig shown here works with a dry grinder or belt sander. Using thin wood as a table extender, drill holes in it as required and use another piece of wood as a rotating arm. With the plane blade attached to the rotating arm with double-faced tape, you can select the amount of crown you want on a blade by picking a suitable point of rotation. About 7-in. radius is fine for a #4½ or #5½ plane blade. For fine adjustment, you can make the rotating arm adjustable in length.

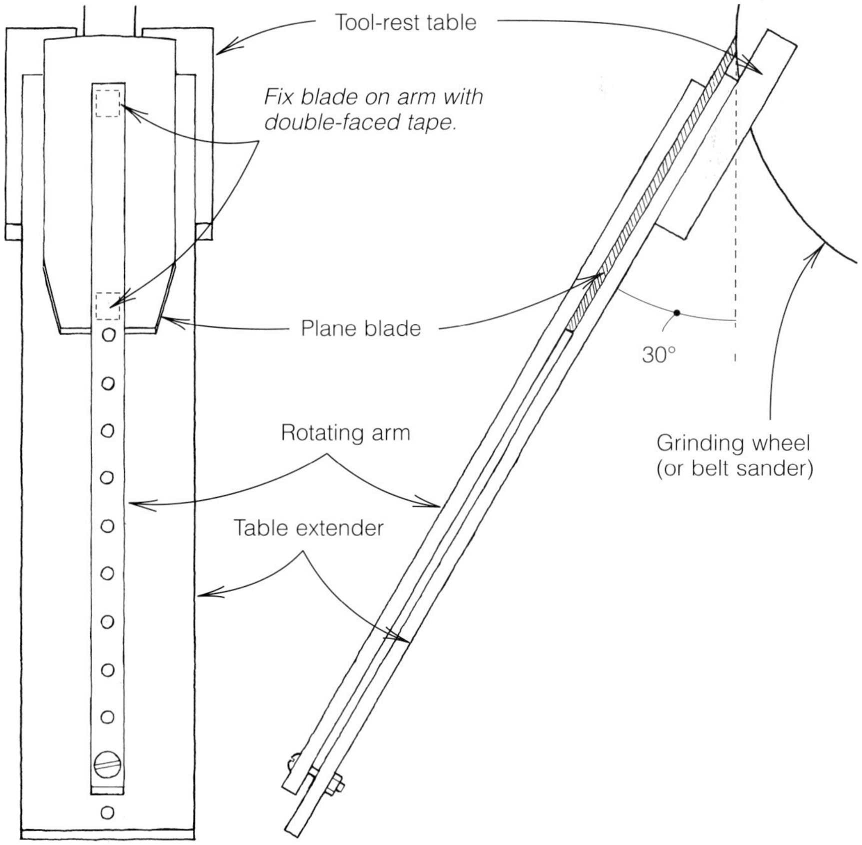

A scrub plane has a convex-shaped blade for removal of large amounts of stock in a relatively short time.

SCRUB PLANE

The scrub plane is the very roughest of the smoothing planes and is used for major stock removal. The blade comes with quite a sharply curved edge, which is fairly easy to maintain using exactly the same principle described in the sidebar on p. 81 (only in this instance a slightly modified jig would be necessary to hold the blade farther up). The grind radius can be as little as 1½ in.

JACK PLANES, JOINTER PLANES AND OTHERS (#5, #6, #7 AND #8)

Most woodworkers use these larger planes (jack, fore, jointer, trying and panel planes) only for working the edge of stock, in which case the blade can be ground and honed perfectly square. For use on surfaces wider than the plane, you would ease the corners of the blade as described under smoothing planes.

A GUIDE TO PLANE NAMES

Planes have many names, but a rough guide by length of plane is: 7 in. to 10 in.–smoothing plane; 12 in. to 18 in.–jack or fore plane; 20 in. and above–jointer or trying plane.

One exception to this structure is the type of plane made popular by Spiers and Norris in England (much like the plane shown second from bottom in the photo at right). These finely made planes, which invariably have steel bodies with wood infill, were used for work of high accuracy. Sized from 14 in. to 18 in., they are universally known as panel planes.

From top to bottom, a Bailey #30 jointer, a Stanley #7 jointer, a 16-in. craftsman-made panel plane and a Record #05 jack.

BLOCK PLANES

Whereas bench planes are generally used with the grain, the block plane was designed to work end grain. Today it is used for all types of cuts, but its name comes from its original use in dressing the top of butchers' blocks. As the various ways to shape the blade are discussed below, keep in mind that the recommendations are aimed at effective end-grain cutting.

Block planes provide an opportunity for some very innovative sharpening, but they are probably among the worst-made planes on the market today. For example, of the four block planes made by Record and Stanley (see the photo at right), only the Record #09$\frac{1}{2}$ has a lever cap that is long enough. Since block planes do not have cap irons, the lever cap has to do double duty whenever a cap iron would be desirable—usually only for face- or edge-grain cutting with a standard block plane; a cap iron is not needed when cutting end grain. Because these planes have only a narrow bed lip and a frog post for the blade to rest on, it is desirable that the lever cap extend at least to a point above the bed lip; otherwise, it will be pressing on an unsupported section of the blade.

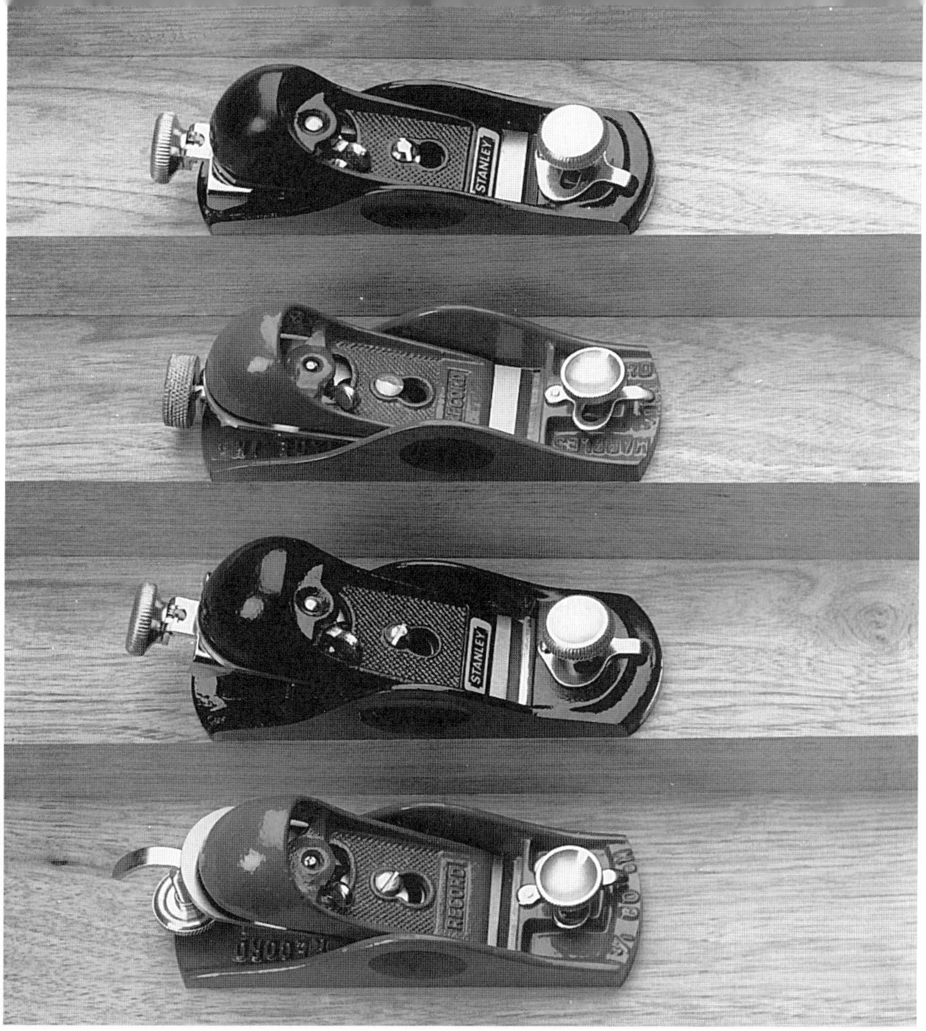

From top to bottom, the Stanley #60, the Record #060$\frac{1}{2}$ (both low-angle block planes), the Stanley #9$\frac{1}{2}$ and the Record #09$\frac{1}{2}$ (both standard block planes). Only the Record #09$\frac{1}{2}$ has a lever cap that is long enough, and then just barely. It would be better if the lever cap were $\frac{1}{8}$ in. longer.

LOWERING THE BED ANGLE ON A BLOCK PLANE

If you have a short lever cap on your block plane, it will apply pressure behind the machined portion of the bed causing the end of the blade to be lifted away from the bed. To reduce blade chatter caused by this flaw, you have to lower the bed angle so that the blade rests on the bed at the mouth, not $\frac{1}{4}$ in. back of the mouth. To dress the bed, strip the plane (removing the adjustable nosepiece) and file the bed, letting the file pass through the open mouth and using the frog post as a guide since it is several degrees below the blade line on all modern block planes. (The low post is another flaw, but at least it works in your favor for this process.)

If you find it too difficult to get even seating of the tensioned blade along the entire bed, you can relieve just the back part of the bed so that the blade only touches at the mouth. That is still better than the condition you are correcting.

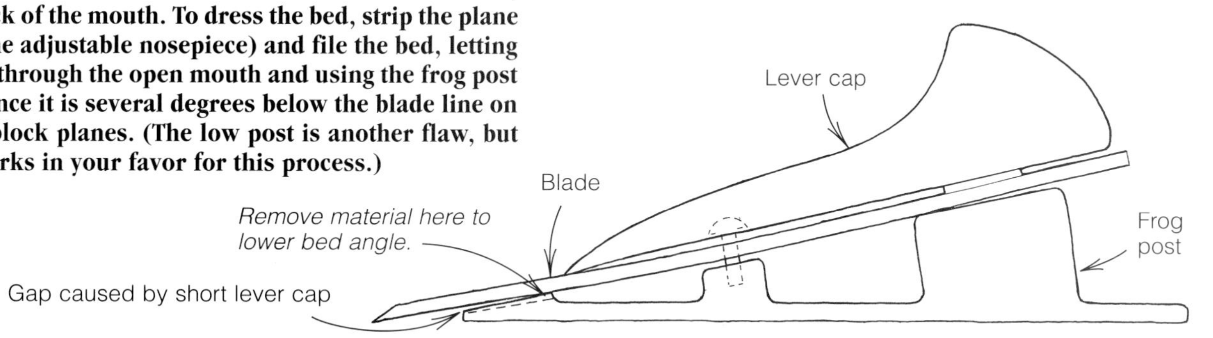

The lever caps on both of the Stanley block planes are about ¼ in. short of what they should be, and the lever cap on the Record #060½ is nearly ½ in. short. To compensate for this, you should lower the bed angle by 1° or 2° to ensure that the pressure of the short lever cap does not cause the blade to arch away from the front of the bed (see the sidebar on p. 83). Assuming that you have done that and all the other necessary tune-up procedures, you can turn your attention to the blade.

BEVEL ANGLES

The standard block plane (#9½) has a bed angle of 20°. Since the blade is used bevel up, if we put a standard 25° bevel on the blade, we will end up with a cutting angle of 45°. This just happens to be the same cutting angle that we have for a smoothing plane, which has a bed angle of 45° but where the blade is used bevel down. So when you sharpen the blade of your standard block plane at 25°, you produce what is in essence a smaller smoothing plane.

But there is nothing to say that you can't put two bevels on a plane blade. You can easily grind and hone a 15° bevel on the blade and then put a 10° back bevel on the face of the blade (as shown in the top drawing at right). This would still leave you with a 25° included angle, but you would now have reduced your cutting angle from 45° to 35°. You are still left with a 10° relief angle, which is perfectly adequate for block-plane use.

Possibly more significant, you have sharpened the blade of your standard block plane in a manner that will give you a lower cutting angle than someone who sharpens a low-angle block plane in a standard fashion (12° bed angle plus 25° bevel, a total of 37°).

All of this dazzling footwork with bevel angles now raises the question, "Why do we bother with a low-angle block plane?" It is a good question. The answer is that lower bed angles not only let you use lower cutting angles but they also align the blade more closely with the direction of cut, thereby minimizing chatter. The lower you make the bed angle, the closer you approach the function of a chisel, which does not chatter.

BEVEL ANGLES FOR STANDARD BLOCK PLANE

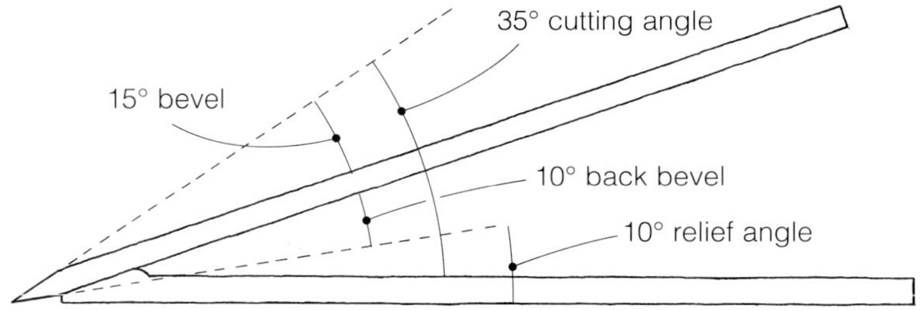

BEVEL ANGLES FOR LOW-ANGLE BLOCK PLANE

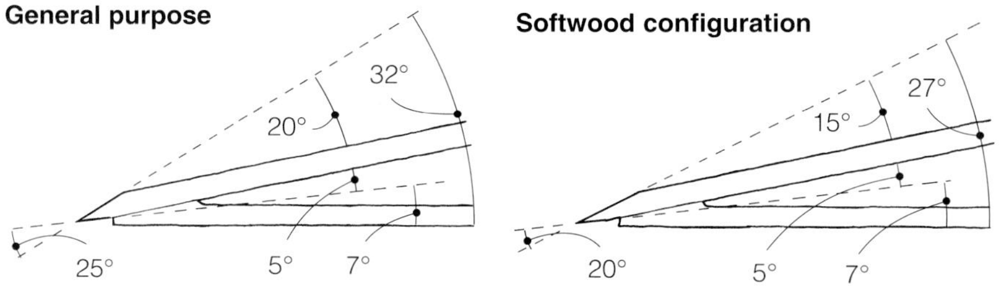

In practice, whether or not you get chatter with a low-angle block plane depends almost entirely on the fit of the blade to the bed and how well you can tension your blade with the lever cap. A well-tuned standard block plane will chatter less on end grain than a low-angle plane with a blade just as sharp but that has not otherwise been tuned. In my view, once the blade is clamped in position properly with a lever cap of the right length, bed angles become a secondary consideration; cutting angles remain significant.

Given the curious state of block-plane production today, I would look first for a block plane that can be tensioned properly (e.g., a Record #09½), get an extra blade, and then have one blade sharpened for regular block-plane use and the other blade sharpened for low-angle use.

LOW-ANGLE BLOCK PLANES

Having undermined the argument for having a low-angle block plane, let's take a look at them anyway. As explained in Chapter 2, you want the lowest possible cutting angle when you are working end grain. One aspect of cutting end grain is that the lighter the cut you make, the lower the relief angle required. This is fairly straightforward because the lighter cut causes less fiber distortion and therefore less springback.

So for fine trimming work on end grain (where you are not going to be taking heavy cuts), I would recommend that you put a 20° bevel on the blade and a 5° back bevel (see the drawing at left above). This will give you a 32° cutting angle. For working softwoods only, you can change this even more. You can put a 15° bevel on the blade and a 5° back bevel (see the drawing at right above). But if you do this and inadvertently use the plane on end-grain oak, you can expect to put some marvelous serrations in your blade.

It is difficult to be definitive about many of these bevel angles. Some people never skew a block plane in use; other people always skew it. If you normally use a block plane in a skewed position, you can get away with lower bevel angles. If you are always working clear pine, you can get away with very low bevel angles. Only you know which wood you will be working and how you will be working it. Experience will tell you what you can and cannot do. All I can do here is provide you with a rough road map.

In all of the block-plane drawings I have shown fairly long back bevels. This was done only to make the illustrations clearer. The back bevels should be very short, only enough to give you the edge strength that is required. In general, this means that a back bevel from 1/64 in. to 1/32 in. is ample. If you make the back bevels too long, they start to interfere with the fit of the blade in the plane.

By now you should also have realized that there is a strong argument for low-angle block planes. Not only can you get the total cutting angle as low as 27° (which is approaching the cutting angle of a chisel), but a block plane is far easier to use in a skewed position than is a chisel. If you then skew a block plane with a 27° cutting angle, you can drop the effective cutting angle further—to 20° at 45° of skew, and 14° at 60° of skew.

Whether or not you do any or all of the things suggested here is almost incidental to my purpose. What is particularly important is that you become comfortable with the principles involved so that you can tune your planes and shape their blades to suit your requirements and your practices.

Blades in planes like the Stanley #99 side rabbet (left) and the Stanley #140 block plane (right) are among the most difficult to sharpen accurately.

SPECIAL-PURPOSE PLANES

Although modern woodworkers are most familiar with the standard bench and block planes, earlier woodworkers had a great variety of special-purpose planes at their disposal. Many of these planes have been supplanted by electrical routers (and indeed some are no longer in production), but they all present some interesting sharpening dilemmas.

SKEW-TIPPED BLADES

The various skew-tipped blades, such as from the Stanley side-rabbet planes (#79, #98 or #99) and the #140 block plane, are sharpened in essentially the same manner as skew chisels (see p. 71).

The need to maintain an accurate skew angle is paramount in a plane such as the #140, because there is very little room to move the blade laterally on the bed in order to adjust for any errors in sharpening angle. The complicating factor with this plane is that the blade corner must be flush with the edge of the body to perform the rabbeting function properly.

The same is true of any of the Stanley side rabbets, but these are even more difficult to adjust because the bed angle is only about 7°. Add to this the fact that there is virtually no lateral adjustment possible because the blade runs in a machined slot and you have one of the toughest sharpening problems of any plane blade.

Since both of these styles have bevel-up blades, they are sharpened at the lowest angle consistent with the wood being worked. You will note from the photo above that the #99 side rabbet has the extra wrinkles of having the blade docked at two places on the corner as well.

To anyone who does not own a plane like these it is not immediately apparent why such planes should present problems. But low bed angles always present adjustment problems because the lower the bed angle, the greater the rotation of the blade on the bed to change depth of cut from one side of the blade to the other. If you combine this with the further limiting factor of having to have the very tip of the blade always flush with the side of the plane, you find that almost all maneuvering room has been eliminated.

Panel-raising planes Panel-raising planes usually have a double-ground edge. These should be treated essentially like two different blades, with each section sharpened separately and then the junction left crisp or slightly rounded as preferred. It is essential that you not change the length of either bevel to ensure that the blade continues to match the plane sole.

SQUARING A SHOULDER-PLANE BLADE

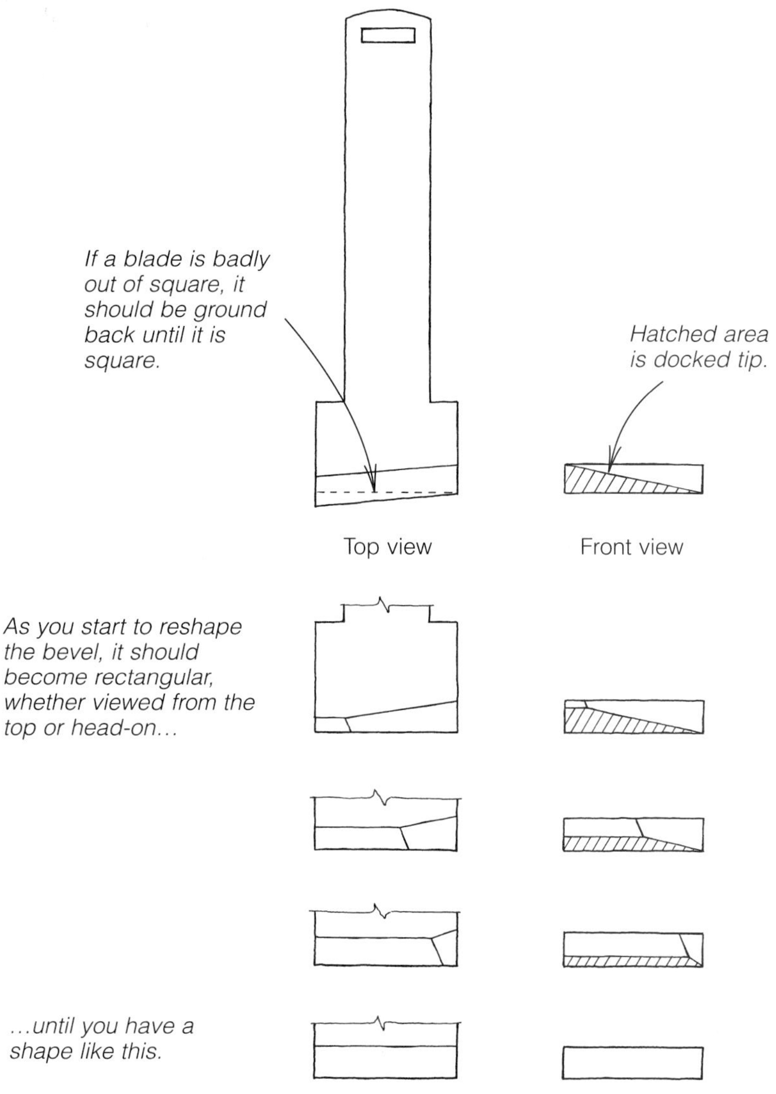

BULLNOSE AND SHOULDER PLANES

Bullnose planes, shoulder planes and standard rabbet planes have blades exactly the same width as the sole. They also usually have fairly low bed angles and limited lateral adjustment. This combination of factors makes it mandatory that these blades be sharpened perfectly square across the front.

Once again, a honing guide makes it much easier to keep these blades square. When you put such a blade in a honing guide and have it set at the correct angle (which involves most of the same considerations as block planes), you should take one or two strokes on the stone and then check whether or not your honing band is of equal width across the bevel. If it is not, you should adjust blade alignment and take another couple of strokes. By such a process, you get the blade perfectly square in the guide.

With a standard bench plane like a #4, you can be off-square by as much as several degrees and still compensate for it by lateral adjustment of the blade in the plane body. This is not the case with the blade of a shoulder plane. If such a blade gets seriously off-square, the best thing you can do is grind it square across the front and then restrike your bevel (see the drawing at left). In such a case, you now watch to be sure that the bevel being created is exactly parallel to the face of the blade. The easiest way to check this is by watching the line of light at the tip of the blade. What starts out as a wedge shape becomes a narrow rectangle if you hone properly and finally disappears as you come to a sharp edge.

ROUTER PLANES

Router planes have largely been supplanted by electrical routers, but they are still used for some types of inletting and restoration work.

Router planes usually come with a square-tipped blade and sometimes with an additional spear-point blade. Both blades must be honed freehand. Router blades are set at a slight angle to the stem in order to give them the necessary relief angle. The blade should be lapped on the flat of the foot, and then the bevel is honed freehand. This is done most easily by letting the blade post overhang the edge of the stone, using one hand to move the blade back and forth and a finger of the other hand to hold the bevel in contact with the stone. Router-plane blades are actually quite forgiving and will tolerate minor variations in geometry without causing large problems in use.

A standard router plane with a spear-point cutter. The plane should also come with one or more square-tipped cutters.

MOLDING PLANES

Molding planes are little used today, both because of the change in the nature of house trim and the advent of routers and ready-made molding. If you have a molding plane, the blade should be sharpened the first time by honing the entire profile bevel with shaped stones and then lapping the face of the cutter. How you perform subsequent sharpenings depends on how long you want your cutter to last.

It can be a tricky business to hone the bevel of a molding cutter. It is far simpler just to lap the face of the blade when you wish to restore the edge. The difficulty with the latter approach is that you make the blades progressively thinner with each lapping. For most users, this thinning process is insignificant since the cutters will not be used that often. For someone dedicated to the use of molding planes on a frequent and long-term basis, honing the bevel each time rather than lapping the face will give longer life to the blade.

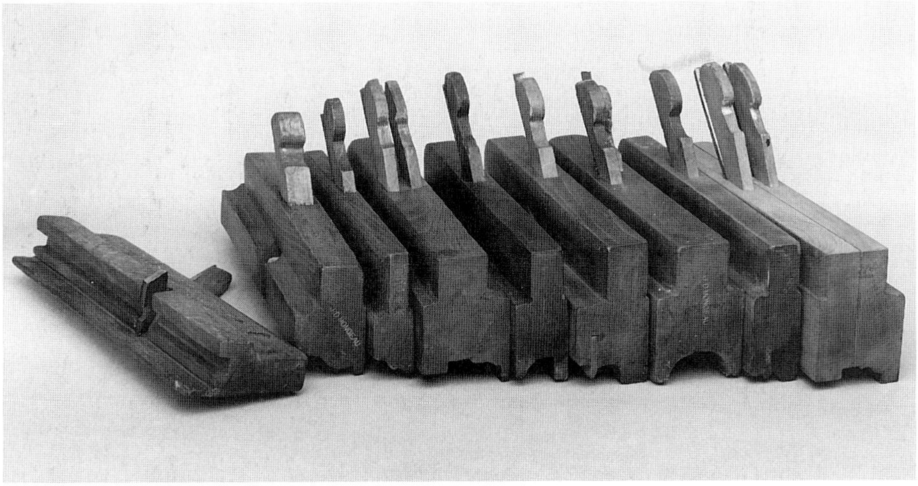

Molding planes like these filled the bottom of carpenters' tool chests before the invention of combination planes.

If you choose this route, you will find that you can hone many of the blades on a molding made by the blade. Just rub chromium-oxide honing compound on the molding and draw the blade along it. This technique works only for the blades with straight bevels. For blades such as ogees or ovolos, you will have to modify the molding slightly to make it a properly shaped hone because the blades are ground at an angle different from the one at which they cut. Therefore the hone will be a slightly different shape than the cut molding. Confusing? Trust me; it's a fact.

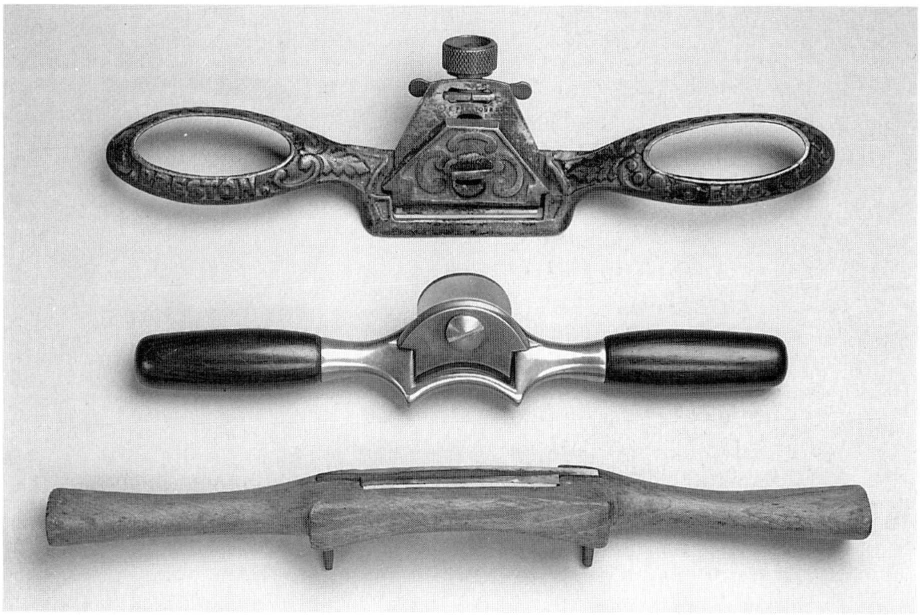

From top to bottom, an ornate, old Sargent spokeshave with a square blade, a modern concave spokeshave, and a traditional wooden model (shown upside-down to reveal the very low cutting angle of the blade).

JIG FOR SHARPENING CONCAVE SPOKESHAVE BLADE

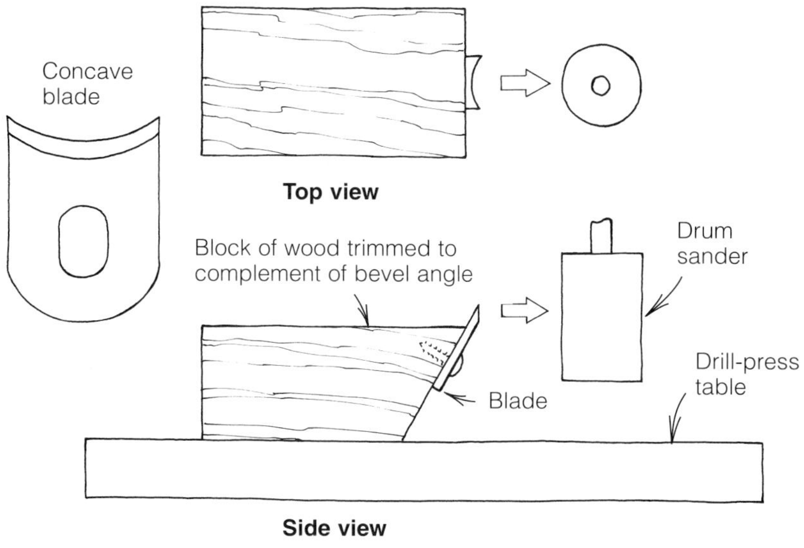

SPOKESHAVES

Square-ended spokeshave blades are sharpened exactly the same as plane blades. Special care should be given to lapping the face of the blade since these are often very poorly ground blades with a very rough surface finish.

Convex blades can be sharpened using the method described in the sidebar on p. 81. Concave blades can best be ground with a small drum sander (see the drawing below), and then honed with a stone or wooden dowel charged with honing compound. The U-shaped blade of the traditional wooden spokeshave is best done on a 1-in. belt sander with a fine sanding belt, followed by honing on a leather belt.

BLIND NAILER

There is no good reason to single out the blind-nailer blade for special attention, except that the proper sharpening of this blade is a good demonstration of applying the basic principles of sharpening.

A blind nailer is used to raise a shaving, leaving one end attached so that a nail can be driven in the trough and hidden by gluing the free end of the shaving back in place. I had been mildly intrigued by the Stanley blind nailer for years before I actually owned one. The first time I used it, however, I was very disappointed with the recommended ¼-in. chisel. Since the blind nailer had a bed angle of 15°, the chisel had to be used bevel up. This relatively high cutting angle created a shaving with frequent, very distinct breaks as well as tears along the edges. In fact, when such a shaving was glued back in place it was highly visible because of these two problems.

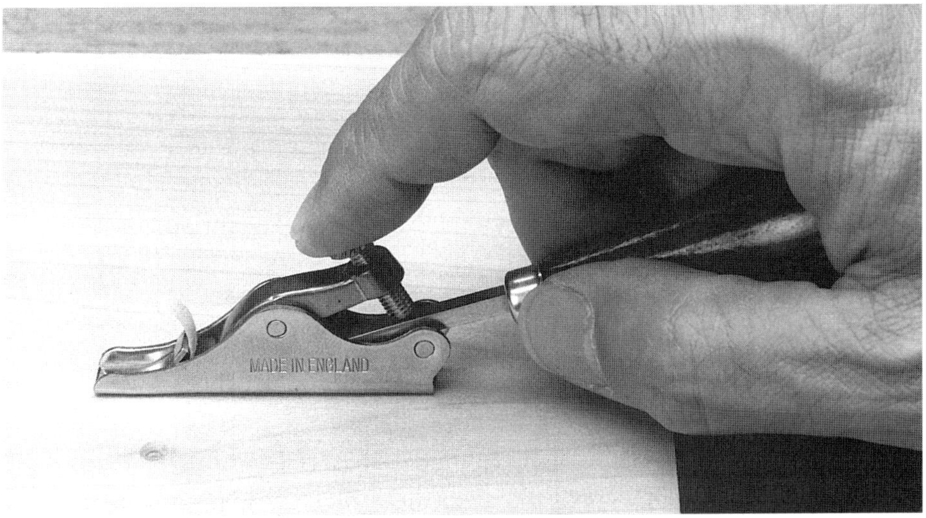

A blind nailer is a specialized small plane used to raise a small shaving of wood wherever a finishing nail needs to be driven. The end of the shaving is then glued back in place to conceal the nail. (Photo by Susan Kahn)

BLIND-NAILER BLADE SHAPE

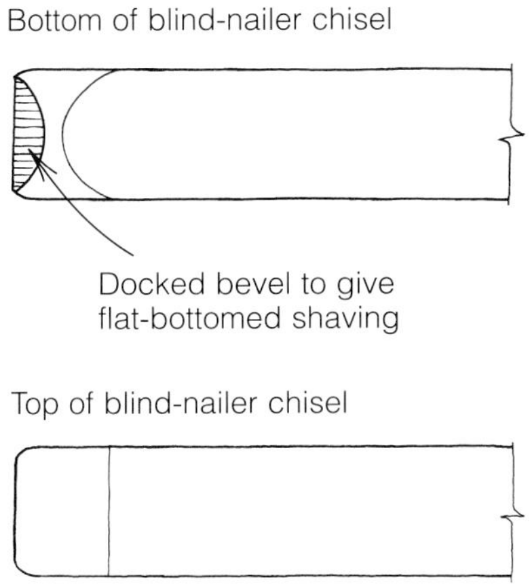

Before testing the blind nailer, the very limited blind nailing I had done had been under chips raised by a low-sweep carving gouge. The basic problem with the carving gouge was that you either had a chip that was too thin to cover a nail head adequately or too thick at the center for easy bending. After sharpening blades at a number of different bevel angles and a number of configurations I arrived at the current design, which is a double-beveled blade rounded on the back in a manner that makes part of the blade act like a chisel and part like a gouge. The key thing is that, like a gouge, it cuts the shaving on the bottom and the sides so that it can be reglued invisibly when carefully done; and, like a chisel, it gives a shaving of constant thickness for most of the blade width. The design is patented.

These blades seldom get dulled because it takes a huge amount of blind nailing to dull a blade. When it is dull, the easiest way to sharpen it is simply to hone the top bevel.

BLIND-NAILER ROADKILL

I was particularly delighted to be given a brand-new Stanley blind nailer by a New York friend a dozen years ago. After tinkering with it for awhile to develop the right blade, I decided to see if it would be economical to produce the tool again. I took it to a firm that specialized in small stampings and asked them if they could make it, and, if so, to quote a price. They wanted to use the Stanley as a model so I left it with them, cautioning them that it had sentimental as well as commercial value.

They made an excellent prototype and quoted a fair price for producing the necessary stamping. A production run was contracted for and everything was going swimmingly until I asked for the return of my Stanley blind nailer. It seems that the message about its value had been lost somewhere along the way. What I got back looked exactly like roadkill. My beautiful nailer had been unpinned and flattened so that the outline could be traced.

It makes absolutely no sense to get upset about a simple little tool, but I know that every tool collector out there will understand exactly how I felt when I saw the splayed carcass.

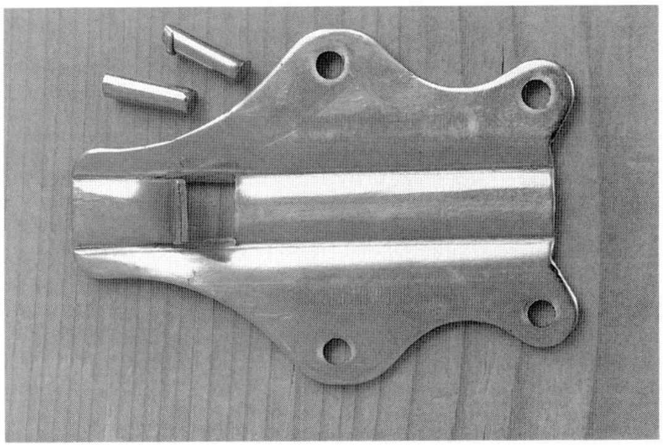

The blind nailer, unpinned and flattened.

CHAPTER 8

KNIVES

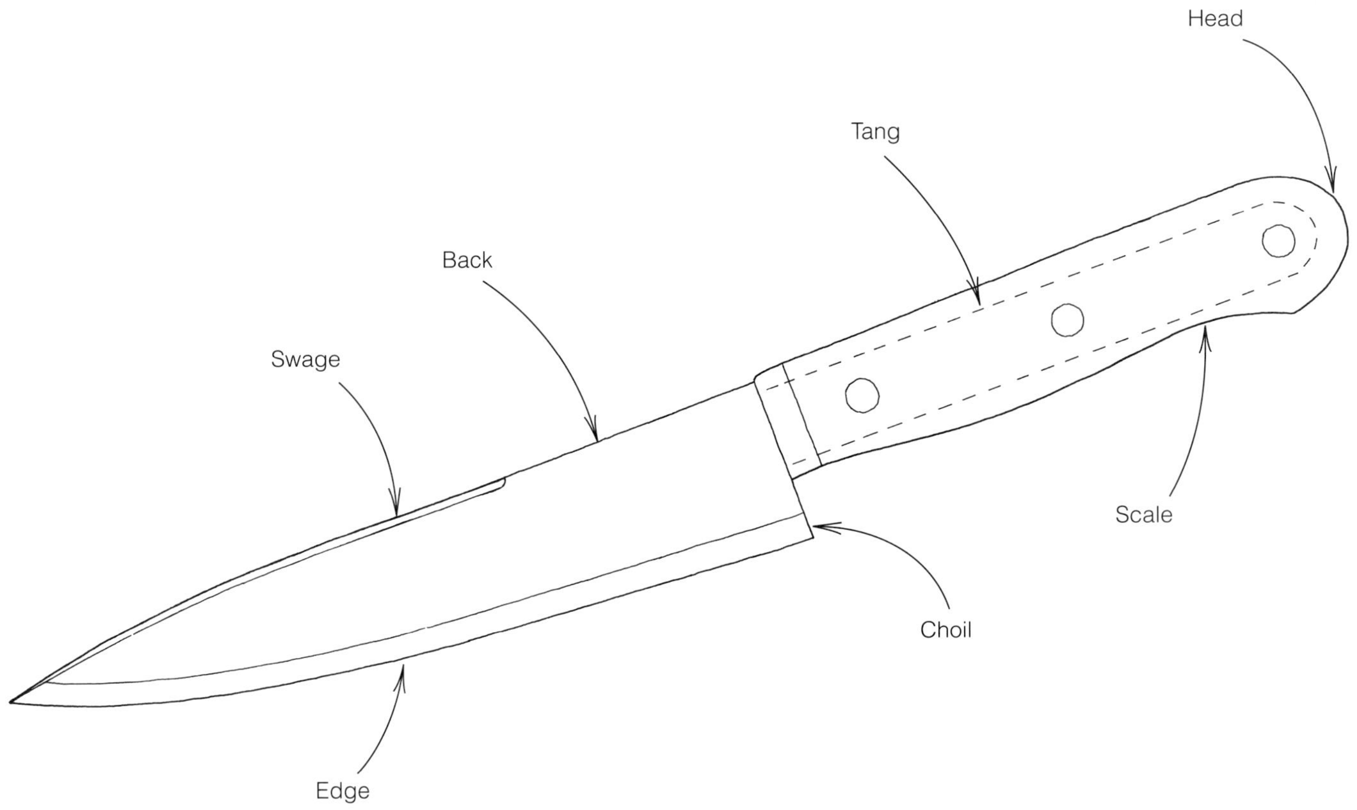

In woodworking, we are basically concerned only with knives that cut wood. But this is a fairly narrow view of the world. Over a lifetime, unless we just happen to be carvers, we will all probably spend more time using kitchen knives than woodworking knives. For this reason, I'm going to talk about kitchen knives first in this chapter.

Actually, there is a second reason. No non-woodworker is going to take a sharpening book seriously if it does not have basic instructions on sharpening kitchen knives. So this next section anticipates the question, "Are you telling me that you bought a book on sharpening and it doesn't even tell you how to sharpen a butcher knife decently?"

Finally, since edge-design considerations are so similar for kitchen knives, belt knives and woodworking knives, this digression into kitchen knives only reinforces the need to adjust edge shape to intended use.

To sharpen a kitchen knife on a belt sander, hold the bevel against the belt in the unsupported area between the platen and the upper wheel. (Photo by Susan Kahn)

KITCHEN KNIVES

Kitchen knives are very easy to sharpen, which is fortunate because most of them are left rattling around in drawers or abused in a variety of ways that dulls them very quickly. However, most kitchen-knife users seem to be satisfied with the condition of the knife as long as the cutting edge is keener than the back of the knife. The tolerance for dull knives is amazingly high in most kitchens.

The practical test of sharpness for a kitchen knife is whether or not it will slice soft vegetables, meat or bread. In all three uses, you do not want a knife with a classically sharp edge such as I have described for chisels and plane blades; you want a slightly serrated edge, a sort of combination between a knife and a saw.

Unlike wood, meat and soft vegetables have little rigidity to their structure. They are about 95% water held together with films and filaments of varying strengths. To cut them, you need an edge that will rend their fabric at very low applied pressure.

The skin of a tomato is sufficiently tough that it will maintain its integrity in the face of pressure from a smooth knife edge. Of course, you can only apply relatively light pressure, otherwise you tend to squash the entire tomato. You will find that a less finely finished edge, one that has many fine serrations in it from a medium-grit abrasive (400x to 1200x) will cut into the tomato much more easily because it is better designed to tear apart a film and sever fibers. Although the desirable amount of serration varies, you want a bit of tooth on any blade used for soft vegetables, meats and bread (see the sidebar at top on p. 92).

BEVEL ANGLES

Since these materials exert minimal forces on the cutting edge, you do not have to police your bevel angles very closely. You can sharpen most kitchen knives freehand and at a reasonably wide range of bevel angles, anywhere from 5° to nearly 20° (10° to 35° included angle) without being overly concerned about edge retention. There is a great deal of flexibility in all of this, and your guide should be an angle in this range that you can consistently reproduce.

There are some exceptions to the above statements. Any knife that will be used for chopping, particularly where bone may be present, should have an included angle (the combined bevel angles) of at least 30°. A cleaver should be at 50° or more to avoid edge nicking. The included angle should be proportional to the force that will be used or, put another way, to the resistance that will be encountered. For a kitchen knife used with hand pressure to divide frozen meat, 30° should be sufficient. For the same knife chopping up chicken or ribs, it should have a 50° or 60° included angle at the edge. In short, it should be sharpened like a cleaver because that is how you are using it.

USING A BELT SANDER

I do virtually all kitchen-knife sharpening on a 1-in. belt sander; a wheel grinder tends to undercut the bevel too much. For something like a meat cleaver, where you need a fairly straight edge or at least a fair curve, you should sharpen opposite the platen of the belt sander. But for all other knives I find it easiest to work in the unsupported area between the platen and the upper wheel (as shown in the photo above). You still have good control, and it naturally gives a slightly rounded bevel for a strong edge (without blunting the overall shape too much). The basic concern is not getting the knife sharp, but getting it sharp without removing too much metal. Even a 240x belt will strip off metal at an alarming rate. Fortunately, you quickly get used to the action of the belt sander and will find that you can easily sharpen knives at the rate of about one a minute on the machine without excessive metal removal.

Unless you are sharpening at a very high included angle, you will almost inevitably get a wire edge no matter how careful you are. This should not be a matter of concern. When you are satisfied that all your knives are well sharpened except for the wire edge, just turn the belt inside out on the belt sander (putting the belt inside the platen to prevent damage) and remove the wire edge with an alternate trailing stroke on the cloth backing on the belt. Alternatively, you can remove the wire edge with a few deft strokes on a stone.

USING STONES

Stones are not quite as fast as a belt sander, but they are kinder to fine knives. Unless a knife needs major reshaping, a water stone in the 800x to 1200x range is fine. Such a stone will remove metal at a good rate and still leave just a nice amount of tooth in the edge.

I find the wooden-based water stones particularly suitable for knife sharpening. There is a 1000x stone in a ½-in. x 2½-in. x 7-in. size that is just right. It is easy to hold safely, is inexpensive and handles the full range of kitchen knives.

BREAD KNIVES

Bread knives should have a bit more tooth than other kitchen knives, because they must cut soft, spongy material. A touch on an 80x belt would be in order; or hone the knife with the coarsest stone you have, stroking directly across the edge. For those bread knives that have one bevel scalloped, it is adequate to hone only the non-scalloped side (at 5° or less).

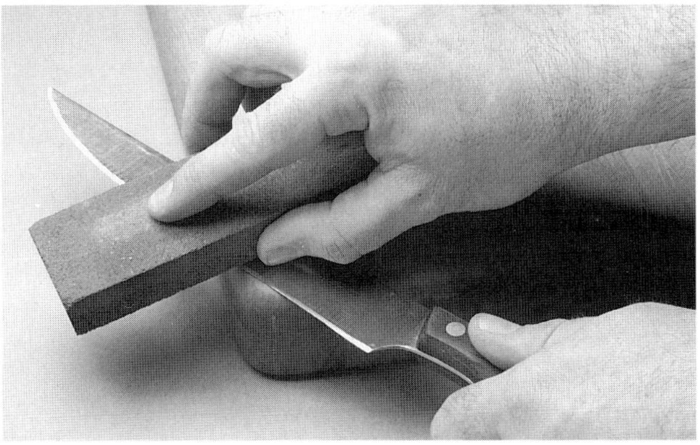

Stroke a coarse stone across the edge of a bread knife to achieve the necessary 'tooth.'

CHECKERING FILES

Back when hand sharpening was done commercially, one file used by the pros was a hand checkering file, also known as a corrugating file. Much like a checkering tool for wood, a checkering file cuts a series of regularly spaced grooves in an edge; in a sense, it degrades an edge rather than improves it. The file was used to dress the edge of hair scissors (if you have tried ordinary scissors on hair you'll know why), and it was used to give tooth to the edge of bread knives. The fine, regular serrations worked equally well in both uses.

Checkering files were traditionally used to groove the edge of a bread knife.

For slicing knives of all kinds, you can use quite low bevel angles for basic edge shape. Bevel angles of 5° (10° included angle) would be about right. Very seldom would the included angle be more than 20°. It is a simple matter to create bevels at 5° and restore them after dulling. Using the 1-in-60 rule (see the sidebar on p. 17), you would raise the back of a 1½-in. wide knife just ⅛ in. off the stone and take slicing cuts on the stone, first in one direction, then the other.

But you don't have to be particularly fussy about these angles. A slicing knife will work well with a 20° included angle, and if you find it easier to sharpen at that angle, do so. Just choose a motion that is comfortable to you and that you can repeat with reasonable certainty. If you imagine that you are trying to peel a layer off the stone with the knife, you should arrive at a fairly consistent sharpening action. If you want an inexpensive guide for knife sharpening, you can use a short section of a plastic spine clamp slipped onto the knife back (see the photo below). The spine clamps are available from stationery stores in several thicknesses, enough to accommodate the normal range of kitchen knives.

EDGE SHAPE FOR A SLICING KNIFE

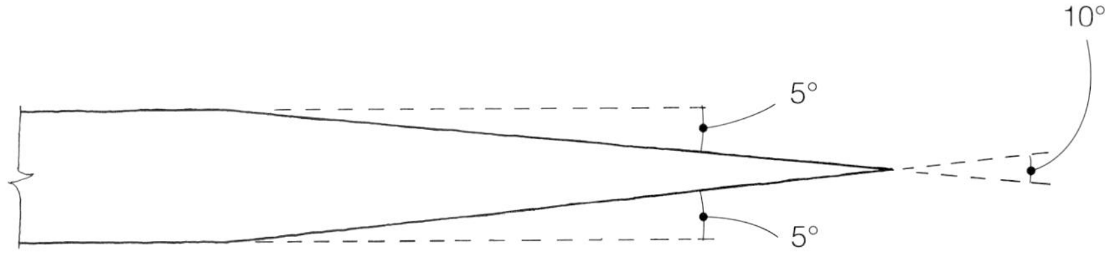

HONING A KNIFE

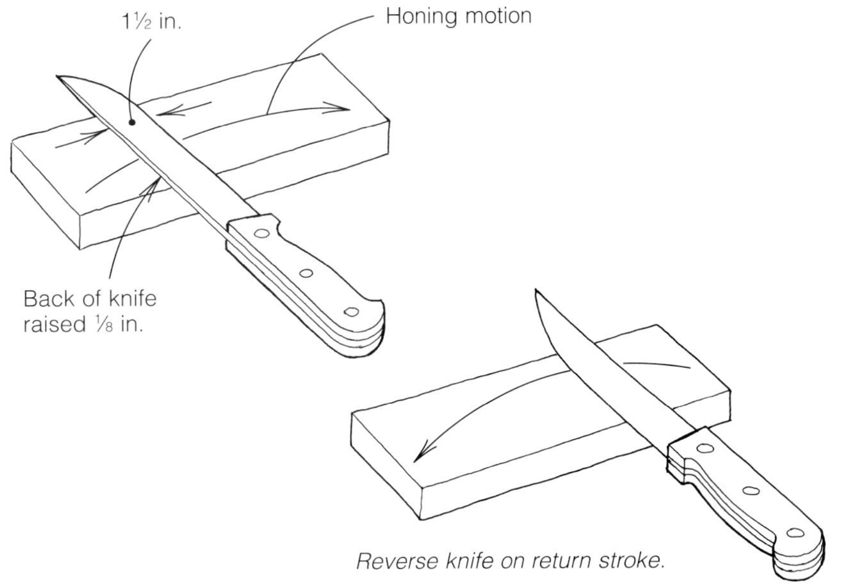

Slipping a plastic spine clamp onto the back of a knife will often raise the blade just about the right amount to hone the required bevel angle. (Photo by Susan Kahn)

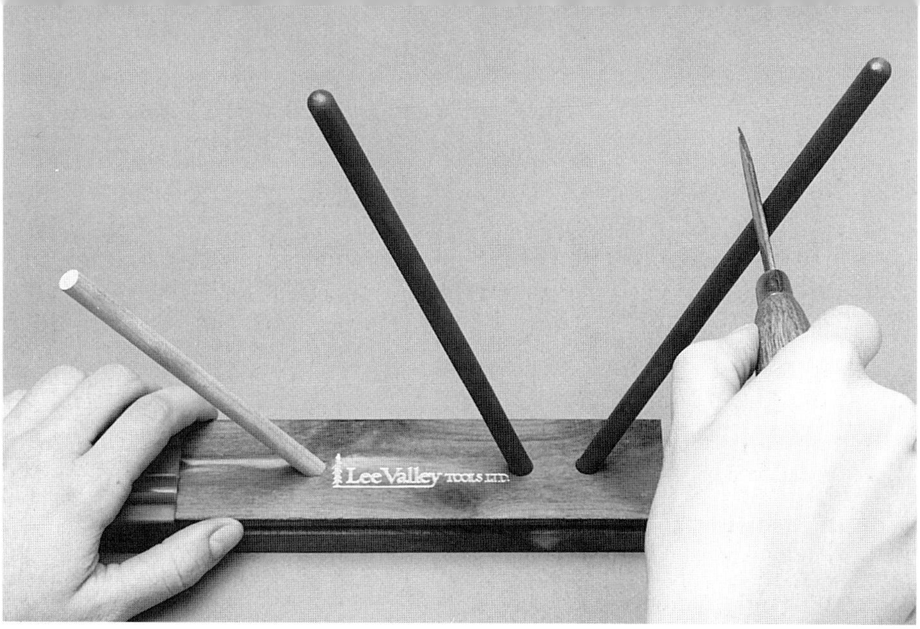

Ceramic honing rods can be used for touching up knives between sharpenings. (The rod at extreme left is for protection only.)

To use a knife steel, hold the steel vertically and take slicing cuts across it with the knife.

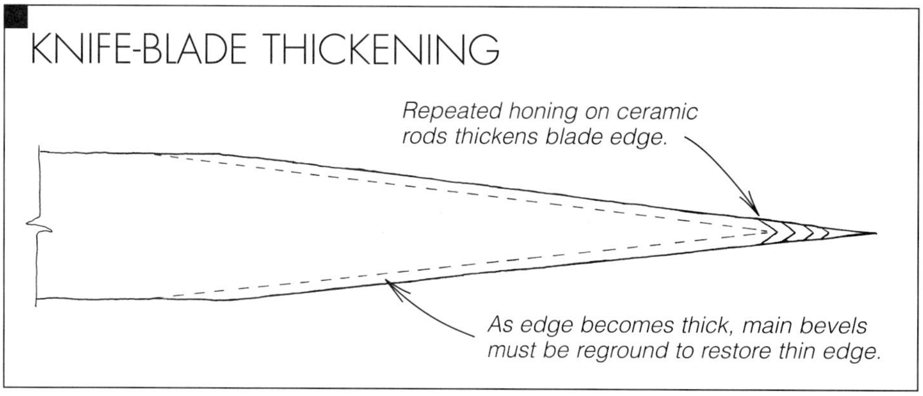

USING HONING RODS

Many people use ceramic honing rods for touching up knife blades between sharpenings. These honing rods are set at quite obtuse angles. The one shown in the photo at top left has rods set at 22½° to the vertical, which, if one follows the instructions for use, would give an included sharpening angle of 45°. This is a fairly blunt angle; while it would be suitable for something like a butcher knife, it would be too obtuse for a slicing knife.

However, it is not necessary to follow the instructions with these rods, which say to hold the knife vertically and draw it against one rod and then the other. Using the ever-handy 1-in-60 rule, you could hone at slightly more than 10° and still find that you were able to restore an edge fairly rapidly. Honing at 22½° as most instructions recommend would lead to fairly rapid thickening of the blade, as shown in the drawing above. This will cause no problems if you are prepared to restore ideal edge geometry on a belt sander regularly.

I prefer to use general-purpose sharpening equipment (stones, belts, micro-abrasive sheets) rather than specialized hones for knives.

USING KNIFE STEELS

A knife steel is a very hard steel rod (Rc 70±) that has a series of fine longitudinal serrations. When a knife is drawn against the rod, the blade touches only the tips of the serrations; the substantial point pressure actually deforms the steel in the blade, smoothing it and displacing it marginally. It is used to create an edge by reforming the steel adjacent to the edge.

The basic problem with knife steels is that they are of hugely varying quality, which is not always reflected in the price. Another problem is that most people use them incorrectly. There is not much you can do about the quality of the steel, other than take the advice of a reputable dealer. Regarding use, I strongly recommend that you adapt the stance shown in the photo above, where you hold the steel in position and draw the knife down and across the steel as if you were going to remove a shaving. The great chefs do freehand steeling of knives with a marvelous show of dexterity. If you are a great chef and have mastered this modified form of swordplay, I commend you. For the more faint of heart who would rather only slit their wrists intentionally, I recommend the illustrated process. It will give far more consistent results.

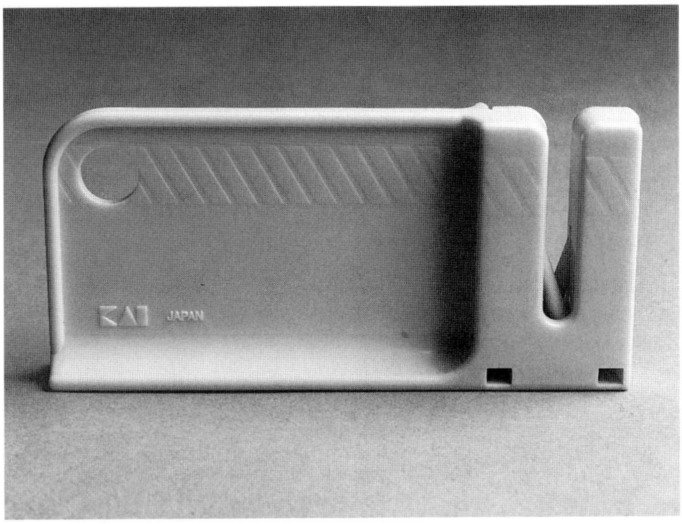

This compact sharpening device with crossed ceramic rods is suitable for Western knives, but not for Japanese laminated-steel blades.

Three pocket knives and, at bottom, a belt knife. The pocket knives are all of modern production, though the French knife in the middle is a style that has not changed in 200 years. (Photo by Susan Kahn)

One final point: Never use a knife steel on a laminated blade with a high-carbon core. It will chip the knife.

JAPANESE KITCHEN KNIVES

There are a number of laminated Japanese kitchen knives on the market today. Like Japanese chisels, these usually have high-carbon steel laminated to a piece of stainless steel or between two pieces of stainless steel. And like most Japanese tools, Japanese knives require a level of care and respect that most Westerners are unprepared to give to such an inanimate device.

Japanese knives will take a very fine edge and can cut paper-thin slices of meat or vegetables. One of the difficulties with them is that the high-carbon steel is very brittle and the knives should generally not be used for chopping of any kind. The edges chip too readily.

You should also be very careful when using honing rods of any kind with Japanese kitchen knives. The high-carbon steel is sufficiently brittle that it can be chipped on honing rods. In particular, you do not want to use one of the small devices with crossed honing rods shown in the photo at left above. The crossed rods are fine for Western knives, but if you draw a Japanese knife between sets of rods like these with any amount of pressure on the knife, you will virtually destroy the edge. It will have a series of small chips all the way along it caused by the wave action of the rods on the brittle steel core.

Some Japanese knives are of the single-bevel type with a flat or slight hollow on the opposite side. These are relatively easy to sharpen, since the basic bevel can be put on one side and the other side need only be given a couple of lapping strokes on the stone.

POCKET KNIVES AND BELT KNIVES

Having already included kitchen knives, there seemed to be no reason not to throw in pocket knives and belt knives as well. Although commonly used by woodworkers, these knives are seldom used for woodworking. Both can be sharpened on oil stones or water stones. The bevel angles chosen would be dictated by the intended use of the knife.

For example, if a belt knife is for general purpose use in camping, it should have quite a sturdy edge for making kindling, cutting rope, whittling tent pegs, and so on. The included angle of the two bevels should be at least 25° and preferably 30°. If the knife were to be used only for skinning and filleting, a 15° included angle would be ample. In both these cases, the sharpening process described for kitchen knives would be followed, but with the additional step of stropping the edge on a leather or wooden hone charged with chromium oxide. You do not need a toothed edge, so you can hone to maximum keenness.

The same general principles apply to pocket knives. The only difference is that if you have a pocket knife with two or more blades, you can sharpen the blades for different purposes.

As a matter of historical interest, traditionally pocket knives were sturdy utility knives with one or more blades pinned at one end of the haft. Penknives were much more refined, with very keen, hard steel blades (to shape pen nibs on goose quills) pinned at opposite ends of the haft. This distinction has now been lost, as evidenced by the photo at right above.

CHIP KNIVES

Chip knives are included here rather than in the chapter on carving tools only because their edge shape is more similar to knives than to the general line of carving tools. Of some ten different kinds of chip knives commonly available, about half are actually chisels rather than knives—relatively small chisels, but chisels nonetheless. The bevels on these can be treated exactly the same way you would treat the bevels on a chisel, leaving them straight and intersecting at whatever chosen angle you desire.

For the styles that are actually knives, the bevel almost inevitably requires a slight rounding in order to give the edge adequate strength and to allow you to change direction while cutting. In practice, all the chisel-like knives are used for stab cuts or straight lines. The rest are used for curvilinear work. Unless abused, these knives almost never need regrinding. All the work that is necessary can be done on a water stone, a bit of 600x silicon-carbide paper glued to a board, and a leather or wood strop with chromium-oxide (green) honing compound on it.

Any basic shaping can be done on 800x to 1200x water stones. This can be followed by stropping the edge either on a hard leather strop with green honing compound or a simple piece of softwood with the same compound on it. For convenience sake, it is useful to have a small piece of wood approximately 1 in. x 6 in. with 600x silicon-carbide paper on one side for thinning out the knife edge after repeated stroppings and a leather strop (charged with chromium oxide) on the other. While carving, it would be typical that the knife would be used for several minutes and then given very light stropping. After this has been repeated

Chip knives are available in a wide range of styles. The knives second and third from left are more popular for carving in the round than for chip carving. (Photo by Susan Kahn)

EMERGENCY HONING COMPOUND

Throughout this book I have recommended chromium-oxide honing compound. The most effective chromium-oxide compounds have an admixture of fine aluminum-oxide particles to speed abrasion, and the best ones are quite a dark green, showing a high ratio of chromium oxide to binders and fillers.

But if you need honing compound and specialized compound is not available, you can use chromium-oxide green oil-based artist's paint. It has a very high chromium-oxide content and can be painted onto any shaped hone you need. It cuts more slowly than the compound but still gives a mirror finish.

Use a carver's hone with 600x paper on one side (above) and a leather strop on the other (top) to maintain a sharp edge on chip knives and disposable-blade knives. (Photos by Susan Kahn)

The thick blade and steep bevel angles of a hacking knife give it the necessary strength for rough work.

a half-dozen times, you might then thin the edge with several trailing cuts on the 600x silicon carbide. Alternating between these two should keep the knife in perfect condition.

DISPOSABLE-BLADE KNIVES

Knives with disposable blades can be sharpened in exactly the same manner as chip knives. The blades may be disposable, but there is no reason that they should not be repeatedly honed to get maximum life from them. As with chip knives, regrinding is unnecessary, and all the maintenance of the blade edge can be done with 600x silicon carbide and a chromium-oxide strop.

HACKING KNIFE

A hacking knife is a substitute for the right tool. It is used in place of bolt cutters, side cutters, a cold chisel or even a small froe. It is always there to be sacrificed to save your good tools.

Because it is almost always used for dividing, edge shape is much more

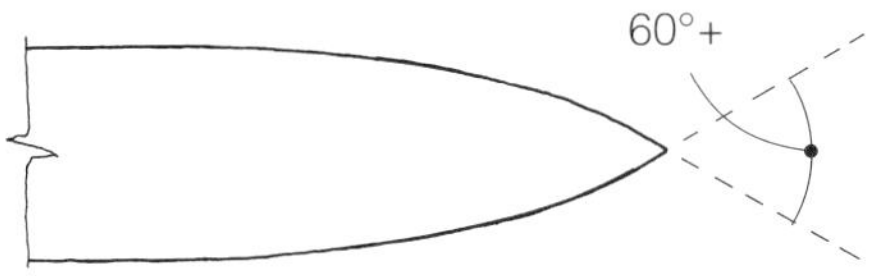

important than keenness. It is an ideal candidate for sharpening on a belt sander since that will give you the profile shown in the drawing above. A rounded bevel with an included angle of 60° or more is suitable.

Two styles of marking knife: the top knife is beveled on one side of the blade only, the bottom knife is beveled on both sides and has an integral scratch awl.

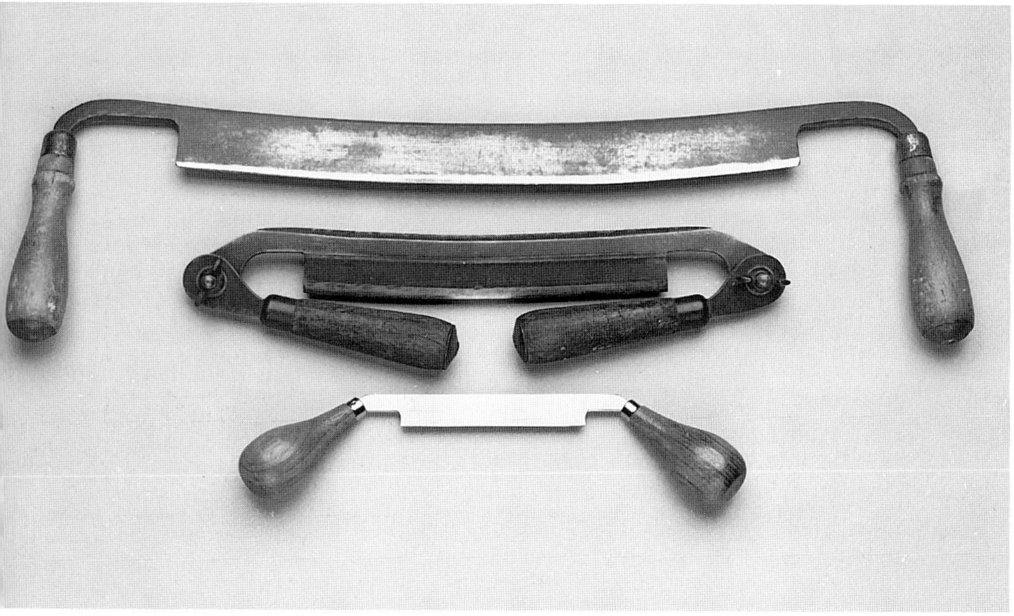

From top to bottom, a long drawknife for bark peeling, a classic carpenter's drawknife with folding handles to act as blade guards and a dainty carver's drawknife for fine work.

MARKING KNIVES

Used to scribe cut lines on stock, marking (or striking) knifes are generally superior to pencils because they mark a narrower line and sever fibers at the same time, preventing splintering during the cutting process.

There are two basic types of marking knife: those beveled on both sides of the blade and those beveled on one side only (see the photo at top). The latter is the easiest to use with accuracy. Available as skews (not shown) or with V-points, the V-point style is the most versatile. It can be used left- or right-handed, and for striking a line away from you as well as toward you. The angle of the V should be about 120°, and the bevel angle about 25°.

Either style can be sharpened freehand on a stone (800x to 1200x). Some users prefer to adjust the skew angle so that the entire cutting edge is normally below the top of the try-square blade; others purposely dull a portion of the blade after honing so that it will not grate along the side of the try-square blade. For anyone using the brass try squares currently on the market, I strongly recommend the second technique to avoid accidentally dimensioning your try square.

FILLING KNIVES

Filling knives are used to place putty or filler and never need sharpening because they are not supposed to be sharp. On the other hand, you will find it worthwhile to buff a filling knife and

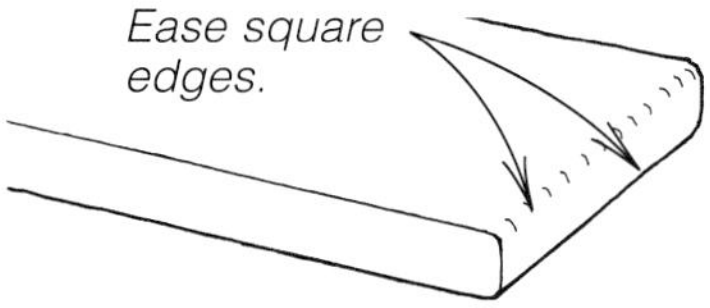

ease any square edges. This will prevent filler from curling up behind the knife as it is being pressed into a hole.

DRAWKNIVES

New drawknives usually require a fairly substantial amount of work to make them usable. As they come from the factory, drawknives usually have a bevel angle of 25° or 30°, which is far steeper than necessary and should be reduced to 20° as a first step in the sharpening process. Depending upon what you are going to do to the knife later, you may even want to start with a bevel angle as low as 15°.

Drawknives are designed to be used bevel up, but if the face of the knife is perfectly flat, only straight cuts can be made this way. Since a drawknife is more frequently used for general shaping than for straight cuts, it is often used bevel down so that you can not only cut into the wood but also change direction and cut out as well. There is an alternative to this. If you put a 15° basic bevel on a drawknife and dub from 2° to 5° off the face of the knife, you will find that it is much more maneuverable (see the drawing below). Only for a very sharp arc would it be necessary to turn the drawknife over and use it bevel down. Even then, you would have to round the primary bevel somewhat or you would still have difficulty making the cut.

So the basic bevel angle that you put on a drawknife is going to depend on the way you later intend to use it. If you bought it solely to remove bark from logs, you might want to hone it at whatever angle it had when you got it.

The standard drawknife can readily be sharpened on a belt sander or with a hand-held stone. I prefer to hone a drawknife by clamping the knife in position on the edge of a bench and then going to work on it with a water stone, stroking the edge at the angle I want. When using an 800x to 1200x stone, I would stroke into the edge, just as you might do with a file. When honing with a 4000x or 8000x stone, I stroke from the back of the knife to the front, because it is too easy to misjudge the angle and put a gouge in the stone.

CARVER'S DRAWKNIFE

A modification of the standard drawknife, carver's drawknives usually have much shorter blades and often have the handles cocked at 45°, which gives them excellent control and makes them very comfortable to use. Also, unlike standard drawknives, these knives usually come with a lower bevel angle. Since they are used almost exclusively in woods with excellent consistency (i.e., woods that are knot-free), they can be sharpened at a 15° bevel angle and hold their edge well. Again, you may wish to put a couple of degrees of back bevel on the blade. Often you will find that just holding a drawknife in position and stropping the edge on the unbeveled side will give you just about the right amount of back bevel. This is all a matter of personal taste, and you should adjust the process to what works best for you.

There are dozens of knife types that have not been covered in this chapter, but all can be sharpened with one or more of the methods outlined. Shape the blade for the action you want and the edge strength you need.

MODIFIED DRAWKNIFE

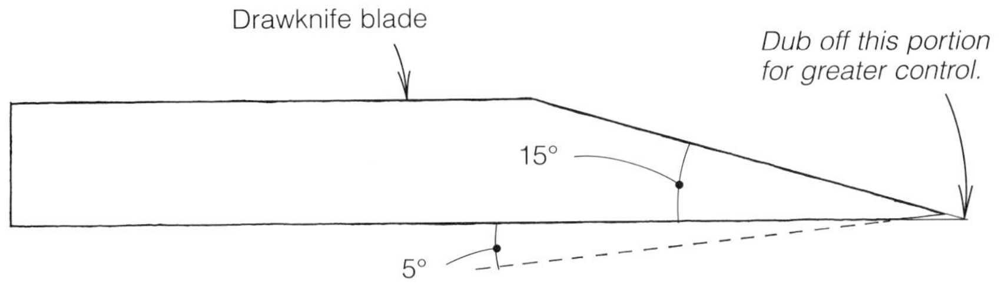

BARK SPUDS

No tool demonstrates the importance of shape versus keenness as well as a bark spud, which is a specialized form of knife used to remove bark from logs (very necessary in log-house construction). Bark spuds usually have handles about 4 ft. long and are used longitudinally on the log. A good spud has a concave edge; it tends to keep the tool centered in use. But a spud is sharpened differently at different times of year.

When there is a choice, logs for lumber are cut in late winter when the wood is at minimum moisture content. On such logs, the bark is intimately bonded to the tree. If you were to use such logs for building, you would need a spud with a decent edge on it to separate the bark from the wood. But if the log is cut when the sap is flowing and is peeled immediately, you want a dull edge on the spud. You want the tool to follow the cambium layer, which is fragile and "sappy" at that time. If the spud is too sharp, it will cut into the wood. You do not want it to cut; you want it to follow the line of least resistance and just separate the bark from the log.

A concave-edge bark spud. (Photo by Susan Kahn)

CHAPTER 9

CARVING TOOLS

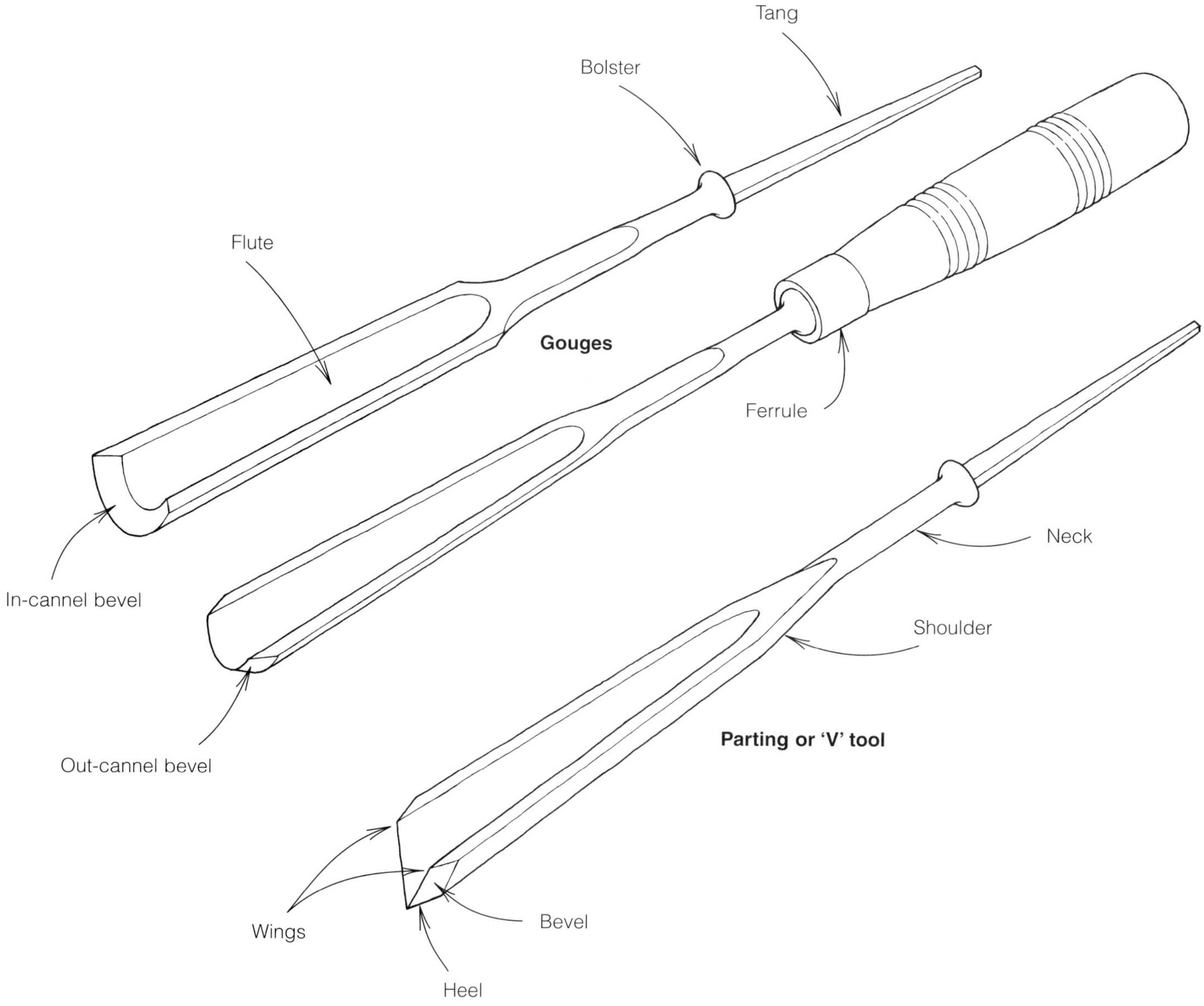

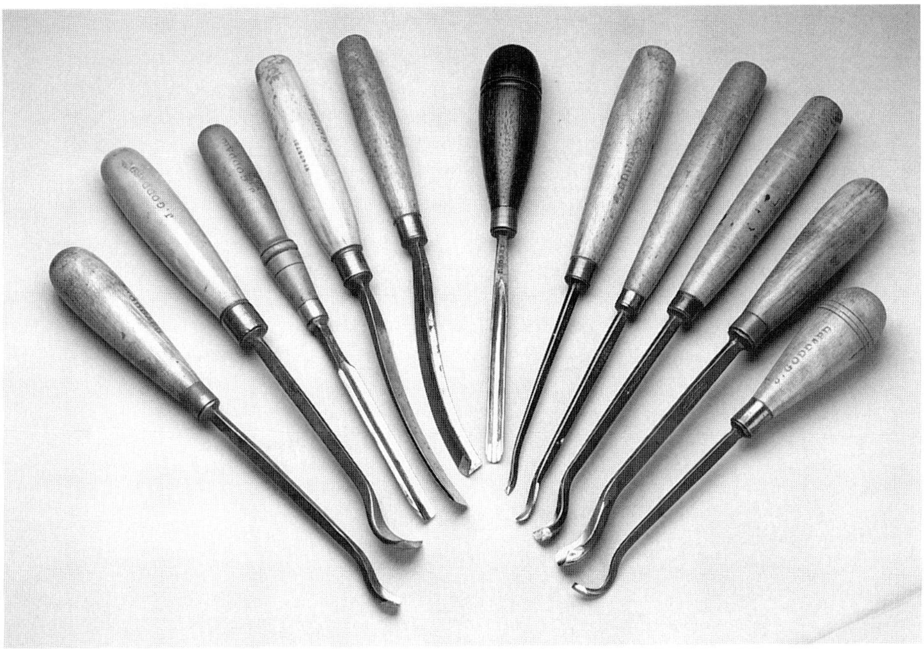

A selection of older carving tools, showing a variety of handle shapes. All but three of the tools were made in the famous Addis factory, the world's foremost maker of carving tools until it closed down a half century ago.

If you learn to sharpen carving tools well, you should be able to sharpen anything. Virtually every hand-tool shape considered in the rest of the book is included in the standard range of carving tools. The wide variety of shapes requires versatile grinding and honing systems. At the same time, the diversity often precludes the use of honing guides and demands the development of freehand sharpening skills in any would-be carver.

To complicate the carver's life, only a very few carving tools can be purchased in a ready-to-use state. Historically, carving tools were supplied with a basic grind only. In Britain, until recently, a sharp tool was considered to be a used tool. Since the supplier could not know how the tool was going to be used or on what woods, honing the tool would have required assumptions in both areas. There was a higher probability of being wrong than being right, so the tool was supplied with a basic grind only.

Today, some carving tools can be purchased in a ready-to-use state, which is a mixed blessing. On the positive side, it indicates to the buyer the degree of sharpness that can be attained, but on the negative side, it implies that the provided shape is the correct one.

As with all tools, edge shape has to be married to technique and the material to be worked; nowhere is this more important than with carving tools. Whether or not tools come from the store sharp or dull, you know that they will eventually become dull anyway, so good sharpening technique has to be developed by every carver. Fortunately, modern technology has provided a vast array of effective and flexible sharpening materials and systems, so the primary problem becomes one of determining what shape you want, not so much how to arrive at it.

GOUGES

The constant refrain of business consultants is to look at products from the customer's viewpoint to determine whether or not the products are appropriate. While this may sound a bit childlike, it is useful to do just that if you want to understand exactly why you should shape certain tools certain ways. You should look at them from the viewpoint of the wood about to be cut.

Consider the standard carving gouge that you might buy in an unsharpened state. You can almost be certain that this tool is incorrectly shaped, so whether or not it has a sharp edge is incidental.

CHOOSING A BEVEL ANGLE

One of the first things to be decided is a suitable bevel angle. For light cuts in cedar, pine or basswood, a 15° bevel angle would probably be adequate. For a bit heavier work you would beef this up to 20°, and for very hard woods you might want to make it 25°. If you are going to be using a mallet on the gouge you may want a 30° bevel or even 35° depending upon the nature of the steel in the tool. As usual, you want the lowest bevel angle consistent with edge retention, so let's assume an angle for general-purpose use of 25°.

Assuming that you have the gouge sharpened at a 25° bevel angle, you would find that it just begins to cut the wood at about a 30° angle of attack. There are times when you might want such a high angle of attack to clear surrounding work, but for most relief carving a lower angle of attack would give better control.

To consider this for a moment, think of using a carpenter's chisel to make a paring cut on wood. Using it bevel up, the applied force will be in line with the direction of cut. But if you are forced to make the cut with the bevel down (because of some adjacent obstruction), you know that this carries with it greater danger of a slip because you will be applying force at an angle (equal to the bevel angle plus a few degrees) to the direction of cut. You now not only have to overcome the resistance of the wood being cut, but you have also substantially increased friction between the chisel and the wood because of the additional downward force. And, as any physics teacher or your own experience in winter driving might tell you, friction is at its greatest just before slipping occurs. These are the ideal conditions for an uncontrolled cut. So, we try to keep the shaft of the tool as closely aligned with the direction of cut as possible.

As you decrease the bevel angle on a gouge, you bring the shaft into closer alignment with the direction of cut. You also weaken the edge of the tool, but this is easily strengthened by putting some bevel on the inside of the gouge. This "in-cannel" bevel not only strengthens the edge by increasing the included angle, but it also makes it much easier to use. To understand this, you have to put yourself in the position of the wood. Consider a gouge that has been sharpened at a bevel angle of 25°: viewed head-on, it would look something like Drawing 1 on the facing page; but as the gouge is lifted up just past the 25° angle so that it can cut into the wood, it would look something like Drawing 2.

Notice that the gouge would be able to cut in this position only if it partially compresses the wood at the same time that it cuts, since, as presented, the gouge is wider than the cut it is going to make (the cutting edge is the smaller of the two semicircles). So to get any significant depth of cut, the gouge has to be tilted above 25° so that a reasonable portion of the gouge can enter the wood before wedging action takes place. This angle might be 30° or more (Drawing 3).

The problem with all of this is that only two points of the gouge have the correct relief angle behind the edge. Over the rest of the surface the relief angle is either too great, as would be the case at the very deepest point of cut, or too shallow, which would require compression of the wood for the gouge to penetrate.

Compare this situation to one where we have part of the bevel on the outside of the gouge and part of the bevel on the inside (see Drawing 4 on the facing page). Of course, now we have only to lift the gouge just above 15° in order to begin the cut because there is only 15° of outside bevel. It is interesting that at the cutting point (see Drawing 5), we see immediately that such a design would have much less side wedging than one where the bevel was entirely on the outside of the gouge. Lifted up to get the same amount of cut as in Drawing 3, we can see that the compromises are not as pronounced (see Drawing 6). There is still a section where the gouge is lifted past the ideal relief angle, and the cut will still be a compromise between some compression at the upper edges of the cut and some tearout at the very bottom of the cut, both combined with some control problems (though these would be substantially less than would be the case when all the bevel is on the outside of the gouge).

MECHANICAL ADVANTAGE

The repeated refrain of "the lowest bevel angle consistent with edge retention" has a special meaning in carving. Anyone who has carved knows that there is a constant threat of a sudden slip that can ruin a piece. For this reason, the carver wants to be able to cut using the least amount of pressure on the tool because this makes it the most controllable.

Well, the degree of sharpness is not the only thing that determines how much pressure must be applied. The carving tool is a wedge that is being driven into the wood. The shape of the wedge determines its mechanical advantage, and the mechanical advantage determines the force required for penetration. Since mechanical advantage equals D/W (depth/width), as you lower the bevel angle on a carving tool, you decrease the force required to use it.

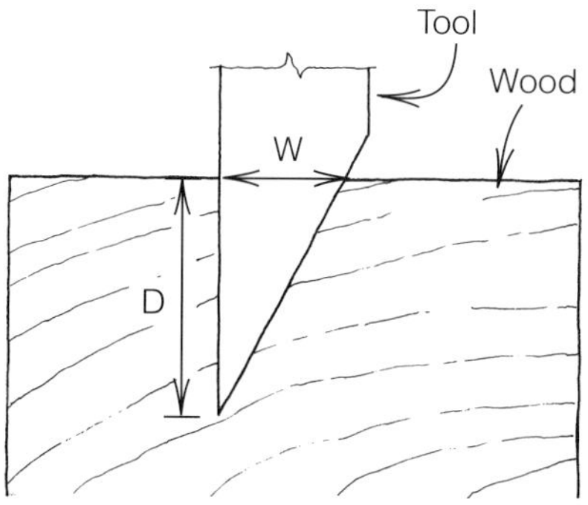

CARVING-GOUGE BEVELS

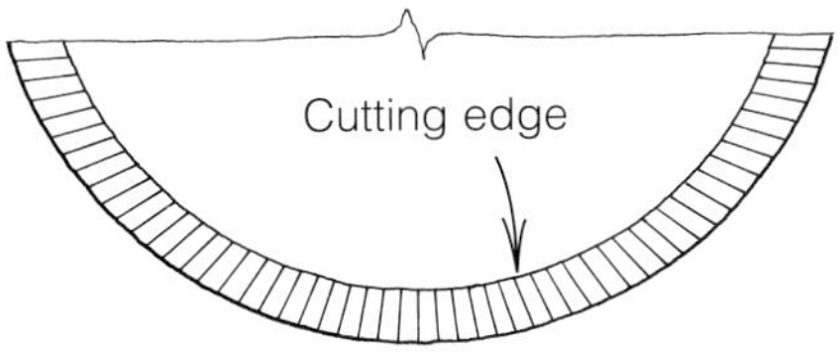

1. Gouge viewed head-on

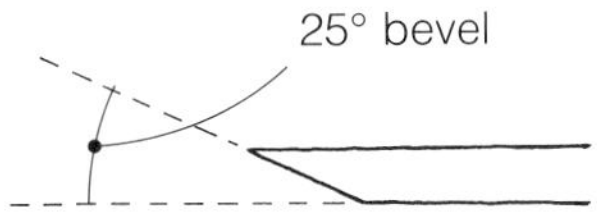

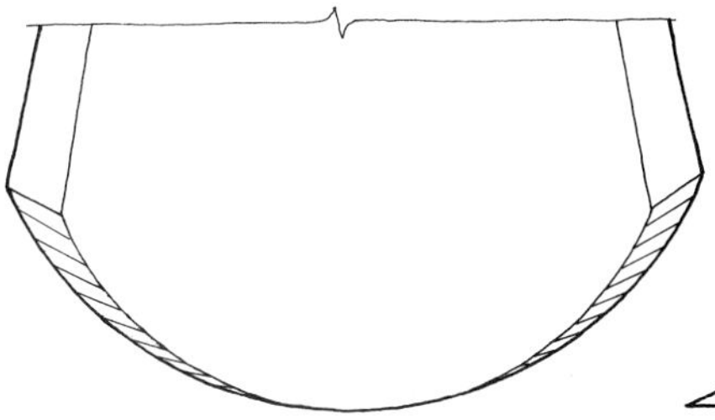

2. Gouge raised to 25°

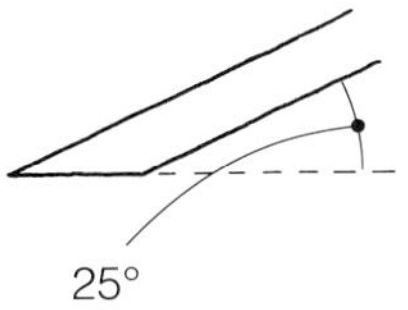

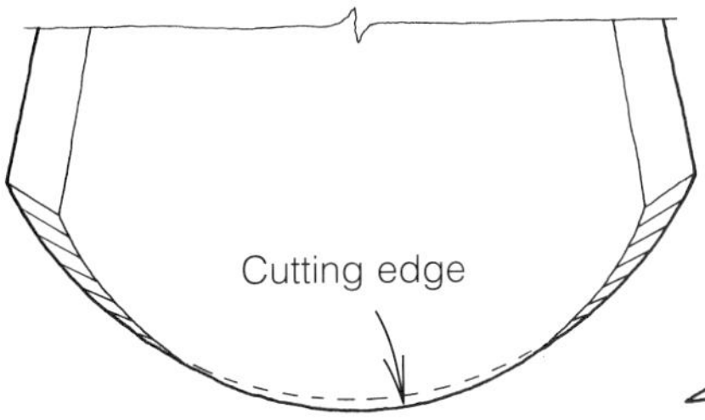

3. Gouge cutting

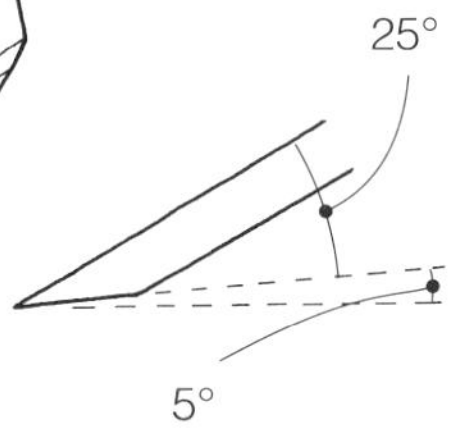

Gouge must be tilted to 30° or more to get significant depth of cut.

Transferring some of bevel to inside of gouge lowers cutting angle...

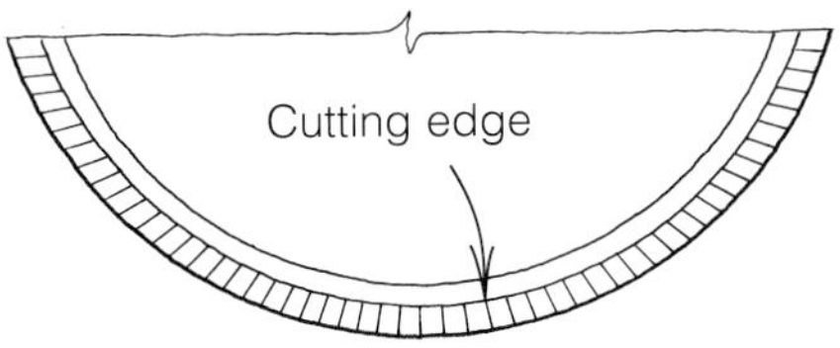

4. Gouge viewed head-on

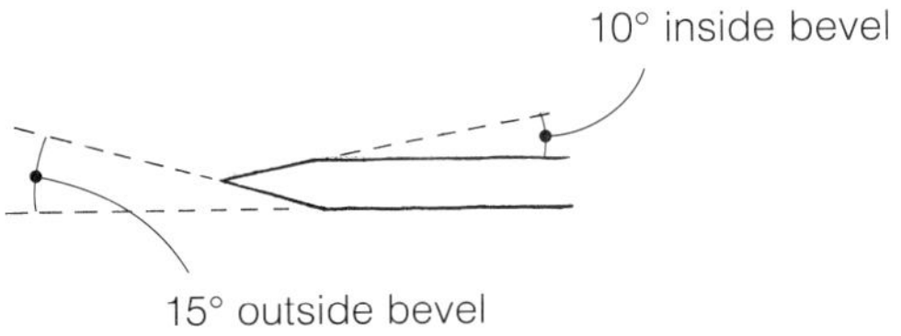

...and reduces wedging action.

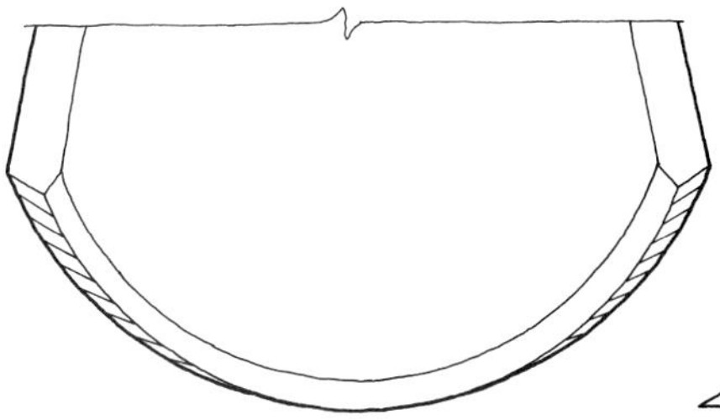

5. Gouge raised to 15°

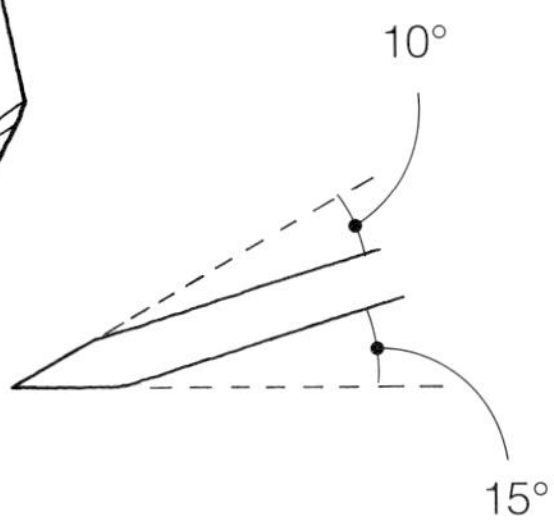

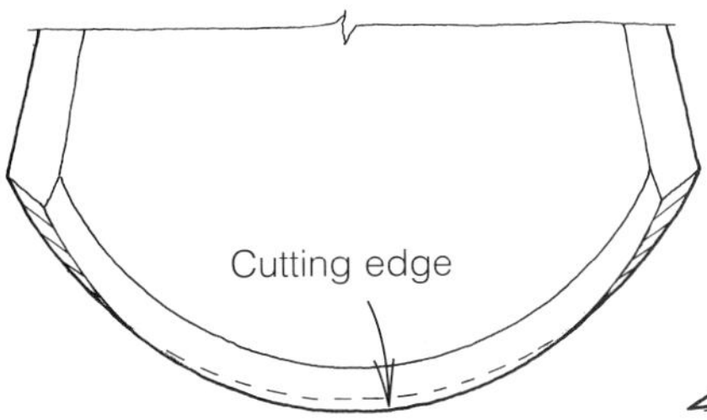

6. Gouge cutting

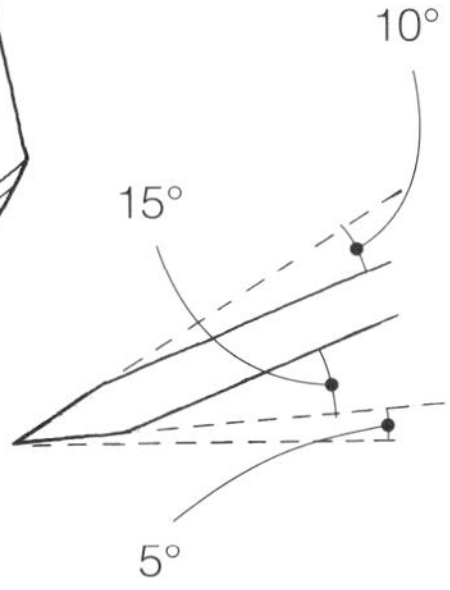

IN-CANNEL AND OUT-CANNEL GOUGES

As a general rule, carving gouges are out-cannel and patternmaker's gouges are in-cannel. Firmer gouges, which are heavier than carving gouges and shorter than patternmaker's gouges, can be either. The primary use for an in-cannel gouge is to make a straight groove of a known radius. This is important in patternmaking, where a shaft or similar machinery feature may have to fit into the groove of the casting made from the pattern. The same thing is true for millwrights who may have to make pillow blocks for shafts and would want in-cannel gouges for good control and a long straight cut.

The increased popularity of routers and the availability of low-cost large-diameter bits have virtually eliminated the demand for in-cannel gouges. They are so rarely used today that the term "gouge" is generally understood to mean an out-cannel gouge. In fact, to many people the term "cannel" is new to their vocabulary.

I bought the small in-cannel gouge being used in the photo below at some long-forgotten tool sale. It is very flexible and can be used just like a cranked-neck gouge. With just a breath of back bevel on it (in this case, back bevel means out-cannel) to compensate for the bend, it will cut dead true on any flat surface. It would be a fairly straightforward matter to make small gouges like this out of drill rod; only the tip would have to be shaped.

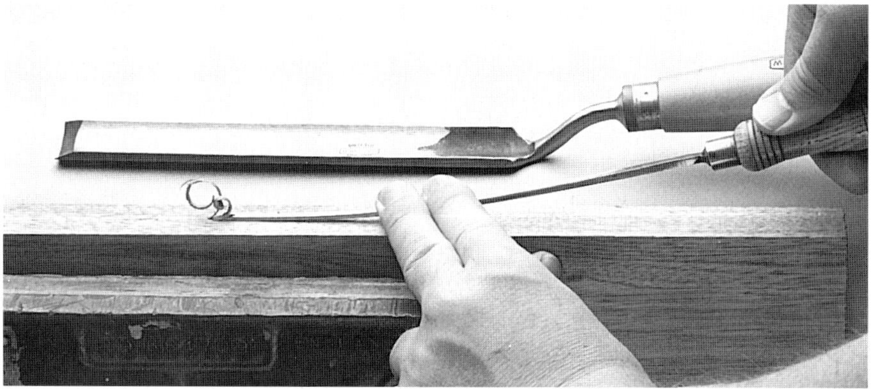

A slim, flexible in-cannel gouge can perform the same function as a cranked-neck gouge.

IN-CANNEL GOUGE

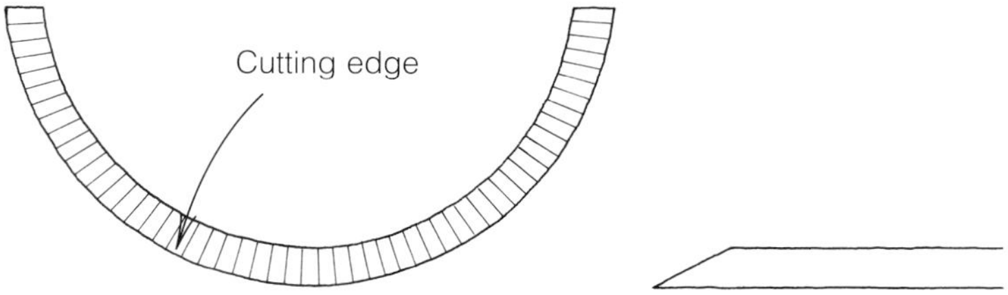

7. Gouge viewed head-on (bevel inside)

If transferring part of the bevel to the inside is a good thing, why not transfer all the bevel to the inside ? Well, if you do that you will have a gouge that can cut only straight grooves. Having no bevel on the outside, you could not change direction with it. This is called an in-cannel gouge, and, while it is much loved by patternmakers, it is virtually useless for carving since it can be used only on a flat surface where the cut is going to start at one edge and run some distance in a straight line at consistent depth of cut. In addition, since it would be used almost flush with the surface, it must either have a cranked neck or be very flexible, as shown in the photo at left.

Viewed head-on, it would look exactly the same as the gouge in Drawing 1 on p. 103, except now the larger-radius circle, not the smaller-radius circle, would be the cutting edge (see Drawing 7 below).

This shows that the need to be able to change direction while cutting can be maintained only by having a decent amount of the bevel on the outside of the gouge. But so far we have been a bit inflexible in the analysis. Why not change the amount of bevel transfer as we change position on the gouge? Taking our earlier example where we transfer 10° of the bevel to the inside so that we could get a 15° attack angle, we see that we could eliminate a lot of problems if we progressively transferred bevel from the outside to the inside until it was totally in-cannel at the top. Viewed head-on the gouge would look something like Drawing 8 on the facing page. Raised to a 15° angle it would look something like Drawing 9.

This looks fine, but there are a couple of cautionary notes. First, the upper edges are quite weak with only 10° included angles. Second, the gouge would not look exactly like Drawing 9 because we have been playing fast and loose with geometry. In fact, if you had a gouge ground like one in Drawing 8, raised to 15° it would look more like Drawing 10.

TRANSITIONAL BEVEL

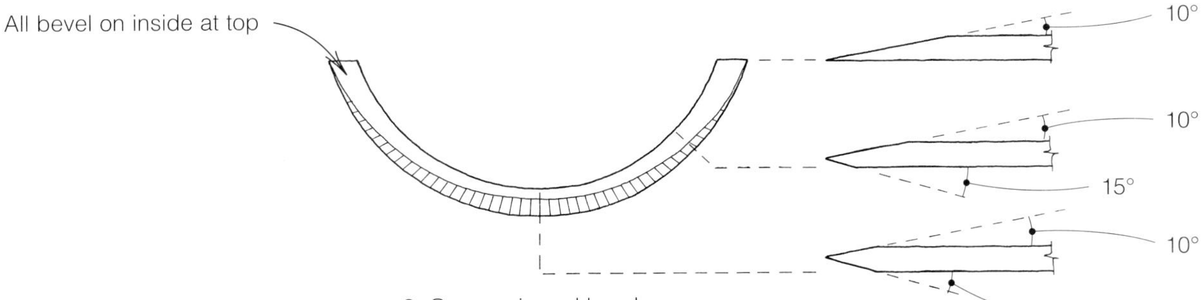

8. Gouge viewed head-on

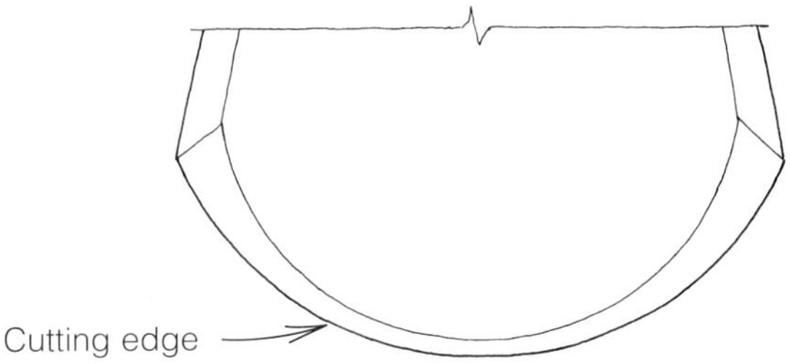

9. Gouge raised to 15° (ideal)

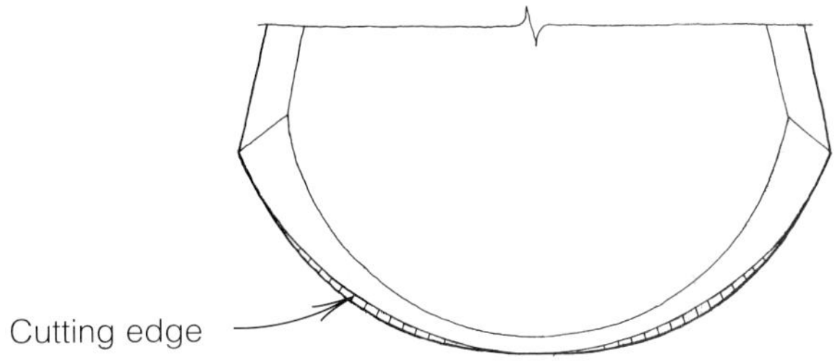

10. Gouge raised to 15° (actual)

There would still be some wedging action, because the cutting edge of the gouge would still be inside the overall profile presented to the wood. The only way to grind the gouge that would look exactly like Drawing 9 would be to have constantly changing bevel angles both inside and out. The outside bevel would start at 15° and be gradually reduced until it would reach 0° just as it disappeared. In the same manner, the inside bevel would start at 10° and continue to increase until it reached 25° at the top of the gouge. It is exactly this sort of transitional bevel both inside and outside that you should strive for when you sharpen carving gouges.

You do not have to follow the above examples slavishly when sharpening your carving gouges, but understanding the principles involved lets you understand what is happening when you are cutting wood. This prepares you for the day when you switch from carving basswood to carving cherry and wonder why your tools are suddenly not working the way you expect them to. You might find that you have been depending on wood compression to make a number of your best moves and that the much more unforgiving cherry will not let you make those moves. Just as you might have to increase the bevel angles to keep edges from crumbling, you might have to pay a lot more attention to relief angles so that you can retain some maneuverability in cherry.

At the other end of the scale, if you are always going to be carving softwoods of consistent density, all of the bevel angles used in the examples are too great. You will get a much better finish if you lower them to something closer to 15° in total. The low bevel angles will give you a much smoother finish with less fiber pulling and crushing.

At the risk of being a bore, I would also say that if you have not understood all of the material in this chapter so far, you should re-read it. The principles explained are of critical importance to effective sharpening of carving gouges.

ROUNDING THE BEVEL

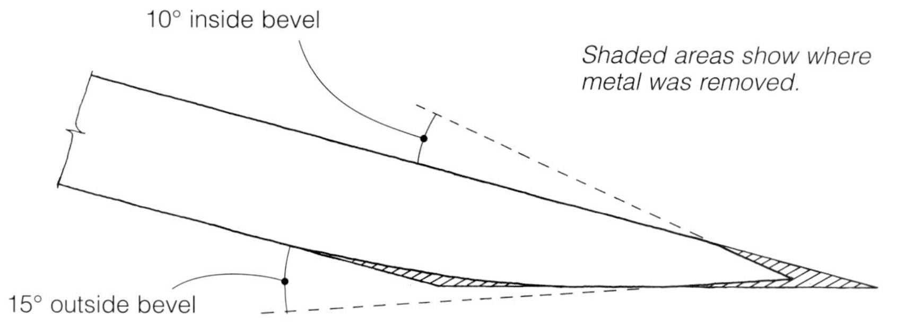

GOUGE TIPS

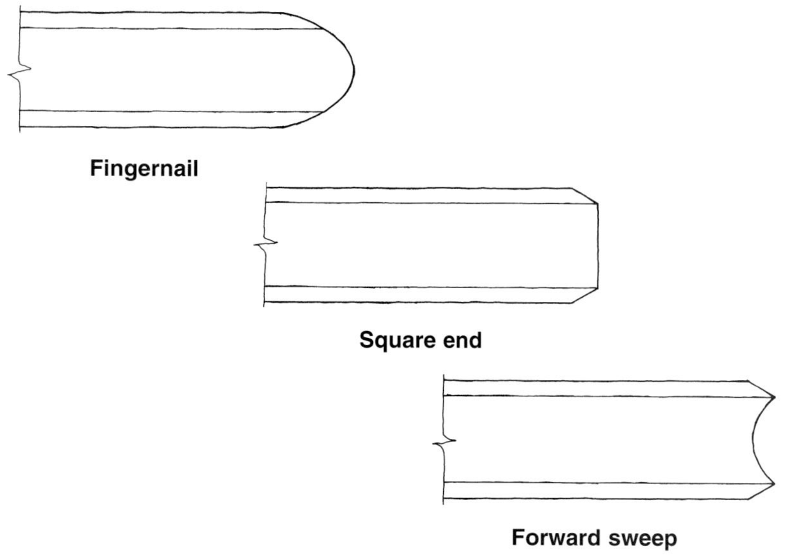

ROUNDING THE BEVEL

Unless you intend to use a gouge for long straight grooves of a constant depth, you are probably going to want some degree of roundness on the bevel. Otherwise, you will have difficulty changing your depth of cut in the wood. That should probably be rephrased; you will have no difficulty continuing to cut ever deeper if you have a flat bevel, but you will find it difficult to level out or to cut out of the wood. Both would require some prying with consequent damage to the wood, the chisel or both. Using the example above where we had 15° outside bevel and 10° inside bevel, you might want to shape the outside bevel as shown in the top drawing at left.

In this case, the outside bevel is more of a long, gradual curve than a flat bevel. You can be sure that this will work better than a flat bevel for most carving requirements. The question for personal technique becomes one of deciding the shape of curve you want. You will also notice in the example that the 10° interior bevel is much shorter than the 15° exterior bevel. This is something you would adjust to your own wood, tools and techniques. It is shown this way just to indicate that the bevels do not have to be of equal length, because any edge crumbling or rolling is going to take place only at the tip of the gouge unless you are making very heavy cuts or abusing the tool. Since it is far easier to grind bevels on the outside of gouges than on the inside, I prefer to keep the outside bevel long and the inside bevel short wherever possible.

GOUGE TIPS—FINGERNAIL, SQUARE END OR SWEPT FORWARD?

Most carvers like to have a slight fingernail on all their gouges because this is the easiest shape to hone. Others will have square-end gouges, and a few will have gouges with a slight forward sweep to the upper edges (see the bottom drawing at left).

Unless you have good reason to do otherwise, I recommend that you keep the ends of your gouges square. The shape is not so significant when you are cutting with the grain. But when you are cutting cross grain it makes sense to sever the ends of the fibers at the same time or slightly before dislodging the central part of the chip (see the photo on the facing page). You will see many sets of carving tools with fingernail ends on all of the gouges. Often this indicates only that the manufacturer found it easier to sharpen a gouge that way than to do it properly.

The clean cut on the left was made by a square-end gouge; there is no tear-out anywhere. The rougher cut on the right was made by a fingernail-end gouge.

DOT AND CROSS PATTERN

1. Use fingernail-end gouge to make two stab cuts. Gouge tip matches dot diameter.

2. Use gouge with swept-forward wings to make sloping cuts that release chips on either side of dot. Gouge should have exactly same flute shape as first gouge.

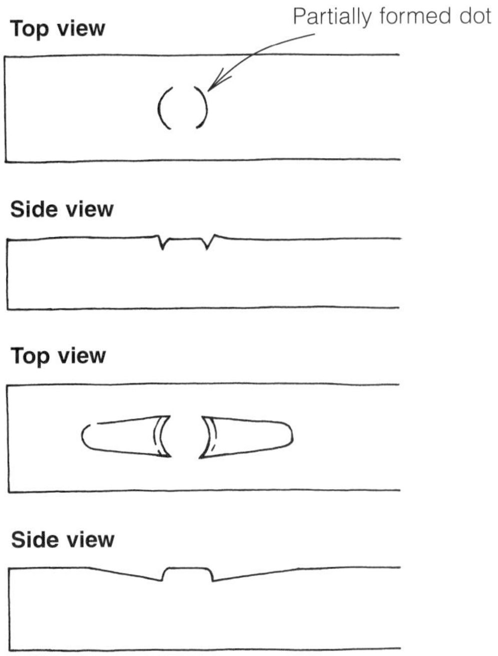

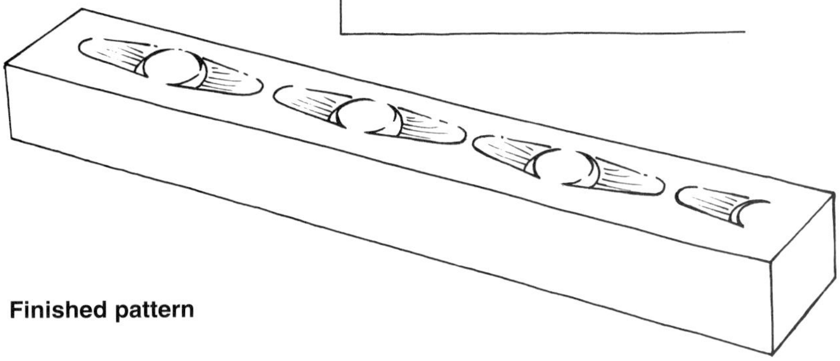

Finished pattern

There are times when you need a fingernail end, however. For example, if you were carving a dot and cross pattern (as shown in the drawing at right), ideally you would want two gouges of exactly the same size and curvature, one with slightly forward swept wings and the other with a fingernail end that exactly matches the sweep (curvature) of the gouge. This would allow you to make stab cuts that would almost exactly match the horizontal cuts. More important, it would prevent popping off any of the dots, which is what would happen if you were using a square-end gouge for the stab cuts. If you have ever tried this type of carving, you will know exactly the advantages described.

TRUING THE SWEEP

In cross section, most gouges are not true segments of circles. They are more often parabolic in shape. This may or may not cause you a problem when you are carving, but it will almost always cause you a problem when you are sharpening.

To deal with the carving aspect first, many carvers like to use a roll cut (see p. 14) when they are working cross grain or end grain. As they push the gouge through the wood, they rotate it. This has exactly the same effect as skewing a plane blade or chisel when cross-grain or end-grain cutting (see the discussion in Chapter 2). It changes the relationship of the forces acting on the wood and on the tool, generally providing a cleaner cut. However, to make an effective roll cut without bruising the wood, stressing the tool or tearing fibers, the part of the gouge in contact with the wood should be a perfect semicircle. Tools with non-circular cross sections do not rotate well as they are cutting.

Fortunately, it is also easier to sharpen a tool with a semicircular cross section than it is with any other curved cross section. It is much easier to roll the tool to grind an even bevel when you are dealing with a regular shape. This happens to be one case where it is both easier and more effective to work on the inside of the tool than the outside. There are a variety of ways to true the sweep. If you have a cylindrical stone of the right diameter, you can true the inside of the gouge with that. Since the odds of this being the case are just

True the outside of a gouge on a belt sander, with the tool held at exactly 90° to the belt in the slack part between the platen and the upper wheel. (Photo by Susan Kahn)

When honing the outside bevel of the gouge on a leather belt, tilt the tool slightly downward so it will not dig into the belt as the belt is turning. (Photo by Susan Kahn)

slightly better than winning the lottery, the next best thing to do is to get a dowel that approximately matches the sweep, coat it with liquid sandpaper, or apply PSA-backed abrasive, chuck it up in a drill press or hand drill and grind the inside to shape. Alternatively, you can just wrap the dowel with abrasive sheet and do it all manually.

It is not necessary to dress the entire flute. It is desirable to grind as much of it as possible, but you have to true only the portion that will be coming into contact with the wood. Whatever you use for truing the sweep can also be used for any in-cannel beveling you may want to do.

After you have the inside true, if you grind the bevel on the gouge at a constant angle you will be able to see where the outside of the tool is out of round. The only reason you would want to true this, since it does not come in contact with the wood, is again to make grinding easier. If you were grinding a bevel on a gouge that is substantially thicker in some places than in others, it is more difficult to keep the edge even. The easiest way to trim up the outside is on a belt sander just above the platen (as shown in the top photo at left).

HONING A GOUGE

You probably thought that we were never going to get to this point, considering all the things that had to be done to the gouge already. For honing the outside bevel, my first choice would be a belt sander with a micro-finishing abrasive belt or a leather belt dressed with chromium-oxide honing compound. My next choice would be a hard felt wheel dressed with chromium oxide, and my last choice would be a manual method using either some combination of the above materials on a wooden backing or a fine Japanese slipstone.

On a belt sander, I prefer to hold the gouge nearly horizontal as I hone (as shown in the bottom photo at left). It is important that it be skewed slightly in the direction of travel of the belt. I prefer using a reversible motor on the belt sander, so that shaping can be done with the belt running from top to bottom and honing done with the belt running from bottom to top. It can all be done with the belt running only one way (from top to bottom, as shown in the photos at left), but it requires a few more contortions.

On a felt wheel, I would again use the same general grip, using a trailing cut on the side of the wheel or the face of the wheel depending upon light conditions. Generally, I use the side of the wheel for fine work because it allows better angular control (see the top left photo below). The face of the wheel is fine for heavy polishing or, if shaped, for honing as well, but you run a higher risk of dubbing an edge. Where shop lighting is directly overhead, it is easier to use the face of the wheel for everything (just another argument for good lighting at your grinding station).

For honing the inside of the gouge (and whether or not you put any bevel on the inside, you have to hone it to a mirror finish if you want a good cutting edge), I prefer a shaped felt wheel charged with chromium-oxide honing compound (bottom left photo below). But a very close second, and in some instances a first choice, is a piece of wood formed by the gouge itself for honing both the inside and the outside.

It is simple to cut the edge of a scrap of wood to shape for the inside of the gouge (top right photo below) and to carve a groove in the face of the same scrap for honing the outside bevel (bottom right photo below). It is a highly effective sharpening device that can be made at virtually no cost. Dressed with chromium-oxide honing compound, the strop can be kept at hand when you are carving so that you can give a tool a quick touchup without having to leave your carving station.

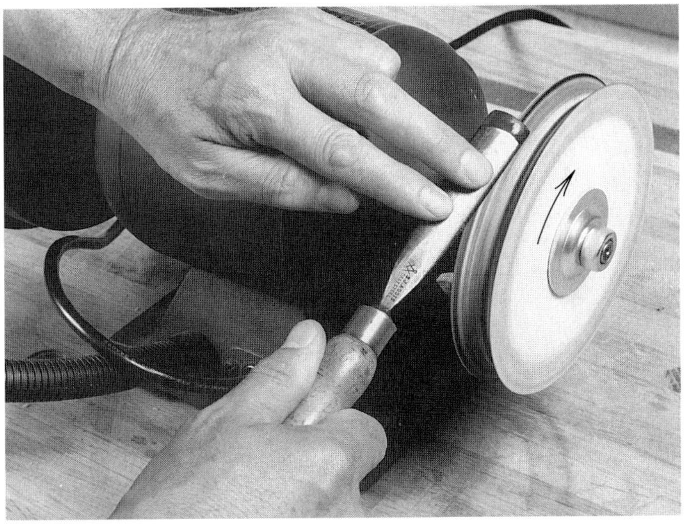

When honing on a felt wheel, hold the bevel flat against the side of the wheel with a trailing stroke.

Hone the inside of a gouge on the rounded edge of a shaped felt wheel charged with chromium-oxide honing compound.

The flute and the outside bevel can also be honed with trailing strokes on a custom-made wooden strop charged with honing compound. (Photos by Susan Kahn)

BENT GOUGES

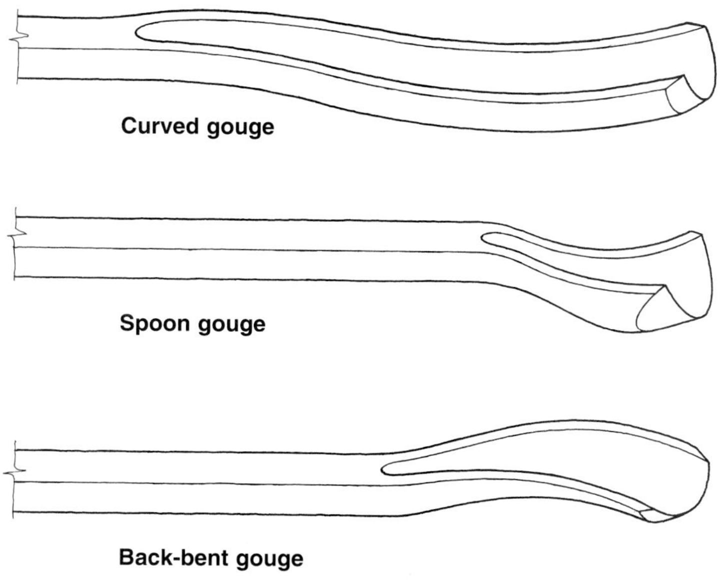

The best method, one that will accommodate the curve of the gouge, is to shape a wooden disk of appropriate diameter to the correct shape and apply liquid sandpaper to it. Like the cone this could be used in a hand drill, clamped in a vise or in a drill press, either method leaving both hands free to manipulate the tool. The same basic shape will do for honing bent gouges, but in this case the wood should be charged with chromium-oxide honing compound only.

BACK-BENT GOUGES

Back-bent gouges present no unique problems that were not dealt with above. Today, only someone carving endless clusters of grapes would bother buying a back-bent gouge, since a small amount of inside bevel will let you use a regular gouge in place of the back bent.

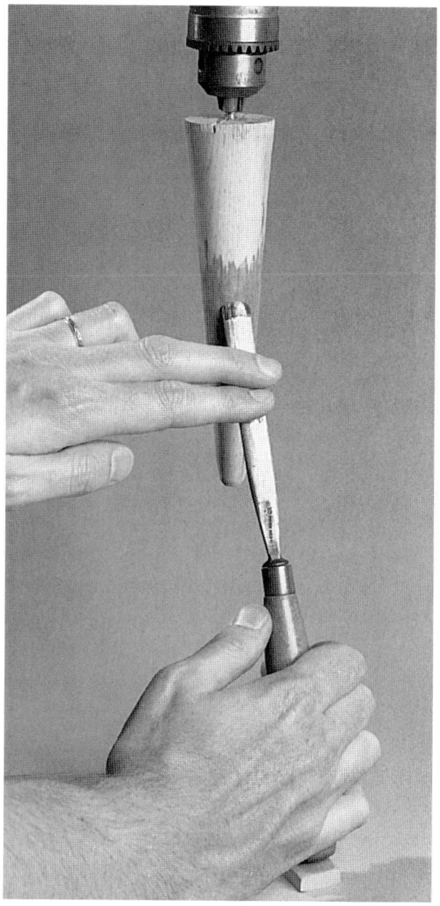

To true the sweep using a drill-press-mounted cone, hold the gouge against the cone at a slight skew so that the cone gives a trailing stroke as it rotates.

BENT GOUGES

Bent gouges, which are used on recessed surfaces, include curved gouges and spoon gouges. A curved gouge is used where there is a reasonable amount of maneuvering room, and a spoon gouge in very restricted spaces. Bent gouges are subject to all of the same considerations as straight gouges, although they do present some special difficulties when it comes to truing the sweep and honing the inside.

You can use the same general principles for truing the sweep on bent gouges as you do with straight gouges, but you must deal with a much shorter section of the tool because the tool is bent. A coating of liquid sandpaper or PSA-backed abrasive on a shopmade wooden cone is the easiest way to address the problem (see the photo at left). This will true only a short section of the gouge, but it can also be used for grinding the inside bevel of the tool.

VEINING TOOLS

Veiners are narrow, high-sweep gouges used for fine grooving. Again, the considerations for gouges in general apply to veining tools. The only difference is that veining tools are so small that it is often easier to deal with them purely manually rather than going near any power equipment. Making your own hones from wood and charging them with chromium-oxide honing compound is a godsend for veining tools. It lets you touch them up without risking geometric rearrangement, which is so easy on tools with such a small cross section.

PARTING TOOLS

For most carvers, these are truly the tools from hell. They are the most difficult carving tool of all to grind and hone and probably the easiest to damage in use. One of the primary problems with parting tools is that they are frequently badly made. They often do not have a crisp V-shaped bottom, and the wings of the tool are often not ground flat on the inside. It seems to me that the primary reason for these defects is sloppy manufacturing processes. Japanese parting tools tend to have good conformation even in the inexpensive sets. It is in the European tools that you will find the most problems.

You have two choices when you get a defective parting tool. You can return it to the vendor or you can correct it. Given the current state of world manufacturing, I would suggest that you keep the parting tool if it only needs a small amount of work to bring it into line. From personal experience, I can tell you that the vendors have a hard time finding perfect ones. The answer is not just to buy Japanese ones (unless you intend carving only softwood) because Japanese parting tools, like Japanese chisels, are usually laminated and can be quite temperamental in Western hardwoods.

Assuming that you have a tool with a defect like the one shown in the drawing at far right, the best way to restore it is with a diamond file. If you can find a 600x diamond file that is not itself defective, it does not take long to true the wing of a parting tool, although you will probably not get an ideally shaped V-bottom. To clean that up, I would recommend either a 75mm (3-in.) feather-edge file or a carefully fitted micro-finishing abrasive on a steel blank. Whatever you do, make sure you have the inside of the parting

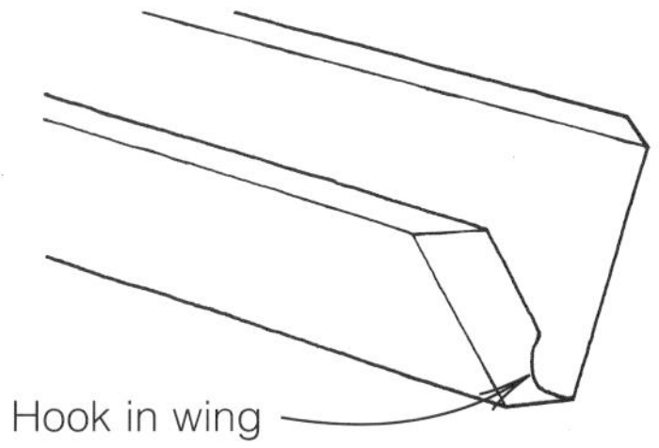

tool dressed properly before you attempt to sharpen it. If you attempted to sharpen the defective parting tool shown in the drawing, you would find that the whole side would fall away in the area of the defect giving you a tool that looks something like the drawing above. The hook in the wing makes the tool impossible to use for anything but cutting parallel to the grain. In cross-grain cutting the fibers will be trapped in the hook and will tear out. The inside of a parting tool must be straight, so that when you sharpen the wing it can be abraded evenly and in a line parallel to the inside of the wing.

SHAPING THE HEEL

The whole purpose of a parting tool is to take advantage of the play of light and shadow on the sides of the cut, with a very clear demarcation line where they meet. For best effect this junction must be kept sharp.

You can make the cut from a parting tool with a rounded V look crisp if you shape the heel carefully, and you can also make a cut from a parting tool with a sharp V look round if you shape the heel poorly. To give yourself the best mobility with a parting tool, you should use fairly short bevels and then relieve the tool for some distance back. You want a fairly short bevel so that you can

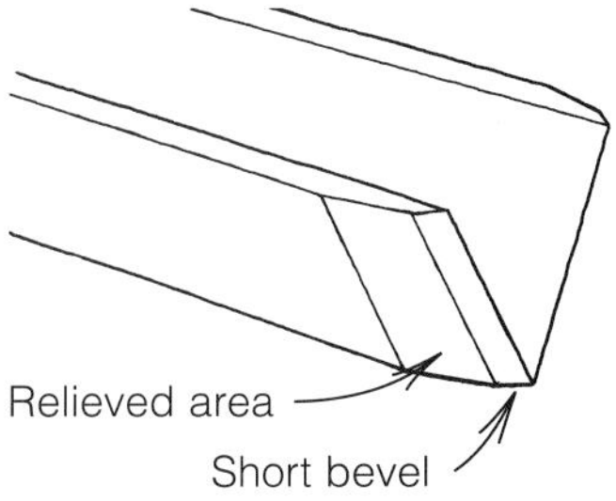

change direction quickly and still make a clean cut.

A parting tool always cuts a more obtuse angle than the angle of its wings. Taking a 60° parting tool as an example, it will cut a 60° V only at a 0° bevel angle. As soon as the tool is tilted, it cuts more than a 60° V. Depending upon the sweep of the wings, it could be cutting as much as a 90° V at a 45° lift angle. In fact, one of the early tricks you learn with a parting tool is to increase the attack angle when you are turning a tight curve, because it gives you a greater relief angle and greater maneuverability. In any event, you want to give yourself ample clearance so that the only mark left on the wood will be the crisp V made by the two intersecting cutting surfaces. However, if you have a parting tool that does not have a sharp V, you can simulate this by shaping the heel into a sharp V so that in use the heel will press into the bottom of the cut and make it appear crisper than it really is. This is only a makeshift solution, and the bottom of the parting tool should be dressed out as soon as possible so that there is a crisp V there.

PARTING-TOOL PROFILE

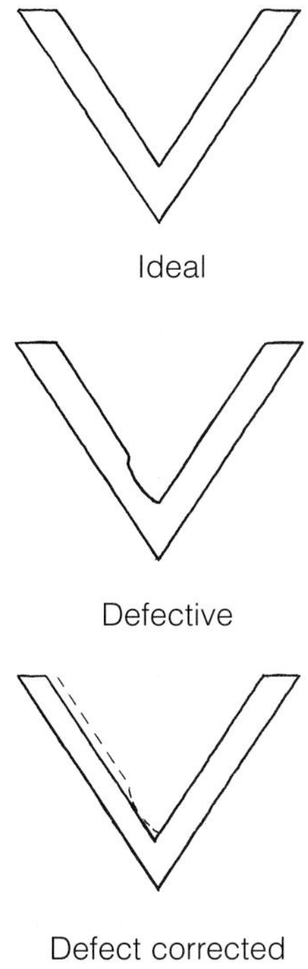

WING SWEEP

For a general-purpose parting tool, you want the wings to rise at 90° to the axis of the tool (see the drawing on p. 112). With the wings square, in use they will always be leading the heel of the tool. This is necessary so that the edges of the chip are severed before the bottom. If the wings were swept backward, the heel of the tool would have to be forced through the wood and, particularly dangerous, as the cut was ending the heel could be snapped off in an attempt to lever out of the cut. Wings that are square to the axis of the tool are actually swept forward in relation to the bevel so that the heel is not trapped as the tool comes out of the wood.

For long and deep cuts where there are no sharp curves, some carvers like to put a fair amount of forward sweep on the wings so that the chip releases more easily. This is more a matter of personal preference than necessity. It is also conceivable that you would want the wings on a parting tool swept back slightly. This would be the case if you were making stop cuts with the tool, cuts that butted some other feature.

As a final consideration, regardless of how you sweep the wings, you will find that reducing the bevel angle as you come up the wing will increase the maneuverability of the tool. The rationale is exactly the same as that given in the shaping of gouges. A reduced bevel angle reduces lateral wedging. In fact, there is no reason that the tool could not have some inside bevel, as recommended for gouges, to strengthen the upper wings.

The inhibiting factor in all of this shaping is that parting tools are so hard to sharpen well that you may want to stop when you have a keen edge and a workable shape, even if it is not ideal. You would not be alone if you did.

WING SWEEP

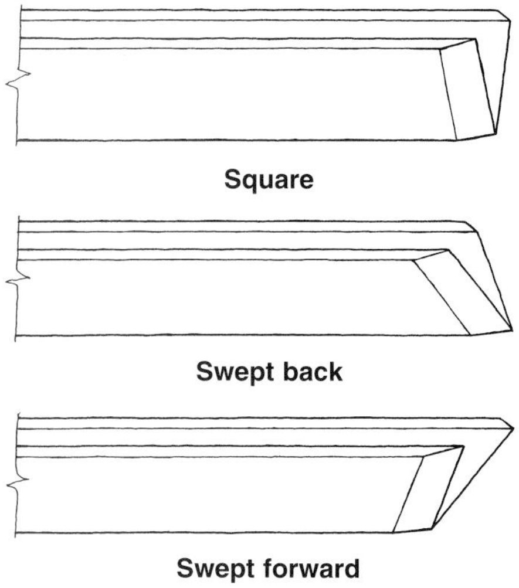

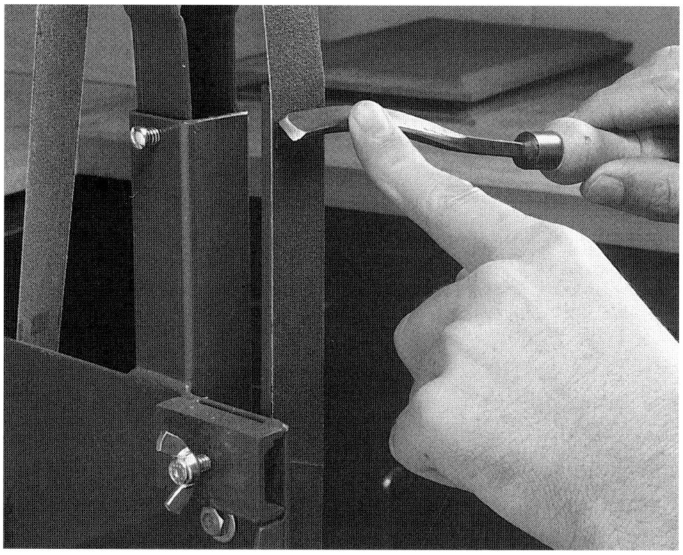

Sharpen the bevel of a parting tool over the platen on a belt sander, with the tool held more or less horizontal and the wing edge roughly parallel to the belt travel.

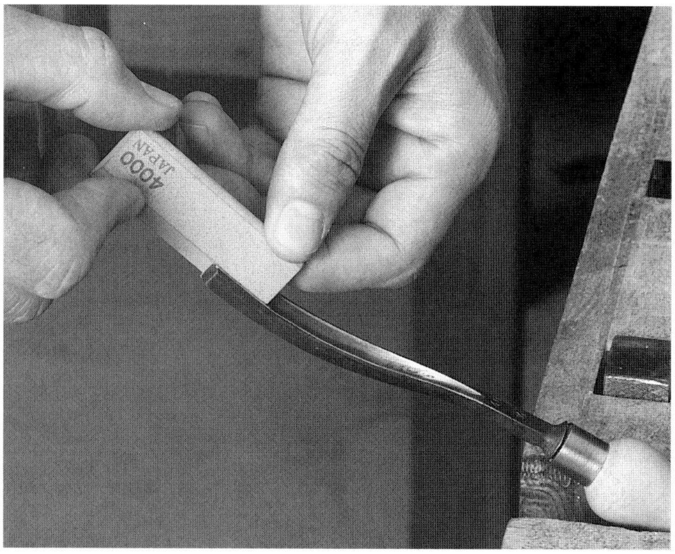

Alternatively, you can clamp the parting tool in a vise and use a slipstone on the inside.

Hone the inside of a parting tool on a custom-made wooden form charged with honing compound. (Photos by Susan Kahn)

SHARPENING PARTING TOOLS

V-tools should be sharpened very carefully, and for this reason I would use a fairly fine belt (no coarser than 120x) on a belt sander. I would also hold the tool so that the wing edge is almost parallel to the direction of travel of the belt, as shown in the top photo on the facing page. This orientation makes it easiest to ensure an even grind along the entire edge. If you accidentally grind past the line of light at the heel, you must square up the wings and start over again. Otherwise, you will have a fiber trap at the heel that will constantly frustrate you in use.

A parting tool cannot be sharpened adequately on the face of a grinding wheel—it's much too finicky a job. If you don't have a belt sander or a horizontal wet wheel, I would recommend clamping the tool at a suitable angle and using a bench stone or slipstone to shape the edge (see the bottom left photo on the facing page). For honing, use a micro-finishing abrasive belt, a leather belt with chromium-oxide compound or custom-made wooden forms charged with chromium-oxide compound. As with gouges, a parting tool will shape its own hone (bottom right photo on facing page).

INSHAVES

Inshaves have a variety of uses, from dressing the inside of barrel staves to forming chair seats. Most inshaves sold in North America today come from a German manufacturer of drawknives. The stock blade is bent into shape, hardened, tempered and then ground only on the outside of the tool. This is probably the best example of the curious belief still held by some that a tool can be sharpened by working on only one of the two surfaces that make an edge.

An inshave is not an easy tool to use, and it must be very well sharpened to be effective. A new inshave of the type mentioned above needs a fair amount of work on the inside. This is best done with a sanding drum, as shown in the photo at left below. Whenever you are using a sanding drum for sharpening, use the largest-diameter drum that will fit in the curves of the tool. The smaller the drum, the more scalloped the edge you will create. Use a confident sweep of the drum on the tool (if it is being held in a flex shaft) or of the tool on the drum (if it is drill press mounted). Hesitation or indecision will leave you with a nasty little groove in one spot on the edge. When the lion's share of the work seems to be done, you can switch to using a gouge cone or a sandpaper-covered wooden form to finish grinding the inside. Then use micro-finishing abrasives or chromium-oxide compound on a wooden form for final honing.

The outside bevel is very easily done on a belt sander or manually. For most uses, the outside bevel should be slightly rounded so that the tool can cut in a gentle arc, as is necessary when making chair seats, for example.

SCORPS

A scorp, commonly used for carving spoons, is a variation of an inshave and should be sharpened in the same manner; obviously the scale of equipment should be reduced to fit the size. Fortunately new scorps come with a far better finish than inshaves and frequently need only honing.

The outside of a scorp can be honed on a belt sander or by hand. I would avoid trying to do it on a felt wheel, because it is not an easy tool to control on a wheel. For the inside of the scorp, I recommend a wooden form, shaped as

Sharpen the inside of an inshave with a sanding drum (left) and the outside bevel in the slack of the belt on a belt sander (right). (Photos by Susan Kahn)

shown in the photo below, charged with chromium-oxide compound and used much like a file, always stroking from the back to the edge.

For the outside of the scorp, a custom-shaped wooden form is fine, only in this case you should have three grooves—one for the center of the tool and one for each edge. Again, always stroke from back to edge. In this case, you would push the scorp through the formed troughs.

The included angle on the edge of both inshaves and scorps can be quite low, somewhere around 15°. Any damage that does occur to the edge in use is usually caused by a scraping or prying action on end grain, both of which are incorrect uses of the tool.

MICRO-SCORPS

These small tools bear about the same relationship to regular scorps as chip-carving knives do to butcher knives. A relatively recent innovation, micro-scorps are the ultimate miniaturization of the spoon gouge. They are unquestionably tricky tools to sharpen. You want to keep a semicircular edge all in one plane. Edge irregularity will cause fiber trapping and make the tool difficult to use.

To hone the inside of a micro-scorp, use a wooden dowel (a bamboo skewer also works well) charged with chromium-oxide compound. The dowel should be just slightly smaller in diameter than the hole of the scorp, and it should always be passed through in one direction only so that there is a trailing stroke on the edge. If you try to run it back and forth in the hole, you will cause edge dulling.

The easiest way to hone the outside of a micro-scorp is with a small wooden-backed leather strop (see the photo at left on the facing page). It has just the right amount of forgiveness to prevent putting flats on the edge, and if you hone with a quartering stroke (diagonal to the edge) you will detect any problems before they become too great.

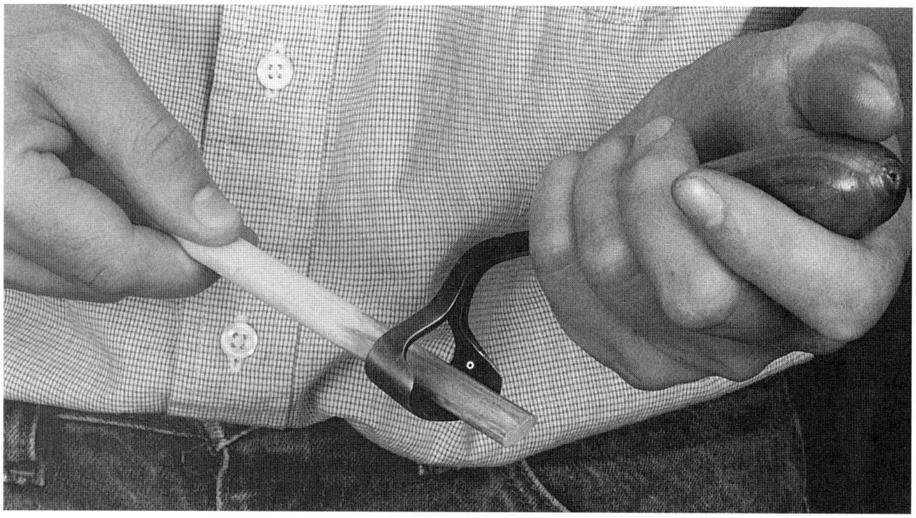

With the cutting edge of the tool facing away, use a chromium-oxide-charged wooden form to hone the inside of a scorp. Move the form much like a file, from the back inside of the scorp toward the edge. (Photo by Susan Kahn)

HONING WITH BAMBOO SKEWERS

Bamboo skewers are wonderful tools in the woodshop. They are ideal for putting glue in dowel holes. They can be pared flat on one end to make an epoxy mixing paddle that is also an excellent applicator. They are useful as small dowels. They are good spacers to keep glue squeeze-out off a bench. The list is endless.

They have a limited use in sharpening as hones for a few tools. Charged with chromium oxide, they make a strong hone for the inside of veiners, small parting tools and micro-scorps. They are just about the right size; if not, they can be pared to fit using the tool itself. In use, it is best to force the skewer into the micro-scorp from the back and pull it through as you might a needle. It works well.

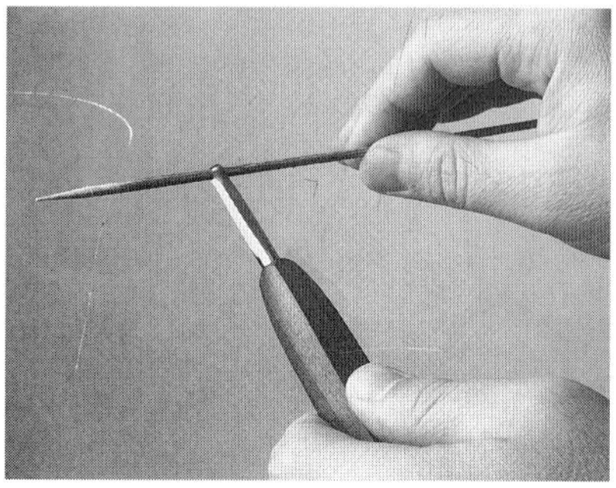

HOOK KNIVES

Hook knives serve similar purposes to scorps and inshaves in hollowing vessels and are sharpened in a similar way. Carver's hooks, which have a gently curved blade with a tight hook on the end, are best sharpened on a belt sander on the convex side and with an abrasive-covered wooden form on the inside. An appropriately sized wooden dowel can be used to hone the inside of a tight hook.

The larger hook knives of the Swedish style are honed similarly on the convex side but require slightly different treatment on the inside. Since these are double-edged knives, inside honing has to be done carefully, otherwise you might dull one edge as you are sharpening the other. A wooden dowel charged with green honing compound will still do the job, but I prefer to use one that is no more than three-quarters the diameter of the inside of the hook. You are honing through what is, in essence, a section of a cylinder. If your hone is the same size as the inside of the cylinder, you cannot tilt it at all to avoid scraping against the entry edge. If you use a smaller hone, you avoid this problem.

You invariably end up putting a small bevel on the inside of the tool, but this is no problem since the outside bevel can be reduced to compensate. When the knife is purchased, the outside bevel is usually a bit too steep anyway. Again, you are looking for an included angle in the range of 15°, 20° maximum for harder woods and heavy cuts. This is definitely one tool that you want to use at the lowest possible included angle in order to maximize your mechanical advantage.

KEEPING CARVING TOOLS SHARP

After doling out all this advice on how to sharpen carving tools, it seems worthwhile to offer some advice on how to avoid dulling them after you have them in the shape you want.

Carving tools do not dull quickly unless:

- they are being forced unnaturally, either through excessive mallet blows or because of prying action;
- they are being used carelessly or stored where they can rattle together;
- they are being used on dirty wood; or
- they are being used on wood of inconsistent texture. Pin knots in spruce cause faster edge deterioration than carving a hard, but consistently dense wood like ebony.

Half the secret of having sharp tools that stay sharp is in shaping the edges correctly; the other half is in not dulling them through ignorance and carelessness.

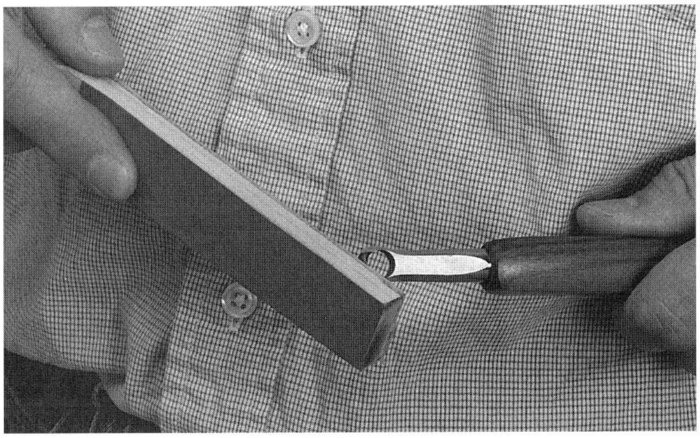

Use a leather strop to hone the outside of a micro-scorp, honing the edge with a quartering stroke. (Photo by Susan Kahn)

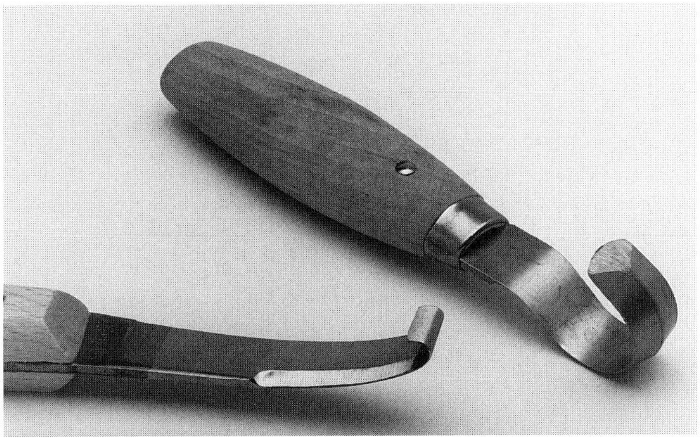

Hook knives include carver's hooks (left) and double-beveled Swedish-style knives (right). (Photo by Susan Kahn)

CHAPTER 10

TURNING TOOLS

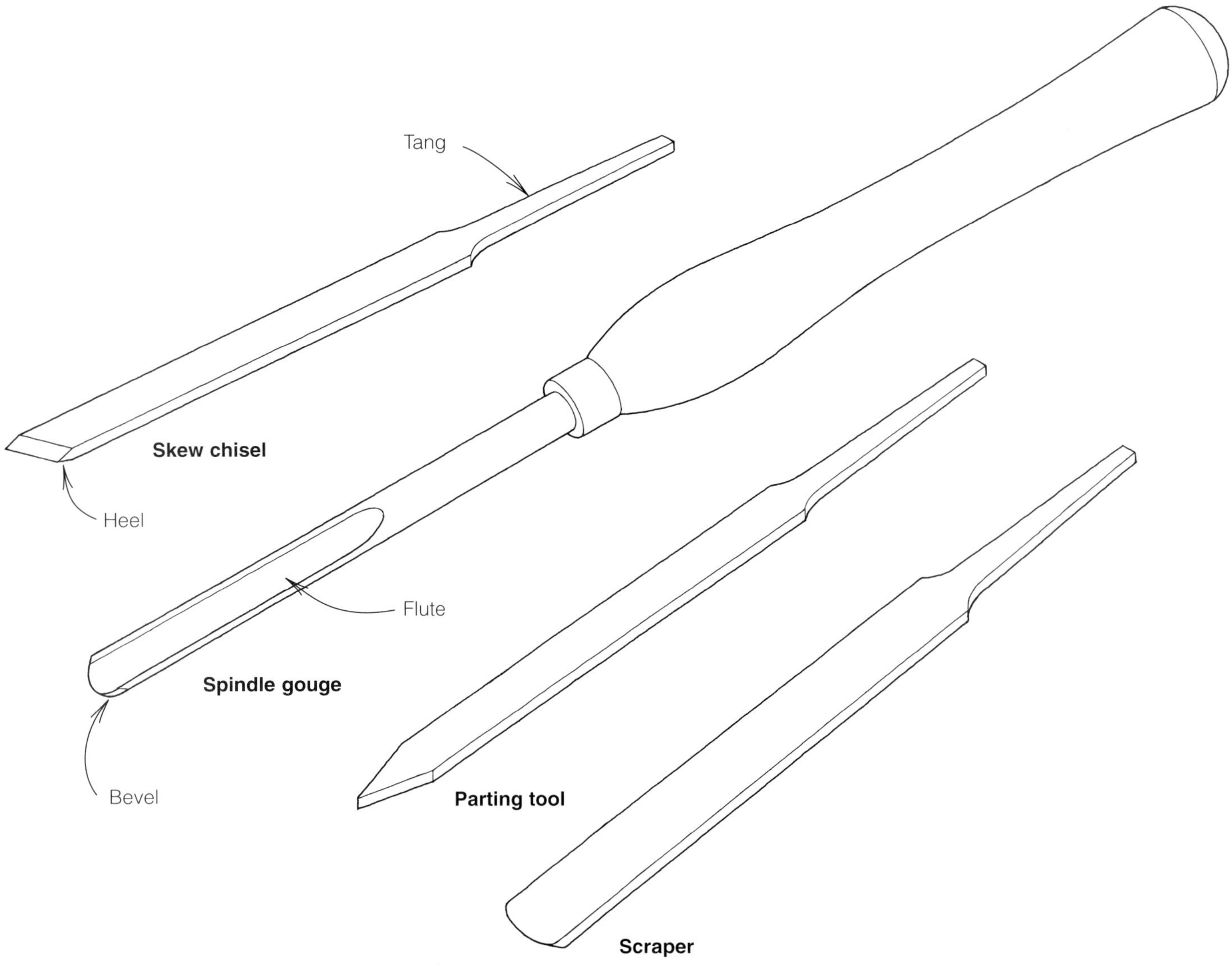

Of all woodworkers, I feel particularly sorry for turners because they not only face conflicting advice on sharpening from the various authors in the field but also are unable to rely on the suitability of any of the grind angles on tools when they buy them. I have seen scrapers come from the factory with an 80° bevel angle, even though a 70° angle is advertised, and skews with a 90° included angle, triple the angle that most teachers would recommend.

After reading a number of books on turning over the years and having listened to a number of turning instructors, I have come to the conclusion that most good turners achieve their results by overwhelming their tools with tremendous innate skill. Unfortunately, many of these same turners who have developed specific techniques to overcome tool-shape inadequacies then go on to recommend these techniques to novice turners, when the novice should be learning good shaping and honing technique instead. In my view, this is the basic reason for the proliferation of techniques that we have seen in the last ten or fifteen years.

In this chapter, I am going to avoid the subject of turning technique entirely. Part of the reason is that good sharpening principles can be adapted to any technique. The other part of the reason is that I do not want to put myself in the same position as some of the turning authors who make very categorical statements about sharpening technique even when they have limited understanding of metallurgy or abrasives. Having drawn a line in the sand, I will try to stay on my side of it.

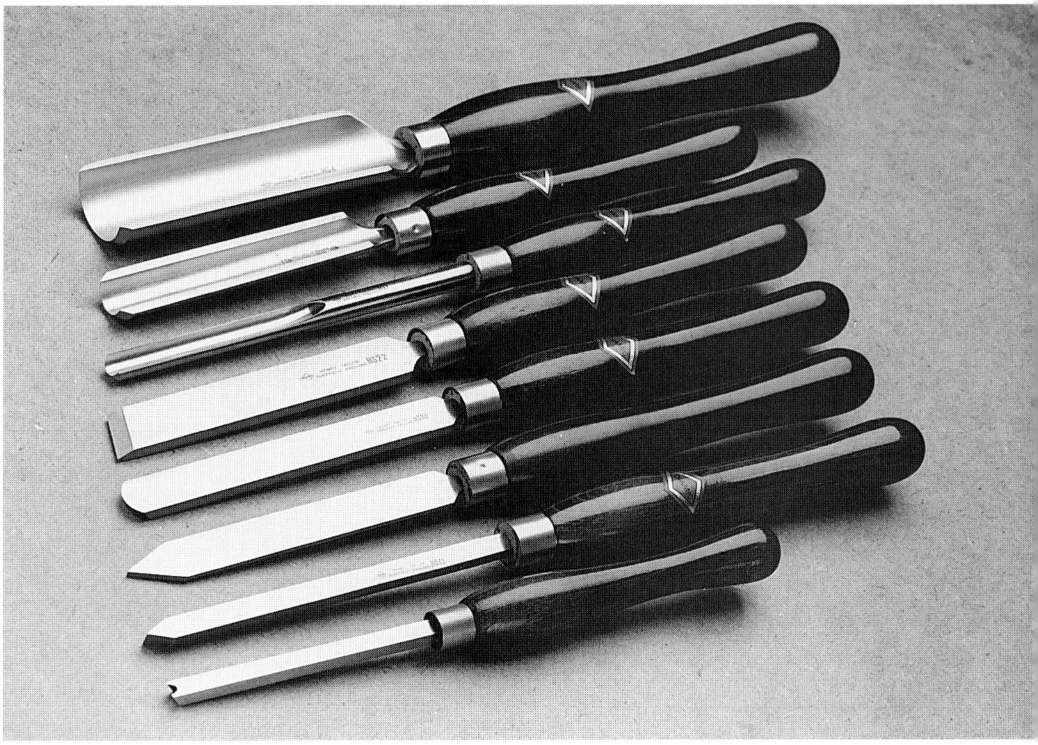

A typical selection of tools for spindle turning.

SETTING TOOL-REST ANGLES

Since you use only a small number of grinding angles for most shop tools, it is worth making a few angle templates to keep near your grinder or belt sander. Use at least ½-in. thick material and make the templates about 8 in. long and 3 in. deep. The angle you use to set your tool rest is 180° less the grind angle, but if you use parallel-sided stock for the template you will have both angles anyway. Mark the angles and give the template a coat of shellac to keep it stable.

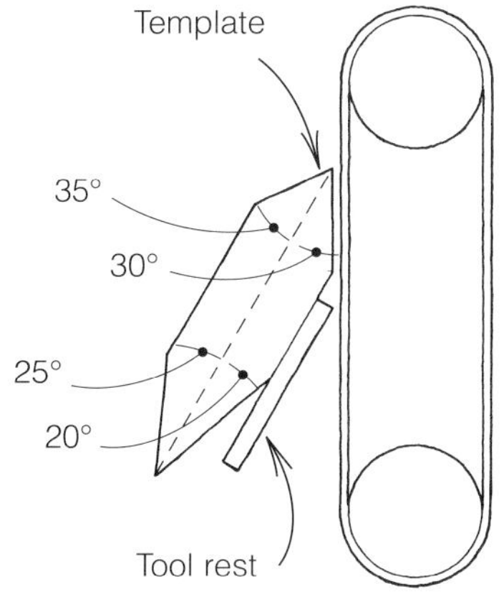

GRIND ANGLES/ BEVEL ANGLES

The same general theory developed in Chapter 2 applies to turning tools just as it does to chisels and plane blades, namely, "a cutting tool should be ground at the lowest possible bevel angle consistent with edge retention." The only difference is that turning tools are much more like power tools than hand tools and are subjected to more severe shocks than chisels or plane blades. This requires some increase in bevel angles in order to withstand the shocks, but the basic principle applies broadly in turning.

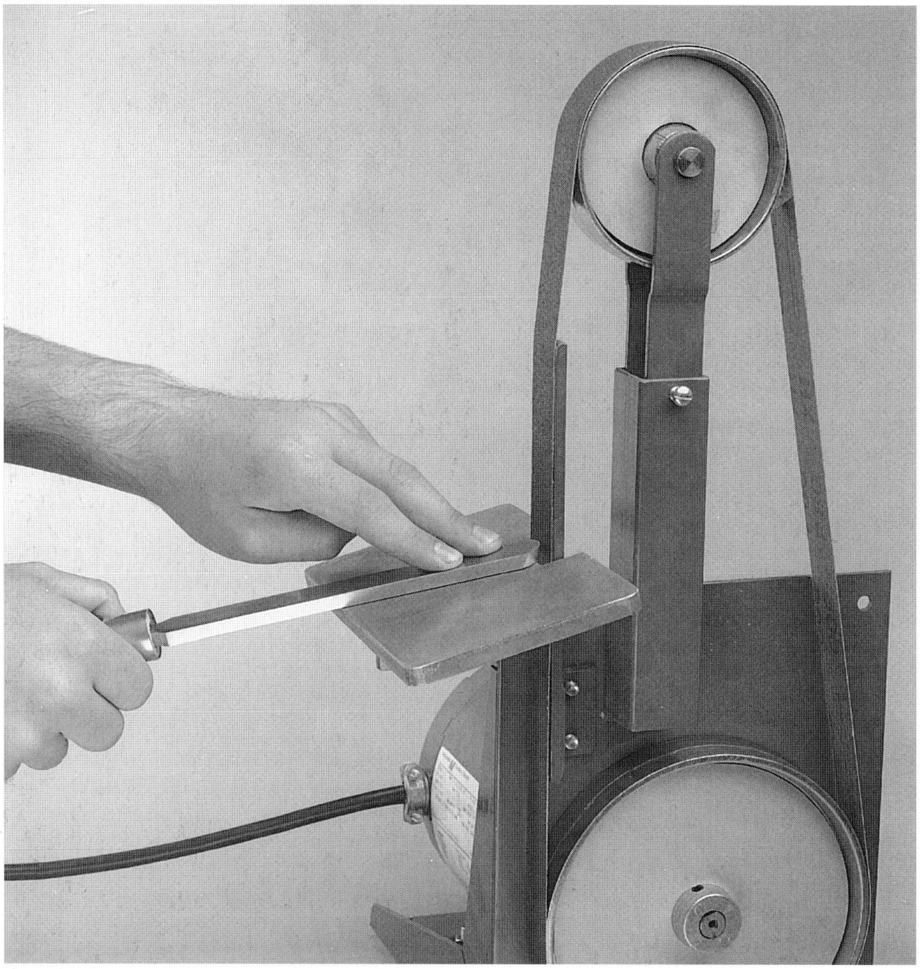

To grind a scraper on a belt sander, set the tool rest at the required angle (usually between 70° and 80°) and grind freehand.

The reason turning tools are more like power tools than hand tools is that they are used to work wood that is under power. In addition to the intermittent shocks experienced, there is generally greater stress and certainly greater heat in the cutting process. But, there are numerous similarities to hand tools; I would use the example of planing cylinders to make the point. It takes a substantial amount of skill to do a good job of planing a cylinder on a lathe using a skew chisel or even a flat chisel. Yet an ordinary bench plane can be applied to the rotating cylinder on the lathe, and you will find that it works very much like using a smoothing plane on wood. With the plane somewhat askew the cylinder, you will find that the wood passing by the plane is much like having the plane passing by the wood. Not, of course, that I recommend this technique because, as stated earlier, I intend to avoid technique and deal only with sharpening. As we look at different tools we will return to the subject of bevel angles repeatedly, but I wanted to emphasize at the beginning of this chapter that the same general theories apply to dimensioning wood in the turning process as they do in other aspects of woodworking.

SCRAPERS

One of the continuing arguments in the turning community is whether or not scraping is an honorable activity. Some turners insist that virtually everything must be done with gouges and skews; they look down on turners who use scrapers to any extent. I believe that this state of affairs came about for two reasons. First, many of the scrapers used traditionally had virtually square edges and tended to pull the fibers out of the wood rather than cut them. Second, there is always a bit of snobbery involved in the competent use of a tricky tool like a skew, whereas virtually anyone can use a scraper acceptably.

Scrapers are far more predictable in use than skews or gouges. It is nearly impossible to get an inadvertent dig, or "catch," when using a scraper. So for all of those woodworkers for whom turning is a very occasional activity and who are just looking for a predictable result from their lathe, scrapers can be a godsend.

If you do a good job of sharpening a scraper, it is no longer a scraper, it is a cutter. Just as you can burnish a hook onto a well-prepared cabinet scraper to make a wonderful small plane, you can put the same sort of hook onto either a carbon-steel or high-speed-steel scraper that will give you clouds of continuous shavings. In fact, you can adjust the size and shape of the hook to make roughing scrapers as well as finishing scrapers.

SHARPENING SCRAPERS

Scrapers are very easy to grind, especially if you use a belt sander. Just set the tool rest at the bevel angle you want (usually between 70° and 80°), lay the scraper flat on the rest and grind freehand, as shown in the photo above.

There are four reasons I recommend using a belt sander. First, it is very easy to set angles accurately between two flat surfaces, and angular control is important here. Second, it is easier to control the grinding process on a belt sander, particularly with oddly shaped scrapers. There is much more maneuvering room than with a bench grinder, where the motor is a limiting factor.

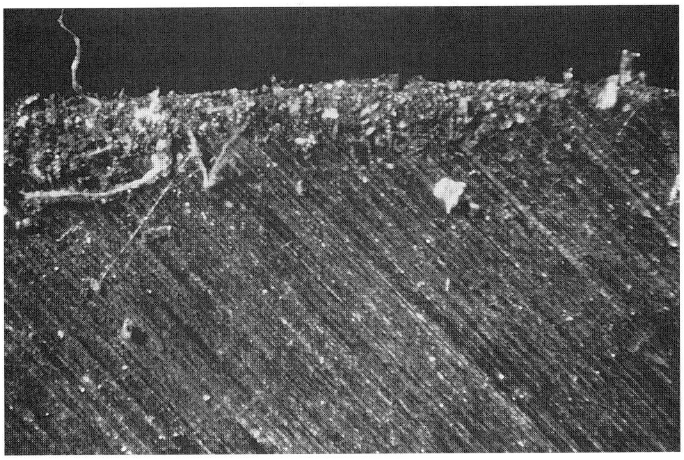

A magnified portion of the tip of a scraper as it comes from the grinder. Bits of broken abrasive particles are visible, as well as the edge burr and portions that are breaking away on the left and right of the photograph.

This is the same scraper after lapping and burnishing. The grind marks are substantially smaller on the scraper and disappear near the burnished edge. The keenness of the edge is apparent. (Photos courtesy Canadian Conservation Institute)

Third, you can change grit sizes in seconds as desired or required, and, fourth, you do not get a hollow grind with a belt sander. Since these scrapers are bevel-rubbing tools in use, a hollow grind is undesirable.

Most turners use scrapers just as they come from the grinding wheel or sander. Even with very fine grit belts or wheels, the scraper will have a burr on the top that creates a tiny cutting edge. As can be seen from the photo at left above, the burr does not vary a great deal in size since it tends to be cut off fairly soon after it is formed. The wire edge that has been released in such a manner is visible on the left-hand side of the photo.

But there is a far better way to get a cutting edge on a scraper that is sharper, stronger, more durable and of more predictable result. You grind the scraper as usual, then strip the burr off the top with a fine honing stone (a 6000x or 8000x water stone, a Black Hard Arkansas, etc.) or, my favorite, the 5-micron silicon-carbide 3M micro-finishing abrasive. It takes the burr off in no time and leaves a mirror finish on the top of the scraping tool. Then you burnish the hook that you want on the scraper.

HOW A BURR FORMS DURING GRINDING

At various times in woodworking literature you will see comments that the burr forms on the top of the scraper by a deposit process; hot chips of steel removed by the wheel are carried around a full rotation and deposited on the top of the scraper, sort of tack welded into position. This is not what happens.

The burr forms on the top of the scraper because a large number of the abrasive particles in a wheel at any one time have negative rake angles. Such particles tend to plow a groove in the steel without removing much material. When the particles first encounter the top edge of the scraper, they deform the steel at that point, raising a lip that is the burr that turners depend on for cutting.

Only a fairly small percentage of particles in a grinding wheel are actually cutting, taking out chips. Many are just scraping or plowing their way through. Scraping or plowing removes material but also generates a lot of heat by deforming the steel. For this reason, you always want a clean unglazed wheel with the maximum number of sharp particles exposed.

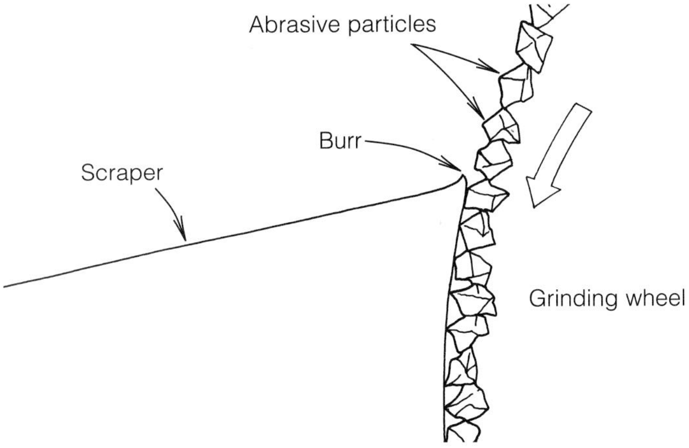

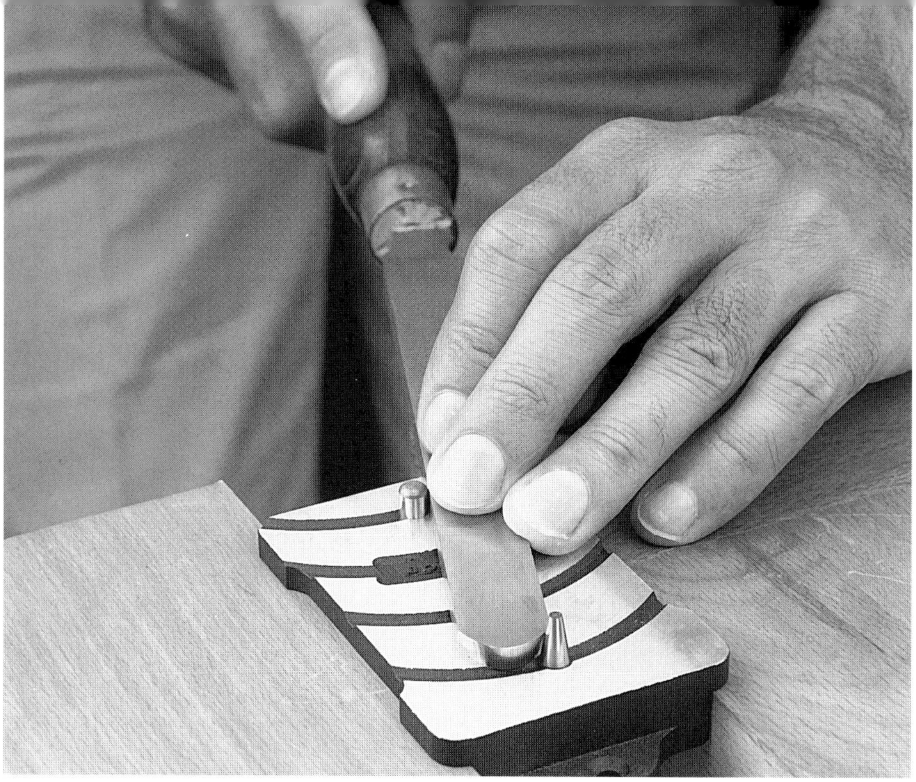

A commercial burnisher for high-speed-steel scrapers.

RPM AND CUTTING ACTION

You will find that the cutting action of any turning tool can be changed by altering the spindle speed. Once a blank has been roughed down to good balance, increasing the spindle speed will make most tools cut more predictably. Whether you notice it or not, you will invariably find that you are taking a lighter cut at the higher speed but removing wood at a faster rate. A tool such as a roughing gouge, which can readily dig at low speeds, becomes more controllable at higher speeds.

Nowhere do you notice this phenomenon more than with burnished scrapers. At sub-optimal speeds, they can catch; at ideal speeds, they will consistently take a beautiful, thin shaving.

So whenever you think that your tool's edge shape may be at fault, check the cutting action at higher and lower spindle speeds before resharpening.

Burnishing the tip Burnishing a turning scraper is not as easy as burnishing a cabinet scraper (see pp. 134-137). The turning scraper is much harder and is often an awkward shape. It can be burnished freehand, but I recommend that you wear gloves for the process since it is easy to slip and give yourself a nasty cut. As a bare minimum, clamp the scraper low in a vise (with wood-lined jaws) so that your hands are less likely to come in contact with an edge.

High-speed-steel scrapers are the toughest to burnish. To deal with these scrapers, I designed the burnisher shown in the photo at left. It is a carbide rod with a 10° conical tip set in an aluminum plate drilled for a lever pin. With the burnisher clamped in a vise, you can set the lever pin in one of several available holes (the one that best suits the scraper at hand) and use both hands plus your body mass to lean into the burnishing process. Even high-speed-steel scrapers are easy to burnish with this system. Scrapers ground at 75° and burnished at 80° with this device serve most turning needs, since the size of the hook can be controlled by burnishing pressure.

If you have never burnished a hook on a turning scraper before, you might be startled by the result. The burnished scraper is a potent cutting tool. If, for example, you have ground the scraper at 70° and burnished it at 80°, you will find that you have a roughing tool, capable of removing a steady stream of thick shavings, even from end grain. You will also find that the scraper tends to be drawn into the work. With a pronounced hook, you can even get digs!

To change from a roughing scraper to a finishing scraper, you just reduce the burnishing angle. This immediately gives you greater control, because you get a wider rubbing bevel. You will find that the process can be adjusted in either direction to accommodate a range of cutting actions. The operative word here is "cutting."

This is no longer a scraping tool; it is a cutting tool capable of giving a very fine finish. Using a light pass at a burnishing angle of 5° or less, you can create a fine hook that is easily controlled in use. You will find that such a scraper can make a substantial difference turning slim stock between centers. The hook draws the work to it, reducing whip by acting like a steady rest. You will find equally that you can get remarkable finishes on face-plate work with such a scraper. The finish

GRINDING WHEELS FOR TURNERS

Books on turning all offer sharpening advice, but only two of the ten in print as this is being written deal with the specific type of grinding wheel that should be used. Both recommend aluminum-oxide stones of medium hardness, 38A80H-8VBE in one case and 38A60J-8VBE in the other. The latter, although coarser than the former, is also harder, so the finished grind will be similar. A J-grade will last longer but grind hotter then an H-grade; it would be fine for high-speed steel but would require a light touch with a high-carbon steel.

For grinding high-speed steel, Jerry Glaser, a California tool designer and manufacturer, uses one of the new seeded-gel stones from Norton (see p. 39). The seeded-gel process bonds small particles together to form larger ones; these are then combined with standard aluminum-oxide particles in ratios up to 1:1. In use, the constructed particles tend to fracture rather than break away, creating a stone that gives a finer grind than the grit size would indicate. Glaser uses a 5SG60KVS, which indicates that 50% of the particles are seeded gel in a 60-grit wheel of K (medium) hardness with some sort of vitrified bond.

Norton recommends this seeded-gel stone for use only where sufficient grinding pressure will be used to ensure particle fracture; it is not for light cuts and is too hot for carbon steel. Used for grinding the basic shape on HSS tools, though, it is ideal.

Since HSS is reputed to have good red hardness, Glaser performed some basic tests to see how tool hardness might be affected by various heat levels (see the drawing below). As the results show, only the area that had been glowing red had serious softening; anything that had not been burned black retained the original hardness or close to it. This is quite different from high-carbon-steel alloys, where you can be certain that anything that turned blue during grinding has been unacceptably softened.

For anyone grinding both carbon-steel and HSS turning tools, I would still recommend a 38A80H-8VBE as the best all-round wheel.

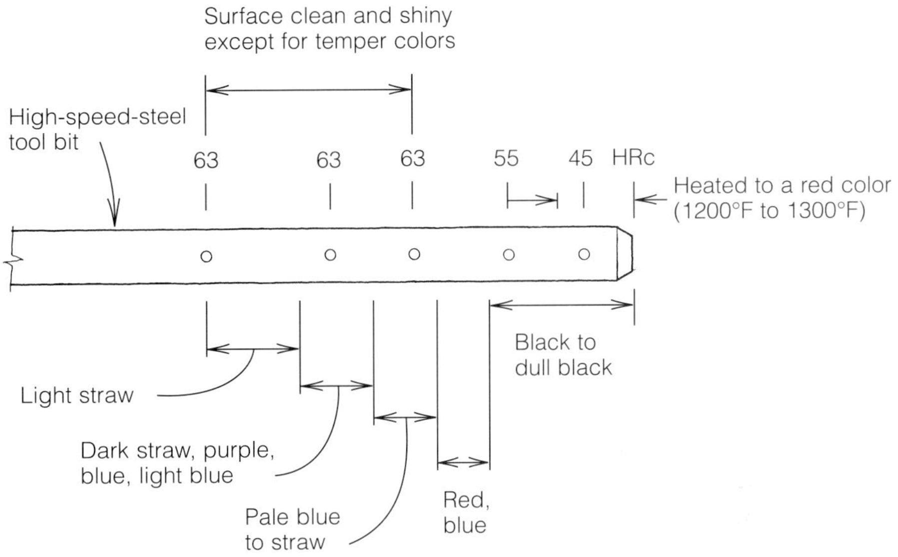

achieved and the degree of control that this system offers is truly remarkable. For example, you will find that you can tilt the scrapers to take shearing cuts. What else you do with them is a function of your technique and interest.

As with any other edge, the smoothness of the two surfaces intersecting to form the edge determines its keenness. Thus far I have mentioned honing only one of the two surfaces, the flat top of the scraper. I am reluctant to suggest honing the ground bevel, because even a slight angular difference can compromise the final hook. Another reason honing is less necessary in this instance is that a burnisher, used at an angle so close to the primary bevel angle, tends to blend the grinding serrations into a smooth plane. It is a bit like a knife-sharpening steel in effect. And the final reason I would dodge honing the bevel is that if you sharpen scrapers on a belt sander as I recommend, you can use a fine belt to refine the grind without actually honing.

GOUGES

The three families of gouges used in turning (roughing, spindle and bowl) can all be ground on a bench grinder or a belt sander. With a bench grinder, you get a hollow bevel and with a belt sander, a flat bevel. Another consideration is that it is generally more expensive to grind with a belt sander, since belts cost more than stones for removing a given amount of steel. Finally, good gouge-grinding jigs exist for grinders but not for belt sanders. Taking all factors into account, I would recommend using a grinder with an 8-in. wheel, with a 6-in. wheel as an acceptable alternative. (See the sidebar above for more on grinding wheels.)

All gouges should have polished flutes. Sometimes it takes a fair amount of work initially to clean up the flute of a gouge. It can be done with successively finer abrasive paper on a wooden dowel (my preference), with slipstones or with a shaped felt wheel with chromium-oxide honing compound. Whatever method is used, you want the flute of the gouge to be as smooth and straight as possible.

You may also want to hone the ground bevel. Many turners take their gouges directly from the grinder to their work without any kind of honing. That is a personal choice, but a honed edge will cut better, longer and cooler than an edge straight from a grinder. Obviously, it will also leave a smoother finish on the wood.

There are two reasons that most turners go directly from grinding to cutting. The first is that it saves time, and the second is that they do not want to risk creating a second bevel on the gouge, which would cause control problems. Both are legitimate concerns for a production turner, but there are ways around the two problems. The tremendous variety of bevel angles and tip shapes for gouges has precluded the development of sharpening jigs and fixtures that can meet all of the various demands, but the Glaser joystick (see p. 125) will solve most of the problems. It is particularly useful for complex grinds such as the side-ground gouge (discussed below), although it also guarantees a regular, single-bevel grind on other tools as well.

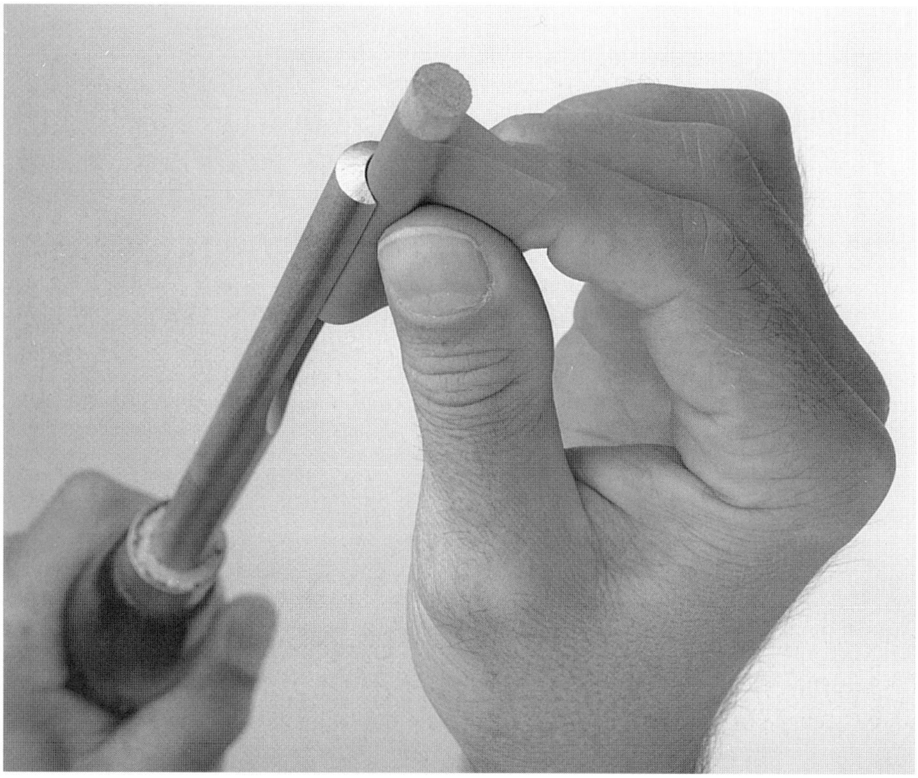

Using fine abrasive paper on a wooden dowel is one of the most effective ways to polish the flute of a gouge.

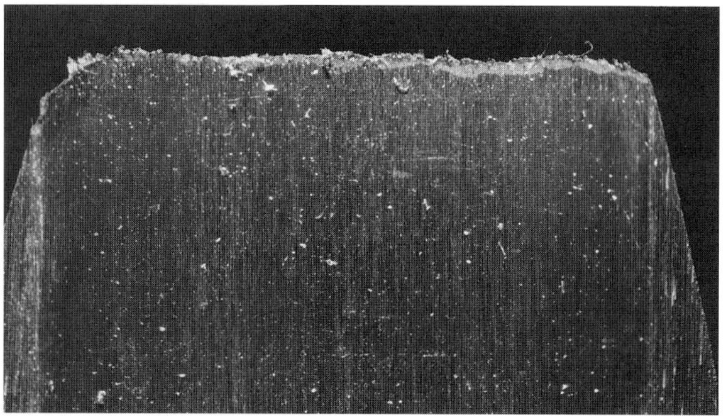

A gouge straight from the grinder has a burr that will cut, but it often has a weak hinge of metal (just visible on the right-hand portion) that will break off almost immediately in use.

A gouge that has been deburred and honed has a stronger and sharper cutting edge. (Photos courtesy Canadian Conservation Institute)

If you have a clean single-bevel grind, you should be able to hand-hone the tool without creating a second bevel. All you want to do is remove the serrations at the edge, not create a wide

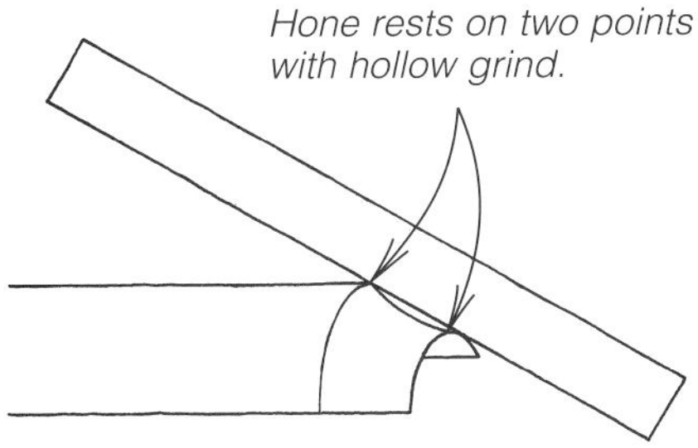

band of mirror finish. Also, if you have ground the tool on a wheel, you will have a hollow grind that makes honing substantially easier since you can rest the hone on two points as you work (see the drawing above).

ROUGHING GOUGES

Roughing gouges should be ground square across the front and have a bevel angle of about 45°. If you turn only softwood, such as clear pine, this bevel angle can be reduced to about 35°. If you turn only hardwood, you may want to increase the angle a bit. Roughing gouges take an incredible beating and need sturdy bevel angles to survive. As usual, you want the lowest bevel angle consistent with edge retention, but with this tool that angle is larger than you might ordinarily expect. As a rough parallel, you can imagine the forces that would be exerted on a carving gouge if you clamped the gouge upright in a vise and tried to carve a piece of wood by striking it against the gouge. This is approximately what happens with a roughing gouge when you use one to rough a square into a cylinder. A constant force is much easier on tools than an intermittent force, just ask any machinist.

WOODEN HONING FORM

For honing both the flutes and bevels of gouges, a wooden spindle can be turned that incorporates the necessary shapes. The wood is charged with chromium-oxide compound before use. The form shown in the photo below includes some shapes for carving tools as well as turning tools.

The form is most easily used on a drill press, with the tool honed on the trailing stroke. Chuck the form in the drill press with a stub in each end (I use lag bolts with the heads cut off). To provide an end bearing, the bottom stud should ride in a lubricated hole in a scrap of wood clamped to the drill-press table.

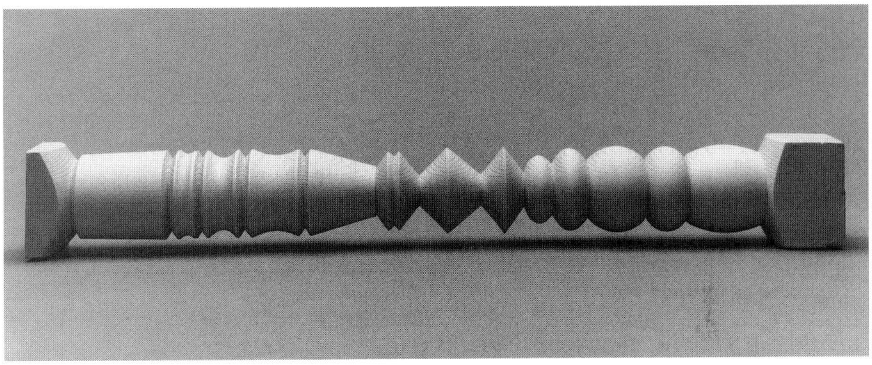

A wooden honing form. (Photo by Susan Kahn)

Roughing gouges, which are ground square across the tip, typically have a 45° bevel angle. These tools exemplify the design principle of form following function: The high wings clip fiber ends to prevent uncontrolled splintering as blanks are roughed down to size.

GRINDING JIG FOR GOUGES

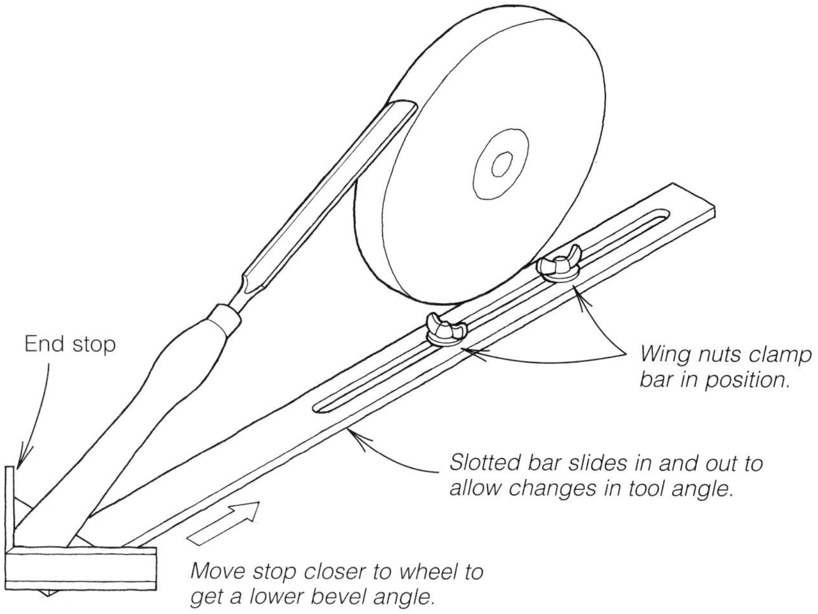

MODIFIED SPINDLE GOUGE

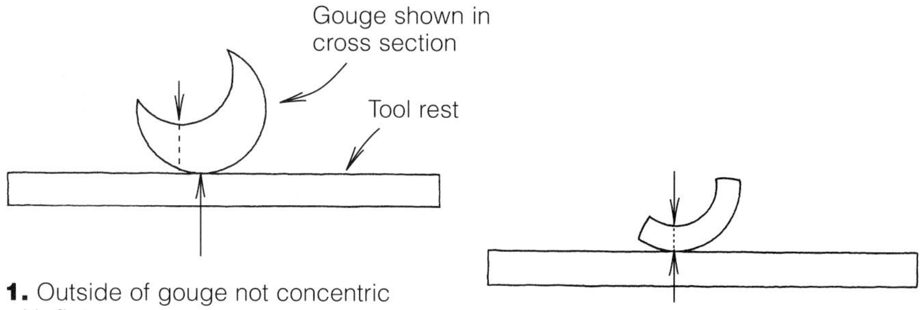

1. Outside of gouge not concentric with flute

2. Outside of gouge concentric with flute

For square-end gouges, such as roughing gouges, a handle end stop to control the bevel angle is a simple and useful jig (see the drawing at top). With the end stop controlling the bevel angle, you need only rotate the gouge, keeping it centered on the wheel. (This jig can also be used to create a fingernail end, if you dwell longer at the limits of the rotation than at the midpoint.)

SPINDLE GOUGES

Spindle gouges have a much easier life of it than roughing gouges and can be sharpened at 25°. As always, for very hard woods this angle may have to be increased a bit, and for very soft woods it can be decreased. There are a couple of things you can do to make your spindle gouges easier to use. First, you should ensure that the tip of the gouge

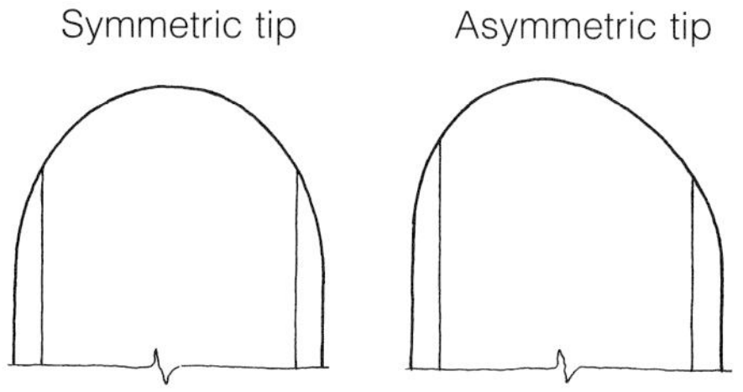

is symmetrical when viewed from the top (see the drawing above). A spindle gouge is so often used like a skew that it makes it much easier to use if the fingernail tip is always centered. Novice turners often find that they are having difficulties with a spindle gouge without realizing that the cause is just bad shape.

As well as ensuring good tip design, you can sometimes improve the functioning of a spindle gouge by adjusting the cross-sectional profile. In his book *The Practice of Woodturning* (The Melaleuca Press, Australia, 1985), Mike Darlow makes some very specific recommendations. As one example, he recommends that the outside of a gouge should be concentric with the arc of the flute, so that the reactive force to cutting is in line with the gouge's point of contact with the tool rest. This eliminates the tendency of the gouge to roll. In Drawing 1 at left, the reactive force must be resisted by the turner or the gouge will roll. But if the outside of the same gouge was concentric with the flute, the reactive force would be in line with the point of contact with the tool rest (as shown in Drawing 2), and the gouge would not have a tendency to roll.

GOUGES

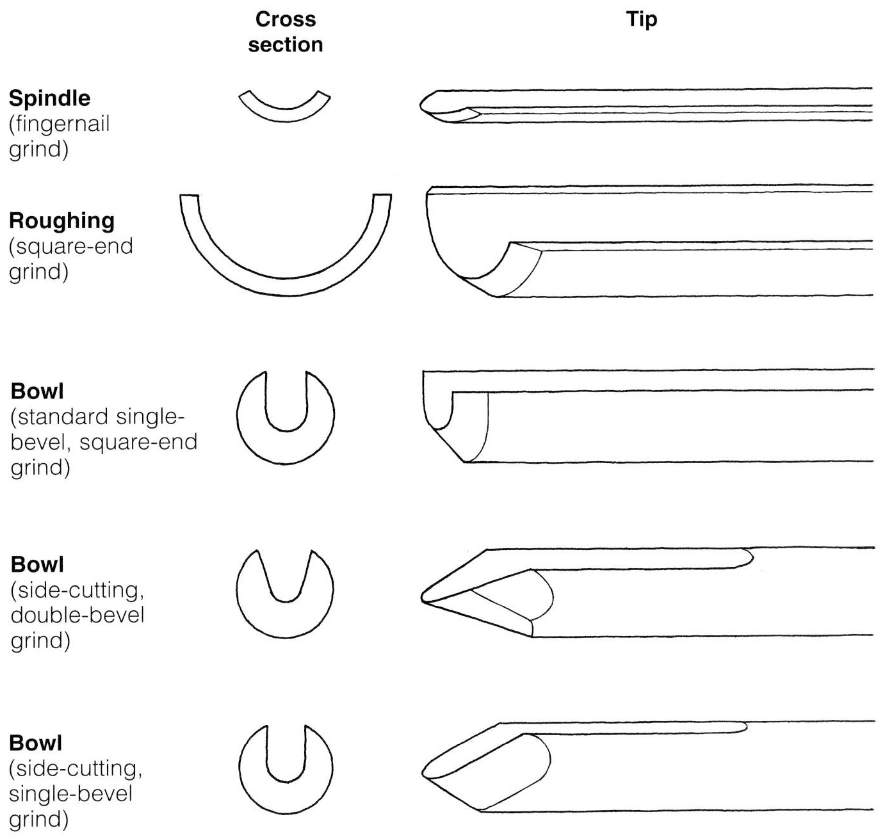

BOWL GOUGES

The angle at which you sharpen bowl gouges depends both on technique and on the nature of the work that you might be doing. Traditionally, bowl gouges were sharpened at a 40° bevel angle and square across the front, but this is one tool that is highly individualistic among turners. The drawing above shows a standard grind and two types of side-cutting gouges.

For a side-cutting gouge like the examples shown (the first use of which is usually credited to the American turner David Ellsworth or the Irish turner Liam O'Neill), it is almost mandatory to use a jig like the Glaser joystick to get a consistent grind. To attempt a grind like this freehand indicates a bravery verging on foolhardiness. It is extremely difficult to avoid creating multiple bevels as you attempt to get a cutting edge with a smoothly flowing line. One is usually sacrificed to attain the other.

There is another factor at play in a side-cutting gouge like this. To have any hope of a good grind, you have to have a smooth, straight flute. If the flute has been ground freehand or has been buffed too enthusiastically on a shaped leather or felt wheel, it will have a rippled surface, which will quickly

GLASER JOYSTICK

One of the most interesting sharpening aids to be developed in recent years is an adjustable joystick designed by Jerry Glaser, a California designer and manufacturer of turning tools. The joystick can be used to sharpen most turning tools (including radiused skews and spindle gouges), but it excels at putting a side-cutting fingernail grind on bowl gouges.

This exaggerated fingernail tip is very difficult to grind freehand. Glaser's device can be adjusted so that the user has to be concerned only about controlling grinding pressure and speed of lateral movement; the compound grind angles are controlled through the various angular and height adjustments in the joystick. Purists might call this de-skilling a process; realists will appreciate the control and repeatability such an aid provides.

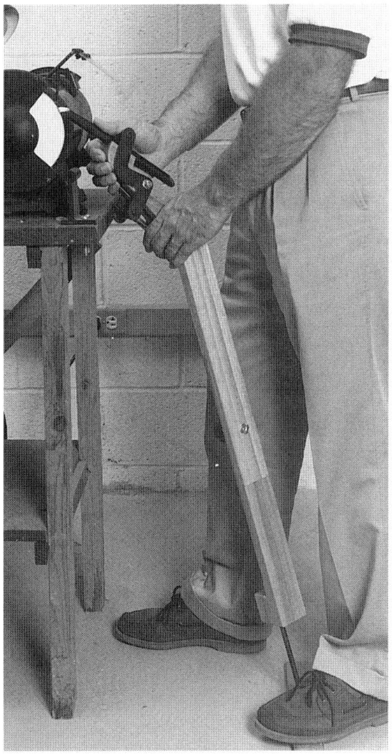

The Glaser joystick in use on a test blank. (Photo by Susan Kahn)

TRUING THE FLUTE

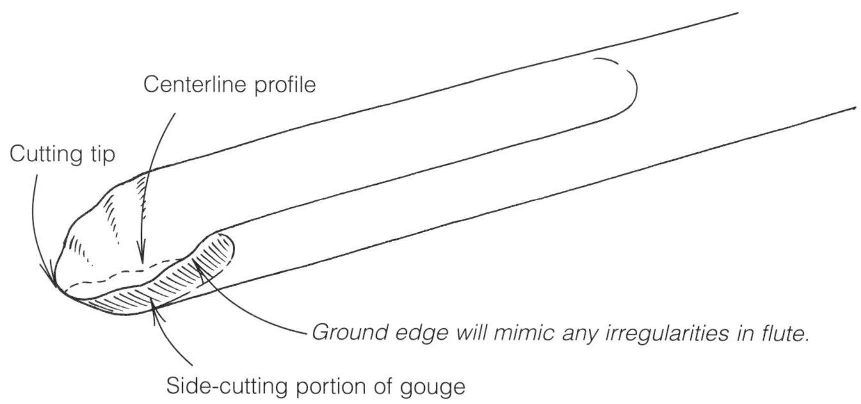

GRINDING A SKEW CHISEL

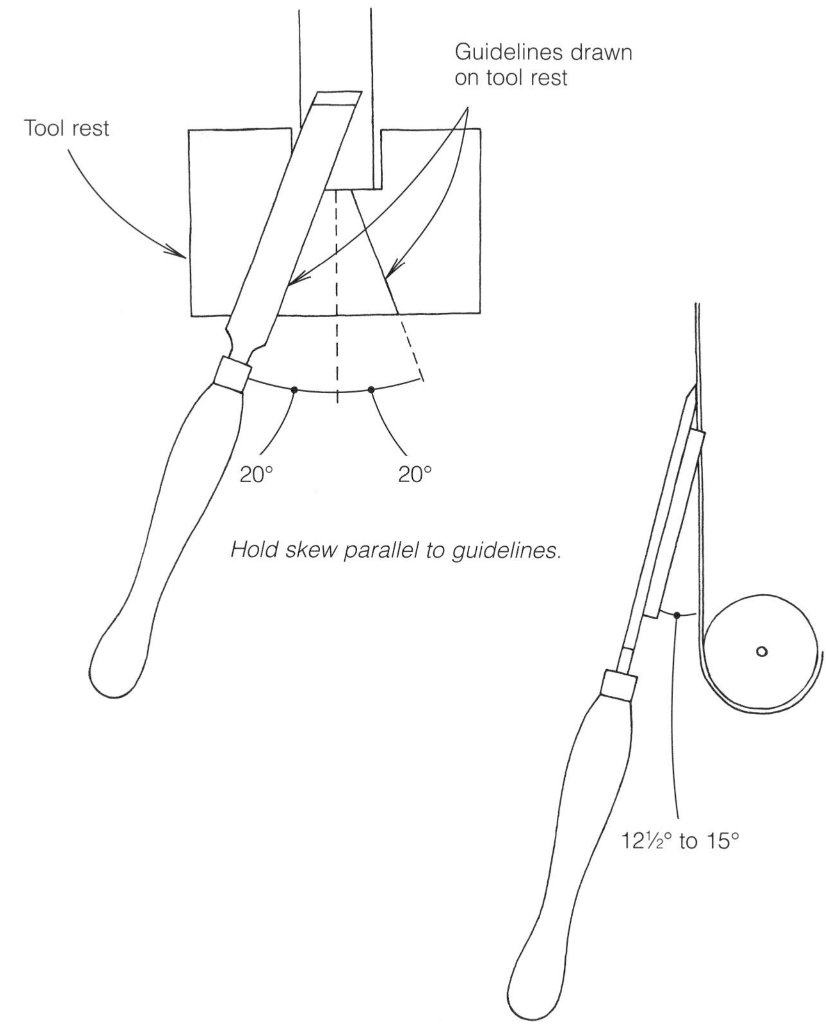

translate into a rippled edge on the side grind (see the top drawing at left). Before grinding, such a gouge would have to have the flute trued. In the home shop, this would best be done with PSA-backed abrasive on a suitably sized dowel or shaped wooden hone.

For a square-end gouge, the flute irregularities would be much less significant since the ground edge would be parallel to the wave crests and troughs. But even in this case the irregularities are seldom exactly parallel to the cutting edge. Inasmuch as they are not parallel, they will introduce edge irregularities unless they are dressed out.

CHISELS

Although many turners insist on using gouges straight from the grinding wheel, almost all turners believe in honing skew chisels. I read one British turning author who felt that it was a waste of time and preferred to drag the skew across the lathe stand in order to remove the burr, but this was an exception to the general practice.

STANDARD SKEWS

The standard skew chisel should be sharpened at about 70° of skew, with bevel angles from 12½° to 15° on each side. At 12½° you would get an included angle of 25°, which would be fine for softwoods. Higher bevel angles might be required for more difficult woods. Grinding a skew is quite straightforward on either a belt sander or a grinding wheel. The same sort of simple jig used for grinding chisels and plane blades will function perfectly well with a skew. Honing can be done with micro-abrasives, either freehand or on a belt sander. Honing can also be accomplished with a simple bench stone.

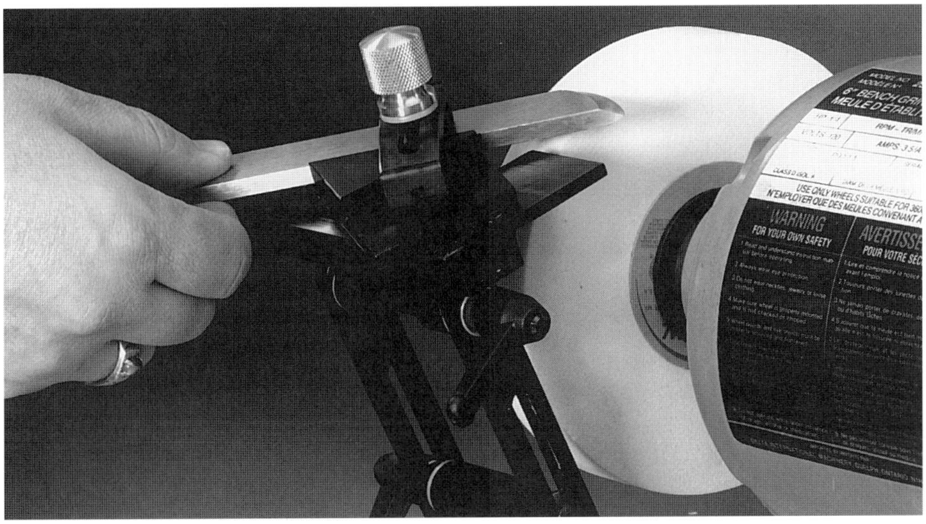

A skew-grinding jig allows you to grind a slight radius on a skew chisel. The radius of the grind is determined by the amount the skew projects from the jig.

RADIUSED SKEWS

A number of turners prefer radiused skews, particularly for turning beads, because they minimize the possibility of digs. You can buy a specially made jig for grinding radiused skews (see the photo above) or make one yourself. If you choose to make a jig, you need only drill a rotation hole in your tool rest and put a matching pin through a tool clamp.

SQUARE-END CHISELS

A standard firmer chisel is often used in place of a skew for planing cylinders or long tapers between centers. The chisel is used askew the turning but, of course, is beveled on only one side. The chisel for this purpose can be sharpened at 25° in exactly the same manner as you would sharpen a regular chisel.

PARTING TOOLS

There are many types of parting tools (the drawing at right shows most of the main types). Sharpening each of these is quite straightforward. The included angles vary from supplier to supplier (anywhere from 30° to 50°), but since they all function by tearing the fibers the angle is not critically important. However, there are a few things you can do to make parting tools function a bit better. These include easing the sharp arrises of the tool and burnishing the tip.

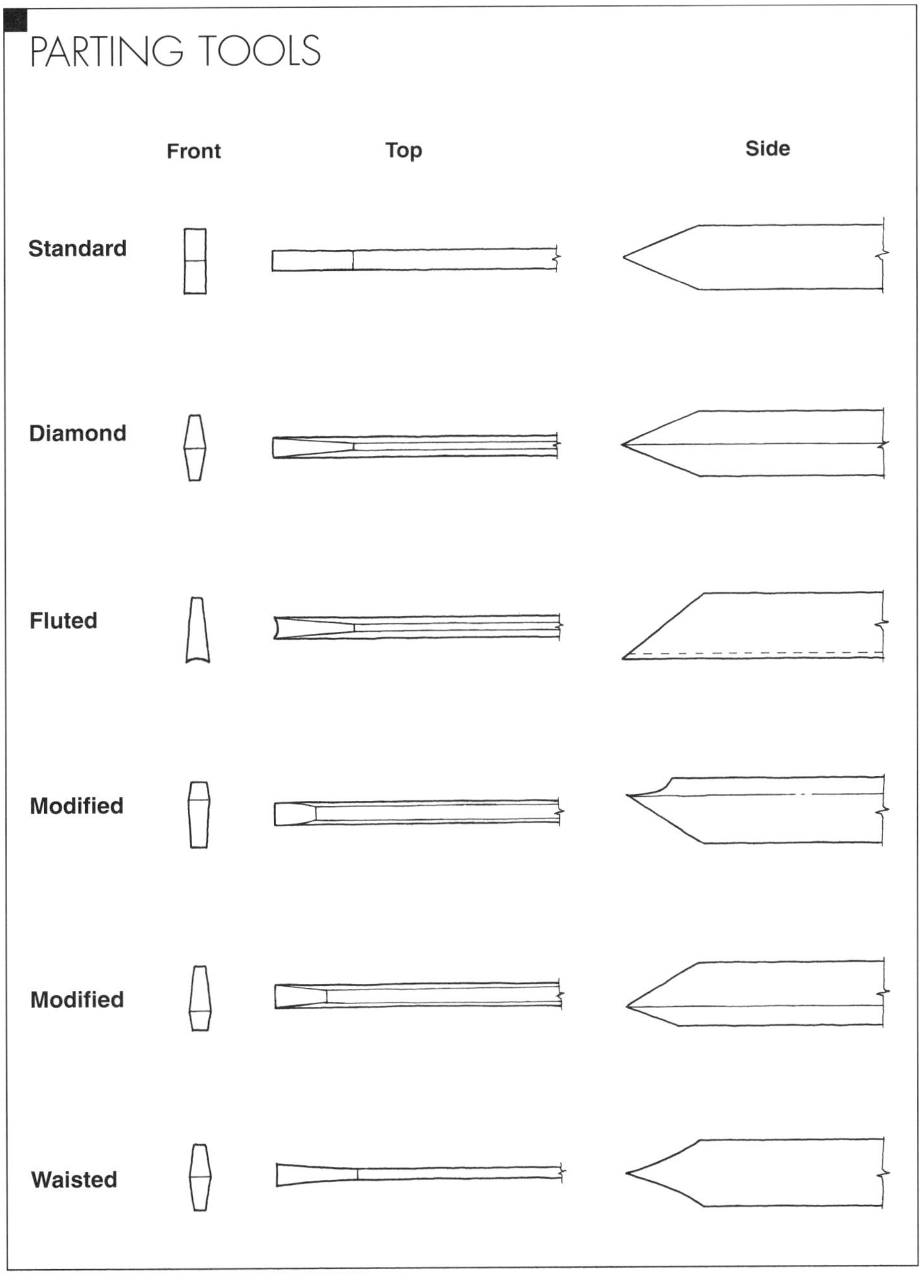

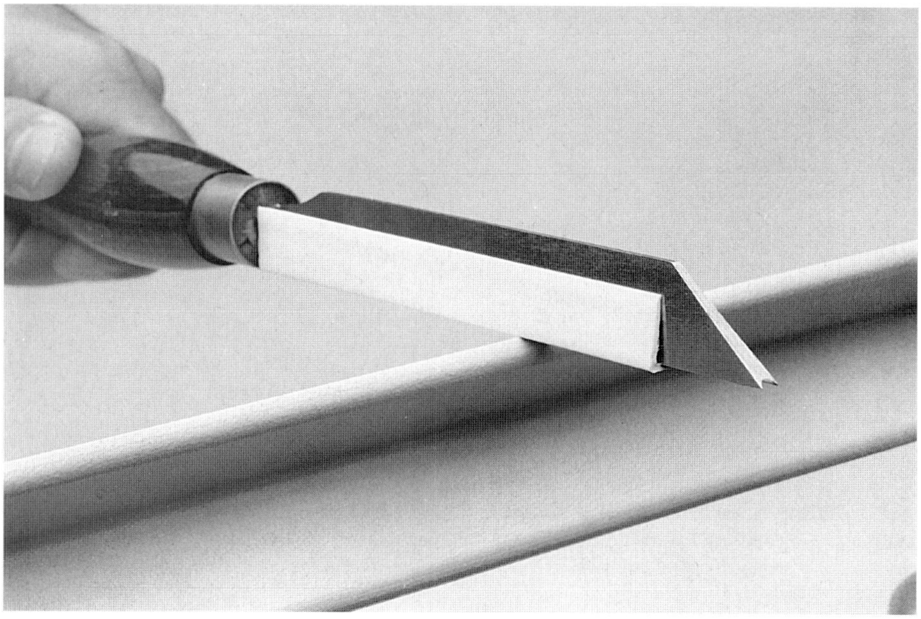

A plastic spline binder on a fluted parting tool prevents the sharp bottom edges from damaging the tool rest.

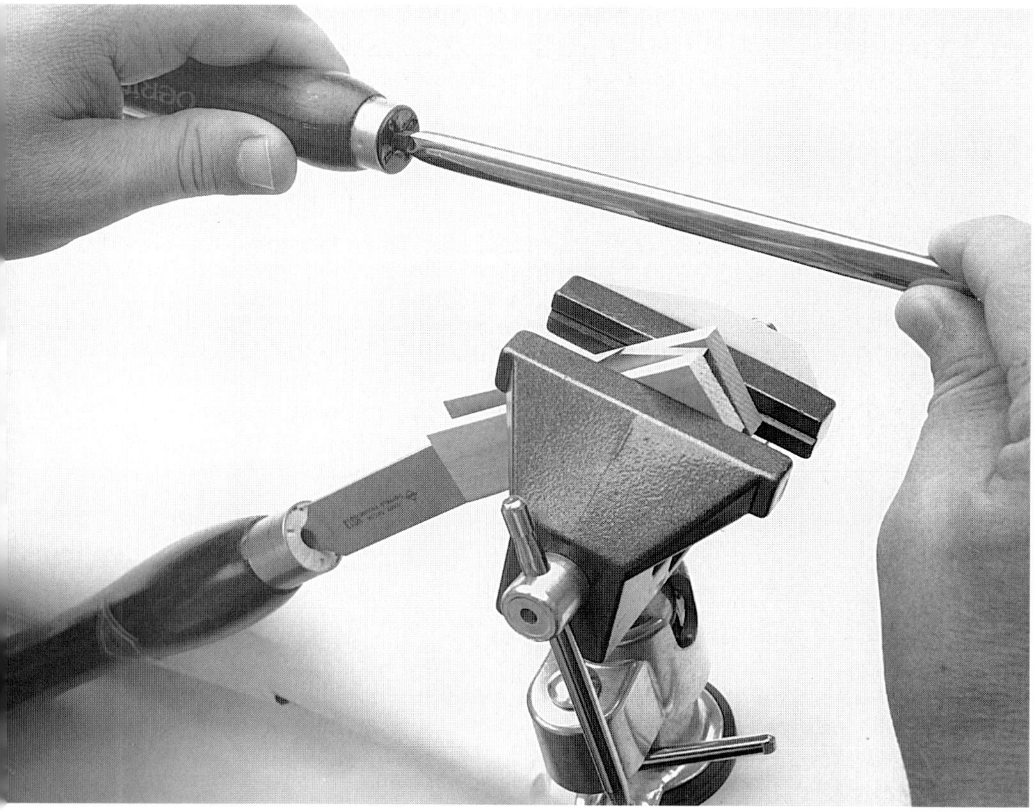

An easy setup for well-controlled burnishing of a parting-tool tip. It may appear that the parting tool is held too deeply in the wood scraps and that the burnisher will not be able to reach it. In fact, the burnisher being used has a teardrop cross-section and will touch all of the edge except the very corners, which is exactly what you want it to do.

EASING ARRISES

All of the samples shown in the drawing on p. 127 except two have tapered upper edges. Of the remaining two, the waisted tool does not require one. With the standard parting tool, it is best to

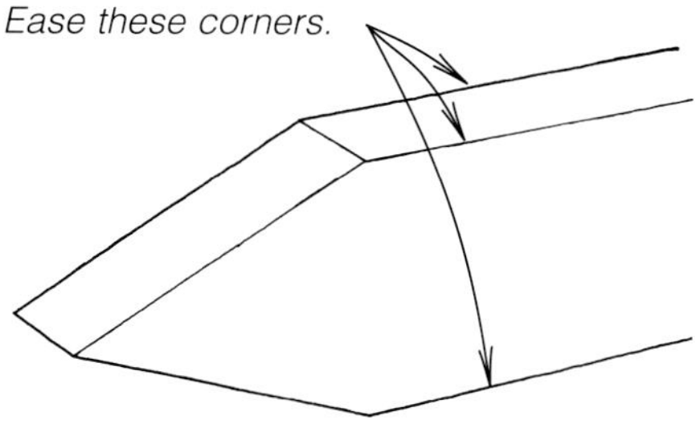

ease the sharp arrises of the tool. Otherwise, it can catch in a deep cut.

All except the fluted parting tool should have the very sharp bottom edges broken so that they do not continually scar the tool rest. In the case of the fluted parting tool, it is a good idea to put a plastic spine binder (trimmed to length) on the tool to keep it from chewing up the tool rest.

BURNISHING THE TIP

Although it does not reduce fiber tearing at the edges of the cut, burnishing a hook on the central portion of the parting tool tip reduces the friction and heat in the cutting process and lets the tool track better. It does not require much of a hook, and the hook should be modified to the central three-quarters to four-fifths of the parting tool. This can be readily done with the parting tool clamped in a vise. If you do not trust your technique, you can put two small wood scraps on either side of the parting tool tip to prevent the hook extending to the outside edge (as shown in the photo at left).

BEADING TOOLS AND OTHERS

Square beading tools are sharpened like parting tools but without the optional burnishing. Shaped beading tools are honed only on the top; the profiles are not touched.

There are many fad shapes in turning that quickly gain in popularity and often as quickly fade. Ones such as ring tools and hooks can be sharpened in the same manner as carving tools of the same design. Others are usually just a variation of tools in the categories already covered in this chapter.

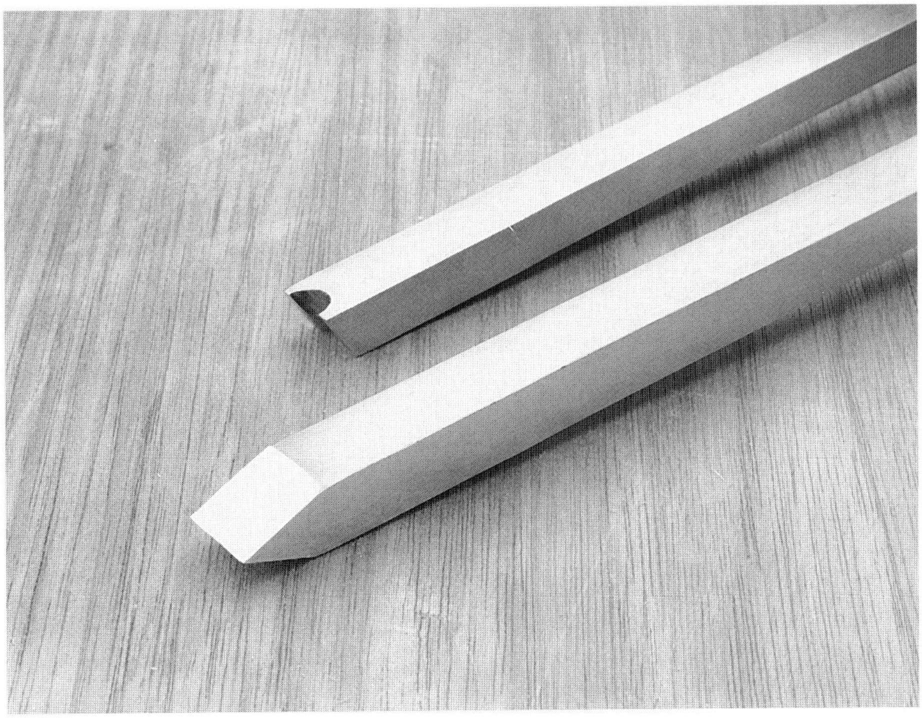

The beading tool at top is a shaped scraper; it is pressed against the spindle to form a bead. The traditional beading tool at bottom is used much like a skew to form a bead.

No area of woodworking has seen greater change in technique and tool design in recent years than woodturning. Some tools that are now considered standard, such as roughing gouges, were barely available in the market twenty years ago. The same period has seen high-carbon steel replaced by high-speed steel in everything but introductory sets.

Fortunately, the new tools, techniques and alloys have been accompanied by advances in abrasives and grinding jigs. But turning tools remain one of the most complex areas of sharpening to master and merit a book, not just a chapter.

CHAPTER 11

SCRAPERS

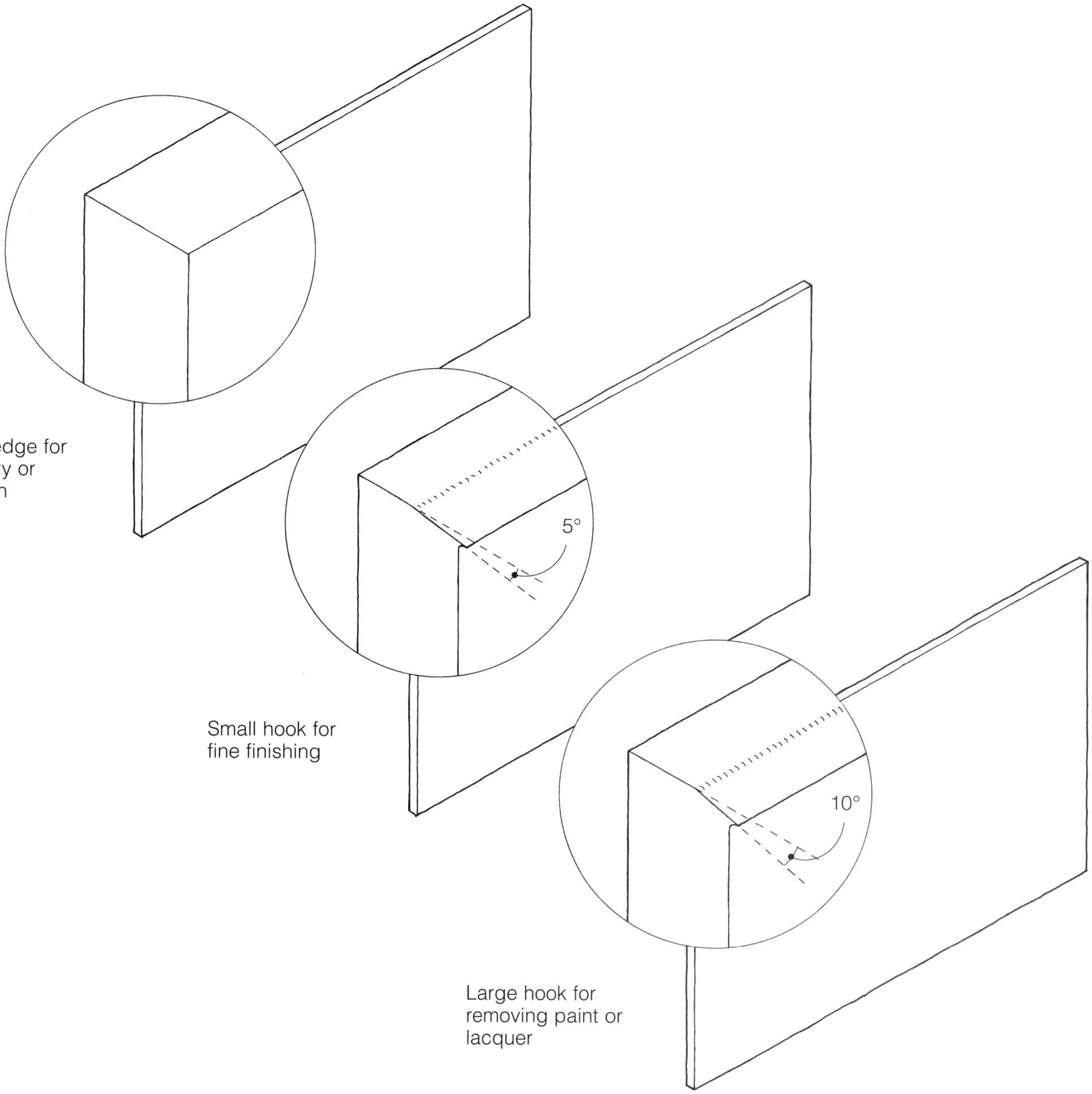

Square edge for marquetry or wild grain

Small hook for fine finishing

Large hook for removing paint or lacquer

Scrapers, a type of hand plane, are the most useful tools in the woodworking shop. No hand tool gives you better control or is more versatile. Scrapers do not cause disasters by suddenly gouging out large pieces of wood and, in fact, are most often used to repair the damage caused by jointers and thickness planers, which are notoriously poor at dealing with varying grain. Scrapers are cheap and easy to sharpen, and they last practically forever. If I am beginning to sound like a revivalist preacher on this subject, it is because the wonders of cabinet scrapers were revealed to me much later in my life than I wish had been the case. I cannot imagine doing any woodworking without scrapers in some form being at hand.

A well-sharpened cabinet scraper should make clean shavings, not dust. (Photo by Susan Kahn)

CABINET SCRAPERS

Among the various scrapers available, rectangular cabinet scrapers are the most versatile and the least expensive. Although they can be made from old handsaws or steel similar in thickness and hardness, they are readily available from a variety of sources at moderate prices. Usually about 2 in. by 6 in., rectangular scrapers vary in thickness from 0.4mm (0.015 in.) to 1mm (0.042 in.). Until recent years, most of them were hardened to Rc38 to Rc42, the same hardness as most Western handsaws (not surprising, since they were frequently made from the same stock of steel). In more recent times, much harder scrapers have become available that are in the Rc48 to Rc52 range and will hold an edge longer than the softer scrapers.

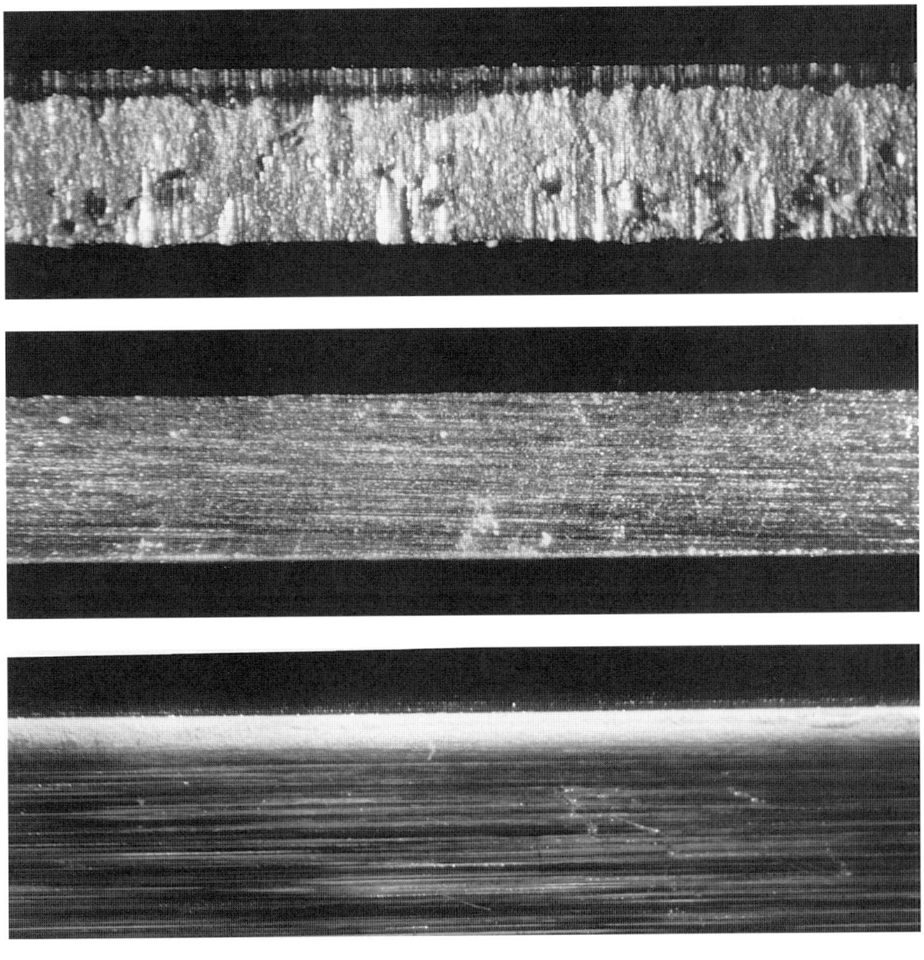

Three cabinet-scraper edges: at top, a sheared edge; in the middle, an edge after jointing with a file; at bottom, an edge (at greater magnification) showing the smoothing effect of stoning and burnishing. (Photos courtesy Canadian Conservation Institute)

JOINTING

Although some cabinet scrapers come with milled edges ready for burnishing (e.g., Sandvik and Veritas), most are just sheared from polished spring steel and have been deburred but do not have milled edges. The first thing that has to be done with such a scraper is to joint it to give it a smooth edge at 90° to the sides.

Jointing a cabinet scraper creates a smooth edge at 90° to the sides.

The scraper should be clamped in a padded-jaw vise and jointed with a mill file. It takes at most a half-dozen strokes at moderate pressure, followed by a couple of strokes at light pressure for the finest possible finish. You can make a simple jointing jig by running a kerf the same width as the file in a block of wood (see the sidebar below), or you can buy one of several jointing jigs that are on the market. You can also joint the cabinet scraper using the file freehand, but this can cause you problems in ensuing steps in the sharpening process if you do not get an edge that is dead flat or if you do not file exactly in line with the scraper.

JOINTING AIDS

There are many ways you can joint a scraper (or a handsaw) without using a commercial jointer. Some are detailed here, others you should be able to invent yourself. As with most things, if you know the principles, you can conceive a solution. In jointing, the principles are: (a) keep the edge flat, (b) keep the edge square.

Option A. Make a jointer from a piece of wood. Make the kerf a press fit for your file, or put two wood screws in it to clamp the file. Clip the sharp ends off the screws so that they have bearing flats.

Option B. If you are so impoverished that you can't afford a mill file, drill a hole that is a drive fit for a triangular file and run a saw cut up to it. Add screws if it would make you feel more secure or if the hole is oversize. Be sure the flat of the file is at 90° to the kerf sides.

Option C. If the first two methods are too complex, just use two scraps of wood. Hold them to the file with finger pressure (thumbs on top of the file). Clamp the scraper between two pieces of hardwood in your vise and file the scraper until it is flush with the wood. (Note that I would not use this system with a handsaw, because it is too easy to slip.)

Option A

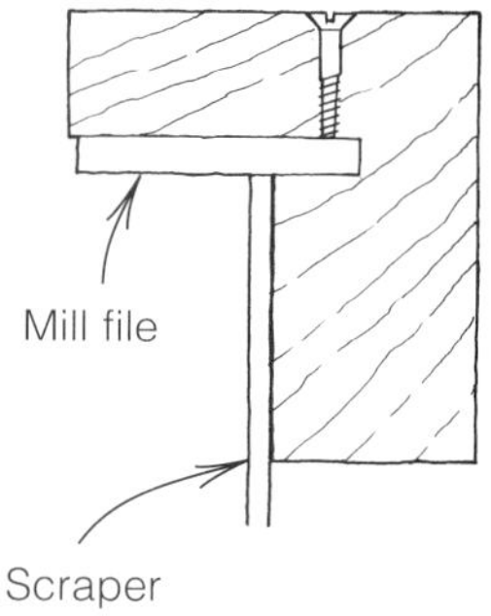

Option B

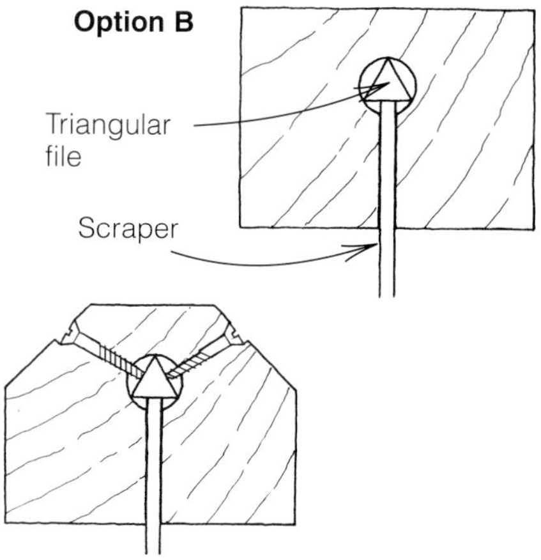

Option C

Hold file against two scraps of wood and rub back and forth along edge of scraper.

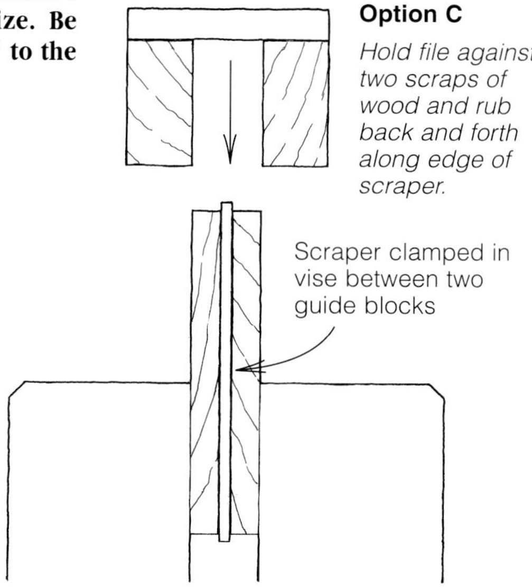

Jointing the cabinet scraper will eliminate the ragged edge caused in the shearing process and replace it with a series of very fine serrations, which will be exactly parallel to the edge if you have used a jointing jig (see the top photo below). If you have done your filing freehand, these serrations will not be parallel to the edge and could result in an uneven interface with the scraper side (see the bottom photo below).

If you have done a good job of jointing the cabinet scraper, you should have a good usable edge that requires no further work for some purposes. For example, if you are removing a layer of crazed varnish in a restoration project or a bit of glue seepage in marquetry, the square edge will do the job nicely without removing much wood (see the drawing on p. 130). But for most purposes, you'll have to go on to burnish the scraper, or better yet, to stone first and then burnish.

Whether or not you decide to stone the scraper depends upon what you intend to do with it and how fussy you are. You can go directly to the burnishing process (see pp. 134-137) if you have filed carefully, or if you are only using the scraper for something like paint removal where the edge will get torn quickly anyway. Stoning is not mandatory, but I strongly recommend that you try it at least once so that you can compare scrapers prepared both ways.

STONING

Just as you want two perfectly smooth surfaces to create a good edge on a chisel, you need the same thing for the best possible edge on a cabinet scraper. It is for this reason that you stone the edge of the scraper. If you have done a good job of filing, you can move directly to a relatively fine stone, something like a 1200x water stone.

For ease of control and to avoid damage to your stones, I recommend that you always stone your scrapers on the side of the stone. This is easily done in a couple of ways. You can set the stone on your bench with a scrap of wood next to it and, holding the stone with one hand, run the scraper back and forth against the edge of the stone using the wood as support (see the photo below). This keeps the scraper at a true 90° to the face of the stone.

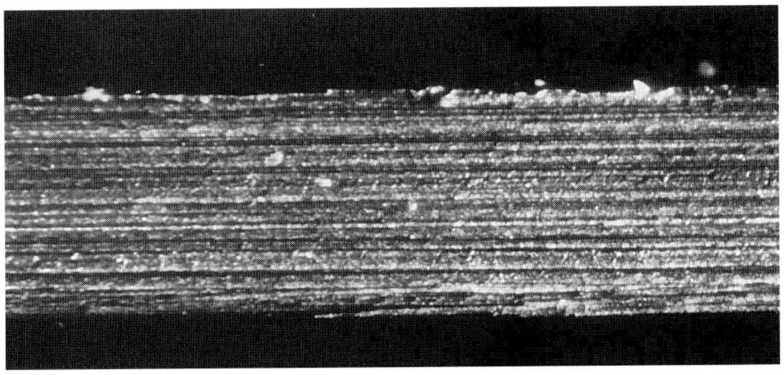

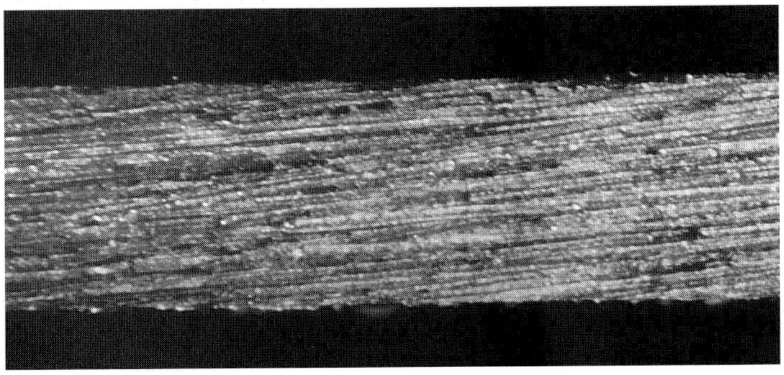

Two magnified scraper edges, one jointed straight (top), the other jointed at an angle (above). After burnishing, the scraper jointed at an angle will have small hooks in the edge wherever the filing grooves intersect it. (Photos courtesy Canadian Conservation Institute)

Using a scrap of wood to support and align the scraper, stone the edge on the side of a stone.

Another method is to set the stone on edge projecting over the side of your bench and use the face of the bench to maintain a 90° angle as you stone the edge.

If you have used a jointer that holds the file perfectly flat in the jointing process, you will find that it does not take long to stone the edge of the scraper. For a fine edge, you should move on to a 6000x or an 8000x stone and repeat the process. Since these stones usually have wooden bases (see the photo at right on p. 133), the first method is recommended as the easiest to maintain a square edge.

Be careful that you stone a scraper only once on any one spot on the stone, since you will develop a groove in the stone that can round the edge of the scraper. As with any stone, you should be sure that the surface you are using is flat before you begin to use it. You can use a stone a number of times on the side before you have to true the side of the stone, since you have only to vary the thickness of the backing block to adjust the height of the scraper to an unused portion on the stone.

With some scrapers that have not been well polished originally, you will also want to dress both faces of the scraper on a fine stone. (You would also do this to remove any burr raised in the general stoning process.) If you do all of these stoning steps carefully, you should have a very crisp edge on the scraper that can be used as is for fine work such as marquetry or you can then proceed to the next step, burnishing a hook on the scraper.

BURNISHING

The purpose of burnishing a cabinet scraper is to deform the steel to create an edge that has an included angle of something less than the 90° that you started with. To do this, you need a burnisher that is appreciably harder than the cabinet scraper you are burnishing. This would be at least Rc60 in steel, or it could be a finely ground carbide rod in the Rc80 range. You also want a burnisher that is smooth so that it is not abrading the scraper at any time; you want the burnisher to mold the steel to shape, not remove any steel.

Some woodworkers recommend using the shank of a screwdriver, the back of a chisel, or even a valve stem to burnish cabinet scrapers. While you may find a screwdriver shank that is hard enough to burnish your cabinet scraper, this is normally only the case if the shank is chrome-plated or nickel-plated. The plating is hard but it is also very thin. As soon as you break through the plating you can cause major damage to the edge of your cabinet scraper. The back of a chisel is the wrong shape, is not smooth enough and is almost never hard enough to be an effective burnisher. Automotive valve stems have nicely formed shanks, but they too are not sufficiently hard, particularly for the modern hard scrapers.

If you want to avoid buying a burnisher, one of the very few things you can use with any confidence is a file that you have very carefully ground to remove the teeth and then completely polished to a smooth finish. In this process, you have to be certain that you don't draw the temper of the file; otherwise, you may soften it below an acceptable level.

There are four basic shapes of burnishers on the market: triangular, round, oval and teardrop (see the sidebar at left). The teardrop-shape cross section is actually a combination of the other three. Historically, the triangular burnisher was used on rectangular cabinet scrapers, and the round and oval burnishers on curved scrapers. The teardrop shape can be used on either.

BURNISHER SHAPES

Although a curve is supposed to touch a line at a point, that is not the case with burnishers. As soon as pressure is applied to a burnisher, it begins to sink into the scraper. Just how far it sinks depends on the applied pressure, the radius of the burnisher at the point of tangency and the hardness of the scraper.

You can roll a hook with light pressure and a small-radius burnisher or use a larger-radius burnisher with more pressure. No burnisher should have any corners; all curves should blend into each other or, in the case of the triangular burnisher, with the plain sides. The round burnisher is the least versatile of the four shapes; the teardrop burnisher is the most versatile because it offers a range of radii.

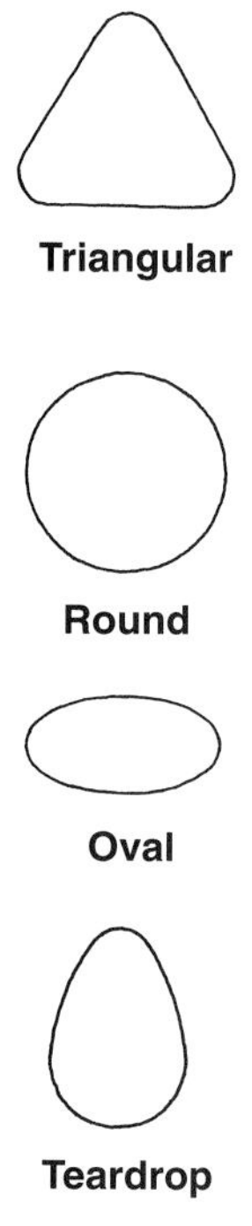

There is a reason for the various shapes. Using the teardrop shape as an example (since it incorporates the others), you would use the largest radius portion for the smoothing strokes on a cabinet scraper and the middle radius portion for burnishing a hook. On very thin cabinet scrapers, which tend to bend when you are burnishing them, you would use the smallest radius so that you would get maximum point pressure without causing the scraper to bend away from the burnisher. In general, you want to use the largest radius that will do the job effectively since it will cause the fewest ripples in the hook. You will quickly learn that by adjusting the pressure you put on the burnisher, you can change the action of it and get exactly the sort of hook you are looking for.

Having chosen your burnisher you are ready to burnish a hook on the cabinet scraper. Before you touch the burnisher to the scraper, you should put some form of lubricant on the scraper. You can use oil (which means you will have to wipe it clean after use), candle wax or whatever machine-top wax you have at hand.

I prefer to rub the tip of my finger along the side of my nose or behind my ear and then rub it along the scraper edge. There is just enough natural oil in either spot to provide the lubrication you need for this process. The great advantage of using this natural lubricant is that it is nearby, there is sufficient supply for almost any amount of burnishing and it will not contaminate your scraper with something that may later end up on your workpiece. If you do not put some lubricant on the cabinet scraper, you will find that the burnishing process generates enough heat to risk damage to either the cabinet scraper or the burnisher. It is a very simple trick, but one that I recommend you always use.

BURNISHER TECHNIQUE

We all have little idiosyncrasies in technique that are important to us but may have greater imagined than real effect on a process. Two of mine are the way I hold a burnisher and the way I always try to travel slightly across an edge as I burnish.

I always hold the unhandled end of a burnisher with the tips of two fingers and a thumb, rather than using a very firm grip. This reduces the amount of pressure that I can apply. If I don't do this, I find myself rolling on hooks that look like tidal waves.

Another habit, which I believe has merit, is to travel just slightly across an edge as you move the burnisher along it. Not only does this feel right, but it avoids overheating the burnisher at one spot with the danger of drawing the temper and then grooving it. It also prevents even minor traveling the opposite way, which seems intuitively wrong to me.

Holding the tip of the burnisher loosely reduces the amount of pressure you can apply and results in a smaller hook. (Photo by Susan Kahn)

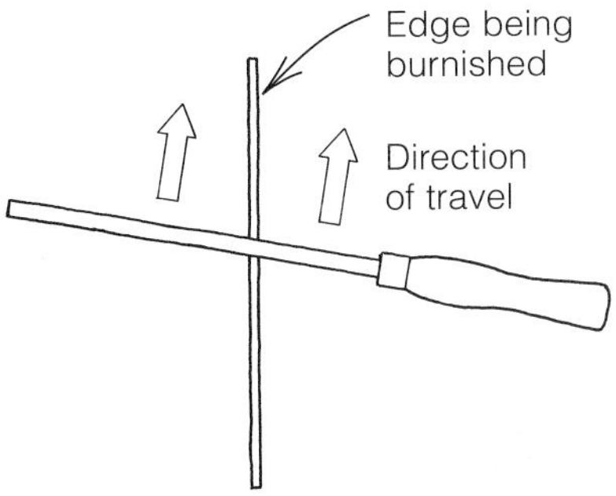

Always let the burnisher travel slightly across the edge as you burnish.

With an unstoned scraper, you should first take one or two strokes using moderate pressure with the burnisher parallel to the scraper edge. This tends to burnish down any serrations left from jointing (which would have caused friction in use later) and will begin to swell the edge of the cabinet scraper. With soft cabinet scrapers (those in the Rc38 to Rc42 range), you may find that this gives you just the right amount of hook, since it is next to impossible to keep your burnisher exactly parallel to the edge without laying on a few degrees of hook accidentally. You'll be able to feel any hook on the scraper by plucking the edge of the scraper with your fingernail. If you have never used a cabinet scraper before, you should now try the scraper on a piece of hardwood before any further burnishing to see what sort of effect you get.

For any substantial wood removal, you are probably going to need more of a hook than you will get with the burnisher parallel to the edge of the scraper. You will probably want to put at least 2° of hook on the scraper and possibly as much as 15°. The amount of hook is highly subjective. I prefer a relatively low angle, almost never greater than 5°. Perfectly competent

SETTING A BURNISHING ANGLE

If you are uncomfortable doing freehand burnishing of a cabinet scraper, there is a very simple jig you can use to control angles. Clamp the scraper in a vise (always with wooden or padded jaws) next to a 1½-in. wide piece of wood. If you let the cabinet scraper project ⅛ in. above the 1½-in. piece of wood and then let your burnisher blade rest both on the cabinet scraper and on the piece of wood, you will have a 5° burnishing angle. For a 10° angle (see the drawing below), have the burnisher project ¼ in. above the block of wood; for a 15° angle, let it project ⅜ in., and so on. This is an application of the 1-in-60 rule discussed on p. 17.

It's well worth trying this technique at least once so that you get a good idea of what the different angles look like from your normal working stance. Whether or not you use the guide all the time depends on your technique. Some people have great hand-eye coordination and can get nearly perfect repeatability when freehand burnishing. Most people cannot.

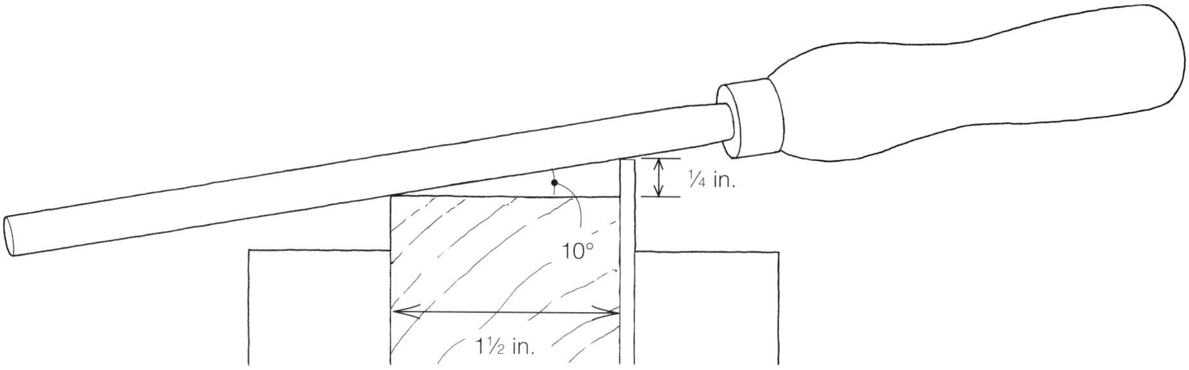

A variable burnisher makes it possible to burnish cabinet scrapers accurately and consistently at angles from 0° to 15°.

cabinetmakers I know prefer to put a much larger amount of hook on a scraper, often going up to 15°. The difficulty I have with such a large angle is that the scraper must be tilted so far forward in use that it makes it far easier to burn your knuckles.

Setting the angle of the burnisher is difficult to do by eye, and I would suggest you use the angle-setting system described in the sidebar at the top of the page. Alternatively, you can use a jigged burnisher like the Veritas variable burnisher, which has a carbide rod that can be dialed to any burnishing angle from 0° to 15° (see the photo above). Incidentally, you never have to worry about overheating the carbide rod. It can take it. But you should still put a dab of lubricant on the scraper edge; although friction will not hurt the carbide, it can cause a tear in the scraper hook.

SCRAPER RELIEF ANGLES

The rolled edge on a scraper works much like a plane but with some significant differences. First, it has a higher cutting angle than most planes. Second, the depth of cut is controlled by the size of the hook and the relief angle. A large hook will let the scraper take a thicker shaving, but the depth of cut can be reduced by tilting the scraper back a bit. The reduced relief angle will reduce the depth of cut.

If you have vigorously burnished your scraper to the point that it will cut only if you lean it forward until your knuckles are scraping the wood, don't despair. Instead of filing the hook off and starting again, take a couple of jointing passes on the scraper. You can often change the relief angle enough that the scraper will work properly. The hook might be a bit weak but it beats starting from scratch again.

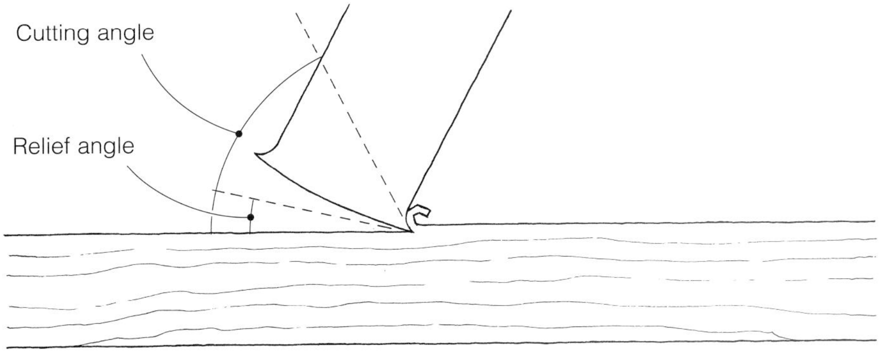

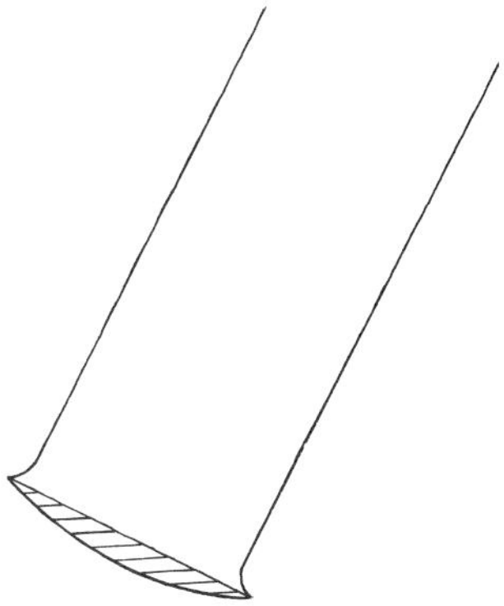

File off hatched portion to change relief angle.

Regardless of the final hook you intend to put on, I recommend that you put it on with as few passes as possible. The number of passes you need depends upon the hardness of your scraper, the pressure you are applying to the burnisher and the shape of that portion of the burnisher that is touching the cabinet scraper. You can arrive at the best combination by experimentation. This is not a process that can be readily detailed for everyone. Whenever possible, I lay on the hook in a single pass, which can be done easily with softer scrapers, though the hard scrapers usually require several passes.

If you have followed the steps reasonably carefully, you should be able to bow the scraper in your hand and take long, virtually transparent shavings from a piece of hardwood. If you only get dust, you have done something wrong. A well-sharpened cabinet scraper is one of the finest planes there is. It automatically controls the depth of shaving it will take, and you should be able to work very difficult grain with it far more readily than you can with any one of your bench planes.

RESHARPENING SCRAPERS

Two cabinetmakers I know say that an edge can be "picked up" once or twice by running a sharp point along it before you have to resharpen the scraper. Both of these cabinetmakers use a jeweler's burnisher for this process. I am not sure why some jeweler's burnishers have a sharp point on them and others don't, but it is only those curved burnishers with a sharp point that can be used for this process. I have found the whole business of picking up a hook to be very tricky and cannot recommend it. Neither am I pig-headed enough to say that it does not work. What I have found is that it is fairly easy to tear the hook with the burnisher point.

Assuming that your scraper edge is dulled and that you have "picked it up" as many times as practical, you now have to resharpen starting at the first step, which is jointing. When you resharpen, you should remove all of the former hook. This may take a dozen passes with a mill file, but you should be sure that all of the old hook is gone before you start once again.

This process is not as ominous as it sounds, since rectangular cabinet scrapers have four perfectly usable edges and you won't have to resharpen them that frequently if you look after them. First, you do not have to put the same degree of hook on all four edges of the cabinet scraper. You can put different angles and sizes of hooks on each of the four corners and mark them accordingly. To avoid having to resharpen more often than necessary, either keep your cabinet scraper in a vinyl sleeve when it is not being used or keep edge protectors on it. Much like files, more cabinet scrapers are rendered useless when they are not being used than when they are. Just like a file, if it is allowed to rattle around in areas where it will come in contact with other pieces of metal, the cabinet scraper will quickly be dulled. Unless sharpening is your main aim in life, you should keep the edges protected.

SOME PROBLEMS WITH SCRAPERS

Although cabinet scrapers are incredibly useful tools, they can cause problems as well as solve them. As you are busily cleaning up a bit of torn grain caused by your planer, you will sometimes find that you have put a dished area in the wood that will be very noticeable once you have applied a finish. You should take longer strokes to minimize this dishing effect.

Another problem you may encounter is a washboard effect—a series of ripples in the wood you are working. Skewing the cabinet scraper as you work, first one way and then the other, will avoid creating washboard. It will usually give you a better shaving as well, for the reasons covered in Chapter 2. When you skew the cabinet scraper it has the same effect as using a bench plane with a longer sole; you are effectively lengthening the sole of the cabinet scraper as you skew it.

Since washboard is caused by the way the scraper is forming shavings or chips, you can also reduce washboard by tilting your cabinet scraper farther forward, essentially increasing the cutting angle so that you get a different type of chip formation. Although this reduces the washboard effect, it also gives a slightly fuzzier finish.

CABINET SCRAPERS AND SOFTWOOD

The very high cutting angles of cabinet scrapers make them unsuitable for softwoods. If you are very careful when you stone and burnish a cabinet scraper, you can get a hook that will almost work on softwoods like pine and butternut, but it never quite makes it. There is a tendency to crush the fibers rather than cut them. The crushed fibers catch on the edge of the scraper and will then strip out of your work, leaving long gouges.

By the very nature of the way they are used, cabinet scrapers apply substantial pressure on wood. Even if you did not tear softwoods, you would compress them with a cabinet scraper. Good as they are, even cabinet scrapers have their limitations.

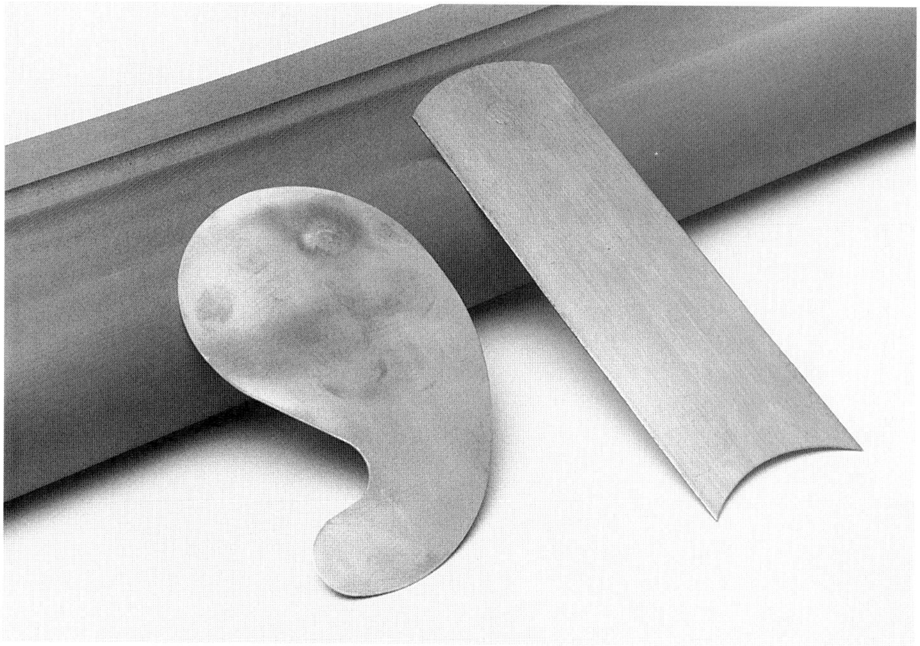

Curved scrapers can handle a wide range of scraping jobs. The scraper with convex/concave ends is suitable for bowl work or for scraping spindles. The comma-shaped scraper is used almost exclusively for fluting and bowl interiors. (Photo by Susan Kahn)

CURVED SCRAPERS

Curved scrapers are used for bowls, some types of fielded panels, turnings—in fact, anywhere that a curved form is necessary or will serve better than a rectangle. There are many shapes on the market; the two most common are shown in the photo at left.

The convex edges are most readily ground in the slack part of a belt sander. If a 280-grit belt (or finer) is used, no stoning is necessary. The concave edges can be ground on a suitably sized sanding drum. With both edges, some sort of fence or rest should be used to maintain a true 90° face on the scraper. If you have neither a belt sander nor sanding drums, you can stone the edges freehand.

Clamping and burnishing considerations for curved scrapers are the same as for rectangular scrapers.

SCRAPER PLANES

Hand-held scrapers tend not only to follow contours but also often emphasize them when used with bad technique. Scraper planes were developed to minimize this effect. A scraper plane is really just a cabinet scraper held in a steel body that makes the process more controllable in some aspects. You won't get the dishing effect mentioned earlier; with a plane the surface will be much more regular. The other great advantage of scraper planes is that you can work a piece of stock vigorously without tiring or burning your thumbs.

Scraper planes are not just jigged cabinet scrapers, however; their blades are designed differently. The blades are usually beveled and require a different burnishing technique than hand-held scrapers.

The bevel angle on scraper-plane blades is usually 45°, although some come with a factory grind of 30°. You might get a marginally cleaner cut in some woods with the lower bevel angle, but you also have a weaker hook and will experience more blade vibration. The 15° difference in bevel angle does not seem to make a great deal of difference when you come to burnishing a hook. Because of the bevel on the blade, a hook can be rolled on very easily. As shown in the drawing below, the burnishing angle should be about 15°. If you go as far as 20°, you get too much scraping and not enough cutting. The higher angle also increases blade chatter. If you go too far the other way (for example, as low as 5°), you risk curling the hook into a semicircle so that it will not cut at all.

If you use very light pressure when you are burnishing, you can get reasonably good cutting action over a fairly wide range of burnishing angles, but I find the tool works best with a fairly pronounced hook put on at 15°.

SCRAPER PLANES

The two types of scraper planes most commonly used today are similar to the Stanley #12 and the Stanley #80, both discontinued by Stanley in 1947, though replicas are now made by others. The Stanley #81 style, with its rosewood sole and nickel-plated body (discontinued in 1941), has not been replicated as far as I know.

The Stanley #12 had the great advantage of having a blade-angle adjustment built in. With this scraper, you can be fairly cavalier about your burnishing angle and adjust the blade angle to compensate. With the Stanley #80 and its cousins, there are no second chances. You have to get the angle right the first time.

From left to right, the Stanley #12, Stanley #81, Stanley #80 and Stanley #80 replica.

BURNISHING A SCRAPER-PLANE BLADE

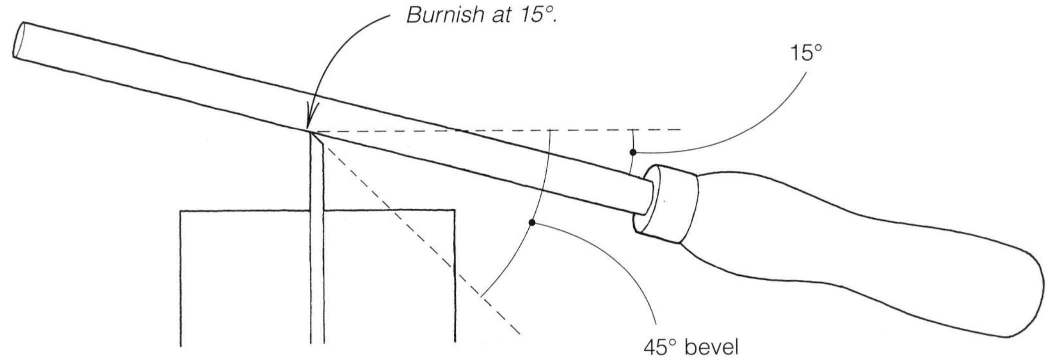

Just like hand-held cabinet scrapers, scraper-plane blades should be face-lapped to take out grinding marks, and the bevel should be honed with as much care as possible. These blades are too wide to fit most honing guides, so they usually must be sharpened freehand. It makes everything much simpler if you have a jointer with a 45° setting as well as the 90° setting for hand-held scrapers. Well jointed, the blades can be honed quickly freehand, or you can hold them next to a guide beveled at 45°, as shown in the photo below.

To hone a scraper-plane blade, clamp the blade against a 45° block and pass the stone across the bevel. The tape wrapped around the stone prevents abrasion of the block.

The craftsman-made scratch stock at left was made to form the cap molding shown. The commercial beading tool at right has interchangeable blades for beading, reeding and fluting. (Photo by Susan Kahn)

SCRATCH STOCKS

Blades for scratch stocks (also called beading tools) are scrapers. You can bevel the edge or you can leave it square. Both edges work well in hardwoods and are more forgiving in softwoods than regular cabinet scrapers. Since blades for scratch stocks are frequently craftsman-made, you should concentrate on getting the profile you want, hone that profile and then turn your attention to the faces of the blade. I say faces specifically because I believe that a square-edge scratch stock is more versatile than a beveled-edge blade since it allows you to cut in either direction. You can always be cutting with the grain.

With the profile finished, it is a simple matter to lap the faces of the blade as required to get a smooth finish and create a sharp edge. The coarseness of stone you start with will be dictated by the nature of the stock that you chose for your blade. Highly polished stock will need little work; coarsely ground stock will need quite a bit. In any event, once you have a crisp edge on the blade you will find that you can use it for quite a long time before it needs to be resharpened.

This is one scraper blade that you lap only, not burnish. In general, you should avoid touching the profile after it has been initially formed and honed; you need only lap the blade to resharpen it. Lapping the blade will make it marginally thinner each time you sharpen, but it is easier than trying to maintain an accurate profile through repeated honings of the profile itself. Besides, the blade is usually made for a specific project and will not see that much use.

PAINT SCRAPERS

Most paints are very abrasive because of the pigments in them, and as a result they are very hard on a sharp edge. The person who coined the term "working edge" must have been thinking of paint scrapers. I always take "working edge" to mean an edge that is not particularly sharp but is functional. That seems appropriate for a paint scraper.

For resharpenable-blade scrapers (including disposable-blade scrapers), I recommend sharpening on a 1-in. belt sander with a 120x belt. You get a remarkably good edge, and you get it quickly.

For people doing a lot of serious paint scraping, there are very inexpensive carbide paint scrapers on the market that are far more durable than steel ones. The blades are reversible and inexpensive. If you must scrape paint, you might as well treat yourself to one of these scrapers as compensation for having to do such a miserable job.

RESTORATION SCRAPERS

Anyone who has had to remove several layers of old finish in any restoration project knows the nightmare of trying to get even a thoroughly softened finish out of nooks and crannies. The easiest way to do it, particularly if you are dealing with a fair amount of reeding and fluting, is to make scrapers to fit the profile of the moldings.

An excellent raw material for making these scrapers is commercial steel strapping. It comes in a variety of widths, but the ½-in. steel strapping seems to be about the handiest. Strapping is spring steel of relatively low Rockwell hardness, which is quite easy to file and grind. The narrow bands are particularly useful for getting into difficult areas. The profiles you need can be made very quickly using files, a belt sander and sanding drums.

As with blades for scratch stocks, it is easiest to leave the edge square so that you can work with the grain at all times. You can even shape a piece to clean up a bit of router burn on new work. A square-end piece of strapping can be used to winkle glue out of corners, and you will also find that you can burnish a hook on strapping to make a small, flexible cabinet scraper. As you may have noticed, all this has very little to do with sharpening, but it's such a useful idea that I could not resist including it. Besides, the strapping can be had free-of-charge almost anywhere that goods on pallets are being handled.

Refinishing scrapers made of steel strapping are handy for removing finish from moldings. (Photo by Susan Kahn)

REFINISHING SCRAPERS

When stripping off an old finish, you can scratch a patina if you use a metal scraper. Often you want to maintain the patina and therefore need scrapers that will not mark the surface in any way. Scrapers made from a close-grained hardwood (boxwood is best) do an excellent job and will not damage the piece being worked on. It is also a simple matter to make small wooden scrapers to fit specific moldings. You can get very crisp edges on such scrapers that will do an excellent job of removing a softened finish.

Hardwood refinishing scrapers. (Photo by Susan Kahn)

CHAPTER 12

HANDSAWS

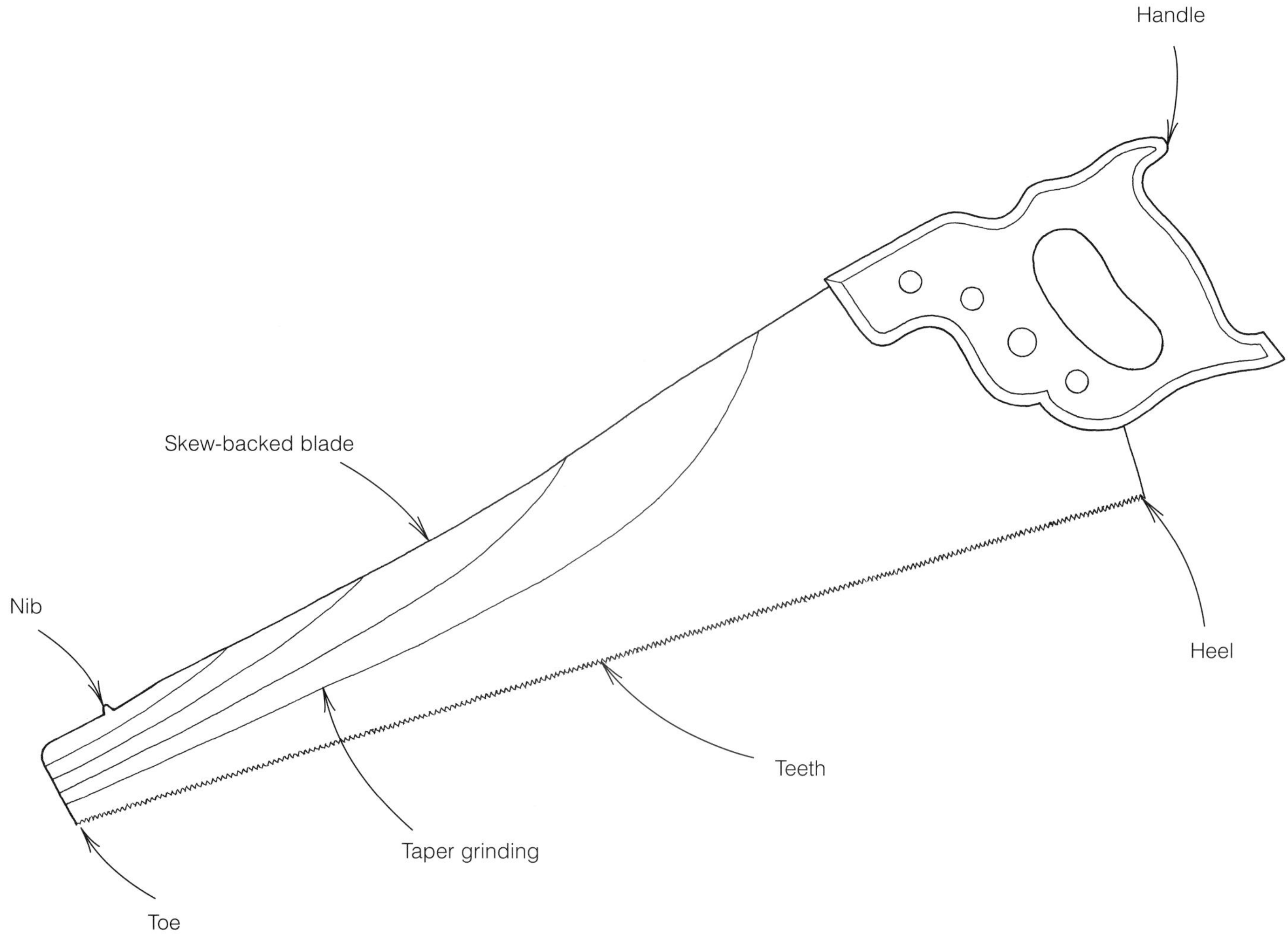

SAW TEETH

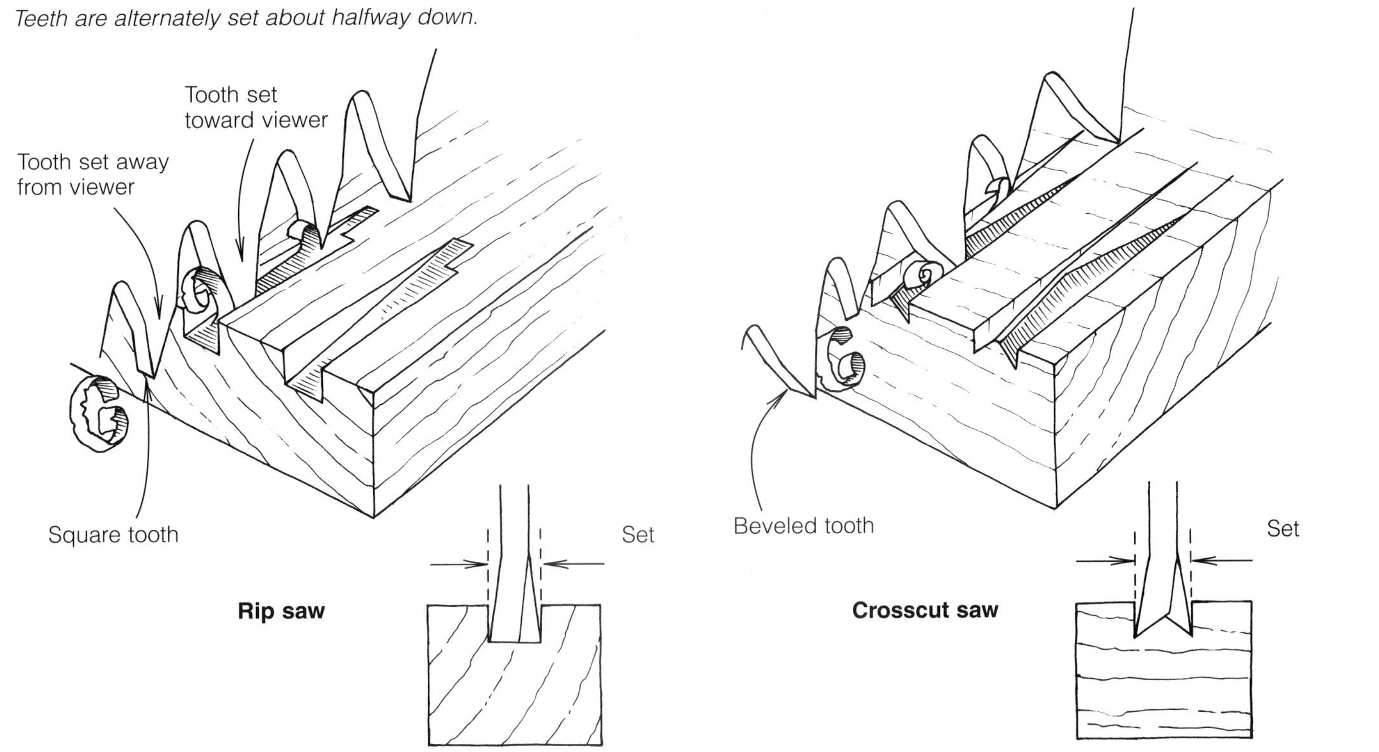

Although most people use powered saws today, a good understanding of handsaws is basic to understanding power saws because power tools are really just hand tools operating at speed.

There is another reason to pay particular attention to sharpening handsaws: It is nearly impossible to find a sharpening service today that will sharpen your handsaws as well as you can do it yourself the very first time you try. If you value your saws or even if you just want them to operate efficiently, it is worth spending some time learning how to sharpen them.

HOW SAWS WORK

A saw is just a number of tiny chisels arranged in a linear pattern designed to cut small chips of wood and carry them out of the kerf. The tips of the small chisels, called teeth on a saw, are shaped according to whether the saw will be cutting with the grain or across the grain, in dry wood or in green wood, in softwood or in hardwood, and so on. In every instance, you want the saw to work as efficiently as possible, with the greatest cutting speed and the least effort.

The two simplest cases to consider are the standard rip saw and the standard crosscut saw. As the drawing above shows, a rip saw has square teeth because it is designed to cut with the grain. A crosscut saw has beveled teeth because it cuts across the grain and must sever fibers, not just divide them. Obviously, a lot of sawing is done somewhere between these two orientations, and this will be dealt with in more detail later. For the moment, a good rule of thumb is that you normally use a crosscut saw if you are cutting across the grain at any angle. Only when you are cutting parallel to the grain do you use a rip saw.

For a saw to work effectively, a few other conditions have to be met:

Adequate set The kerf that the saw makes in wood must be wider than the thickness of the blade to prevent the saw from binding. To attain this wider kerf, the teeth are bent, or "set," slightly outward. How much set the teeth are given depends on the saw type and the wood to be cut. On a fine-toothed backsaw for use with dry hardwood, 0.005 in. would be adequate; for a two-man crosscut saw in green wood, 0.020 in. would be more appropriate. There is much more fiber springback in green wood than in dry.

Jointed teeth Teeth performing the same function should be at the same height in order to do the same amount of work. Uneven heights create inefficiency and uneven wear. Regular jointing keeps teeth even.

Adequate gullets The space between teeth has to be large enough to carry the accumulation of chips created by the sawing process until the chips can be dumped outside the kerf. The total space is determined by the distance between teeth and the depth of the gullets.

Effective rake The leading edge of the tooth must be formed at the most efficient angle for creating the chip.

GENERAL SHARPENING PROCEDURES

To ensure that saws meet these various requirements, the sharpening process involves the following steps: jointing, shaping, setting and pointing. Although not all steps are necessary each time, they are always performed in the same sequence. For example, if a saw requires only setting and pointing it should be done in that sequence, not in reverse.

JOINTING

A saw should be jointed every time that it is filed. I can hear the rustle of rising eyebrows out there, but keeping even tooth height is so basic to good saw operation that it should be constantly maintained. This is not a big deal. If a saw needs sharpening, it obviously has dull teeth. Passing a jointer over the teeth is not going to dull them much more, but it will ensure that they are all the same height. Besides that, any time you joint a saw you should only joint it until you just touch the shortest tooth. Any jointing past that point is a waste of saw and a waste of sharpening time. Often, a single pass with the jointer is all that is needed.

To maintain even tooth height, a saw should be jointed every time it is sharpened. This backsaw shows the uneven tooth pattern that can result if a saw is not jointed.

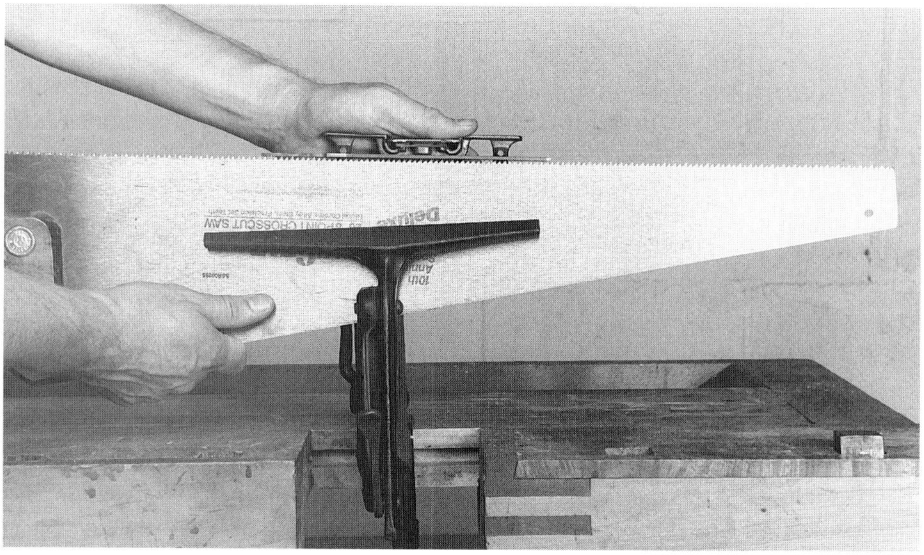

Joint a saw by passing a mill file over the teeth. A jointer holds the file at 90° to the blade. (Photo by Susan Kahn)

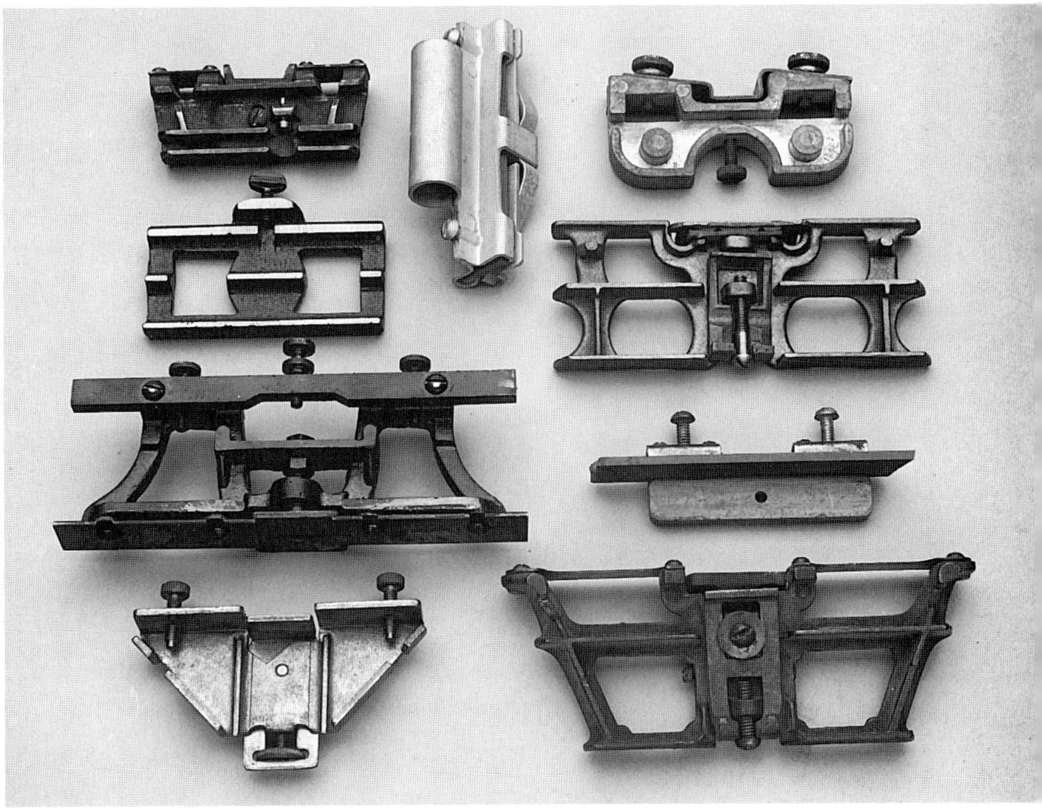

A selection of saw jointers. Each one will clamp a file, but some have integral screws that allow you to bow the file and some have raker gauges.

Jointing a saw is much like jointing a cabinet scraper. If you turn to the sidebar on p. 132, you'll find a variety of suggestions for making jointers. Alternatively, you can buy one from any specialty tool dealer; you can also find excellent saw jointers in flea markets, garage sales and antique shops. A few styles are shown in the photo at right. The really exotic ones will not only do flat jointing but have an integral screw that can be used to flex a file to match the crown (or circle) of a saw. Such a jointer might also include a raker gauge and setting gauge, as well as the facility to mount a file for side-dressing a saw. I have never been able to resist buying just one more jointer; the result of my decades of weakness is that I had no trouble at all trotting out the selection shown in the photo.

SHAPING

If you perform all the other sharpening functions well, you should never have to worry about shaping teeth. However, if you have been slovenly (or if you want to restore or convert a saw), you will have to address the question of tooth shaping.

After jointing, you may be faced with a tooth pattern that looks something like that shown in the drawing below. This pattern is evidence of bad previous sharpening technique, and the only thing you can do with a blade like this is to shape the teeth properly before you go any further in the sharpening process. To shape the teeth, file directly across the blade. Only after you have all the teeth properly shaped should you go on to bevel them. Experienced saw filers can do both at once, but I suggest that you try the two-step method first.

Bad tooth pattern requires reshaping of teeth.

For crosscut saws that are going to be used both in hardwood and softwood, the rake angle of the teeth is negative, varying from 15° for quite an aggressive cut to 30°, which is the standard peg-tooth pattern (see the drawing at right). The 30° angle will give a smoother cut than a 15° rake but will also sacrifice some speed and sawdust-clearing ability. When we look at two-man crosscut saws and Swede saws later in this chapter, we will deal almost exclusively with the higher negative rake angles because these saws have raker teeth that handle the bulk of sawdust clearing.

Rip saws usually have 0° of rake, though they are sometimes given a bit of negative rake for better control in difficult grain conditions.

Dealing with a messy tooth pattern of the type shown in the drawing on p. 145 is a bit tricky. The best thing to do

RAKE ANGLES

Rake for crosscut teeth

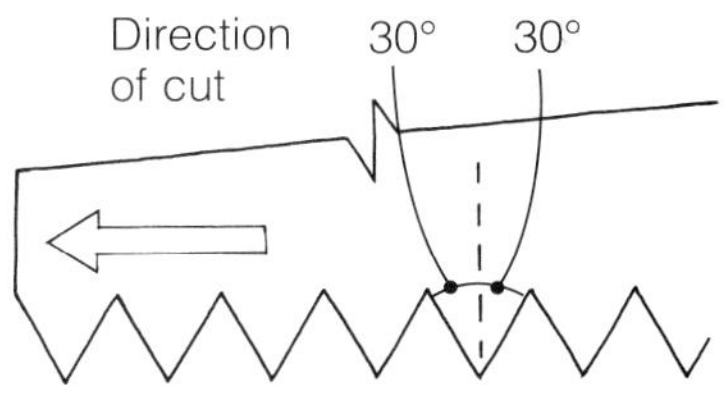

Standard peg tooth

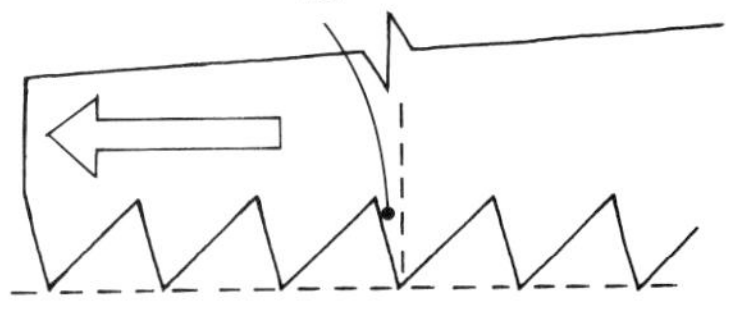

Aggressive pattern

Rake for rip teeth

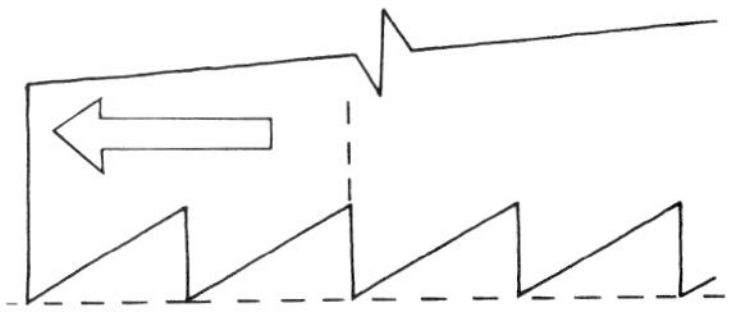

Standard 0° rake

Use a rake-angle guide held horizontally to maintain the correct tooth rake angle. The guide is a small, flat block, drilled to accept the file tip, that press-fits onto the end of the file. (Note that for better illustration the filing stance shown here is more open than usual.)

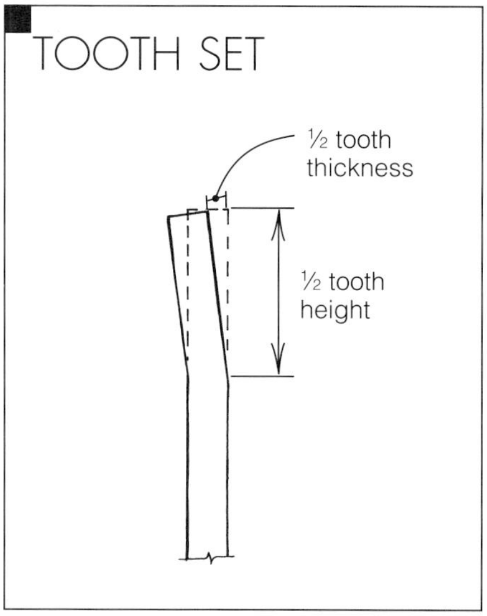

Dealing with a messy tooth pattern of the type shown in the drawing on p. 145 is a bit tricky. The best thing to do is mark a new gullet-bottom line and cut all the gullets down to a common base line. To establish greater control of the process you should make a rake-angle guide to slide onto the tip of your file, as shown in the photo above. You will quickly find in filing saws that it is very handy to have handles on both ends of the file. You are always controlling at least two angles when you are filing (the rake angle and the 90° angle to the blade), and most people can use all the help they can get. As you are reshaping the teeth you need only keep the guide horizontal to ensure that you are putting the correct rake angle on the front of every tooth. Using the guide and a scribed base line, you should be able to recreate a regular tooth pattern.

As you are filing, you will find that one face of the file will cut more aggressively than the other. You can compensate for this with hand pressure, equalizing the amount of bite when desirable. This is one of the few times that you will do all the filing from one side of the saw. The only thing you are worried about in shaping is getting the correct rake angle and depth of gullet, and this can all be done from one side where you have marked the base line for the gullets.

After you have completed shaping the teeth, it is a good idea to pass the jointer over the saw again. You do this for two reasons: first, because you've probably not done a perfect job of shaping, so a light jointing would be useful anyway; and second, because you need tiny flats on the tips of the teeth in order to guide you later in the sharpening process.

SETTING

Most saws have too much set for cabinetmakers. They are set for general-purpose use in both hardwoods and softwoods at all sorts of moisture contents. If you are going to be using a saw only for dry wood, it requires less set, and if you are going to be using it only for dry hardwood, you require less yet. In general, a saw cuts the straightest with the least amount of set. Excessive set allows the blade to flop about in the kerf, changing cutting angles as it does so.

A couple of other points worth noting are that you should never reverse the direction of set of a tooth; it weakens the tooth unacceptably and could even break it. Also, set only the top half of a tooth. The depth gauge on your saw-setting tool should regulate this quite easily. An amount of set equal to half the thickness of the tooth should be ample. This will give a kerf that is double the thickness of the saw blade, which is more than enough in anything but the wettest and softest of woods.

There are numerous tools for setting saw teeth, but the most practical one is the commercial pistol-grip sawset. The sawset should have a dial anvil that is adjustable for the number of teeth per inch and for the setting height on the tooth. When you are buying such a sawset, try to find an old one that has a range from 4 to 16 tpi. Most, if not all, on the market today have a range from only 4 to 12 tpi. If you have one of the latter sawsets, you can cheat your way up past 12 tpi by reducing the amount of tooth that you set. A given set angle applied to the top quarter of a tooth will result in half the amount of offset that would be the case if it were applied to the top half of the tooth. With this knowledge filed away, you should be able to adapt your sawset to your needs even if it is a 4 to 12 tpi model.

To set the teeth, clamp the saw in a vise and set every other tooth. Squeezing the handles of the sawset together drives a beveled punch against an anvil, bending the teeth outward. When half of the teeth have been set, reverse the saw in the vise and set the balance of the teeth. Try to use the same amount of pressure for setting each tooth and ensure that the sawset is resting squarely on the teeth each time.

Like jointers, sawsets were (and still are) available in a wide range of styles, from the pistol-grip models at left to the plier styles at right.

With the saw clamped in a vise, use a sawset to bend the top half of the teeth alternately to the left and right.

POINTING THE TEETH

Normally called "sharpening" (even though the word should refer to the whole shaping process not just one step), pointing the teeth is the step in the process where you establish the cutting bevels and eliminate the flats from the jointing process, all without changing the tooth outline. Filing of a Western saw is always performed after the teeth are set; with Japanese saws, the teeth are sometimes set first.

Of particular importance in this process is to use a vise that clamps the saw firmly. There are various

CLAMPING A SAW

All saw filing except jointing requires a vise that will clamp the saw as close as possible to the teeth (to minimize vibration) and not get in the way in any of the filing processes. The best saw vises are the old ones that clamp to a table top and are jointed for tilting (see the photo on the facing page). These vises are slim at the top and ground slightly hollow so that clamping pressure is equalized across their width.

You can readily make a wooden clamp that drops into a bench vise or mechanic's vise to serve the same purpose. Since the hinges are not mortised, the jaws will tilt inward slightly on any saw being held. This should compensate for any bowing of the clamp as pressure is applied to it by the vise. If your woodworking vise does not have a jaw that is slightly canted in at the top (as it should be), you may have to apply a few layers of tape just below the riding ledge on one side to ensure that sufficient clamping pressure is transferred to the jaw end of the clamp.

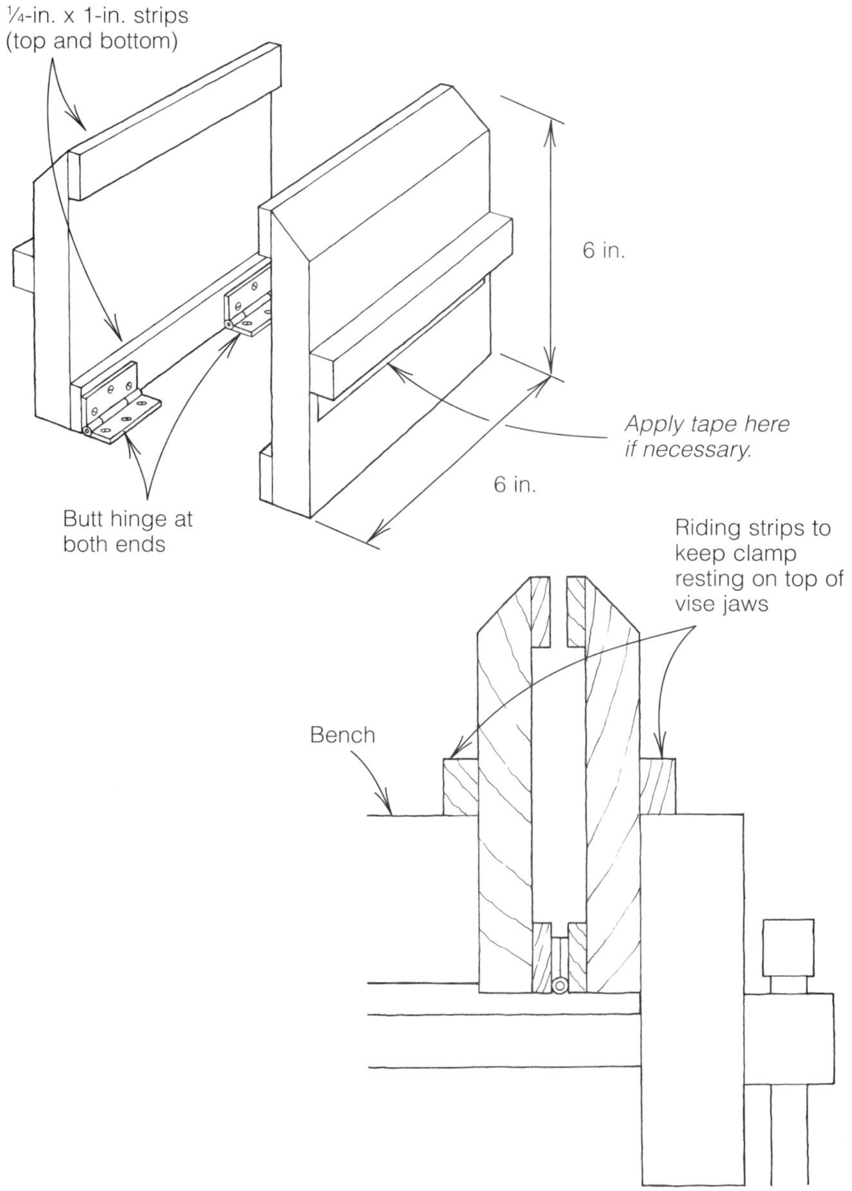

commercial vises available, or you can make a simple wooden one as shown in the sidebar at left.

As a minor complication in the filing process, you should use files that are specific to the number of teeth per inch in the saw, as detailed below:

7-in. regular	5 to 5½ tpi
7-in. extra slim	8 tpi
6-in. extra slim	10 tpi
6-in. double extra slim	12 tpi
4-in. extra slim	15 tpi
4-in. double extra slim	22 tpi

This advice may seem somewhat odd since these are all triangular files, all have 60° face intersections and all will fit between the teeth of any of the saws listed. But there is a logic to it all. As the files reduce in size, the cut becomes finer. In addition, the flats on the files are equal to slightly more than double the face length of the teeth for which they are specified. In essence, this gives you three complete files in one. This gradation system balances the wear on the file, because you are never using more than half of the adjoining flats at any one time (see the drawing below). If, on the other hand, you were to use a 6-in. extra slim to file a 5-point saw, the file would be useless once two of the flats were dulled.

USING THE CORRECT FILE

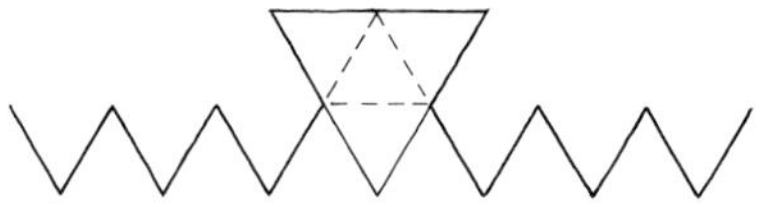

As this file becomes worn in use, it can be rotated to an unused corner with fresh, sharp teeth.

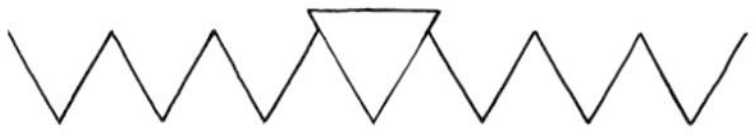

This file is useless after it becomes worn in one orientation. Rotation will give you one sharp side and one side that is two-thirds dull.

Obviously, you do not have to hew religiously to the table on the facing page, but you would certainly find it difficult to sharpen a dovetail saw with a 7-in. regular saw file. The cut would be too coarse, and you would have a hard time seeing what you were doing.

A variety of other files are used for sharpening saws (e.g., web-saw files, great American crosscut files), but triangular files are all you need for rip and crosscut handsaws.

CROSSCUT SAWS

Crosscut saws are the most commonly used style of saw and will therefore be the ones most frequently sharpened. Regardless of the size of saw or the number of teeth per inch, the procedure is the same, although some of the equipment might change.

JOINTING

The only variation from the standard jointing process is if you have a saw with a bit of crown in it (such as breasted handsaws, flooring saws and many log saws). You have three choices in jointing such a saw.

If you have a jointing jig with an integral screw to set file camber, set the camber to a point just less than the crown of the saw. Some jointers have outrigger shoes to accommodate saws with camber. If you have such a jointer, you can use it, or you can make outrigger shoes to retrofit an existing jointer. The easiest approach, and an eminently practical one, is to run the jointer over the teeth in a nice, even sweep; you will find that you can maintain the crown quite adequately in the process.

As always, joint only until you have touched the shortest tooth.

CARING FOR YOUR HANDSAW

Just like a chisel or a plane blade, you cannot afford to have rust on a saw. You will not get a crisp junction between the side of the blade and the filed portion of the bevel if the blade is rusted. Any rust on a blade should be removed before the sharpening process starts, because most methods of removing the rust will also cause some dulling.

Depending on the design of the saw and the amount of rust, the rust can be removed by stoning, steel wool or emery cloth. Emery cloth is usually the most practical. Unlike a stone, it can be used on a saw that has set in the teeth and, unlike steel wool, will fracture and remove any rust blisters on the steel. Only very fine emery cloth should be used to leave the saw with the smoothest possible finish.

After removing any rust and sharpening the saw, you should get in the habit of giving your saw a thin coat of wax. The wax will not only reduce any friction in the kerf but also protect the saw from rust between uses. There are many good waxes on the market for treating machine surfaces (jointer beds, table-saw tops, etc.), and all will serve well with saw blades.

Finally, if handsaws are taken out of the shop, they should be protected with blade guards or a suitable saw case. As with most other tools, they are dulled more frequently through carelessness than through cutting wood.

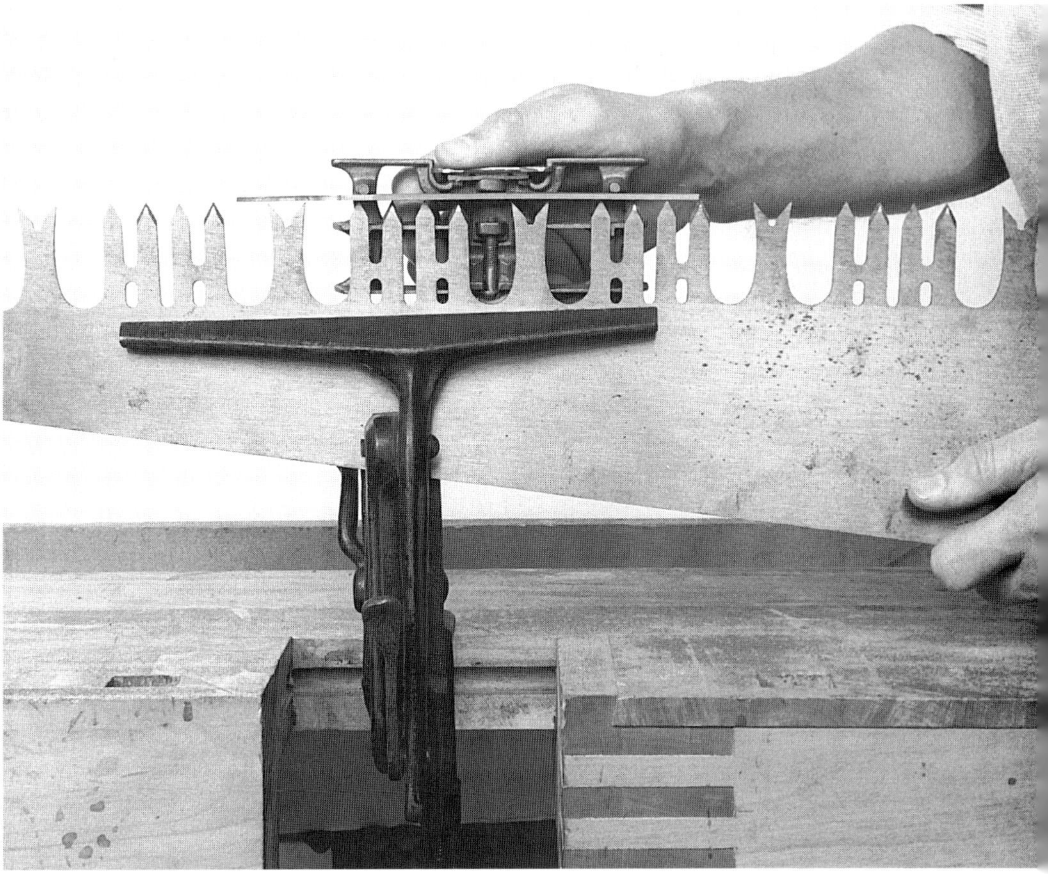

One way to joint a saw with a crowned blade is to use a jointer that has a screw to set file camber. (Photo by Susan Kahn)

TOOTH BEVEL ANGLES

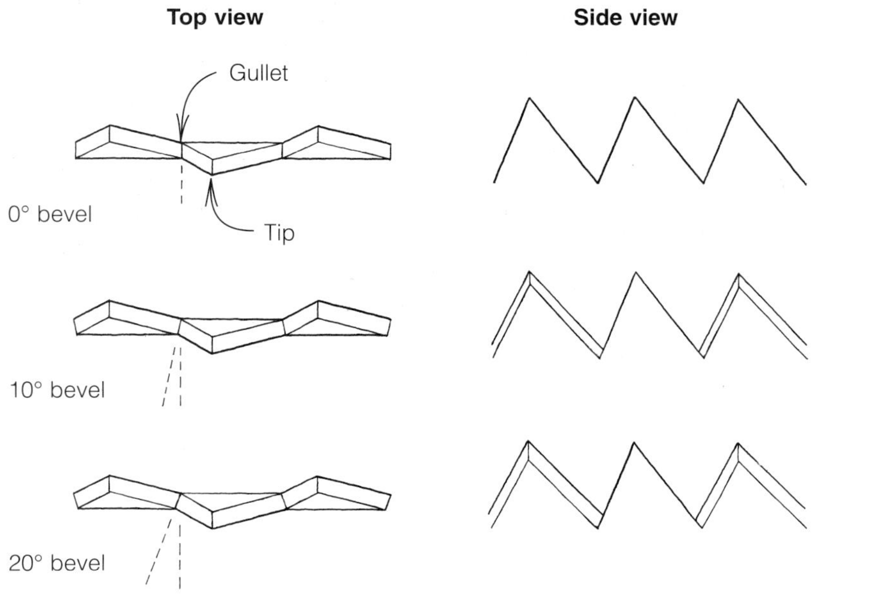

GULLET ANGLES AND FILES

For Western saws, gullet angles are always stated as 60° because triangular saws (with equal face widths) are standard. For accuracy, it should be noted that the gullet angle is only 60° for saws with no tooth bevel (i.e., rip saws). As bevel is introduced, the gullet angle increases. For example, at 45° of bevel the gullet angle is about 81° (see the drawing at right).

This increase becomes quite significant when you get to higher bevel angles, for example, what you might need on a Swede-saw blade. If you intend to maintain a 60° gullet angle, it is only possible to use a triangular saw file if you also drop the file handle the same number of degrees as the bevel angle. With 10° of bevel, drop the handle 10° below horizontal; with 30° of bevel, drop the handle 30°, and so on.

In practical terms, this is not worth the effort. It is better to set your rake angle and bevel angle and then file at whatever angle to the horizontal you find comfortable. You will not have 60° gullet angles, but it is doubtful that the variation from 60° will materially affect the performance of your saw. In fact, as you use higher bevel angles the tips of the teeth have a more fragile configuration. If the included angle at the tip increases (as it would if the file is not tilted enough to compensate), it tends to strengthen the tip.

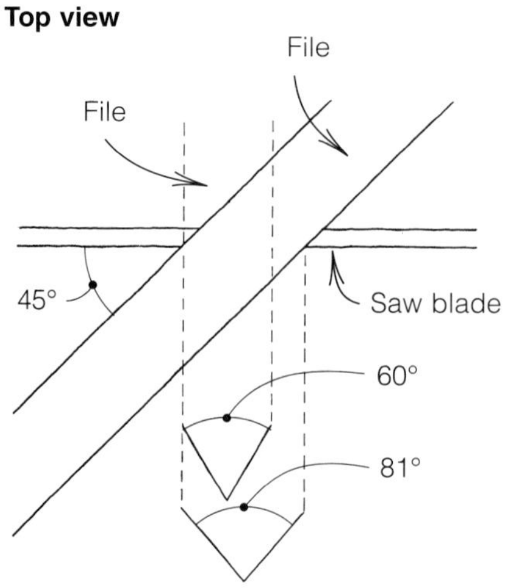

SHAPING AND SETTING THE TEETH

Very seldom is reshaping necessary in the full process dealt with earlier, but it is useful each time you sharpen a saw to check the general tooth pattern to see if any irregularity is creeping in. A bit of adept filing can often correct the problem in time to avoid a full-blown reshaping session. If you joint the saw regularly, you will maintain tooth shape effortlessly.

Set the teeth as explained on p. 147, making sure that you have the dial anvil set for the correct number of teeth per inch and that you use equal pressure on each tooth.

POINTING THE TEETH

To point the teeth, put the saw in the vise with the teeth no more than ¼ in. above the vise jaws. Choose the amount of bevel (or "fleam") that you want for the teeth. This is usually around 10° but could be as much as 45° depending upon exactly what you are going to use the saw for.

At 10° you really just have a modified rip saw, whereas at 45° you will have a crosscut saw that goes through wood like butter but will require frequent sharpening. It will also work best cutting directly cross grain and will diminish in effectiveness in angle cuts as it approaches the parallel grain (or rip) configuration. As a general rule, you will find that anything between 10° and 20° will give you a general-purpose crosscut. Above that, it becomes a faster-cutting saw but one that is more intolerant of variable grain alignment.

With your file aligned with a bevel guide, drop the handle the same number of degrees as the amount of bevel you are using (see the sidebar at left). This means that you will be filing up toward the tips of the teeth. Not only does this tilt maintain the 60° gullet angle, but it also substantially reduces vibration. If you did not file upwards in this way, you would find that no matter how careful you were the saw would vibrate annoyingly just as it tends to do when filing rip teeth.

Remember that you are sharpening two faces at once (the back of one tooth and the face of another) and that you want to remove only about half of the flat on the tip of any tooth (the other half will be removed when you file from the other side). File confidently with a smooth, firm stroke. You will very quickly develop the pattern and find after a while that you do not need the bevel guide—you will be too busy checking tops of teeth to pay any attention to it anyway.

Tremendously helpful in all of this is the correct light. Natural light is best, and you should have your vise set up facing a window, not a point source of light. If you sit at the right height, flats on the tip of the teeth will shine like beacons and you will have no difficulty gauging your progress (see the bottom photo at right).

Once you have filed half of the teeth, reverse the saw and do the other half.

DRESSING THE BLADE

Filing a saw leaves a burr on the teeth. This wire edge is usually left on, but it can be removed if you wish. Before you even think of deburring the blade, try a test cut. If you have been a bit light with your set, you may want every scrap of burr on the teeth for kerf clearance.

Another reason to take a test cut first is to see if the saw has any tendency to run in the cut. If this is the first time you have ever sharpened a saw, there is an excellent chance that you filed off a bit too much when you reversed the saw in the vise. You not only filed until the flats disappeared but you took an extra little poke just to be sure. Having all the teeth set one way just a bit shorter than all the teeth set the other way is virtually guaranteed to cause the saw to fade to the side with the longer teeth.

If this is the case with your saw, take a fairly fine stone (1200x or finer) and dress the saw teeth on the side to which the blade is running. Dressing removes the burr on the teeth and will also remove a bit of the set.

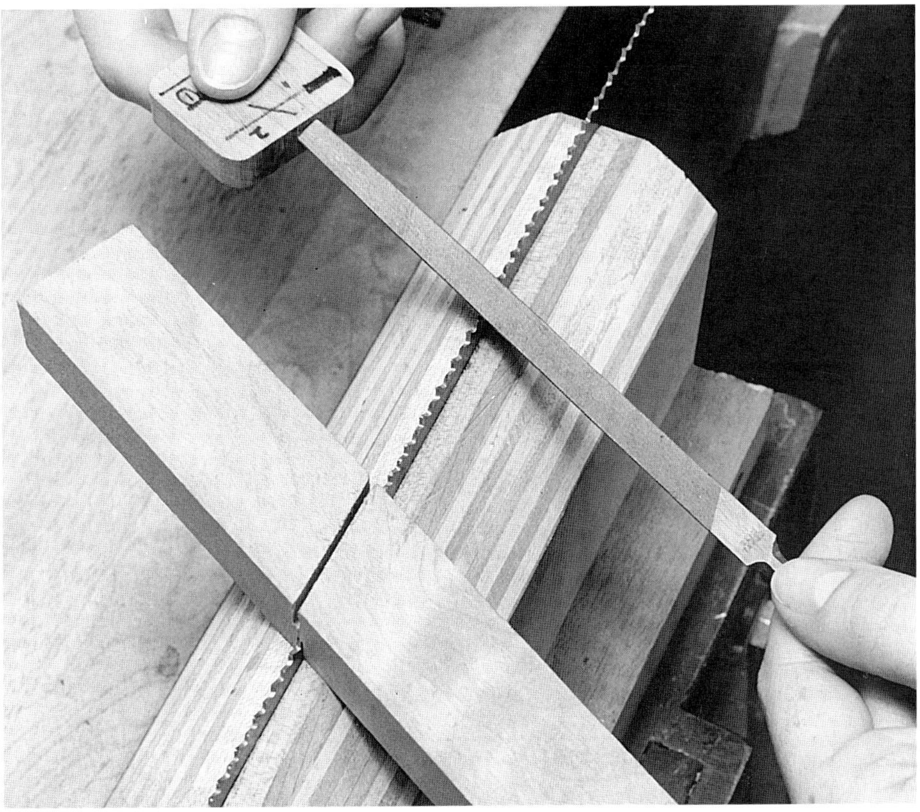

A bevel guide slipped over the blade helps you maintain the correct bevel angle when filing crosscut saws.

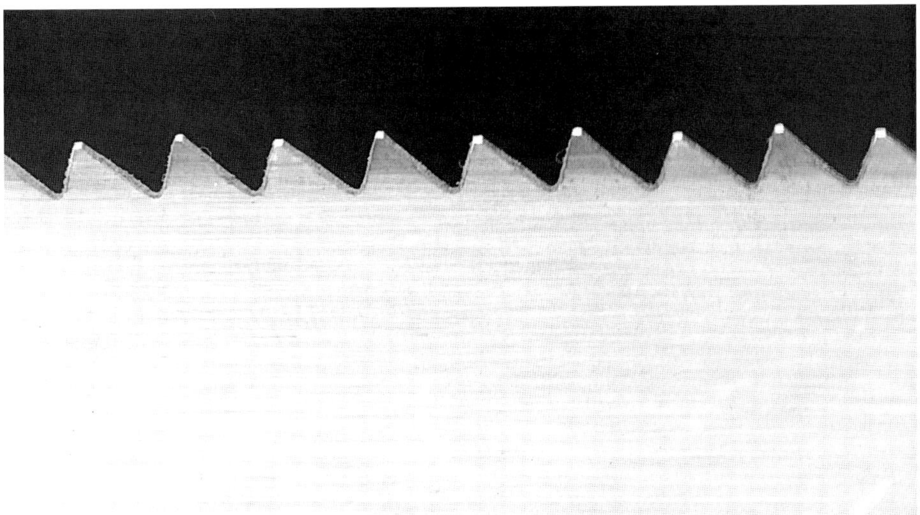

Light reflected from the jointed teeth serves as a visual reference when pointing tooth tips.

Take another test cut. If the saw now runs true, be grateful that you got out of trouble so easily. If it now runs to the other side, take a light dressing off the opposite side of the teeth. If this is done carefully, you should not have to go past dressing one side only. At worst, you should go only as far as a light dressing on the second side. If it still runs, rejoint, reset if necessary and take greater care in filing.

RIP SAWS

Rip saws are jointed and set in the same manner as crosscut saws, but the teeth are pointed differently. Rip teeth usually have 0° of rake and are filed straight across the saw. Keep the file horizontal and at 90° to the blade (see the drawing below). The saw should be clamped low in the vise with no more distance between the bottom of the gullet and the top edge of the vise than you need for filing room.

It is easy to get vibration when you file straight across the saw, and you will end up putting an edge on your own teeth as well as the saw's teeth. It is just marginally more pleasant than fingernails on a blackboard.

Theoretically, you could file all the teeth from one side of the saw, but it is a good idea to file every other one, reverse the saw in the vise and then file the balance. This puts an even amount of burr on both sides of the saw and also compensates for any bias that you have in the system. You might be dropping the file handle 5°, or you might be filing at 85° instead of 90°. In either case, if you make the same errors on both sides of the saw they will tend to balance out.

For ripping very dense wood with wild grain, you may want to put some bevel, or fleam, on the tooth of your rip saw (about 10° should do). Not only does a little bit of fleam help with wild grain, but it allows a rip saw to work better in a cut that is slightly diagonal to the grain.

POINTING RIPSAW TEETH

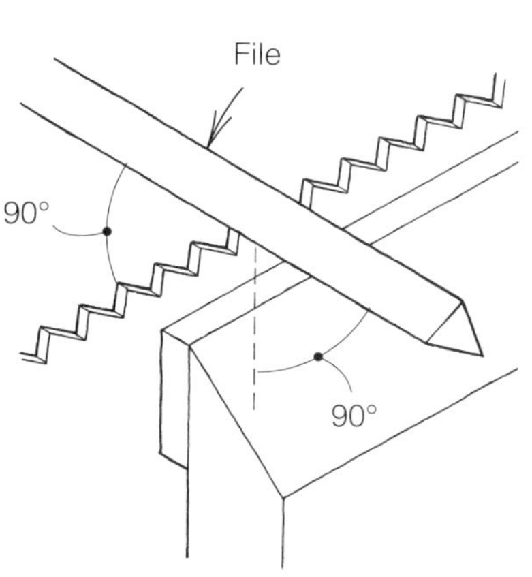

TROUBLESHOOTING A RIP SAW

If you find that your rip saw is hard to use—you have a hard time starting the cut, for example—you may want to modify the tooth pattern. As well as putting a bit of fleam on the tooth to handle difficult grain, you may also want to put up to 10° of negative rake on the tooth as well. In essence, what you are doing is converting the rip saw into a combination rip and crosscut saw. There is nothing particularly wrong in this. It will make the saw a little slower in the ripping process but more controllable in difficult woods or in bias cuts. You do what you have to do to make it work for you.

FINE-TOOTHED SAWS

Filing and pointing saws with very fine teeth can present some problems. Since most pistol-grip sawsets will not accommodate saws with more than 16 teeth per inch, you either have to use an alternative setting technique or cheat in the manner mentioned on p. 147, where you use the sawset at the 16 tpi setting but set a smaller portion of tooth.

An alternative is to clamp the saw to a piece of hardwood and set the teeth with a pin punch and a small hammer. This is not as difficult as it sounds, and the minor variations in set can be corrected with side dressing after the teeth have been pointed.

For pointing very fine teeth (as on a gent's saw), you may find that a 4-in. double-extra slim saw file is still too large and it may be necessary to use either a feather-edge file or a very fine (#3 or #4 cut) triangular needle file. For extremely fine saws (such as blitz saws and slotting saws), you might have to use a magnifying glass and the teeth should be filed square across the blade. Filed alternately, you will find that the amount of burr left from filing gives the blade adequate set, which is a good thing because it is nearly impossible to do a competent job of setting teeth finer than 25 tpi with normal shop equipment.

DOVETAIL SAWS

If you use a saw only for dovetail work, you will find that rip-sharpened teeth with 10° of negative rake, 10° of bevel and minimum set will work very well. I recommend this bias toward the rip pattern, because you will undoubtedly have other saws for crosscutting but this might be your only choice for dovetailing; you want to be sure that it works as well as possible in this use even if that limits its use elsewhere. And since dovetailing is essentially ripping, the saw should be sharpened accordingly.

Many years ago I asked a Scottish cabinetmaker if he would tell me exactly how he went about sharpening his dovetail saw. He laughed and said that he had never had the nerve to try. He had been using it for some fifteen years for cutting dovetails, and at his current rate of production he felt he would never have to sharpen it and he certainly had no intention of doing so. He said that it took him long enough to adapt himself to its idiosyncrasies and that he had no intention of introducing new ones. I have thought of his comments many times since and have found other cabinetmakers who did not have the nerve to touch their dovetail saws. I leave it to you to determine where the line is between bravery and stupidity in this field.

VENEER SAWS

The two most common types of veneer saws are the French style, which has a curved blade with the teeth raked toward the center from either side, and the standard, rest-of-the-world style, which has peg teeth cut to chisel tips. Regardless of which type you own, you will probably never have to file either one because you need to cut a huge amount of veneer to wear the teeth down to the point that they need filing.

If you should ever need to file a veneer saw, file it straight across like a rip saw. You are not really sharpening the teeth when you file the saw but redefining them. You sharpen the teeth by stoning the bevels. With the French-style, the teeth are beveled on one side only. Stone the flat and the bevel with the finest, hardest stone you have. With the rest-of-the-world style, stone both bevels with a trailing stroke.

Two styles of veneer saws: at left, a French veneer saw; at right, a standard veneer saw. (Photo by Susan Kahn)

VENEER-SAW BEVELS

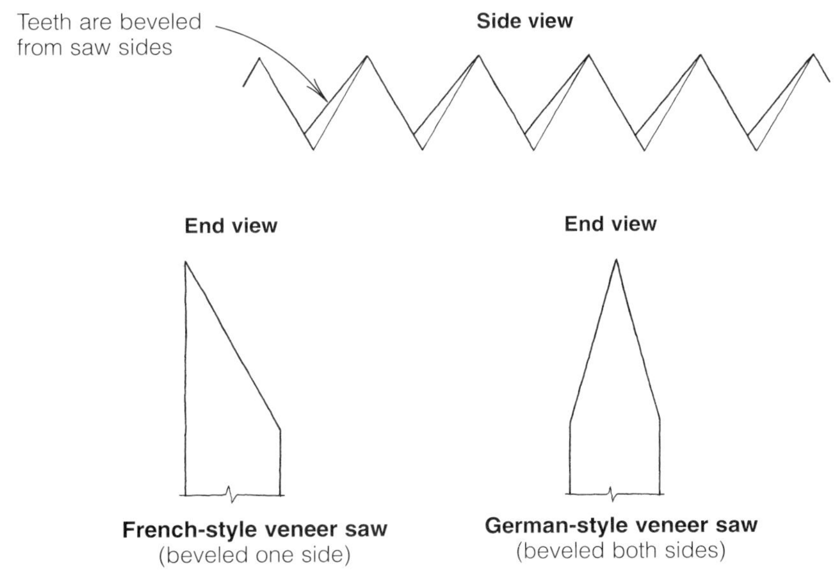

TWO-MAN CROSSCUT SAWS

Two-man crosscut saws are little used today, although they were a vital part of the logging industry well into this century. There are two reasons to include them in this book. First, a good understanding of two-man crosscuts gives us a better understanding of Japanese saws (see pp. 158-161), which are very popular today. Second, there is a renewed interest in logging-arts competitions in North America, and competitors desperately search for detailed sharpening information in the hopes that they can knock a couple of seconds off their best log-buck time.

Although two-man crosscuts come in two basic styles, felling and bucking, only the bucking saw will be dealt with here. The sharpening considerations for a felling saw are almost exactly the same, since the only real difference is that a felling saw is much thinner and more flexible, reflecting the

THE ONE-MAN SAW

There were numerous inventions in the 1800s aimed at easing the lot of the sawyer who either had to or wanted to work alone. One device that left little imprint in the sawdust of time was Giles' Drag Sawing Machine (shown at right). It is hard to conceive of a device more difficult to move around in the bush.

But the one enduring tip for the feller was to use a "rubberman." Most felling saws were too thin and flexible to be used by one man. They could not be pushed through the cut; they had to be pulled. A shop tip of the 1800s was to use a strong rubber band on one end of the saw to draw the saw back and to keep the end from flopping in the dirt. This assist was called a rubberman.

Giles' Drag Sawing Machine.

CROSSCUT-SAW TOOTH PATTERNS

Lance tooth

Lance-perforated tooth

Champion tooth

requirements of its specific use and the fact that it was almost invariably a two-man saw.

The bucking saw, on the other hand, is used as a two-man saw in competition today but was made stiffer and heavier than the felling saw so that it could be used by a single sawyer. The rigidity was needed for the push stroke in one-man use, and the weight was needed to increase the speed of cut.

Further simplifying things, the only tooth pattern that will be considered here is the lance-perforated tooth (see the drawing at left). The considerations are nearly the same as those for the champion tooth, the other popular style. The lance-tooth pattern is also popular, but it is exactly the same as the lance perforated except that the cutters are less rigid and less predictable.

CLEANING THE SAW

The sharpening sequence for a two-man crosscut is quite straightforward. Begin by removing any pitch from the saw with saw-blade cleaner, and any rust by stoning the entire saw. The stoning serves two purposes. It will remove any rust that has accumulated and reveal any kinks or bumps in the blade. Without going into great detail, it is usually better to have the kinks removed by an experienced saw doctor than attempt it yourself.

JOINTING THE SAW

The saw should be jointed exactly the same way as a handsaw. Since most two-man crosscuts are crescent-shaped, either a jointer with outriders should be used or one of the cast-iron jointers that has the curvature adjustment screw (see the photo on p. 149).

RAKER SHAPING

Raker teeth in a crosscut saw remove fibers from the center of the kerf that have already been clipped at the ends by the cutting teeth. The trick is to set the rakers at a height that will remove all of the central ridge of wood but not tear any fibers. A crosscut saw that works well will yield clean, curly shavings. When the rakers are too long, the fibers will be torn along the edge and the shavings are said to have whiskers (see the bottom drawing at right). Obviously, this would increase cutting resistance.

Because the cutting teeth compress fibers as well as sever them, there is some fiber springback after the cutting tooth passes, much like the springback that is experienced behind a plane blade (see pp. 16-17). To set the raker height properly the amount of springback has to be calculated. This is not particularly simple since the springback varies between wood types, is very dependent on moisture content and is affected by the shape of the cutter, the weight of the saw and the technique of the user.

Optimum raker height can vary from as little as 0.005 in. short of the cutters for a light saw in dry hardwood to as much as 0.035 in. short for a heavy saw in green softwood. For competitions

JOINTED CROSSCUT TEETH

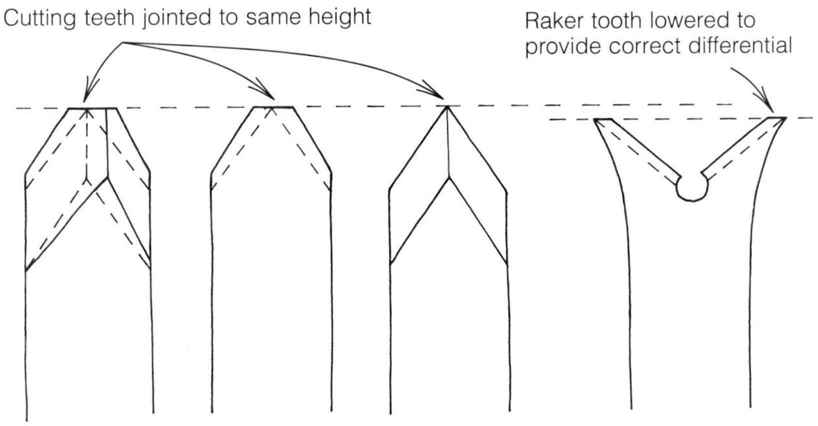

With the teeth jointed, the next step is to point the teeth and file the relief angles on the rakers. In the example shown here, the tooth on the far left will require more filing on the right-hand side than on the left to recenter the tip (the dotted lines show the new tooth design). This is one exception to always filing away half of the jointing flat from each side.

CROSSCUT-SAW SHAVINGS

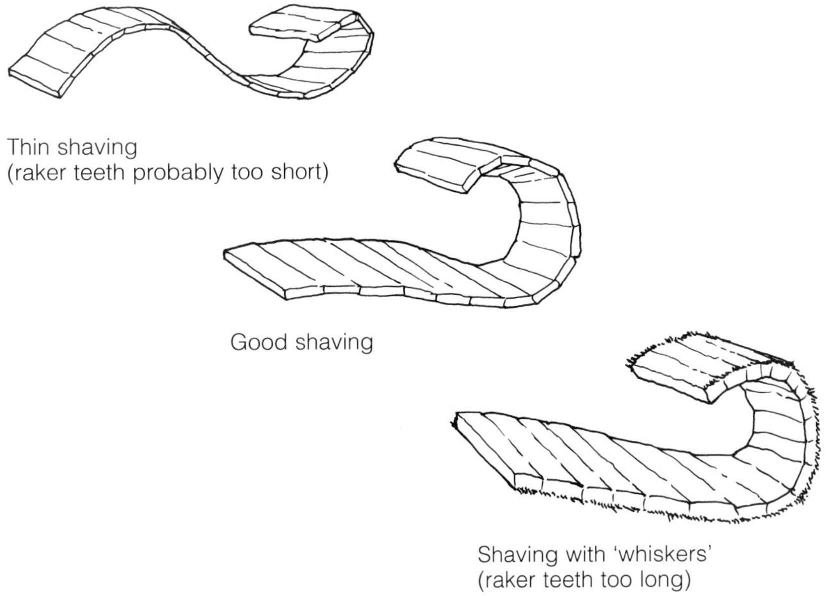

MAKING A RAKER GAUGE

A simple raker gauge can be made from channel stock or material bent in a brake. It can be filed in steps or in one continuous slope for calibration.

Another method is to use a simple L-shaped piece of angle drilled and tapped for a large diameter (¼ in.±) ¼-20 or M-8 bolt. The bolt is used as a simple micrometer. For example, one full turn of a ¼-20 bolt is 0.050 in. If you want rakers that are 0.025 in. below the cutters, you first set the bolt flush with the inside top of the angle and then advance it one half turn. You would then file rakers until they would just clear the bolt tip.

Gauge made from channel stock

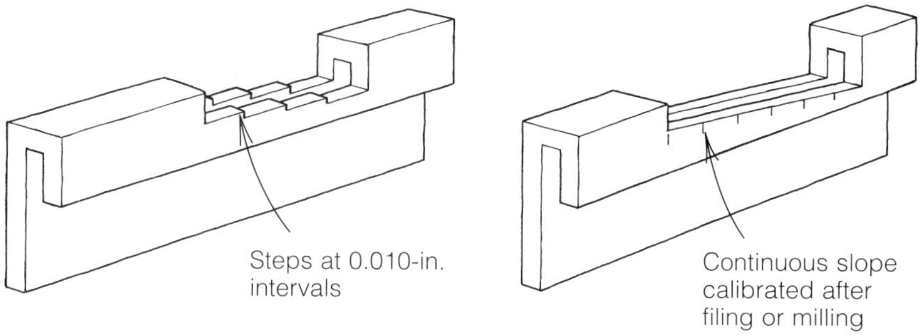

Gauge made from L-shaped angle

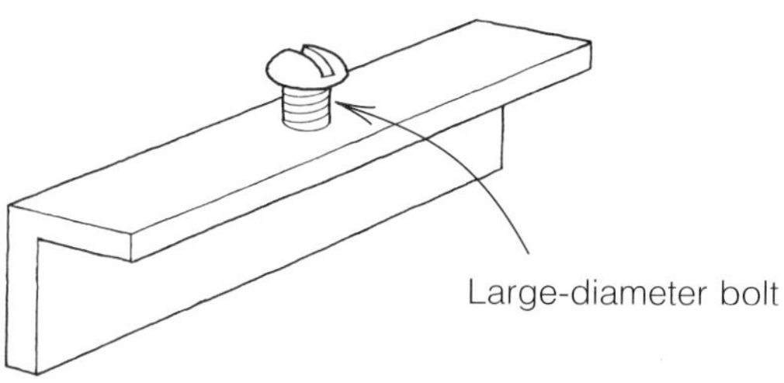

Use a swaging hammer to set the rakers below the height of the cutting teeth. (Photo by Susan Kahn)

where the material being bucked is a turned bolt, raker height will have to be about 0.015 in. below cutter tips. Rakers should not be set there initially; they should be set higher and dressed back by experiment just until they produce no whiskers. One of the many secrets to fast sawing is to have the rakers remove the maximum amount of wood but not tear any fibers. This reduces the friction of the cutting teeth and creates the most efficient combination of tooth action possible.

There are many ways to measure raker height in a two-man crosscut. The various jointers mentioned on p. 145 often have raker gauges. If it is not possible to find one of those, it is a simple matter to make a raker gauge, as shown in the sidebar at left.

Rakers can be filed to height, or they can be swaged. If a swaging hammer cannot be found, a 16-oz. riveting hammer or Warrington hammer will do the job. The tip of the raker should be struck as shown in the photo at left and checked against the pin of the raker gauge.

SETTING THE TEETH

There is a fair amount of discussion among logging-arts competitors about whether setting or filing should come first. The argument for filing first is that you get a better shape if you are filing an unset tooth. In fact, a tooth always has some set in it so it makes very little difference whether it is filed first or set first. What does make a great deal of difference is whether you end up with a short tooth. For that reason I would set the teeth, give them a preliminary dressing and then file them.

It is very important in competition sawing that the setting be highly regular. For this reason, if the teeth are set and then given an initial dressing, the dressing will remove a portion of the flat spot and guarantee that the filed tooth will not accidentally be dressed short later. If the procedure is reversed, side dressing could cause some teeth to be shorter than others.

Crosscut teeth can be spring set, though it is difficult to maintain a regular setting. (Photo by Susan Kahn)

STAKE SETTING

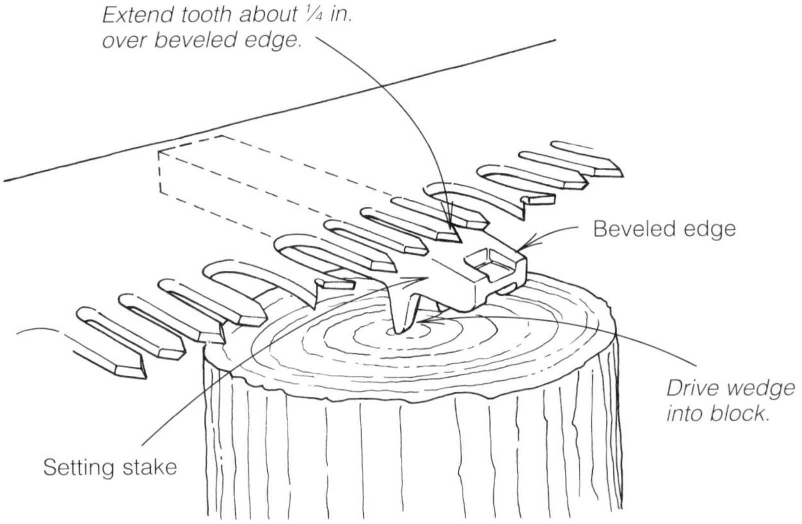

Teeth can be spring set with a wrest, or hammer set. Spring setting (see the photo above) is too much of an uncontrolled process to give good results. The most common method is to use a setting stake, letting the tooth extend about 1/4 in. over the beveled portion (see the drawing at right) and striking it with a hammer. The same hammer used for swaging is quite acceptable. For narrow teeth (which is exactly what you have with a lance-tooth pattern), an 8-oz. hammer may be necessary to avoid interference with adjoining teeth. An 8-oz. Warrington hammer is suitable.

There is one difficulty with this process; it means that there is a lot of saw handling as the teeth are set and then checked. Every tooth should be checked with a spider gauge (see the sidebar at right) and must be lifted off the setting stake each time, which is somewhat cumbersome. The alternative is to use a hand anvil, which requires more skill. The final choice is usually determined by what is available.

If the saw has consistent steel in it, you should be able to come very close to the right amount of set after you set the first two or three teeth. For an overset tooth, draw it back from the

MAKING A SPIDER GAUGE

A spider gauge is used to check the set in saw teeth. A gauge can be made in minutes with four screws and a scrap of wood. To set a spider gauge for use, put a feeler gauge under one tip and adjust the screw at the other tip.

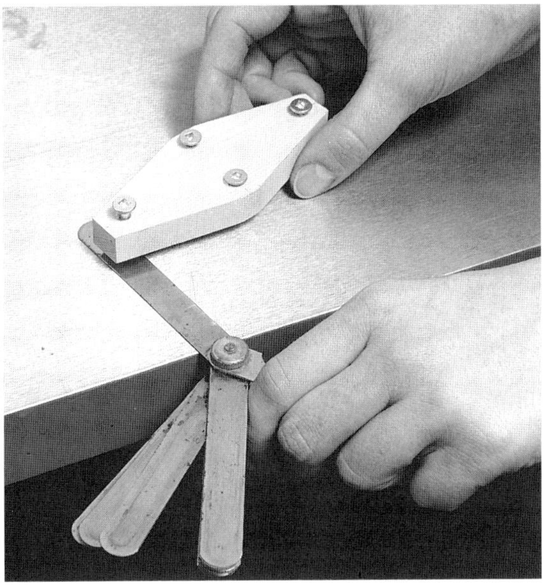

Setting a spider gauge.

CUTTING LOGS SOFT SIDE UP

To ensure logs of exactly the same diameter for logging-arts competitions, it is a common practice to have a plywood factory or a veneer mill peel a log to the exact diameter. Often this is done as much as a week before the competition, and the peeled logs are left in the open air at the competition site.

When these logs are lashed up in the frame for the bucking competition, it is important that they be soft side up; otherwise, the tips can be broken off the cutters that have been so carefully shaped and honed. A log lying in the sun for even a couple of days can develop an extremely hard shell on the top half of the log. In a well-run competition, this shell is placed at the bottom when the log is lashed up. But since the log has to be constantly relashed, competitors should be aware that they might be sandbagged by a log that is hard side up.

beveled portion and give it a tap to straighten it partially, and then carefully reset the tooth with several light blows, checking each time with the spider gauge.

POINTING THE TEETH

For competition sawing you want "hungry" teeth, that is, teeth with low bevel angles that come to a finely honed point at the tip that will slice into the wood. The secret is to get the teeth as thin as possible so that they slice deeply into the wood yet with enough strength to stand up to the aggressive pace of competition sawing.

The V-tip should be somewhere between 35° and 45°; the bevel should be 30°. It is possible (but risky) to

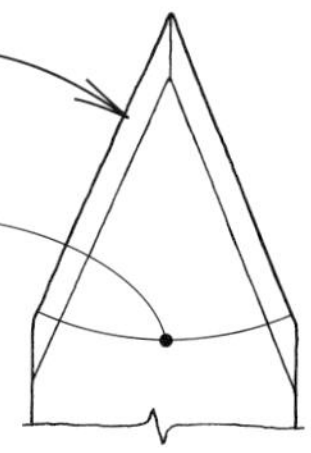

reduce both of these angles. (Note that in this case bevel is being used differently than earlier in the book, where 30° of bevel was 60° off a square edge; in saw filing, 30° of bevel is 30° off a square edge.)

The teeth are easiest to see if the saw has been clamped in a vise that is tilted toward the light. The filing is best done in an enclosed area facing good light. The teeth should be filed until there is just the tiniest flat left at the tip; the flat will be removed when you hone the bevels with a stone.

After filing, the final strokes on the teeth are done with a fine stone. A hard Arkansas knife file is best for this purpose, although a small water stone can be used if handled carefully. In general, water stones are a bit soft for this type of work and the swarf too readily obscures the edge. The back of the tooth should be deburred before stoning is complete so that the finest possible tip is made on the tooth.

CAUTIONARY NOTE

If you are going to be at all serious about competitive sawing, you should have two saws, one for practice and one for competition. It takes several hours to do a first-class job of sharpening a competition saw, and it usually needs to be done at home not at the competition site. A second saw lets you practice your timing to get it down pat at any time without risking any last-minute damage to your competition saw.

SWEDE SAWS AND BUCK SAWS

Where I grew up, a saw with a wooden frame and a turn-buckle tensioner (with a 32-in. or 36-in. blade) was called a buck saw. A saw with a tubular-steel frame, a lever tensioner and a standard 42-in. blade was known as a Swede saw. Nobody took buck saws seriously with their funny little peg-tooth blades, and everybody used Swede saws with the standard four-cutters-and-a-raker pattern. Properly sharpened and tensioned, Swede saws cut quickly with very little effort. With reasonable set in the teeth, it was possible to make cuts that would not even have been attempted with a two-man crosscut because it would have bound in the kerf for sure. The slim Swede-saw blade was next to impossible to trap in a cut. It was the standard cordwood saw.

Buck saws are sharpened exactly like crosscut handsaws, and Swede saws are sharpened like two-man crosscuts.

JAPANESE SAWS

With some minor exceptions, I do not recommend that you attempt to sharpen Japanese saws. Almost without exception, the teeth have been formed and sharpened with diamond wheels, and it is not possible to get as fine a finish using a file. Even if you could create as fine a finish, it is unreasonable to expect that you could develop reasonable competency without sacrificing several saws.

The geometry of Japanese saws is far more complex than that of Western saws. It is rare to find a Japanese saw where two bevels extend from gullet to tip to form a point. There is usually a third bevel and sometimes a fourth bevel incorporated in the tooth. It is not reasonable to expect that you could perfectly recreate this geometry by freehand filing.

Cutting dovetails is probably a good parallel. I doubt that you did a decent job the first time you cut dovetails or even the second time. Yet with dovetails you are dealing with a fairly simple shape in a size that is readily

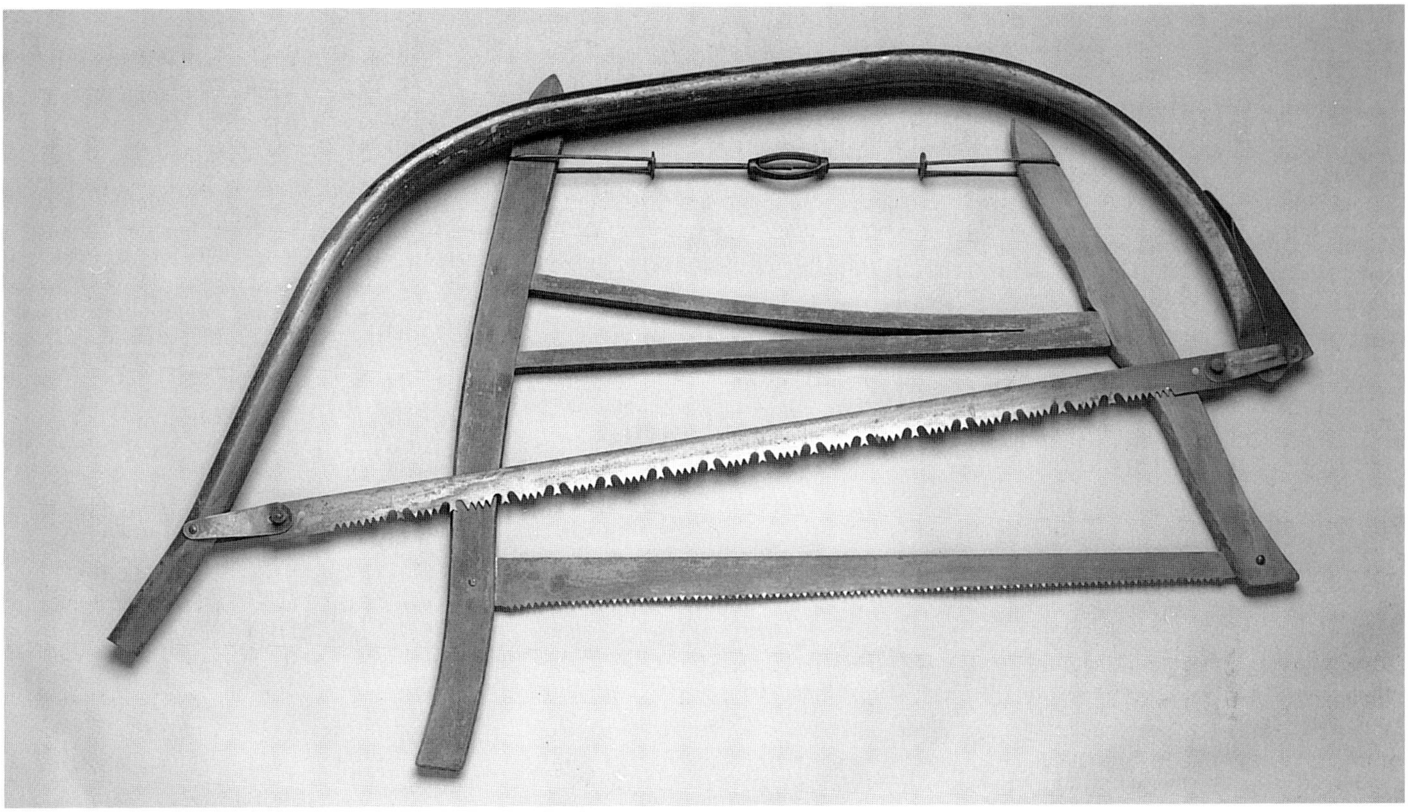

A Swede saw with a typical four-cutters-and-a-raker blade and a buck saw with a peg-tooth blade. Buck saws look nicer hung on a wall; that's where they should stay.

seen, and the shaping is done with tools that are quite controllable. If you contrast that with using a feather-edge file on flexible steel under a magnifying glass with the prospect of the tiniest slip seriously damaging an adjoining tooth, I think you will agree that your time might be better spent practicing your dovetailing.

There is some cause for hope in all of this. Virtually every type of Japanese saw is now available in a disposable-blade model. The blades are very durable and generally represent very good value for the money. And there are some Japanese saws that you can resharpen or at least touch up several times without having to apprentice to a temple builder for five years.

JAPANESE-SAW TEETH

Typical Japanese crosscut-tooth patterns

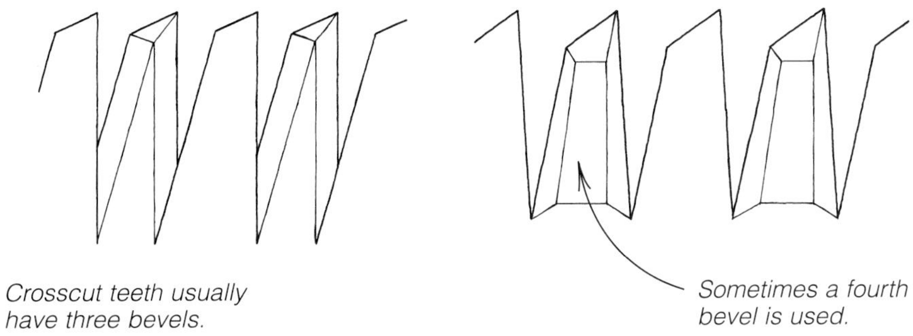

Western crosscut-tooth patterns

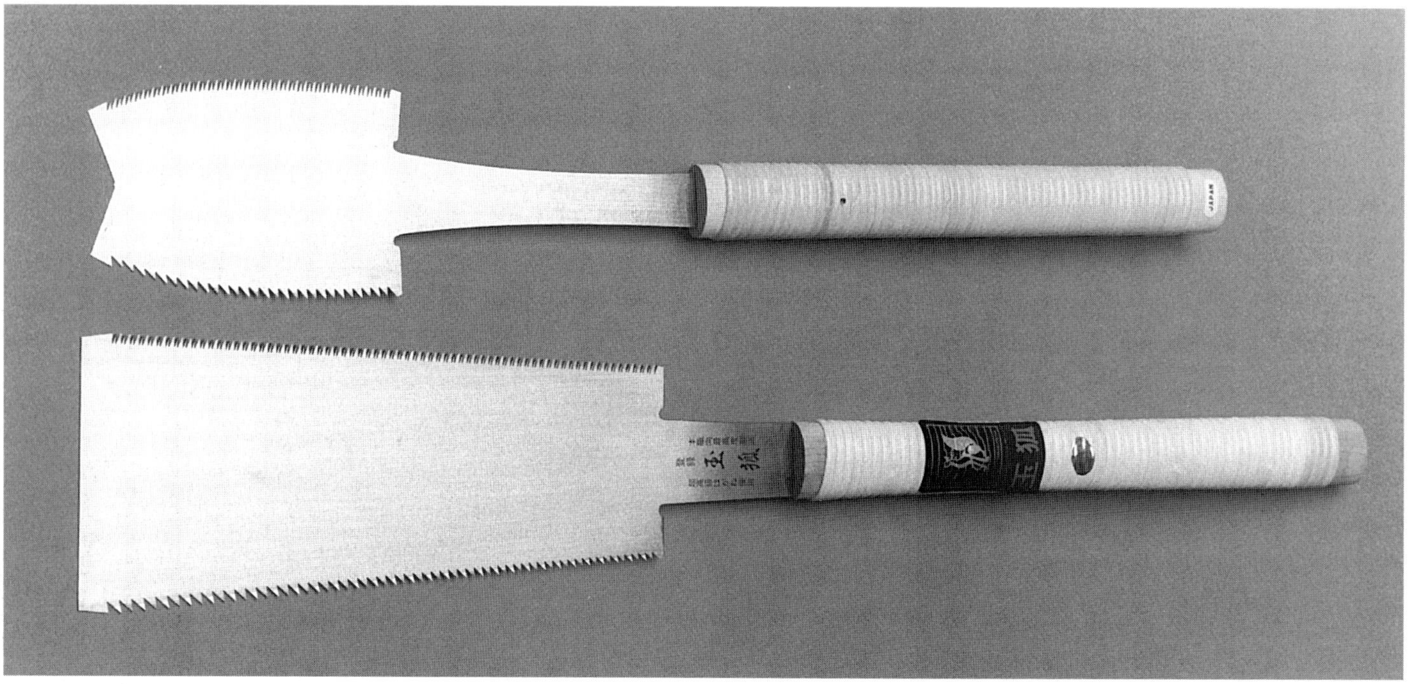

An azebiki saw (top) is used for cuts in restricted areas; it is particularly appreciated by boatbuilders. A ryoba (bottom) is the standard carpenter's saw in Japan. Both saws have rip teeth on one edge, crosscut teeth on the other. (Photo by Susan Kahn)

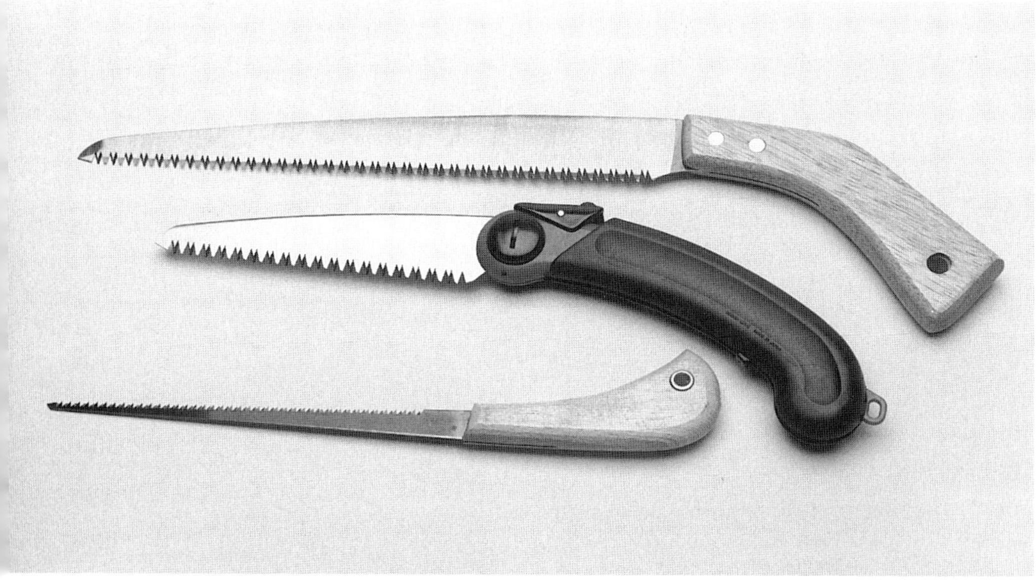

Two pruning saws and a keyhole saw. The saw at top, which has set teeth, is typical of Japanese pruning saws (though made in Taiwan). The middle saw, which has a tapered blade, is a top-of-the-line folding pruning saw made in Japan. The keyhole saw at bottom is just as effective in plasterboard as in wood. (Photo by Susan Kahn)

RIP SAWS

Several Japanese saws (ryoba, azebiki, etc.) have rip teeth fashioned in much the same manner as the rip teeth in Western saws, though the geometry is quite different and the blades are quite a bit thinner. These saws should be clamped close to the gullet and sharpened with a feather-edge file, a 4-in. file for larger teeth, and a 3-in. file for the balance. Otherwise, use the same sharpening sequence as you would for a Western saw.

KEYHOLE SAWS

Japanese keyhole saws usually have no set; they do not require any because the blade is radically tapered from tooth to back. These saws can be sharpened much like Western crosscuts—all you have to do is maintain the original geometry.

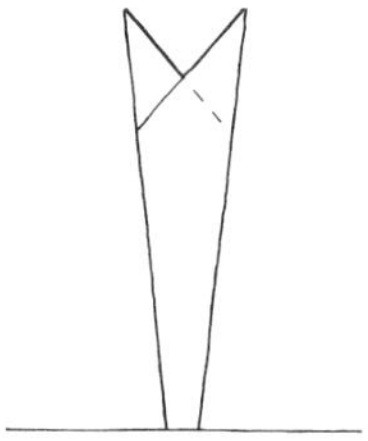

Cross section of keyhole saw with tapered blade

PRUNING SAWS

With their large teeth, Japanese pruning saws are relatively easy to touch up. They come in two patterns: a fairly standard pattern with set teeth, and a rigid blade pattern that has no set (the blade is tapered from tooth to back). Both usually have secondary bevels at the tips of the teeth to make a stronger tip.

To sharpen one of these saws, it is usually not necessary to touch either of the primary bevels; you need to file only the secondary bevel to redefine the tip of the tooth. Despite the complex geometry, if you clamp a Japanese pruning saw in a saw vise between you and the light and tilt the vise until the light reflects directly into your eyes from the secondary bevels when you are in your filing stance, you will be able to file these bevels quite handily with a 3-in. feather-edge file. You will quickly become accustomed to the filing angle because you have the light reflection to guide you.

I am seldom able to file a Japanese saw without having the file slither off at least one tip and grate down the side of an adjoining tooth. For this reason, I prefer a safe-edge file. I also prefer to hold the file in one hand while I put my other thumb on top of the file and a fingertip behind the blade. This dampens the vibration of the blade and it also provides a brake for the file. I find that the file does not go astray nearly so often if I hold my finger behind the tooth. With a safe-edge file, even if you do slip off the tooth tip you cause minimal damage.

There is one final benefit to touching up these saws by filing only the secondary bevel. You will find that you can maintain even tooth height by keeping the secondary bevels the same size. When you file a bevel it becomes slightly larger with each stroke. The size difference is sufficient that you can use this as a guide to maintain tooth height without having to resort to jointing. Since the teeth are very hard, particularly in the rigid-blade pruning saws, I always find it a very unnerving process to joint the saw. The file dances all over the place unless you swap your normal bastard-cut mill file for a #2-cut Swiss pattern. Even then it is an uncomfortable feeling to joint a hard-tooth saw. I have touched up the disposable blades of pruning saws three or four times without a discernible difference in tooth height developing.

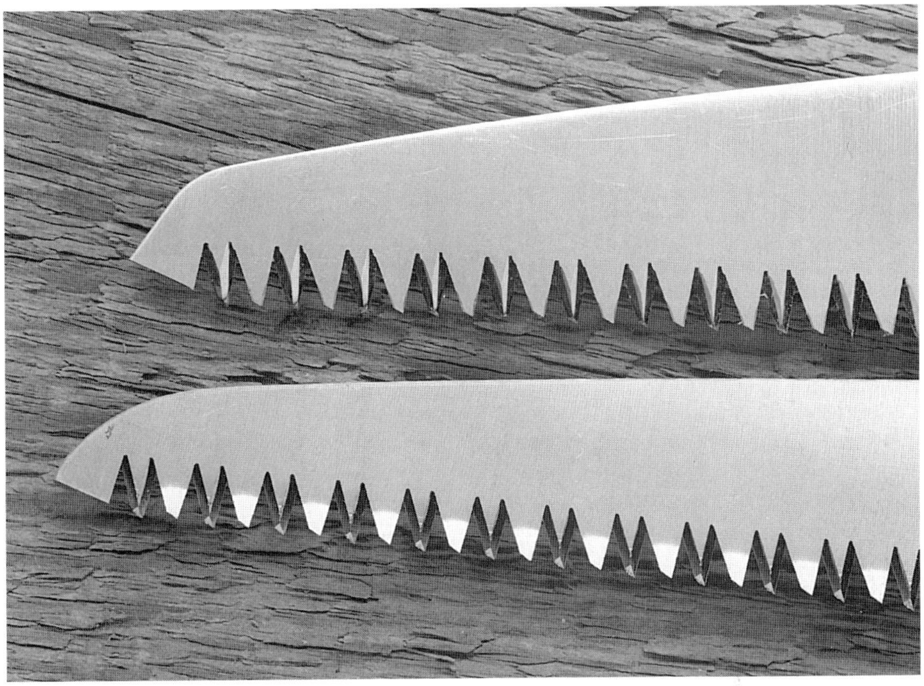

The pruning saw at top has a tapered blade to prevent binding; the saw at bottom has set teeth.

Incidentally, if you have never used a Japanese pruning saw you should treat yourself to one. They are a joy to use. Many years ago, I tried to convince Western saw makers to buy Japanese sharpening machinery so they could make similar saws, or at least saws that were as sharp and had accurately formed teeth. This plea was always greeted with a bemused promise to "look into it." They never did. It is doubtful now that many of them will be able to make up for lost time. Several Taiwanese firms are soaking up a large part of the market with very well made saws, sharpened on Japanese equipment but sold at a fraction of the price of Japanese saws. Even Stanley now offers a Japanese-tooth-pattern saw made in Asia.

CHAPTER 13

AXES, HATCHETS AND ADZES

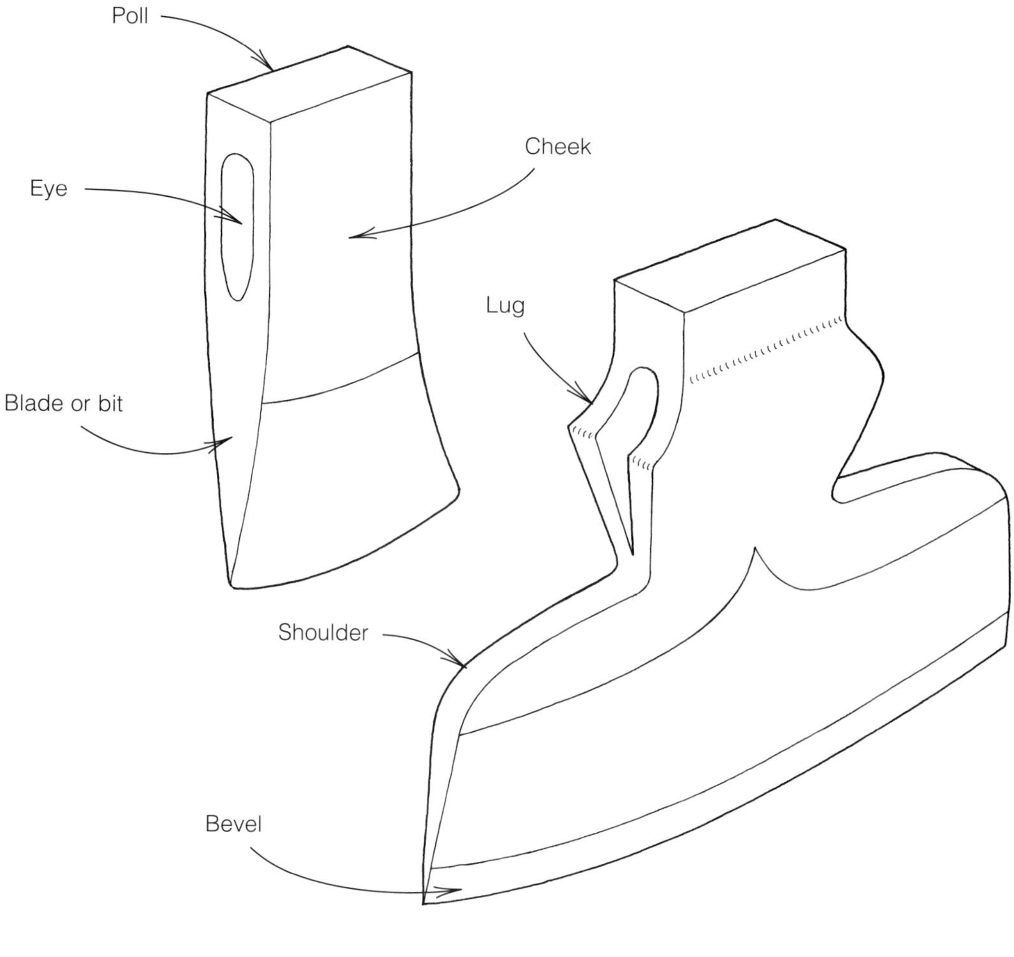

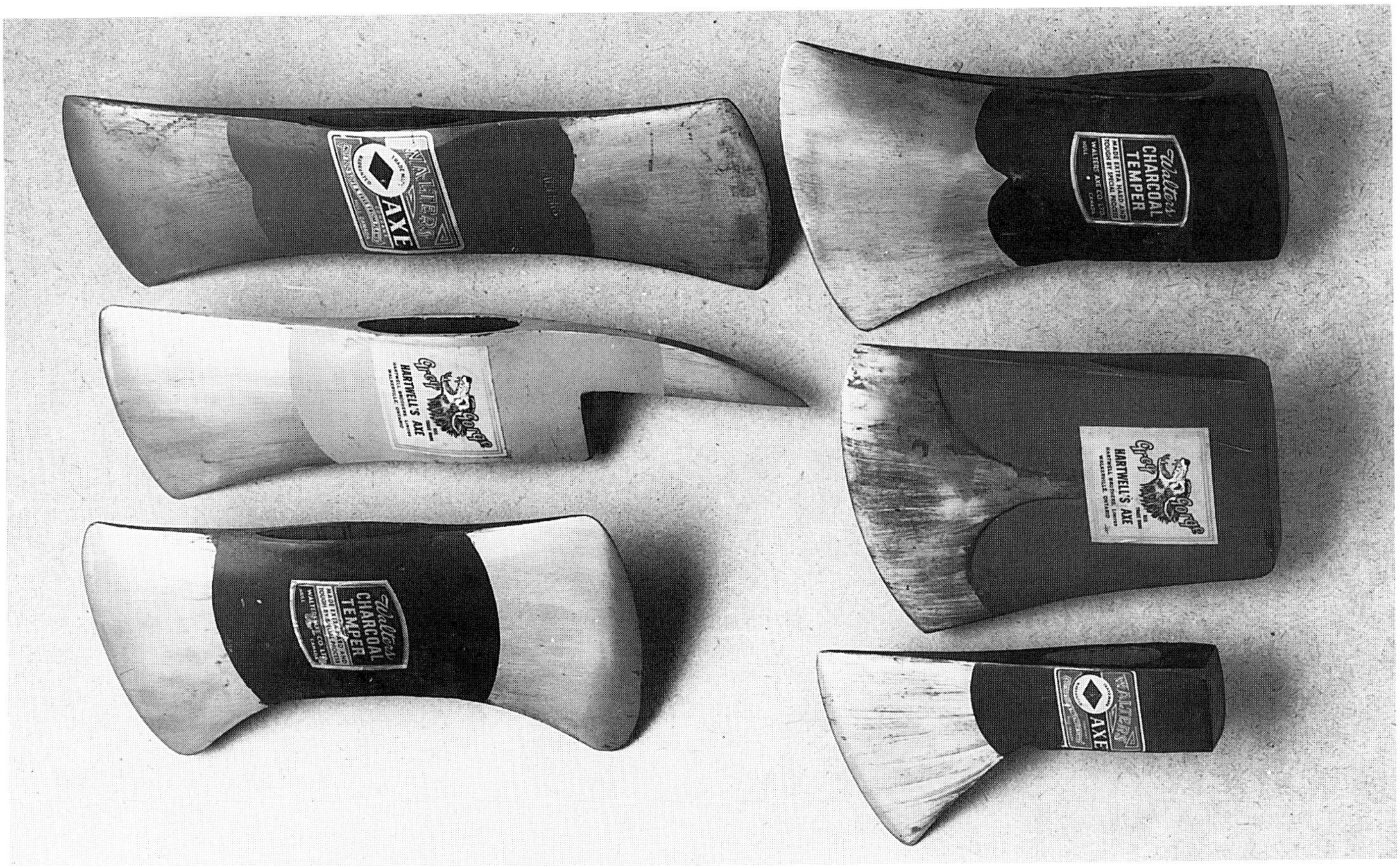

A selection of felling and notching axes. The three double-bit axes at left are (from top to bottom) felling, rafting and swamping styles. The three single-bit axes are (top to bottom) general purpose, full-wedge notching and carpenter's tomahawk pattern.

This book is devoted to the shaping and honing of the wide variety of wedges that we use as cutting tools. If edge tools were separated into the categories of basic and advanced wedges, axes, hatchets and adzes would be considered basic wedges. This is the only category of woodworking hand tool where applied force and direction of cut are both determined before the tool touches the wood. The effectiveness of the wedge is controlled solely by its mass and shape and the skill with which it is flung at the wood.

There are two basic types of ax: those with a centered cutting edge (the most common kind), and those where the blade has a single bevel and the cutting edge is not on the central axis of the head (side axes).

Of the centered-edge type, there are three basic shapes—one for felling or general shaping, one for splitting and, most ubiquitous of all, the utility ax. Describing how to sharpen a utility ax is a bit like describing how to sharpen a handsaw for both crosscutting and ripping; it is hardly worth the effort. The tool becomes such a mass of compromises that it performs no single function well. All that can be said of a utility ax is that you have two choices: either you continue to sharpen it the way it came from the factory, concentrating on a keen edge and ignoring edge geometry, or you can bias the shape to suit the work most frequently demanded of the tool (that is, rework the basic shape as required). Actually, there is a third choice. Get rid of the utility ax and buy what you really need.

FELLING AND NOTCHING AXES

Felling and notching axes are the ballerinas of the ax world, graceful, delicately shaped and a joy in performance. A well-shaped felling ax can drop a 4-in. diameter tree with two strokes. It will notch a tree for felling in seconds, or shape timber more rapidly than a power tool. To use a good felling ax on green wood is to experience the origins of the Paul Bunyan stories.

AX ABUSE

The ax face in the block of wood is mute evidence of abuse. The user tried to split a block of wood with a felling ax. When the ax became seized in the wood, he first hammered on the poll to drive it deeper, hoping to split the wood and free the ax. When he saw that the ax cheeks were beginning to distort, he switched to hitting the ax on the side to free it. The ax head snapped at the point of most stress, next to the wood.

If you are ever faced with a similar problem, saw partway through the block just below the face; this will allow the wood to open and free the ax. Better yet, if you use tools for their intended purpose, you can avoid such problems.

A felling ax is designed for maximum penetration and minimum wedging action. It excels at severing fibers and should never be used to split wood. It is not just that it splits wood poorly, but it can become lodged so solidly in the end grain that it might have to be cut out. Any attempt at levering it out using the handle would only break it.

For working dry wood, either milled timbers or deadwood, the edge should have an included angle of about 20° to 25°, 10° to 12° per side. For green wood, this can be reduced to an included angle of 15° to 20°. These angles may seem low compared with something like a mortise chisel, which performs basically the same function, but the forces experienced by an ax blade are normally more balanced. A chisel has the bending forces applied primarily to the beveled side. With an ax, the forces are applied more evenly to both sides of the blade; the head tends to follow the path of least resistance as it penetrates the wood.

There are exceptions to this general rule. In notching a tree for felling, an ax is used somewhat like a mortise chisel.

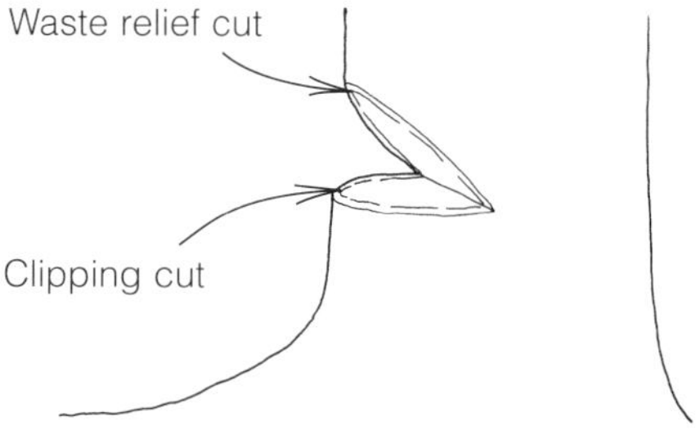

Waste is relieved from the upper part of the cut and then clipped off at the bottom with a horizontal cut (see the drawing above). The horizontal cut most closely imitates the action of a mortise chisel. The difference is that the direct cross-grain cut is usually made first when mortising but last when deepening a notch with an ax. The forces on the ax edge are still uneven but less so than in the case of the mortise chisel.

The other case where extraordinary forces are applied to a felling ax is in trimming dead branches, where there is deadwood encased by the branch collar. Just as pin knots are the enemy of the smooth plane, dead branches are the enemy of the ax.

If you watch experienced woodcutters limb trees, they will use the back of the ax head to knock off dead branches. In cold weather, they will also use the same technique with small live branches, as long as the wood is frozen so that the branches will snap off readily just at the branch collar. Partly this is done for general efficiency, but also to avoid cutting into dead branches, which have the same effect on an ax blade as pin knots have on a plane. The concentration of resisting forces on a small section of blade can cause the section to curl or crumble.

If after shaping an ax head you find the edge too weak in use, just increase

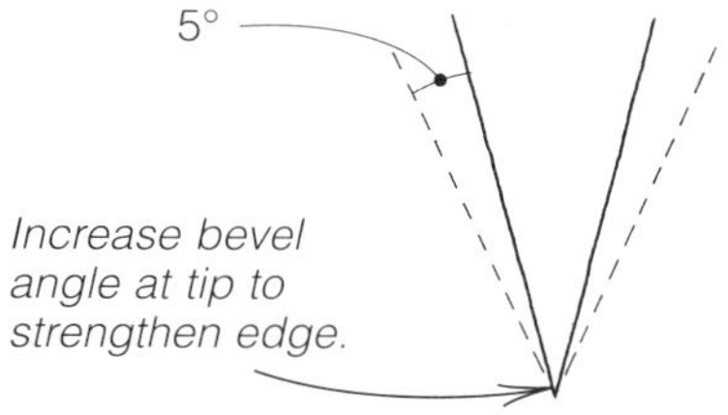

the bevel angle a few degrees (no more than 5°), for the last 1/16 in. or so, as you would with a chisel (see the drawing above). This will strengthen the edge without materially affecting performance. The ax will not penetrate quite as deeply with each swing, but it will work consistently without the need for constant maintenance.

DOUBLE-BIT AXES

Double-bit axes (shown in the photo on p. 163) are seldom seen today, but they were in common use a century ago. In fact, they were more commonly used as felling axes in North America than were the single-bit style.

There were three main reasons that double-bit axes were preferred. First, they have better balance than single-bit axes; the center of gravity of the head is at the middle of the eye. With a single-bit ax, there is usually more mass forward of the eye. Second, double-bit axes have two edges; if one is dulled accidentally, it is not necessary to stop and sharpen that edge immediately. And, third, the two edges were often used for different purposes and accordingly were often shaped differently.

A double-bit ax has quite a different feel from a single bit. The handle is straight and usually more oval in cross section. The perfect balance makes it easier to aim accurately and generally lets you do more precise work. To be efficient in using any ax you should be able to strike the same point repeatedly. This is particularly true in large-diameter work where a cut may have to be extended some distance around a log. Unless it is extended in a single plane, a lot of effort is expended in tearing fibers rather than severing them.

For the modern user, probably the most important feature of the double-bit ax, next to the wonderful balance, is the ability to shape two edges differently, one for felling and one for limbing. The edge for limbing would have a higher included angle than the edge for felling. To avoid confusion, it is useful to have a handy visual indicator that tells you which edge is which. Initially, the label on the ax head can be used as a guide, but if that has been removed either intentionally or with wear, put a dot of paint on the head or the handle as a guide.

THE DESTRUCTION OF A BEAUTIFUL AX

When I was growing up in northern Saskatchewan in the 1940s, the main source of cash for my parents was wood. We cut our own firewood for cooking and heating, and we cut endless hundreds of cords of spruce (usually 8 ft. long) for pulp mills as well as 4-ft. lengths of poplar to be split and dried before selling as firewood. It was all done with hand axes and Swede saws.

My father looked after his tools well; they were always well cared for and sharp. They had to be since they represented a substantial investment. It took over a day's woodcutting income to buy an ax in 1945.

I remember as yesterday when my father bought a new felling ax for my uncle, who lived with us. It had the slimmest blade of any ax I'd ever seen. Two inches back from the edge that ax would have been no more than ¼ in. thick, and the face must have been a full 6 in. wide. I was jealous because I always had to use some hand-me-down ax with a handle frayed from limbing overstrikes and bound with a makeshift guard of stovepipe wire wrapped around the first 2 in. back of the head. It was suited to my skill if not my aspirations.

My father was never very thrilled about the way my uncle looked after his ax; in retrospect, I suspect that he coveted that ax because it was unquestionably the best in our diverse collection.

We always had to travel somewhere to cut wood. Anything larger than 6 in. in diameter had long since been cut on our homestead, so we would cut wood on crown land or the section of land owned by the Hudson's Bay Company, both several miles away. We would set out in the morning with a team of horses and a bare-bunked sleigh, the axes slung in their holders on the back side of the bunks (the front sides plowed snow!) and the Swede saws hanging from a bunk post.

Saskatchewan winters were always cold; there was no hint of global warming in the '40s. By the time we got to the bush, we were often half-frozen and the tools might be at a cool -40°F. My father knew the danger of using an ax at that temperature, so he would tuck his under his backside on the sack of straw that he used as a cushion and insulator when driving and warm the ax for the last ten or fifteen minutes of the trip. My uncle never warmed his ax before using it, and my father would grumble about this carelessness but, being a gentle man, never forced the issue.

One particularly cold morning (memory makes it even colder than it was and the bush even farther away from home), my uncle unslung his ax from the sleigh bunk, walked over to a poplar, cleared snow from a spot on the ground for solid footing and prepared to notch the tree. With the first swing, he took the entire face out of his ax. I can still remember the huge crescent-shaped piece of steel stuck in the tree. I can also remember how angry I was because I had never had the chance to use that beautiful ax and now it was no more.

I have bought many axes since that incident and, just as the weather used to be colder then, I am equally certain that axes used to be more beautiful than they are today.

Using an 8-in. mill file, file the ax away from the edge.

To get a consistently shaped wedge, it will probably be necessary to remove more material from the center portion of the head than at the tips of the face (see the drawing below). Among older axes you will often find a substantial

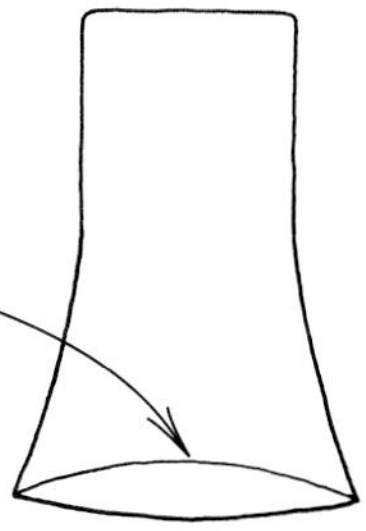

swelling toward the center of the head, feathering off both fore and aft. When you file such an ax you will get a much wider bevel in the center of the head than at either tip. One log builder I know files his felling ax by resting the tip of the file at the center of the ax head near the poll and then using a draw-filing technique in a semicircular motion to shape the face. It seems to work well for him, although I find it to be an uncomfortable motion and prefer striking a basic bevel angle at the center of the face and extending it in each direction.

There is a tendency to file a steeper bevel angle at the center of the face than at either tip. Partly this is dictated by the above-mentioned swelling at the center and partly by the tendency to file the lowest bevel angle where it is easiest to file the lowest bevel angle. There is no great harm in doing this unless the included bevel angle near the edge becomes too small and weakens the edge. More usual is that the bevel angle is too great at the center of the ax, causing too much wedging action in use and reducing penetration.

FILING AN AX HEAD

An 8-in. mill bastard file is ideal for shaping most ax heads. The steel in the head is usually no harder than Rc55 and can be filed readily. A mill file will remove stock quickly and controllably. With a bit of practice, it is easy to maintain angles, particularly when you use the height of the file above the ax eye as an indicator of angle. It is also safest to file an ax from the eye side of the edge, although almost every woodsman I have known files directly toward the edge with cavalier abandon.

HONING THE EDGE

Honing the edge of an ax is similar to honing a drawknife or any other tool that requires freehand stoning. For reasons of tradition, this is still one tool that I prefer to hone with an oil stone. Unquestionably a large part of this is the memory of my father honing axes. He used a bit of 3-In-One or neat's-foot oil, whichever was handiest, and an easy rotary motion with the stone. This technique leaves a surface finish a bit like the geometric pattern that you find on the inside of an old pocketwatch case. After honing with the oil stone, I finish off in a highly untraditional manner—a chromium-oxide-charged felt wheel on a power grinder. It would have made my father shake his head, I'm sure.

There is no reason that all of this could not be done with water stones in sequence, or with just one water stone in the 1000x range and a rigid strop charged with chromium oxide. You could also hone the edge with several grits of belt on a belt sander.

MAINTAINING THE EDGE ON AN AX

As well as shaping the face properly and using an ax only for its intended purpose, the next best thing you can do is keep it in a sheath to avoid accidental dulling. In the same vein, be aware that there is often a lot of grit embedded in the bark near the base of a tree. In books on early logging practices, you will see photographs where the bark has been removed in a ring around the tree where the saw cut will be made. This was done to remove the grit-impregnated bark so it would not dull the saw blade. You can do the same in the area where you intend to notch the tree with your felling ax, but since you would normally have to use an ax to remove the bark this all gets very fussy. With some trees it is very easy to strip the bark from a safe cut a foot or more up the tree, with others not so easy. The degree of fussiness you bring to your woodworking activities I leave to you.

SPLITTING MAULS AND SPLITTING AXES

The two basic types of splitting instruments are splitting mauls and splitting axes. A splitting maul is a cross between a post maul and an ax; it has a maul eye, oval-shaped and much smaller than an ax eye. Like a splitting ax it has very thick cheeks so that the head can be reversed and the tool used as a maul to drive splitting wedges. Some people believe that the thick cheeks on these tools are designed so that a lodged head can be driven through the block with a post maul. All I can say to these people is that I hope they enjoy replacing handles, because there is no easier way to ruin handles on either of these tools than by driving them through wood with another sledge. The vibrations caused in the undamped handle will soon cause it to split between the annular rings.

Splitting tools available today are seldom ideally shaped. The splitting maul at left comes closest to an ideal shape but is heavier than most people can comfortably use. The splitting ax at right is easier to use but could benefit from fuller cheeks.

SPLITTING MAULS

It is virtually impossible to lodge a splitting maul in sound wood. The face is formed by two intersecting arcs, which result in minimal surface contact as it splits the piece of wood. The two pieces of the block are tangent to the maul head so there is only a very narrow band of contact on either side of the head (see the drawing at right).

Anyone who has split a great deal of wood by hand will recognize the advantage of this shape. The only time it is difficult to remove a splitting maul from a block of wood after an unsuccessful blow is if there is a punk section in the block. Wood that has just begun to rot will deform readily and virtually mold itself around the head of the maul. Otherwise, you will seldom have any difficulty removing a splitting maul for a second strike.

There is not much to say about sharpening a splitting maul. Remove any major flat spots from the edge and give the head a shot of wax, Dri-Cote or other lubricant to reduce friction. Unless you are very careful, you will shortly have another flat spot on the edge anyway so there is no use spending a great deal of time dressing it.

SPLITTING-MAUL SHAPE

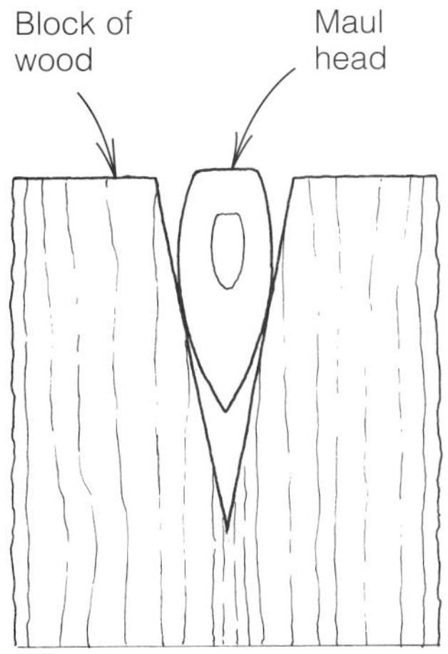

Because of the shape of the maul, there is minimal surface contact with the wood.

SPLITTING-AX SHAPE

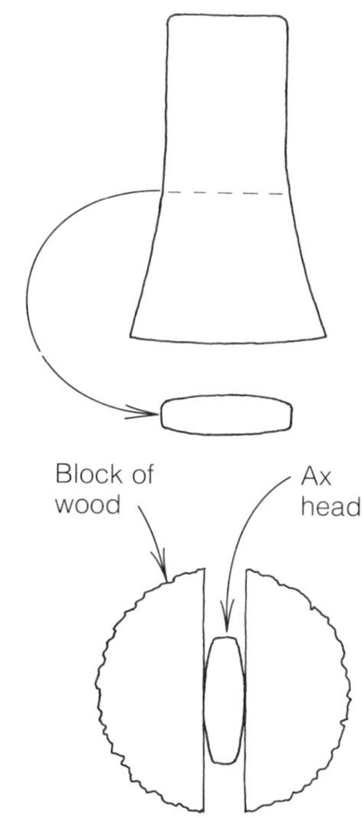

Swelled axis of ax head reduces surface contact with the wood.

SPLITTING AXES

A splitting ax is shaped differently from a splitting maul; it is much closer to a utility ax in shape, although usually much heavier. A well-shaped splitting ax will also be swelled substantially along the vertical axis of the head (see the drawing at left). Once again the principle is to reduce surface contact with the two halves of the block being split, only this time the line of tangency is at 90° to that of the splitting maul. That is not quite true since a well-shaped splitting maul strives for point contact rather than line contact, and it would be swelled along both the horizontal axis and the vertical axis.

The swelling at the center makes it possible to lever a splitting ax out of a block of wood after an unsuccessful strike. If it cannot be levered out, the ax should have sufficient eye strength that it can be driven through but, as mentioned above, this risks breaking the handle. If you must drive it through, strike the head dead-center with a one-handed blow while the other hand is on the handle dampening vibrations.

Like the maul, the splitting ax is basically a blunt instrument for primitive work. Maintain the bevels so that there are no flat spots on the edge and forget any fancy honing. In use, the cutting edge comes in contact with wood only as the head first enters the block; otherwise, the splitting crack runs well ahead of the edge. Your time is better spent concentrating on reducing friction along the sides of the head rather than worrying about the keenness of the edge.

MAINTAINING THE EDGE

The main concern you have with a splitting tool is to keep it from striking the ground and becoming dulled on pebbles or stones. To prevent this, and to make the whole splitting process a lot easier, find a good-sized block of unsplit wood, bed it solidly in the ground and use it as a splitting base. Many people do not appreciate the importance of getting the block on a solid base. The base is important since you do not want the inertia of the descending head to be absorbed in deformation of any material other than the block you are trying to split. Using a splitting base that is sitting on springy turf will waste a lot of your effort.

WEDGING AN AX HANDLE

A loose handle in an ax can be tightened easily with hardwood wedges. If the handle can be removed completely, do so, and make saw cuts where you intend to wedge. If the handle cannot be removed easily, use a chisel to open the wood where you want to wedge. In general, the wedges should be driven parallel to the minor axis of the eye. This best resists the usual compressive forces exerted on the handle when it is "levered" out of a cut, and, equally important, it avoids the danger of distorting the eye.

If some spreading across the minor axis is required, make the wedge cuts at a 45° angle to each axis. Avoid wedging parallel to the major axis. A wedge is a powerful device; it can damage the eye permanently if misapplied.

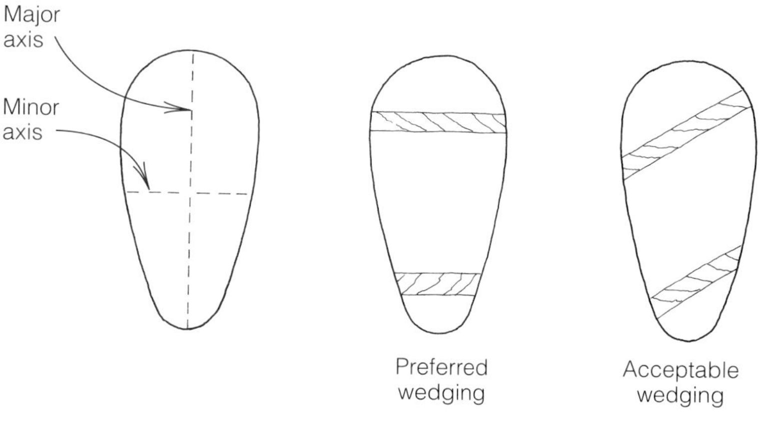

The European bearded ax (left) and the Canada-pattern broad ax (right) are the two most common styles of broad axes.

This classic old Canada pattern broad ax (made by Lyman Perkins, Hull, Quebec, sometime prior to 1834) shows rust pitting and a typical scarf weld.

SIDE AXES

A side ax is any ax that has a bevel on one side of the blade only. The two most common types are broad axes and bench axes. In general, they differ only in size. The broad ax is intended for two-handed use, the bench ax for one-handed use.

BROAD AXES

Of the various styles of broad axes, the two most common today are the Canada-pattern broad ax (the style most used in North America) and the bearded ax, a European style.

Both types are used for squaring timbers, but the European ax is not nearly as heavy, weighing about 6 lb., and is more suited to the European style of building construction. The North American ax was used for heavier work, in working the generally larger pines for log houses and hardwoods for railroad ties. Some Canada-pattern axes weigh as much as 12 lb. They also usually have a cambered face, whereas the European axes are normally flat. Both styles have offset handles to avoid knuckle-barking.

The North American style can be used to make cross-grain cuts; the European style always has to be used askew the grain to avoid the tips digging in. As a final difference, the European axes have thinner blades and usually lower bevel angles, reflecting the more delicate nature of their use. The North American axes needed beefier edges to slash through the knots in hardwood.

Because of the tremendous variability in the steel of these old axes, it is a good idea to start out with a bevel of about 30° and work your way either up or down in bevel angle according to your intended use and the quality of the steel in the ax head.

SHARPENING A BROAD AX

As with any single-bevel tool, you should focus your attention first on the back side of the blade. It should be flat, smooth and free of defects. The latter point is particularly important if you have bought an old broad ax (see the photo at right). Almost without exception, these have been left to rust in a shed, barn or damp basement. You have to remove the rust and then eliminate any pitting on the back of the blade. Since you want to keep the back

EARLY AX MANUFACTURING

Like early chisels and plane blades, the major parts of ax heads were made from mild steel or iron with forge-welded, higher-carbon-steel bits. There were three basic methods for attaching the steel bit to an iron ax head: the overcoat method, the insert method and the scarf joint.

All began the same, with a flat piece of iron that had the two halves of the eye partially formed in it and a bit of end treatment. The iron was then formed over a removable mandrel before forging the two halves together. The steel bit was welded to the iron, and finally the edge was formed.

With broad axes, the iron body was feathered to an edge and then the steel bit was scarfed onto the blade. Oddly enough, some of the scarf joints were the reverse of the one illustrated below. This meant that you would run into the iron faster with repeated sharpening.

All this is not just of historic interest; it has application for today's tool buyer. Anyone who wants a cambered Canada-pattern broad ax has to buy an antique. The smart buyer will ensure that there is still enough of the steel bit left to give reasonable service.

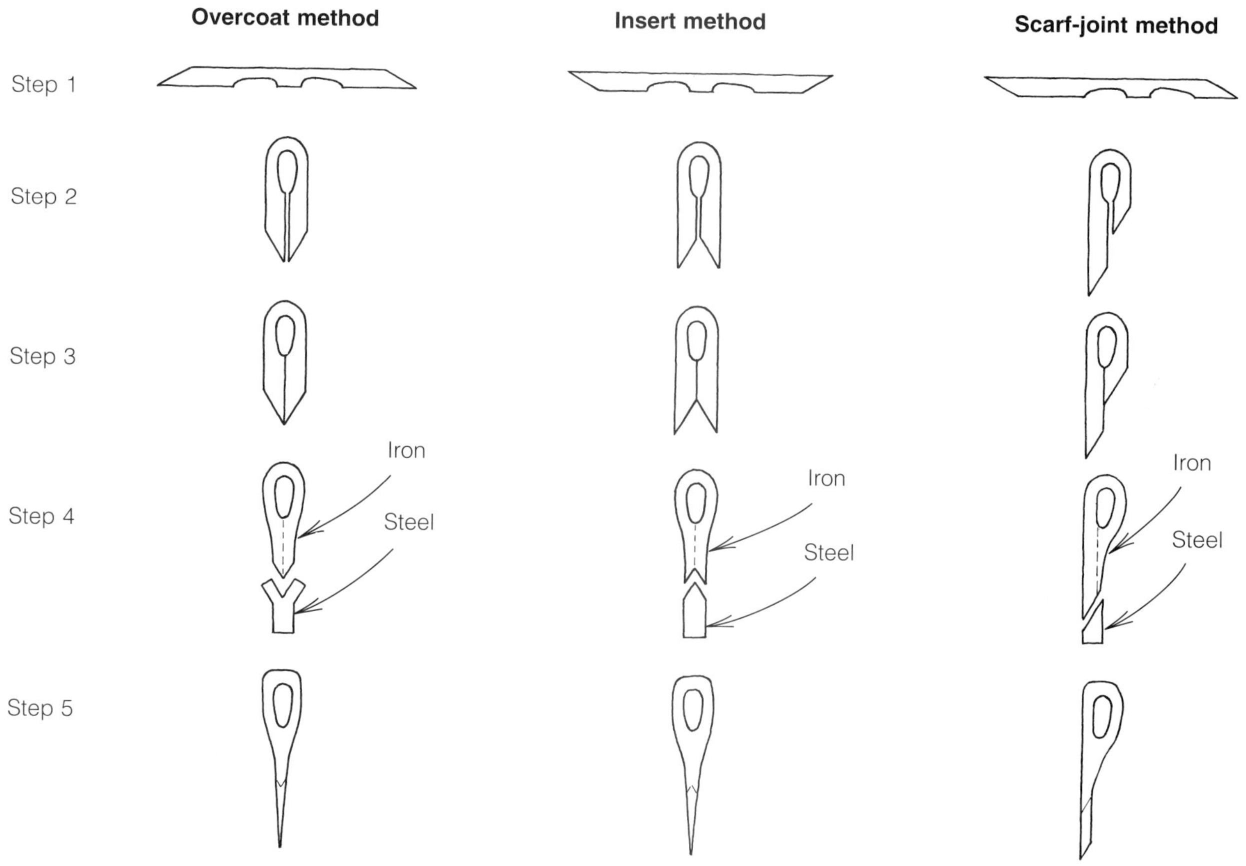

of the blade as regular as possible, the fastest way to dress the back of the blade is on a 3-in. (or larger) belt sander mounted upside-down in a vise. Using a sequence of belts from coarse to fine, strip the back of the blade until you have a defect-free surface and a smooth plane. For the final touches, a medium-grit water stone (800x to 1200x) works well.

Depending upon your individual technique and the nature of the work you will be doing, you may want to put just a touch of back bevel on the blade. This may seem like heresy to some of you, but it can make a difficult tool much easier to use for the novice. The inertial mass of a vigorously swung broad ax exerts a tremendous amount of force on the blade edge. Because the force is all from the beveled side, any deflection of the blade will cause it to bite into the wood more deeply than intended. It is far easier to prevent damaged work by using an ax that has a slight tendency to cut away from the line than it is with an ax that tends to cut toward the finish line and possibly past it.

There is no easy rule of thumb for putting back bevel on a broad-ax blade. For knot-free pine, buffing the back of the edge will usually give you enough back bevel to make the ax highly controllable. The amount of bevel is almost invisible to the naked eye. For heavier work in hardwoods, you may want to stone a visible bevel on the back of the blade. Until you have some experience with back bevels, approach them the same way you would a porcupine. You can cause damage if you become too aggressive. Avoid long shallow back bevels unless you are absolutely certain that is what you want. It takes a long time to dress away an unwanted bevel, even with a belt sander. It may even be necessary to take an extra $1/16$ in. or $1/8$ in. off the main bevel in order to restore a blade that has been the object of overexuberance.

Other than the above considerations, a broad ax can be sharpened with the same equipment used for a felling ax. The steel is usually fairly soft in a broad ax and will file readily. The edge can be refined with stones and strops as necessary.

HATCHETS

Hatchets are miniature axes. They come in center-bevel and side-bevel (or broad hatchet) styles. They are little used in most types of woodworking today, although they remain as handy as ever for one-handed shaping. The sharpening considerations for hatchets are exactly the same as for axes. Kindling hatchets should be shaped like splitting axes; camping hatchets like felling axes; and broad hatchets like broad axes. The same equipment is used to shape and hone them.

The shingling hatchet (see the drawing on p. 172) is one special case worth mentioning. Although originally designed for use with wooden shingles and lath, it is more commonly used today with asphalt shingles. Instead of being used in the classic manner to split and shape shingles, it is used much in the manner of a cutting knife. The back corner of the blade is used to cut or deeply score an asphalt shingle so that a portion can be removed; the poll is used to drive roofing nails.

It is difficult to keep the handle tight in a traditional hatchet (center) because the eye is short. Any levering on the handle causes fiber compression, which quickly loosens the head. For axes subject to lateral leverage, the cheeks can be extended fore and/or aft to form lugs that create the effect of a deeper eye. The two hand-forged hatchets at left and right have this feature.

MODIFIED SHINGLING HATCHET

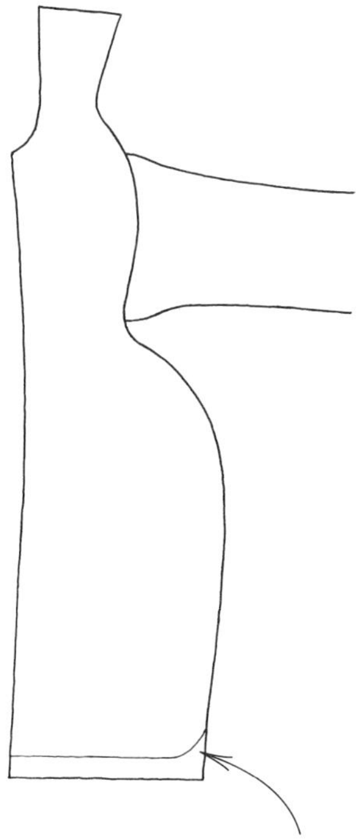

Sharpen back edge at about 10° center bevel for ½ in.

For anyone using it in this manner, it is worthwhile paying particular attention to the back corner of the blade to keep it sharp and as friction-free as possible. To improve the cutting action, the bevel can be reduced to about a 10° included angle for the last ½ in. of the blade; the back edge should be center-beveled at about 10° for ½ in. as well (see the drawing at left).

After the corner has been shaped, honing is still worthwhile, not because the sharp corner will last longer than a few hours in use but because the smooth surface (particularly when coated with a dry lubricant) will reduce friction in the cut. In short, it should be adapted to its new use.

ADZES

Adzes are one step up the evolutionary ladder from axes. Traditionally, they were used to refine many of the rough shapes created by axes. As an example, old timber-frame houses will often have exposed joists that show very fine adz work. The builder would use a broad ax to square the beam and an adz to dress it. Although use of either tool took skill, there is an inherent danger in using a foot adz to square a beam that separated the user from others in the trade, much like the difference between a trim carpenter and a framing carpenter today.

A foot adz is so called not to differentiate it from a hand adz but to reflect the nature of its use. The carpenter would make cuts directly under one foot, using the foot pressure on the shaving as a check-stop. There are many apocryphal stories about carpenters betting workmates that they could separate the sole of their boot from the upper without cutting a thread of their sock. Whether or not these stories have any factual basis, there is no question about the developed skill of some users.

STRAIGHT ADZES

A straight foot adz compares most directly with a broad ax. It is sometimes used parallel to the grain of the wood or askew the grain, but most commonly cross grain to achieve a reasonably flat, regular surface.

A selection of straight adzes: from left to right, a pin poll adz (railway style); a half-head adz, or sledge poll; a standard adz (whole head or flat head); and a half-head variation.

Like a broad ax, an adz sometimes has a slightly cambered face so that the corners do not catch and cause the head to twist. Some crown is put on the edge for the same reason (see the drawing at right). It tends to keep the blade moving in a straight line. The amount of camber is usually dictated by the tool, although you can vary it slightly, but the amount of crown is your choice. For cutting with the grain, you need little or no crown; for cutting cross grain, you want as much as is necessary to control splintering. Almost all users put a slight crown on an adz edge, except for a lipped adz, which is used with a straight edge.

Like most single-bevel tools, the unbeveled side of the adz is often ignored. It should not be. The back of the adz should be linished, or stoned, until it is a smooth plane. A 120x belt sander or disc sander will do the brute work; use 240x to refine it, and then stone it or use a power buff to finish.

The basic bevel angle should be 25° to 30°, depending on whether you intend to use the adz for roughing or finishing and whether or not you like back bevel on the tool. Like most single-bevel impact tools (broad axes, carpenter's hatchets, etc.), an adz can benefit from some back bevel. It allows the tool to cut a shallow scallop rather than a straight plane. For roughing, I recommend a 25° bevel for softwood and 30° for dry hardwood, if you intend to have no back bevel. If you want back bevel on the blade, these angles can be dropped by as many degrees of back bevel you intend to use. For example, with 5° of back bevel you could drop the primary bevel to 20° for softwood and 25° for hardwood. For work where you would be making shallow cuts to achieve a fine finish, the bevel angle could be dropped another 5°.

The back bevel should be very shallow and slightly rounded. Use a stone to set the bevel, resting the stone on a 1/16-in. thick piece of material about 2 in. back of the edge (see the sidebar on the 1-in-60 rule on p. 17). This will give you a 2° back bevel. Then strop the bevel to refine the surface. The stropping will tend to round the bevel a bit. It is usually enough.

As always, your desired result combined with your technique of use will determine the degree of back bevel you want. Start with a very shallow angle (about 2°) and make the bevel short. You can always take more off, but you can't put it back on.

These are starting points only. The nature of the work you intend to do and the nature of the steel in your adz could dictate a stronger edge. Starting with a fairly low basic bevel as we have here, it is easy to beef it up with a steeper micro-bevel if needed.

With a new adz, or one new to you, simply hone the edge in the shape you found it. Then test the tool and your technique. If it cuts well and you are happy with the action, there is no need to tinker with it. If you find it digging in uncontrollably, then adjust the bevel.

LIPPED ADZES

A lipped, or shipwright's, adz (see the photo on p. 174) presents special sharpening problems. It is designed specifically for cross-grain work. The turned-up lips clip off splinters that the main edge has raised.

Like other adzes, lipped adzes were once made by a number of manufacturers in several variations of width, eye angle, and so on. To my knowledge, there is only one factory in Europe that makes lipped adzes today, and they do not make them well. The adzes are drop-forged but are not smithed afterward. Smithing is a hand process whereby a tool is refined in some way on an anvil. For example, paring gouges need smithing to straighten them after they are forged. So do lipped adzes.

In the adz-forging process, the head is formed in steps; the last step is to turn the lips. But there is some springback, which causes the adz face to arch upward next to the lips. The thicker

ADZ SHAPE

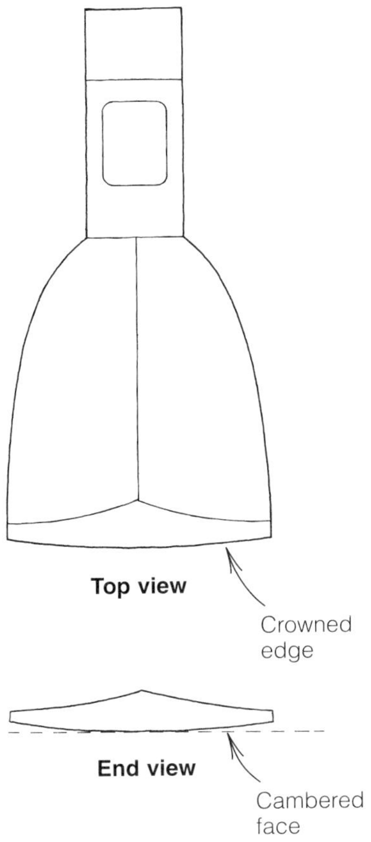

If this lipped adz does not have the recurve removed from the center, it will always be difficult to use because the corners will catch first, twisting the adz.

On a lipped adz, use a sanding drum matched to the inside radius to sharpen the bevel in the lip area. (Photo by Susan Kahn)

central portion of the blade resists the pressure, and the result is a bit like the recurved shape of a hunting or target bow. (The photo at left shows the recurve.)

To make such an adz usable, you first have to rework the back. This can best be done with a belt sander or a sanding disc with a coarse belt (start at 80x). As you approach flatness (or a fair curve, whichever you want), change to finer grits as necessary, ending at 240x with a light touch. Only after this major reworking can you turn your attention to detailed shaping of the edge.

In all probability, you'll be faced with a nasty, ragged-looking edge after you have reworked the back of the adz. In particular, you will probably have fairly deep indents in the areas of the lips. The entire edge should be ground back until it's straight; then you can re-establish the bevel.

A lipped adz is particularly tricky to sharpen in the area of the lip. The brute work can be done with a flex shaft and a sanding drum of a radius just smaller than the radius at the corner of the lip. Use a light touch to prevent overheating and when the line of light becomes uncomfortably narrow, switch to slipstones or cylindrical hones.

Whether or not you choose to put some back bevel on the main part of the edge, you do not want any on the lips themselves. There should be no back bevel from the top of the lips to the point at which they become tangent to the flat part of the face. Any back bevel in this area would cause the adz to wedge laterally in the cut. Since this adz is designed for trenching cuts, you do not want it to be wider at any point than the trench that it is cutting.

ADZ-HEAD DESIGN

There are two immutable features of an adz that should be considered before purchasing. The first is head curvature. The curvature you want depends on your height, since you want the head curvature to match the arc that the head makes when you are swinging the adz.

This curvature is closely allied to the second thing that you cannot change about an adz, the angle of the eye to the blade. Most adzes do not have heads of constant curvature. They usually have a shallow curve in the forward part of the head and then either a progressively tighter curve or a break point where the shallow curve intersects with a sharper curve. The minimum arc through which the adz can be swung is determined by the shallower of the two curves. The center of this arc is called the true rotation point (see the drawing at right).

If you want to use a fairly full swing with a lipped adz, you will want a rotation point at least 25 in. from the edge. Fortunately, most lipped adzes are designed that way. Most foot adzes, on the other hand, are designed with tighter curvatures so that at least one forearm can be braced against the front of a thigh to control the cutting action. It would be very difficult to take anything near a full swing with such an adz. It has to be used with a short, choppy swing.

The true rotation point varies from adz to adz but is important to its use. If this point is too close to the head you will have to choke up on the handle to get a controlled cut. You would also find it hard to get a shallow, relatively flat cut without using unusual technique. At the other end of the scale, if the rotation point is too far from the head, substantial back bevel could be necessary to bring the rotation point closer to the head.

While some of this discussion may seem peripheral to sharpening, it is not. The purpose of the tool and the technique of the user are key to shaping the edge for effective use. If a tool cannot be shaped to fit the user's style and to meet the user's purposes, there is little point in putting a keen edge on it.

ADZ ROTATION POINTS

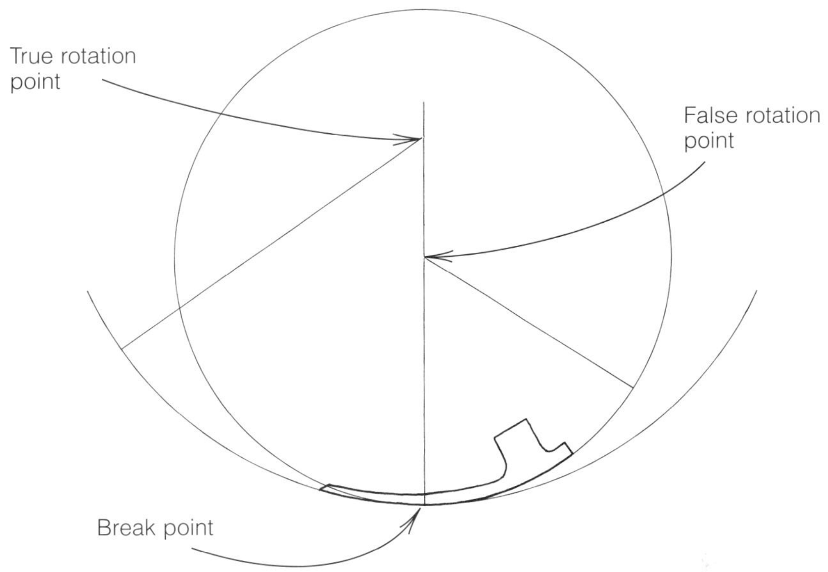

CHAPTER 14

POWER-SAW BLADES

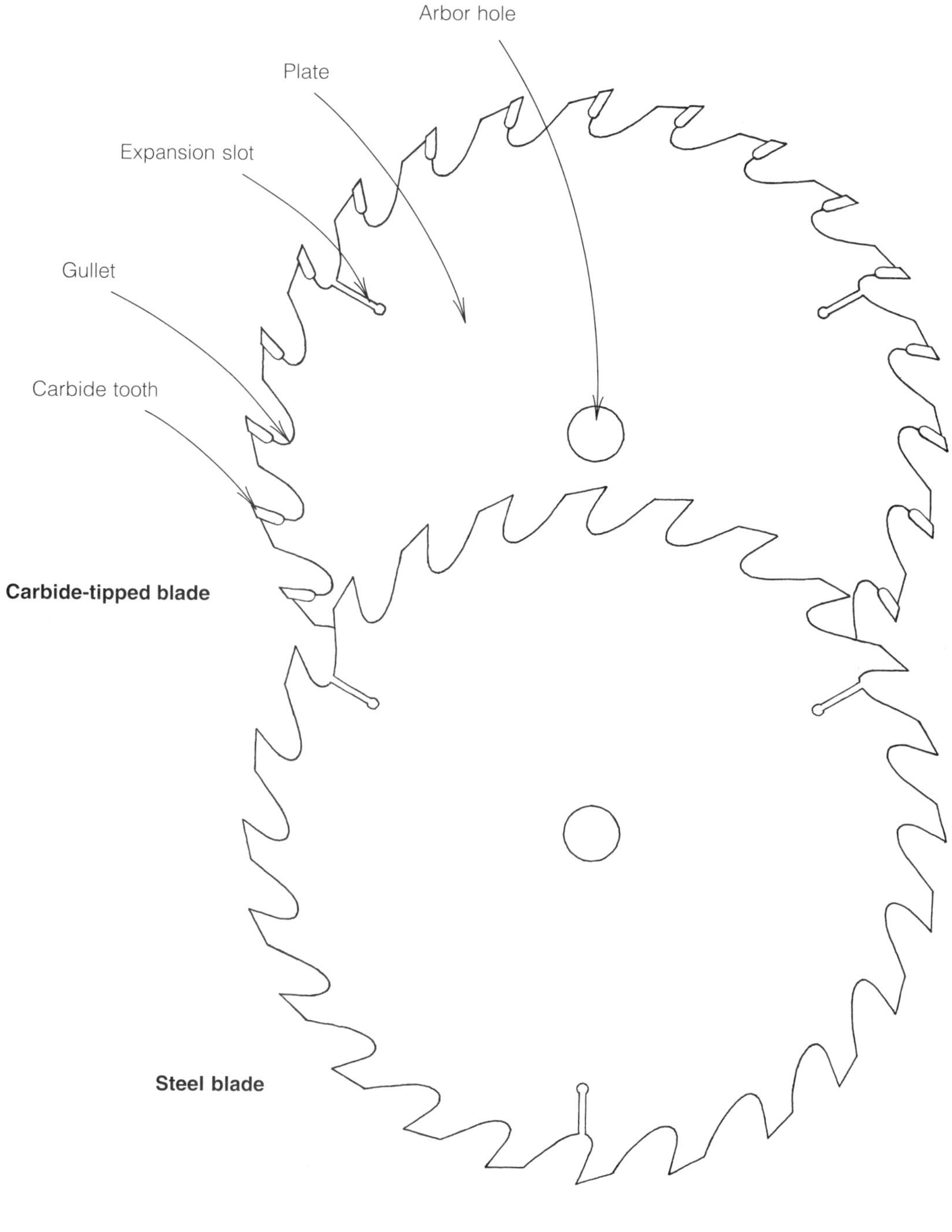

Although very few craftsmen sharpen their own circular-saw or bandsaw blades today, some understanding of saw sharpening and tooth shape is necessary to understand how a saw functions. Whether or not you ever intend to sharpen your own saw blades, an understanding of the principles will help you identify and solve problems with them, as well as guide you in blade selection.

Very few all-steel blades are used today; tungsten-carbide-tipped blades have taken over the market. For this reason, some of the information in this chapter will have limited application for many readers. It will be useful for instrument makers and model makers, who still use small-diameter all-steel blades. At the other end of the scale, it is equally applicable to the blades still used in cordwood saws and some small mills.

FACTORS IN BLADE PERFORMANCE

A circular-saw blade is basically a plate with chisels fashioned in the rim. Saw teeth cut like miniature chisels, and the forces on them are similar. There are several complicating factors with circular saws, however. Unlike a chisel, where your primary concern is a single keen edge at a suitable bevel angle, sharpness of a circular-saw blade is only one of several factors that affect the cutting action.

BLADE STIFFNESS

A blade that runs true is necessary for a clean cut. Assuming a perfectly functioning drive mechanism, there are still a number of factors related to blade stiffness alone that contribute to true running. These include the thickness and tensioning of the plate, and the speed of rotation.

Plate thickness A thick plate is usually stiffer than a thin plate. Unfortunately, it also makes a wider kerf and wastes more material. The trade-off becomes one of waste versus minimum required thickness. While you can usually afford some additional thickness in a cutoff-saw blade (because most material needs to be docked anyway), a thick rip-saw blade wastes an amazing amount of material. Just how thin you can make a rip blade depends to a great extent on the consistency and thickness of the material to be worked. Inconsistent material such as knotty pine causes more problems than a consistently hard material like birch. A saw blade naturally tends to dodge a hard spot in the wood, particularly when the knot is encountered tangentially. Cutting straight through the center of a knot causes fewer problems than clipping the edge off one.

Stiffening washers, also called blade stabilizers or blade flanges, are useful on any blade but particularly on thinner ripping blades. You should always use the largest size of stiffening washer that is feasible given the depth of material you want to cut; washers should be at least one-third the diameter of the blade. Good stiffening washers contact the blade only in a narrow band at the edge of the washer. The centers of the washers should be relieved so that pressure is focused at the perimeter band. Washers substantially improve the performance of thin blades by forcing the blade to cut in a straight line instead of dodging hard spots.

Plate tensioning All-steel saw blades must have properly tensioned plates, otherwise they will run untrue as soon as the rim begins to heat from cutting action. As the rim heats, it expands and if the plate cannot accommodate the expansion, the rim will adopt a snakelike shape. A well-tensioned plate will be slightly loose in the center. On blades over 18 in. in diameter this looseness can be visible; the portion between the arbor hole and the rim will bow away from a straightedge just slightly. As the rim heats, the loose portion will firm up with rim expansion. The blade will then run true at its normal operating temperature.

Because it is very difficult to tension small-diameter saw blades adequately by any automated process, manufacturers cut expansion slots in the rim of the blade. In some cheap blades there are no slots. In others the slots terminate in round holes to avoid stress risers that would cause blade cracking. Unfortunately, blades with holes in them tend to be exceptionally noisy because the holes act like whistles when the blade is running at speed. Some manufacturers have attempted to solve this problem by putting soft copper slugs in the holes to reduce the noise. This is only a satisfactory solution when the holes are slightly countersunk on each side first so that the slug can be riveted into position. Otherwise slugs can shift, causing rubbing on the end of the slug and throwing the blade off. Some blade manufacturers have now gone to a type of laser-cut expansion slot much like an inverted question mark that avoids stress risers and still allows the blade to run relatively quietly. Better blades have expansion slots.

Speed of rotation High rotation speeds tend to make a blade run cooler because of the increased cooling action of air on the teeth. This, in turn, reduces expansion at the rim. Blades sometimes have recommended operating speeds but almost always have maximum rotation speed limits. Contrary to what you might think, speeds beyond the rated limit make a blade looser, not tighter, causing dangerous flutter with reduced quality of cut and substantial risk of blade damage. You should never run a blade beyond the stated limit.

TOOTH HEIGHT

If the teeth of a saw blade are not all exactly the same height in relation to the center, not only will some teeth be doing more work than others but the uneven force will cause spindle stress, resulting in minute lateral displacement of the teeth. This will cause a slightly serrated finish on the wood as well as increased wear on the drive train.

GULLET SIZE

Most steel-tooth saws can be sharpened a number of times before you have to be concerned about the size of the gullets. Nonetheless, it is necessary to have gullets of a sufficient size to carry away the chips cut by the tooth. Undersized gullets will cause sawdust packing, which will quickly cause a number of other distortion problems. Gullets are usually dressed out with a suitably shaped file.

FINISH DRAG

Any part of the tooth or saw blade that touches the wood during cutting should be as smooth as possible. Numerous research projects have shown that a rough finish substantially increases rate of wear as well as increasing heat through friction. Sharpened teeth should be finished as finely as possible, even to the point of stoning them if required. The saw blade should be kept free of any gum or glue buildup and should be lightly waxed or sprayed regularly with a low-friction coating.

DRIVE MECHANISM

The best-maintained blade cannot cut well if the drive mechanism is worn or untrue. Spindle bearings have to be maintained; untrue spindles should be corrected or replaced, and worn saw collars should be refaced as necessary. Problems with the drive mechanism are more frequently the source of poor performance than bad saw blades.

STEEL CIRCULAR-SAW BLADES

Steel circular-saw blades require essentially the same treatment as handsaw blades (see Chapter 12): jointing, gumming, setting the teeth, filing the teeth and side dressing. Sharpening technique differs somewhat for rip blades and crosscut blades.

SHARPENING RIP BLADES

Circular rip blades, like the hand rip saw, have chisel-tipped teeth designed for cutting with the grain. The first step in sharpening a rip blade is to joint the teeth.

BASIC EQUIPMENT FOR SHARPENING

A typical bench setup for sharpening steel circular-saw blades includes:

1. A saw-blade vise, either commercial or shopmade.

2. Tools for spring setting the teeth: either a pistol-grip sawset for relatively thin, small-diameter blades of 4 tpi or more, or a commercial or shopmade stake-and-anvil for setting larger, heavier-gauge teeth. Swaged teeth will require a swaging tool and hammer.

3. Files for sharpening: these might include feather-edge files, triangular or square-section files, round-edge flat mill files or round files; and a stone for jointing.

4. A set gauge, raker gauge and gullet compass (all of which can be shopmade) to control tooth-shape tolerances.

5. For frequent blade sharpening or reconditioning, a grinder or other powered arbor, plus a diamond-point dresser to shape your own abrasive grinding wheels for saw-blade gumming.

Jointing Jointing accomplishes three things: it removes the rounded shoulders on tooth tips caused by prolonged cutting; it levels the teeth in preparation for the filing of crisp, new tips; and it ensures that the blade is round.

To prepare for jointing, rip partway through a hardwood board, clamp the board in position and adjust the blade height until the teeth are just proud of the board, as shown in the photo at right. Unplug the saw and rotate the blade by hand, bringing one tooth to apogee. Using the horizontal top surfaces of the board as a guide, file or hone the tip of the tooth to create a very small, new flat. Then rotate the blade to move on to the next tooth.

Gumming Gumming is the process of enlarging tooth gullets to maintain chip-carrying capacity. Gumming is not usually required until a blade has been sharpened several times.

The shape of the gullet contour also establishes the rake angle of the tooth. In the case of a rip blade, "half pitch" describes the geometry where the lead edge of a tooth, extended toward the center portion of the blade, falls halfway between the center hole and the perimeter (see the drawing at right). Well-rounded gullet lines are needed to clear chips and to prevent cracks from forming. Gullets must be uniform to ensure balance as well as even distribution of heat and stress. To establish a new line for gullet bottoms, scribe a circle with a pair of trammel points or a compass.

STEEL CIRCULAR RIP BLADE

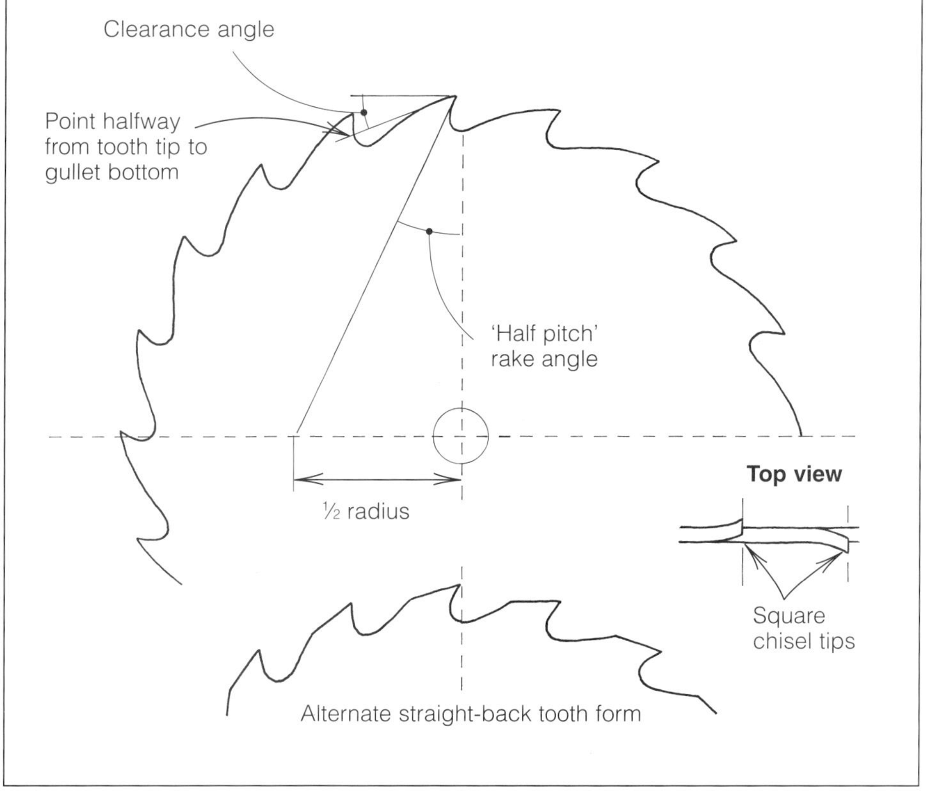

With the saw teeth just proud of a kerf in a hardwood board, joint the tips with a stone.

Gum rip-tooth gullets to half pitch with an 8-in. or 10-in. round file (second-cut), deepening and shaping the gullet lines by eye down to the new line. The blade should be held in a saw vise (as shown in the photo at top left below). Take the same number of file strokes per gullet to ensure balanced metal removal.

A power-driven abrasive gumming wheel will also do the job, potentially faster and more uniformly. Use a diamond-point dresser to shape an abrasive wheel to the proper profile. Then mount the wheel on a table saw, radial-arm saw, bench grinder, mandrel or electric drill and make a jig to control the angle of attack and ensure square-edged gullets as you move from tooth to tooth (see the photo at top right below). Power gumming should be done very slowly to prevent heat buildup.

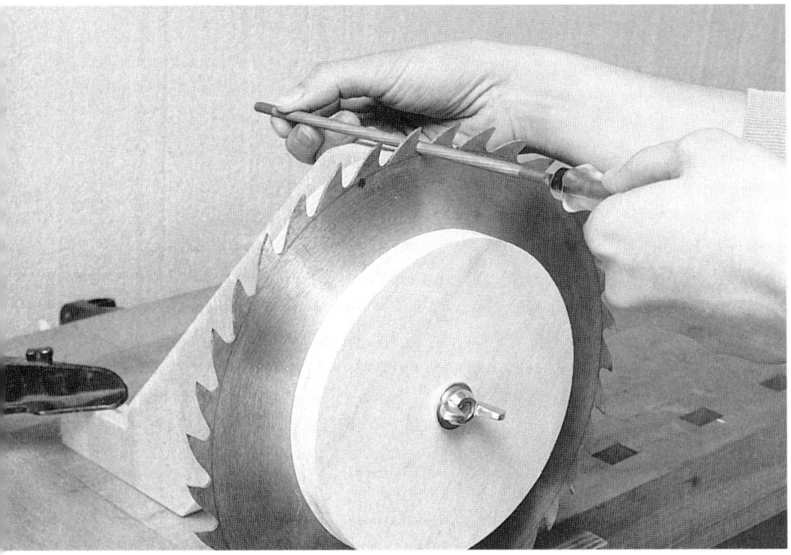

Gum rip-tooth gullets to half pitch with a round file.

Power gumming can be done with a thin, round-edge abrasive wheel mounted on a radial-arm saw. Note the clamp and indexing pin to register successive teeth.

A saw wrest is a traditional saw-setting tool used on large, thick blades.

File across the backs of the rip teeth, sliding the file up toward the tips.

Setting the teeth The alternate bending over of tooth tips called "set" creates the kerf clearance that prevents binding and the dangers of stock kickback. The set must be even to reduce strain, chatter, vibration and the tendency of the blade to lead to one side during the cut. The amount of set should be no more than half the thickness of the tooth, and can be less when dry hardwood is being cut.

In the past, for large, relatively thick blades, a wrench-like notch tool called a saw wrest was used to bend teeth over, with the amount of tooth set judged by an experienced eye (see the photo at bottom left on the facing page). More common, however, and much easier to control is a commercial stake-and-anvil with a spring-loaded punch or hammer.

To measure the amount of set, make a four-bolt side-set gauge called a spider, which can be read or preset with the help of a feeler gauge on a flat surface (see the photo on p. 157). It's advisable to duplicate the amount of set noted when the blade was new, though cutting thin, dry hardwood will permit considerably less set than that required for thick, wet softwoods. To keep the amount of necessary bending force to a minimum and to avoid setting up strains that might endanger the gullet bottoms, don't set more than one-third of the way down the tooth set. Set alternate teeth in one direction; then turn the blade over and set the remaining teeth in the other direction. Never reverse the set of a tooth.

Swaging In production ripping operations, especially where green lumber is sawn in quantity, teeth on larger-diameter blades are sometimes swaged rather than set. This is a technique whereby the steel tip of each tooth is spread so its extra width at the flared point is given clearance on both sides, allowing fast ripping and high feed rates, but a rough cut. This is done with swaging anvils, eccentric swaging machines or simple upset swagers. After swaging, the tooth sides must be taper-dressed with a file to create tip-to-body clearance, and to even the set in preparation for the final filing of the tips.

Filing the teeth Rip teeth need square chisel tips for proper cutting. After gumming and setting, mount the blade in a saw vise. File straight across the backs of the teeth, sliding the file upward toward the point during each stroke to create the curved back slope of the tooth, as shown in the photo at bottom right on the facing page. Depending on the size of the teeth, use a triangular taper file or a flat mill file (bastard cut). To maintain an adequate clearance angle and ensure that the backs of the teeth don't end up higher than the points, keep in mind a line from the tip of the tooth back to a point halfway between the bottom of the gullet and top of the next tooth. Maintain the original factory clearance angle, which should be in the range of 12° to 20° near the tooth tip.

File alternate teeth (*with* the set to avoid chatter), knocking off the burr with a scrap of wood to see more clearly the results of filing. Then turn the blade around and complete the remaining teeth. File the backs of the teeth until the flats resulting from previous jointing have just disappeared. Note that on some rip blades, the back of each tooth is a straight line that finally dips into a gullet contour (see the drawing on p. 179). Maintain this straight back during filing. Don't file the leading edges of the teeth. Commercial file guides are available to regulate the filing stroke, but they are not really necessary if you're prepared to do a little practicing to minimize the arm's natural tendency to arc during the freehand filing stroke.

Side dressing To even the set and remove burrs, do a very light side honing with a flat stone on the side of the blade after sharpening. A more accurate dressing can be accomplished by laying the blade flat on an abrasive disc or on a supported sheet of silicon-carbide sandpaper or fine emery cloth, then slowly turning the blade backward for one revolution.

SHARPENING CROSSCUT BLADES

The crosscut-blade category includes plywood- and veneer-cutting blades, as well as blades designed for some cutoff saws and smooth trimmer saws. Unlike rip-saw blades, crosscut blades tend to be fine-toothed with alternately beveled tips to sever the fibers during the cut. Teeth may be spring-set on a flat-blade body, or without set when the blade is hollow-ground. Because of the sheer number of cutters to sharpen on these blades, and the fact that equally smooth cuts can often be made with a more versatile combination planer blade, steel crosscut blades are playing a dwindling role in woodworking shops. They tend to be reserved for small-scale work in thin materials, typically by musical-instrument makers and model makers.

Jointing Joint only enough to create small flats on all teeth, using the method described for rip blades.

Gumming In the smaller diameters of crosscut blades, gullet-shaping (gumming) occurs as part of the final filing step, described below. On larger-diameter blades with rounded gullet bottoms, use a round file for gumming, in a manner similar to that described for rip blades.

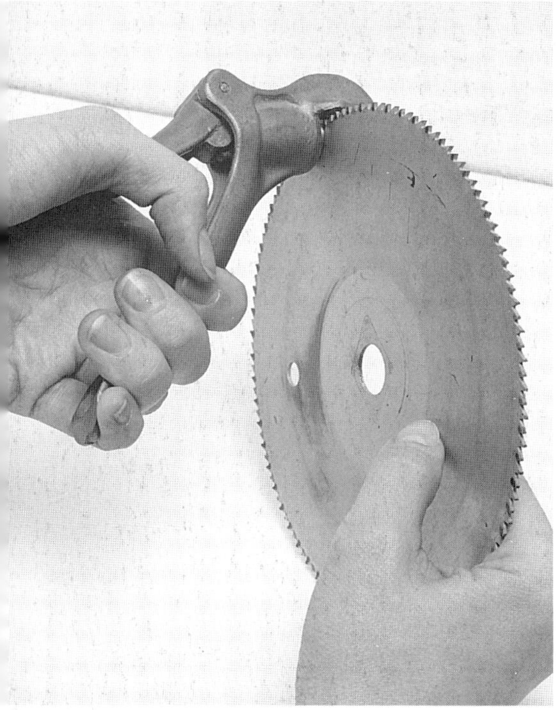

Set teeth on a steel plywood blade with a pistol-grip sawset.

Setting the teeth Blades with relatively coarse teeth (more than ¼ in. point to point) will require the use of a stake-and-anvil for setting. Finer teeth (below ¼ in. pitch) on thinner, smaller-diameter blades can be set with a heavy-duty pistol-grip sawset, as shown in the photo at left.

Filing the teeth To file the teeth, first clamp the blade in a saw vise. In general, try to maintain the original factory bevel angles and tooth profiles when filing crosscut saw teeth. As with crosscut handsaws (see Chapter 12), the teeth must be beveled on the face opposite the set. Orient the file handle to conform to the factory gullet shape and bevel angles, then file alternate teeth. Reverse the blade and file the remaining teeth until the jointing flats disappear.

On large, coarse-toothed crosscut blades, where the teeth are more than ⅜ in. from point to point and the gullets are rounded, use an 8-in. or 10-in. mill bastard file with two rounded safe edges. Tooth pitches below ⅜ in. will require a thinner section flat file, an 8-in. cant saw file or a tapered triangular file, depending on tooth configuration and gullet shape.

To cut through the cross-banded layers, plywood blades must function as combination rip/crosscut blades. As such, their fine teeth will have relatively small tooth bevel angles (around 10°) and can be sharpened with triangular files, handled according to the same technique as for crosscut handsaws, where the file dresses the face and back bevel angles of adjacent teeth at the same time.

Rake angles Rake angles of crosscut teeth vary considerably with different styles and applications. Some coarse cutoff saws have V-teeth ("peg" teeth) with equal 30° back and negative rake angles (see the drawing below), while others have a milder 10° negative rake angle. One common style incorporates what are called "center pitch" teeth,

RAKE ANGLES FOR STEEL CIRCULAR CROSSCUT BLADES

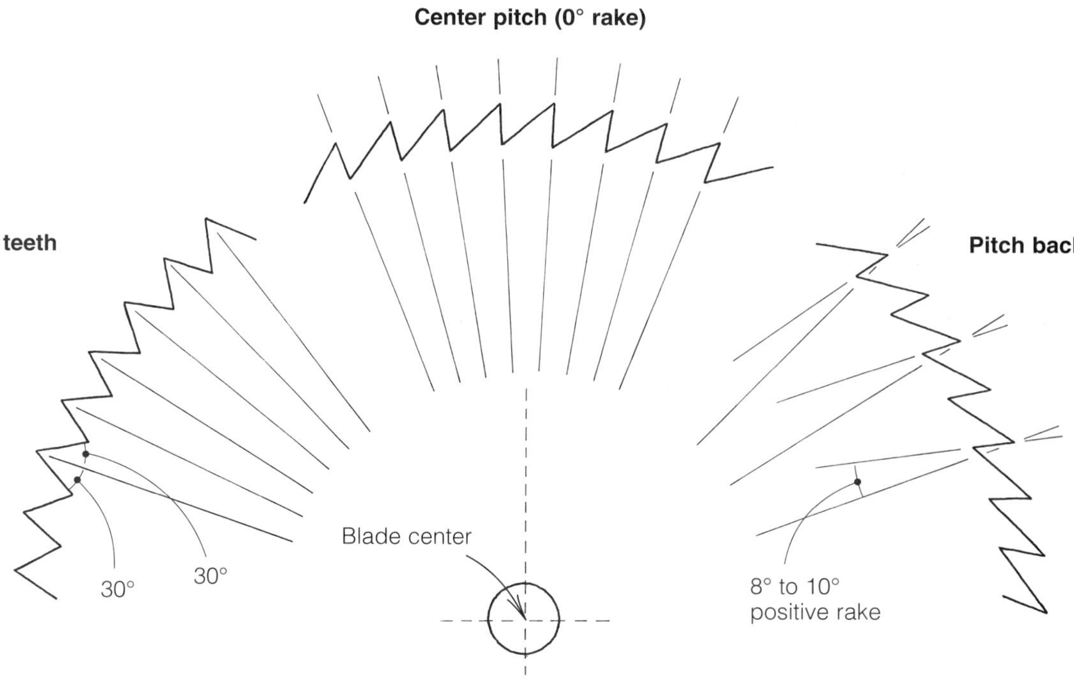

where the rake angle is zero. All these teeth have 60° gullet angles and can be sharpened with triangular files. However, blades whose teeth have a *positive* hook angle (e.g., 10° back from center pitch), such as are found on some smooth trimmer saws, have gullet angles less than 60° and won't accommodate triangular files. Instead, they require either a feather-edge file or grinding against a narrow, profiled abrasive wheel.

SHARPENING COMBINATION BLADES

There are a number of different styles of steel combination rip/crosscut blades (see the drawing below), each with its own sharpening requirements. Fortunately, all the teeth are either rip or crosscut teeth and would be sharpened accordingly.

SHARPENING DADO-BLADE SETS

Steel dado-blade sets consist of two outside cutting blades and a set of inner chipper blades (see the drawing on p. 184). The outside blades have repeating groups of cutters separated by a deep-gullet raker; the inner chippers, usually with blade-body thicknesses of ¼ in., ⅛ in. and $^1/_{16}$ in., have two diametrically opposed raker teeth. The two outer blades, in combination with one or more chippers plus suitable shims, allow accurate dado and groove cutting of any width from about ¼ in. to 1 in.

Though the pair of outer steel dado blades superficially resemble combination planer blades, they differ in that the groups of cutting teeth are all set one way and filed alike. Rakers and inside chipping teeth are filed straight across, $^1/_{64}$ in. lower than the cutters. The rakers on the two outside blades are left unset, while the chippers have swaged chisel points.

The first step in the sharpening sequence is to joint all the teeth of the outside blades, as well as the inner chippers, to the same height. (This step may not be necessary for a minor touchup.) Next, gum the raker gullets on the outside blades to about one-third pitch.

If necessary, set the outer-blade cutter teeth (sometimes called the spur sections) in groups, all on one side, left or right, in an alternating pattern. Use a pistol-grip sawset or, on thicker, larger-diameter blades, a stake-and-anvil.

After setting, file the outside cutter groups with either a triangular file or a mill file held at a low angle, to achieve about a 20° face bevel angle, while maintaining the factory rake angle. Note that some dado sets use a different geometry, with outer blades having chisel-pointed spur sections ground straight across rather than beveled edges.

File the backs of the outer-blade rakers and the inner chipper teeth straight across until the flats produced by jointing disappear. Then add one or two strokes to bring all rakers and

STEEL CIRCULAR COMBINATION BLADES

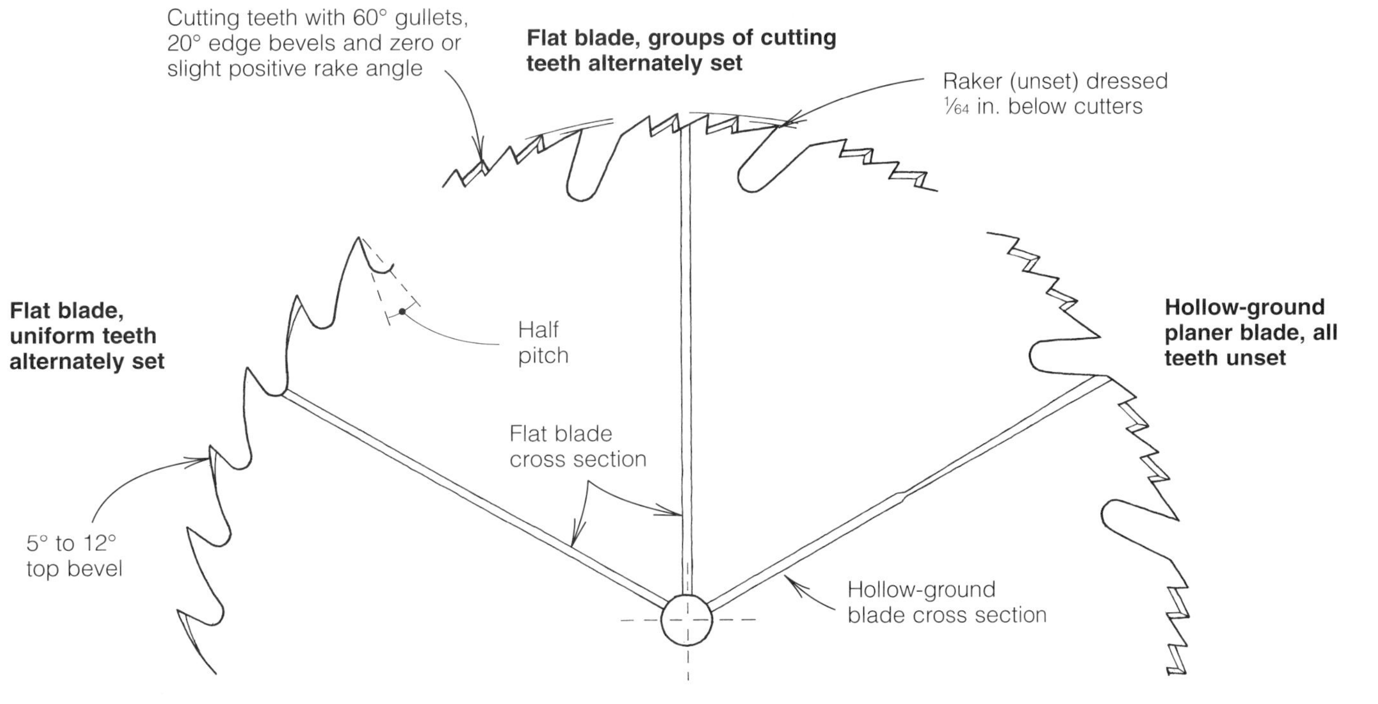

STEEL DADO BLADES

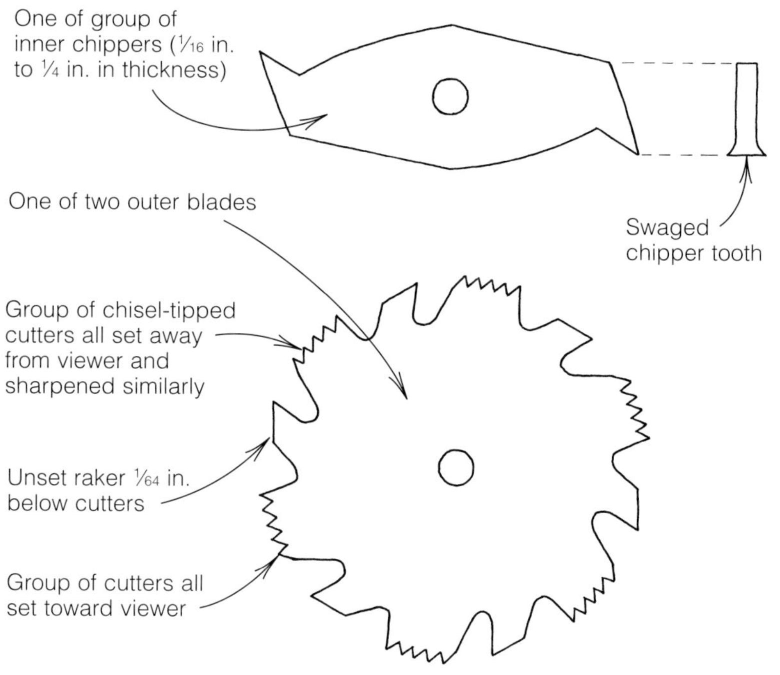

chippers down 1/64 in. below the level of the cutters. Use a shopmade raker gauge (see p. 156) to check this distance.

When setting up dado blades for use on the saw, be sure to stagger the chipper blades in relation to one another, and to nest the chipper teeth in the gullet spaces of the two outside blades, so that all blade bodies rest flat against each other. When the inner chippers have lost too much swage to refiling, send the complete set out for professional reconditioning. Some things are better left to the professional.

The wobble dado The wobble, or quick-set, dado is a single blade with an adjustable body core that can be turned and locked to cut a given width of dado, which is characterized by a somewhat concave floor. These blades come in the various tooth patterns described above. If you have not yet bought a dado set, do yourself a favor and buy a stacking model. They put less stress on your machine than wobble dadoes and are capable of much greater accuracy.

CARBIDE-TIPPED CIRCULAR-SAW BLADES

In recent decades tungsten-carbide-tipped circular-saw blades have generally replaced steel blades in both commercial and home woodworking shops. Though expensive, they cut smoothly, stay sharp much longer and can stand up to hard abrasive materials such as particleboard, medium-density fiberboard (MDF) and woods with silica content.

Tungsten carbide is a manmade alloy made through a sintering process, whereby tungsten, carbon and other ingredients are mixed, heated and fused together under pressure. The resulting compound is almost diamond-hard and can work at high temperatures, but it is too brittle to be shaped into very thin or finely tapered sections for working wood. The sections must be fairly blocky to survive shock.

High-quality carbide-tipped circular-saw blades have a number of features in common. Teeth are made from the appropriate grade of carbide, for the best balance between shock resistance and wear resistance. They have precisely machined blade bodies, balanced and tensioned for smooth, safe operation, and are rated for the rpm at which they'll be used. Good blades have adequate expansion slots and teeth of generous thickness, brazed into plate pockets (see the top drawing on the facing page). The brazing will be gap-free and non-porous.

Low-quality carbide blades have untensioned plates, the carbide teeth are not in pockets but are just brazed to the flat face of the tooth, and the brazing is often porous, causing a weak bond between plate and tooth. They can have a host of other problems as well, but lack of pockets and poor brazing are the immediate indicators.

A wide variety of carbide blade types are available for specific applications, including basic rip, crosscut and combination cut, as well as blades designed for plastics, particleboards and laminates. The various blade types are available in a range of diameters and numbers of teeth per blade.

The geometry of carbide teeth is generally more complex than that of steel blades. The effects achieved by setting and swaging in steel teeth are achieved through grinding with carbide teeth. Not only is it possible to have a variety of tooth patterns on the same blade, but the teeth often have both top and side clearance angles to improve cutting action while reducing friction in the kerf. In addition, huge strides have been made in the formulation of carbides. At one time, you had only to be concerned with the grade of carbide suitable to your purpose. The grades ranged from C1, which is the most shock resistant but the least wear resistant, to C4, which is the least shock resistant but has maximum wear resistance. Today you also have to take into consideration micro-grain carbides, which, like finely grained steel, hold an edge better because of the very fine grain structure that can be sharpened to a more perfect edge. More about that later.

TOOTH PATTERNS

Some of the basic tooth patterns for carbide blades are shown in the bottom drawing at right. They include:

Flat top These teeth have chisel-like tips particularly suited to ripping. They give a square-bottomed kerf. Although very effective in ripping solid woods, flat-top teeth tend to be dulled easily by abrasive materials such as MDF and particleboard.

Alternate top bevel (ATB) Alternately beveled, these teeth are effective in shearing fibers and reducing tearout, giving a smooth cross-grain cut even in stringy materials. They are a standard choice for cutoff work.

Combination This is a multi-purpose blade suited for the user who wants a single blade for both ripping and crosscutting. The usual design features five closely grouped teeth with a deep gullet between groupings. The first tooth in the group is a raker tooth followed by four alternate-topped bevel teeth. Although a compromise design, combination teeth give an acceptable finish in crosscutting and are still quite efficient in ripping. This is the blade to have if you can afford only one.

Triple-chip grind (TCG) Specifically designed for dense abrasive materials such as MDF, particleboard and plastic laminates, these blades have a unique cutting action. The triple-beveled chippers knock out a central groove, and the ensuing flat-top raker dresses it out to full width. This not only minimizes the shock on an individual tooth but also substantially reduces blast-out in laminates.

Hollow-ground teeth This is another design that strives to reduce blast-out in laminates. Teeth that are ground hollow on the face encourage material to collapse toward the center of the kerf. Teeth alternately clear the center of the cut then the edges. This design is particularly effective in reducing chipping of double-faced melamines, but it is not a style that can be sharpened by all sharpening services.

CARBIDE-TIPPED CIRCULAR BLADES

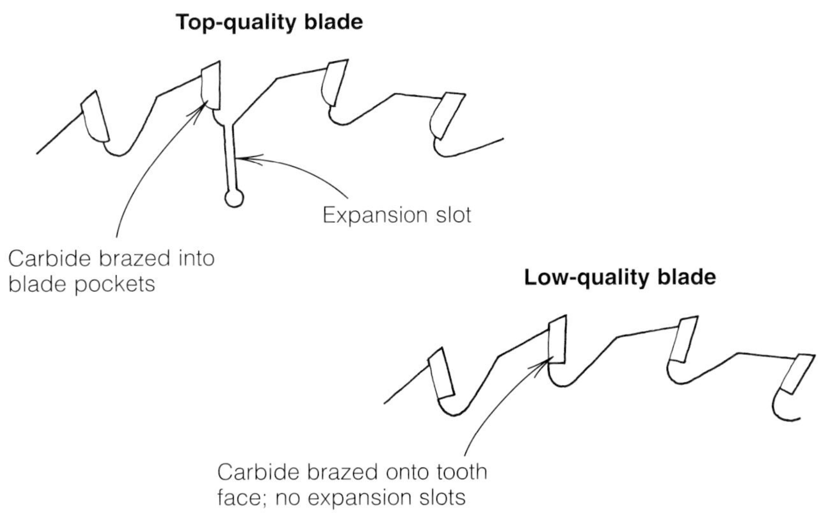

TOOTH PATTERNS FOR CARBIDE-TIPPED BLADES

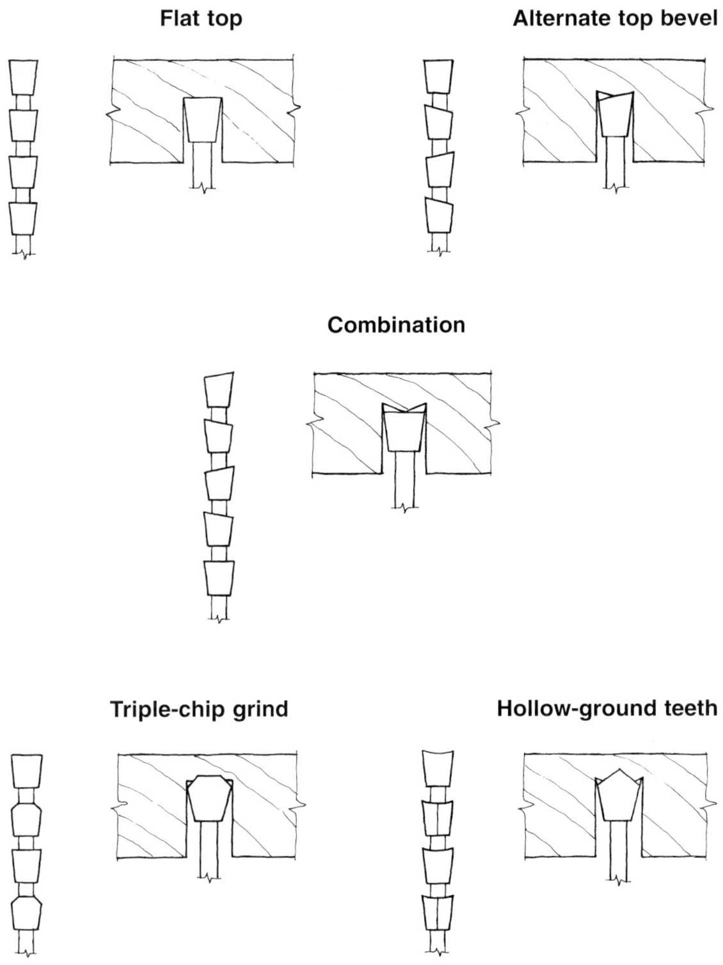

SHARPENING CARBIDE SAW BLADES

In general, you should not attempt to sharpen your own carbide saw blades. The hardness of carbide requires that you do it with a diamond hone. If you use a hone coarser than 600x, you risk fracturing the carbide. Regardless of the care you take, you also risk all the other problems of inadvertently changing clearance or bevel angles, causing uneven tooth height, and so on.

If you absolutely must touch up a blade to finish a project, do the absolute minimum of work and do it carefully. You will change tooth height and affect tooth geometry the least if you work only on the face of the tooth (except for hollow-ground teeth). Use a good quality 600x (or finer) diamond hone.

Even with a 600x hone you will leave a much rougher surface than is achieved with a 600x power wheel. A power wheel tends to leave a fine finish if it is set to remove a given amount and then traverses the tooth. The set amount will be removed in the initial stage of the traverse, and the balance of the wheel will refine the surface, just removing the high spots.

You will protect your investment best if you send or take the blade to a reputable sharpening service. The service should use 600x diamond wheels with flood coolant. Dry grinding can cause cracking from heat buildup. The coefficient of expansion of carbide is much less than steel; the differential can be deadly if heat is not minimized.

Most services use 400x for facing the tooth and 600x for topping. This should be the minimum; 600x for both is better. Some teeth are now sharpened with an 800x wheel, but that fine a grit is uncommon.

Unless a tooth is chipped, in which case it may have to be replaced, sharpening should remove no more than 0.005 in. from the tooth face and 0.010 in. from the top. A good service will remove the minimum amount of carbide, sometimes as little as 0.003 in.

AN OUNCE OF PREVENTION...

Good sharpening technique goes hand in hand with tool care that minimizes dulling in the first place. There are many things you can do to avoid dulling your saw blades.

1. Choose the appropriate blade for the material and for the type of cut being made.

2. Don't run a blade beyond its rated rpm, and use an appropriate feed speed that keeps the blade cutting without bogging down.

3. Try to use a setup that keeps at least three teeth in contact with the stock.

4. Examine blades routinely for sharpness, cracks, runout, warp, imbalance and rust. Don't store blades in direct sunlight that can heat and distort the body. Use a light coat of oil, wax or water-displacement chemical to keep invisible rust from nibbling away at the teeth.

5. Don't touch the teeth unless it is necessary. Many people have acidic perspiration that causes rust almost instantaneously. With carbide teeth, perspiration can etch the teeth.

6. Some blades come from the factory coated with lacquer to prevent rust. Strip off this coating, taking particular care in the area of the arbor hole and support flanges to ensure smooth seating and to reduce the chance of blade flutter. Accumulated gum and pitch can cause binding, kickback, friction and heat. To remove sticky resins, soak your blades in kerosene or use a commercial gum and pitch remover. Don't scrape off accumulations with an edged tool, however, since the scratch marks will attract more residues.

7. Keep the table-saw top aligned with the plane of the blade.

8. Check that support flanges are clean and flat, and that they are at least one-third the diameter of the blade in use.

9. Don't overtighten the arbor nut.

10. Ensure that the rip fence is aligned and that the throat-insert plate is flat and flush with the table top.

11. Don't try to bore out the arbor hole on your circular blade since this can adversely affect tensioning and concentricity.

12. Never let the teeth touch steel. If you lay the blade down, lay it on wood. Be very careful when changing blades.

13. Never let a carbide blade overheat. The cobalt in the carbide can virtually evaporate. At temperatures as low as 300°C (572°F) chemical reaction, particularly when cutting MDF, can cause the cobalt to sublimate.

14. Always use a steady, controlled feed rate for work. Blades usually last longer in production shops with power feeders than at the hands of hobbyists, who often feed work at alarming rates and then puzzle over bad cuts.

Variable feed rates cause two problems. First, a fast feed rate can cause shocks that will fracture the teeth. Second, because a saw blade is just like a gyroscope, reaction is at 90° to applied force. An uneven feed rate causes the blade to waver laterally as it reacts to the force differences.

from the face and 0.005 in. from the top. If there are no chipped teeth, such light removal can often fully restore a blade.

SOME FINER POINTS OF CARBIDE SAWS

Carbide teeth are brazed onto saw blades by various methods, the two most common being either freehand with an oxyacetylene torch, or in a more controlled manner with induction heating coils. The traditional brazing material was silver solder in wire form, which wicked into the joint by capillary action. One problem with both methods is that the metal plate expands much more than the carbide during the brazing process. This can cause microscopic cracking of the carbide even when a high-silver-content solder is used.

Tri-met brazing More recently, some manufacturers have begun using a tri-metal sandwich between the pocket and the tooth. This is a silver-copper-silver sandwich 0.012 in. or 0.015 in. thick that prevents the fracturing by providing some flexibility; it also provides a cushion to absorb shock. The technology originated in the manufacture of shaper bits and larger router bits, where the problems are magnified.

Micro-grain carbides Just as with steel, the finer you can make the grain in tungsten carbide the better the edge you get and the finer the finish you can put on it. The micro-grain carbides are all in the C4 category, which means that they have good wear characteristics but are subject to shock fractures. In some ways the toughness is increased as particle size is reduced, because it provides a greater number of inner-connective bonds. In general, as the cobalt content is reduced in micro-grain carbides, the hardness and wear characteristics are improved. Some have as little as 4% cobalt and in the sub-micron range as little as 3%.

One of the difficulties here is to know just what a micro-grain carbide is. The measure used is 1 micron, but it is used differently in different parts of the industry. Some carbide manufacturers say that it is micro-grain carbide if the majority of particles are less than 1 micron in size. Others say that it can be called micro-grain if 20% of the particles are less than 1 micron, and still others say that all the particles have to be 1 micron or less. In fact, some manufacturers offer coarse, medium and fine micro-grain carbides but tend to be a bit vague about the particle size. If you want to unnerve your blade supplier, you might want to ask the size of the micro-grain carbide in their saw teeth. Most suppliers cannot answer the question. As an aside, these teeth must be sharpened with at least a 600x diamond wheel, otherwise much of the edge effect of the finer structure will be lost.

BANDSAW BLADES

At one time, bandsaw blades were routinely resharpened, but their relative cost has dropped to the point where it is more economical to replace them than send them out for resharpening. In addition, bandsaw blades almost universally have flame-hardened tips, and while it is possible to resharpen several times it is not possible to set the teeth without breakage. Each time the blade is sharpened you lose a bit more set.

If you should want to sharpen your own bandsaw blades, there is really only one practical approach—using an appropriately sized diamond burr in a flex shaft or a small Dremel-type hand grinder.

In general, you want to retain the original tooth geometry of the blade. This is most easily done if you remove the blade from the bandsaw and clamp it in a vise, as you would a handsaw. Selecting a diamond burr of the right diameter, you will find that you can sharpen each tooth quite quickly with very little experience.

CARBIDE AND CHEMICALS

Most woodworkers are familiar with the non-wood constituents of chipboard and particleboard. These materials are notorious for high levels of grit and the occasional piece of metal. Only affluent woodworkers would use their best saw blades on them. But most woodworkers are unaware of other problems lurking in these reconstituted materials, such as the chemical composition of glues and binders.

Medium-density fiberboard (MDF) is a popular woodworking material today. It is equally popular with sharpening services, since blades can be dulled at an alarming rate when working MDF. One of the unanticipated problems in working MDF is that there are occasional resin globules encapsulated in the material. These are particularly hard and can cause a substantial shock to a carbide tooth. Combined with this is the high density of the material, which causes heat buildup through friction, and, finally, the nature of the binders themselves, which can cause chemical interaction with tungsten carbide, even with high-speed steel.

A substantial amount of research has been done in this area of hot corrosion, and three phenomena have been studied in detail—high-temperature oxidation, high-temperature halogenation and high-temperature sulfidation. These chemical effects outstrip the normal wear effect of cutting the material. The extent of these problems is leading the industry into the development of new carbides and has already been instrumental in the introduction of ceramic router bits.

CHAINSAW TEETH

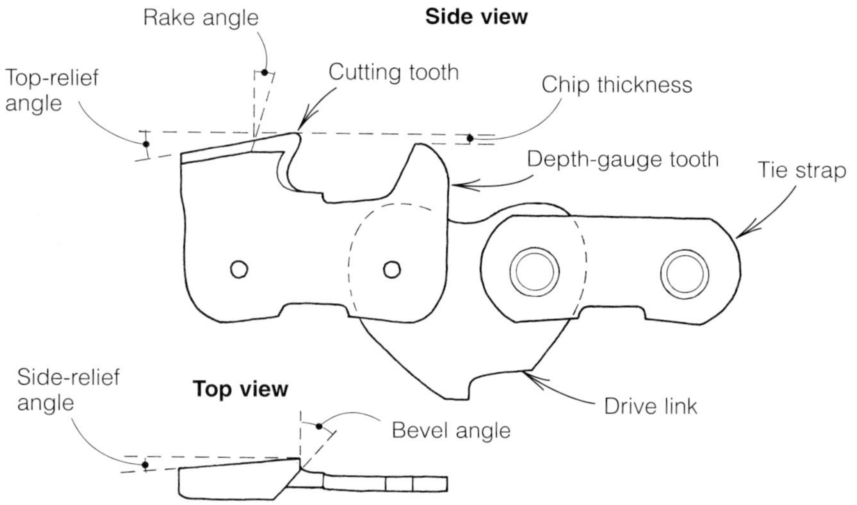

FILE ANGLE FOR SHARPENING CUTTERS

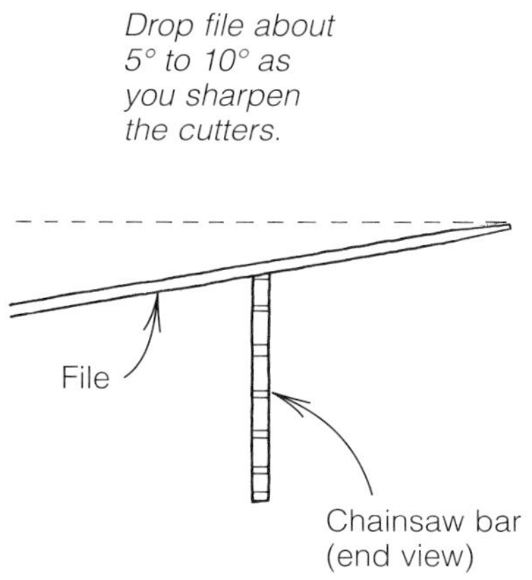

Set up for sharpening a saw chain by clamping the chainsaw bar in a mechanic's vise, with the chain tightened until you can just rotate it with a stick by hand. (Photo by Susan Kahn)

CHAINSAWS

I have always found it curious that people who will quite cheerfully sharpen their own chisels and plane blades will take their saw chains to a commercial sharpening service. In my opinion, it's easier to do a competent job sharpening saw chains than sharpening plane blades.

Your chain specifications (rake angle, bevel angle, gauge-tooth height, pitch, etc.) will all be specified in the operator's manual. The manual will also tell you what diameter round file you should use for sharpening.

There are several hand-held electric chain sharpeners on the market, as well as several filing jigs. All come with instructions for use. Here, I will cover only the basic method using an unjigged file by hand.

SHARPENING A SAW CHAIN

Begin by clamping the center of the bar of the chainsaw in a mechanic's vise, as shown in the photo at left. Tighten the chain until you can just rotate it using a stick of wood on the chain with one hand on each end.

Using the round file recommended in your operator's manual, take as many strokes as necessary to sharpen a cutting tooth, maintaining the original rake (or "hook") angle and bevel angle (typically 30° and 35°, respectively). The file should be held with the handle just slightly dropped (5° to 10°) as you do this (see the drawing at right above). Repeat for two or three more teeth, advance the chain and then repeat the operation until you have sharpened all the teeth that can be sharpened from one side. Reverse the chainsaw in the vise and do the other half of the teeth.

Once every two or three sharpenings, you may also have to file the depth-gauge teeth. The indications that these need attention are reduced rate of cut and fine, not chunky, sawdust. For this job, you'll need to slip a depth-gauge tool over the chain to check the setting. You can either buy a gauge specific to your saw, or make one as described in the sidebar on p. 156, using the gauge-height information in the operator's manual.

Be careful not to overfile gauge teeth or the chain will grab and cut roughly. It's better to leave them a bit too high than too low. Also, always restore the curved profile after shortening the teeth; otherwise, they will grab in the cut causing chain chatter.

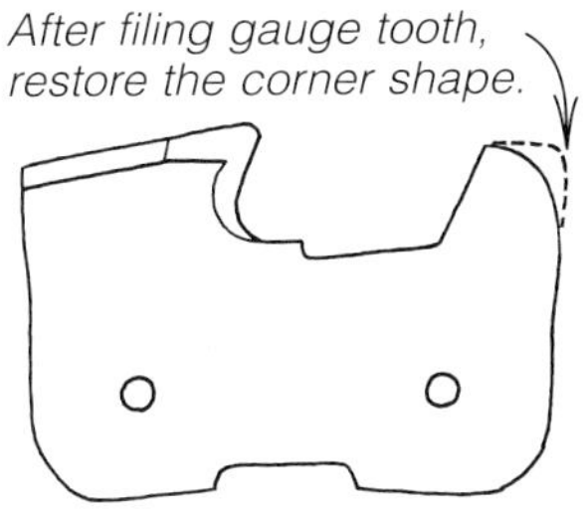

Restoring damaged teeth Unless you have hit a stone, one or two file strokes should be enough to sharpen each tooth. You have to be fairly ham-handed to change the tooth geometry significantly with one or two strokes. However, if you have dulled the chain by hitting a stone, you may have to take a half-dozen strokes or more to remove all tooth rounding (see the top drawing at right).

For this many strokes, more care will have to be taken to maintain the original tooth geometry. It is fairly easy to maintain the bevel, though if you cannot do so by eye you can make yourself a bevel guide (see p. 151). The real trick is to maintain the rake angle. The natural tendency is to press down on the file rather than drawing it laterally into the tooth; the result of downward pressure is that you increase the rake angle by undercutting the tooth. An increase in rake angle (like a short gauge tooth) causes the chain to grab and run rough in the cut.

To prevent this problem, position yourself almost directly over the chain and note how much of the file is covered by the link tooth and how much is exposed before you start filing (see the bottom drawing at right). As you file, keep the same amount exposed and you will not change the rake angle.

RIPPING CHAIN

The vast majority of chainsaws are used in crosscut work only. To do a competent job of ripping, they require a different chain sharpened quite differently. The most common need for ripping with a chainsaw is in chainsaw lumbermaking. A crosscut chain can be modified for efficient ripping by converting it to 0° bevel and 50° rake, but it is better to buy chain designed specifically for ripping. Ripping chain is generally available at specialty chainsaw dealers, who can also provide the necessary filing specifications.

SOME CHAINSAW DOS AND DON'TS

Because of the relief angle built into the top of a cutting tooth, each time you sharpen it you lower the cutting edge. The secret to keeping teeth all the same height is to keep them the same length. Every few touchups on a chain you should measure the length of the teeth and, exactly as you would do if you were jointing a handsaw, file them all to the length of the shortest tooth. This will automatically make them all the same height.

The allowable depth of cut of an individual tooth can be greater in softwood than in hardwood, and greater in green wood than in dry. If you intend to use your chainsaw for general-purpose work, you should file the gauge teeth to accommodate the hardest, driest material that you will be cutting. This will slow you down a bit in green wood or softwood, but you will have a far safer tool with substantially reduced risk of kickback.

Throughout this book, I have generally avoided repeating the phrase that you shouldn't run with sharp objects in your hand because it is self-evident. But a chainsaw is potentially the most dangerous tool you can use. You should not even think about starting up a chainsaw unless you are wearing safety pants or chaps. You should also have a hard hat, hearing protectors and other safety equipment suitable to the work you are doing.

You add a substantial margin of safety to the operation of your saw if the chain is properly sharpened.

FILING DAMAGED TEETH

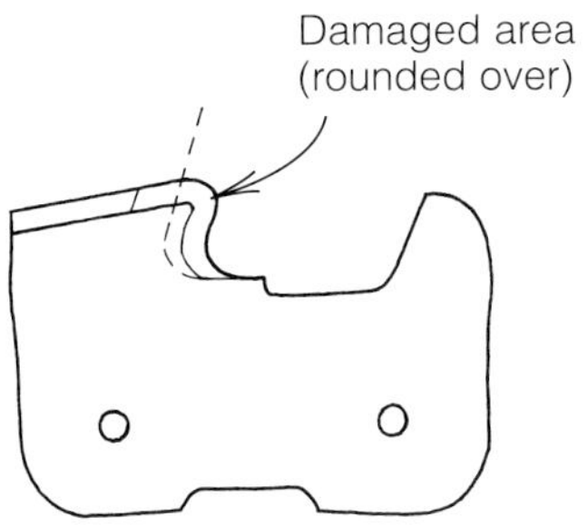

After striking a stone, damaged teeth must be filed back to eliminate any rounding.

MAINTAINING RAKE ANGLE

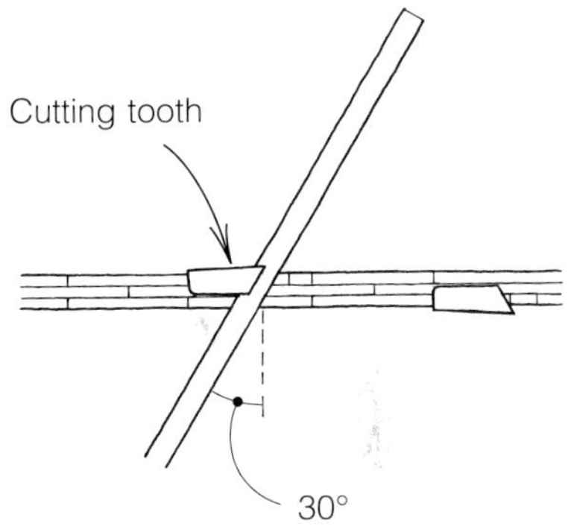

Learning how to sharpen your own chain is a bit like learning how to pack your own parachute—it's your health that's going to be involved in the use of this tool, and you should rely on yourself to protect it.

CHAPTER 15

DRILL BITS

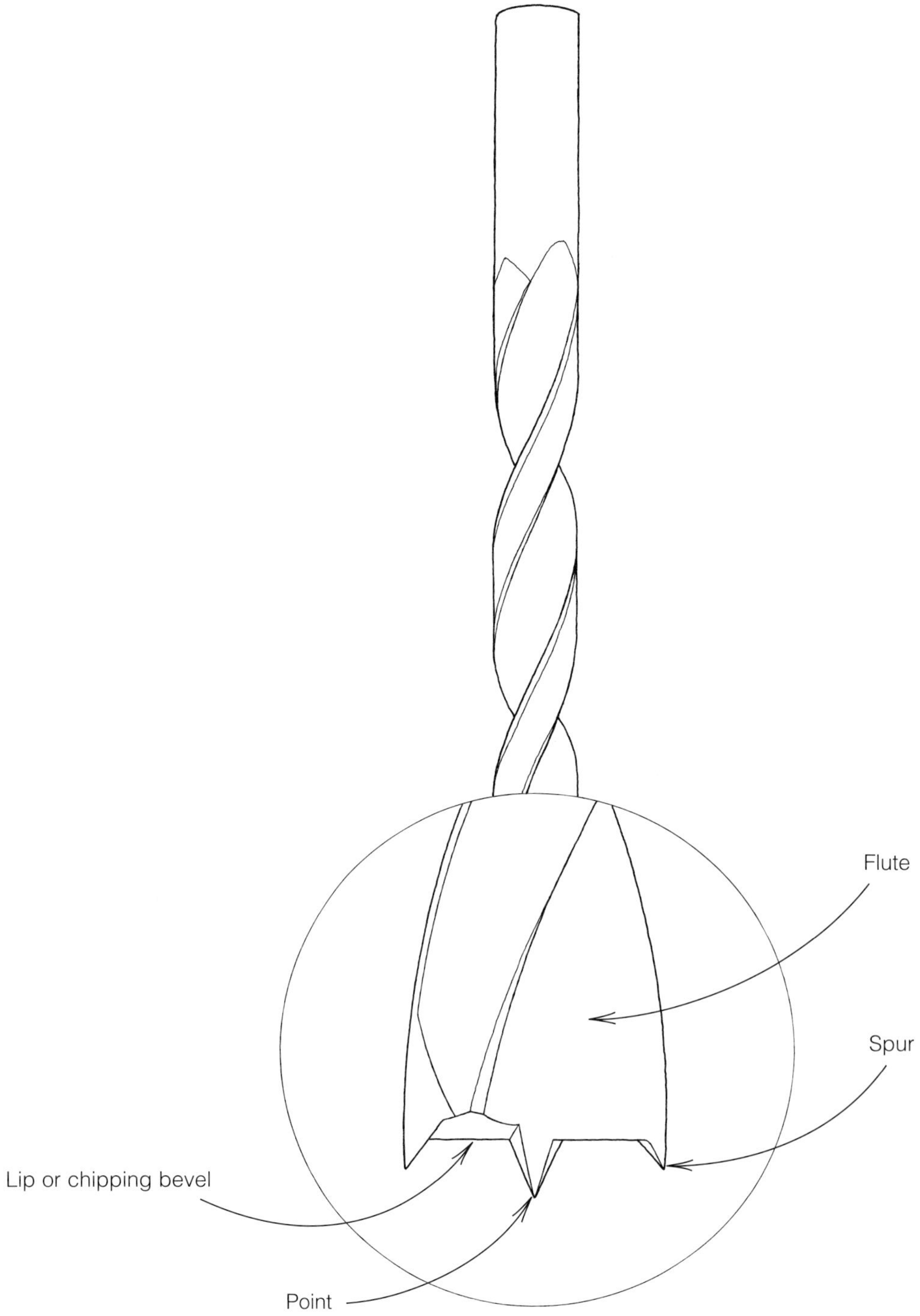

Of all the cutting tools that woodworkers use, drill bits have more demanded of them and less attention paid to them than any others. We expect them to drill end grain and cross grain equally well and are immediately suspicious of them, not ourselves, when we find that holes we drill are untrue or oversize. But the ultimate insult to drill bits is that we do not bother sharpening them as long as increasing amounts of pressure will still cause them to cut.

We do the most damage to our bits when we underfeed and overspeed. All drill bits, from inexpensive carbon-steel bits to top-of-the-line carbide-tipped bits, will last longer and hold their edge better if they are not overheated. Almost without exception, woodworkers run their bits at excessive rpm for the feed rate that they are using.

If you think about the way you use a brace and a bit, you will realize that you never produce such thick chips when you are using an electric hand drill or a drill press. This is because you are almost invariably underfeeding for a given rpm. You should either increase the feed rate or cut back on the rpm. Otherwise, you stand a good chance of overheating the bit from a lot of unnecessary friction. Anybody who owns Forstner bits will know exactly what I mean. If Forstner bits are not used at low speeds and maximum feeds, the chances of generating enough friction to burn a rim are very high. Yet properly used, Forstner bits cut the cleanest, most accurate holes of any bit in the shop. There is an incentive to act intelligently.

GENERAL SHARPENING CONSIDERATIONS

Unlike chisels, planes, turning tools and many other cutting tools that you buy today, drill bits are usually ready to use when they are new. Also, unlike the other tools just mentioned, it is usually wise to honor the manufacturer's geometry. In other words, you should maintain the same cutting angles, the same clearance angles and the same rake angles that the manufacturer used originally. You will be considered no less of a craftsman for not introducing your own idiosyncrasies to these particular tools.

Honoring the geometry of the bit also means that you should leave the center of the bit where you find it. The two fastest ways to ruin a drill bit are to grind the tip off-center and to tinker with the circumferential surface. Either can change the effective cutting diameter of the bit and render it useless for anything other than drilling approximately sized holes.

One last cautionary note is that you should always do the least amount of sharpening possible. This is one place where more is not better. You will find it sufficiently challenging to maintain bit geometry using a minimalist approach. If you approach the problem determined to regrind, rehone and restore every visible surface, you will be dead in the water before you know it. In many ways, it is fortunate that most woodworkers ignore their drill bits since undue attention brings with it substantial potential for damage.

DRILL-BIT METALLURGY

In no category of tools do we find a broader range of metals than in woodworking bits. Bits range from the simple carbon tool steel of an auger bit through complex alloys, various varieties of high-speed steel, surface treatments like nitriding, inserted tips of various types, to bits that are solid tungsten carbide from shank to tip. Just as this wide range of materials has a wide range of edge-holding abilities, heat tolerances and purchase prices, each requires different sharpening materials and tactics.

In general, the ease of sharpening is inversely proportional to the complexity of metallurgy. You can easily touch up a steel auger bit with an auger-bit file, whereas your entire sharpening arsenal will probably be useless to you when you are facing a badly chipped carbide bit. Just as you should not feel inadequate for neither wanting to nor knowing how to reorganize the geometry of your drill bits, you should recognize that some things are best left to specialized services. Excessive sharpening zeal can cause you as much trouble as do-it-yourself surgery.

TWIST BITS

Everybody owns a set of twist bits. They are used for drilling wood, metal, plastic, plasterboard, virtually anything that needs to be perforated around the house. Twist bits are sharpened differently for different materials. For example, a much more acute point angle is used for wood than for metal. Since this book is all about sharpening woodworking tools and twist bits are far from being the best choice for woodworking, I think that it makes more sense to deal with the general-purpose style, still a very necessary set of bits in any shop.

The vast majority of twist bits are ground in the standard configuration shown to the left in the photo on p. 192—that is, 118° point angle and 30° of rake. These are perfectly fine bits and will give good service. A variation that I prefer for general-purpose use is the split-tip style shown at right in the photo. These bits have the same rake angle with a somewhat more oblique point angle (140°), but the primary difference is that this style has greater chip-carrying capacity because of the parabolic flute design; it also tends to drill a tighter tolerance hole because of the wider edge margin. These bits seem to work equally well in metal; in fact, the split-tip point virtually eliminates skating. A center dimple is usually not needed to start a hole.

STANDARD TWIST-BIT GEOMETRY

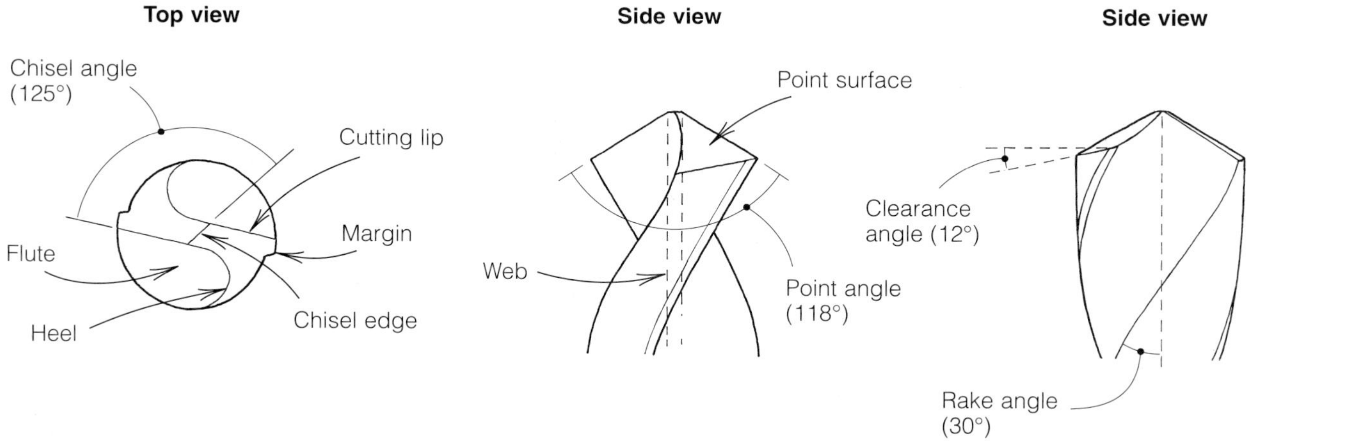

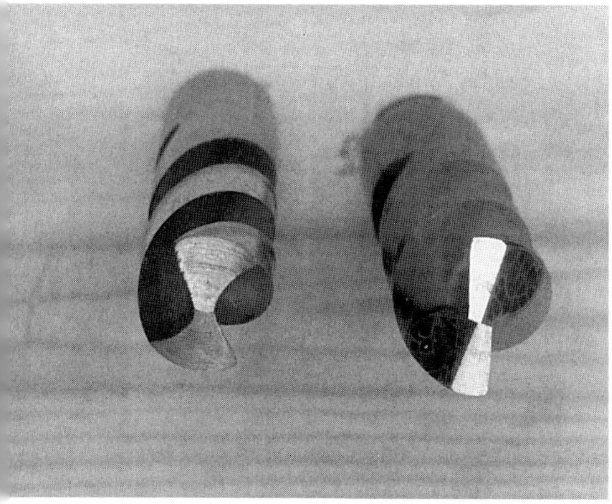

Two styles of twist bits: standard tip (left) and split tip (right). The split-tip bit has less tendency to skate on entry. (Photo by Susan Kahn)

Rather than spending a great deal of time describing shopmade jigs and devices that give indifferent results with twist bits, or telling you how to go about the freehand grinding of twist bits (which is a direct road to hell!), I would make two strong recommendations. First, buy only American-made high-speed-steel twist bits. They are still the best of any made in the world and will stay sharp for an incredible length of time if not abused. Second, buy a twist-drill sharpening jig and follow the instructions. For bits up to ⅜ in., I prefer the curious little hop-along model made by Eclipse in England, but the bench-mount models for use with a grinding wheel are also serviceable (see the top photo on the facing page). There are also a number of electric-drill-powered models that do a reasonable job.

If you absolutely must do freehand sharpening of a twist bit, deal only with the flute side of the bevel using small abrasive rods or a conical bit in a powered hand unit (see the photo at bottom left on the facing page). You will probably change the rake angle a bit, but this will cause fewer problems than you will undoubtedly create by freehanding your way around the bevel.

TAPER-POINT TWIST BITS

Taper-point twist bits are a very specialized version of twist bits adapted for drilling tapered holes for woodworking screws. They are normally used in combination with countersink/counterbore units to drill holes for screws so that the head will be flush with the surface of the wood or, in the case of counterboring, below the surface of the wood so that the hole can be plugged.

These bits rarely need sharpening. They are high-speed steel (if you have bought American ones) and will drill thousands of holes before showing any discernible wear. Only boatbuilders are likely to use taper-point twist bits enough to need to sharpen them (and even then the bits are more likely to break than become dull).

If you should find that you need to sharpen a taper-point twist bit, whether it be the tip or the edge of the margin, I recommend that you use a thin, round-edge slipstone in the flute (see the photo at bottom right on the facing page). This will properly hone the margins and restore the tip to serviceable condition. You might be able to use a sharpening jig for the tip, but the taper usually eliminates this alternative.

Sharpening jigs for twist bits include a drill-powered sharpener (left), a 'hop-along' model that supports the bit as it is rolled over a sheet of sandpaper (middle) and a bench-mounted guide for use with a grinding wheel (right). (Photo by Susan Kahn)

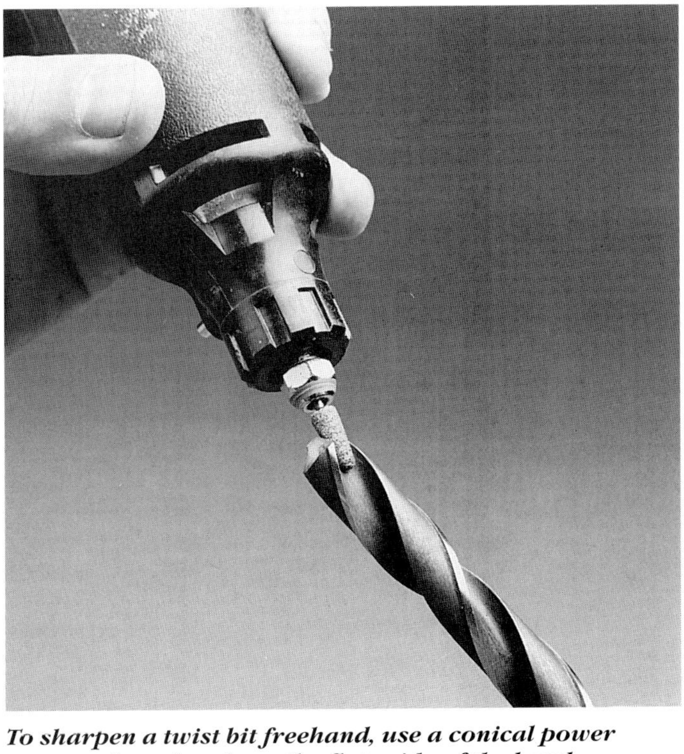

To sharpen a twist bit freehand, use a conical power stone and work only on the flute side of the bevel.

Taper-point twist bits can be honed with a thin, round-edge slipstone.

SPADE BITS

These inexpensive flat bits are ideal for rough work where you need approximately sized holes. Spade bits do not enter wood very cleanly, and the holes that they drill are often slightly oval. They have a strong tendency to wander in end grain. Most are designed with a zero rake angle, although some manufacturers have incorporated a groove in the face of the bit immediately above the bevel that does give the bit a positive rake angle. Most flat bits have a clearance angle of about 10°. On some bits, the cutting lips are at 90° to the axis of the tool; on others, they are canted slightly to ensure scoring of the circumference of the hole before chipping action starts.

Spade bits can be sharpened freehand with an auger-bit file, or you can make a simple jig for sharpening them, as shown below. The problem with freehand sharpening is that you run the risk of getting the cutting lips at slightly different heights, causing one to do more work than the other. This will tend to make the holes even more oval than they might ordinarily be.

The point of the spade bit is normally sharpened by lapping the flats on either side (see the top photo below). Sharpening it this way you do not run the risk of sharpening the point off-center. On bits with a V-groove running back from the point, the V-groove can be touched up on the inside with either a square or triangular stone file (see the bottom photo below).

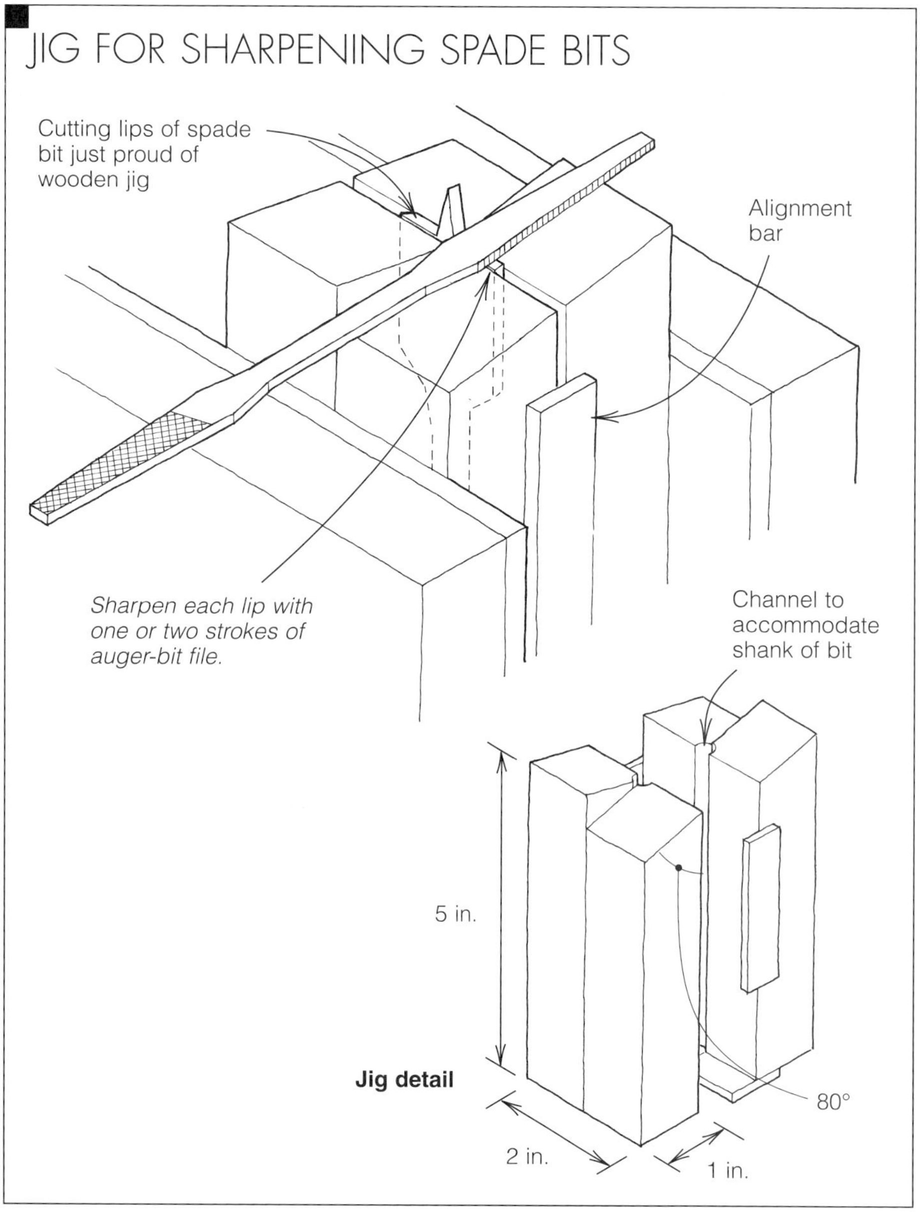

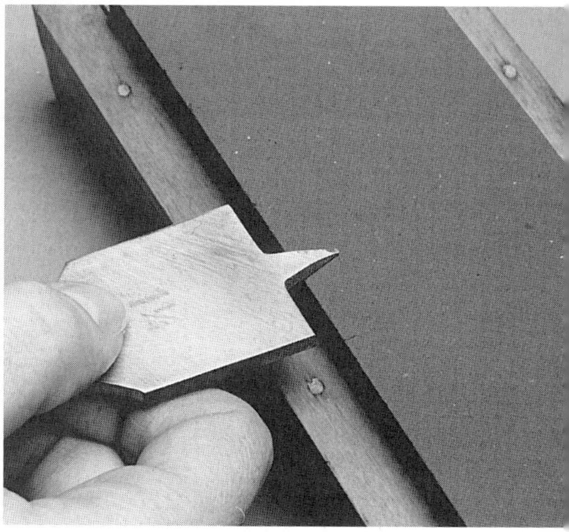

Sharpen the point of a spade bit by lapping the flats on either side.

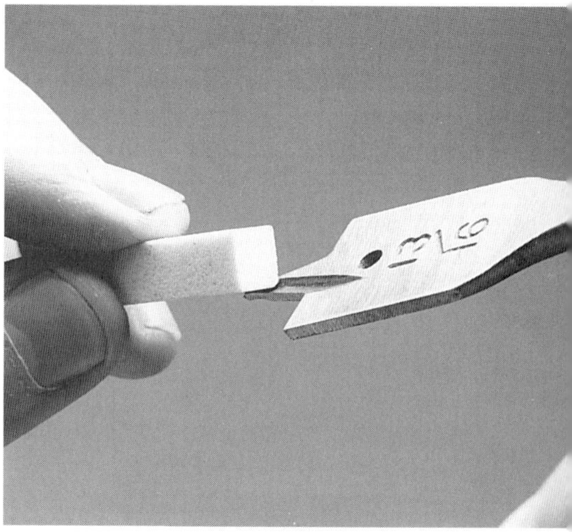

Touch up the inside of a V-groove on a spade bit with a stone file.

AUGER BITS

Auger bits used to come in a bewildering array of styles, with great variety in type of shank, tooth pattern, lips, spurs and lead screws. The one common feature was the auger flutes to carry away chips.

As with all other bits, the original geometry of the bit must be respected in the sharpening process. In fact, it was to maintain this geometry that the auger-bit file was developed, so that some surfaces could be abraded while adjoining ones could be preserved.

LEAD SCREW

Unless the bit has been abused, the lead screw will never require work. If it has been damaged, the grooves can be chased using a feather-edge file or a suitable Swiss pattern file (see the bottom photo below). This should be done lightly. It is relatively easy to do with a bit intended for use in softwood, which has a coarse lead screw, but is a much trickier process on an auger bit intended for hardwood, which has a fine lead screw. In either case, though, the screw should be kept in good condition, since it is the screw that pulls the bit into the wood.

If a screw is beyond repair, or if you want to convert an auger bit to machine use, the screw point can be converted to a brad point. In making the conversion, be sure that the tip of the brad point extends past the spur(s) of the auger bit if it has any. When used in a drill press or driven by a power hand drill, auger bits should be used at very low rpm.

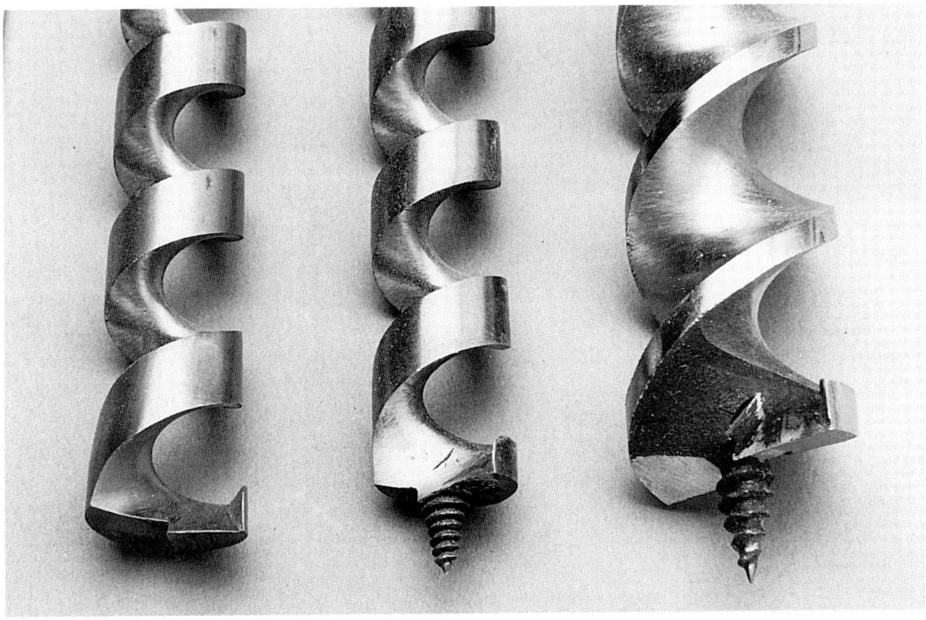

The auger bit at far left, a single-twist 'barefoot' (or bullnose) style, is prized for end-grain boring since it has no tendency to grain-follow. The center bit is for rough work; the sharp wing partially compensates for the lack of a spur. The double-twist auger at right would cut the smoothest hole and has the greatest chip capacity.

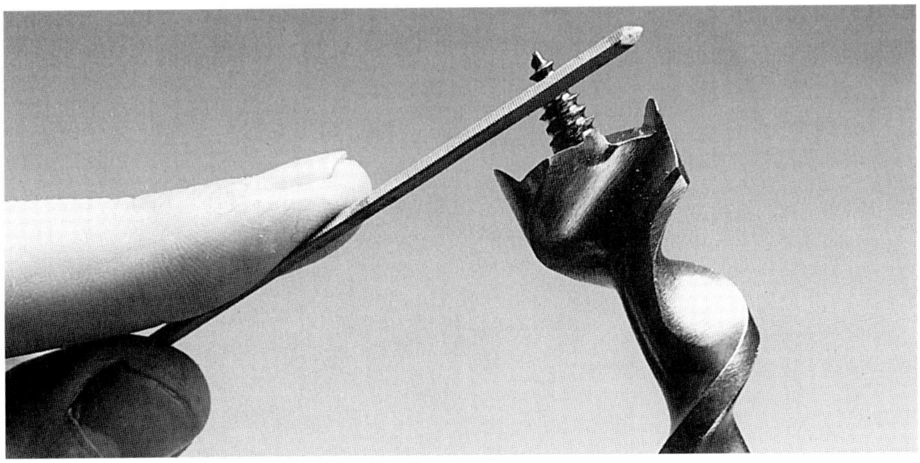

The lead screw on an auger bit can be touched up lightly with a feather-edge file.

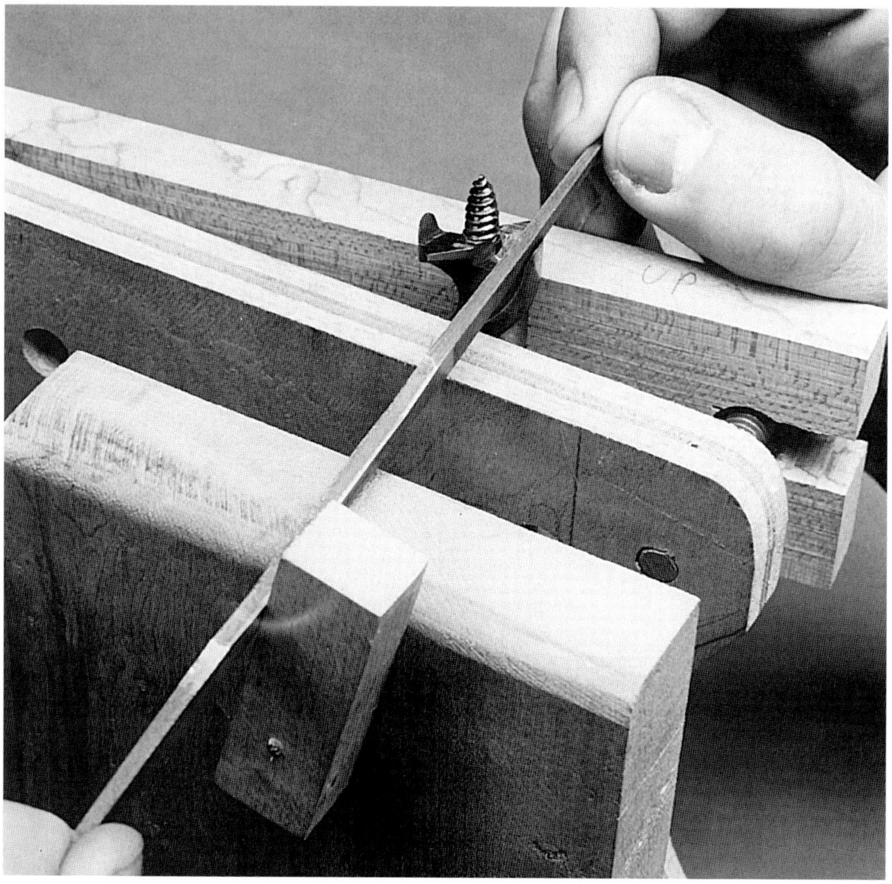

Use an auger-bit file to file the inside of the spurs (making sure the safe edge of the file is against the lip).

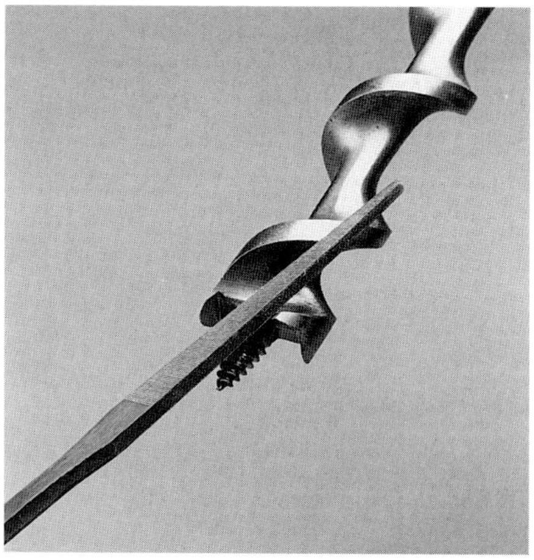

File the cutting lip of an auger bit with an upward stroke through the throat of the bit.

Use a slipstone to sharpen the inside lip of a shell auger.

SPURS

Only file the inside of the spurs, not the periphery. Using an auger-bit file, the safe edge of the file can be against the lip with the cut edge against the spur (as shown in the photo at left). If stoning is sufficient, a thin piece of plastic or similar material will protect the lip while the spur is being stoned. Never take off any more than is absolutely necessary, since an auger bit without spurs is limited in use.

CUTTING LIPS

The cutting lip of the auger bit is filed with an upward stroke through the throat of the bit at the original bevel angle (see the photo at bottom left). Be careful to maintain the chipping bevels at the same height so that they do the same amount of work. As with the outlining spurs, the cutting lips can be stoned as long as the lips are protected.

SHELL AUGER

I don't know how this tool came to be named a shell auger since it is not an auger at all. It is a shell bit and is normally sharpened on the inside of the lip in large sizes, although it can also be sharpened on the outside since the geometry is fairly straightforward to maintain.

BRAD-POINT BITS

Also referred to as brad-point spur bits or brad-point drills, these bits have generally replaced auger bits in woodworking. (This went hand-in-hand with power hand drills replacing braces.)

As shown in the top photo on the facing page, there are three basic types of brad point. The bits at far left and far right are examples of the single-lip, single-flute style, a very direct imitation of classic auger-bit design. This style is still available but uncommon.

The two most common styles are the utility brad point and the double-lipped brad point (usually just called "lipped brad point"). The utility brad point is an inexpensive model, whose entire tip geometry (lips, spurs, brad) is created by two passes of a 90° milling cutter through the tip at an angle of 20° to the

Brad-point bits developed hand in hand with portable drills. Initially, they mimicked auger bits (far left and far right), but now they are almost all made in one of the two center styles (lipped brad point, center left, and utility brad point, center right).

axis of the bit. Essentially the outer limits of the chipping bevels become the outlining spurs.

Lipped brad points have a more complex tip grind. As shown in the photo above (second bit from left), an actual outlining spur is ground on the tip, which gives a somewhat slimmer brad point. In use, the lipped brad point almost invariably enters the wood more cleanly than the utility model, but a slight hesitation on entry will give a clean hole with either one. A more basic problem with economy models is that they are usually made offshore; just as the best twist bits are made in the United States, lipped brad points are ground from twist bits and the best lipped brad points are still made in the United States. This is not rampant nationalism (I'm Canadian, after all), just the simple truth. (There are some bits, including Forstner-style bits and sawtooth bits, where the best bits, in my view, are not made in the United States. Given the rapid transfer of technology in all fields, it will be only a very short time until good brad points start flowing in as well.)

There is a variation of the double-lipped brad point that has lips shaped a bit differently from the model just mentioned. This type of lip is not highest at the leading edge but has a parabolic tip. Bits of this type give very clean entry but are prone to overheating, since there is much more friction on this type of lip as it presses its way into the wood. Not much different in style, there are now also

UTILITY BRAD-POINT GEOMETRY

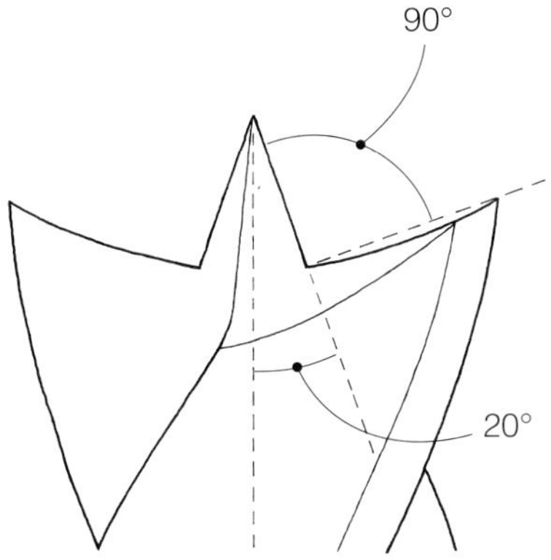

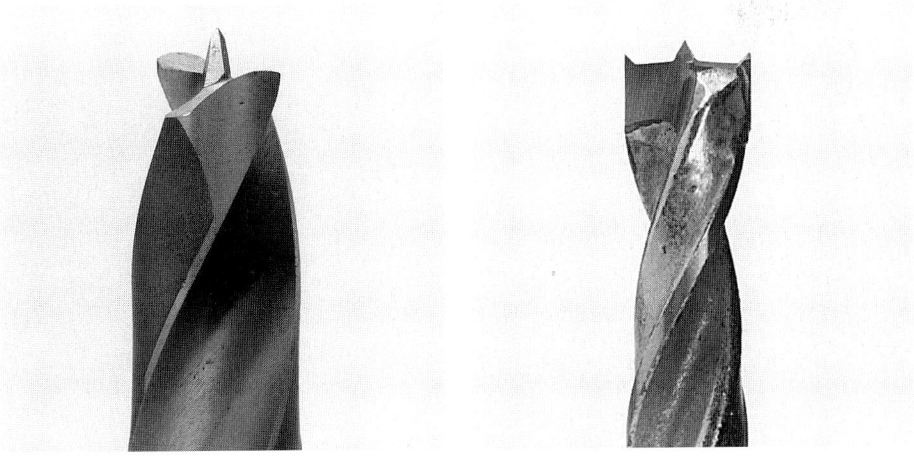

Variations of standard brad-point bits include the parabolic-spur brad point (left) and the carbide-tipped brad point (right). (Photos by Susan Kahn)

carbide-tipped brad points on the market. These tend to have somewhat finer lips and are very durable.

SHARPENING BRAD-POINT BITS

The easiest of all brad points to sharpen is the utility brad point, which can be filed with an auger-bit file along the chipping bevels, or honed in the flute as shown in the photo at left. These are usually carbon-steel bits, and by the time they have become dull they have usually been overheated once or twice so they are quite easy to file. They can be filed a number of times before the center brad becomes both too wide and too long for the bit to function properly. When the bit gets to this condition, rather than tinker with the center brad you should treat yourself to a new bit.

But if you must tinker, first file a small flat on the point and then sharpen it as you would the tooth of a saw, filing from one side until half of the flat is removed and then filing from the other just until the rest is removed. This will leave a narrow chisel tip that can be used as is, or you can file half of the chisel away from one side and half from the other to recreate a point.

Use a small, round stone in the flute to hone a utility brad-point bit.

Sharpening is not quite as straightforward for lipped brad points as it is for the utility brads. It is difficult to come up with sharpening gear that is both fine enough and small enough to hone the flats of the chipping bevels and the flutes. I prefer to use a conical power stone or abrasive rods if the bit is very dull, but otherwise use a wooden dowel, slightly undersized to the flute, well charged with chromium-oxide honing compound. The bit can be drawn along such a dowel held in a vise with a trailing stroke; the dowel will polish the inside of the flute and restore the lip to razor-sharp condition.

The basic geometry of the bit is maintained almost in total. Over time, you will decrease the rake angle slightly, but only by a negligible amount. Don't worry if in either grinding or honing the inside of the flute you happen to put a mark in the trailing edge of the margin farther up the bit. This will not affect the action of the bit one iota. If you have created any roughness, smooth it but otherwise don't be concerned about it. As always, it is better not to tinker with the brad point itself unless you absolutely have to.

Lastly, in sharpening the carbide-tipped brad points (should you ever have to) it is best to use a very fine diamond abrasive. The 9-micron size of 3M abrasive seems to do a good job.

FORSTNER-BIT ANATOMY

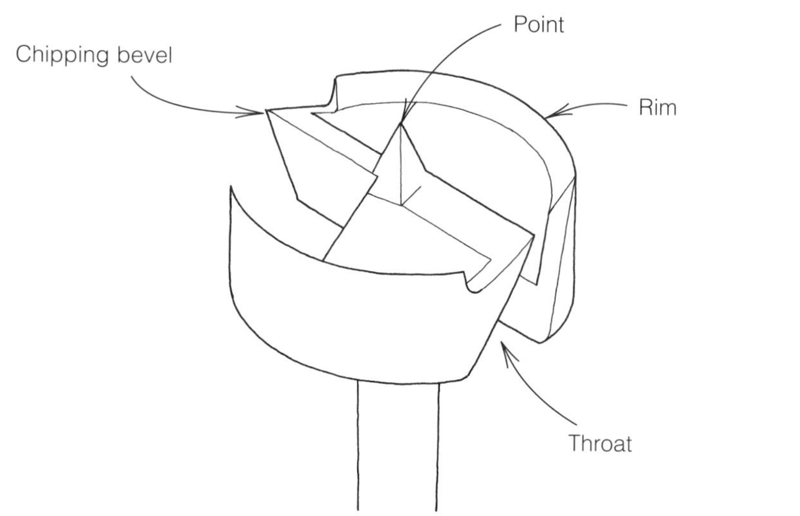

FORSTNER BITS

Forstner bits are a joy to use, but they carry with them the seeds of their own destruction. Since the rim on a well-ground Forstner is about 0.005 in. higher than the chipping bevels, it scores the circumference of the hole before the chipping bevels begin to remove wood. Therein lies the problem. It is easy to generate a lot of rim heat as these bits are used. Even when they are used properly, it is very difficult to avoid overheating in hard, resinous woods. It is mandatory that Forstner bits be used judiciously and be kept free of resin. They should be cleaned frequently and have a dry lubricant applied to them.

SHARPENING FORSTNER BITS

Forstner bits are not particularly difficult to sharpen. The inside of the rim can be sharpened with a small, round honing stone, and the chipping bevels can be dressed with a fine file or stone directly through the throat. The periphery of the bit should never be touched, and the back of the chipping bevels should be touched only when they need to be dressed down below the rim. When working on chipping bevels, it is easiest to do a major portion of the relief with a small power hone brought in from the end (see the drawing below), and then complete the job with a fine needle file or diamond file. For repairing major damage, see the discussion under sawtooth machine bits.

Use a round honing stone, with the aid of a jig that keeps the stone at the correct angle, to sharpen the inside rim of a Forstner bit (top). A slipstone can be used to touch up the chipping bevels (above).

SHARPENING FORSTNER-BIT BEVELS

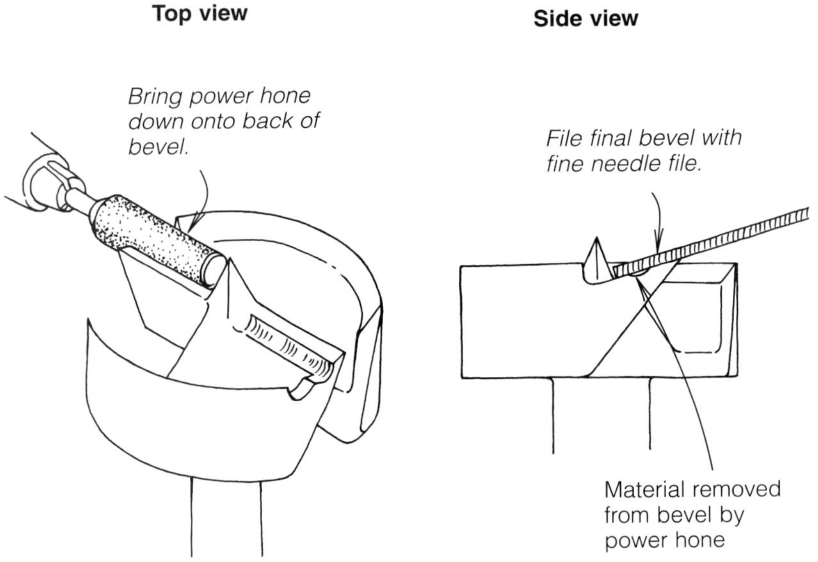

SAWTOOTH MACHINE BITS

The classic sawtooth bit (also called a multi-spur bit) has one or two chipping bevels and a ring of outlining spurs patterned after rip-saw teeth—usually flat-topped teeth at zero rake angle. Because they cut with a sawing rather than slicing action, sawtooth bits tend to heat less than Forstner bits. At the same time, they do not enter as cleanly because the unbeveled teeth cause some cross-grain splintering.

Partly to resolve the entry problem and partly for economy of manufacturing, manufacturers began producing multi-spur bits by modifying standard Forstner patterns. There are at least three different patterns of this new style of bit (see the drawing at left), and all have slicing tips on the spurs rather than narrow chipping bevels like the classic sawtooth. As a result, they require some of the sharpening techniques of Forstner bits with adjustments according to tooth variation.

SAWTOOTH BITS

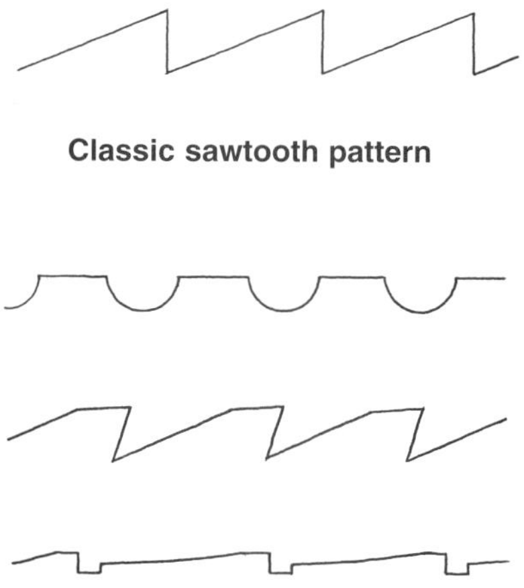

SHARPENING SAWTOOTH BITS

In general, I would recommend that you sharpen all styles the same as a classic sawtooth. Over time, this means that the spurs will develop narrow chipping bevels like the classic sawtooth. You can restore the original slicing tip if you wish, but it is an incredibly fiddly business and I recommend that you use good drilling technique (i.e., a slight hesitation on entry) to compensate for the changed geometry.

The main chipping bevel(s) on a sawtooth can be sharpened the same as on a Forstner bit. For sharpening the teeth, a triangular file is best (see the photo at left below); a feather-edge file can be used where a triangular file will not fit. It is usually sufficient to address the leading face of the tooth only. The file should be held level, with one edge aimed directly at the center brad.

If major work has to be done on a sawtooth bit, the entire face of the bit has to be jointed first. The photo at right below shows a sawtooth mounted in a drill press being jointed on a sharpening stone sitting on the drill-press table. The center brad must be

Sharpen the teeth of a sawtooth bit with a triangular file.

With the sawtooth bit mounted in a drill press, joint the face of a the bit on a bench stone. (Photo by Susan Kahn)

kept clear of the stone and only the balance of the bit jointed just until the shortest tooth is touched. The top left photo at right shows the newly jointed bit with fairly substantial flats on some teeth but lesser flats on others; the shortest tooth has just been touched by the stone. The stone has also touched the chipping bevel, partly eliminating the relief angle.

To restore the bit, first the rim teeth have to be front filed until flats on the top just disappear. Since the center brad has been damaged on the bit shown in the photos, it needs some attention. Fortunately, it can be filed flat across and still function. It will not be reduced in height by very much, and, rather than risk destroying the centricity of the brad by filing the edges, it is simplest to create some sharp edges by filing it straight across the top. The brad will still penetrate quite well, and it will not have lost its centricity.

Finally, the relief angles have to be restored to the chipping bevels, and the chipping bevels have to be brought to a level 0.005 in. below the teeth. Rather than try to get the entire chipping bevel 0.005 in. below the teeth, it is best to file the chipping bevels at a slight angle, upward toward the center. It will not matter if the center of the chipping bevels are at the same height as the teeth as long as they slope off to a point approximately 0.005 in. below the teeth at the perimeter.

A handy device for gauging your progress in all of this is a small piece of hardwood with a good flat surface that has a hole drilled in it to accommodate the center brad. File the chipping bevels at about a 10° angle until you can just slide a piece of good-bond typing paper under the end of the chipping bevel when the teeth are flush against the face of the hardwood jig (see the photo at top right). If you are going to err on one side, be conservative.

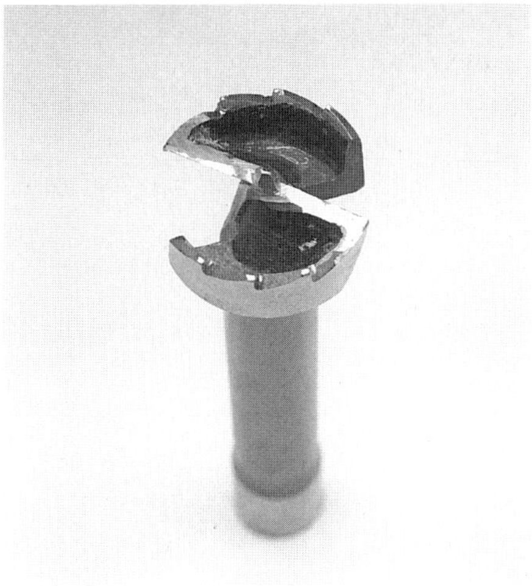

A sawtooth bit that has been jointed to make all teeth the same height.

The chipping bevels of a sawtooth bit should be filed slightly lower than the perimeter teeth. Gauge the height by setting the bit on a piece of hardwood and sliding a piece of typing paper under the bevel.

Although this wood bit does not have the versatility of a Forstner bit, it is much more practical for production work. (Photos by Susan Kahn)

WOOD BITS

These bits do not have a distinctive name on the market. Called different things in different countries, wood bits originated as installation bits for European hardware and are now available in a full range of sizes. They are also available in a full range of materials from high-carbon steel through high-speed steel to bits with carbide inserts. As with all bits of this type, the periphery is not touched. The outlining spurs are honed on the inside flats with an abrasive suitable to their metallurgy, and the chipping bevels are honed through the throat the same as one would do with a Forstner bit or a sawtooth bit.

Sharpen the teeth of a sawtooth hole cutter with a triangular file, just as you would sharpen a ripsaw.

HOLE CUTTERS

Sawtooth hole cutters usually have an adjustable twist bit that acts as a pilot for the ring of rip-sharpened sawteeth. The rim teeth are sharpened just as you would sharpen a rip saw. They are usually sufficiently fine teeth that a double extra-slim saw file can be used. For harder, high-speed-steel versions, either a triangular honing file or a triangular diamond file would be used. Do not try to set the teeth in these saws.

EXPANSION BITS AND ADJUSTABLE HOLE CUTTERS

There are a host of expansion bits on the market. In every case, they are some variation of an auger bit, a wood bit, a sawtooth bit or a Forstner bit. You can check under each of these to see how to sharpen the various components. For adjustable hole cutters, it is usually just a case of filing the cutter bevel and lapping the face of the cutter.

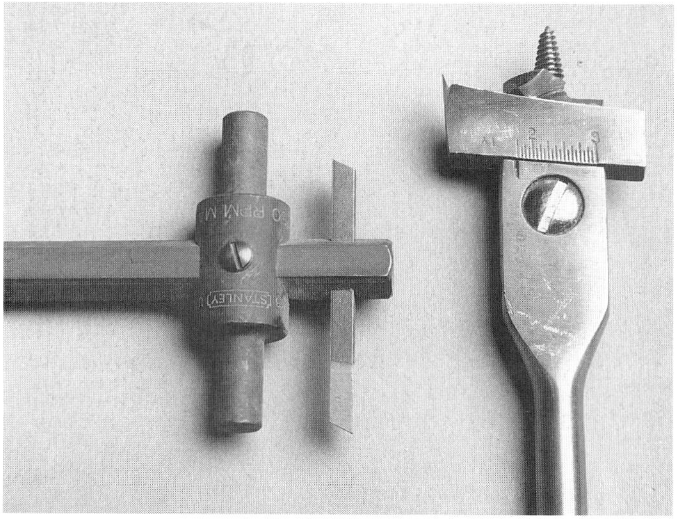

The adjustable hole cutter at left (used in a drill press) and the expandable auger bit at right are typical of bits that adjust to cut a range of hole diameters.

Lapping the face of a cutter for an adjustable hole cutter.

PLUG CUTTERS

Plug cutters require quite a different sharpening philosophy from virtually all other bits, because the concern with these cutters is not the periphery of the bit but the central core. Since plug cutters are used for cutting plugs of a predetermined size, it is not the outside diameter of the hole they make that is of concern but the inside diameter of the hole, where the plug is formed. There are two basic types of plug cutters: fluted cutters and barrel-type cutters.

FLUTED PLUG CUTTERS

There are three subdivisions of fluted plug cutters: the two-flute cutter, the four-flute cutter and the four-flute Snug-Plug cutter. The first two make cylindrical plugs, the third makes a plug that is one-quarter cylindrical and three-quarters tapered, like a cork. All are sharpened the same way. The tips of the teeth can either be filed or stoned; be sure to maintain the relief angle as you do it. You can increase the relief angle without materially affecting the function, but decreasing it even slightly could cause bevel rubbing.

To form the best point on the individual teeth, it is also a good idea to hone the flat leading edge of the tooth (as shown in the photo at right). With the tapered plug cutters this is mandatory, because the teeth cut the major diameter of the plug and the minor diameter is formed by the scraping action of the upper part of the teeth. This action creates the smoothest plug of this type but does require that the leading edge of the tooth be maintained; there must be a crisp intersection with the inside of the tooth for good scraping action.

Fortunately, there is not much danger that you will be tempted to tinker with the inside of the plug cutter since it is awkward to get in there. There are times, however, when it may be necessary to do some deburring on the inside, particularly if the plug cutter has been dropped. If any of the teeth tips are bent over, they are invariably bent toward the center of the plug cutter and, if they are not dressed back

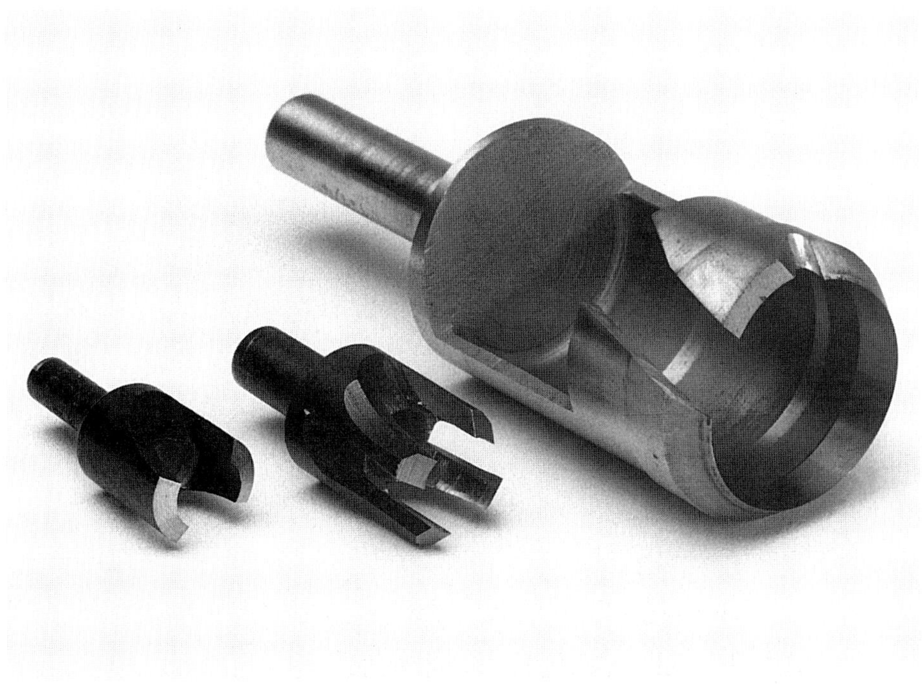

The two basic types of plug cutters are fluted cutters and barrel-type cutters. Shown from left to right are a two-flute cutter, a four-flute Snug-Plug cutter and a barrel-type plug cutter. (Photo by Susan Kahn)

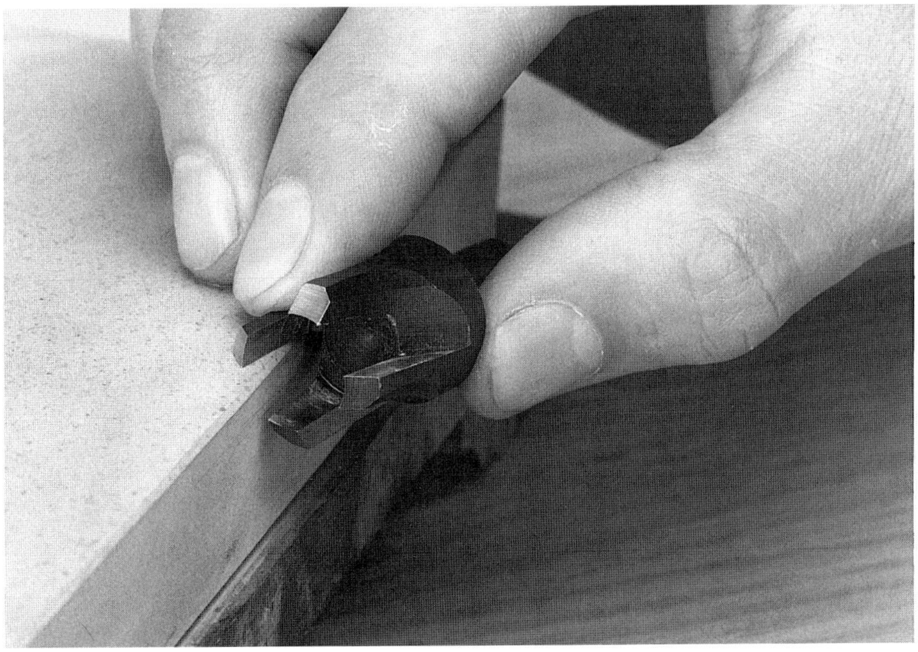

With the cutter pinched up against the stone, hone the flat leading edges of the teeth of a tapered plug cutter. (Photo by Susan Kahn)

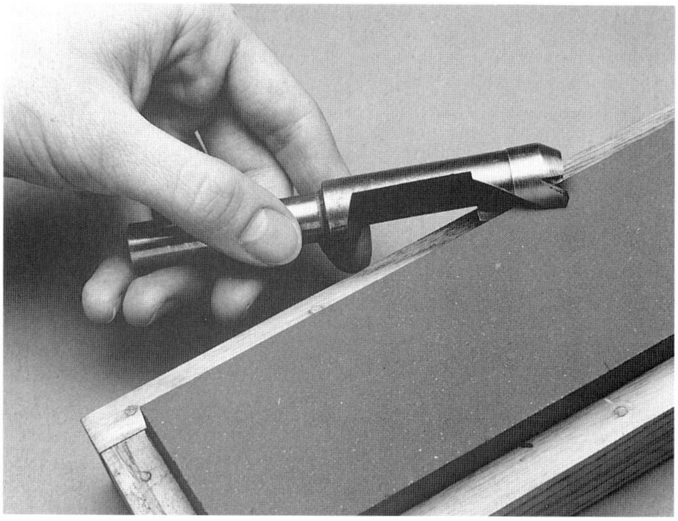

To sharpen the chipping bevel of a barrel-type plug cutter, hone the face on a stone.

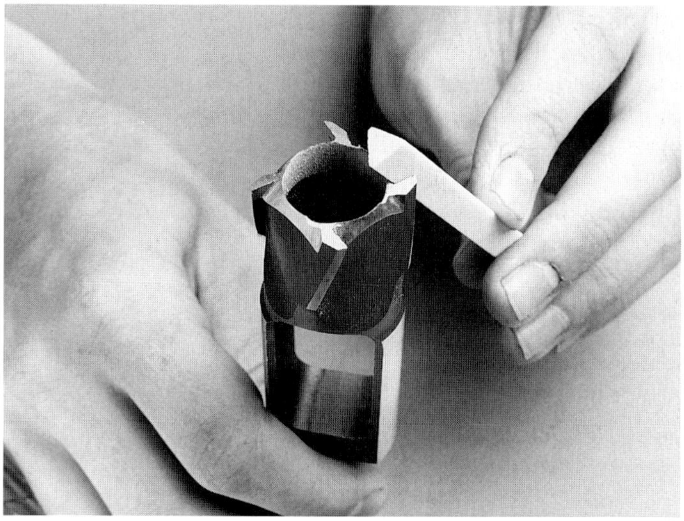

On barrel-type cutters that have four chipping bevels, use a triangular stone to hone the bevels.

A tenon cutter. (Photo courtesy W.L. Fuller, Inc.)

to the original interior diameter, the cutter will always cut undersized plugs. Fortunately, it is quite easy to dress them back using a round honing stone and a bit of care.

BARREL-TYPE PLUG CUTTERS

There are several makers of barrel-type plug cutters, but the cutters have common geometry. These are almost like Forstner bits turned inside out. They have a raised lip that scores the outside perimeter of the plug and a chipping bevel that removes wood from outside the scored circle.

Barrel cutters are not bits that you want to damage because they are not much fun to sharpen. Sharpening the chipping bevel is very straightforward since you need only hone the face (as shown in the photo at top left). There is no easy way to hone the rim of the cutter. You cannot touch the interior since that would change the diameter, so you are limited to honing the outside bevel of the rim with a small hand-held stone or a bench stone. Fortunately, this very seldom has to be done. Some barrel-type plug cutters have four chippers; these have to be honed with a triangular stone, as shown in the photo at top right.

TENON CUTTER

A tenon cutter is just a specialized type of plug cutter. The basic difference is that the tips of the teeth are shaped so that they form a clean shoulder on the tenon. Otherwise, it is sharpened exactly the same as a plug cutter—the leading edges of the teeth are lapped, and the tops of the teeth are honed, maintaining the original relief angle.

A drill-press mortising attachment.

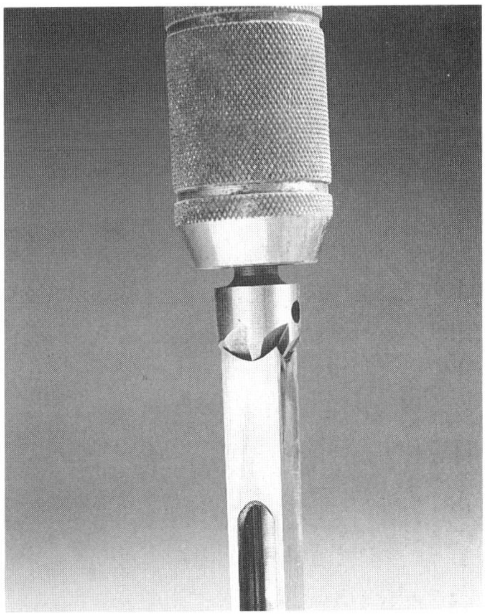

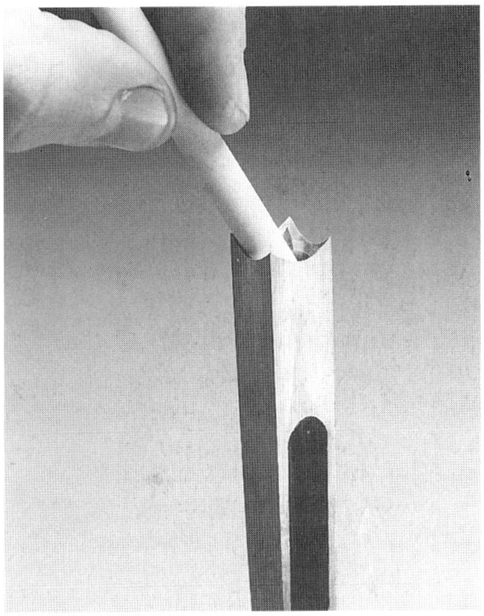

The hollow chisel of a drill-press mortising attachment is sharpened with a countersink-like device (top) and then honed with a round stone (above).

DRILL-PRESS MORTISING ATTACHMENT

The drill-press mortising attachment is a combination of a hollow square-mortise chisel and an auger bit. The auger bit is sharpened in the same manner as any auger bit, but the hollow square mortise chisel presents a shape problem. To overcome this problem, the chisel manufacturers have designed a special countersink-like sharpening device with either solid or interchangeable pilots to fit the inside diameter of the various hollow chisels. The cutting lips of this bit dress the inside bevels of the mortise chisel. To complete the sharpening of the chisel, you should then hone the interior.

If you find that the chisel requires excessive pressure to penetrate, you can dress each of the inside corners with a very fine cut round or oval file. With the chisel clamped in a vise you should stroke toward the inside and remove only enough to reduce the wedging action of the inside corners. To remove any remaining burrs, it may be necessary to lap the four outside faces of the hollow chisel. This is readily done on a bench stone.

CHAPTER 16

PERIPHERAL MILLING CUTTERS

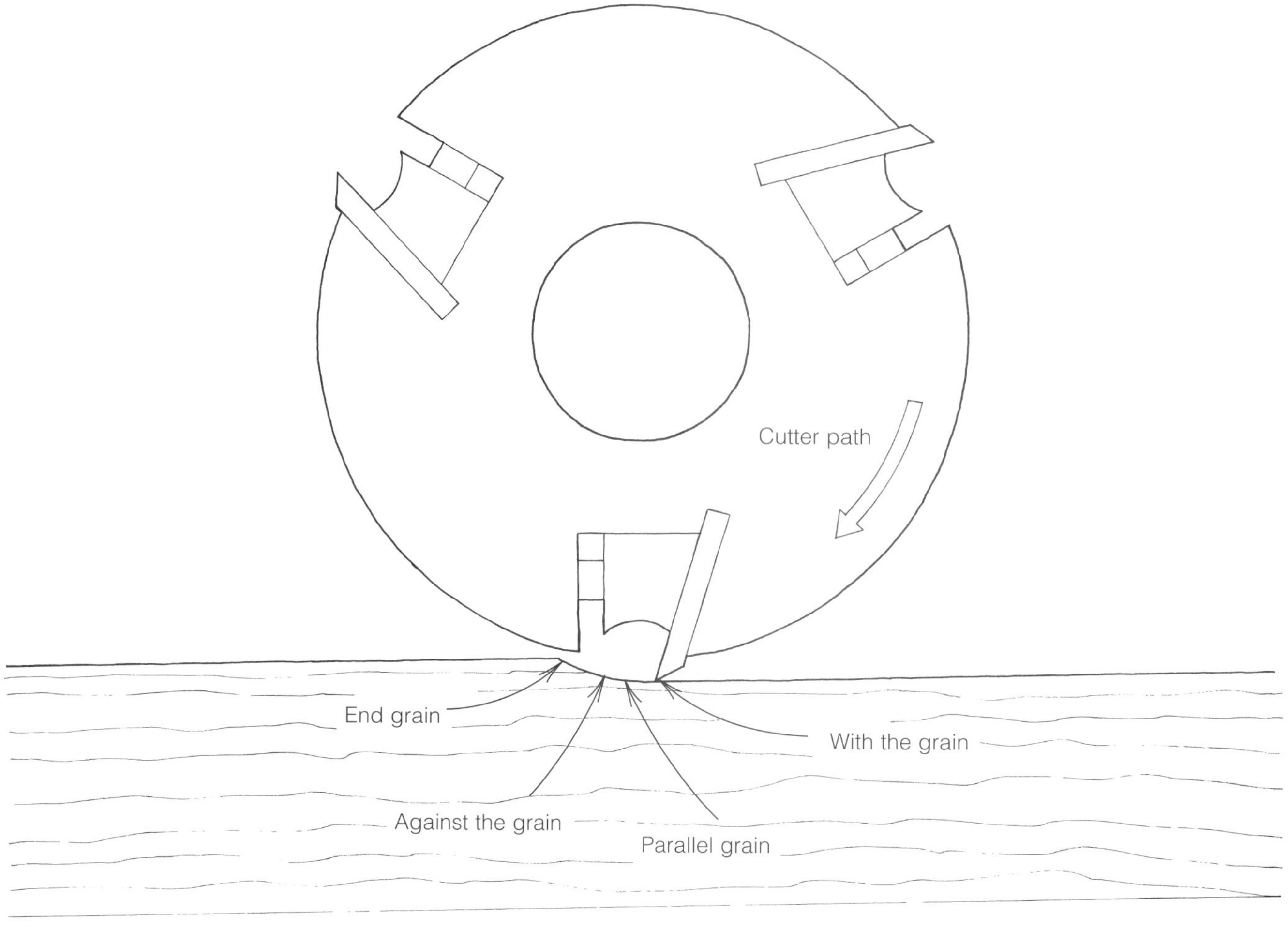

Peripheral milling is the phrase used to describe the cutting action of knives attached to a rotary cutterhead. This could be at low speed (e.g., a cutterhead used in a drill press) but usually refers to the high-speed, high-torque machines such as routers, jointers and shapers. With all of these machines, the cutting action is a series of overlapping arcs taking evenly spaced bites out of the wood.

Because these machines work at very high speed and the cutting edges have to deal with all grain configurations (see the drawing on the facing page) as well as withstand substantial shock, all edges are formed to cut at very low rake angles and have relatively high included angles.

It is beyond the scope of this book to deal with all of the considerations that go into deciding the appropriate rake and relief angle for these cutters, since they vary by cutterhead diameter among many other things. Thus, it is assumed here that all edges will be resharpened honoring the original blade geometry.

JOINTER AND PLANER KNIVES

Most woodworkers have the nagging feeling that they should be sharpening their own jointer and planer knives rather than buying extra sets and having their knives sharpened commercially. However, unless you are doing a huge amount of milling or are living in a remote area, sharpening your own knives really does not make sense. The time consumed is usually out of all proportion to the money saved, and the end result is usually of lower quality than that you could expect from even a run-of-the-mill sharpening service. This is truly one area where equipment overwhelms technique by a substantial margin. If you do not have an excellent system for holding a blade straight and rigid, you will be in trouble from the opening gun.

KEEPING KNIVES SHARP

There are a couple of ways to minimize the amount of sharpening you have to do with jointer and planer knives. First, you can keep your lumber clean so that it does not have grit on the surface. Second, if you have to deal with dirty lumber, make all the roughing cuts with one set of blades and then either resharpen or change to a new set of blades for final dimensioning. Otherwise, you will often find that one set of blades will last for only half the job because of the very rapid deterioration from grit on the lumber. Although the second set of blades may complete the job for you, you will find that you have two sets of dull blades when you are finished. If you make all of the roughing cuts with one set of blades, they will certainly be dull, but the replacement set should still be perfectly usable after the rest of the dimensioning passes.

It is worth stressing that the cause of blade dulling in a small shop almost invariably is not the abrasive effect of the wood itself on the blades; it is the damage caused by the dirt on the surface of the wood.

While I am sure that none of you do it, absolutely one of the most abrasive things you can put through your equipment is lumber with old paint on it. It does not matter how clean it looks or how free of nails the lumber is, paint will dull your knives in minutes. Many paints have metallic oxides in them that are very abrasive. (As mentioned on p. 96, the artist's color chromium-oxide green makes a good honing medium.)

But all of this is begging the question. There are some of you out there determined to sharpen your own knives regardless of the economics. Fortunately, there is one thing that most people can do that will probably save both time and money: touch up the blades while they are still in the machine.

SHARPENING KNIVES "IN SITU"

Blades that are not removed from a machine do not have to be put back. This is an obvious but important fact. With the exception of the Tersa quick-change cutterhead, systems for fixing and adjusting blades in jointers and planers have changed little in the last fifty years. For most machines, changing a blade is an aggravating process and one to be avoided if possible. Thus, any time you can bring blades back to usable condition without removing them from the machine you should do so.

One system that can be used is shown in the top photo on p. 208. This system operates on the same principle as the manual honing system, except that a trim router and a cup wheel with the appropriate rpm rating are used. This is not a system for the faint-of-heart, and I do not recommend it. It is possible to grind jointer knives well with this system, but it requires very close control of the depth of cut and it is easy to burn a blade through minor inadvertence.

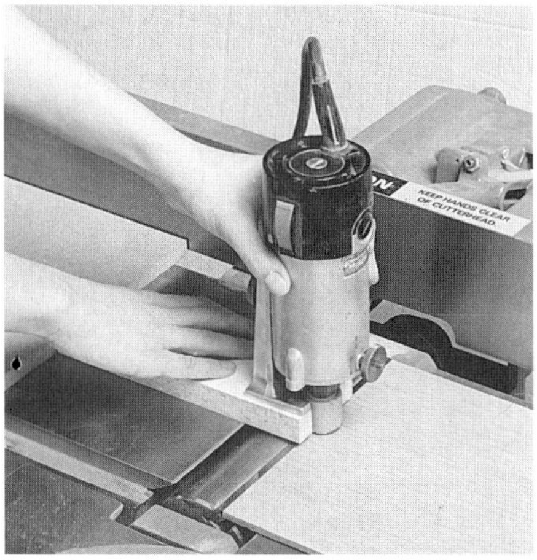

This sharpening system for jointer knives uses a trim router and a cup wheel.

On jointers with feed belts, lock the cutterhead in position by clamping the belt.

SETUP FOR BLADE HONING

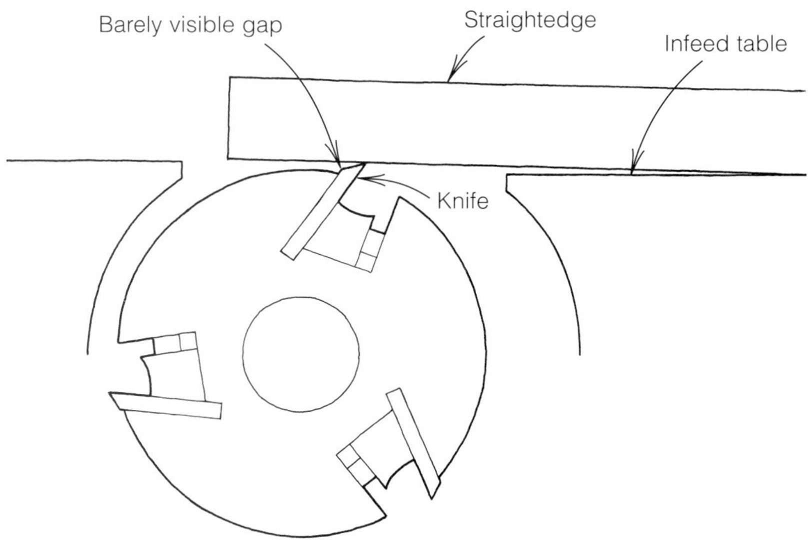

Some large thickness planers are designed with built-in tracks to accommodate a cross-feed electric grinding head to grind the knife bevels. If you have such a planer, read no further. If not, however, you can mimic this activity in a low-tech way by taking advantage of high-tech abrasives to achieve a similar result.

First, unplug your machine. Then adjust the infeed table until you can lay a straightedge on it that will also rest on the knife bevel, which should be just shy of parallel to the infeed table and slightly above it (see the drawing above). Parallel to the infeed table would be fine, but this is not easy to judge by eye so I recommend erring on the side of increasing the bevel angle slightly. Since this reduces the relief angle, you have to be careful. But this is a touch-up process, and the original relief can be fully restored the next time the blades are sharpened commercially.

With the blade bevel as close as possible to parallel to the infeed table, lock the cutterhead in position. Depending on the make of your machine, this could be done by clamping the feed belt as shown in the bottom photo at left.

Now comes the fiddly part. Since you are going to hone the blade with a standard bench stone (and you do not want to abrade the infeed table), you need to wrap tape around the stone in two places. The infeed table should be lower than the knife edge by the thickness of the tape you are going to use plus a couple of thousands of an inch.

This is really not that complex. Put the tape on the stone and rest the stone on the knife so that the stone is supported by the knife and the tape at the other end of the stone. Now slowly raise the infeed table until the other strip of tape just touches the table (see the drawing on the facing page). Before you start honing, you should make a wedge gauge (see the sidebar on p. 210) and mark it so that you can set the other knives in exactly the same position when the time comes. The distance to measure is the distance between the infeed table and the knife edge. When the head is rotated to the next knife, you want to maintain this distance exactly.

In the honing process, you do not want the honing stone going directly across the knife; otherwise, you risk either loading the stone in that one spot or wearing a groove in it. To avoid this,

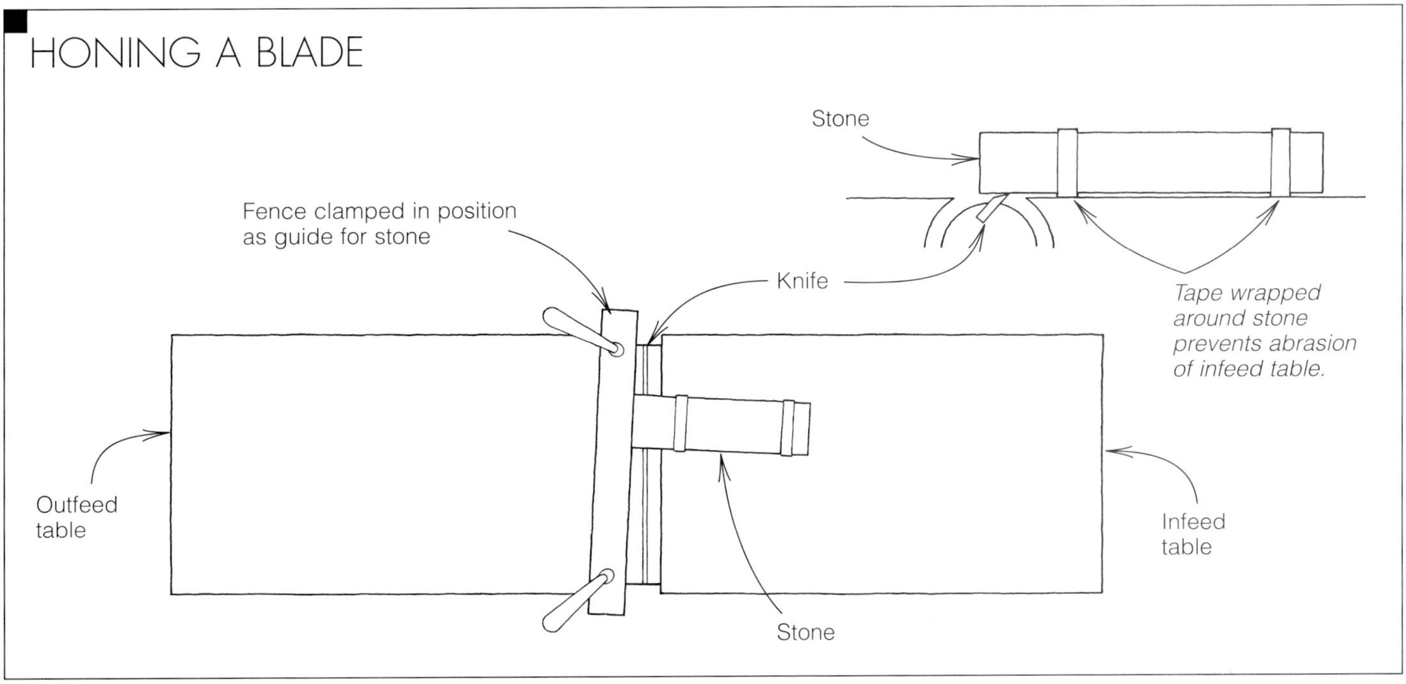

clamp a fence askew the infeed table an appropriate distance away from the knife, as shown in the drawing above. Then hone the knife. If, when you have finished honing, the knife is not yet sharp, remove one layer of tape from each band on the stone and continue honing. If that does not do the job, the knives did not need a touchup in the first place—they needed to be reground. In any event, you will quickly learn how many layers of tape to put on. Tape is amazingly consistent in thickness, which makes this a very accurate method. You do have to remember to finish each blade with the same number of layers of tape on the stone. This keeps all blades the same height.

If you have honed with a fairly coarse stone (600x or coarser), you should refine the edge with a finer grit before rotating the cutterhead to the next blade. To do this, put tape only on the end of the finishing stone away from the guide fence; make sure that the tape is in the same position on the finishing stone (relative to the fence) that it was on the coarse stone. If you use one less layer of tape, you will have made a tiny angular change at the blade. With the finishing stone (1200x to 6000x) resting on the tape at on end and the blade at the other, take a half-dozen passes over the blade and you will have honed a small micro-bevel.

Use a small stone to deburr the face of the knife after honing.

After you have honed all the blades, it is a simple matter to remove any burr from the face of the blade with a small stone if necessary. Just slide the stone along the blade, ensuring that it is perfectly flush with the face (see the photo above).

Commercial honing devices can be used to hone the bevel and deburr the knife edge. (Photo by Susan Kahn)

ACCURACY OF A WEDGE GAUGE

There are dozens of situations in the shop where you want to measure the size of a gap and it is either impossible to use a dial caliper or you do not have one. You can make incredibly accurate gauges from hardwood or scrap aluminum by a very simple process.

Cut a gently tapered piece of material, mark it off with thicknesses and then put graduation marks between them. If, for example, you use a wedge that has a rise of 1 unit for every 25 units of length, you have effectively enlarged your measurement scale by a factor of 25. It is the principle of the dial caliper in linear form. By magnifying the scale, you can take readings to an accuracy that would be impossible to take in any other way. You may need to borrow a micrometer or caliper to establish the major thickness accurately, but from there you can interpolate the rest. The system is just as effective with a V-gauge as it is with a wedge gauge.

Using the example of the wedge between the cutterhead and the infeed table, you do not care what the distance is as long as you can replicate it accurately. A wedge gauge best lets you do that because it is more accurate than any other means you can devise.

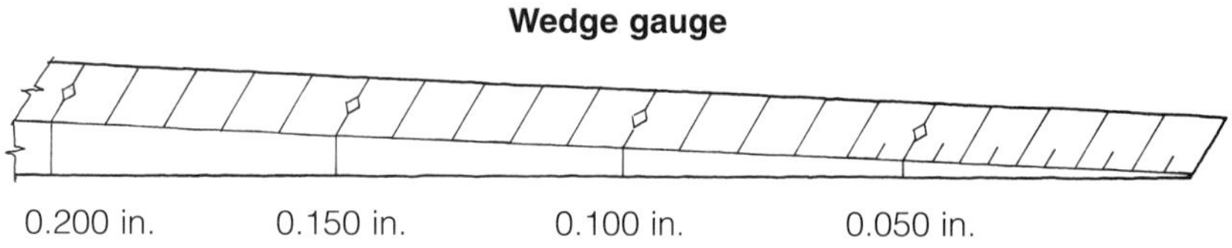

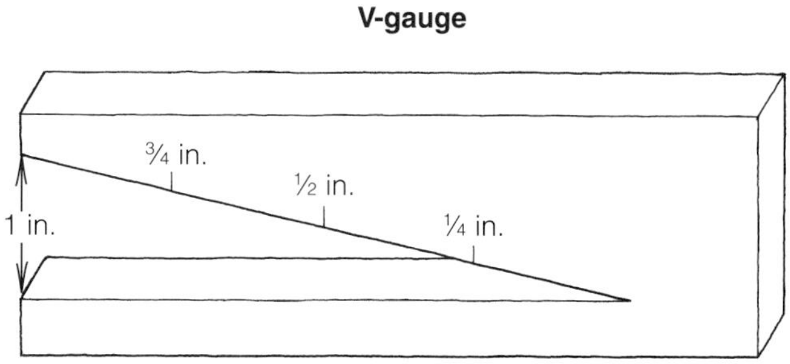

There are small honing devices on the market that can be used to hone the bevel and to deburr the knife edge (see the photo above). Most of these have pitifully coarse abrasives in them; they do not create a very fine edge and tend to weaken the knife edge because of the grooves that they score in the bevel. I suspect that these hones would work much better with a tiny strip of the 3M diamond micro-finishing abrasive (9-micron size) stuck to a block of aluminum in place of the honing stone. The diamond would cut quickly but still leave a very fine finish. This could be followed up with an even finer micro-finishing abrasive on another face of the block.

SHARPENING KNIVES REMOVED FROM THE MACHINE

Once you have removed the knives from the machine, you have several choices. My first choice is to send the knives out to a good professional sharpening service. Unless you have a high production shop where the knives of several machines have to be sharpened, it is hard to justify the investment in a system that will do a good job with jointer or planer knives. Whatever system you use, you want to ensure that all knives in a set are treated the same, so that their dimensions are the same and they weigh the same amount. The latter point is often ignored and can lead to an unbalanced cutterhead. Another reason to keep the dimensions the same is to provide some automation to the sharpening process.

A good shop grinder for jointer knives could be of the style shown in the photo at right, or it could be one of the various wet-wheel horizontal grinders on the market that have special jointer-knife honing jigs. The advantage of the latter unit is that other tools can be ground and honed on it as well.

There are various designs of jointer-blade sharpeners that you can make, but they all require a substantial investment of time and effort to get second-class results. If you cannot justify the cost of a good manufactured system, your best bet is to develop good technique for honing blades but leave the regrinding to the specialists.

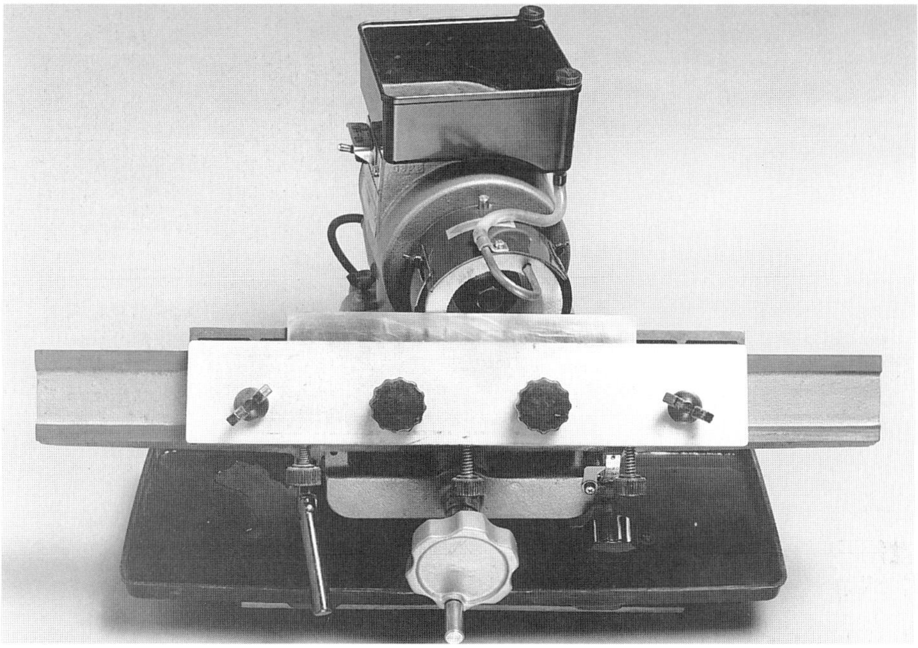

A typical shop grinder for jointer knives.

ROUTER BITS

A few bits used in a router, such as spiral bits and burr-cut bits, must be sent out for professional precision grinding; this will remove the least amount of metal while still maintaining bit geometry and overall balance.

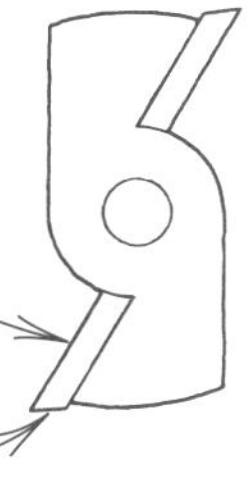

But the vast majority of router bits used today are double-flute bits with carbide inserts. With some minor exceptions (e.g., very small bits), these bits can have the flat face of the carbide insert lapped on a diamond hone to restore the edge. Under no circumstances should you attempt freehand grinding of router-bit profiles, and only with single-flute bits should you ever consider honing the bevel.

DON'T TOUCH THAT BEVEL!

You will often see a photo in tool catalogs something like the one shown below extolling the virtues of some particular honing device for router bits. A photo like this is misleading. First, it indicates that you can readily do freehand honing of the bevels on a straight bit. This is not the case. Second, it implies that there is nothing wrong with honing the bevel on a router bit; this is equally misleading. It is important that router-bit cutting edges be equidistant from the axis of the cutter. If not, one edge will be doing more work than the other, but, more important, it will no longer be balanced if more is taken off one cutting edge than the other.

You can also cause imbalance in a router bit by lapping one face more than the other. Whenever you are honing a router bit, you should take approximately the same number of strokes on each face to avoid introducing any imbalance in the bit.

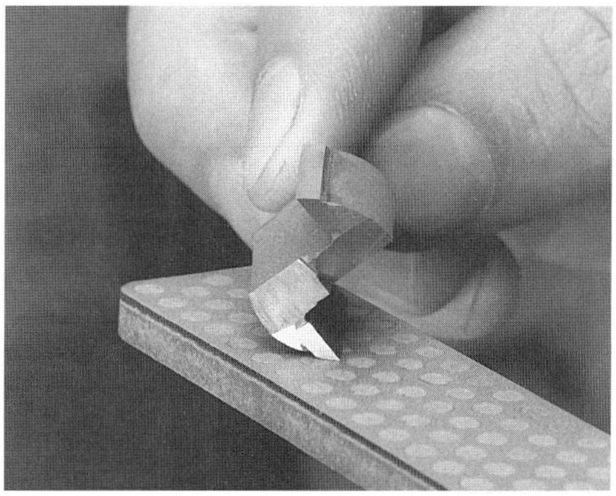

NEVER hone the bevel of a double-flute router bit! (Photo by Susan Kahn)

If you have a bit that cannot be restored by lapping the face, it should be sent out to a professional sharpening service or it should be replaced. In today's world, it is often less expensive to replace the bit than it is to have a nick ground out of it.

SHARPENING CARBIDE ROUTER BITS

For standard bits, the face of the carbide can be lapped on a diamond stone, but you will need a diamond file for honing the new style of chip-limitation router bit that has a slot next to the carbide insert rather than an open 90° quadrant. Just slide the bit back and forth on the file using light to moderate pressure and a touch of very light oil, such as WD-40. Heavy pressure puts deep score marks in the carbide and can dislodge diamond crystals from the file.

Craftsmen frequently feel that they should get the same degree of finish using a 400x diamond hone as the manufacturer did when originally grinding the router bit with a 400x diamond wheel. This is an unrealistic expectation, since a wheel taking a specific depth of cut will cut to the predetermined depth on entry and then essentially knock the peaks off all the ridges as the cutting wheel is withdrawn. In a more sophisticated form this is called cutting to "spark out." This means that you pass the wheel over the work at a predetermined height (or run the work past the wheel) until no more abrasion is taking place (i.e., there are no more sparks).

When honing by hand, the router bit and the diamond hone are not in any fixed relationship. The diamond hone will continue to cut as long as it is pressed against the router bit or, conversely, the router bit is pressed against it. The process by which the tops are knocked off the ridges never occurs, so the finish is always rougher than it would be with a power system using the same grit size.

In view of this, if you want a finish on your router bit that is as fine as the factory one, you are going to have to use finer-grit diamond than the manufacturer did to achieve it. Most router bits have had the insert face lapped with a 400x diamond wheel. A few use a 600x wheel, and at least one uses an 800x wheel. You can achieve about the same surface finish as a 600x wheel using a 1200x diamond stone. Just as you would do if you were sharpening anything else, you may want to start lapping the router bit on a 400x or 600x diamond and finish on a 1200x to save time. This depends on the amount of sharpening that has to be done to restore the edge.

As you reduce diamond particle size, also reduce honing pressure. The very fine diamond particles can be dislodged more readily than the larger ones. The basic reason is that the nickel plating must be thinner to avoid masking the cutting action.

HIGH-SPEED-STEEL ROUTER BITS

Steel router bits are almost a thing of the past, which is unfortunate since much higher rake angles are possible with steel bits than with carbide bits. Because of the higher rake angle, they do a much cleaner job on end-grain

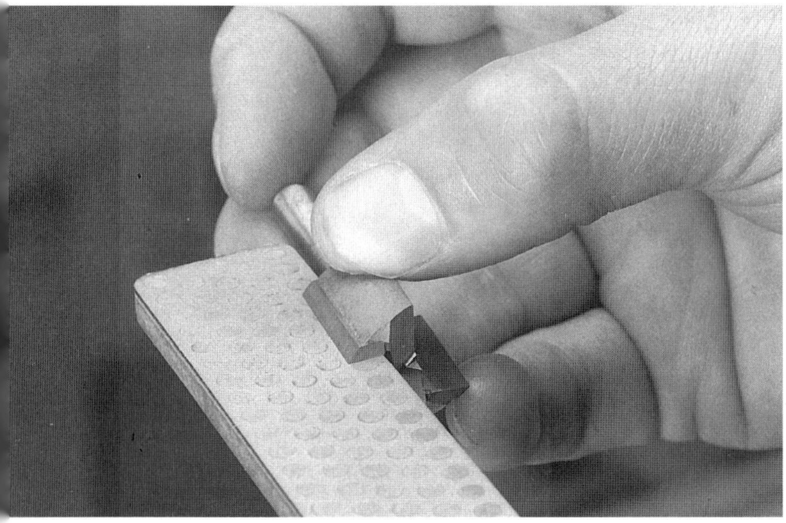

Lap only the flat face of a carbide router bit. (Photo by Susan Kahn)

Chip-limitation router bits (left) have a narrower gap between the carbide insert and the body than do standard bits (right) and require a diamond file for honing. (Photo by Susan Kahn)

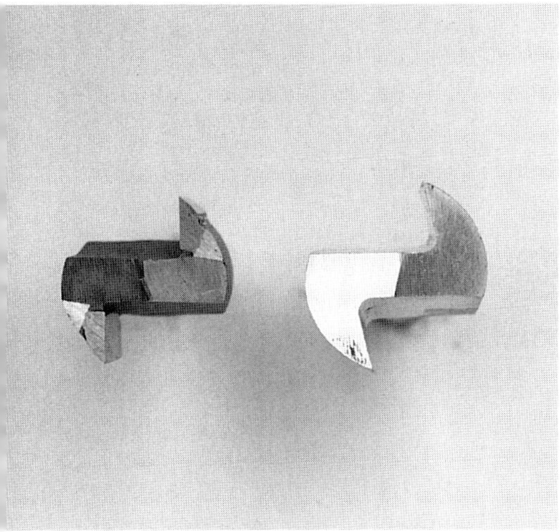

The rake angle of the cutting edge can be higher with a high-speed-steel router bit (right) than with a carbide bit (left) without prejudicing the strength of the edge. (Photo by Susan Kahn)

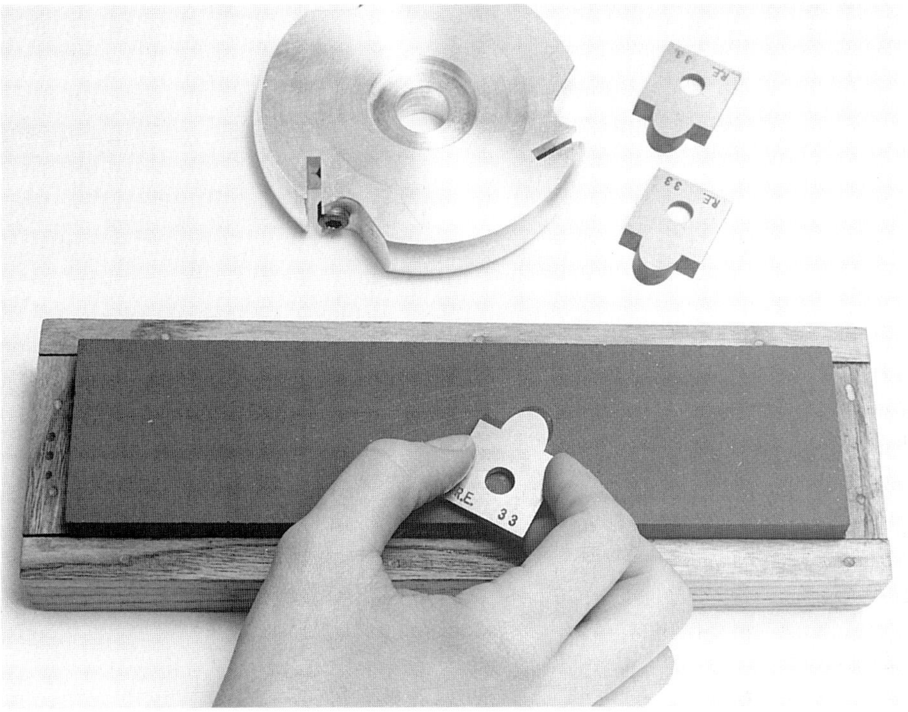

Molding-head cutters can be lapped on a stone.

softwoods; they cause far less fiber pulling. Although the higher rake angle could cause problems in highly variable grain, it gives a smoother finish working with the grain and on end grain.

High-speed-steel router bits can be sharpened in exactly the same way as carbide-insert bits, but you have a greater choice of abrasives—it is not necessary to use diamond stones.

OTHER PERIPHERAL MILLING CUTTERS

Each year several more designs of milling cutters come on the market, usually to fade away within a few seasons. But three basic styles that have been with us for decades are shaper blades, molding-head cutters and mortising bits.

The sheer size of shaper blades often makes it impractical to consider lapping the face with a diamond hone. It can be done, but it is a time-consuming process. It is generally more practical to have shaper blades custom-ground on a profile grinder.

Simple molding-head cutters, on the other hand, can be touched up fairly readily. Just remove the knives from the head and lap them with finger pressure on a suitable stone, as shown in the photo at top right.

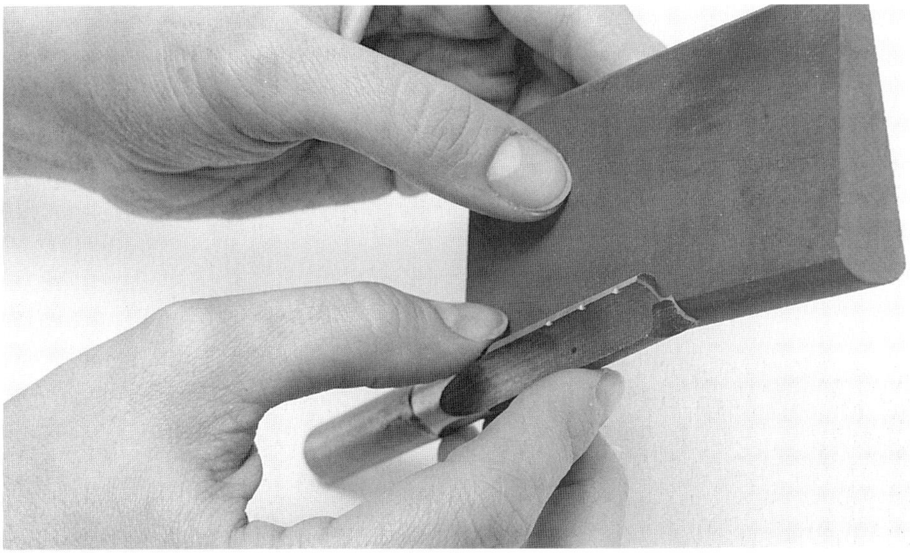

Use a slipstone to hone a chair mortising bit.

Mortising bits come in a variety of styles but have similar shapes to router bits. A chair mortising bit can be honed with an appropriately shaped shop stone (see the photo above), and a miller bit can be done on the edge of a diamond lap the same as one would hone a router bit.

CHAPTER 17

OTHER SHOP TOOLS

In many parts of this book as much time has been spent on shaping and conditioning tools as on putting a keen edge on them. Nowhere will this be the case more than in this chapter. Here we will be dealing with fettling tools more than sharpening them. "Fettle" is a fine old English word that means to trim, clean or adjust something to put it in good condition. Or, as it would have been said a century ago in North America, to put it in fine fettle.

An ideal example is a standard pair of tweezers. Most tweezers that you buy are made to look like tweezers but almost never act like tweezers. They have clubbish, malformed tips that are barely capable of gripping a matchstick let alone the fine splinter of wood that has just been driven under your fingernail. Such tweezers require fettling, not sharpening. We do not want them to cut, we just want them to work properly. So it is with many of the other tools discussed in this chapter. Some will require sharpening, but many others will require only pointing, serrating or shaping in some way to perform their task better.

TWEEZERS

Having introduced the subject of tweezers, besides wondering what they are doing in a book of woodworking tools, you might also be wondering just how tweezers should best be shaped to perform their tasks.

Most tweezers look like they should work but often will not. If you were to try to grip something with the tweezers shown in the top drawing below, you would find that the tips do not meet well originally and become progressively worse as pressure is applied. In addition, the surface is far too rough to provide a good grip. It actually has the potential to crush and sever a sliver where the excessively large ridges meet rather than clamping it properly for removal.

To shape the tips properly you have to grind back the serrated faces to make them more or less flat but with many fine cross serrations. The coarse work can be done on a belt sander. To finish off you have only to fold a piece of sandpaper and run the tweezers back and forth on either side with a firm grip, as shown in the photo at left below. This will abrade the inside of the tips so that they are approximately parallel under firm grip and will therefore always touch first at the extreme limit of the tip, just where you want the first contact to be made.

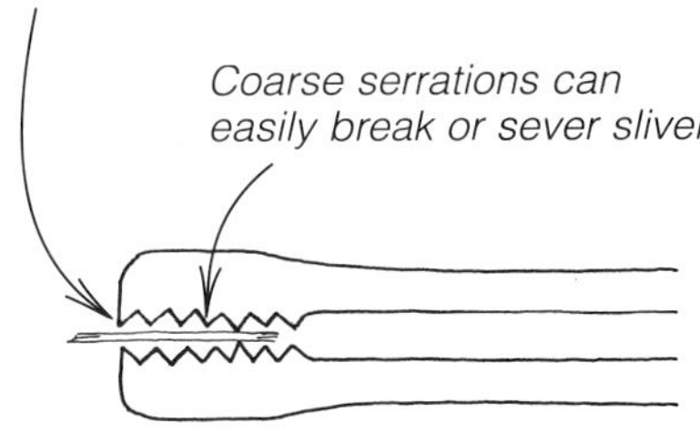

Bad tips

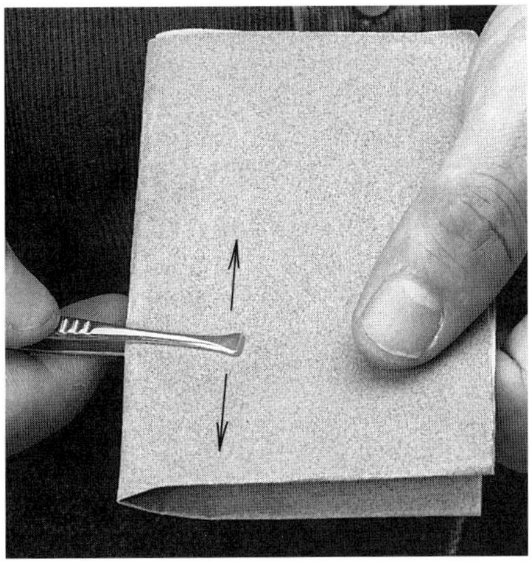

Once the serrated faces of the tweezers have been ground back, finish off by passing the tweezers back and forth over a piece of sandpaper. (Photos by Susan Kahn)

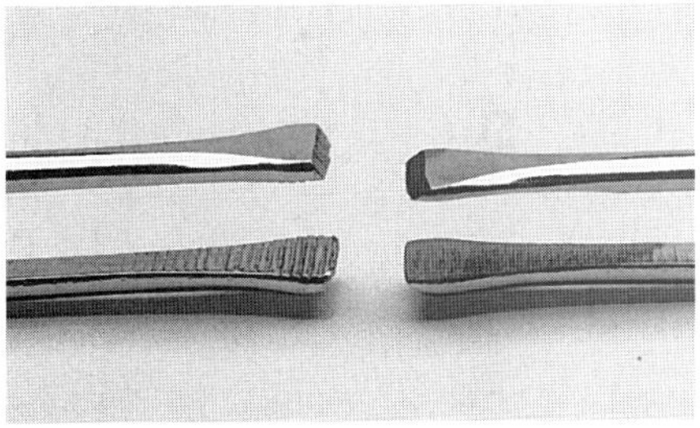

Tweezer tips, before and after interior shaping.

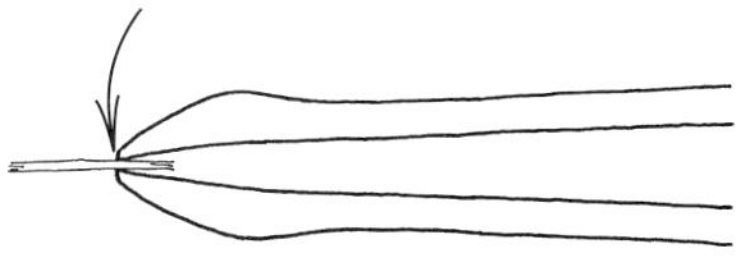

Good tips

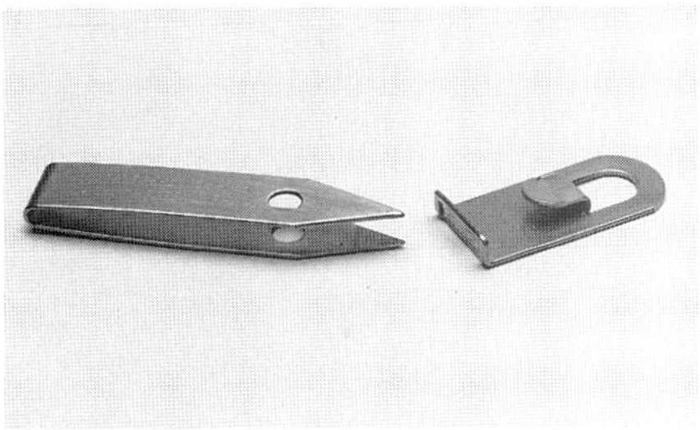

These tweezers, the best design in the author's opinion, have tips ground to a fine point with a light cross-score on the inside to grip slivers. (The device on the right is a tip guard.)

MAKING AN ECCENTRIC TRAMMEL POINT

Cheap trammel points have symmetrical pins, and all length adjustment must be made by tapping and sliding the clamp heads. More expensive trammel sets have one eccentric point so that fine adjustments can be made by rotating the eccentric point.

It is quite simple to make an eccentric pin if you are making yourself a set of trammel points. All you have to do is chuck a pin between two jaws of your hand drill and adjust the pin tip until it just crosses the centerline axis of the drill, as shown in the drawing below. Now go to your belt sander and sharpen the rod just as if it were a regular conically tipped tool. You will find it very easy to make the eccentric pin you want.

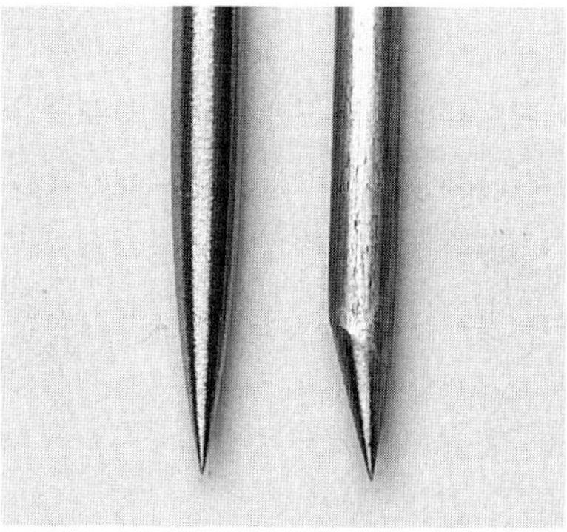

Concentric and eccentric trammel points. (Photo by Susan Kahn)

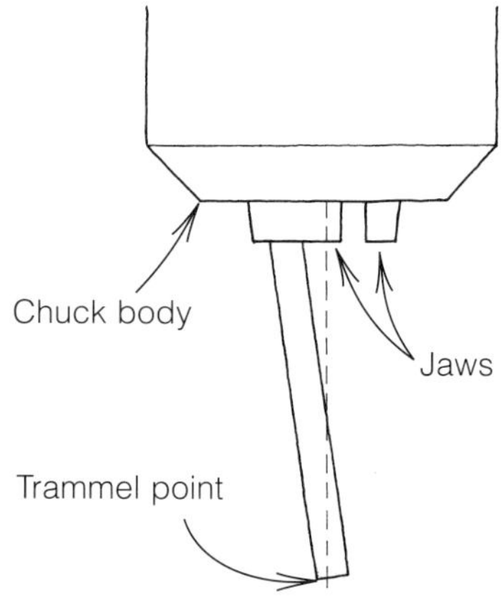

To sharpen a concentric trammel point, chuck the tool in a drill press and hold a stone against the point as it turns. (Photo by Susan Kahn)

TRAMMEL POINTS, CENTER PUNCHES, AWLS

The secret to sharpening any conical-tipped tool is to have the tool rotating while you are sharpening it. For tools that have no handle, like a trammel point or a center punch, the easiest way to sharpen the tool is to chuck the blade directly in a drill press and use a bench stone to shape the tip as the tool is rotating, as shown in the photo above. You can use the same technique for tools that have easy-to-remove handles (often the case with scratch awls and garnish awls).

Alternatively, you can chuck the tool directly in a hand drill and sharpen it on a wheel or belt sander. If the handle cannot be removed, the tool can be rotated by hand against a belt sander.

AWLS WITH BEVELED TIPS

The traditional brad awl has a double-beveled tip with the bevels meeting at the axis of the awl. Pressed into wood with the wedge at 90° to the grain and rotated back and forth slightly, the tip tends to sever fibers and minimizes splitting. An awl like this can be sharpened in a variety of ways, but the simplest is probably on a bench stone. The geometry is not particularly critical,

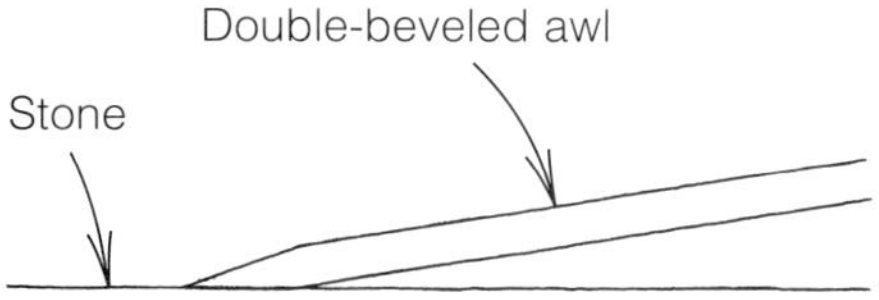

although wood penetration is better with shallower bevel angles.

A less common but very effective tool, particularly for working in hardwood, is the square awl. You twist the awl as you push it in and it drills a hole. Once a square awl has been ground, it needs lapping of the four faces on a bench stone only occasionally. For this

To convert a round awl into a square awl, use a square piece of wood on the awl as a visual guide while you grind. (Photo by Susan Kahn)

SCREWDRIVER TIPS

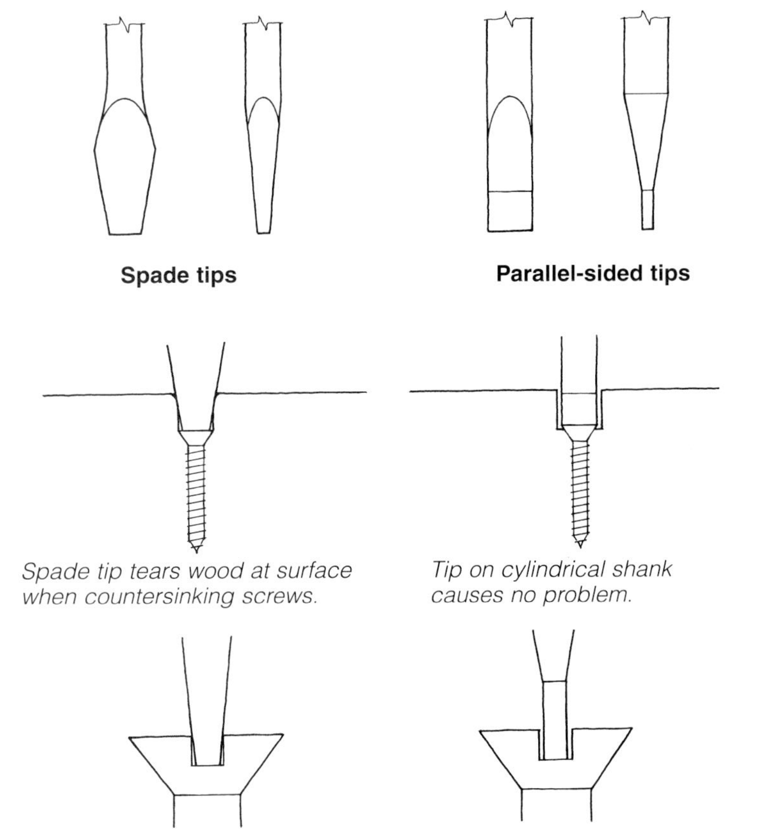

process, it is not difficult to keep the awl properly oriented by feel alone. Because the awl drills by scraping the sides of the hole, it should be lapped whenever the facet intersections have become at all rounded.

If you want to make a square awl from a round awl, it is most readily done by pushing the round awl through a thin square piece of wood and using the edges of the wood as a visual or physical guide while you grind. Using the wood square as a visual template, you have a far better chance of getting a square cross-section than if you tried to gauge everything by reference only to the tiny flats on the tool.

SCREWDRIVERS

Restoring screwdriver tips is not strictly sharpening, but you can have more effective tips if you apply a bit of sharpening cunning to them.

Probably fewer than 1% of the readers of this book have ever tried regrinding any screwdriver other than a slotted one. I suspect that fewer than one in ten of you have even done that. I am always amazed at the number of screwdrivers in people's shops (including my own) that are virtually useless but are kept around "just in case." I have no intention of trying to reform the world on this issue, but it is not beyond the wit of man to repair a screwdriver tip. Slot screwdrivers are particularly easy to repair; in fact, you can usually make them better than new. Other tip shapes present more problems.

SLOT SCREWDRIVERS

Not only are slot screwdrivers the easiest to reshape, but they are also usually the ones most in need of it, even when new and unused. Just like chisels, slot screwdrivers do not come out of the package ready for use: the tips are invariably wrongly shaped for woodworking. They are wedge-shaped in both axes, when what you need is a tip of constant diameter with the flats parallel for a distance at least as great as the depth of slot of any screw they are to be used on.

MODIFIED SCREWDRIVER TIPS

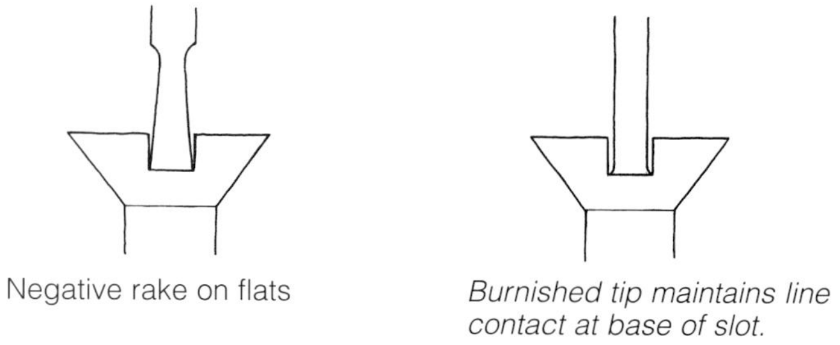

JIG FOR HONING SCREWDRIVER TIPS

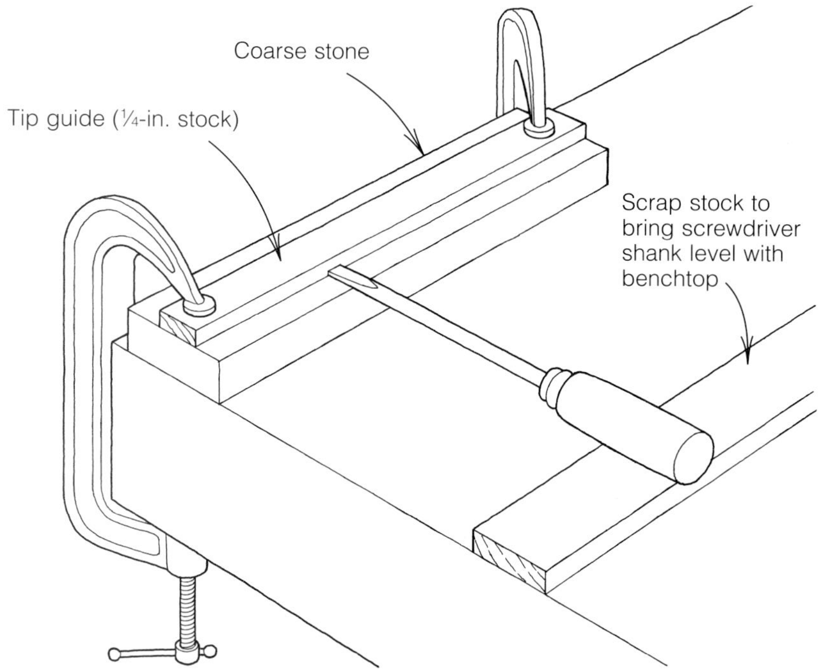

For woodworking use, it is important that no part of the screwdriver be wider than the tip. The best example of the need for a parallel-sided tip is when you want to countersink screws for plugging. A spade-shaped tip can score the sides of the counterbore, making it impossible to do a decent job of plugging because of the damage done to the walls of the countersunk hole (see the drawing on p. 217).

A cylindrical shank will follow the screw without damage. The same is true when driving a screw next to some protruding detail; a cylindrical shank will not mark an adjoining surface as a spade tip can. In the other axis, a wedge shape encourages the screwdriver to cam out of the slot. Parallel sides do not.

If you want to be particularly cunning, there are two ways you can redesign the tip to improve the grip even more. One is to put a slight negative rake on the flats (see the top drawing at left). The rake has to be very slight since the modification weakens the tip. However, it ensures that the line of contact is always at the bottom of the slot.

But the easiest and most effective method is to form the tip with parallel sides and then burnish the end. It takes a fair amount of pressure (use a triangular burnisher or the small-radius edge of a tear-drop burnisher), but you need only a slight swelling to achieve your purpose. You now have a tip that will tolerate minor misalignment and still maintain line contact at the base of the slot.

This design is particularly effective with brass screws. The burnished edge cuts into the brass at the bottom of the slot, virtually locking the tip in position as long as there is torque on it. Incidentally, if you find the tip too hard to burnish, you can clamp the screwdriver in a vise and roll the hooks on the tip by tapping the tip with a hammer.

Whatever you do to the tip of a new screwdriver will probably improve its shape, but you should be careful not to overheat the tip and soften it. Reshaping can be done on a coarse bench stone with minor jigging (see the drawing at left), or with a file if the tip is soft enough. The minor serrations from the bench stone improve tip grip by resisting cam-out. Do not polish them off. In fact, this is what is called a cross-ground tip in tool catalogs.

SQUARE-RECESS SCREWDRIVERS

Unlike slot screwdrivers, square-recess (or Robertson) screwdrivers usually come with properly shaped tips. If well hardened originally, they seldom deform in use because they seldom slip. Square-recess power bits, on the other hand, can be more readily damaged in use (just like all power bits).

The power bits are made to be disposable, but not so the screwdrivers. To restore their shape, they have to be docked at the tip and the flats extended at the original angles and cross-sectional dimensions. Since the tips are usually milled originally, the flats will be tangential to the arc left by the milling head. This may require you to remove a fair bit of metal the first time you reshape the tip.

With care, this shaping can all be done on a grinding wheel; alternatively, you can use a diamond file. The tips are usually too hard for a steel file. To guide your eye when filing, clamp the screwdriver between two pieces of wood with the flat to be filed parallel to and just proud of the wood (see the drawing at right).

RESTORING SQUARE-RECESS SCREWDRIVER TIPS

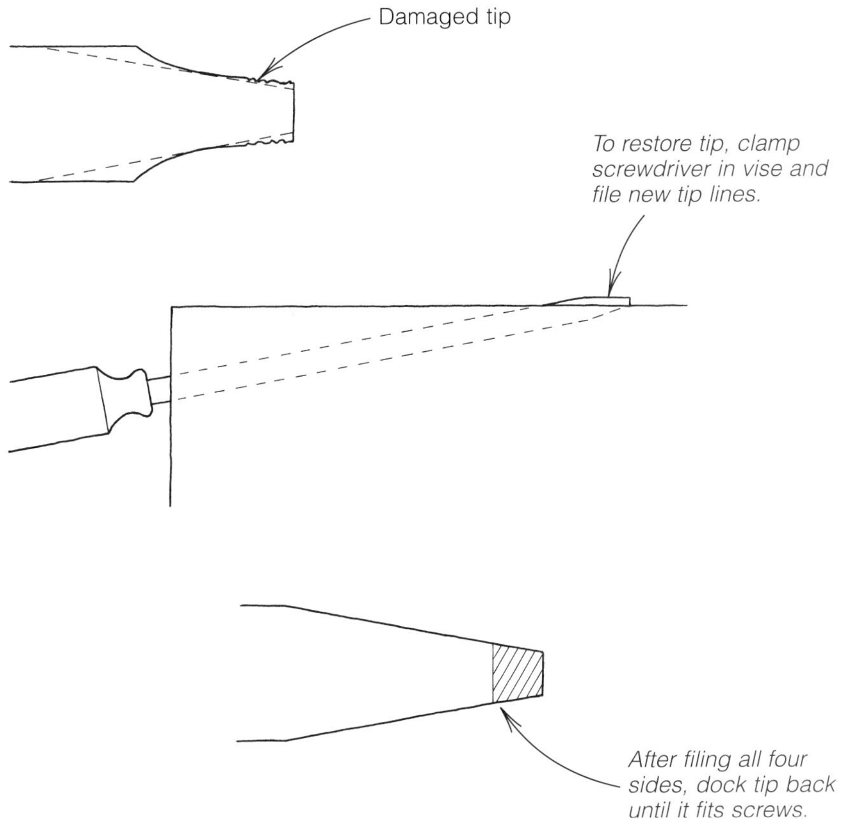

WOODEN VISE JAWS

Whenever you have to use temporary wooden jaws in a vise and the jaws have to be even (as when reshaping a screwdriver tip), there are at least three easy ways to do it.

Option A. Put double-faced tape on the outside of the wooden jaws, line them up with the vise jaws and close the vise. You can then open and close the vise at will, and the jaws will stay tacked in position.

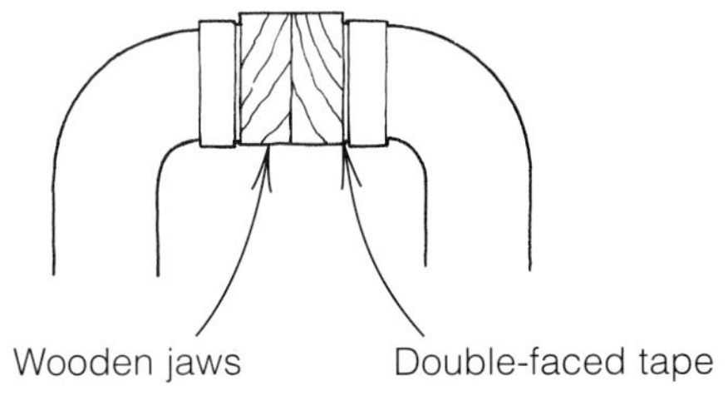

Option B. Kerf a piece of wood just slightly narrower than the item you want to hold. Press the item into the kerf and put the whole thing in the vise.

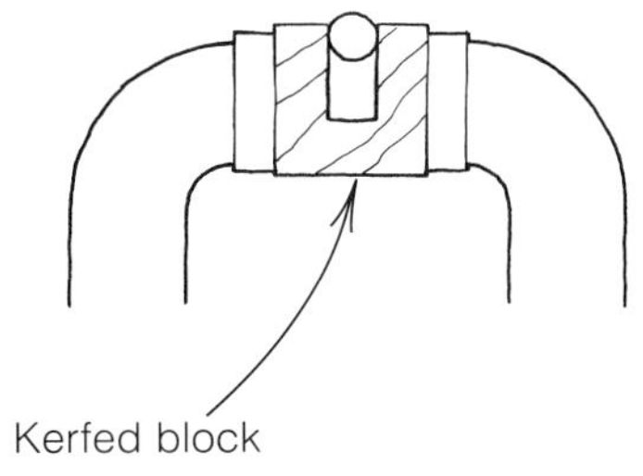

Option C. For very wide items, tack thin stock on a base that is the same width as the item you want to hold.

Any of these methods is easier than trying to hold two jaws with something positioned between them as you try to close the vise.

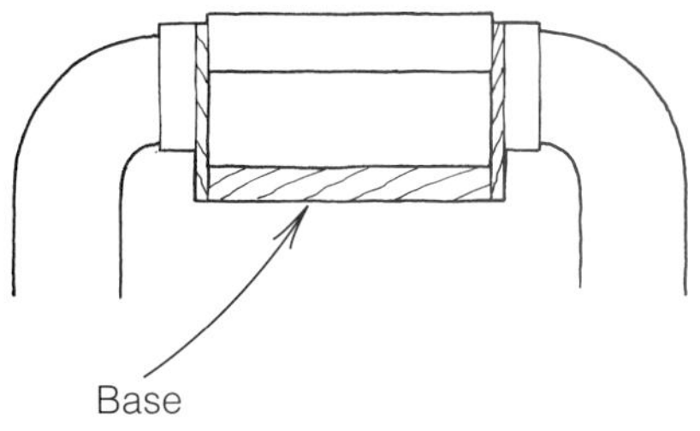

PHILLIPS SCREWDRIVERS

Restoring a Phillips screwdriver tip is just a matter of restoring the original geometry. Well, not quite. The first thing you find as you apply a square file to the tip grooves is that the manufacturer did not create the grooves this way, because you find the file cutting only at opposite ends of the groove. The groove was originally formed by a radius-tipped die or cutter. This means that you have to do a bit of filing before you get to the area that needs restoration. No matter, the grooves are easy to file.

If you are questioning why anyone would file the grooves first rather than the four flats, the primary reason is that you want as much reference face as possible on the groove sides to orient the file, particularly because the file touches initially only at the groove ends. Once the grooves are evenly filed, you can address the flats. File the flats back to the width required (i.e., the original width). Finally, dock the end of the screwdriver so the driver will seat properly in screws.

Filing a Phillips tip is all a bit awkward the first time, but you quickly get the hang of it and find that you can restore tips to a condition at least as good as the original and often better. To make filing as easy as possible, clamp the screwdriver in a vise with the grooves approximately horizontal.

To reshape a damaged Phillips screwdriver tip (top), first file the grooves, then the flats (middle) and finish by docking the tip (bottom).

OTHER SCREWDRIVER STYLES

There are several other types of screws on the market, but the shaping principles for their drivers are the same as those already described, only the shapes differ.

MARKING AND CUTTING GAUGES

Marking and cutting gauges are frequently used for the same purposes. Only occasionally does a woodworker use a cutting gauge for cutting something to depth; more commonly it is used for some purpose like marking tenon shoulders, where it is prized for the crisp shoulders it makes.

In Western tradition, a cutting gauge had a knife beveled on one side as a cutter, and a marking gauge had a conical pin as a marker. In Japan (possibly in other countries) knives were used in all woodworking gauges. The question of which style to use is nearly irrelevant since there is a huge amount of evidence in used gauges to show that most Western marking-gauge owners spent a great deal of time trying to make their gauges cut better by filing the pins to double-beveled points that looked suspiciously like knives.

For those of you unfamiliar with cutting gauges, they are always used with the knife bevel to the waste side of the marked cut. In this manner, it is possible to eliminate the width of the cutter as a consideration in marking a line. It also severs the fibers so that any tearout from a saw will be on the waste side of the cut.

SHARPENING CUTTERS

The knife in a cutting gauge should be sharpened as you would any knife beveled on one side. Remove the cutter from the gauge, grind and hone the knife bevel, then lap the other side.

If you have a Japanese marking/cutting gauge and use extensive central heating during the winter, you will find that the knife will probably be seized in the gauge stem. Japanese manufacturers often make these gauges from wood with 10% or more moisture content; as this dries down in winter, the knife gets locked in place.

It is a good idea to open the knife slot a bit, cut a wedge mortise and fashion a small wedge to hold the knife, just the way Western cutting gauges are designed. Otherwise you might snap

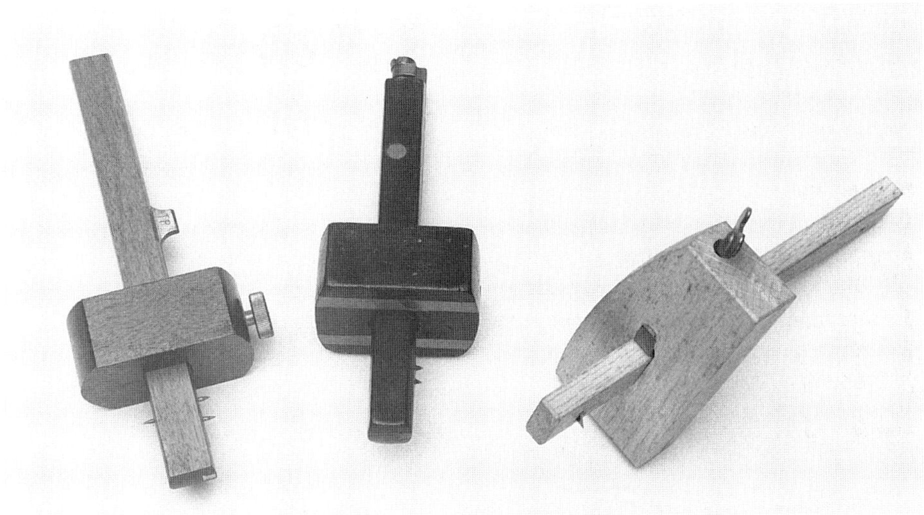

From left to right, a slide-mechanism mortise/marking gauge, a screw-mechanism mortise gauge and a simple Japanese marking/cutting gauge. (Photo by Susan Kahn)

The knives in Japanese marking/cutting gauges can be difficult to remove for sharpening. The knife shown here snapped when removal was attempted.

the knife trying to remove it, as has happened to the knife in the gauge shown in the photo at top right.

SHARPENING PINS

With many marking gauges, it is not possible to remove the pins for sharpening. Since removal and replacement would tend to loosen them anyway, sharpening the pins in place is common.

There are at least three schools of thought on sharpening marking-gauge pins. The first, to maintain the conical point, is the least-followed practice. The second is to file both sides of the pin to bring it to a sharp point. The last is to file the side next to the gauge head vertically and put all the bevel on the side away from the gauge head. I call this "knife envy"; it is an attempt to convert a marking gauge into a cutting gauge.

One problem with sharpening pins in place is that there's a danger of filing grooves in the gauge stem at the same time as you shape the pins (see the photo at right). However, there are several ways to avoid this problem. You can: use an auger-bit file that has safe edges; use a feather-edge file, after grinding (and buffing) the apex to make it safe; use a square-edged file with tape covering the edge; modify a cheap needle file for the purpose; or make a safe-edge file with PSA-backed abrasive.

Once a pin becomes too short and it is not possible either to drive it out farther or remove it, just file it close to flush, tap it back into the stem out of the way, drill a hole next to it and put in a new pin. Only with a graduated-stem gauge does it matter exactly where the pin is on the stem.

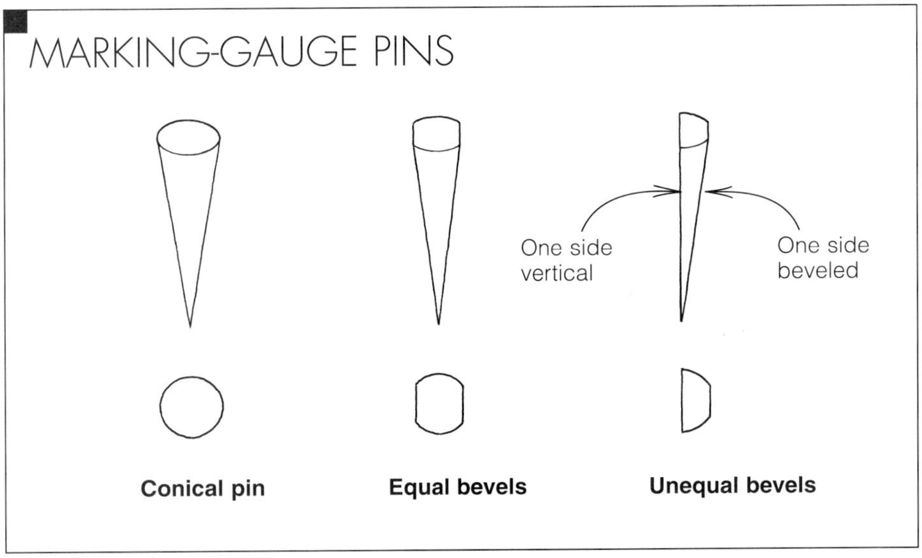

The stem of this old marking gauge has been scored by repeated filing of the marking pin.

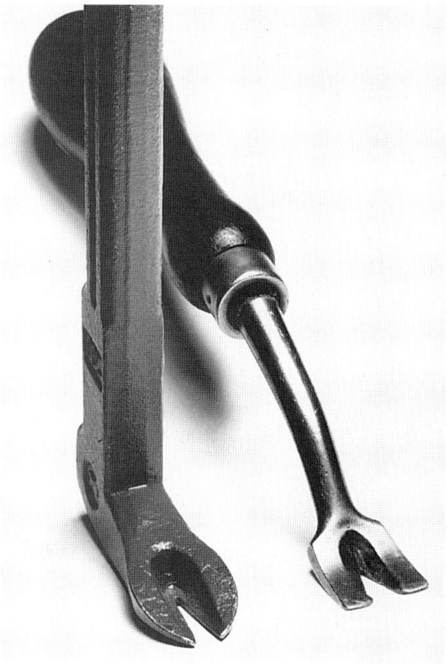

The claws of a Japanese cat's paw (left) are quite different from those of a traditional Western tack lifter (right). The relief grinding in the nail slot, the pointed tips and the rounded bottom differentiate them.

Hammer claws should be ground to smooth strong wedges, as shown on the hammer at front. The tips of the claws on the back hammer are much steeper than necessary. (Photos by Susan Kahn)

CLAW TOOLS

Hammers, renovator's bars, cat's paws and tack lifters are all likely to need some redefining of their claw tips at some time. In each case, the shape of the claws should be related to the force that will be applied to them.

For example, the claws on most tack lifters are much thicker than necessary for removing tacks and small brads. If the claws are not thinned at the tips and brought to a finer wedge shape, they will always be more destructive in use than is necessary. With a fine tip, they can be slipped under a tack head without gouging large chunks out of the wood.

CAT'S PAWS

A Japanese cat's paw shows how a tool can be effectively designed to be pressed under a nail head with minimal disturbance of surrounding wood. Whereas a Western tool might have flat chisel-tipped claws, a Japanese cat's paw has claws that are pointed on the tips as well as being relief-ground away from the nail slot. It is far easier to force such claws under nail heads. The design manages to give precision in use with substantial strength. That is what you should aim for when you sharpen any claw tool.

HAMMERS

Since hammer claws are as often used for prying as they are for nail removal, they should not be ground to mimic cat's paws. They have a dual purpose, and both purposes should be served. In the photo above, one set of claws has been ground to smooth strong wedges; the other has been docked abruptly, weakening the very tip and making the first ¼ in. or so a much steeper wedge than necessary.

RENOVATOR'S BARS

The prying tips of bars should be ground to suit their purpose. Two well-designed tips are shown in the top photo on the facing page. The large tip is on a Swedish renovator's bar, so called because it is as useful in construction as it is in demolition. The tip is designed to be driven into very narrow cracks to wedge apart fastened structural members with minimal damage to either. The other tip (on a Japanese renovator's cat's paw) has the same objective, but for smaller-scale work like room trim or cabinetry.

Both tools are designed in relation to their length as well as to their purpose. They are as thin as they can be given the width of their tips and their

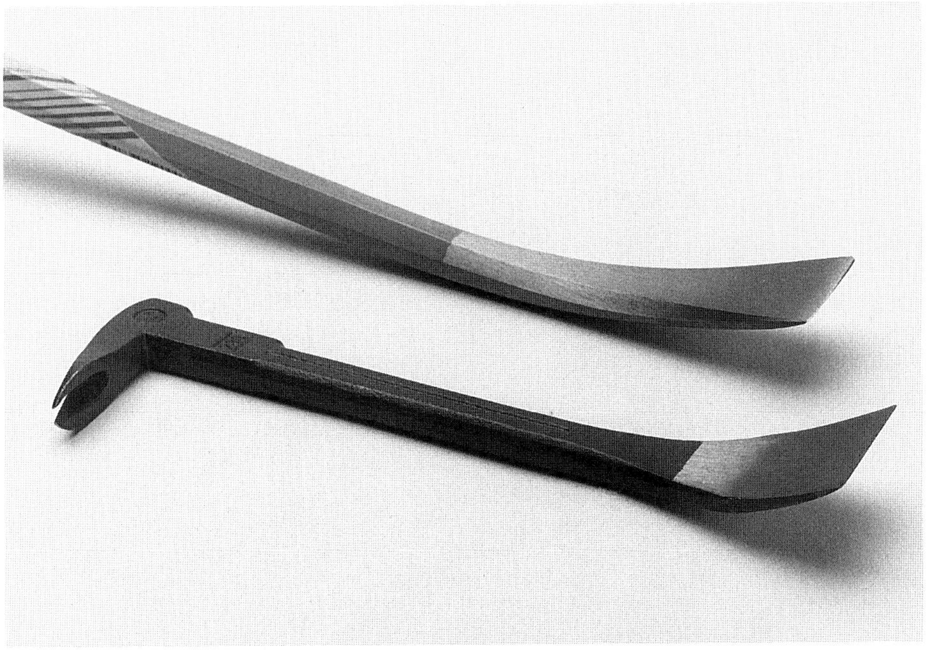

The prying tips of renovator's bars (back) and renovator's cat's paws (front) should be ground as thin as possible. (Photo by Susan Kahn)

NAIL-SET TIPS

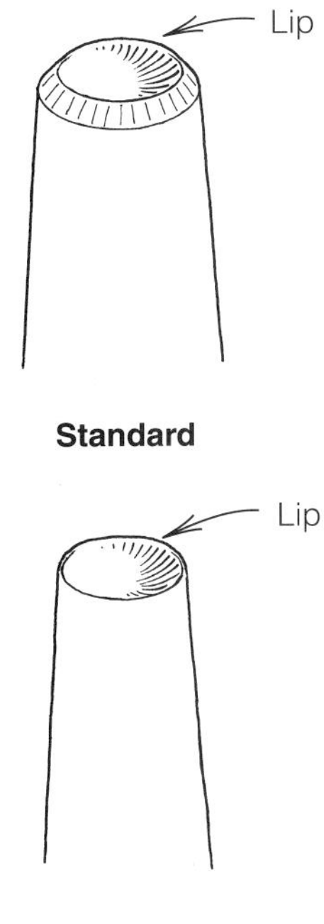

length. Whenever you regrind a tool like this you should keep the length of the tool in mind, because someone will eventually use all of the leverage afforded and the tool has to be able to withstand the force.

There is one particularly difficult grinding problem with claw tools. This is the set of claws that has a "hole" worn in them; all but the largest nails escape their grip. The only thing that can be

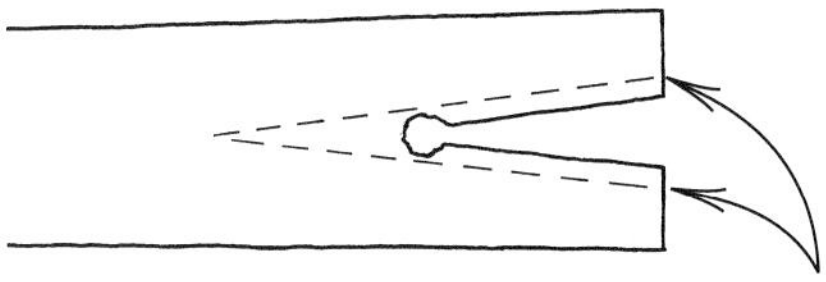

Restore claws by grinding back to dotted lines.

done in this case is to lengthen the claws, moving the nail slot farther back in the head as shown in the drawing above. Although time-consuming, this can be done with grinding burrs and/or discs. There are now inexpensive and aggressive diamond burrs and discs on the market that are ideal for this sort of job.

NAIL SETS

Nail sets have a conical or spherical depression in the tip; they depend on a sharp lip for their grip on a nail head. There are two styles: the standard tip and the European tip (see the drawing at right).

The standard tip is stronger than the European tip but will not follow as cleanly when you want to countersink nails. With either style, once you flatten the lip, the set will not grip a nail head securely. On a larger nail set, you can recreate the tip with a ball-tip or flame-tip diamond or carbide burr (see the photo at right). On a very small nail set where you might not be able to do that, I would recommend that you first try to make a crater with a center punch and then do some judicious peripheral grinding. You will need some magnification if you attempt this.

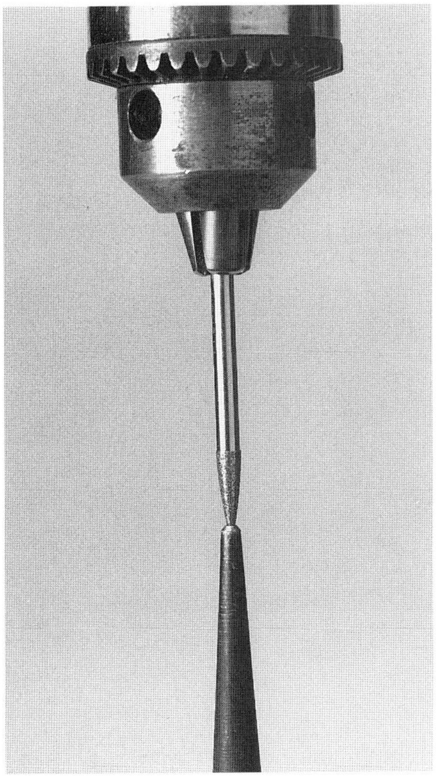

Use a flame-tip burr to recreate the tip of a flattened nail set. (Photo by Susan Kahn)

A very easy fix, although not quite as good as the ones described, is to grind the nail set flat on the tip and then drive it against a double-cut file. This will create several points on the tip of the

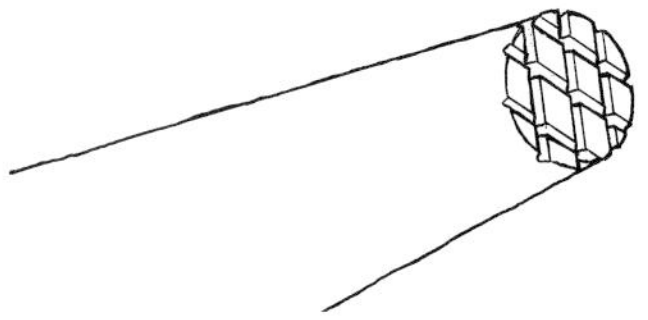

set (see the drawing above) that will grip a nail head.

But the best thing you can do, as usual, is to look after your nail sets in the first place. Nail sets are hard. Nail heads are soft. If you avoid using your nail sets as pin punches, they will probably never dull unless you happen to be a finish carpenter and use them every day.

PLIERS

About the most you can do for a pair of pliers is to sharpen the teeth when they get dull. A triangular diamond file works well. The jaws would normally be case-hardened and be too hard for a steel file.

If the pliers have side cutters, they can usually be sharpened once before the rest of the jaws interfere with complete closure. It is generally best to sharpen the outside bevel only, respecting the original geometry and ensuring that the cutting edges remain straight and meet evenly. Altogether, this is a daunting task and there are no handy jigs to take the skill out of it.

END CUTTERS, NAIL PULLERS

End cutters and nail pullers look so similar that it is tempting to use them in the same way. I did and took a huge chunk off the corner of one jaw of my favorite end cutters as I was trying to wrench a reluctant spike from its moorings. In general, end cutters are harder than nail pullers and have a slimmer jaw profile. They are designed to cut (not to have substantial lateral pressure applied as I did) and can therefore afford a lower included angle on each jaw than can nail pullers.

Pliers' side cutters can usually be sharpened once or twice before the serrated jaws meet.

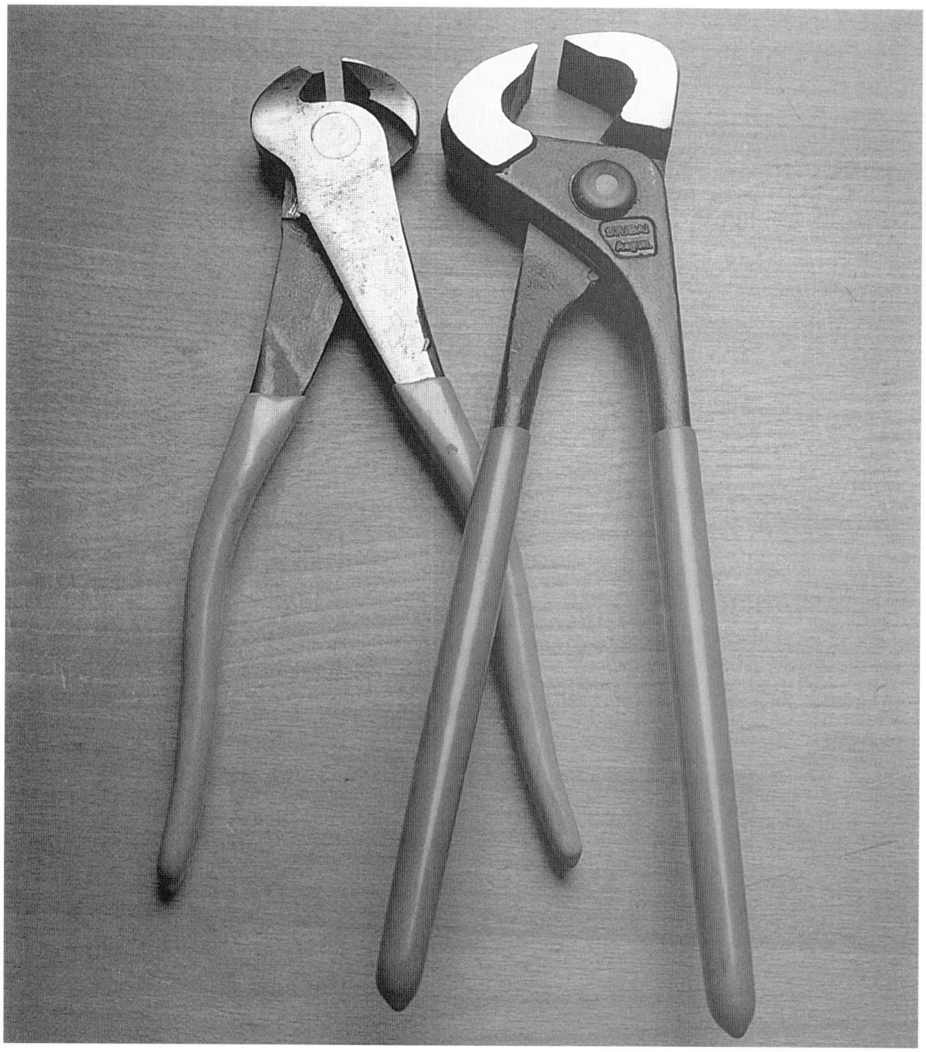

A nail puller (the longer-handled tool at right) can be used as an end cutter, although it is not as efficient because it is hinged well back from the jaw edges. However, an end cutter (at left) cannot be used as a nail puller because the jaws are too brittle (note the corner off one jaw).

Either tool can have the jaws restored by judicious work on a belt sander (a 1-in. belt sander lets you work around the jaw limitations quite

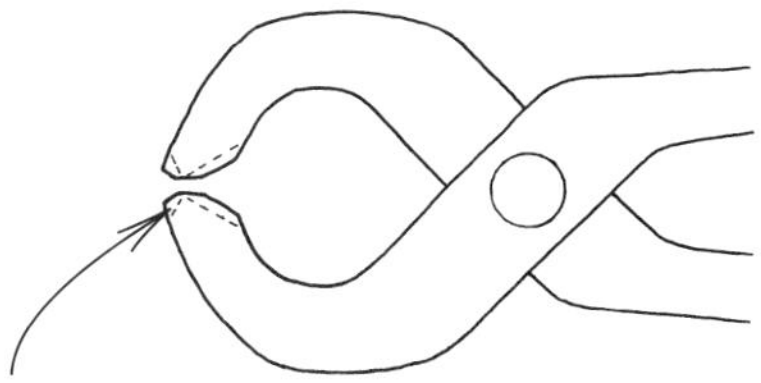

Joint worn jaws before filing bevels.

easily) or by filing. In either case, the original jaw geometry should be maintained and, to ensure that the jaws continue to meet evenly, they should be jointed before the bevels are filed.

It is fairly easy to joint the jaws and then adjust the flats so that they meet evenly. Only then should you file the bevels to recreate an edge. With the flat to guide you, it is straightforward to file a bevel correctly; just keep the flat of even width as you file. And, finally, do not file the bevel to the point that the jointing flat disappears entirely; leave a narrow line of light the complete length. There are two reasons for this. First, you want the jaw edges not only to be parallel to each other, but to meet, not bypass. So, when you file the second jaw, you may find that a bit more must be filed off one edge or the other of the first jaw so that the two can meet properly. Second, you should leave a very slight flat on each jaw anyway to maintain edge strength.

SCISSORS AND SHEARS

Top-quality scissors and shears should be sharpened professionally; sewing centers frequently provide the service. But for the under $10 variety, the kind most of us have in our shops, there is no reason not to have a go at them. With a bit of care, you can do a perfectly serviceable job.

Scissors are most easily sharpened on a belt sander. With the table set at whatever bevel angle was originally on the scissors and the scissors open, grind one side, then the other, always with the belt running into the edge. Usually a single pass on a 120x belt will do it. After grinding, very carefully deburr the edge by taking a light pass on a fine stone (1000x or finer) with the flat of the blade.

Scissors usually dull as a result of the blades abrading each other; the material being cut is usually the lesser cause. As the blades pass each other they wear off a tiny amount each time.

Grind blades back to dotted lines.

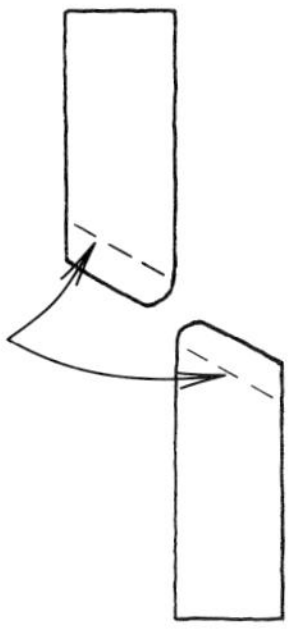

In the drawing above, the blades would have to be ground back to the dotted line to be restored.

In general, you can regrind scissors at the found bevel angle, but this should not be less than 45° for utility use. For cutting very thin materials, a narrow flat on the edge is sometimes used.

PUNCHES

It is just possible that one in a thousand readers might be faced with the task of sharpening a veneer punch some day. More probable is that you will need to sharpen a leather punch or a punch-style washer cutter. Sharpening any style of punch is a challenge, but with care anything is possible.

The most difficult aspect of sharpening a punch is keeping the cutting edge in one plane. It has to be flat to work properly. The first thing to do is joint the punch edge on a bench stone—800x to 1200x is fine. Joint it only until you can see a line of light all the way around the punch. Then, starting at the thickest part of the edge, work your way around the edge with a slipstone or a small bench stone, sharpening it the same way you would with a gouge until there is a barely discernible or no line of light left.

Using a hard leather strop or a wooden strop charged with chromium oxide, carefully finish the edge. If you accidentally go too far in one spot, lightly rejoint the punch and start again.

Although not possible with a veneer punch because of its irregular shape, a circular punch can be honed and stropped on a belt sander if you are confident of your technique. But since

Punches like the two above are used for cutting leather, cork or any soft, nonmetallic material. The punch head on the left has a cam-lock mechanism; the one on the right threads into the holder. (Photo by Susan Kahn)

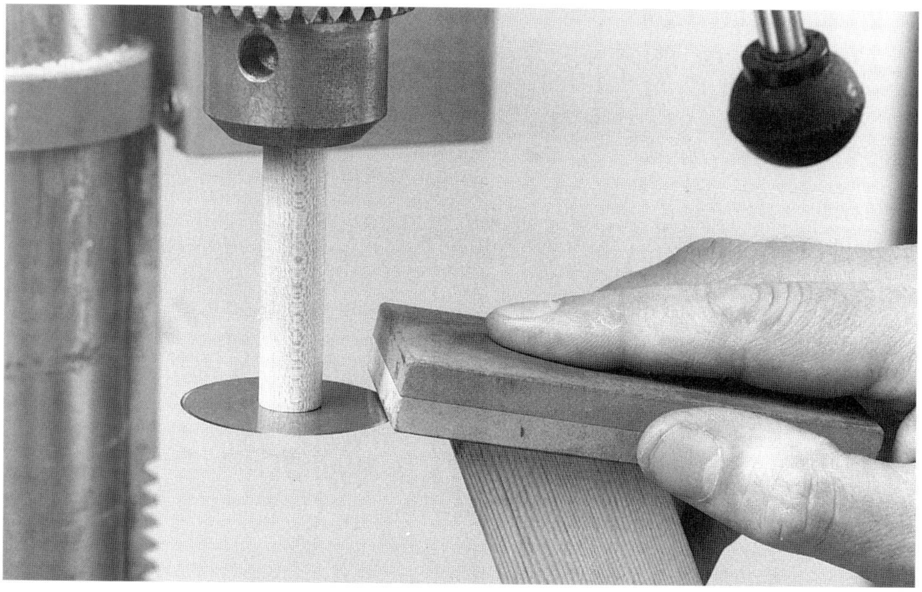

To sharpen a rotary cutter, mount the cutter on a mandrel in a drill press and hold a stone against the bevel while the cutter is turning. Use a steady rest to support the stone at the correct angle. (Photo by Susan Kahn)

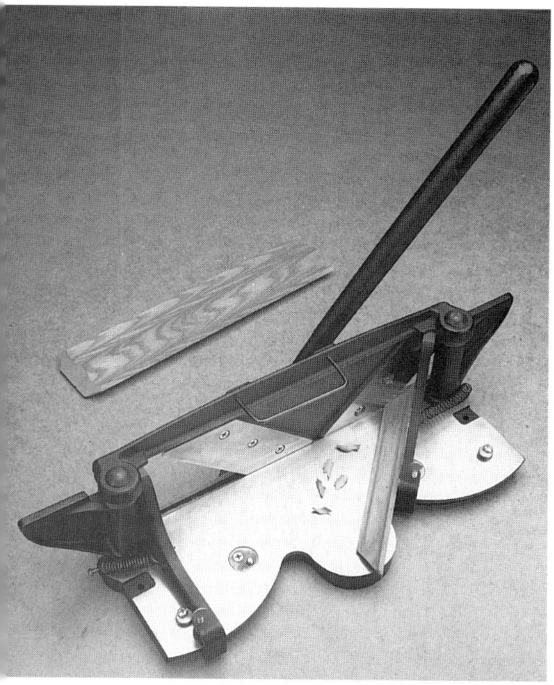

Miter trimmers are used only for trimming stock, usually taking off less than 1/8 in. per pass.

it is so easy to overshoot the mark with power equipment, I recommend hand honing.

ROTARY CUTTERS

Rotary cutters have long been popular for cutting fabric but have only recently infiltrated the woodworking shop for veneer cutting. Most rotary cutters have disposable cutter wheels, but these can also be resharpened.

The secret is to mount the cutter on a mandrel in a drill press, or in an electric hand drill clamped in a vise, and sharpen the cutter while it is turning. For a very dull cutter, use a medium-grit stone (e.g. 800x) followed by a 4000x or 8000x stone.

In both instances you should use a steady rest of some kind that lets you hone at the original bevel angle of the cutter, as shown in the photo at top. Be particularly careful in this process since the rotating cutter can give you a serious cut.

It is a simple matter to make a mandrel from a piece of dowel and use a screw to hold the cutter in position. The neck size of the screw should be the same as the center hole of the cutter.

MITER-TRIMMER BLADES

Fortunately, miter-trimmer blades do not need frequent sharpening. Since they are large, awkward tools and have to be exceptionally keen to work well, that is a good thing. As with jointer and planer blades, if a good sharpening service is available, these blades are as well left to professionals. They can use a traversing jig for grinding, something you cannot readily duplicate.

If the blades need only honing and are not nicked, this is something that you can readily do. The blades are thick enough and long enough that the bevel provides quite a large reference surface for a sharpening stone. It is time-consuming, but the entire bevel can be honed. You should start with an 800x water stone for good speed of cut and do 90% of the work with that stone, finishing off with a 6000x or an 8000x stone.

A shopmade honing jig that works well is a piece of wood sliced at the bevel angle of the trimmer blade (see the drawing on the facing page). Screw the blade to the block with small-shank screws and washers (to give yourself lots of adjustment room) and clamp the block in a vise. With the blade projecting just above the block and a wrap of tape on the far side of the stone to prevent abrasion of the wood, you can control the honing process. You may increase the bevel angle by a few minutes, but not enough to be concerned about. You can fine-tune everything by adding or removing layers of tape on the stone.

When you have finished honing the bevel you will probably have created some burr on the edge, however minor. Of paramount importance in removing this burr is that the face of the blade be kept dead flat. Even minor buffing on the inboard face can cause the blade to veer off-line, unless it is done very carefully. The best system is to put a sheet of 0.5 micron chromium-oxide lapping film on a piece of flat hardwood plywood. With the blade flat on the sheet, draw it across with a trailing stroke; that will refine the edge sufficiently. Any more than that could introduce error in the cut.

CORNERING TOOLS

The easiest way to sharpen a cornering tool is not to touch the convex side at all. The geometry is fairly involved, and it is simpler if the convex side be left alone once it has been properly honed once.

A 1-in. diameter sanding drum is ideal for the concave side of a cornering tool. All you have to do is press the cornering tool against the rotating sanding drum to grind the inside. If a fair amount of work has to be done, start with a coarse sleeve and then move to a fine sleeve for finishing.

To put a very fine edge on the cornering tool, finish off with a 1-in. dowel and green honing compound. One end of the dowel can be turned down so that it can be chucked in a drill press, or the dowel can be mounted between centers on a lathe to speed everything up. Alternatively, it can be used just as one uses a slipstone.

At various times, cornering tools that are incorrectly ground come on the market; usually the bevels of the two cutting edges are in the same plane. This fault can be corrected with time and effort, but it is wiser to return the tool to the vendor. Although you often have to accept tools that need honing, you should never have to accept tools that have manufacturing defects.

JIG FOR HONING MITER-TRIMMER BLADES

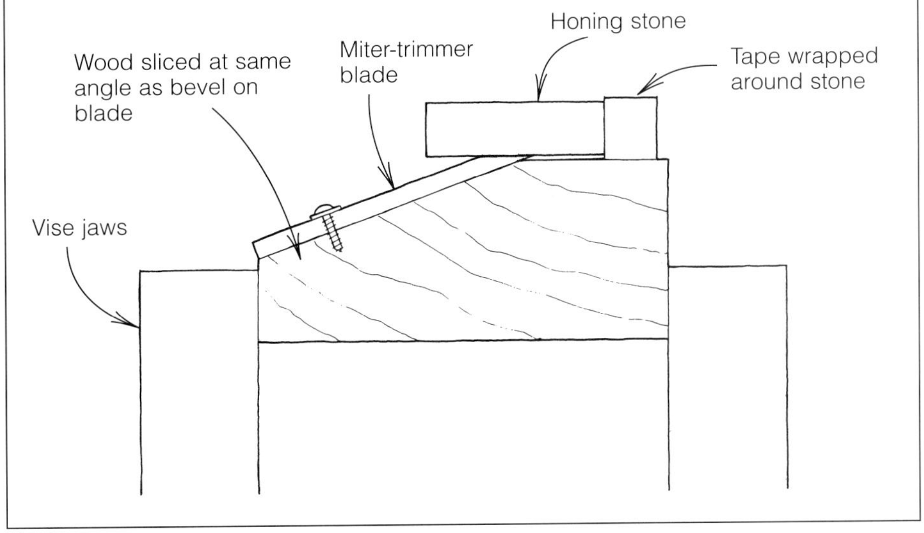

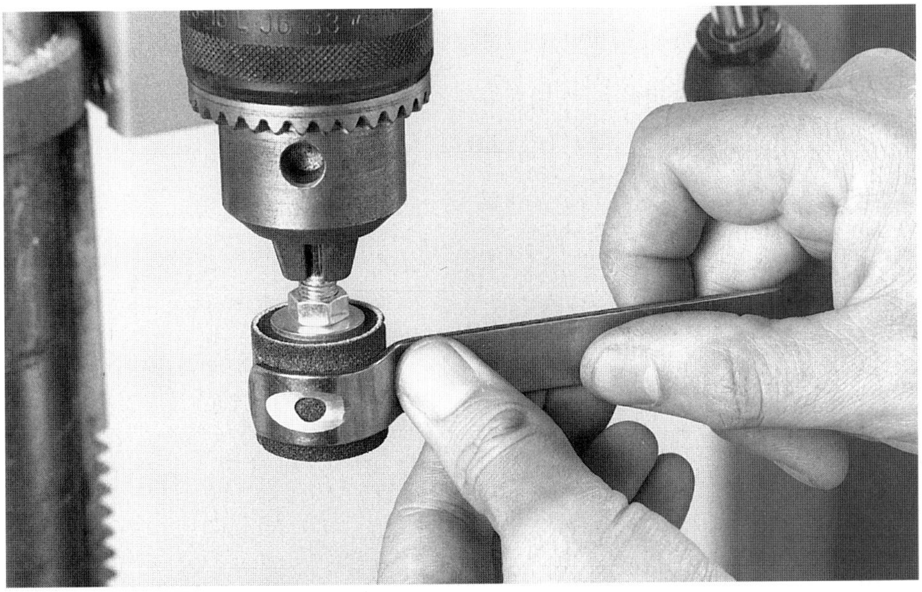

Sharpen a cornering tool by pressing the inside curve against a rotating 1-in. sanding drum. (Photo by Susan Kahn)

AFTERWORD

There is no question that I have failed to cover some tools in this book. As I was reading the final draft, I realized that I had missed nicker spurs, those miserable little cloverleaves screwed to the sides of combination planes. I could launch into an explanation of sharpening a nicker spur, but, after 227 pages, I would hope that you could gaily seize the wretched thing, deftly shape the bevel, lap the face and be plowing a clean groove seconds later.

All this should be possible because you should now know that sharpening is mostly common sense augmented by a few basic principles, some standard abrasives and a few cunning jigs. Be assured that your sharpening skill will increase with confidence. Also be assured that once you have used really sharp tools, you will be happy with nothing less; both your tools and your craftsmanship will benefit from your new knowledge and confidence. And remember, even if you apply your new knowledge only to kitchen knives, you can still be a neighborhood hero.

APPENDIX 1
CHIP CLASSIFICATION

Dr. Norman C. Franz, now retired and living in Vancouver, was a Professor in the Dept. of Wood Technology at the University of Michigan for many years. Although he contributed a great deal to the literature of wood machining over the years, his 1956 doctoral thesis is of particular significance to tool users since it established a framework for chip (or shaving) classification that made it possible to understand many aspects of wood cutting and wood-cutting tools that had been poorly explained in the literature until then.

It was never Dr. Franz's intent to light the way for hand-tool users. He was trying to analyze what happened during rotary power cutting but found the complications of setting up adequate test equipment so great that he chose to use orthogonal cutting (cutting in a straight line) instead to develop his analysis. If you have a rotary cutting device of infinite diameter, you have straight-line cutting anyway. Dr. Franz used rake angles, relief angles, and so on, that are common primarily to power tools not to hand tools, but the results he obtained are still applicable to hand tools in many ways. It is unfortunate that his work was not given greater publicity before now, because it so clearly explains many of the effects we see when using tools like bench planes and chisels.

It is not possible to do justice to a 150-page thesis in these few pages, but, with Dr. Franz's assistance, I have extracted those parts that would be of greatest interest to non-industrial tool users.

Dr. Franz used this modified milling machine for most of his test cuts. It allowed him to control depth of cut at the same time as he measured forces and photographed the action with the movie camera mounted opposite the cutter. All of the photographs that show chip formation on the following pages were taken on this equipment.

CHIP FORMATION

Throughout this analysis, wherever you read the word "chip" you can substitute "shaving," if that makes you feel more comfortable. For definitional reasons, Franz used "chip" to describe removed wood whether or not it was in the continuous form of a shaving or in smaller particles that laymen might call chips. He classified chips in three basic types.

TYPE I

This is the type of chip that is formed when the wood splits ahead of the cutting edge, then rides up along the front of the cutting tool until the bending force breaks the chip. It is the type of chip that is typical of bench planes with bed angles of 50° or 55°. Such a chip gives a very smooth surface when cutting with the grain (or exactly parallel to the grain, as shown in the top photo at right), but it gives a very rough surface when cutting against the grain (as shown in the middle photo), because the chip repeatedly breaks below the intended cutline.

Top: A Type I chip produces a very smooth surface when cutting parallel to the grain.

Middle: When cutting against the grain, the same chip produces a very rough surface.

Bottom: The rough surface produced by Type I chips when cutting against the grain.

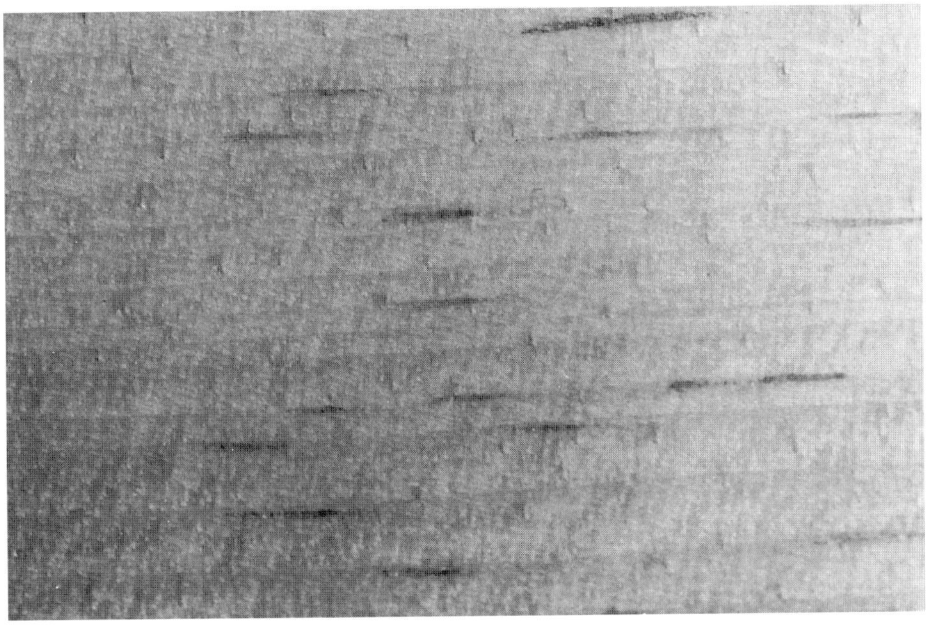

TYPE II

With this type of chip, the wood fails in a plane (extending from the cutting edge to the work surface) that roughly bisects the angle between the rake face and the direction of travel. This is the type of chip that you could expect from a scraping plane or other tools with a low rake angle (see the top photo at left).

At times, Type I and Type II chips occur in combination with each other, as shown in the middle photo. When cutting with the grain or parallel to it, the resulting finish is excellent, as shown in the bottom photo.

However, when both chip types occur cutting against the grain, the resulting surface would be more similar to that shown in the bottom photo on the facing page.

Top: A Type II chip.

Middle: Type I and Type II chips occurring in combination in parallel-grain cutting.

Bottom: The smooth surface produced by Type I and Type II chips occurring in combination when cutting parallel to the grain.

TYPE III

This type of chip occurs when conditions produce compression and shearing failures in the wood ahead of the cutting tool. As with the Type I chip, this is a cyclical, not a continuous, process. The Type III chip is associated with very small or negative rake angles where the ruptured wood does not freely escape up the front of the advancing tool (see the top photo at right).

In some instances, a built-up edge of compacted material develops at the edge, creating a false edge with a positive rake angle that momentarily produces a Type I chip before the process begins again (see the middle photo). Because the surface generated with the Type III chip is determined by wood failures ahead of the tool, these failures can extend below the intended cutting line and the damage remains prominent in the finished work, producing what is commonly described as fuzzy grain (see the bottom photo). The false edge that develops with a Type III chip is encouraged by negative rake angles, a high coefficient of friction between the chip and the tool face, and tool dullness; the rounded edge of a dulled tool has the effect of creating a greater negative rake angle because of the rounding.

Top: A Type III chip showing a built-up edge.

Middle: A built-up edge that exhibits a large positive rake angle about to create a Type I chip.

Bottom: Fuzzy grain resulting from Type III chips.

THE WORK OF DR. WILLIAM MCKENZIE

Because Dr. Franz's intent was to analyze rotary cutting, none of his experiments used very high rake angles (low cutting angles), thin shavings or the very sharp edges that we associate with low-angle hand planes or paring tools that most woodworkers look to for a very fine finish. In fact, this shortcoming was brought home to him by an Australian, Dr. William McKenzie, who pointed out that there was actually a Type 0 chip that could be created by a very sharp blade with a very low cutting angle cutting with (or exactly parallel to) the grain. The chip created was a continuous shaving of the type we associate with low-angle planes.

Dr. McKenzie had been schooled well. He studied with Dr. Franz at the University of Michigan from 1958 to 1960, when he presented his own doctoral thesis on a subject that directly paralleled Dr. Franz's and had in fact been inspired by Franz's earlier work. Using much the same equipment that Franz had used, McKenzie analyzed the factors at play when cutting end grain.

In classifying the types of chips created when cutting end grain, McKenzie found two basic types, each with a variant. Because McKenzie, like Franz, was attempting to simulate machining conditions (in this case, sawing), he used relatively high cutting angles (low rake angles) and work-sharp edges. So, once again, the effect of very low cutting angles that one might find when using a low-angle block plane or a paring chisel with a keen edge was not encompassed by the study. Rather than dealing with chip type, McKenzie dealt with the nature of the failure of the wood, so it is the failures that are classified by type rather than the chips.

TYPE I FAILURE

McKenzie found that the distinguishing feature of a Type I failure is that splits occur parallel to the grain below the cutting plane. In Type I(a) failures, as shown in the top photo at left, such splits are short and regular, leaving comparatively high surface quality. In Type I(b) failures (bottom photo), several short splits occur between fairly regularly spaced longer splits that leave a substantially poorer quality of surface.

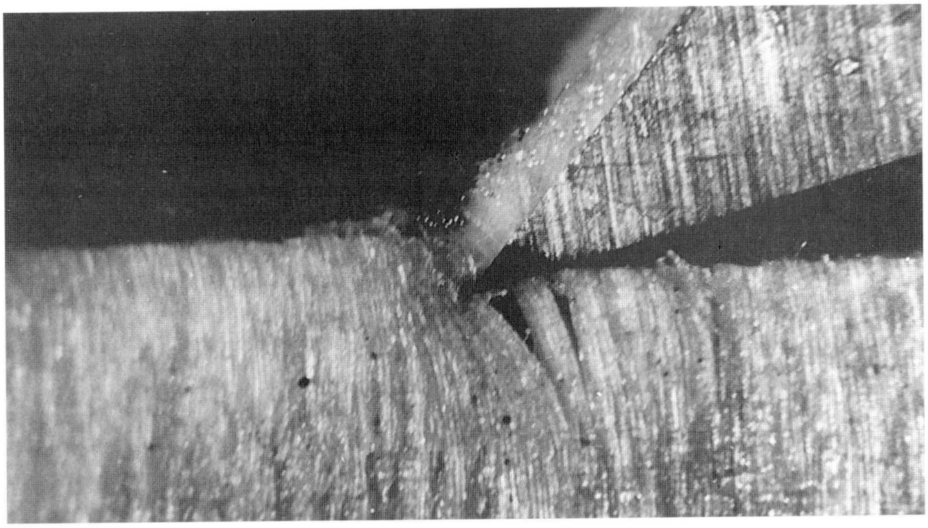

Top: Type I(a) failure in saturated eastern white pine; 40° rake angle; 0.010 in. chip thickness; 30x magnification.

Bottom: Type I(b) failure in eastern white pine at 5% moisture content; 30° rake angle; 0.030 in. chip thickness; 30x magnification.

TYPE II FAILURE

The distinguishing feature of a Type II failure is that the wood fails at some distance below the cutting plane but parallel to it. In a Type II(a) failure (top photo at right), the failure is intermittent, but in a Type II(b) failure (middle photo), it is continuous.

In this testing, McKenzie found that moisture content had a great effect. The bottom photo shows the quite different effect of the cutting action on end-grain maple at 5% moisture content and 14% moisture content.

In all of the above material, careful note should be taken of the rake angles of the cutting tools and the fact that the cutting edges were not as sharp as those that would normally be used on hand tools today. They are probably still reflective of the general keenness of power tools. In spite of such differences, there is a wealth of information to be drawn from this research that could inform further research.

Top: Type II(a) failure in yellow poplar at 5% moisture content; 40° rake angle; 0.030 in. chip thickness; 10x magnification.

Middle: Type II(b) failure in common persimmon at 5% moisture content; 40° rake angle; 0.030 in. chip thickness; 10x magnification.

Bottom: The effect of moisture content on the rupture pattern in cutting sugar maple: back sample, 5% moisture content; front sample, 14% moisture content.

APPENDIX 2

INTERNATIONAL GRIT STANDARDS

Of the various grit-grading systems in use today, three dominate. The most familiar to North Americans is the U.S. standard used for grading loose grit, sandpaper and stones. The P-grade (or FEPA) system used in much of Europe is very close to the U.S. standard in grits below 240x but varies widely above that. The same is true of the Japanese standard (JIS-grade).

The Japanese standard above 1000x has become dominant worldwide in bench stones, because the Japanese are virtually the only manufacturers of fine-grit stones.

Eventually, measurement of grit size in microns will likely dominate, because it is the only system that is both rational and readily understandable by anyone, anywhere.

WHAT IS A MICRON?

A micron is one millionth of a meter. There are 25 of them in one thousandth of an inch. In more practical terms, a human hair is between 20 and 40 microns thick, and this page is about 100 microns thick.

ABRASIVE-GRADE COMPARISON

Size in Microns	U.S. Industrial Mesh	European P-Grade	Japanese JIS-Grade	Emery
100	#150	-	-	-
80	180	-	-	-
60	220	P240	#240	-
50	240	-	280	-
40	280	-	320	-
-	320	P360	360	-
-	360	P500	400	1/0
30	400	-	500	2/0
20	500	P1000	600	3/0
15	600	-	1000	-
-	800	P1200	1200	-
12	-	-	1500	-
9	-	-	2000	4/0
5	-	-	2500	-
4	-	-	3000	-
3	-	-	4000	-
2	-	-	6000	-
1	-	-	8000	-
0.3	-	-	10000	-

GLOSSARY

ABRASIVE A substance used for wearing away a surface.

ARRIS A sharp edge created by the junction of two surfaces in different planes. In short, a corner.

ATTACK ANGLE *See* Cutting angle.

BACK BEVEL A bevel ground on the clearance face of a cutting tool.

BED ANGLE The angle between the bed of a plane and its sole.

BEVEL A sloping surface. With edge tools, it is the primary part of the tool tip that is abraded to create a sharp cutting edge.

BEVEL ANGLE The angle between the face of a tool and the bevel.

BOB A small, shaped buffing head.

BOND The material holding abrasive particles together. Could be rubber, resin, fused clay (vitrified), etc.

BORT Diamonds (or diamond fragments) not of gem quality used as abrasives.

BREASTED Shaped like a breast, proud in the center. Used to describe handsaws where the line of teeth is convex.

BRUZZ Another name for a corner chisel.

BUFFING One method of polishing using cloth or felt wheels charged with compounds.

BURNISH To form or refine a surface or edge by pressure rather than abrasion.

BURR The ridge or flap of metal created at an edge during an abrading process.

CAMBER The condition of being slightly convex.

CANNEL A flute or gutter. Gouges are said to be in-cannel if the bevel is inside the flute and out-cannel if the bevel is on the outside.

CAP IRON A strip of metal reinforcing a plane blade to reduce vibration in use. Usually it is tightly fitted to the plane blade and shaped so that it causes shavings to bend sharply as they are formed. It can then also be called a chip breaker.

CHATTER The porpoising of an edge creating an uneven surface.

CHIP BREAKER *See* Cap iron.

CLEARANCE ANGLE The angle between the relief face of a cutter and the generated surface that is necessary to accommodate fiber springback. Also called the relief angle.

CROWN The amount of central projection of an edge.

CUTTING ANGLE The angle between the generated surface and the rake face of the tool. Also called the attack angle. It is always the complement of the rake angle.

DAMP To reduce the amplitude of motion.

DIG A term used in turning to describe a rapid, unplanned penetration of the tool into the work.

DOCK To shorten.

DRAW-FILE To use a file at 90° to its usual path of travel.

DRESS To restore a grinding wheel to its desired condition by selectively wearing away part of the wheel.

DUB To increase the included angle of a cutting edge beyond its effective limit. Usually done by accident.

FLEAM A beveled tooth on a saw is "fleam cut." Named after a surgeon's lancet (or fleam) for blood letting.

FLUTE A channel resembling half of a musical flute split lengthwise.

FLUTTER The degree to which a grinding wheel does not rotate in a plane at 90° to its axis.

GENERATED SURFACE The work surface created by the action of a cutting tool.

GLAZE The loading of a bench stone or wheel with metal and/or crushed abrasive.

GRAIN The direction of orientation of transportation cells in wood.

GRIND To give an edge a basic shape by rapid abrasion.

GRIT Particles of abrasive.

GULLET The hollow behind a saw tooth that provides space for chip accumulation.

GUM To deepen and enlarge the spaces (or gullets) between the teeth of a saw.

HOLLOW GRIND To grind a concave face or bevel on a tool.

HONE To refine an edge that has already been given a basic shape.

HOOK The wave-crest edge created by burnishing a tool.

HOP Lack of concentricity of a grinding wheel about its axis.

INCLUDED ANGLE The angle formed by the rake face and the clearance face of a cutter tip.

JOINT To render true by flattening or straightening.

LAND The portion of a chisel side that is vertical to the face, the unbeveled portion.

LAP A bed of material (cast iron, copper, plastic, etc.) used to hold abrasive particles to refine the surface of a tool. Also the act of using a lap.

LINISHING Freehand abrasion of tools on a belt sander to dimension the surface and/or give it a consistent surface.

MICRO-BEVEL Any small secondary (or tertiary) bevel, usually to strengthen an edge or facilitate honing.

MICRO-GRAIN Small grains. Vaguely used to describe grains of which some are one micron or less in diameter.

MICRON One millionth part of a meter.

PARING CUT Any light cut, but typically of the nature of using a kitchen paring knife.

PERIPHERAL MILLING Any milling using the periphery of a wheel or cylinder for cutting.

PITCH The angle of the leading face of a saw tooth in relation to the axis of the saw.

PLATEN The flat backing plate on a belt sander.

POLISH To refine a surface by reduction of the depth of scratches in it.

PRIMARY BEVEL *See* Bevel.

QUARTERING STROKE A honing motion where the path of travel is at 45° to the line of the edge. Most commonly used with a curved edge (like a scimitar) where a stroke at 90° to the line of the edge would create a localized flat.

QUENCH To cool by immersing in water or other liquid.

RAKE ANGLE The angle between a line drawn normal to the cut surface and the steepest part of the rake face of the cutter.

RAKER A tooth whose primary function is to remove fibers severed by another tooth.

RELIEF ANGLE *See* Clearance angle.

ROCKWELL HARDNESS Symbolized HRc or Rc. A standard measure of tool hardness on the Rockwell C scale. Other scales (A, B, etc.) are used for other materials.

ROLL CUT The rotation of a gouge around its longitudinal axis as it is being forced through wood.

SAFE-EDGE Said of files when an edge is uncut.

SECONDARY BEVEL A second bevel ground on the primary bevel of a tool. Normally done to strengthen the tool tip or to change the cutting action.

SET The deflection of metal (or other material) to another shape. Used to describe the amount of deflection of saw teeth from the plane of the blade.

SHEARING CUT The same as a skew cut.

SKATING The erratic movement of a bit tip as it moves away from the intended point of penetration.

SKEW BLADE A blade ground at an angle other than 90° to the intended path of travel.

SKEW CUT Any cut where the cutting edge is at an angle other than 90° to the path of travel.

SLICING CUT Any cut where the cutting edge is not pressed into the work at an angle 90° to the line of the edge.

SLICK Any large, long-handled chisel used to make paring cuts with body pressure only.

SPUR Usually a tooth that scores the edge of a cut on a bit or combination plane. A spur section is an outside blade of a dado set.

STROP To refine an edge with a trailing stroke.

SWAGE To spread, mold or bend with force. Also, the tool used to do it, and sometimes the item acted on.

SWARF The bits of metal and fractured abrasive created in the sharpening process.

SWEEP A measure of curvature of a gouge flute. The most gradual sweep is #1 and the tightest is #11.

TEAROUT Fibers torn from below the cutting line.

TEMPER To bring steel to a suitable degree of hardness by heating it to the required temperature and then cooling it in a controlled manner, usually by immersing (quenching) it in a liquid.

TRAILING STROKE A honing motion where the edge is trailing, not leading.

WIRE EDGE The narrow edge section that bends back rather than submit to being abraded. So called because it looks like a fine wire when removed.

WREST To twist or bend. A saw wrest is used to put set in teeth.

INDEX

C

EDITOR PETER CHAPMAN

DESIGNER/LAYOUT ARTIST HENRY ROTH

ILLUSTRATOR LEE HOV

ART ASSISTANT SUZANNA YANNES

PHOTOGRAPHY LEE VALLEY TOOLS (EXCEPT WHERE NOTED)

TYPEFACE GARAMOND

PAPER WARREN PATINA MATTE, 70 LB., NEUTRAL pH

PRINTER QUEBECOR PRINTING/KINGSPORT, KINGSPORT, TENNESSEE

Features

July/August 2005 — Volume 29, Number 4

Page 32

Page 42

Page 56

Woodworker's Journal

Departments

July/August 2005 Volume 29, Number 4

Page 18

Page 19

Page 28

Page 68

Woodworkers

Techniques

Tools

Page 22

What's the Secret to Flawless Glue Line Rips?

NEW Anti-Vibration Glue Line Rip Blades by Freud

1 Rip

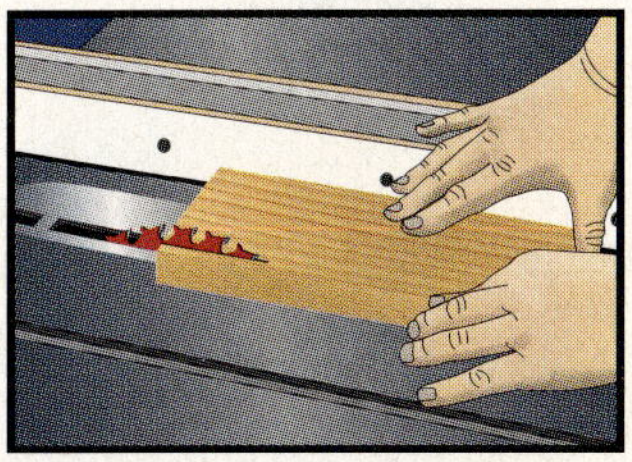

2 Glue

3 Clamp

Put your jointer away when you use these Freud Blades

In the past, producing flawless glue joints required jointing or sanding.

Not any more!

Freud's new Anti-Vibration Glue Line Rip Blades are designed to improve workmanship as well as eliminate unnecessary rework.

Standard saw blades that vibrate cause swirls that lead to poor joints. Freud's unique Laser-Cut Anti-Vibration Slots virtually eliminate vibration and sideways movement of the cutting edge against the material. Now, you can rip, glue and clamp your project eliminating the need for sanding or jointing.

The triple chip teeth feature special micrograin carbide manufactured and designed by Freud to withstand the impact encountered when ripping hard and softwoods. These blades are ideal for ripping 1/8" to 1" Maple, Oak, Pine and even exotic hard and softwoods and are available either with Perma-SHIELD® coating (non stick coating that prevents heat and pitch build up increasing the cutting life of a saw blade) or polished finish.

Whether you're a production shop or a custom woodworker, Freud makes it easy for you to create strong, flawless glue joints.

Rip Cut with Freud Blade

Rip Cut with Other Blade

freud®
The Psychology of Woodworking

ISO 9001
VISION 2000

FOR MORE INFORMATION CALL 1-800-472-7307
IN CANADA CALL 1-800-263-7016
www.FreudTools.com

Red saw blades are a registered trademark of Freud America, Inc.

(Circle No. 28 on PRODUCT INFORMATION form)

Workshop Wonder Tool

Watching a new woodworker use a hand plane with ease and comfort is a thing of beauty for this grizzled ol' woodworking editor. Twenty-something LiLi Jackson handles her #4 Stanley in much the same way that her grandfather, Norton Rockler, might have 60 years ago. It's a curious thing. My generation (50-something) has always been enamored with power. If you could put a motor on it ... plug it in ... add a battery ... well, that just had to be a good thing, right?

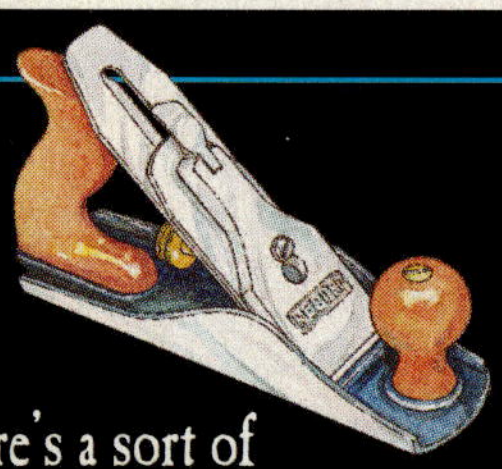

"There's a sort of immeasurable satisfaction that comes when you glide a finely made and tuned hand plane across a board and nearly effortlessly a thin shaving curls up in the throat of the tool." — *Bruce Kieffer*

Not so for LiLi. As she notes in her article about building a Pencil Post Bed *(see page 42)*, she enjoys power and hand tools equally, each at its own time and for its own purpose. Woodworking, she has discovered, is a process ... and there is pleasure in that process.

The other day, I was talking with Bruce Kieffer on this very topic. *(Bruce built the stunning Arts & Crafts Hutch featured on page 32.)* He's of my generation and, until recently, eschewed hand planes. Now, he's downright poetic about them. "There's a sort of immeasurable satisfaction that comes when you glide a finely made and tuned hand plane across a board and nearly effortlessly a thin shaving curls up in the throat of the tool," he told me. Whoa! Is this the same Bruce who said (not too long ago) that he is one of those die-hard woodworkers who shuns hand planes. "They are," he explained back then, "too slow compared to 'plugged-in' tools." Today he owns a half dozen hand planes and, he notes, "It seems that I use at least one of them on every project I build." Ian Kirby said it best *(in Techniques, see page 28)* when he observed: "If you had just invented a bench plane, it would be heralded as the wonder tool of the workshop."

# # #

Elsewhere in this issue, I take great pleasure in introducing Betty Scarpino, woodturner extraordinaire. She'll be writing our turning column *(see page 22)*, and we couldn't be more delighted to have signed up such fine talent. You've got to love her point of view *("Create with intent ... but don't forget to have some fun!")*. She's going to fit in just fine around here.

JULY/AUGUST 2005
Volume 29, Number 4

LARRY N. STOIAKEN *Editor in Chief*
JOHN KELLIHER *Art Director*
ROB JOHNSTONE *Editor*
JEFF JACOBSON *Associate Art Director*
JOANNA WERCH TAKES *Associate Editor*
LINDA HAUS *Techniques Editor*
SIMON WATTS *West Coast Editor*
STEVE HINDERAKER *Photographer*

ANN ROCKLER JACKSON *Publisher*
CHARLA SCOFIELD *Circulation Director*
KELLY ROSAAEN *Circulation Coordinator*
SARAH M. GREER *Advertising & Production Director*
ALYSSA TAUER *Advertising Assistant*

Editorial Advisors
NORTON ROCKLER STEVE KROHMER

Contributing Editors
MICHAEL DRESDNER RICK WHITE
CHRIS MARSHALL MIKE McGLYNN

ADVERTISING SALES
J.F. Van Gilder Company
P.O. BOX 802405, Dallas Texas 75380
DAVID BECKLER *david@jvgco.com*
TERRI MATHIS *terri@jvgco.com*
JIM VAN GILDER *jim@jvgco.com*
Phone: (972) 392-1892
Fax: (972) 392-1893

Audit Bureau of Circulations Member

SUBSCRIPTION INQUIRIES
(800) 765-4119 or *www.woodworkersjournal.com*.
Write *Woodworker's Journal*, P.O. Box 56583, Boulder, CO 80322-6583. E-mail: *woodworkersjournal@neodata.com*. Include mailing label for renewals and address changes. For gift subscriptions, include your name and address and your gift recipient's.

BACK ISSUES & REPRINTS
Woodworker's Journal or Today's Woodworker
Call: (800) 610-0883
www.woodworkersjournal.com

Woodworker's Journal (ISSN: 0199-1892), is published in February, April, June, August, October and December by Rockler Press Inc., 4365 Willow Dr., Medina, MN 55340. Periodical postage paid at Medina, Minnesota and additional mailing offices. Postmaster: Send all address changes to Woodworker's Journal, P.O. Box 56583, Boulder, CO 80322-6583. Subscription Rates: One-year, $19.95 (U.S.); $25.95 U.S. funds (Canada and other countries). Single copy price, $5.99 (U.S.); $7.99 (Canada/other countries). Reproduction without permission prohibited. Publications Mail Agreement Number 0861065. Canadian Publication Agreement #40009401. Printed in the USA.

WEB SITE: www.woodworkersjournal.com

Consider it an investment in your free time.
How you spend your personal time is the truest reflection of your values. You can waste it. Or make the most of it. But if you'd like to have something to show for it consider picking up a Dremel 400 Series XPR. The XPR Multi-Saw attachment enables you to bring your visions to life in exacting detail. Saw intricate patterns and create original designs. You can also use the XPR to sand, carve and perfect projects. Which ensures your time is always well rewarded. Should questions arise call 1-800-4DREMEL or visit dremel.com.
DREMEL 400 XPR

Enjoying the Woodworking Journey

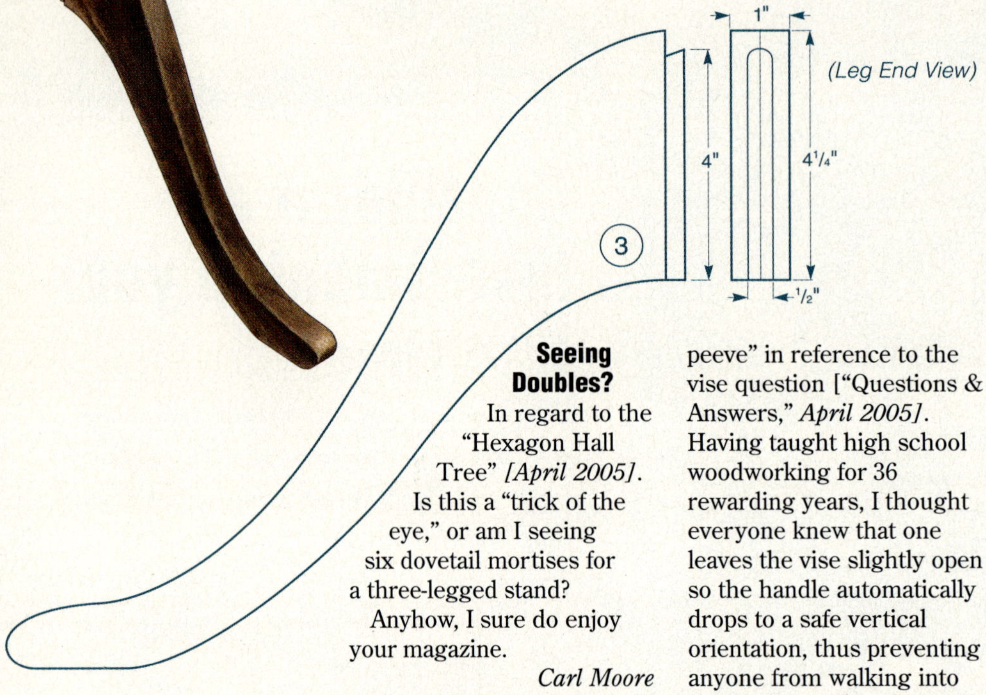

Seeing Doubles?

In regard to the "Hexagon Hall Tree" *[April 2005]*. Is this a "trick of the eye," or am I seeing six dovetail mortises for a three-legged stand?

Anyhow, I sure do enjoy your magazine.

Carl Moore
Rochester, Illinois

WJ Responds:

Our illustrator apparently enjoys drawing dovetail mortises so much that he put one on every facet of the hall tree instead of on every other facet. The correct number of mortises is three.

No Scraps in Her Stove

I just read your article in the Q&A section in the *April 2005* issue on saving scraps. I almost cried when I heard that woodworkers are burning their scraps! What is waste to one woodworker is gold to another. When a woodworker who builds large projects gets the scrap bin full, he/she should make a friend of an intarsian and recycle that wood into intarsia projects.

Barbara Rhoades
O'Fallon, Missouri

Proper Vise Etiquette

I must respond to Mr. Ian Kirby's snide remark about "the daily dose of some thoughtless woodshop teacher's pet peeve" in reference to the vise question ["Questions & Answers," *April 2005]*. Having taught high school woodworking for 36 rewarding years, I thought everyone knew that one leaves the vise slightly open so the handle automatically drops to a safe vertical orientation, thus preventing anyone from walking into the handle were it locked in a horizontal position.

Jim Vasi
Williamsville, New York

Dare I say I'm sure you've given some bad ad"vise" before?

Steve Jennings
Holmen, Wisconsin

… walk into an open vise or the handle sticking out from the edge of the bench parallel to the benchtop, just once, and you may forever be changed. Safety ... it's always about safety.

David Mathias
Brookfield, Illinois

One woodworker's stove fuel is another's beautiful intarsia raw material....

Appreciating the Journey

Ian Kirby's article "Harvesting the Parts" from the *April 2005* issue was fantastic! This article has shown me how to look at and select wood from a whole new perspective. For more than 30 years, I've been conscious of a wood's color and grain, but I never really looked at wood the way he has shown us. I guess that's why he's a master!

I, for one, look forward to Ian's articles every issue. He makes me think more about "why" I'm building and getting it completed. He has helped me more appreciate the "journey" of building something instead of just getting to the end.

John E. Brady
East Berlin, Pennsylvania

RIDGID Takes the Full Dado

I have a comment regarding the RIDGID® table saw in your *[April 2005]* comparison ("Today's Shop"). I work part-time for Home Depot™, and I often tell customers about the RIDGID saw's many qualities, one of which is its ability to accept a full 13/16" dado blade. This saw has the same arbor as the larger RIDGID contractor saw, and I've used a full

Mail Call! Contact us by writing to "Letters," Woodworker's Journal, 4365 Willow Drive, Medina, Minnesota 55340, by fax at (763) 478-8396 or by e-mail: letters@woodworkersjournal.com We ask that all letters, including e-mails, include a mailing address and phone number. We reserve the right to edit for length and clarity.

dado many times with no problem. I went on to read the owner's manual for the model tested and, in fact, a full dado can be used and only the nut is required to secure the blade — not the washer as used with a regular saw blade.

Pete Araujo
Fort Montgomery, New York

WJ Responds:
Oops! Good catch, Pete. I missed the full width dado function on the RIDGID saw. It's one more good feature on a very nice benchtop table saw.

Rob Johnstone
Editor

Easy Access; More Storage
I enjoy your magazine very much and was inspired by the "Easy-access Storage Bins" project *[February 2005]*. I made a couple of changes: I used 1/2" plywood, and my back was 24" x 24", which gave me an extra row of bins. Thanks, and keep up with the great projects.

Rudy Bartol
Dinwiddie County, Virginia

"You say Lectern, I Say Podium, Let's Call the ..."
In your *February 2005* issue, you have plans for a podium. A podium is a small, usually square, raised platform for a band director to stand on to direct a band or orchestra. *Pod* = Latin for foot.

A lectern is a stand with a usually slanted top to hold the speaker's notes. *Lect* = Latin for speak.

Your plan = Lectern.

Colonel John Polesky
Sagamore, Pennsylvania

Joanna (Dictionary Girl) **Werch Takes Responds:**
From the *American Heritage® Dictionary of the English Language*, Fourth Edition, 2000: "Podium: 1. An elevated platform, as for an orchestra conductor or public speaker. 2. A stand for holding the notes of a public speaker; a lectern." (From the same source):" Etymology [of "lectern"]: from Latin *lectus*, past participle of *legere*, to read."

Safety First: Learning how to operate power and hand tools is essential for developing safe woodworking practices. For purposes of clarity, necessary guards have been removed from equipment shown in our magazine. We in no way recommend using this equipment without safety guards and urge readers to strictly follow manufacturers' instructions and safety precautions.

Glue: Why More Isn't Better

There's a reason waterbased white and yellow glues don't work when flooded on a joint.

THIS ISSUE'S EXPERTS

Dale Zimmerman *is a technical specialist at Franklin International, the manufacturers of Titebond® glue.*

Chris Marshall *is a contributing editor to* Woodworker's Journal.

Rob Johnstone *is the editor of* Woodworker's Journal.

Q Why does a glue-up with Titebond® type yellow glue lose considerable strength if the parts are not in intimate contact and the glue layer is increased in thickness even a few thousandths of an inch? (For example, a loose fitting mortise and tenon joint is not as strong as a snug joint.)

Dick Faunce
East Palatka, Florida

A White and yellow glues are waterbased, and that water makes up slightly more than half the volume of glue applied. These glues gradually become less fluid, and develop strength, as the moisture in the glue is drawn into the surrounding wood. If the glue dries without clamp pressure, voids or holes left by the departing water make up about half of the resulting layer of glue. Less voids obviously mean more strength.

The second issue is the thickness of the layer of glue. The voids that exist in every bondline take away from its potential strength, and create some "give," or potential for lateral movement, in the joint. Given this fact, a thicker layer of glue, with collectively more holes or voids, is also weaker because the increased number of holes or voids progressively increases that potential for lateral movement.

— Dale Zimmerman

Q If batteries of various voltages all fit my cordless drill, can I use any voltage I want?

Rod Wolfington
Arlington, Washington

A I've wondered the same thing. To get to the bottom of the issue, I asked Jeff Wilkinson, cordless product marketing director at Bosch Power Tools. He says that it's never a good idea to match a larger voltage battery with a smaller voltage tool or vice versa.

Calibrations within the motor combined with specific battery voltage expectations allow cordless power tools to perform at optimum levels. Mixing tools and batteries can damage both the tool and the battery.

Motors can overload and battery cells can be damaged from excessive power drains. So, stick with the specific batteries that come with your cordless tools for optimum performance and long tool life.

— Chris Marshall

continues on page 14 ...

Oops: While our Jan/Feb 05 issue pictured a 14.4-volt battery on a 12-volt tool (middle), such mix-ups can damage both the tool and the battery.

Contact us by writing to "Q&A", Woodworker's Journal, 4365 Willow Drive, Medina, MN 55340, by faxing us at (763) 478-8396 or by e-mailing us at: QandA@woodworkersjournal.com Please include your home address, phone number and e-mail address (if you have one) with your question.

Use the right clamps, and you'll never find gunky black stuff on your wood again.

Q Yuck! Recently, when I laminated several good size pieces of red oak into a big panel, I got a bunch of black marks where the glue and the clamps touched the wood. How come? (I am guessing it has something to do with my rusty old pipe clamps.)

Felicity Huffman,
Oxnard, California

A You are right about the glue-clamp-oak connection. Moisture (glue), black iron pipes and tannin-rich wood (red oak) will combine to create those black marks, and they are a real pain. (They go right into the wood fibers rather than just sitting on the surface.) You can avoid the problem by applying less glue and keeping the pipes clear of the surface of the wood. Or, you could move to the newer type of pipe clamp with a zinc-coated pipe. (Rockler's Sure-Foot™ is an example.) K-body clamps or aluminum bar clamps will also avoid that nasty problem.

— Rob Johnstone

WINNER! *For simply sending in his question on glue strength, Dick Faunce of East Palatka, Florida wins a* **Hitachi 2¼ HP Fixed/Plunge Base Router Kit.** *Each issue we toss new questions into a hat and draw a winner.*

Getting a Grip in the Shop

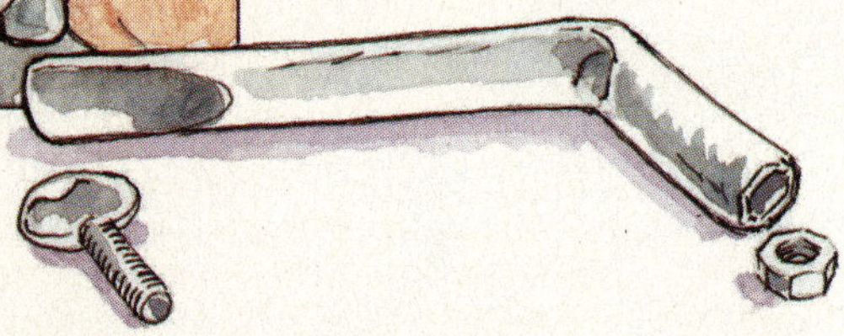

Taming the Thumbscrew

The guide blocks on my 14" JET band saw have thumbscrews (wing nuts) that can be hard to get at — especially the lower ones. My solution is to cut an 8" section of 1/2" electrical conduit, then flatten one end in a vise so it fits neatly over a thumbscrew. Next, I put the hex head of the band saw's table pin in the other end of the conduit and shape it with a hammer until it forms a wrench. Finally, I bend the conduit to about a 70° angle as shown. Adjusting the saw is much easier with this little shop-made tool.

Jim Doering
Pekin, Illinois

Ultimate Sanding Block

How can anything as basic as a sanding block be improved? Easily: saw a 3/8" slot in one face, about 3/4" from the side. Insert one edge of the sandpaper into the slot and wrap it around the block. Just your grip on the block will now keep the paper secure. I keep several sanding blocks on hand, some with square edges, others rounded to different radii. I also like to have blocks of hardwood, such as maple, and softer ones made of pine or poplar.

Mike Michael
Lexington, Virginia

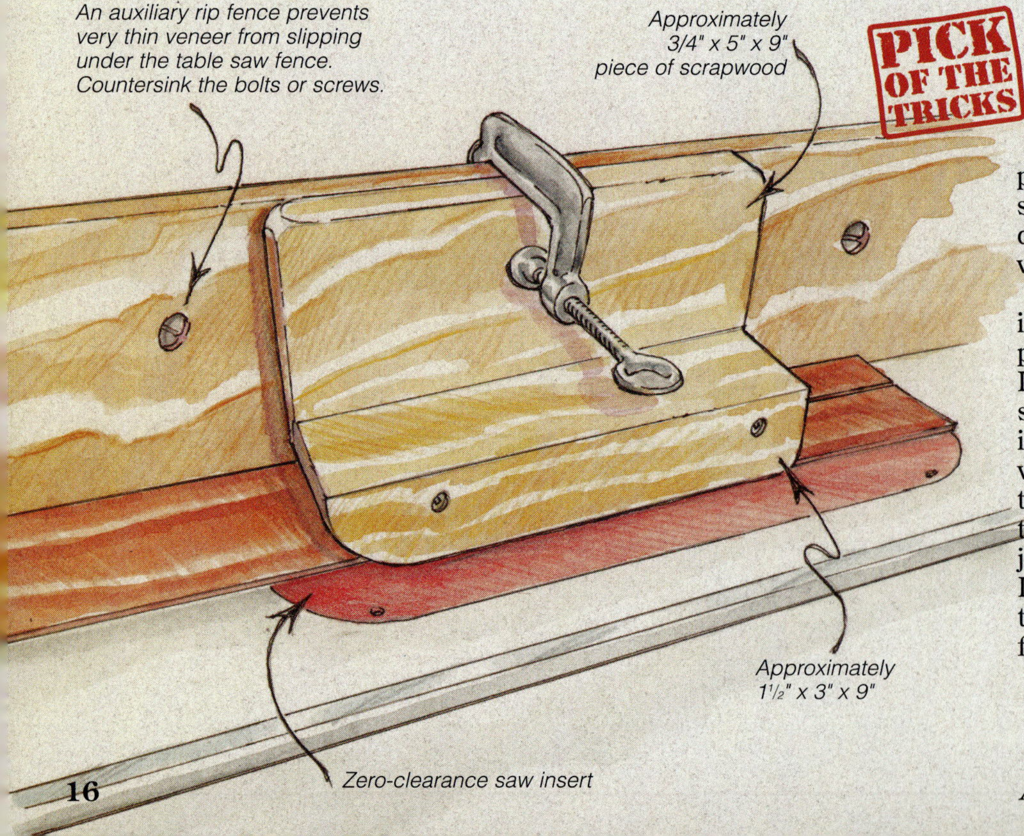

PICK OF THE TRICKS

Cutting Thin Wood on the Table Saw

I make Shaker oval boxes using thin bands of wood. Cutting these pieces on the table saw without some type of hold-down is dangerous so I came up with this version of my own.

First I lower the saw blade and install a zero-clearance insert. Next, position a piece of veneer, put the L-shaped hold-down on top of the stock and clamp it in place, as shown in the sketch. Then I remove the veneer, turn on the saw and raise the blade until I hear it just touch the hold-down. I back off the blade just a bit and start cutting veneer. If the veneer tends to slip under the regular fence, clamp a wooden fence to it as shown.

Larry Underrinwer
Westminster, Maryland

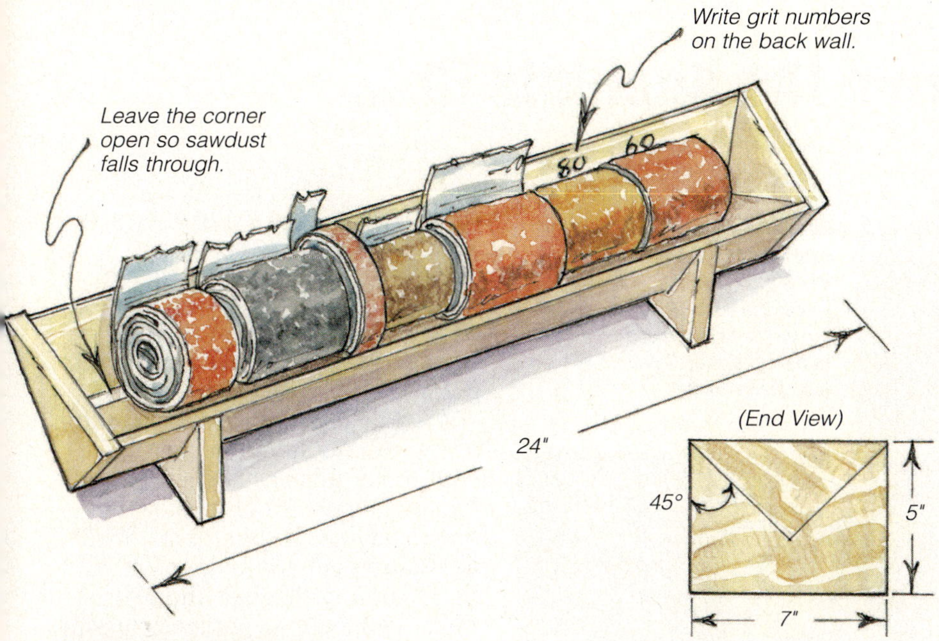

Sandpaper Roll Storage

I often buy end-rolls of sandpaper, either locally or from a catalog supplier. Such rolls vary in width and diameter, and storing them so they are easily accessible is a challenge. My solution is to make a simple cradle, or trough, as shown above. I used 1/2" scrap plywood and left a gap in the bottom to prevent wood dust from accumulating. For convenience, I write the numbers of the grits on the far side of the cradle.

David Carlson
Cary, North Carolina

More On Magnets

Automobile speakers have strong magnets and can usually be picked up at wrecking yards for little or nothing. I use them around the shop for holding chuck keys, small tools, drill bits, etc. If they have protruding rivets, simply grind them flush.

Paul McKibben
Norcross, Georgia

Table Saw Hold-down

I like to use a table saw sled when my work requires an accurate, 90° cut. I devised the hold-down shown in the sketch below to keep my fingers well away from the blade and also prevent the work from "creeping" as it is being cut.

Joseph Raber
Louisville, Ohio

WINNER! *In addition to our standard payment (below) Larry Underrinwer of Westminster, Maryland, will also receive* **a Drill Docter DD400PK** *for being selected as the "Pick of the Tricks" winner. We pay from $100 to $200 for all tricks used. To join in the fun, send us your original, unpublished trick. Please include a photo or drawing if necessary. Submit your Tricks of the Trade to Woodworker's Journal, Dept. T/T, P.O. Box 261, Medina, MN 55340. Or e-mail:* **tricks@woodworkersjournal.com.**

Wood from the Ancients On ...

Bob Teisberg, left, is bringing to the U.S. the world's oldest wood: the kauri preserved underground in New Zealand swamps (see photo below).

Buried Treasure:

World's Oldest Wood

Bob Teisberg lives on an island in Lake Superior, where underwater logs are regularly recovered. He always thought the 10,000-year-old lake was "the age of the ages," but then he visited New Zealand.

It was a "quantum leap" for his mind to encompass the 40,000-plus years of the ancient kauri wood he found in gift shops and museums, Bob said. That special wood came to mind a few months later when his cabinetmaking business got a special commission. Since then, he and a partner in Seattle, Washington, have formed Ancientwood, Ltd. to bring the world's oldest wood to the U.S.

Ironically, Bob said, his Asian associates don't have a lot of respect for the old stuff. "Swamp kauri," it's called in New Zealand, where modern growth of the Pacific Rim tree provides "beautiful, crystal-clear" wood. In that case, Bob summarized, "Why bother pulling it out of the ground?"

For himself, though, the age and the "intensity" of the wood do have a special quality. Technically, the wood works easily and is as forgiving as cherry or teak, "but it just demands a lot more attention."

Part of it is the age. New Zealand scientists at the Kauri Museum in Matahoke *(www.kauri-museum.com)* have attributed prehistoric dates, and the Beta Analytic Lab in Florida carbon dated one sample to greater than 43,000 years; the other, greater than 47,000. "This is wood that has been underground since before Lake Superior existed," Bob said.

Bob's own "unscientific" theory, for how the kauri survived in such good condition — developed with some help from the New Zealand associates he mentioned earlier — is that "it was in the perfect chemical slurry of swamps." The kauri tree, as it grows, continually sheds its bark. Bob says it's likely that, ages upon ages ago, a grove of kauri trees grew near a river that somehow became blocked. As the ground softened, the trees on the edge fell over, while those still standing continued to shed their bark. Over the next, say, 500 years, as the pond lost its water, the trees and shredded bark eventually became buried, but the water table stayed close to the surface. "The bark that was preserving the tree as it grew was the same in the water: the right chemical soup," Bob speculated.

While the kauri tree grows in several countries along the Pacific Rim, New Zealand is the only spot where the right phenomenon occurred to preserve the ancient swamp kauri. And, "we don't know how long our business will last," because "nobody knows how much there is," Bob said.

What he does know is that some of the wood has "an amazing iridescent quality," Bob said. "About 80 percent of it, once the finish goes on, it shimmers." While this quality is hard to describe, he said, sanding through the grits, then finishing it — particularly with varnish — sets it off.

As the kauri wood gives off this shimmering characteristic, Bob said, "you go past it and you do a double-take, and then you find out it's the world's oldest wood — it's 'oh-my-God!'"

For more info, call 888-201-7544 or visit *www.ancientwood.com.*

— Joanna Werch Takes

Bob's first project with ancient kauri wood was this cabinet commissioned to hold a Ming vase.

d Duane Gemelke used
ve weeks in the classroom.
too, is interested in
rking education,
arly in Minneapolis, where
up and started his
y, Rockler Woodworking
rdware, 51 years ago.
contemporary 9- and 10-
d fourth and fifth graders
l about safety, then made
projects: an ice cream scoop,
ning top and a pen.

Alan found it a rewarding experience. The kids turned on a dead cup center in head stock instead of tail stock, allowing the instructors to control the drive of the lathe "like drag on a fishing reel," he said, "The kids weren't intimidated by the machine. I had them doing some cuts that adults I've taught couldn't learn in weeks."

— Joanna Werch Takes

continues on page 20 ...

Pull Up A Chair:

Design on the HOTSEAT

With its first HOTSEAT design competition, Indiana furniture company OFS reached out to up and coming designers for what "we think will be an ongoing conversation," said marketing director Chris Rogers. The competition also drew attention from woodworking teachers, who had their students view and critique designs as they were posted on the web site. The education component pleased OFS, Chris said, and judging criteria of aesthetics, sustainability, accessibility and use of wood included issues that are discussed "on a constant basis."

OFS will manufacture the winning entry. For more info and pictures, visit *www.ofsthehotseat.com.*

Cory Grosser's HOTSEAT chair design submission "Outside In" (right and above) has a CNC-routed nature pattern on the bent plywood back to remind us of the source of wood products.

Various veneer colors were among the design possibilities for the Doberman chair entry in the HOTSEAT competition.

Finalist Ralph Bremenkamp said the inspiration for the design of his contemporary plywood chair came from the butterfly stool.

Timothy Murphy of Saugatuck, Michigan's KLM Beam Seating — a formed plywood seat with an ebony stained veneer finish — won the contest.

Anatomy of a Bowl

By Betty Scarpino

The *Journal's* new woodturning expert, Betty Scarpino, takes us through the basics of designing and turning a bowl.

No doubt you have seen hundreds of bowls in your lifetime, but have you really considered what elements make up a bowl? Before you try to turn one, you should. At breakfast, take a look at your cereal bowl. Then line up all the bowls in your home, ceramic, glass, wood, metal, and figure out which ones you like; then ask yourself why you like them.

A bowl has three basic elements: a rim, a body and a base. Once you begin to critically consider the elements of bowls, you'll find that you have more control over your own creations, and I dare say have more fun making them! When designing a bowl, I find it helpful to draw or sketch different forms. Determine the size of the wood you will be using, then consider each of the three elements — rim, body and base — in terms of how they fit together in concert with the size and shape of your bowl blank. In many ways, this process is a bit like putting together a puzzle, but it's a puzzle of your own design.

Considering the Rim

When designing a bowl, the rim is very often overlooked by woodturners, yet it is a critical segment. A rim can be thin or thick, narrow or wide, natural-edged or finished. It can also be curved or flat, concave or convex, and can flow toward the inside of the bowl or slope outward. An inward flowing rim invites the eye into the bowl, an outward sloping rim leads the eye out and away.

Wide rims are great for adding decoration such as carving or texturing. If you have selected wood that does not have a stunning grain pattern, consider making a bowl with a wide rim, then adding some texturing and/or coloring. If painting wood does not suit your fancy, perhaps bleaching a section to lighten an area is more your style. One advantage to bleaching is that it simply removes color, so the grain pattern remains visible.

On the other hand, if you have a large piece of two-inch thick curly oak and you want to show off the grain, consider a bowl with

Three basic elements make up a bowl.

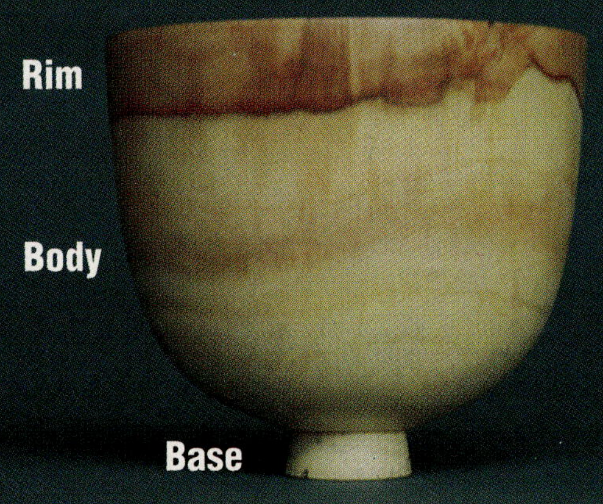

a wide, curved rim and a small body. The rim will certainly be noticed, and you'll have made the best of nature's bounty.

When selecting a rim for your bowl, considering function will help narow your choices. A natural-edge bowl with the bark left on does not function well for eating popcorn. It does, however, look lovely as a decorative item on a shelf.

Body Building

The body of a bowl is the prime focus of our turning efforts , where the majority of the wood will be removed to create the cavity of the bowl. The scope and variety of possible forms and shapes for this section are vast, with some shapes more personally pleasing than others. The size of the bowl blank often limits your options for the body of a bowl. I prefer curved, round bodies for bowls. Curves in wood often show off grain patterns better than flat surfaces and are organic and sensual. Flat, straight sections are seen as formal.

Once again, it's important to consider the purpose or function of your bowl. If it is to contain fruit or popcorn, a curved body is more compatible. If your bowl is purely decorative, anything will work. Curves can be slight or exaggerated; one- or multidimensional such as an 'S' curve. As before, the size of your blank will constrain your options.

For flat or straight bowl sides, consider the look of an outward sloping side versus an inward sloping side. One is inviting, while the other gives the feeling of protection and secrecy. Often, a beginning turner will attack a bowl blank and cut straight in … leaving no option but to have a flat-bottomed bowl. While this design isn't bad,

Wide, Short, Tall or Round

A wide bowl with a narrow rim invites the eye into the bowl and the contents within. This stained ash example is a very practical shape.

This 8" wide bowl is taller than the example above with a more defined base. It is bleached maple ... a light-colored wood made even lighter.

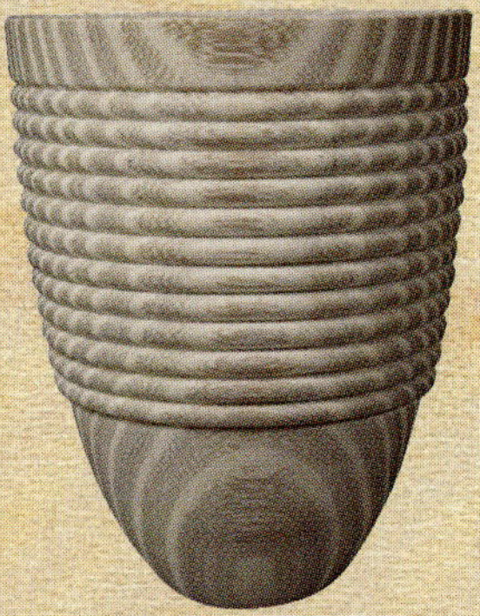

Tall, narrow and inscrutable, this osage orange bowl features concentric rings or beads to break up its long body. Its base is very mimimal.

A shape that is somewhat between the bleached maple bowl above and the osage orange bowl. Notice how the symmetrical groove details stop, bringing focus to the rim of the vessel.

many beginners who end up with straight-sided bowls did not really want a flat bottom. A great way to overcome this tendency is to shape the outside profile of your bowl first, then remove the wood on the inside of the bowl. You will not be breaking any secret turning laws.

The Lowly Base

Here's an important tip … don't overlook the importance of the base of your bowl! Even though the bowl may not be picked up and closely examined, its base determines how the bowl will be presented to the viewer. A fun exercise to try is experimenting with different bases quickly made from leftover pieces of wood. Pair them up with those not-quite-good-enough bowls you'll likely have littering your shop. (You'll find them in my shop!) Start with a tall, thin base and then a very tall, thin base. What would it look like with a tall, thick base instead? Consider a wide, thin base. (I'm sure you can see where this is leading.) As with a bowl's rim and body, bases can slope inward or outward, be straight or curved, convex or concave. You can model some of these shapes by cutting profiles out of 1" lumber using your band saw. These three-dimensional visual aids will give you a fair idea if the shape works well with your design.

But, after saying all that, your bowl could actually look quite elegant with the body serving as the base of the bowl … sort of a bowl-with-no-base. This type of treatment is particularly useful when your bowl blank is not very thick, and it is easy to achieve with just a bit of sanding (off the lathe) or by reverse turning. I find this type of base very functional in large offerings like a popcorn bowl. It sits in your lap comfortably, as well as on a table, and it feels welcoming in your hands.

Actually putting a knife to wood is the second or third step in creating a bowl. After going through the design steps related above, the author shapes a bowl from a cherry blank.

Designing and Turning with Intent

Here's an example of how I'd approach making a salad bowl: My client likes color and carving on kitchenware, so I will make a medium-thickness rim. It functions well, and it also leaves room for a small amount of decoration. I can either paint the rim and/or carve it. I will make this salad bowl slightly larger than I think will be needed: tossing a salad, especially for messy folks, requires plenty of contained space. (I know that the recipient of this bowl tends to be a bit wild when tossing a salad.) So, I will make a bowl body that is round and slightly curved inward to help contain the greens, peppers, mushrooms, onions and olives as they are enthusiastically prepared. It's only after this thought process that I select the wood, sketch a simple form and proceed to the lathe.

A quick aside about wall thickness: By now the turning community is fairly well in agreement that thin-walled vessels and bowls are not necessarily a measure of perfection. I prefer to think in terms of intent. If your intention is to make a thin-walled, even-thickness bowl, then strive for that … but if you like thick walls, make them that way. I think the goal is to "make it look like you meant to do what you just did"! To do that, you need to carefully consider your options and create with intent. But while you are doing that, don't forget to have some fun!

Betty Scarpino is our new woodturning columnist. She has been turning wood for almost 30 years.

A Barrel of Fun

What's This?

George Resing of Novato, California found these pieces of a tool in his granddad's shop. Know what it is — or how it goes together? Send in your answer for a chance to win a prize!

If you have your own woodworking mystery tool (or the answer to this issue's entry), send it to Stumpers, *c/o Woodworker's Journal, P.O. Box 261, Medina, Minnesota 55340. Or send us an e-mail:* jtakes@woodworkersjournal.com

Of a Certain Vintage ...

The tool in the *April* issue *Stumpers* is called a "scorp." My father used one in the 40s and 50s to refurbish the insides of barrel staves in summer just before he began the family winemaking in September. The scorp and an old, curved wooden plane were all he needed. He secured the wooden stave in a vise, gripped the scorp in his right hand, pressed down on it with his left and pulled!

Tony Lazzaretti
Andover, Massachusetts

What a scorp isn't used for (see the suggestions in the story) is more interesting than its intended purpose.

Scraping the Barrel

Yup, **Cliff Thomas** of Austin, Texas's tool is a scorp (also called an inshave plane — **Bill Vernier** of Leonard, Michigan, or a cooper's one-handed adze — **Curtis Brainard** of Glendora, California). Coopers used it to shave curved surface like barrels — or buckets, added **A.G. Delgado** of Walnut Creek, California.

Also, said **Gary J. Leon** of Covington, Georgia, chairmakers used it "to begin carving out the contour in wooden seats to fit a person's bottom." It could also "scoop out dough bowls," said **Carl Heimiller** of Buffalo, New York.

Besides such standard uses, the mail from WJ readers introduced us to a few, umm, exotic, options. **Margaret R. Maddox** of Dallas, Texas, guessed it was for "scraping out the belly of a canoe." That's possible: **Donald Murphy** from Dansville, New York said his grandfather used it to make wooden gutters.

Bill Sorrell of Corona, California, tried to convince us it was "for separating and carrying stacked sheets of plywood." Maybe that idea isn't so far-fetched, since **Jack S. Pooley** of Tampa, Florida reminisced about his job at a hardware store 30 years ago, where, "We had several of these 'nail rakes,' used to scoop [loose nails] into the scale bin before weighing them."

Jack did admit that he "[didn't] know if this was the intended use." **Dr. Tom Del Pico** of Smithville, Missouri, had no such compunction when stating, "This tool has to be one of a variety of 'hoof knives' used by farriers and veterinarians" to gouge soles on horses and mules.

Both **Cheryl Ali** of Long Beach, California, and **Larry McDaniel** of West Carrollton, Ohio guessed it was an Asian gardening implement. With a different region in mind, **Peter Kongevold** of Huntington Station, New York, said it was "used to hollow out the heel in wooden clogs."

Several answers followed **Rick Tjoekler** of Everson, Washington's theme that the tool "is commonly referred to as a fleshing tool." To elaborate, **William A. Watson** of Pineville, Oregon, said, "The tool has two uses: 1. to remove the hair from a scaled hog during butchering. 2. to remove unwanted tissue from a hide that is to be dried and tanned."

While we always appreciate woodworkers' ingenuity, we hope those of you who use your scorp for this purpose have **not** also been employing it for its intended one, which **Frank Tyler** of Jacksonville, Florida describes thusly: "rounding the inside of staves to ensure a good, **clean** product for the distiller or vintner who ultimately would use the barrel." (Emphasis added.)

— Joanna Werch Takes

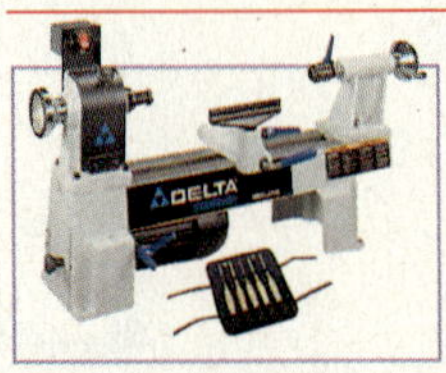

WINNER! *Peter Kongevold of Huntington Station, New York wins* ***a Delta ShopMaster Model LA200K MIDI LATHE® and Turning Tools.*** *We toss all the Stumpers letters into a hat to select a winner.*

Introducing the
K3 Kreg Jig®
NEW AVAILABLE SOON!
Packed with Innovative NEW Features...
The Fastest way to Join Wood!
Quickly switch Drill Guide Block between Portable and Benchtop bases!
2 TOOLS in 1
INTERCHANGEABLE DRILL GUIDE DESIGN
PATENT PENDING
Material Support Stop
Material support stop allows you to quickly repeat pocket hole locations and swings out of the way when drilling panels.
Unlimited Material Thickness
Sliding upright design is extremely fast to adjust with the ability to center a screw in ½" up to 1-1/2" thick material in 1/8" increments.
Dust Collection
Dust collection shroud attaches to any standard 1-1/4" hose for a "chip-free" work area.
Front Side Clamping
Front side clamping puts the clamp handle on the same side as your drill. No more reaching around panels to clamp the workpiece!
The Kreg Jig® Master System is the ultimate package for Pocket Hole Joinery!
Includes Benchtop base, Portable base, (1) Interchangeable Drill Guide Block, Dust Collection Shroud, Drill Bit, Material Support Stop, Premium Face Clamp, Driver bits, and Self-tapping screws.
Kreg Jig® Master System
ITEM# K3MS
US Suggested Retail
$149.99
Kreg™
800-447-8638
www.kregtool.com
The Blue Mark of Quality.
(Circle No. 43 on PRODUCT INFORMATION form)

In Praise of Bench Planes

By Ian Kirby

If you had just invented a bench plane, it would be heralded as the wonder tool of the workshop.

A modest but powerful tool kit. Same-width blades are interchangeable, so buying several would guarantee a sharp backup ready for either plane.

Set coarsely, it will hog off shavings that are 1/8" thick from the edge or face of a sawn board. Set fine, it will remove a shaving that is just one to two thousandths of an inch thick, leaving a cut surface that is smooth enough for the most discriminating touch. With the aid of a straightedge, winding sticks, and a try square, you can hand plane parts to deliver total dimensional and geometric accuracy.

In short, a plane has a greater range of capabilities than any other single hand or machine tool. It's worth every bit of time and energy it takes to develop the skills that allow you to take advantage of all it can do.

Bench planes come in different sizes and different widths, indicated by a number. Although you can make a case for owning half a dozen or more of these sizes, practically all flat furniture parts can be accomplished using only two, an 07 and an 04½ (shown above).

The 07 is 22" long and the 04½ is 10" long. They are both 2⅜" wide, which provides the advantage of interchangeable blades.

Preparing The Plane

To successfully use a plane, you must first have two things right:

- the blade must be sharp
- the set must be correct

Sharpening and setting, while beyond the scope of this article, are thoroughly covered in a handbook I wrote some time ago, *Sharpening with Waterstones*, published by Linden Press.

A bench stop controls the workpiece and provides instant feedback if you are planing incorrectly.

Using The Plane

There are three aspects to skillful plane use:

- grip — how you hold the plane in your hands
- stance — how and where you stand
- movement — what you do with your body to press and push the plane to make a controlled cut.

The tool is used to plane wood in a variety of ways and situations: each requiring a slight variation of grip, stance, and movement.

The face of a workpiece is planed flat on the bench; long edges and ends are planed held in a vise. Short edges — say, 24" long and less, 3/4" thick and more, and up to 3" wide — are also planed on the bench. You need a flat bench and a bench stop. The bench stop is the most fundamental of holding devices. It's about 1½" x 3" in section and usually 4" - 5" from the end of the bench. It can be raised and lowered from zero to 5". Not only does the bench stop control the workpiece, it advises you how well you are planing with instant feedback. If you skew the plane when planing a face, the workpiece will abruptly rotate from its anchored position against the bench stop, at worst landing on the floor! If you apply uneven side to side pressure when planing an edge, the workpiece will tip over. Another advantage of benchtop planing is that you can immediately lift the workpiece to inspect by eye and touch and to check with a straightedge and try square.

A common alternative is to trap the workpiece between bench dogs. This is a bad idea because it removes your instant feedback from incorrect planing. Also, over-tightening may distort the workpiece, which, when planed "flat," becomes "unflat" once it's released.

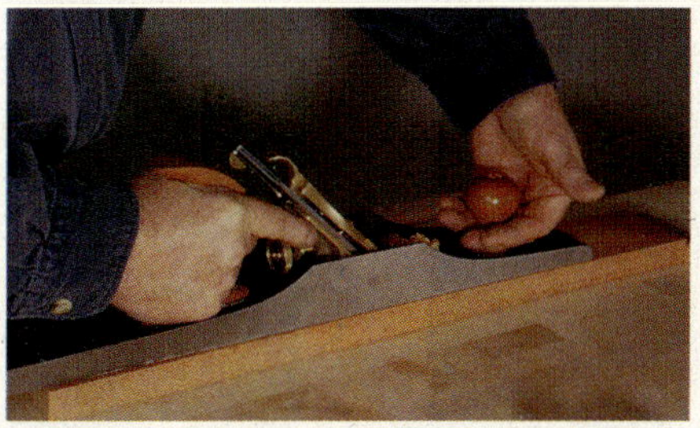

Grip

Grip the handle with the right hand. Press the index finger against the cast frog under the blade. When you grip tightly, there is diagonal tension between your index finger and your little finger, which is bearing on the other side of the handle at the bottom. This grip provides maximum control of the plane. To remove a wide shaving from the face of the workpiece, apply firm left-hand pressure on the toe of the plane at the beginning of the stroke. Grasp the tote between your second and third finger and press down with the heel of your hand. By mid-stroke, apply pressure with both hands. Apply right-hand pressure at the end of the stroke.

Stance and Movement

The photo sequence shows that four feet is about the maximum length you can plane without taking steps.

Stance and movement go together. The most common mistake is to exaggerate arm movement. In the early stages of the stroke, only lower body and leg movement propel the plane forward.

In the beginning stance, the feet are about 18" apart and the back foot more at right angles than a walking step to enable a strong push off.

To plane an edge, grip the sole between thumb and fingers; the thumb presses firmly down.

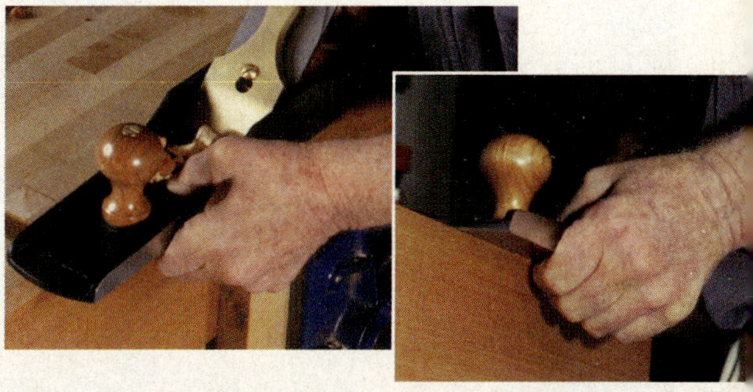

Body mechanics are essential to success ...

Stand almost at the end of the board, left arm as far back as it will bend. Press down with both hands and arms and start the cut by pushing with the legs — no arm movement.

You will move halfway along the stroke by transferring weight to the front foot, with the back foot pushing forward, turning and lifting onto the toes.

The stroke is finished almost entirely by extending the arms. Downward pressure on the plane has shifted entirely to the right hand.

Lamello Top 20S Biscuit Joiner

CHARLES KURALT

ARTS & CRAFTS HUTCH

By Bruce Kieffer

Building an exquisite piece like this is a labor of love. It's not a reproduction, but a totally new design incorporating many elements found on traditional Mission era furniture.

I have been building furniture for over 25 years, and I always feel lucky when I get a commission of this caliber. At first glance it may look fairly simple to build, but don't be fooled: it's a complex piece. If you decide to build one for yourself, be prepared to devote about 200 hours to complete the job. During the construction there's a lot to consider and ponder. I found myself scratching my head often, even though I designed the piece! If you take it slow, things will work out fine.

This piece belongs to a very nice couple who live in downtown St. Paul, Minnesota. They are redecorating their home with newly manufactured Mission pieces. They were looking for a "top-notch" small hutch to be the centerpiece of their remodel, but they couldn't find one they liked. That's when they called me. We spent a lot of time designing this piece. All of us think it turned out great.

Design Details

The hutch consists of a bookcase attached to a cabinet. They're built as two separate pieces which are joined during the final assembly of the hutch. This makes it easier to move around and work on the smaller sections.

The sides and doors of the cabinet are frame-and-panel construction. The panels are veneered with book-matched "tiger ray" white oak with the rays oriented about 45° to the grain. The results are stunning panels with chevron patterned grain. I bought my veneer from the site *wood-veneers.com*. They e-mailed me pictures of the sheets so I could see them before I bought them. It worked out great.

These pulls are handcrafted by Gerry Rucks. *(www.arts-n-craftshardware.com)* The style we chose is called "Square Cutouts." You'll need to ask for them by name. The hinges are ball-tipped, loose pin and solid brass, darkened with "Super Blue" Liquid Gun Blue *(www.birchwoodcasey.com)*.

This hutch is made mostly from solid quartersawn white oak lumber. The interior panels of the cabinet are riftsawn white oak plywood edged with solid white oak. The cabinet back and drawer bottoms are also riftsawn plywood. Many of the parts are attached with hidden screws so the pieces can "float" when the wood changes size from seasonal relative humidity changes. The bookcase upper rail is attached with screws and desktop fasteners, but no glue. This allows that rail to expand and contract without exposing any gaps or unfinished areas or, worse yet, causing a crack in the piece.

The bookcase back is 15 pieces of tongue and groove, straight-grained riftsawn white oak lumber. I enhanced the vertical lines by creating faux "V"-grooves by chamfering the edges of the tongue and groove joints. Five different widths are used to make the back pieces, but they look equally sized when installed. The drawer sides and backs are solid riftsawn white oak, too.

The doors and drawers are set back 1/8" into the cabinet to create shadow lines. To make the doors look and operate properly, the cabinet hinges need to be mounted on 1/4" strips of oak, where they can be mortised just like flush-mounted

Veneering "Sandwich" Exploded View

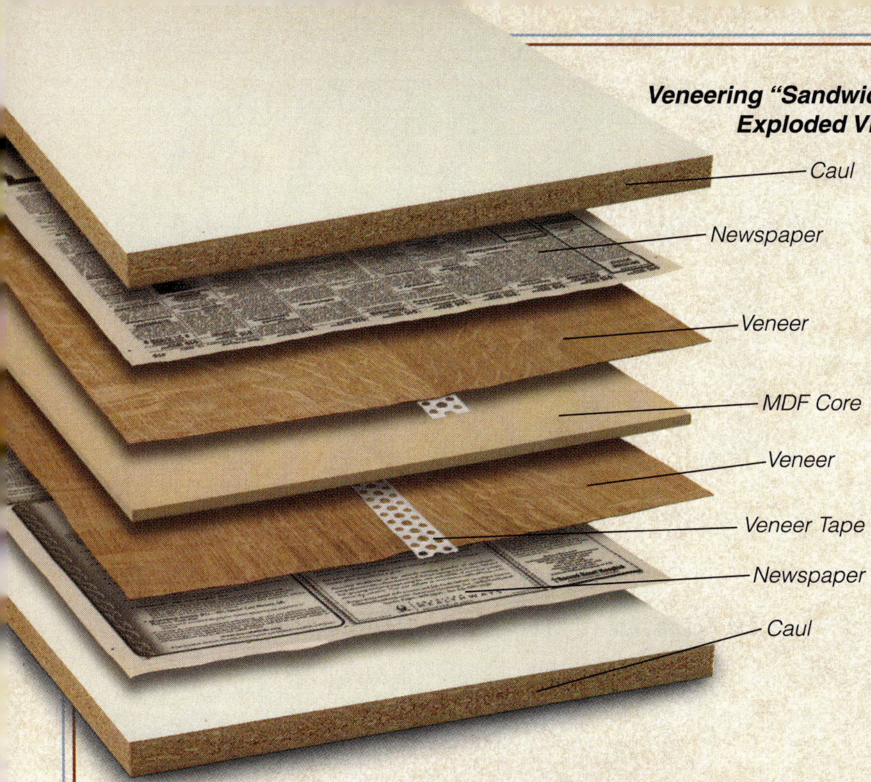

SEVEN STEPS TO VENEERING SUCCESS

Making your own veneered panels adds another dimension to your woodworking arsenal, and it's fun to do. The woodworking techniques used for veneering are similar to those used with solid wood. Saw, joint, glue, clamp, trim and sand are all familiar woodworking tasks. In this case, narrow sheets of veneer are edge joined to make wider sheets that are then applied to a substrate (the core the veneer is glued to). I prefer MDF for my substrates since it's smooth, flat, and very stable. I find it easiest to use wood glue, cauls (flat panels that spread the clamp pressure) and clamps. For small veneered panels like these I use slow-setting yellow glue. Getting the glue on fast enough is always a problem, so glue up one panel at a time, and get some help if you can.

You must make "balanced" panels (a core with veneer on both faces in this case), and you need to put both pieces of veneer on the core at the same time. Oversize the veneer pieces so you can cut them to their finished sizes after the veneers are glued to the substrates.

STEP 2: I use my jointer and a jig to joint the edges of the veneer sheets.

STEP 1: Use a veneer saw and straightedge to cut the lengths and the widths slightly oversize (cut the substrates oversize, too). Cut to their finished sizes after the veneers are glued to their substrates.

STEP 3: Lay the veneer sheets face up, pull the book-matched edges together, and temporarily join the sheets with masking tape.

STEP 4: Flip the joined sheets over and apply a piece of gummed backed veneer tape down the joint. Lay a scrap flat panel over the taped sheet so it dries flat. Remove the masking tape.

STEP 5: Lay the sheet with the tape side down over the edge of your table. Open and glue the joint. Lay the sheet flat again to close the joint and place sticks aside the joint to hold it flat.

STEP 6: Assemble the glue-up "sandwich" as shown in the exploded photo (above left). Using a narrow paint roller, apply a moderate coat of slow-setting glue to both sides of the core and to each veneer.

STEP 7: The glue-up requires a few deep reach clamps. They are very important because the clamping pressure needs to be applied to the center first so no excess glue gets trapped there. Let the glue cure 24 hours before removing the clamps and trimming the panels to their finished sizes.

doors. It's more work, but much more forgiving if a mistake is made.

The drawers are guided by under-drawer, center-mounted tracks and guides. The tracks are complex fabrications that are assembled loose in the web frames. The guides are just strips of wood glued to the drawer bottoms. The tracks are not "locked" in place until the drawers are finished. It's easier to align them that way. Also, the drawers are stopped using small flipper style drawer stops recessed into the underside of the upper web frame.

There are edging pieces attached to the fronts of the under-drawer web frames 1/16" below the level of those frames. This prevents the wear areas that most inset wood-on-wood tracked drawers exhibit when the bottoms of the drawer sides rub on the wood piece below the drawer. By moving the edging down, I create a 1/16" reveal under the drawer, eliminating the rub areas and, as a bonus, creating a lip to align the door latch blocks to later.

Construction Notes

Careful wood selection has a huge effect on the final results. I picked my best pieces for the wide front rails and the drawer faces. I selected stock to insure that the ray pattern was balanced with the flakes displaying equally in both directions. I also carefully picked the wood for the corbels so their rays were at 45° pointing down and out, to match the door panels. It also made them mirrored images of each other. I started by resawing some 8/4 boards to try and get a book-match look for the corbels, but I found that unpredictable. So instead I searched through all of my 4/4 stock until I found the right

A Freud® Adjustable Tongue and Groove Router Bit Set was used to cut the cabinet frame and panel joints, and the bookcase back slat joints.

pieces. It helped to have my corbel template made with lines drawn on each side indicating the pattern I wanted.

I made sure that the show edges of the edging pieces used on the cabinet bottom, uprights and web frames were plainsawn to match the edges of the quartersawn legs and top.

All of the casework joinery is done with 1/4" deep blind dadoes. I used a shop-made template and a guide bushing to rout the dadoes. All the dadoes are stopped 1/2" back from the front edges except the dadoes for the web frames under the drawers. Those are stopped 1 7/16" from the front edges of the cabinet sides and uprights. The web frame edging pieces are fit and attached after the cabinet is assembled.

Rout the blind dadoes using a 1/2" straight bit, a guide bushing and shop-made templates. One template is used to fit the solid wood parts, and another for the plywood parts.

Assembling this bookcase and cabinet can be a nightmare if you don't anticipate the effects of cumulative error and deal with 3/4" thick plywood that's really closer to 11/16" thick (one of my pet peeves). Oversizing the interior pieces slightly and fitting them during the assembly is my solution. When dry fitting the parts, you'll have to hold the panels back from the front edges a bit since the "blind" notches aren't cut yet. I always use a joint cutting and dry fitting sequence of: inside to outside, and then top to bottom. Once

The author uses a band saw to cut the notches at the fronts of the shelf and web frame pieces that fit in the dadoes.

everything fits right, then the notches are cut on the front edges to complete the blind dadoes.

The cabinet's lower curved front and rear curved rails are glued to the bottom and screwed to the sides. I used my mortise machine to chop square holes in the sides so I could cover the assembly screws with square end grain plugs. This worked great until I applied the stain and the plugs essentially disappeared! Even so, the only way to make them show up better under the dark stain would be to use a darker species of wood, and I would never do that. So it is what it is.

I made sure to elongate any screw holes where I knew there could be movement of the joined parts. For the bookcase and cabinet tops, I held them tight at their front edges and let their back edges expand and contract. For the bookcase's upper rail and the cabinet's lower curved rails, I secured them at their top edges, letting the bottoms float.

This hutch is stained with an Onondaga Mission Brown colored NRG (non-grain raising) dye stain which I purchased from the web site *www.woodfinishingsupplies.com*. I had this color custom mixed for this hutch, but they have the same color available on the web site now. It's a very rich and dark hue. I applied three coats of Danish oil for the top coats of this hutch.

Building the Cabinet

Make the veneered panels for the sides and doors, then make the sides of the cabinet. I used a Freud® Adjustable Tongue and Groove (T&G) Router Bit Set to rout the joints (*photo* page 35). It worked great, but what's unusual about it is that it cuts 7/16" deep. The *Material List* dimensions for the tenoned rails and the bookcase back slats all include the 7/16" dimension. If you use another method to cut the tongue and groove joints,

Upper Web Frame Assembly
(Bottom View)

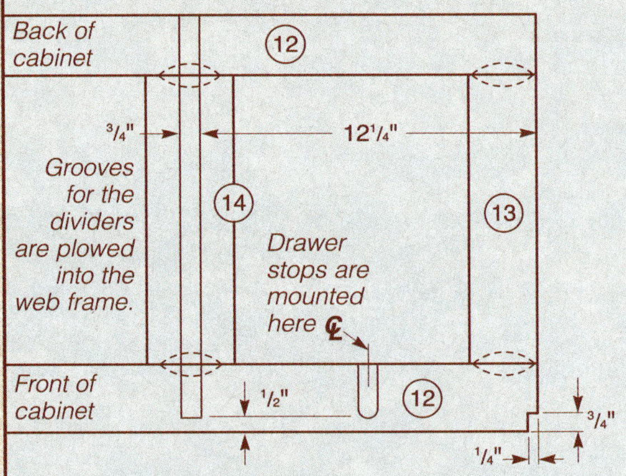

Leg Dado and Back Rabbet
(Top View)

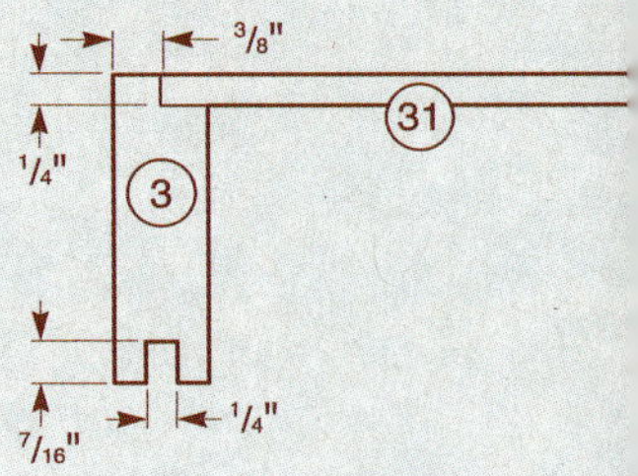

Side Panel Assembly
(Inside View)

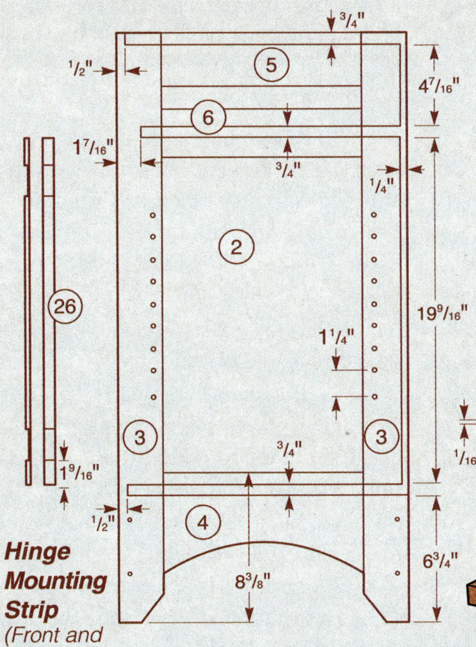

Hinge Mounting Strip
(Front and Side Views)

Leg and Side Lower Rail
(Front View)

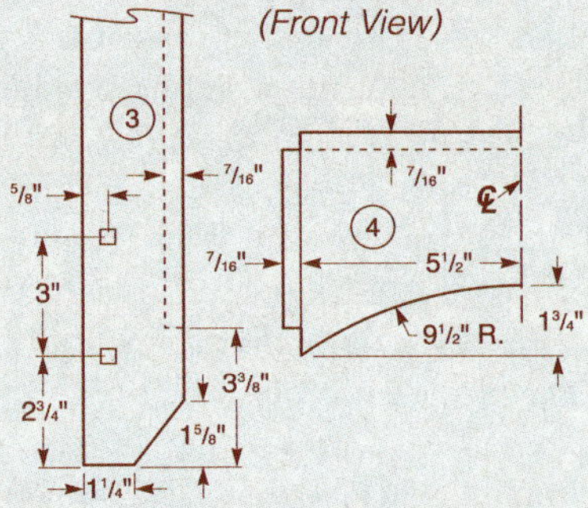

Web Frame, Web Frame Edging and Drawer Track
(Section View)

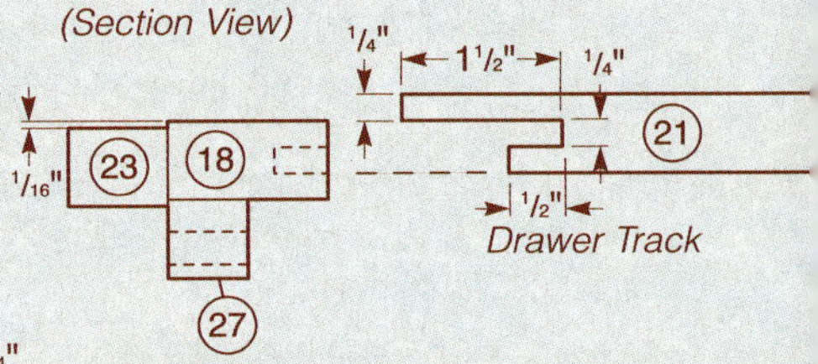

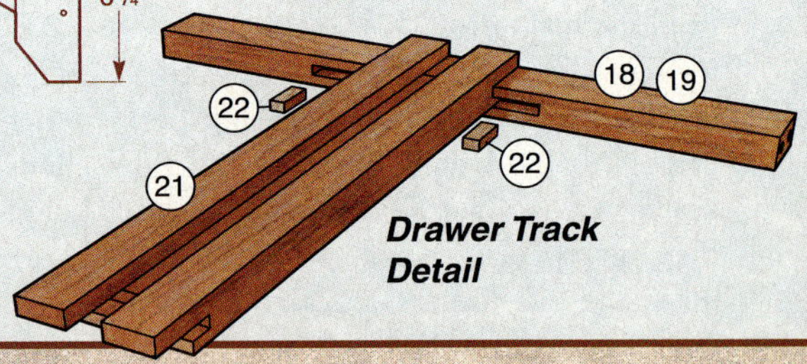

Drawer Track Detail

Sand the long, sweeping curves of the lower rails smooth with a sanding block cut to match the curve's radius. Do the same for the other curved pieces.

MATERIAL LIST Cabinet

		T x W x L
1	Side Panel MDF Substrates (2)	1/4" x 11 7/8" x 22 1/2"
2	Side Panel Veener (4)	1/32" x 11 7/8" x 22 1/2"
3	Legs (4)	3/4" x 2 1/2" x 33"
4	Side Lower Rails (2)*	3/4" x 5 5/8" x 11 7/8"
5	Side Upper Rails (2)*	3/4" x 3" x 11 7/8"
6	Fill Strips (2)	1/4" x 2 1/4" x 11"
7	End Grain Plugs (8)	3/8" x 3/8" x 1/4"
8	Bottom (1)	3/4" x 15" x 44"
9	Bottom Edging (1)	3/4" x 3/4" x 43 1/2"
10	Dividers (2)	3/4" x 15" x 25 1/4"
11	Divider Edgings (2)	3/4" x 3/4" x 24 3/4"
12	Upper Web Frame Stiles (2)	3/4" x 2 1/2" x 44"

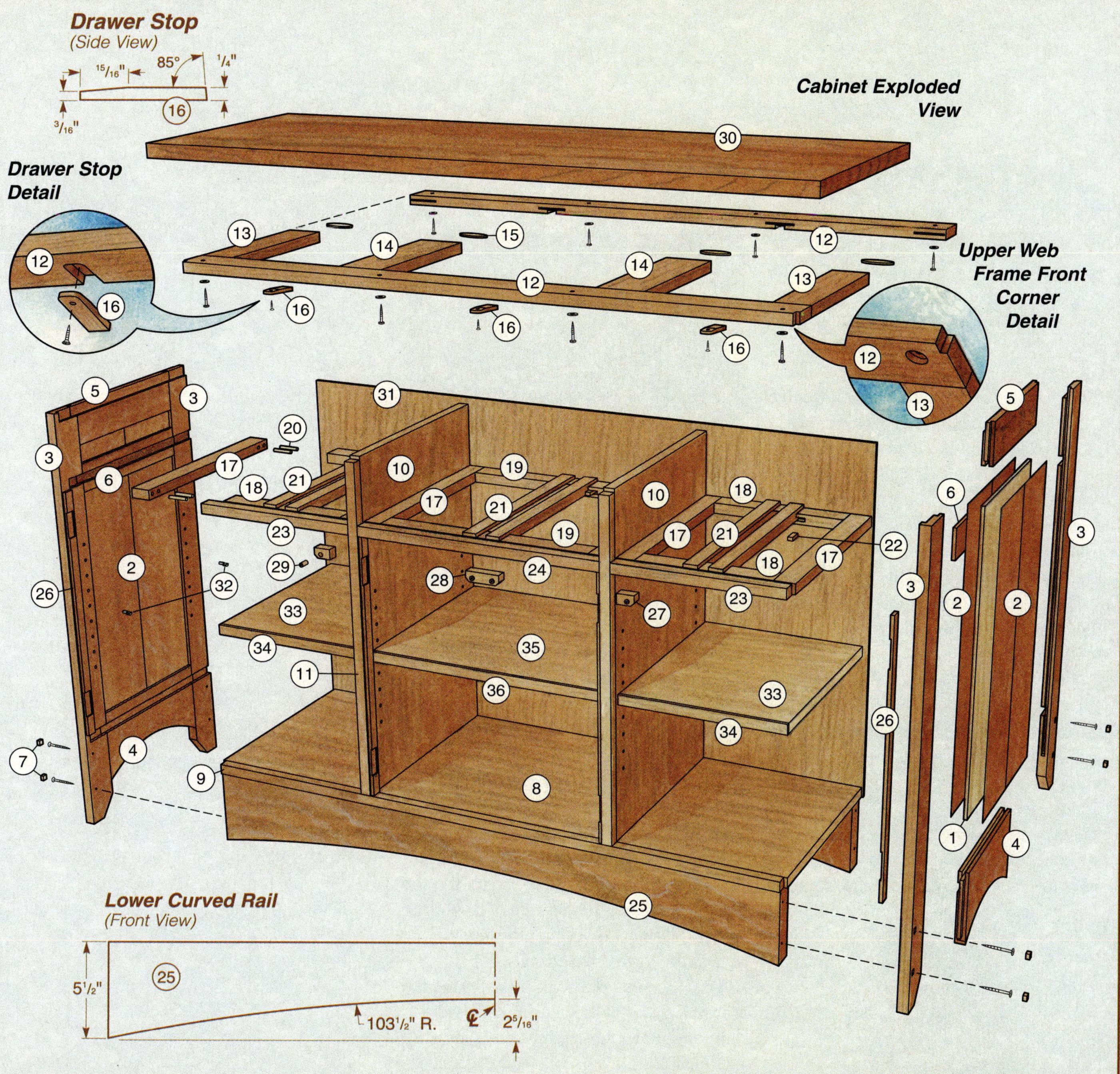

		T x W x L
13	Upper Web Frame End Rails (2)	3/4" x 2 1/2" x 10 3/4"
14	Upper Web Frame Middle Rails (2)	3/4" x 3 1/4" x 10 3/4"
15	Biscuits (8)	#20
16	Drawer Stops (3)	1/4" x 3/4" x 2 1/2"
17	Lower Web Frame Stiles (6)	3/4" x 1 1/2" x 14 13/16"
18	Lower Web Frame Rails (4)	3/4" x 1 1/2" x 9 1/2"
19	Lower Web Frame Middle Rails (2)	3/4" x 1 1/2" x 15 1/2"
20	Dowel Pins (24)	1/4" Dia. x 1 1/2"
21	Drawer Tracks (3)	3/4" x 2 3/4" x 14 3/4"
22	Drawer Track Locks (12)	1/4" x 3/8" x 1"
23	Short Web Frame Edging (2)	3/4" x 15/16" x 12"
24	Web Frame Edging (1)	3/4" x 15/16" x 18"

		T x W x L
25	Lower Curved Rails (2)	1 1/2" x 5 1/2" x 43 1/2"
26	Hinge Mounting Strips (4)	3/4" x 1/4" x 19 1/2"
27	Single Door Latch Blocks (2)	3/4" x 3/4" x 1 1/4"
28	Double Door Latch Blocks (1)	3/4" x 3/4" x 2 1/2"
29	Magnetic Door Catches (4)	5/16" Dia.
30	Top (1)	1" x 16 3/4" x 47"
31	Back (1)	1/4" x 44 1/4" x 26 1/4"
32	Antique Brass Shelf Pins (40)	5 mm
33	Small Shelves (2)	3/4" x 14 9/16" x 11 7/8"
34	Small Shelf Edgings (2)	1/4" x 3/4" x 11 7/8"
35	Shelf (1)	3/4" x 14 9/16" x 17 7/8"
36	Shelf Edging (1)	1/4" x 3/4" x 17 7/8"

QUARTERSAWN BEAUTY

you may need to compensate for the change. I find the Freud T&G set works best if you make a shallow scoring pass first, and then a full-depth pass to cut the remainder of the joint. I also leave the rails slightly wide, cut the end tenons first, then cut the rails to their final widths. Only then do I cut the rail grooves.

The grooves in the legs (pieces 3) are stopped short of the leg bottoms. As well, the tenon bottom ends of the side lower rails (pieces 4) are cut off so that when the sides are assembled, there is no visible joint (it's called a blind tenon). Wait to cut the curved shape of the side lower rails until after cutting the tongue and groove joints.

Next, assemble the rest of the casework parts for the cabinet. Don't forget to set the drawer tracks (pieces 21) loose in the web frames as they're assembled. Cut the blind dadoes in the sides, bottom and upper web frame. Remember that the fronts of the under-drawer web frames are set back farther than the rest of the parts. Rout the rabbets in the sides for the back

Desktop fasteners hold the upper rail tight to the bookcase uprights but allow it to "float" with movement caused by humidity changes.

and the upper web frame. Dry fit the parts and make the necessary adjustments, then go ahead and cut the notches on the front ends of the web frames, dividers and bottom to complete the blind dado joints (*photo* page 35). Fabricate the drawer stops (pieces 16), rout their grooves in the underside of the upper frame, and mount them to see that they work correctly. Cut the curved shapes of the lower curved rails (pieces 25). Drill the screw assembly holes in the sides for the lower rails, and those in the web frame to attach the top (piece 30). Chop the square holes for the plugs (pieces 7) that cover the screws that attach the lower curved rails.

Drill the shelf pin holes. Finish sand the show surfaces of the interior cabinet parts and assemble the cabinet casework. Fit and attach the web frame edging (pieces 23 and 24). Make sure you position them 1/16" down from the top of the under-drawer web frames. Cut the back (piece 31) and screw it to the cabinet. Make the door latch blocks (pieces 27 and 28) and glue them in place. Make and attach the top (piece 30), and make the shelves (pieces 33 through 36).

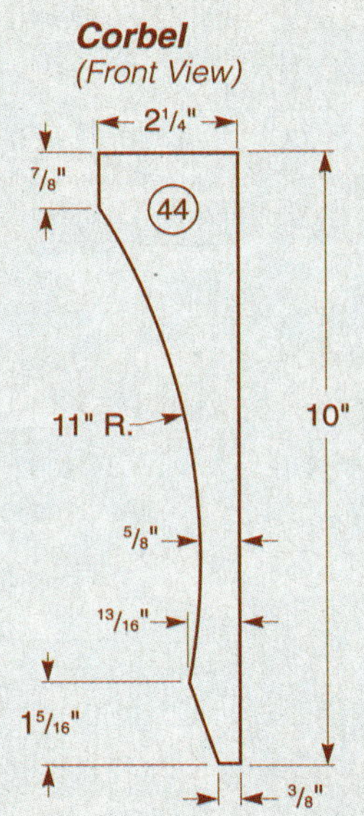

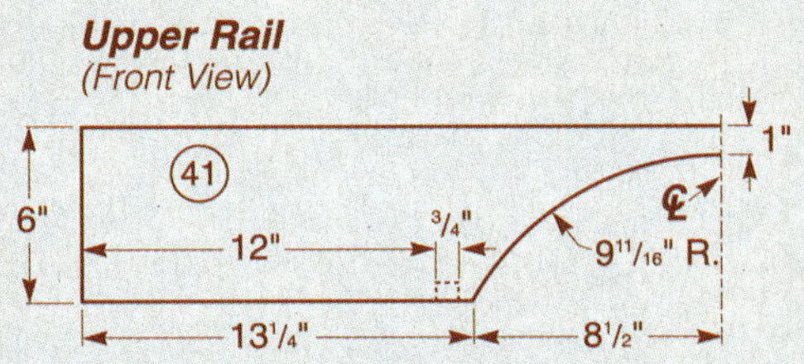

Notches are hand chopped in the back of the upper rail to allow it to expand and contract without showing evidence of that movement.

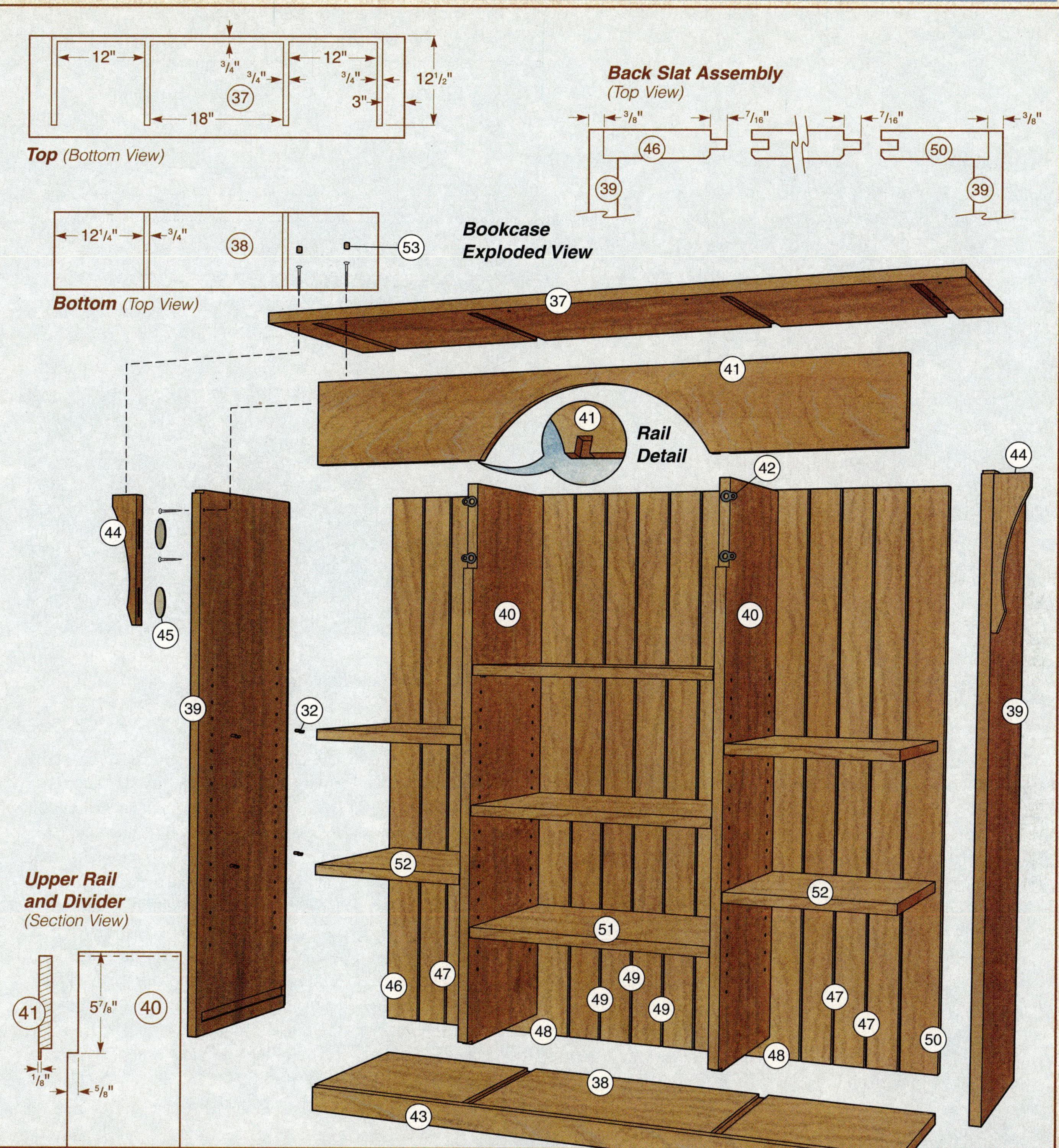

MATERIAL LIST Bookcase

	T x W x L
37 Top (1)	3/4" x 13 3/4" x 51"
38 Bottom (1)	3/4" x 11 1/4" x 44"
39 Sides (2)	3/4" x 13" x 41 1/2"
40 Dividers (2)	3/4" x 12" x 40"
41 Upper Rail (1)	3/4" x 6" x 43 1/2"
42 Desktop Fasteners (4)	"Figure 8" style
43 Lower Rail (1)	3/4" x 1 3/4" x 43 1/2"
44 Corbels (2)	3/4" x 2 1/4" x 10"
45 Biscuits (4)	#20

	T x W x L
46 Left End Slat* (1)	3/4" x 3 3/16" x 41 5/8"
47 Side Section Slats* (6)	3/4" x 2 7/8" x 41 5/8"
48 Slats on Dividers* (2)	3/4" x 6 1/8" x 41 5/8"
49 Center Section Slats* (5)	3/4" x 3" x 41 5/8"
50 Right End Slat (1)	3/4" x 2 3/4" x 41 5/8"
51 Center Shelves (3)	3/4" x 17 7/8" x 12"
52 Outer Shelves (4)	3/4" x 11 7/8" x 12"
53 Screw Cover Plugs (16)	3/8" Dia. x 1/4"

**Tongues are 7/16".*

Door Exploded View

MATERIAL LIST Doors and Drawers

	T x W x L
54 Door Stiles (8)	3/4" x 2 1/2" x 19 3/8"
55 Small Door Rails* (4)	3/4" x 2 1/2" x 4 9/16"
56 Door Rails* (4)	3/4" x 2 1/2" x 7 1/2"
57 Small Door Panel Substrates (2)	1/4" x 4 9/16" x 15 1/4"
58 Door Panel Veneer (4)	1/32" x 4 9/16" x 15 1/4"
59 Door Panel Substrates (2)	1/4" x 7 1/2" x 15 1/4"
60 Door Panel Veneer (4)	1/32" x 7 1/2" x 15 1/4"
61 Brass Ball-Tipped Butt Hinges (8)	2" x 1 1/2"
62 Small Drawer Fronts** (2)	3/4" x 4 3/8" x 11 7/8"
63 Drawer Front** (1)	3/4" x 4 3/8" x 17 7/8"

The chevron patterned white oak rays are achieved on the doors by means of book-matched veneer.

ATTENTION TO DETAILS MAKES THE DIFFERENCE

Building the Bookcase

When making the bookcase, keep in mind that the upper rail and the corbels (pieces 41 and 44) are set back 1/8" from the front edges of the sides (pieces 39), and the lower rail (piece 43) is set back 1/4" from the front edges of the sides. The front edges of the dividers (pieces 40) are flush with the front of the lower rail.

Edge glue together boards to make the sides, top, bottom and uprights of the bookcase. Make the upper and lower rails. Glue the lower rail to the bottom. Rout the blind dado grooves and the rabbets for the back slats (pieces 46 through 50). Drill the shelf pin holes and the screw assembly holes in the top, bottom and sides. Cut the biscuit groove for and in the corbels.

Form the notches on the upper ends of the sides and bottom ends of the uprights for the blind dadoes. Also cut the notches at the tops of the uprights for the upper rail. Dry assemble the bookcase, fit the upper rail, and mark where the uprights land on its back. Chop the deep but short grooves in the back of the upper rail (*photo* page 38). Finish sand everything and assemble the bookcase. Attach the upper rail with desktop fasteners, but without any glue (*photo* page 38). Glue and screw the top on and plug the screw holes (pieces 53). Fabricate the back slats and fit the entire back so there are 1/32" expansion gaps between each back slat. Screw the back in place. Place screws at the top and bottom of each slat, on the edges of the end slats, and in the center of the slats that bridge the dividers. Make the shelves (pieces 51 and 52).

Making the Doors and Drawers

All I can say is, if you've gotten this far, making the doors and drawers should be a snap! The doors are made just like the cabinet sides. Make them slightly large so there's something to trim when you fit them in the cabinet. I cut the hinge mortises with a router and a template

The author uses a router with a bottom-bearing hinge mortising bit and a hinge template to rout the hinge mortises. Before the template is removed, he chops the mortise corners square using the template as a guide.

		T x W x L
64	Drawer Sides (6)	1/2" x 4 3/8" x 15 3/16"
65	Small Drawer Backs*** (2)	1/2" x 3 13/16" x 11 3/8"
66	Drawer Back*** (1)	1/2" x 3 13/16" x 17 3/8"
67	Small Drawer Bottom (2)	1/4" x 14 5/8" x 11 3/8"
68	Drawer Bottom (1)	1/4" x 14 5/8" x 17 3/8"
69	Drawer Guides (3)	5/16" x 3/4" x 14 5/8"
70	Drawer Pulls (3)	Handmade brass
71	Door Pulls (4)	Handmade brass

*Tenons are 7/16"
**Cut from one piece.
***Cut width to fit.

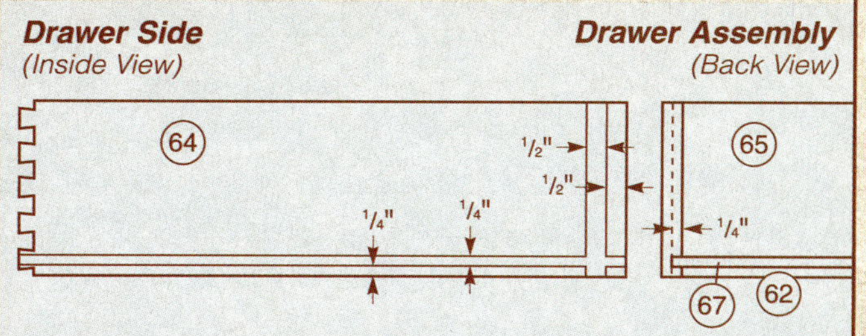

Wonderful stock selection and dovetailed joints add beauty to the drawers.

(*photo* below left). To make the hinge mounting strips (pieces 26), I routed the hinge mortises on the edge of a wide board that was 3/4" thick. Then I sliced off the 1/4" wide strips. Glue the hinge mounting strips in place, and attach the hinges and doors. The loose pin hinges make it easy to mount and unmount the doors during the fitting. Even so, it will take hours to get your doors fit perfectly.

The drawer fronts are joined to the drawer sides with jig-cut, half-blind dovetails (*photo* below right). The drawer backs are set into dadoes in the sides. I plowed grooves in the drawer fronts and sides for the drawer bottoms. The drawer guides are centered and glued to the undersides of the drawer bottoms. I made MDF spacers to center them perfectly. Cut the drawer backs short to allow the drawer bottoms to slide in place. Then screw them to the bottom edge of the drawer backs. When the drawers are finished, set them in the cabinet. Adjust them so all the gaps are right, and "lock in" the drawer tracks by gluing the drawer track locks (pieces 22) in place in the web frame grooves.

Staining and Finishing

Be warned, staining a large piece like this hutch is difficult enough, but staining it with a dark dye stain is about as tough as it gets. If you've never used a dye stain like this before, then practice on some large panels until you get the feel of it. Oddly enough, dye staining an inside corner doesn't seem as hard to do as with oil stain, but you should practice that as well.

To make this stain, or for that matter any stain, look good, the wood must be sanded evenly and thoroughly. I random orbit sanded everything to 220 grit. I found the most successful method for applying the stain was to brush it on, let it soak in a bit, and then blend it in with a dye-soaked rag. I was also careful not to allow the dye to pool in the inside corners. If that happened, I would have trouble getting those areas colored evenly.

To finish the hutch, I applied Danish oil over the stain. I put one sealer coat on everything, two coats on the cabinet interior surfaces and three coats on all of outside show wood surfaces. It really popped the grain and is silky to the touch.

Then I delivered the hutch to my clients and enjoyed a job well done.

Bruce Kieffer is a professional woodworker and project designer from St. Paul, Minnesota.

The half-blind drawer dovetail joints are cut with a router and dovetail bit and a dovetail jig. Every dovetail jig is a little different. This jig leaves a half pin at the top and bottom of the 4 3/8" wide drawer fronts. You may need to adjust for your jig.

Pencil Post Bed

By LiLi Jackson

We spend more than a third of our lives sleeping (and personally, I feel like I could use a lot more). While I can't figure out a way to spend more time in bed, perhaps I can make the time I do spend there ... opulent. With that in mind, I thought "what could possibly be more lavish than a beautiful handmade bed!"

The next morning, I set out to build one.

The Pencil Post design is one of the oldest American bed forms, dating back as far as 1690, but the main reason I chose to build this Shaker style piece is its understated elegance. It will fit with furnishings of nearly any decor or era and, with this design, can be easily knocked down, always a benefit with large pieces of furniture.

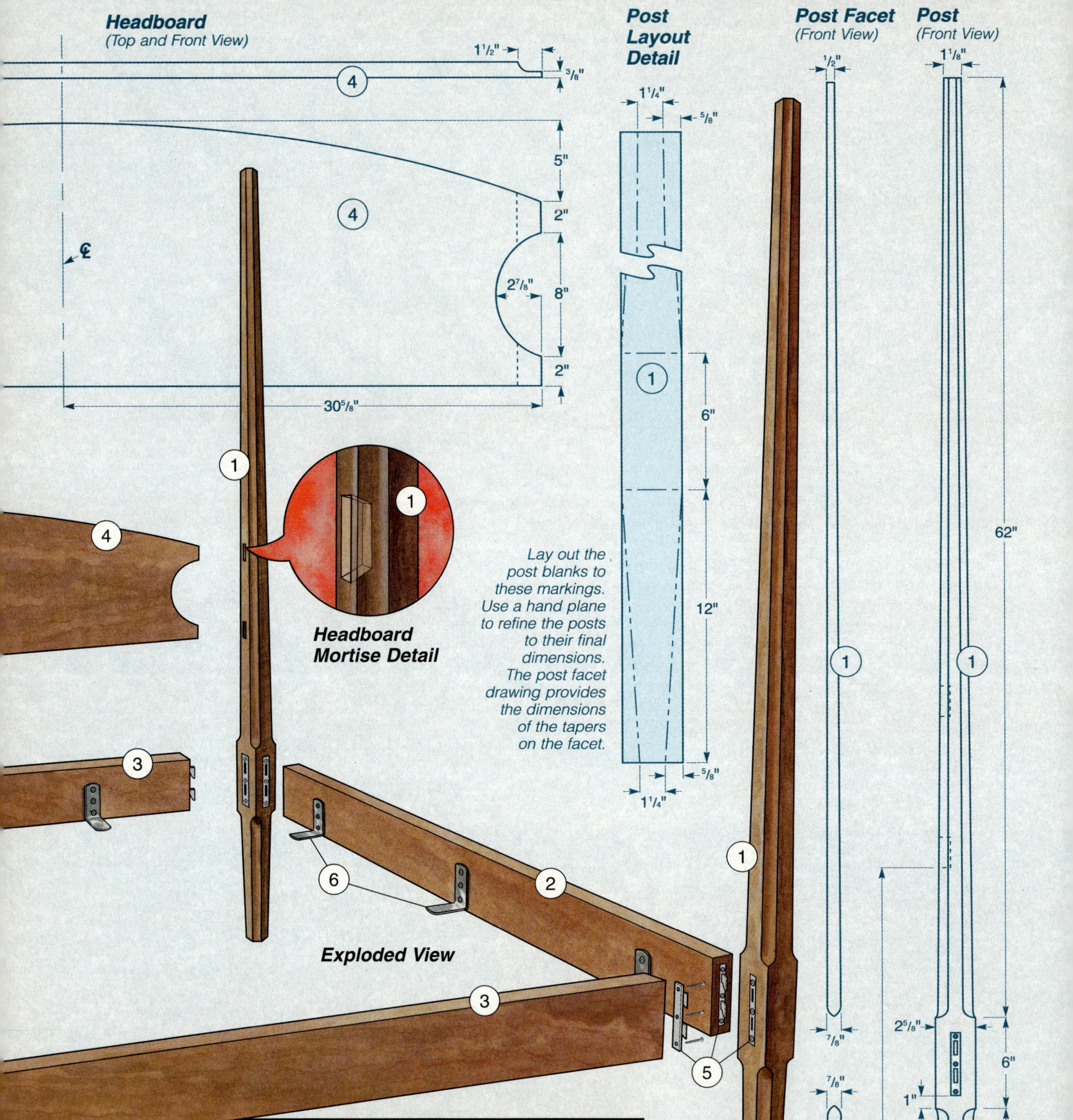

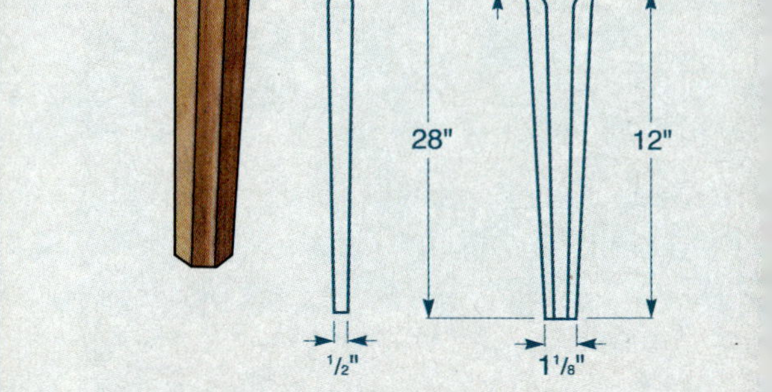

Material List

		T x W x L
1	Posts (4)	2⅝" x 2⅝" x 62"
2	Long Bed Rails (2)	1¾" x 5⅜" x 81"
3	Short Bed Rails (2)	1¾" x 5⅜" x 60¼"
4	Headboard (1)	1" x 17" x 61¼"
5	Bed Rail Fastener Sets (2)	4" x 5/8"
6	Box Spring Fasteners (10)	1¼" x 3⅝"

Pencil Post Bed Supplies

The following supplies are available from Woodworker's Journal.

4" Bed Rail Fasteners #28589..........$10.99*
*Box Spring Fastener Set** #38593.......$2.99*
**Two sets (4 per set) are required.*
***10 recommended.*

To order your supplies, call 800-610-0883 and mention code W5084.

The first step in machining the pencil posts is done on the band saw. Slice off the tapered sections from the leg blank. Reserve the drop and tape it back in place. Repeat the cut-and-tape process on successive faces of the post until you've cut all the tapers.

Getting Underway

After selecting an excellent stack of cherry lumber and milling it all to size, I glued the most highly figured boards together to create blanks for the posts and the headboard (see *Material List* for their dimensions). After the glue had cured, I began laying out the posts (pieces 1). Starting from the bottom, measure 12" up each post and mark a line bisecting its width. From there, measure up another 6" and draw a similar line. Use a square to extend the lines completely around the post blanks. At the top and bottom of the post blanks, mark points 5/8" in from each corner. Use a long straightedge to connect these points to the lines bisecting the post. (See the *Post Layout Detail* at left.) This describes the tapers on the posts. Repeat this process on the long face of each post blank to prepare for slicing the tapers.

I find it most pleasing to use a combination of power and hand tools on my projects. Often, I will use power tools at the beginning of the project to speed it up, and end up using hand tools to get more of a feeling of precision. With the posts, I started my milling on the band saw. This is a very simple cut: just aim down the lines you just marked and start sawing. After cutting the first face, I taped the waste back in position to recreate a flat surface to cut from (this is much like the initial cuts on a cabriole leg).

After sawing the tapers on all four posts, I took them back to my workbench and smoothed out the tapers with a 04½ bench plane. Then, with the post held between bench dogs, I rotated it 45° and planed down each of the long edges to form the octagonal "pencil" shape. The wood I selected had a lot of figure to it and, consequently, the grain would often run in different

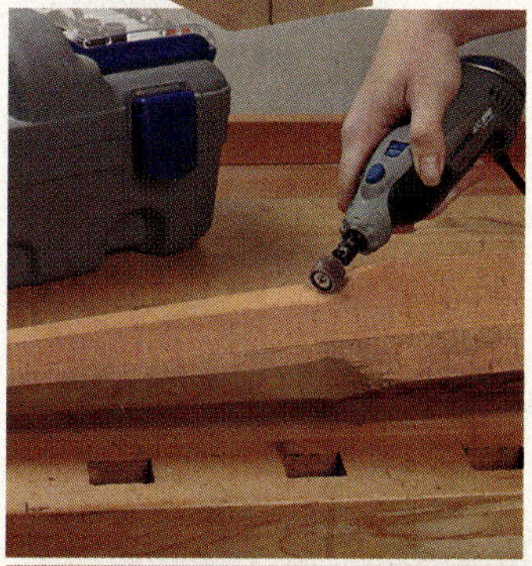

Shaping the posts requires a series of steps combining both hand and power tools. After the initial tapers are removed on the band saw, additional facets are created using a plane and spokeshave. The curved details that end the facets are carved with a rotary tool.

A mortising machine is just the ticket to form the two-step mortises on the posts. The segment of the bed where you mount the hardware remains sticked up (square and rectangular). This makes it much easier to chop the mortises. Alas, the mortises on the ends of the bed rails must be chopped the old-fashioned way, with a couple of sharp chisels.

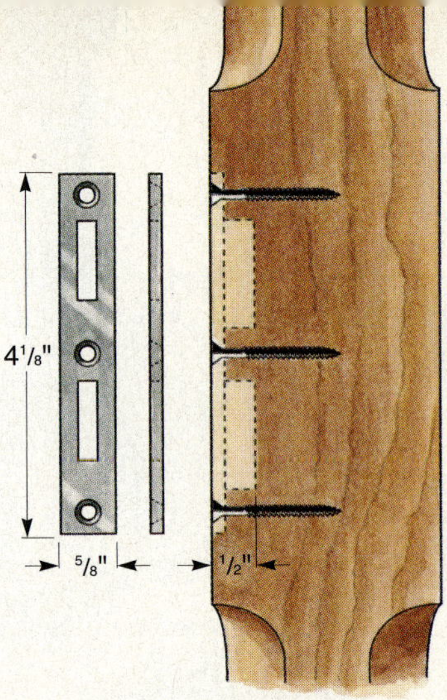

directions. So I turned to a spokeshave (often cutting in the exact opposite direction as I was with the plane) to handle that wild grain. As is common with the pencil post design, I wanted the octagon to merge into a squared up section where the bed rails (pieces 2 and 3) would join the posts. To achieve that shape, I used a Dremel® rotary tool and my trusty spokeshave to merge the taper up into the squared-up rectangular post segment. Take your time and form symmetrical curves ... these small details add a grace and elegance to this simple design.

Bed Rail Hardware

In order to connect the posts together, you need bed rails, and to link the bed rails and posts, I used bed rail fasteners. To chop the two-level mortises for the hardware in the post, I used a mortising machine (see the *photo*, above). Later, when I made the bed rails (ultra simple rectangular shapes), I formed matching mortises using a couple of bench chisels. The only step remaining with the bed rails is to knock down their long edges, so I won't hurt myself when I get out of bed! I completed this with a roundover bit in my router table.

A combination of careful layout and trial-and-error test fittings are required to fit the headboard tenons in their mortises. The bed rail hardware holds the bed together so firmly that you do not need to glue the headboard in place. Thus, the bed knocks all the way down to its nine pieces when it's time to move.

> "Dream no small dreams for they have no power to move the hearts of men."
>
> – Goethe

Technically, I now have a working bed, but what would a bed be without a headboard? (That was a rhetorical question.) Since I was going for that gracefully simple Shaker look, I drew out a rather traditional headboard shape. (It easily prevents my pillows from falling behind the bed.) Once again, I stepped over to the band saw to slice out the overall shape and then to the the belt sander to remove the band saw marks. Look to the *Drawings* on page 44 for all the construction details on the headboard (piece 4) and for details on shaping its tenons. I used a four-in-hand file to scoop out the back of the tenons.

One of the most satisfying aspects of making things yourself is that you can design them to fit your needs. Depending on the height of your mattress and boxspring — and the overall appearance you want the bed to have — you can locate the headboard to suit your needs. Back at the drill press, I chose two posts and mortised them for the headboard using a 1/2" Forstner bit (see the *photos* on the previous page). Then I cleaned up the mortises with a sharp chisel. You will need to do some trial-and-error fitting on both the mortises and the headboard's tenons.

Subtle Finishing Additive

Yay! The bed is built. On to my absolutely favorite part: sanding and finishing (just kidding). There is a lot of surface area to cover, but for environmental and traditional design reasons, I chose to brush on shellac. I mixed up a batch of blonde shellac mixed with some powdered mica and brushed it on with a good natural bristle brush. I sanded between coats with 320-grit paper. One trick I used for shellacking the posts was tapping a small finishing nail into both ends of each post. Now you can rest them on the nails to create a "rotisserie effect" while you apply the finish. After four coats, I lightly buffed all of the pieces with steel wool, and then, still using steel wool, rubbed on a coat of wax.

Have you ever heard the saying "Good night, sleep tight; don't let the bed bugs bite?" In olden days, people used to weave rope through the bed rails to create a surface for their mattress to lie on. Every so often, they would have to tighten the rope to keep the bed from sagging. (Hence the sleep tight ... oh, you got that.) If you have a box spring to put your mattress on, you can get off easy by screwing in a few box spring fasteners (pieces 5) to each bed rail. (Although this will do nothing to prevent the bed bugs from biting.)

This wasn't the hardest project I've ever built, but all that sanding sure left me needing a nap. Now that I've made my bed I intend to sleep, perchance to dream up my next "must build" project. And remember, "Dream no small dreams for they have no power to move the hearts of men." — *Goethe*

Lucky enough to be born into a woodworking family, Woodworker's Journal *reporter LiLi Jackson has recently been traveling the country and attending some of the best woodworking schools around. Look for her occasional reports in our* Shop Talk *department.*

The author used blonde shellac mixed with a small amount of powdered mica to add a subtle sparkle to this traditional finish.

The Building Blocks of Furniture Making

By Ian Kirby

Part 2: Frame-and-panel Variations

An exploration of the rich possibilities using solid wood and manufactured sheet material.

In the *June* issue *(The Building Blocks of Woodworking,* pp. 66 - 70), I explained that once a way of dealing with the shrinkage and expansion of solid wood was devised using frame-and-panel construction, woodworkers had the fundamental building block that allowed for the making of durable furniture. Here I'll explore the practical adaptations of the frame-and-panel.

In terms of solid wood, little has changed with the concept of making a strong frame with a groove around its inner edge to hold a loose panel. However, the solid wood version now has a rival in the form of manufactured sheet material (MSM).

Plywood, particleboard, and medium density fiberboard don't shrink or expand to any appreciable degree. Dimensionally stable, they don't need to be held within a solid frame, yet this is how they are used in the manufacture of furniture and cabinets. The MSM making method may be seen as the reverse of the solid wood making method — the panel, firmly glued into the groove of the dimensionally stable frame, is the structural element.

Solid Wood Frame-and-panels

There are two types of frame-and-panel structures. One type sits inside the frame, for example, a typical raised-and-fielded panel.

Hand feeding the frame parts past a router bit will inevitably incur some slight dimensional deviations. A vernier caliper is invaluable for finding them.

The other sits over the frame, and is commonly called a plant-on panel, although it's held in a groove just like its cousin.

The panel inside the frame is the one preferred by carpenters and house builders for paneling walls.

The plant-on panel was preferred by furniture makers (see the Gimson's sideboard story on page 53). Its construction method makes the frame subordinate to the panel. The panel's simplicity strips away all the visual fuss of raised-and-fielded construction and encourages the maker to select and display the beauty inherent in wood.

Variations on a theme

Beaded panel

Handmade raised-and-fielded panel

Machine-made raised-and-fielded frame-and-panel

Plant-on frame-and-panel

A typical raised-and-fielded panel sitting inside a frame (left). The highlights and shadows define the center field, helped by the rabbet which is not the same width all around. The 15° slope on the reveal of the frame makes a more appealing transition between frame and panel than would the severity of a square-edged reveal.

The four plant-on panels (above) are divided by three muntins which are the same length as the stiles. The alignment of shoulders is a small detail in the pursuit of a simpler whole.

Plant-on Panel

The plant-on panel offers the designer a radically different opportunity with which to work.

If, for instance, you can find a board or two that comes from the crotch of a tree that displays stunning colour and grain pattern, the plant-on panel is the ideal way to present it because its surface won't be disrupted by raising and fielding.

Sadly, such material was never plentiful and is becoming scarcer by the day. Fortunately, quartersawn and spalted material in narrow widths and all sorts of species is less scarce, so you can design the piece with an elegant pattern of multiple long and narrow panels. Adding additional muntins barely increases the making time and stiffens the frame structure.

Making the Plant-on Frame-and-panel

The groove on both the frame and panel is filled with a tongue, a simple solution I like both conceptually and technically. The thickness of the

Cut back the panel tongues, as shown in the bottom drawing, to allow room for expansion.

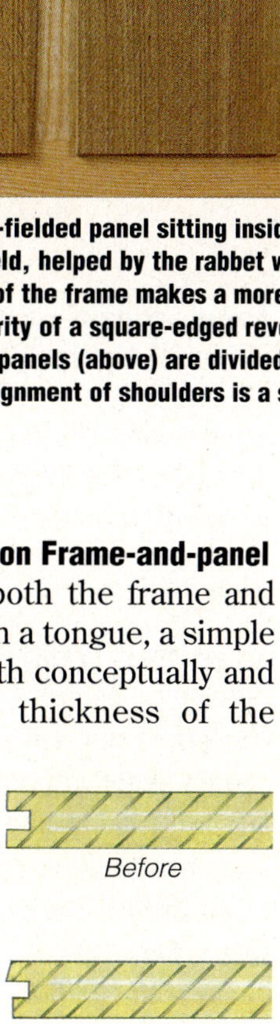

tongue equals the width of the groove. So, in cutting the desired groove with the correct cutter setting, you simultaneously make the tongue.

Slot cutters come in 1/16" increments, an ample range to create the groove you want. My practice is to set the cutter to its own width above the table. Make the panel groove with the inside face down on the table. Make the frame groove with the outside face down on the table. Made to this setting, the tongue is the same dimension as the groove, which is too tight, but once you remove the machine marks by hand planing both faces, the two parts will slot and slide neatly into each other. Make test pieces to confirm the cutter settings are correct. Once you have cut all the parts to dimension, the order of work is:

- joint the frame structure
- cut the grooves in the frame and panel
- fit the panels in their grooves
- dry clamp the whole assembly.

Two router bits do the job. The grooves in the frame and the panel are made with a slot cutter, which come with three or four wings. The taper bit puts the chamfer around the edges of the panel.

Chances are that test fitting will reveal that the joint shoulder lines on the frame are no longer flush. If so, remove the panels, put the frame back together dry, and plane the frame flush on the outside face. It's impossible to get at the shoulders with a plane and difficult with a sander after glue-up. However, you can plane the inside shoulders.

There's no need for the panel to project above the frame more than 1/4" for furniture purposes, thicker perhaps for architectural interiors. Because a panel left square-edged looks coarse, I taper it to 15°, a simple operation on the router table with a chamfer cutter. Alternately, the edge can also be refined by a small rabbet to halve its thickness.

To make an allowance for shrinkage and expansion, cut back the tongues on the edges of the panel. Set your table saw to the height of the tongue plus 1/16" and to the correct width (see *Drawing*, previous page). This cut is best done before tapering the outside edge.

You can see from the drawing that the mortise joint line is cut back to the line of the edge taper.

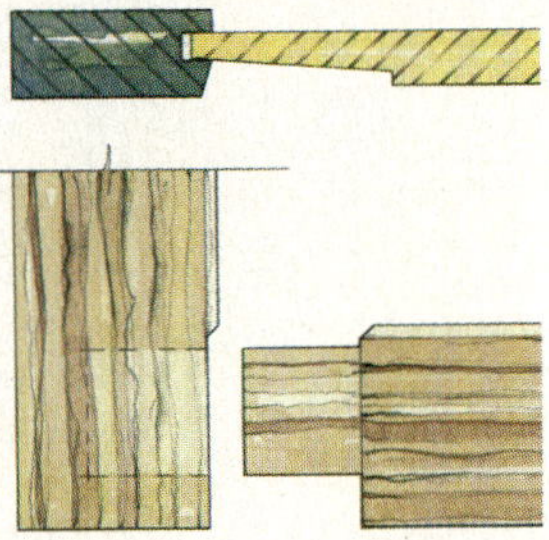

Panel Inside the Frame

What likely springs to mind when we think of a panel inside the frame is the raised-and-fielded panel door ubiquitous in even the most inexpensive kitchens (see *photo* page 49).

The popularity of this construction arises from the ease with which matching router cutters, with the same setup, shape the edge of the frame all around, make the groove all around, and make the four corner joints by coping the ends of the rails. A second cutter raises and fields the panel.

The downside is that you are stuck with the same set of profiles until you acquire more cutters, and even then the range of profiles for both frame and panel is limited.

Because of the widespread use of modern router bits, the fact that the raised-and-fielded panel was traditionally a carpenter's wall paneling construction technique is, as they say, history. It has been used on too many kitchen cabinet doors and in too many magazine projects for me to do anything but acknowledge that

Frame-and-panel Router Cutters

Here again, like the role reversal of a solid wood panel and a MSM panel, we see a reversal in the design method when using router cutters. Using traditional tools and methods, panel dimensions plus the angle of the raising and fielding were variables to be decided at the design stage. Using fixed profile router cutters, these decisions are already made; they therefore become the starting point of design decisions. Visual success depends upon designing the width of the rails and stiles and the width of the panel to best accommodate the cutter profiles. Because the work of milling each workpiece is now the easy part of the process and because interesting selected wood comes in ever narrower dimensions, by using it you have the perfect opportunity to produce more elegant furniture.

Because it's so easy to buzz around all four sides of the panel to make a tongue to fit the grooves, the practice is, unfortunately, much over-used. Carrying the molding across the ends causes considerable grain deflection and a confusing visual effect, especially if you have chosen a piece of flat-sawn wood with a cathedral figure for the panel. The solution? Don't shape the top and bottom edges. Simply put a shoulder and tongue on the ends of the panel as shown in the photo at right. The joint shoulder line adds to the verticality of the composition. The rails are left square on the reveal.

The absence of molding across the top and bottom edges of the panel emphasizes the vertical lines of the raised-and-fielded side edges.

Hand-cut or Router-cut

The chamfer on the reveal edge of the rail and stile meet as a miter in the corner. The joint shoulder is in line with the outer edge of the chamfer.

The back side of the joint shows how the shoulder on the mortise was re-cut to accommodate the 15° chamfer on the reveal of the frame at the front.

it's become an accepted furniture detail. Before I deal with its construction and to keep some historical order, I will discuss its predecessor, the handmade version.

Handmade Frames

Determine the overall design by drawing the frame-and-panel at full size or, better yet, making a mockup. Frame dimensions, more than any other element, establish the overall appearance of the work.

Four decisions are necessary when designing the frame:

- the dimensions of the stiles and rails
- the joinery
- the groove
- the outside reveal of the frame.

Dimensions of stiles and rails — 3/4" or better is a typical off-the-shelf thickness. However, most of what is made at 3/4" would look better at 9/16" and still be plenty strong. Try using 1/32" as the increment by which you make thickness decisions!

On a door the width of stile and rail stock are generally the same. When there are a number of panels divided by muntins, they usually vary in width. Get the dimensions right at the design stage.

Joinery — The traditional joint is a stopped mortise-and-tenon.

When the frame was made entirely by hand, the groove was cut with a plow plane. Because you can't make a stopped groove with a hand plow plane, the tenon on the rail was made with a haunch to fill up the groove on the stile. A machine-made groove can be stopped, so in this case you don't have to make a haunched mortise-and-tenon.

How you make the joint is your call, but smooth mating faces and accurately aligned parts is the aim. With 3/4" stock, make the thickness of the tenon 3/8" ... with 9/16" stock, a 1/4" tenon is strong enough.

Groove — Even though we say "handmade" you are unlikely to make the groove with a plow plane. The groove is usually made on the table saw or with a slot cutter on a router table. The dimensions of the groove and its location on the edge of the part are entirely dependent on the panel design. It must be deep enough to allow the panel to shrink and expand. Most panels will shrink when they leave the shop, so allowing for 1/8" movement on a 10" panel is fine.

Outside Reveal of the Frame — The reveal on a handmade frame-and-panel is normally sloped to an angle of 15° rather than left square, which affects the shoulder line of the joint.

On the edges of rails and stiles the angle is planed after the joint and groove are made. It could also be

The frame can be machined using two (right) separate cutters or one cutter that has both profiles on the same shank (left).

The horizontal cutter can be used with the router held on top of the work, or in a router table where you feed the work across it.

This bit gives us a slope that was never contemplated by traditional furniture makers. The author considers it fine for painted work.

To hold the panel securely vertical, extend the height of the fence. With any router bit, you don't have to make the cut all at once. To reduce the cutting load on you and the bit, remove about half the material on the first pass, then make a second and final cut.

That the raised-and-fielded panel is a carpenter's wall paneling technique is, alas, history. It's been used on too many kitchen cabinet doors and in too many magazine projects for me to do anything but acknowledge that it's become an accepted furniture detail.

–Ian Kirby

done with a taper bit on a router, though it will need a pass with a plane to remove the cutter marks. The shoulder of the mortise has to be cut back to the line of the chamfer. Both parts of the chamfer are cut at 45° to meet in the corner.

Alternative Panels

An alternative to a raised-and-fielded panel inside a frame is seen on the cabinet below. It has English brown oak panels inside an ebonized ash frame. The panels have a single bead on each side edge that sits about 1/2" from the stile to offer a clear view of the profile. The top and bottom have a clear shoulder with a tongue into the common groove.

Manufactured Panels

The upside to manufactured panels is that they are dimensionally stable. The downside is that their surface is visually bland.

One solution is to cover a piece of 1/2" MDF on both sides with some extraordinary veneer that would be impossible to match in solid wood. Put flat into a frame, it wouldn't need any raising or molding in order to look terrific. Its dramatic appearance belies how easy it is to make a veneered panel, yet I rarely see it used in small shops.

Where MDF really comes into its own is for interior wall paneling with a painted finish. Its dimensional stability and smooth surface make it ideal for this purpose. Although it's a three-layer board — the outer surfaces are denser and harder than the core — the cut surface when primed takes paint very well. Cutting a raised-and-fielded motif isn't a problem. The problem is exhausting the waste from the cutter. The dust is fine, makes a terrible mess, and is bad for your lungs. Effective dust collection is a must.

In Part 1 of this article *(June 2005),* I emphasized the importance of the correct proportions of the parts in a frame-and-panel system. A painted, paneled wall underscores this point. Suppose you paint the whole thing the same color, say, white or some calm variation. You will immediately realize that the proportions stand out in stark simplicity because there is no wood grain pattern or different wood tones to distract you from the effect. Under these conditions you may find that raising and fielding the panels creates too much detail — an excess of highlights and shadows.

The sides and back were made with similar panels. The simple tongue and bead are, to my taste, the best of what a machined panel has to offer. The strong highlights and shadows made by the profiles on the edges emphasize the vertical lines of the piece but don't intrude upon the width of the panel or disrupt the grain pattern.

Here you can see how the end shoulder meets the frame. It's at this point that the edge molding is shown clearly in profile.

Sideboard with Plate Stand

This sideboard was designed by Ernest Gimson in 1915. It is made of English walnut and ebony and is typical of Gimson's Arts and Crafts style.

Clearly, it is a magnificent piece of work with many features of interest to modern furniture makers, but I will confine my comments to the doors.

They are curved squares with an overlay panel set on a wide frame. The frame itself has a raising on it made so that the top and bottom edges of the raising coincide with the raised center panel of the drawers on either side of the doors. The pattern on the square overlay panel is made up of four raisings. The first raising is aligned with the raising on the flanking drawers, giving the illusion of a narrow door frame. The inner square contains a raised octagon, which was a common way of terminating the raisings.

Each raising is less than 1/16" high, but there is no doubt about its presence and its effect by way of reflected light.

The sideboard is owned by the Art Gallery and Museum in Cheltenham, England, which kindly gave me permission to use the photograph. The piece is currently on exhibit in the U.S.

This corner of a half-paneled room is a good example of manufactured sheet stock put to attractive paneling use. My thanks to David Grosz, the maker. — *Ian Kirby*

It's perfectly acceptable to leave the panels flat, as in the photo at left, and attach moldings to the edge of the frame. In this example, the molding projects above the frame, as you can see by the highlights, which helps to strongly define the panel shape. Another simple detail is to further emphasize the window by wrapping it around the corners. Yet another way to emphasize the proportions of the parts is to paint the panel and frame in different tones.

Ian Kirby is a master woodworker and author and regular contributor to the Woodworker's Journal.

Veneer Jointing Jig

By Bruce Kieffer

Once the edges are straight, the author tapes them together ... glues the joint and lays them flat until the glue cures.

To achieve a tight joint on his book-matched veneer the author needed to get a perfectly straight edge on his two flitch pieces.

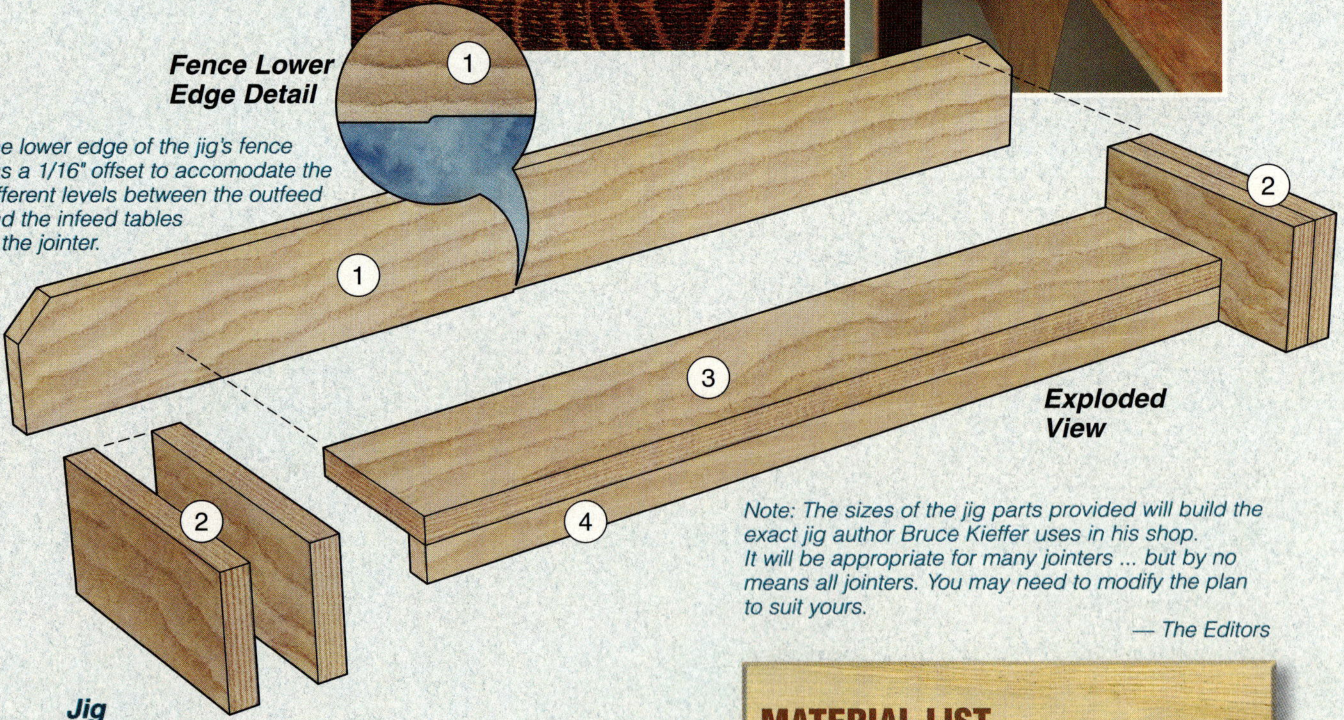

The lower edge of the jig's fence has a 1/16" offset to accomodate the different levels between the outfeed and the infeed tables of the jointer.

Note: The sizes of the jig parts provided will build the exact jig author Bruce Kieffer uses in his shop. It will be appropriate for many jointers ... but by no means all jointers. You may need to modify the plan to suit yours.

— The Editors

Jig
(End View)

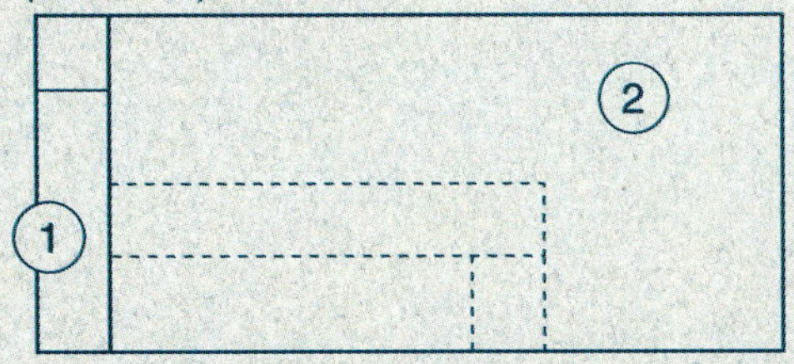

The author added a small piece of material to fit into the rabbet notch on his jointer. See photo, opposite page.

MATERIAL LIST

	T x W x L
1 Fence Face (1)	3/4" x 3½" x 32"
2 Support Blocks (2)	1½" x 3½" x 7"
3 Knife Guard (1)	3/4" x 4½" x 24½"
4 Fill Block (1)	3/4" x 1" x 24½"

Our author used this jig to create dramatic book-matched white oak panel doors for his Arts & Crafts Hutch project featured in this issue. We thought you might find it handy, so here's the skinny on this slick jointer-jig.

I've been veneering for many years, and I've tried just about every imaginable method to quickly and accurately joint the edges of the veneers I want to join together. I tried router jigs, table saw jigs, and hand planes. I didn't like any of those ways, so I settled on using the common method of sandwiching my veneer sheets between two pieces of solid wood, clamping that all together, and passing the entire mess over my jointer. That method works OK, but it's really slow and you have to deal with clamp heads interfering with the jointer's fence and other problems.

Channeling Inventiveness

So there I am some years ago using the sandwich method when it hits me … why not make an auxiliary fence that creates a narrow channel next to the jointer's fence and just pass the sheets through the channel! I quickly whipped together a prototype jig, tested it, and found it worked better than I had imagined.

As you can see, this jig is simple to make. I used Baltic birch plywood for mine, MDF would work fine, too. The outfeed side of the jig is stepped up 1/16" to accommodate the different heights of the infeed and outfeed tables. I added some material to the bottom of the left support block to fill in where my jointer's rabbeting notch is cut in the outfeed table. You'll need to modify your jig to work best with your jointer.

To use the jig, turn off and unplug the jointer, make sure the jointer's knife head is not spinning, set the cutting depth to 1/16", and remove the jointer's guard. Clamp the auxiliary fence over the knives and to the jointer's tables. Adjust the jointer's fence so there's a narrow channel between the fence and the auxiliary fence. To do this, I place two sheets of veneer between the fences, pull them together tightly, and then snug down the jointer's fence. The gap is then large enough for jointing one piece of veneer at a time.

Give it a try and I think you will find this is a great way to joint the edges of your veneer.

Bruce Kieffer is a professional woodworker from St. Paul Minnesota. If he's not in his shop, look for him in the Boundary Waters Canoe Area.

The author uses an auxiliary fence to support the veneer sheets while jointing their edges. Just like when jointing solid wood, it's important to orient the grain direction correctly to avoid edge tearout.

Innovations in Woodworking Basics

SPACE-SAVING CLAMPING SOLUTION

"The sky's the limit" when it comes to how high you can clamp with Rick and Randy Glaser's stacking clamps, says Rick. Like many woodworkers, the brothers were cabinetmakers short on shop space about 10 years ago when they first wondered about how great it would be to have clamps that stacked up. They soon developed their own, and R&R Clamp, Inc. was born.

With their starter system, you get six of these clamps, two alignment bars, two stabilizer bars, three packs of rubber guards and a drill adapter. Once the alignment bars have been mounted to a workbench and checked for square, they can be left in place to ensure squared-up clamping in the future. The drill adapter, Rick says, is a hit with older woodworkers. With it they can use a cordless drill to tighten the clamps so that the entire glue-up assembly is clamped evenly.

Once you have the boards stacked in the clamps, it's possible to take out a board — anywhere in the assembly — while leaving the rest of the clamping assembly intact. Just use caution, says Rick. The starter system comes in 2- and 3-foot clamp lengths which sell for $195 and $250, respectively.

For more information, call 920-863-2987 or visit the web site — www.rrclamp.com.

Elmer's Adds Stainable Wood Glue

It's very likely that you used Elmer's® glue for your very first woodworking project (the kind that might have involved gluing wooden Popsicle® sticks together). At that point, you didn't worry much about squeeze-out, let alone staining your wood. Now that you've grown into a higher aesthetic appreciation, though, Elmer's has, too. Elmer's Stainable Wood Glue is just what it sounds like: a glue specially formulated to hold wood together and also accept a wood stain.

The nontoxic ANSI Type II water-resistant glue has a set time of one hour. According to Elmer's, it's made with real wood fibers, accepts solvent-based stains and paints and has a strength rating of 2,000 - 2,200 psi. The 7.625 oz. bottle sells for about $4, and the 16 oz. bottle for about $6. *For more info, call 888-435-6377 or visit* www.elmers.com.

Elmer's new stainable glue is catching the imagination of woodworkers.

JET's New Line of Parallel Clamps

This summer, JET is introducing something big: the JET Parallel Clamp, which the company claims has the largest clamping surface in the industry. They're basing that claim, says marketing manager Tim Shipley, on a jaw face gluing/clamping surface area that is 4⅛" x 1⅞", for a total surface area of 7.73". The clamping surfaces are on glue-resistant, non-marring resin jaw faces attached to clamps that vary from 12" to 98" in length and offer 90° clamping at up to 1,000 pounds of pressure. Patented or patent-pending features abound, including a clever release lever and rapid action slide-glide trigger, which makes fast adjustments with the flick of a finger. An XACTA™ Rule Measurement System on the bar aids in consistent setup. A moveable end stop also helps to preset clamping capacity, while versatility comes from a side profile that allows narrow clamping and jaws that reverse for use as a spreader. The handle on the Parallel Clamps is designed for ease and comfort, too, with an Acme thread to allow it to turn without binding and an ergonomic SUMOGRIP™ soft grip for comfort and increased torque. The various sizes of JET Parallel Clamp have market prices ranging from $33 to $70, while the framing blocks sell for $30 and the bench dogs for $16. *For more info, call 888-804-7129 or visit* www.jettools.com.

Accessories for the new JET parallel clamps abound.

continues on page 62 ...

10 Minute Tool Test: Blast Off With Baking Soda

Imagine a sandblasting rig that uses baking soda instead of sand. Fully assembled out of the box, I merely filled the bright red tank of the smallest $250 rig with baking soda, plugged in the quick change from my air compressor, and was soon stripping everything from shellac and lacquer to the ultra-durable powder coatings on microwave ovens and tractors.

After experimenting with different air pressures, I went from eroding away soft wood at full blast, to stripping just one layer of paint. The tiny nozzle on the smallest rig means slow going, but it shines in difficult to reach areas. The blast pattern is small, stripping only a tiny area at a time. Think of it like using a pressure washer as opposed to a scrub brush. It's not really faster, but it is a whole lot less laborious.

I'd use a heat gun first to remove the bulk of thick paint, then grab this blaster for flutes, carvings and remaining residue in other hard-to-reach places. It will erode wood, especially soft woods, and rather quickly once the finish is off, so you must keep your wits about you with anything other than very hard woods. It will also leave most woods rough and in need of sanding.

Cleanup is a dream, since the white powder it leaves is safe and water soluble. Various size rigs (starting at $250) are available online from *www.ace-sandblasting.com/soda-blasting.html.*

— Michael Dresdner

WHAT'S IN STORE

BOSCH'S New Fine Line

Bosch accessorizes a top-flight saw, the latest in the laser-race.

Last year, Bosch changed things around on its miter saw line, putting the controls in the front. This year, they've added something new: a laser. Still selling for the same price as the saws without, the Precision Laser-Tracking System saws create a literal "fine line." The laser line is "fine and easy to see," says Bosch rep Jason Feldner, including in the glare of outdoor light, rather than "fuzzy" and hard-to-follow.

The laser on the 4410L 10" Dual Bevel Sliding Compound Miter Saw, as well that on its sibling saws the 5412L 12" — and the 4212L 12" compound miter — is trigger-activated. It comes on when you're ready to make the cut, Jason said — and goes off when you're finished, meaning you can't accidentally leave it on and wear your battery down.

Just like the non-laser saws introduced last year, the new 4410L bevels 47° left and 46° right, with 10 positive detent stops. Sliding fences and standard extensions expand up to 37¼" from either side of the saw. The range selector knob, bevel lock lever, four-position handle and lock-off switch are all on the front of the saw.

Even with the addition of the laser, the price for the 4410L remains the same as that for the laser-less version: around $600. *For more information, call 877-267-2499 or visit* www.boschtools.com.

A Brute of a Dust Collector

With its latest cyclonic dust collector, Oneida is targeting small shops that want powerful dust collection. "Dust Gorilla" incorporates a 35-gallon dust bin, with a high efficiency 2 HP cyclone collector. It's easy to clean and to empty the pleated cartridge filter. An internal silencer on the Dust Gorilla keeps things quiet.

In addition to the Dust Gorilla's cast aluminum fan wheel, dust bin, filter, silencer, motor starter and wall mounting brackets, Oneida also provides support that includes a customized ductwork design for your individual shop. With your Dust Gorilla comes a CD containing a CAD design of your personal ductwork system, with an itemized listing of all the elbows, branches and fittings.

The Dust Gorilla sells for $845. *For more info, call 800-732-4065 or visit* www.oneida-air.com.

ATF 55 E Plunge Saw with Guide Rail

Guide Rail will not mar the workpiece surface

Guide Rail lets you cut directly to the scribe mark – no more measuring

Precision cutting with the adjustable depth-stop

Festool CT Mobile Dust Extractors keep the air clean
HEPA filtration now available

888-337-8600
www.festoolusa.com

Straighter, Faster, Cleaner

The ATF 55 E Plunge Saw and Guide Rail make quick work of straight cuts. You work cleaner and finish faster.

NO CLAMPING. Just place the Guide Rail and cut along the edge. Leaves no marks.

NO CHIPPING. The splinter guard protects the cut edge.

NO CLEANING. Extremely effective dust collection when used with a dust extractor.

Call us or go online to find out more.

FESTOOL®

(Circle No. 26 on PRODUCT INFORMATION form)

Marketplace

To request and receive FREE information on any of the products or services shown in the **Marketplace**, circle the appropriate reader service number(s) on the **PRODUCT INFORMATION CARD** between pages 66 and 67.

To place your advertisement in the **Woodworker's Journal Marketplace,** contact David Beckler, ***david@jvgco.com.*** Call: 800-878-7137 or 972-392-1892 Fax: 972-392-1893

PRODUCT INFORMATION

To receive information about the items advertised in this issue, fill in the postcard, circling the appropriate number(s). Allow 4 to 6 weeks for delivery.

The Voice of the Woodworking Community:

Projects, tips, tools, techniques and more!

PLEASE
PLACE
STAMP
HERE

Name

Address

City State Zip

WOODWORKER'S JOURNAL

MEDIABRAINS COM
PO BOX 12079
NAPLES, FLORIDA 34101-2079

Act Fast: WIN A PORTER-CABLE ROUTER KIT

See other side for details

FREE Tool Giveaway...

We'll select one product info card (below) from the first 100 we receive from this issue. If we pick yours, you will win the **Porter-Cable 895PK Fixed Base Router with Plunge Base and Micro Height Adjuster** shown at right. No purchase is required to participate, but you must answer the survey questions below and send in your card today!

Product Information

To receive information about products and services featured in this issue of **Woodworker's Journal**, fill in your name and address below and circle the appropriate product info number(s).

Name

Address

City State Zip

E-mail Address

Phone Number (optional)

E-Z INFO: To save time and receive product information on a group of advertisers, circle **one** of these numbers.

All advertisers in issue	All power tools	All shop supplies	All showcases
500	**501**	**502**	**503**

1	2	3	4	5	6	7	8	9	10
11	12	13	14	15	16	17	18	19	20
21	22	23	24	25	26	27	28	29	30
31	32	33	34	35	36	37	38	39	40
41	42	43	44	45	46	47	48	49	50
51	52	53	54	55	56	57	58	59	60
61	62	63	64	65	66	67	68	69	70
71	72	73	74	75	76	77	78	79	80
81	82	83	84	85	86	87	88	89	90
91	92	93	94	95	96	97	98	99	100
101	102	103	104	105	106	107	108	109	110
111	112	113	114	115	116	117	118	119	120
121	122	123	124	125	126	127	128	129	130
131	132	133	134	135	136	137	138	139	140
141	142	143	144	145	146	147	148	149	150
151	152	153	154	155	156	157	158	159	160
161	162	163	164	165	166	167	168	169	170
171	172	173	174	175	176	177	**178**	**179**	**180**
181	**182**	**183**	**184**	**185**	**186**	**187**	**188**	**189**	**190**

JA05

Woodworker's Survey

(Answer by circling numbers at left)

How did you receive this issue of *Woodworker's Journal*?

I am a subscriber ....(No. 178)
I bought at newsstand ....(No. 179)
Other (friend, library, etc.) .....(No. 180)

About how much will you spend on woodworking projects, tools and supplies in the next year?

$4,000 or more ....(No. 181)
$1,000 to $3,999....................(No. 182)
$999 or less...........................(No. 183)

How do you use the advertising in *Woodworker's Journal*?*

To make purchasing decisions ....(No. 184)
To visit companies' web sites ....(No. 185)
To find updates on new tools ....(No. 186)

Would you like to receive information and special offers from *Woodworker's Journal* via e-mail?* (NOTE: You must fill in your e-mail address on the card at left.)

Woodworker's Journal eZine ....(Circle No. 188)
Information about your subscription ....(Circle No. 189)
No ....(Circle No. 190)

*Please check all that apply.

Expiration: You must mail this card by the 30th of the month following the cover date.

(Circle No. 59 on PRODUCT INFORMATION form)

Clamping Those Cantankerous Angles

By Chris Marshall

Get a grip on tricky angle joints with these nifty clamps.

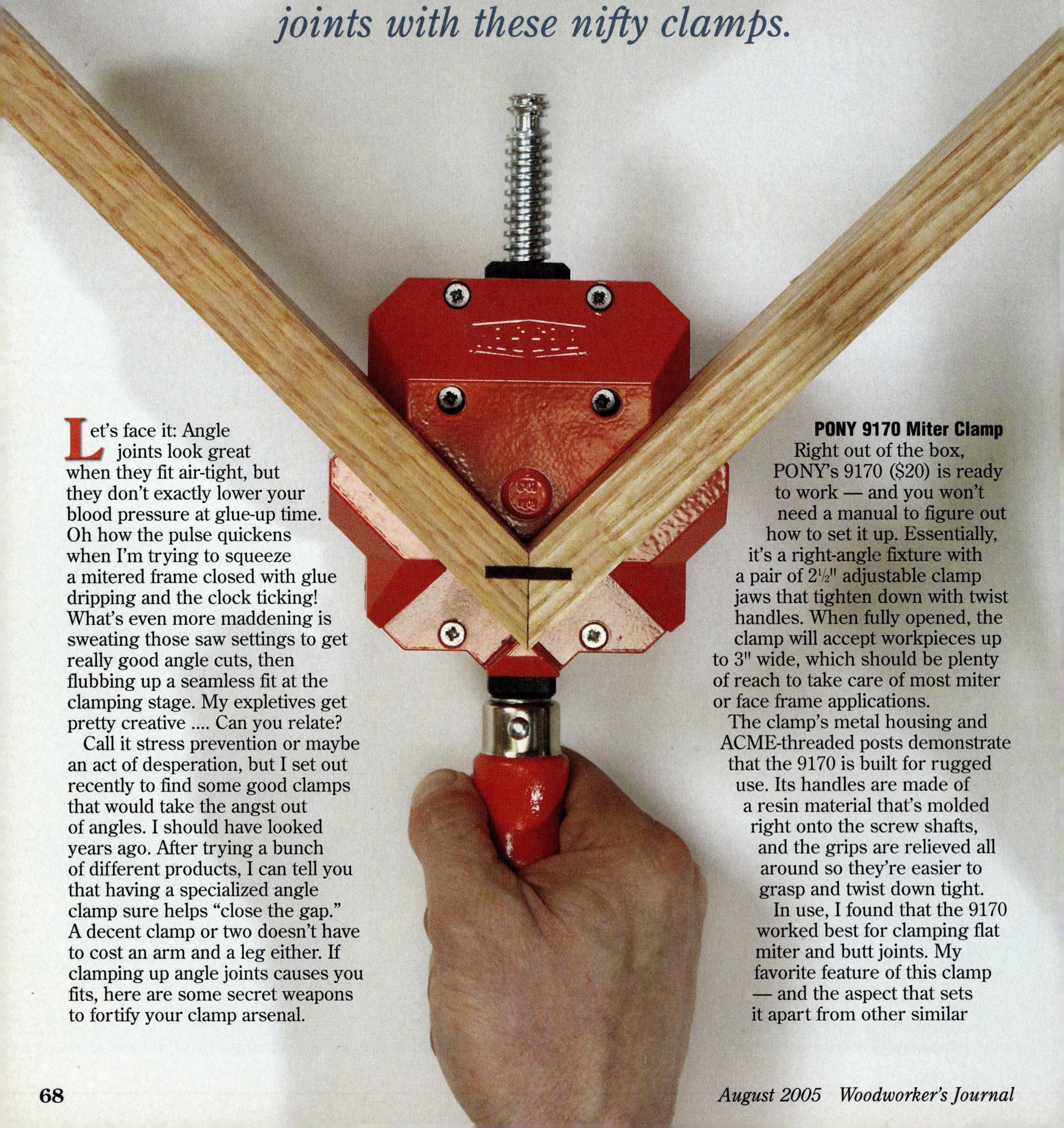

Let's face it: Angle joints look great when they fit air-tight, but they don't exactly lower your blood pressure at glue-up time. Oh how the pulse quickens when I'm trying to squeeze a mitered frame closed with glue dripping and the clock ticking! What's even more maddening is sweating those saw settings to get really good angle cuts, then flubbing up a seamless fit at the clamping stage. My expletives get pretty creative .... Can you relate?

Call it stress prevention or maybe an act of desperation, but I set out recently to find some good clamps that would take the angst out of angles. I should have looked years ago. After trying a bunch of different products, I can tell you that having a specialized angle clamp sure helps "close the gap." A decent clamp or two doesn't have to cost an arm and a leg either. If clamping up angle joints causes you fits, here are some secret weapons to fortify your clamp arsenal.

PONY 9170 Miter Clamp

Right out of the box, PONY's 9170 ($20) is ready to work — and you won't need a manual to figure out how to set it up. Essentially, it's a right-angle fixture with a pair of 2½" adjustable clamp jaws that tighten down with twist handles. When fully opened, the clamp will accept workpieces up to 3" wide, which should be plenty of reach to take care of most miter or face frame applications.

The clamp's metal housing and ACME-threaded posts demonstrate that the 9170 is built for rugged use. Its handles are made of a resin material that's molded right onto the screw shafts, and the grips are relieved all around so they're easier to grasp and twist down tight.

In use, I found that the 9170 worked best for clamping flat miter and butt joints. My favorite feature of this clamp — and the aspect that sets it apart from other similar

When it comes to clamps, who says square isn't cool?

clamps — is the quick-release mechanism on the screws. Just press a button alongside each clamp, and you can slide the jaws into place without turning the handles. Initially, the quick releases were a bit stiff, but they loosened up after awhile. Another helpful part of this clamp's design is that the metal body stays clear of the joint, giving you plenty of working room to drill, nail or drive in reinforcement screws. All things considered, here's a no-nonsense clamp you'll reach for again and again.

Rockler Clamp-It™ Assembly Square Combo Pack

Rockler's Clamp-It Assembly Squares are another good option for holding miter or butt joints square. Made of polycarbonate plastic, the Clamp-It Squares come in 4" or 8" sizes with inner ribbing for greater strength. Their inside corners are clipped to keep these fixtures from affecting the fit right where the joint parts meet.

Clamp-It Assembly Squares will work for any right-angle application, whether you're building picture frames, face frames, boxes or a whole room full of cabinet carcasses. These babies won't deflect, no matter how large the joint members are, and they register a dead-square corner. They also take loads of abuse — I've dropped mine off the bench more than once without damaging the plastic, and the inner ribbing withstands some brutal pressure.

Rockler sells the Clamp-It Squares individually for $8 or $12, depending on the size. (You will need eight to clamp up a cabinet box adequately.) They're also packaged in kit form with one of each Clamp-It size plus four mini bar clamps for $43. I was sent the kit. While the Clamp-It Squares are bulletproof, the tiny 5" bar clamps need a gentler hand. They're not designed for heavy-duty use. But ordinary C- clamps work fine for applying greater amounts of force.

Gross Stabil Multi-Spanner MSP

Gross Stabil's Multi-Spanner ($30) is a nifty little clamping fixture in my book. The body of the clamp is a die-cast framework with a deep slot that accepts one joint member and an open-sided flat surface for clamping the other part. The arrangement of this frame allows for clamping square corners as well as T-shaped joints. The frame walls are about 2½" tall, so there's adequate backing for building small casework or for clamping up standing, end-grain bevel joints.

To hold the joint, the MSP is fitted with a pair of heavy-duty clamp screws with wooden handles and plastic pucks to protect the wood. One screw mounts in a fixed position on the slotted part of the clamp frame, and the other screw is moveable on a pivoting bar — it looks like half of a conventional bar clamp. As far as capacities go, the slotted portion of the clamp frame will accept stock up to 1³⁄₁₆" thick, and the open side can handle 2⅜"-thick material.

The design of the MSP is helpful not only for holding a square corner but also for pressing the parts together to improve the fit. I like the pivoting clamp member: you can direct clamping pressure right where the parts meet or off to the side when you need to beef up the joint with other connectors. I'm also a fan of all-in-one fixtures like

Tool Review continues on page 70 ...

The PONY 9170 Miter Clamp holds right-angle miters firmly, and quick-release jaws promote faster set-ups.

Rockler's Clamp-It Assembly Square and miniature bar clamps hold either inside or outside corners square. They work well for clamping frame or carcass joinery.

A Pinch is All It Takes

The wedged legs of Lee Valley's pinch dogs draw joint parts together as you hammer them in.

There must be a cooper or patternmaker somewhere in history to thank for a couple more stone-simple clamping products you should know about. Lee Valley sells pinch dogs (a set of 18 sells for $22), which basically look like staples on steroids. They're sold in 1" to 2½" lengths and are made of heavy-gauge steel with a galvanized coating, so a set should last for a long time. The legs on these dogs sharpen to a point and taper inward. When you hammer a pinch dog across a joint, the legs function like wedges to pull the joint tight. These dogs work best when sunk into end-grain and softwoods — they'd be a great choice for outdoor projects where a few puncture marks here or there wouldn't matter much.

Rockler sells another pinch-style option called the Maestro Clamp-All Clamp Set ($42). The kit includes four large wire spring clips with pointed tips and an expander pliers. The pliers opens the clip so you can position and sink the points in. You'll also need the pliers for removing the clips to minimize marring. I tried the Maestros on cedar and pine with great results. These clamps will leave tiny indentations, just like the pinch dogs, but if you're building garden planters or birdhouse roofs, these could be the perfect clamps for the job. You can also cover the tips with suction cups for doing finer work or for use on harder woods. I had better luck using the pointy tips and sticking to softer woods.

Just squeeze the expander pliers to open Rockler's Maestro clamps, and let the pointed tips dig in for a firm hold on awkward angle joints.

Gross Stabil's Multi-Spanner MSP is tailor-made for securing butt or T-joints as well as end-bevels and narrow miters. One clamp is fixed; the other swivels to apply clamping pressure just where you want it.

this one that don't have a bag of extra parts to misplace or store.

PONY 90° Corner Clamp (9166) and Corner & Splicing Clamp (9133)
Adjustable Clamp offers two lighter-duty versions of the 9170 Miter Clamp. The PONY 90° Corner Clamp ($9) is a miniature, stripped down version of the 9170. It will still handle pairs of workpieces up to 3" wide, but the clamp jaws are half the size of its larger cousin, and there are no quick-release mechanisms. This version would be handy for building mitered picture frames or smaller face frames, but it isn't designed for larger work or heavy clamping applications. The shallow depth of the clamp surfaces also makes the 9166 too small to hold tall parts adequately. In use, my 9166 held flat miter joints accurately, and the parts didn't shift under pressure.

PONY's 9133 Corner and Splicing Clamp ($12) is basically an adjustable version of the 9166. The clamp body is shaped like a protractor, and one jaw swivels from 45° up to 180° in relation to the other jaw. The all-metal clamp body is marked on either side of square with indexes for setting up 60° or 45° angles, or you can lock the clamp anywhere in between

Tool Review continues on page 72 ...

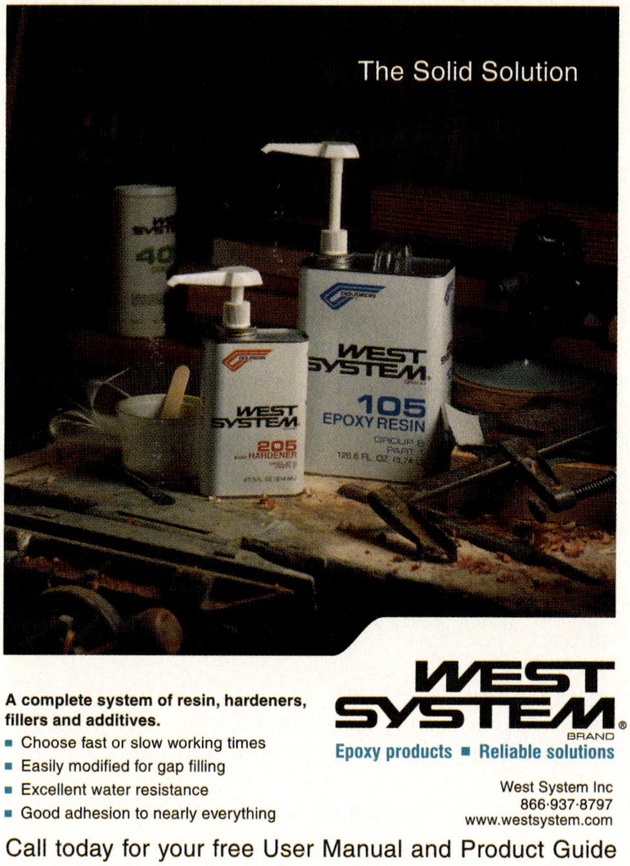

(Circle No. 70 on PRODUCT INFORMATION form)

(Circle No. 10 on PRODUCT INFORMATION form)

(Circle No. 75 on PRODUCT INFORMATION form)

(Circle No. 40 on PRODUCT INFORMATION form)

PONY 9166 and 9133 clamps offer low-cost holding power for either square or angled joints.

No Angle Left Behind

with a set-screw. The index marks are fairly accurate but not really important; just swivel the clamps to suit whatever angle you've got.

If small, light-duty clamping is all you need, these two miniature PONY angle clamps should give satisfactory results at low cost.

Gross Stabil MGS 100 Multi-Angle Clamp

A number of innovative clamps, like the MGS 100, open up your options for clamping both square and non-square angles effectively. This Multi-Angle Clamp is a substantial affair; the base consists of two platforms that slide together on a pair of steel posts. A large ACME-thread screw adjusts the spacing between the platforms when you twist a handle on the side.

Here's how the system works: The inner clamp jaws are a pair of glass-reinforced polyamid blocks that pivot on the base platforms. An Allen screw on each jaw locks it into five different registration holes from 0° to 60° so you can adjust the jig for a variety of joint angles. You can also flip the jaws for clamping 22.5° joints. On the outboard side, a pair of swiveling plastic clamp heads press the joint parts against the inner jaws. They're mounted on steel rods that slide easily into place, and a cam-activated lever locks them tight.

The adjustability of this fixture makes it more versatile than some other clamps, and the quick-set sliding rods and cam levers are no-fuss and lock down solidly. You can gain more access for "working" on the joint by opening up the spacing between the base platforms. Be careful when squeezing on the glue — one of the base rods falls right under the joint area where glue is likely to drip on it. At around $125, the MGS 100 is expensive, but it seems built for tough use.

Standing end-grain bevel joints are easy to lock down with cam levers and swiveling clamp heads on Gross Stabil's MGS 100 Multi-Angle Clamp.

Bessey GS-11 Miter Clamp

Bessey takes an unusual approach to clamping up flat angle joints with the GS-11 clamp ($150). Here, the inner backup surface for supporting workpieces is a trapezoidal-shaped block that pivots completely around to form 90°, 120° or 75° angles, depending on which faces you point toward the outer two clamp jaws. A large T-handle on top of the block makes it easy to lock the block down firmly.

Outboard, there are two foam-lined clamp faces that move laterally when you turn the clamp handle. These jaws pivot to accommodate workpieces that meet the inner block at its various angles. Some clamps in this test allow you to hold workpieces of differing thicknesses or widths, but the GS-11 only grips same-size parts.

In the fully open position, this fixture will accept workpieces up to about 3¼" wide, and the ACME-thread center screw provides stout clamping pressure. The fly-style movement of the outer clamp jaws also helps to draw miter joints tight. The only real limitation to this clamp is that the inner block limits you to just three angle options.

Tool Review continues on page 74 ...

Gross Stabil GSP gives you full control of lateral clamping pressure with a side handle that pulls the joint parts together.

The GS-11 is a heavy fixture with three rubber feet underneath to keep it from shifting on the bench. The weight of the clamp is beneficial when driving attachment screws or nails into the joint. I also like the broad platform that supports joint parts underneath. If you glue your miters, be prudent with the glue: squeeze-out could drip down into the screw mechanism where it would be hard to clean out.

Gross Stabil GSP Miter Clamp

Here's an ingenious clamping fixture that gives you the best of both worlds for angle clamping: it provides a tight hold on both joint parts and sets up to grip an unlimited range of joint angles.

What you get with the GSP is a pair of deep-jawed, 8" bar clamps and a third threaded unit that pulls a pair of aluminum cylinders together. The cylinders work like jaw extensions on the bar clamps.

The genius of this design lies in how simple it really is. The bar clamps hold each of the joint parts solidly, and the side screw draws the joint together. That's really all there is to it. The open, base-free design of the GSP means you can clamp up either acute or obtuse joint angles, but you may want to use splines or other interlocking connectors to ensure that joint parts stay flush.

Another big plus for this clamp is that nothing gets in the way of the joint. Whether you're splining, doweling, nailing or screwing the joint together, the bar clamps are easy to move clear of where you'll want to work. And, glue squeeze-out isn't an issue either because all the clamp threads are located above the joint instead of below it. At $65, the GSP Miter Clamp isn't a cheap investment, but it seems well worth the money, and you'll have two more bar clamps to boot.

Gross Stabil MCX Miter Clamping System

Gross Stabil offers another unusual clamp for drawing 22.5°, 30°, 60° and square miter joints tight. The MCX Miter Clamping System ($32) uses pairs of rubber-lined plastic jaws with a metal crossbar to straddle each joint part. A lock knob holds each set of parts in place. Then, the outside, larger clamp jaws are pulled together with a bar clamp to create the lateral clamping pressure. It functions a bit like the MGS 100 clamp reviewed here, only without the substantial base assembly to back things up.

To keep clamping pressure evenly distributed and make the MCX more versatile, it comes with plastic adapters that switch the gripping angle for the bar clamp. You select from four different pairs of adapters and press them into place on the outer clamps before installing the bar clamp.

There are a couple advantages to the MCX System and a few drawbacks worth mentioning: On the plus side, it will grip joint parts up to 4" wide, and the parts don't have to match widths to still work in the clamp. The clamp design also keeps workpieces flat on the bench, so you can hammer in corrugated or other metal cross connectors without damaging the clamp or throwing the joint out of whack. It also grips the most common miters we use, and the cost isn't outlandish. That said, I found the MCX harder to set up and use than other clamps here. The clamp assemblies tended to slide along the joint parts until the crossbar wedged them in place, and the hand knobs were difficult to

Tool Review continues on page 76 ...

A trapezoid-shaped inner block on Bessey's GS-11 clamp swivels to back up three different joint angles. The outer jaws are self-adjusting to correspond to different angles. One handle draws them together.

(Circle No. 45 on PRODUCT INFORMATION form)

(Circle No. 53 on PRODUCT INFORMATION form)

(Circle No. 61 on PRODUCT INFORMATION form)

(Circle No. 71 on PRODUCT INFORMATION form)

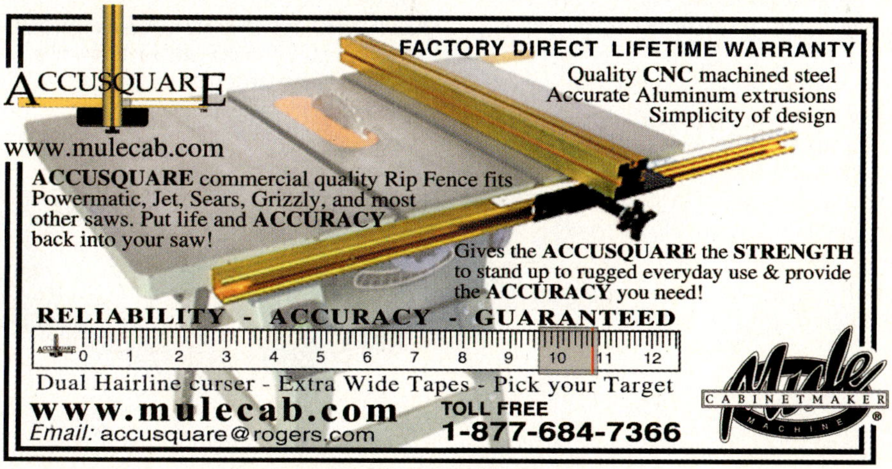

(Circle No. 49 on PRODUCT INFORMATION form)

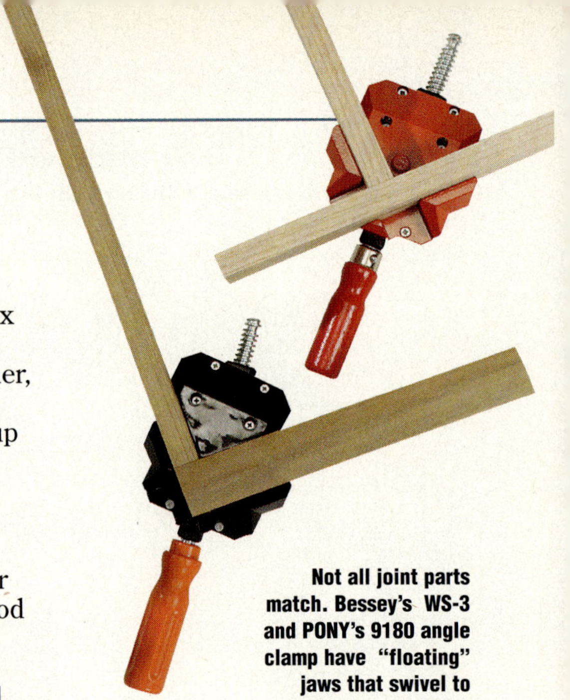

Not all joint parts match. Bessey's WS-3 and PONY's 9180 angle clamp have "floating" jaws that swivel to account for varying material thicknesses.

tighten down. Hang on to the box if you buy this clamp: there are small, loose parts to keep together, and you may need a visual reminder for getting things set up if you don't use the clamp often.

Bessey WS-3 90° Angle Clamp/ PONY 9180 Angle Clamp
Except for changes in paint color and the option of a plastic or wood handle, these two clamps are virtually identical. The Bessey version sells for around $25, and the PONY goes for $20. A central ACME screw draws a wedge-shaped inner jaw into a V-shaped outer jaw to pull joints tight. The

One advantage to the MCX Miter Clamp is that joint parts still remain on the bench during clamping, so you can tap in cross connectors or other reinforcements without damaging the clamp.

cool aspect of both of these clamps is that the jaws swivel and "float" on the screw, so they can shift and equalize clamping pressure as you tighten them down. The swivel feature also makes it possible to grip parts of different thicknesses: For variable-thickness parts, capacities are 7/8" and 2½". For same-thickness material, these clamps have 2" jaw capacity.

You can use these clamps for securing miter joints, joints with beveled ends, butt joints and T-joints. The design of these clamps makes it a little tricky to sneak a nail gun or a driver bit down inside, but it's not too difficult. All in all, these clamps are solidly built and work effectively, whichever color clamp you buy.

Strap Clamps with Tidier Tails
You've probably used a strap clamp for pulling together picture frames, a wooden column or of course, that loose kitchen chair. The trouble I have with strap clamps is what to do with 10 or 15 feet of strap when I'm done using it. My strap clamps form a spaghetti junction in the tool drawer — and I bet yours do, too.

Bessey takes care of the problem with its nifty VAS-23 Variable

continues on page 78 ...

Rockler's low-cost strap clamp has a retractable 12-foot strap and comes with seven corners that fit three different joint angles.

Low-tech Tension

Strap clamps are good options for pulling together closed shapes, but don't forget a few other really cheap clamping solutions for these sorts of applications. Large rubber bands or a length of rubber surgical tubing can come to the rescue during those late-night or weekend glue-ups. Masking or stretchable packing tape also works wonders for temporary clamping, especially tape with a "memory" that shrinks and tightens. Lee Valley sells rubber tubing in 25" lengths for around $15, and Rockler offers a dozen jumbo rubber bands for about $6.

(Circle No. 66 on PRODUCT INFORMATION form)

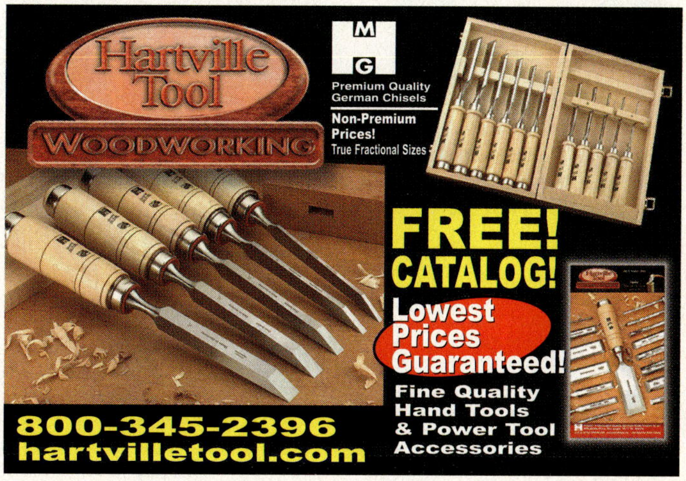

(Circle No. 33 on PRODUCT INFORMATION form)

(Circle No. 63 on PRODUCT INFORMATION form)

Details, Details...

For more technical information or to inquire about sources for purchasing these clamps, contact the manufacturers:

Adjustable Clamp Company (PONY)
312-666-0640;
www.adjustableclamp.com

Bessey Tools North America:
800-828-1004;
www.besseytools.com

Gross Stabil Tool:
866-231-7438;
www.grossstabilclamps.com

Lee Valley Tools:
800-871-8158;
www.leevalley.com

Rockler Woodworking and Hardware:
800-279-4441;
www.rockler.com

All 23 feet of strap on Bessey's VAS-23 clamp coil up neatly right on the clamp for storage. No tangles here.

If your strap clamp doesn't have corner supports, Lee Valley sells some rugged Variable-Angle Web Clamp Corners worth trying. The inner faces swivel past one another, so they adjust for any angle from 30° up to almost 180°.

Angle Strap Clamp ($35). All 23 feet of polyester strap stows neatly on a winding spool right on the clamp body. In fact, the extra strapping never gets in the way; you hand-wind the loose strap after positioning the strap, then twist the bottom handle to tighten things up. It's neat, neat, neat.

The VAS-23 is made for heavy-duty applications. The 1"-wide strapping has a tensile strength of 1100 lbs. Its inner gear mechanism tightens the strap evenly from both ends to prevent joints from shifting out of alignment. If one strap clamp is all you really need, pick this one.

For light-duty work, Rockler also sells an inexpensive strap clamp (item 33822, $12) that won't cause you fits. All 12 feet of the 1/2"-wide strapping wind inside the clamp's housing, and you tighten the clamp down with a hand knob. It comes with seven plastic corners to help distribute the strap pressure.

I've tried to highlight some good clamps in this article. If you want the information and specs that cover all the angles on all of them, check out the spreadsheet for this story on our web site at the URL *www.woodworkersjournal.com.*

Chris Marshall is a Woodworker's Journal *contributing editor.*

Build a Better Frame Clamp...

You've probably seen or used the threaded-rod style frame clamps for making picture frames. What's good about these old standbys is that they offer decent holding power, and you can tweak the pressure on each corner of the frame by tightening four nuts on the clamp. Trouble is, the nuts have to thread all the way on and off the rods to set up or take down the frame — and that involves a lot of twisting. Lee Valley is making the threading process much easier with the Veritas Four-Way Speed Clamp ($23). Instead of the typical round threaded hole in the nuts, Veritas designed "speed nuts" that are actually cross-drilled so the holes look oblong. Only a portion of the bore is threaded; the rest is smooth. With these modified frame nuts, you can slide the nuts right up the rods without turning. The threads only engage when the nuts meet resistance at the frame corners. Loosen the nuts a tad, and they slide off the rods just as easily. Very clever and convenient.

Veritas makes a faster frame clamp using cross-drilled speed nuts that slide in place, then thread down tight.

Complete Dust Collection System for Under $850!
Ask about our exclusive, optional Bag Hold-Down System!
NEW!
The DUST GORILLA™
2hp Cyclone Collector / U.S. made Baldor Motor / Filter / Drum / Brackets / Internal Silencer / Magnetic Switch included.
FREE duct design with system purchase!
"I found your staff excellent to deal with and the packaging of your unit was probably the best I have ever seen. As for performance, the Gorilla has far exceeded my expectations. Amazing suction. I can't say enough about your collector. Your product is number one!"
A.L. - Halifax, Nova Scotia
The DUST GORILLA™
See Us at AWFS 2005 Booth 3283 July 27 - 30th Las Vegas!
Magnetic Switch and Brackets Included!
Oneida Air Systems
Order On-Line!
www.oneida-air.com
Call Today for FREE Brochure!
1.800.732.4065
(Circle No. 52 on PRODUCT INFORMATION form)
Still Proudly Made in the USA!
Oneida Air Systems, Inc. 1001 W. Fayette St., Syracuse, NY 13204

Finishing Flow Chart

By Michael Dresdner

An annotated flow chart for your workshop's wall

In previous columns, I've explained virtually every step of the finishing process in detail. Today, I bring it all together with an annotated flow chart that shows the order of those steps, which steps are mandatory and which are optional, and what questions you should ask in order to tell the difference.

I will assume only two things: that you are starting with clean, new wood, and that you have already made samples. The last thing you want during finishing is a surprise, and making samples of your intended finish steps on scraps of the wood you plan to finish will go a long way toward avoiding unpleasant surprises.

In this chart, all mandatory steps are yellow (rectangles), all optional steps are red (circles), and all questions are blue (diamonds). This running text contains a bit more clarification. For in-depth explanations of each step, you should read the past columns that covered those topics. One thing that should be comforting is that there are only four mandatory operations in a simple finish, half of which are preparation steps involving sanding and cleaning.

The Workflow

Glue spots: Check for glue spots by wetting wood with either water or mineral spirits to make the spots more obvious. Remove the glue by scraping or sanding.

First sanding: Hand or machine sand with at least three successive aluminum oxide grit sizes: 80 (or 100), followed by 120 (or 150), followed by 180 (or 220).

Wood putty: Fill dings or nicks with wood putty that matches the color of the wood, or so that when stained, it will ape the stained wood. Leave the putty slightly

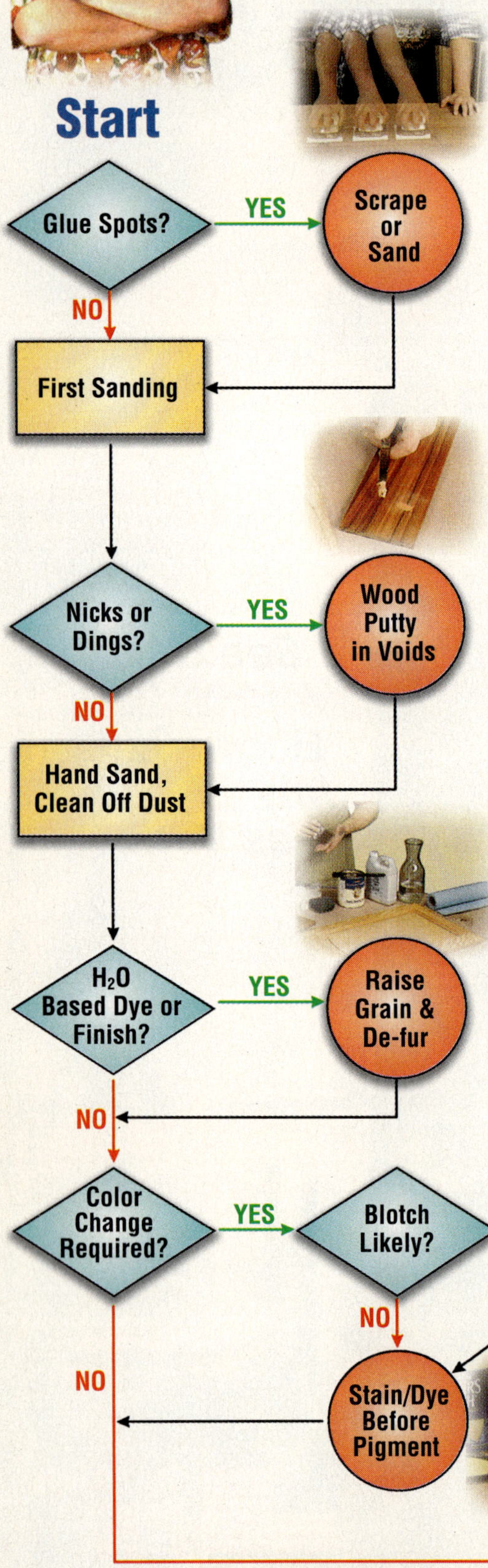

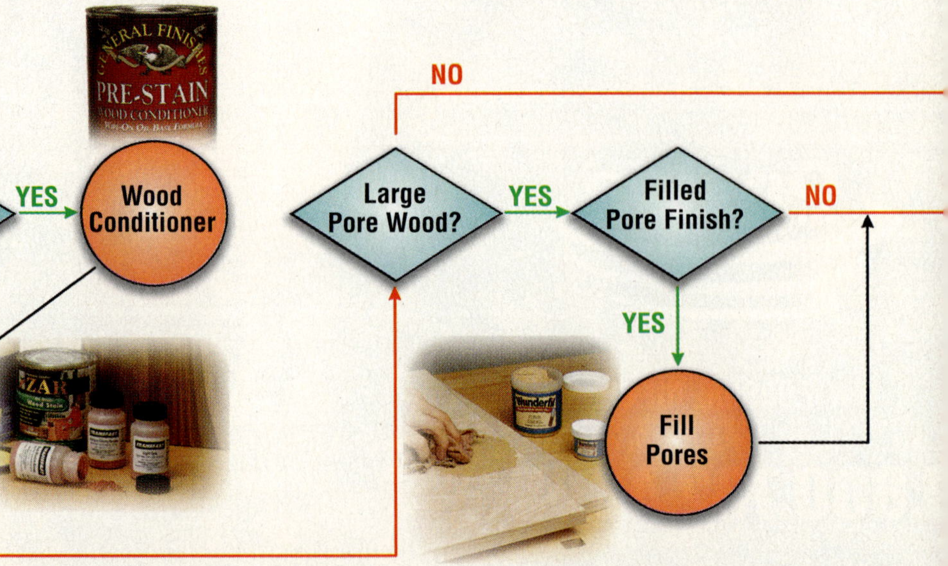

> *“In this chart, all mandatory steps are yellow (rectangles), all optional steps are red (circles), and all questions are blue (diamonds).”*

proud. After it has dried, sand flush during the next step so that the sanded area reveals the exact shape of the original void.

Hand sand & clean off dust: This time, sand by hand, going with the grain when possible, using 180- or 220-grit garnet paper (as opposed to aluminum oxide paper). This step also sands putty flush. Always sand all areas of the piece the same way, in the same sequence, using the same size and type of grit. Wipe, blow or vacuum off sanding dust.

Raise grain, de-fur: Sponge wood liberally with clean water, wipe it all off, and let it dry overnight. Sand very lightly the next day with 400-grit paper. Sand only enough to remove the raised fur.

Conditioner: Apply wood conditioner only when necessary. Some woods and stains require it, while others do not. Making samples will tell you if you need it. Flood conditioner on, wipe it off, and stain while the conditioner is still wet.

Stain: Flood stain on liberally, and wipe it off while still wet. When using two types of stain, dyes go on first, followed by pigment stains. Let each application dry completely before proceeding to the next step.

Fill pores: Open pore finishes on large pore woods are both common and attractive. However, if you prefer the look of a glass smooth surface, fill the pores with inert pore filler. Seal the wood with a very thin coat of dewaxed shellac or Zinsser SealCoat™, or use a thinned coat of your intended topcoat. Apply the filler, remove it, and when it's dry, sand lightly to remove any filler residue on the surface. Let waterbased filler dry overnight, and allow three days for oil-based filler.

continues on page 82 ...

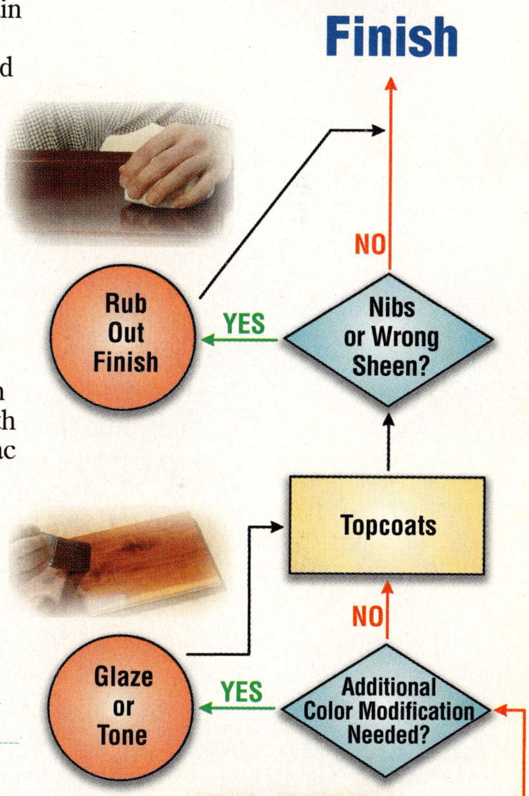

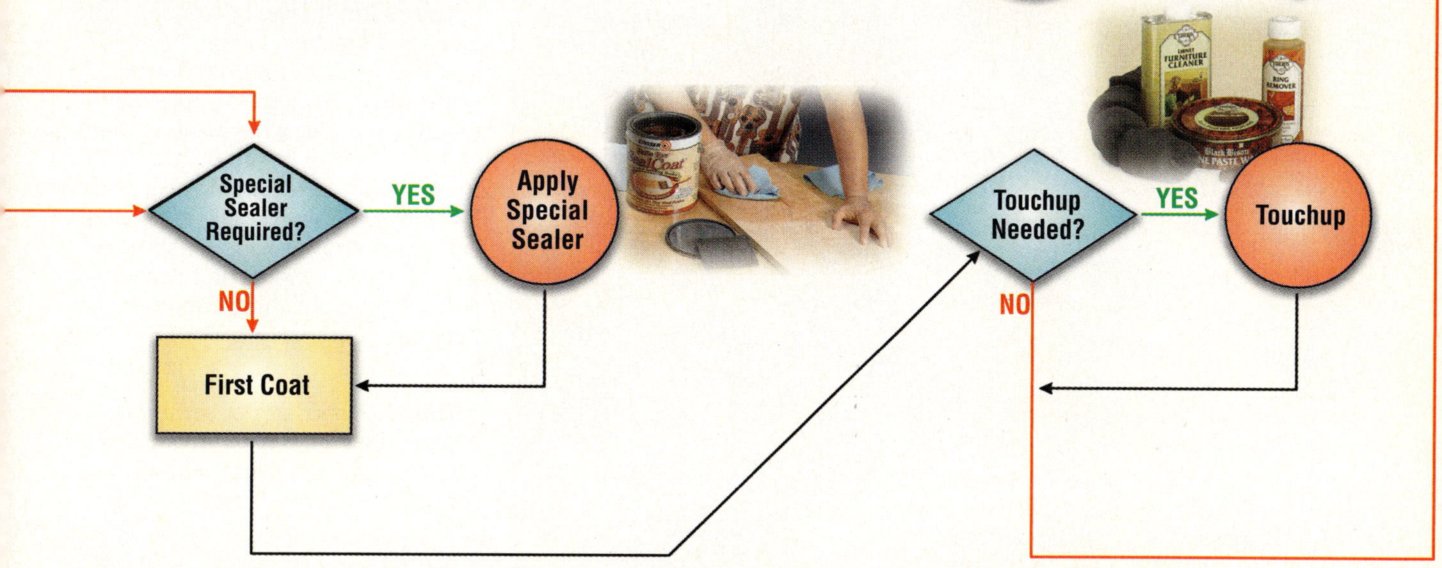

I intend to make a pair of Adirondack chairs to replace a pair, made from white pine, that deteriorated from the elements. The original chairs were carefully painted and repainted with exterior paints, but the wood still rotted after a few years. I had planned to make this pair from oak, but because of the price and poor availability of oak, I decided to use pine again. What type of paint or sealer can I use to protect the chairs from the elements?

— John P. Cirelli

It is a peculiar sort of optimism that allows us to repeat the same actions that previously resulted in failure, yet expect a different outcome. If there was one thing to be learned from chairs that rotted in spite of the best protective finish possible, it is this: Finishes do not change the nature of the wood they cover. If you want rot-resistant furniture, you must start with rot-resistant wood. I'd use Western red cedar. To give these benighted stalwarts the best shot at longevity, start by potting the feet. Prior to finishing, seal the ends of the feet, where end grain meets the ground, with epoxy. The epoxy will prevent water from wicking up under the finish. Use a good exterior primer on the freshly sanded wood, and follow that with exterior acrylic trim paint as opposed to exterior latex house paint. In this case, good priming is as important as the paint. After finishing, use glides or caps to further prevent the feet from standing in water.

— Michael Dresdner

For simply sending in his question about exterior finishes, John P. Cirelli of Barre, Massachusetts wins the **Olympic Wood Finishing Kit** *at left.*

FINISHING THOUGHTS

Applying Sealer and Topcoat

Sealer or first coat: Usually, the first coat of finish will act as the sealer, but in some cases, special sealers are helpful. Zinsser SealCoat is a good choice for the following situations: refinished (as opposed to new wood) surfaces, woods that contain anti-oxidants (all dalbergias and some cedars), extremely porous woods, knotty or resinous woods, surfaces emitting odors, dyed woods and any surfaces that may have been contaminated with wax, dirt or grease. If a special sealer is not needed, simply apply the first coat of finish at this point.

Touchup: Here's where you touch up any missed glue spots, putty spots that came out too light or color irregularities. Putting touchup under glaze or toner coats helps hide it better. Applying it after the first coat prevents it from seeping into the wood and spreading, and allows subsequent coats to seal in the touchup.

Glaze or tone: You can add color between layers of finish with glaze, a thick pigment stain, or with toner, a clear finish laced with dye.

Topcoats: Apply as many coats of your favored finish as is needed for durability and appearance. Sand lightly between coats to remove nibs, brush marks or spray pattern marks. Sand to improve adhesion only if you have waited more than a week between coats of varnish, polyurethane or waterbased coatings. Adhesion sanding is never required for shellac or lacquer. With catalyzed finishes, follow the specific manufacturer recommendations.

Rub out: It is almost impossible to get a final surface smooth enough, so I always plan to rub out the finish. Sand lightly with very fine paper to level nibs. Rub with 0000 steel wool and paste wax for satin finishes, or use finer grit sandpaper, followed by rubbing and polishing compounds, for gloss.

Michael Dresdner is a nationally known finishing expert and author. His latest book is Wood Finishing Fixes *by Taunton Press.*